# TAKING SIDES

Clashing Views in

# Lifespan Development

# TAKING SIDES

Clashing Views in

# Lifespan Development

Selected, Edited, and with Introductions by

**Andrew M. Guest**
*University of Portland*

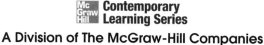

**Mc Graw Hill** **Contemporary Learning Series**

A Division of The McGraw-Hill Companies

Photo Acknowledgment
Cover image: Lori Jelinek

Cover Acknowledgment
Maggie Lytle

Manufactured in the United States of America

First Edition

123456789DOCDOC9876

0-07-351494-2
978-0-07-351494-9
ISSN: 1559-2642

Printed on Recycled Paper

# Preface

**W**e all have a vested stake in the study of life span development because we are all experts in the ages and stages of our own lives. Yet our experiences, and our understandings of those experiences, vary dramatically from person to person. Where some of us are sure that our childhood interactions with our parents shaped everything about the way we function in the world, others are convinced that we are living out a biologically or genetically determined destiny. While many people see childhood as a period of risks and challenges, others appreciate the joy and opportunity of being young. Where we often focus on adulthood as defined by careers and family, we also recognize that well-being in adulthood depends on abstract qualities such as happiness and success. In one sense, these types of contrasts show how the study of life span development is inherently controversial. The purpose of this book is to make that controversy useful by providing educated and intelligent perspectives on issues that are important to everyone's life, not to mention being important to academic study of the life span.

This first edition of *Taking Sides: Clashing Views in Lifespan Development* presents 20 issues that challenge students and scholars to think deeply about issues confronted through the ages and stages of our lives. Each issue is framed by a question about what, why, or how we develop, and each question is addressed from two distinct perspectives presenting different views. These 40 views represent high-quality contemporary work by scholars and experts. Each of the 20 issues also has an introduction with an explanation of how and why it is important for the larger study of life span development, and a postscript contextualizing the views presented through a general discussion and suggestions for further reading.

The materials and ideas dealt with in this book derive from diverse fields of study including psychology, sociology, biology, cognitive science, gerontology, and pediatrics. In fact, one appealing aspect of studying life span development is that it is an interdisciplinary subject focused on answering interesting questions. Thus, while the materials provided with each issue allow an understanding of what experts in diverse subjects think, the challenge for readers is to use the evidence and opinions to answer the questions for themselves. The book explains, for example, why understanding how much our development depends on our parents is important, but it is up to readers to take that explanation and the available evidence to establish their own educated position.

Although the perspectives presented in this book represent educated thinking on these issues, the reason the issues are controversial is because that thinking is still evolving. Researchers are always developing new techniques for studying our biological development, individuals are always adapting to the different challenges faced at each stage of life, and societies are always changing the way they treat children, adults, and the elderly. Likewise, readers of this book, as experts in their own life span development, will have valuable experiences and perspectives that complement those discussed in the book. In the end, what is most important is to have a point of view on these issues that is educated and informed—sometimes that point of view will match earlier beliefs; other times it will represent a dramatic change. In all cases, however, the most valuable understandings derive from using controversy as an opportunity to think through the challenges of our lives.

**A word to the instructor**   An *Instructor's Manual With Test Questions* (multiple-choice and essay) is available through the publisher for the instructor using *Taking Sides* in the classroom. A general guidebook, *Using Taking Sides in the Classroom,* which discusses methods and techniques for integrating the pro-con approach into any classroom setting, is also available. An online version of *Using Taking Sides in the Classroom* and a correspondence service for *Taking Sides* adopters can be found at http://www.mhcls.com/usingts/.

*Taking Sides: Clashing Views in Lifespan Development* is only one title in the Taking Sides series. If you are interested in seeing the table of contents for any of the other titles, please visit the Taking Sides Web site at http://www.mhcls.com/takingsides/.

**Acknowledgments**   I greatly appreciate the opportunities for learning about the life span provided by my former teachers and colleagues at the University of Chicago's Committee on Human Development and by my current students at the University of Portland (who allowed me the opportunity to draft all the material with an intelligent and critical audience). Beyond those groups, I owe the most thanks to Sara Brant for her friendly feedback, dedicated support, and constant understanding.

**Andrew Guest**
*University of Portland*

# Contents In Brief

**PART 1   General Issues in the Study of Life Span Development   1**

Issue 1.   Does Culture and Environment Influence Human Development More Than Our Genes?   2

Issue 2.   Are Peers More Important than Parents During the Process of Development?   25

Issue 3.   Do Significant Innate Differences Influence the Success of Males and Females?   49

**PART 2   Prenatal Development   67**

Issue 4.   Does Prenatal Exposure to Drugs Such as Cocaine Create "Crack Babies" With Special Developmental Concerns?   68

Issue 5.   Is a Natural Childbirth, Without Pain Medication, Best for Development?   86

**PART 3   Infancy   101**

Issue 6.   Is There a "Myth of the First Three Years"?   102

Issue 7.   Are Infants Born With an Innate Ability to Make Symbolic Mental Representations of Objects?   115

**PART 4   Early Childhood   133**

Issue 8.   Does Exposure to Music, including Mozart, During Early Childhood Have a Special Capacity to Enhance Development?   134

Issue 9.   Does Emphasizing Academic Skills Help At-Risk Preschool Children?   152

**PART 5   Middle Childhood   177**

Issue 10.   Has Promoting Self-Esteem Failed to Improve the Education of School-Age Children?   178

Issue 11.   Is Attention Deficit Disorder (ADD/ADHD) a Legitimate Medical Condition That Affects Childhood Behavior?   205

**PART 6   Adolescence   229**

Issue 12.   Are Boys More At-Risk Than Girls as They Develop Through Adolescence?   230

Issue 13.   Does Violent Media Cause Teenage Aggresion?   249

**PART 7   Youth and Early Adulthood   267**

Issue 14.   Should We Use Medication to Deal With the Angst of College and Young Adulthood?   268

Issue 15.   Are College Graduates Unprepared for Adulthood and the World of Work?   286

## PART 8   **Middle Adulthood**    **303**

**Issue 16.** Are Contemporary Adults Overlooking the Importance of Marriage as Part of Successful Development?   304

**Issue 17.** Is One General Intelligence Factor Responsible for Career Success?   321

**Issue 18.** Is Religion a Pure Good in Facilitating Well-Being During Adulthood?   344

## PART 9   **Later Adulthood**    **371**

**Issue 19.** Can We Universally Define "Successful Aging"?   372

**Issue 20.** Is Anti-Aging Technology a Cause for Societal Concern?   394

# Contents

Preface   v
Introduction   xvi

## PART 1   GENERAL ISSUES IN THE STUDY OF LIFE SPAN DEVELOPMENT   1

### Issue 1.   Does Culture and Environment Influence Human Development More Than Our Genes?   2

**YES:   Paul Ehrlich and Marcus Feldman,** from "Genes and Cultures: What Creates Our Behavioral Phenome?" *Current Anthropology* (February 2003)   *4*

**NO:   Gary Marcus,** from "Making the Mind: Why We've Misunderstood the Nature-Nurture Debate," *Boston Review* (December 2003/ January 2004)   *13*

Stanford University professors of biology Paul Ehrlich and Marcus Feldman argue that human behavior exhibits such complexity that genetic programs simply can't explain the way people develop. Psychologist and researcher Gary Marcus asserts that research clearly demonstrates how a relatively small number of genes influence our environmental learning by "cascading" to determine the paths of our behavioral development.

### Issue 2.   Are Peers More Important than Parents During the Process of Development?   25

**YES:   Judith Rich Harris,** from "How to Succeed in Childhood," *The Wilson Quarterly* (Winter 1999)   *27*

**NO:   Howard Gardner,** from "Do Parents Count?" *The New York Review of Books* (November 5, 1998)   *36*

Developmental psychology writer Judith Rich Harris presents a strong and provocative argument suggesting that parents do not influence child development to any significant degree, while peers and social groups have a primary influence. Harvard psychologist Howard Gardener reviews Harris' work and suggests her argument is overstated and misleading—parents do matter.

### Issue 3.   Do Significant Innate Differences Influence the Success of Males and Females?   49

**YES:   Steven Pinker,** from "Sex Ed: The Science of Difference," *The New Republic* (February 14, 2005)   *51*

**NO:   Cynthia Russett,** from "All About Eve: What Men Have Thought About Women Thinking," *The American Scholar* (vol. 74, 2005)   *56*

Cognitive psychologist and author Steven Pinker considers the loud response to the suggestion of Harvard president Lawrence Summers that differences between the numbers of men and women in science might be partly related to innate abilities. Pinker asserts that this possibility is well grounded in research, but provokes reactions based on flawed assumptions of gender equality. Cynthia Russett, a professor at Yale, argues that harmful assumptions of innate deficiencies in woman have a long, and significantly flawed, historical precedent without basis in fact.

# PART 2   PRENATAL DEVELOPMENT   67

### Issue 4.   Does Prenatal Exposure to Drugs Such as Cocaine Create "Crack Babies" With Special Developmental Concerns?   68

**YES:**   **Sherri McCarthy and Thomas Franklin Waters**, from "A Crack Kid Grows Up: A Clinical Case Report," *Journal of Offender Rehabilitation* (vol. 37, 2003)   *70*

**NO:**   **Mariah Blake**, from "The Damage Done: Crack Babies Talk Back," *Columbia Journalism Review* (September/October 2004)   *80*

Sherri McCarthy and Thomas F. Waters, educational psychology and criminal justice professors at Northern Arizona University, review the research on "crack babies" suggesting a link between pre-natal cocaine exposure and serious physical, socioemotional, and cognitive effects requiring special care and attention. Journalist and editor Mariah Blake contends that the idea of "crack babies" with special needs is more a media creation than a medical fact; her investigation does not support the popular idea that prenatal exposure to cocaine determines permanent negative developmental effects.

### Issue 5.   Is a Natural Childbirth, Without Pain Medication, Best for Development?   86

**YES:**   **Lennart Righard**, from "Making Childbirth a Normal Process," *Birth* (March 2001)   *88*

**NO:**   **Gilbert J. Grant**, from *Enjoy Your Labor: A New Approach to Pain Relief for Childbirth* (Russell Hasting Press, 2005)   *93*

Pediatrician and professor Lennart Righard draws from research and from his experience attending to natural childbirth in Sweden to assert that natural childbirth is vastly preferable to the artificial interventions of medical technology. Obstetric anesthesiologist Dr. Gilbert Grant asserts that social pressure toward natural childbirth and misplaced anxiety about risks to the baby lead many pregnant women to unnecessarily suffer through the birthing experience.

# PART 3   INFANCY   101

### Issue 6.   Is There a "Myth of the First Three Years"?   102

**YES:**   **Gwen J. Broude**, from "Scatterbrained Child Rearing," *Reason Magazine* (December, 2000)   *104*

**NO:**   **Zero to Three: National Center for Infants, Toddlers and Families**, from "Zero to Three: Response to the Myth of the First Three Years," http://www.zerotothree.org/no-myth.html   *108*

Gwen J. Broude, who teaches developmental psychology and cognitive science at Vassar College, reviews, supports, and augments John

Bruer's idea that a "myth of the first three years" has falsely used neuro-science to claim that infancy is the only critical developmental period. Zero to Three, a national organization devoted to promoting healthy infant development, contradicts Bruer's idea by asserting that a great deal of diverse research supports the idea that the first three years are critical to development and success in adulthood.

### Issue 7.   Are Infants Born With an Innate Ability to Make Symbolic Mental Representations of Objects?   115

YES:   **Elizabeth S. Spelke,** from "Core Knowledge," *American Psychologist* (November 2000)   *117*

NO:   **Bruce Hood,** from "When Do Infants Know About Objects?" *Perception* (vol. 30, 2001)   *125*

Harvard professor Elizabeth Spelke draws on a large quantity of infant research to suggest infants have an innate understanding of the properties of objects, which is part of what she considers core knowledge systems that are the foundation of thought. Developmental psychologist Bruce Hood points out that the type of research Spelke relies upon is controversial—learning what infants are thinking requires potentially unfair assumptions.

## **PART 4**   EARLY CHILDHOOD   133

### Issue 8.   Does Exposure to Music, including Mozart, During Early Childhood Have a Special Capacity to Enhance Development?   134

YES:   **Gordon L. Shaw,** from *Keeping Mozart in Mind* (Academic Press, 2000)   *136*

NO:   **Michael Linton,** from "The Mozart Effect," *First Things: The Journal of Religion, Culture, and Public Life* (March 1999)   *144*

Neuroscientist Gordon L. Shaw acknowledges that the effect of Mozart on infants is not yet known but argues that the generally positive effect of music on spatial-temporal reasoning supports efforts to endorse music for children. Michael Linton, professor of music at Middle Tennessee State University, asserts that the idea of music having special brain-enhancing powers has been recycled historically and consistently proven an inaccurate myth.

### Issue 9.   Does Emphasizing Academic Skills Help At-Risk Preschool Children?   152

YES:   **U.S. Department of Health and Human Services,** from *Strengthening Head Start: What the Evidence Shows* (June 2003)   *154*

NO:   **C. Cybele Raver and Edward F. Zigler,** from "Another Step Back? Assessing Readiness in Head Start," *Young Children* (January 2004)   *166*

The U.S. Department of Health and Human Services, which is responsible for Head Start—a preschool program for at-risk children—argues that preschool programs can most help young children by emphasizing academic and cognitive skills. Professors C. Cybele Raver and Edward F. Zigler (a founder of Head Start in the 1960s) respond by arguing that overemphasizing academic and cognitive skills at the expense of social, emotional, and physical well-being is a mistake dependent on misguided efforts to make the entire educational system focused on concrete assessment.

# PART 5  MIDDLE CHILDHOOD     177

### Issue 10.  Has Promoting Self-Esteem Failed to Improve the Education of School-Age Children?   178

YES:  **Roy F. Baumeister, Jennifer D. Campbell, Joachim I. Krueger, and Kathleen D. Vohs,** from "Does High Self-Esteem Cause Better Performance, Interpersonal Success, Happiness, or Healthier Lifestyles?" *Psychological Science in the Public Interest* (May 2003)   *180*

NO:  **Neil Humphrey,** from "The Death of the Feel-Good Factor? Self-Esteem in the Educational Context," *School Psychology International* (vol. 25, 2004)   *196*

Social psychologist Roy F. Baumeister and his colleagues engaged in an extensive review of research on the popular idea that self-esteem produces academic achievement and conclude that it does nothing of the sort. Educational psychologist Neil Humphrey asserts that reviews concluding self-esteem does not contribute to achievement are not definitive because they ignore the contextual nature of self-esteem and its importance in creating a generally healthy learning environment.

### Issue 11.  Is Attention Deficit Disorder (ADD/ADHD) a Legitimate Medical Condition That Affects Childhood Behavior?   205

YES:  **Michael Fumento,** from "Trick Question," *The New Republic* (February 3, 2003)   *207*

NO:  **Jonathan Leo,** from "Attention Deficit Disorder: Good Science or Good Marketing?" *Skeptic* (vol. 8, no. 1, 2000)   *214*

Science journalist and writer Michael Fumento suggests that despite the extensive political controversy, it is clear that ADHD is a legitimate medical condition disrupting childhood. Professor of medicine Jonathan Leo suggests that there is no good science to support ADHD; rather, pharmaceutical advertising has taken advantage of the often extreme behavior of school-aged children.

# PART 6  ADOLESCENCE     229

### Issue 12.  Are Boys More At-Risk Than Girls as They Develop Through Adolescence?   230

YES:  **Christina Hoff Sommers,** from "The War Against Boys," *The Atlantic Monthly* (May 2000)   *232*

NO:  **Michael Kimmel,** from "A War Against Boys?" *Tikkun* (November/ December 2000)   *241*

Author and philosopher Christina Hoff Sommers asserts that feminist concern for girls has had the ironic effect of leaving boys behind. She notes that in most high schools it is boys, rather than girls, most at risk. Professor of sociology Michael Kimmel responds to Sommers' argument by noting that her statistics are spun so as to make a particular case, and ignore the real disadvantages faced by girls in contemporary society.

**Issue 13.   Does Violent Media Cause Teenage Aggresion?   249**

YES:   **Dave Grossman,** from "Teaching Kids to Kill," *National Forum* (vol. 80, 2000)   *251*

NO:   **Jonathan L. Freedman,** from *Media Violence and Its Effect on Aggression: Assessing the Scientific Evidence* (University of Toronto Press, 2002)   *257*

Researcher, author, and former military officer Dave Grossman argues that the contemporary media teaches youth to kill in much the same way that the military prepares soldiers for war. From his perspective both use psychological foundations to develop an appetite for aggression. Professor of psychology Jonathan L. Freedman argues that, despite many research efforts to demonstrate a link between media violence and teen aggression, the data does not support that case.

# PART 7   YOUTH AND EARLY ADULTHOOD   267

**Issue 14.   Should We Use Medication to Deal With the Angst of College and Young Adulthood?   268**

YES:   **Harold S. Koplewicz,** from *More than Moody: Recognizing and Treating Adolescent Depression* (G.P. Putnam's Sons, 2002)   *270*

NO:   **Joli Jensen,** from "Let's Not Medicate Away Student Angst," *The Chronicle of Higher Education* (June 13, 2003)   *281*

Psychiatrist Harold S. Koplewicz asserts that antidepressants have a major role to play in reducing genuine distress in college students and young adults. Communications professor Joli Jensen argues that medicating young adults when they are facing the inevitable challenges of young adulthood primarily serves to diminish valuable developmental experiences.

**Issue 15.   Are College Graduates Unprepared for Adulthood and the World of Work?   286**

YES:   **Mel Levine,** from "College Graduates Aren't Ready for the Real World," *The Chronicle of Higher Education* (February 18, 2005)   *288*

NO:   **Frank F. Furstenberg, Jr. et al.,** from "Growing Up Is Harder to Do," *Contexts* (Summer 2004)   *293*

Professor of pediatrics, author, and child-rearing expert Mel Levine argues that contemporary colleges are producing a generation of young adults who are psychologically "unready" for entering adulthood and the world of work. Distinguished sociologist Frank Furstenberg and his research colleagues assert that major social changes have extended the transition to adulthood, and college graduates are the group most apt to cope with these social changes.

# PART 8   MIDDLE ADULTHOOD   303

**Issue 16.   Are Contemporary Adults Overlooking the Importance of Marriage as Part of Successful Development?   304**

YES:   **Linda J. Waite,** from "The Importance of Marriage Is Being Overlooked," *USA Today Magazine* (January 1999)   *306*

NO: **Dorian Solot and Marshall Miller,** from "Unmarried Bliss: Living Happily Ever After Doesn't Necessarily Require a Marriage License," *Providence Phoenix* (January 7–14, 1999) *313*

Sociologist Linda J. Waite presents extensive data to suggest that marriage provides innumerable benefits to adults that believe its declining popularity. Dorian Solot and Marshall Miller, directors of the Alternatives to Marriage Project, assert that the push to promote marriage does not make sense when adults find satisfaction in having the choice to pursue alternative lifestyles.

### Issue 17. Is One General Intelligence Factor Responsible for Career Success? 321

YES: **Linda S. Gottfredson,** from "Where and Why *g* Matters: Not a Mystery," *Human Performance* (vol. 15, 2002) *323*

NO: **Robert J. Sternberg and Jennifer Hedlund,** from "Practical Intelligence, *g*, and Work Psychology," *Human Performance* (vol. 15, 2002) *333*

Psychologist Linda S. Gottfredson asserts that one core intelligence factor akin to IQ—called *g*—is primarily responsible for being successful in the world of work. Professors of psychology and criminal justice Robert J. Sternberg and Jennifer Hedlund argue that efforts to establish one general intelligence factor as the cause of success are misguided because many different types of practical intelligence determine how well one does at work.

### Issue 18. Is Religion a Pure Good in Facilitating Well-Being During Adulthood? 344

YES: **David G. Myers,** from "Wanting More in an Age of Plenty," *Christianity Today* (April 2000) *346*

NO: **Julie Juola Exline,** from "Stumbling Blocks on the Religious Road: Fractured Relationships, Nagging Vices, and the Inner Struggle to Believe," *Psychological Inquiry* (vol. 13, 2002) *355*

Psychologist and author David G. Myers asserts that religion is an anecdote to the discontent many adults feel despite incredible relative material wealth. Professor of psychology Julia Juola Exline asserts that research suggesting religion to be a pure good for adult development neglects to account for the fact that it can also be a source of significant sadness, stress, and confusion.

## PART 9 LATER ADULTHOOD 371

### Issue 19. Can We Universally Define "Successful Aging"? 372

YES: **John W. Rowe and Robert L. Kahn,** from "Successful Aging," *The Gerontologist* (vol. 37, 1997) *374*

NO: **Martha B. Holstein and Meredith Minkler,** from "Self, Society, and the 'New Gerontology'," *The Gerontologist* (vol. 43, 2003) *383*

With a drastically increasing population of the elderly, professors of medicine John W. Rowe and Robert L. Kahn suggest that a unified model of healthy aging is necessary to guide work with the elderly. Martha B. Holstein and Meredith Minkler, professors of religion and public health, respectively, counter that a unified model of successful aging is based on particular values and assumptions that may not be fair to marginalized populations.

## Issue 20.  Is Anti-Aging Technology a Cause for Societal Concern?  394

YES:  **Chris Hackler,** from "Troubling Implications of Doubling the Human Lifespan," *Generations* (Winter 2001/2002)  *396*

NO:  **Ronald Klatz,** from "Anti-Aging Medicine: Resounding, Independent Support for Expansion of an Innovative Medical Specialty," *Generations* (Winter 2001/2002)  *403*

Chris Hackler, professor of medical humanities, argues that advances in medical technology raise as many dilemmas as they solve. If we were able to extend the life span for many years, both society and individuals would face dramatic new challenges. Ronald Klatz, a medical doctor promoting anti-aging technology, asserts that any technology to extend the life span will be both welcome and safe.

Contributors  409
Index  415

# Introduction

## Thinking About Change

The study of life span development centers on a question of great intuitive interest: Do people ever really change? Can an introverted child who is full of worry become a confident and composed adult? Might an apathetic student go on to become successful in the world of work? Do relationships with those we care about inevitably shift across the years?

These types of questions weighed heavily on my mind many years ago when I was a 17 year old preparing to leave the only home I had ever known to attend college. On the night I was leaving, I rode to the airport with my father, a well-educated and thoughtful man. We were rushing so that I could board an overnight flight from the West Coast to the East Coast, bringing with me all my worldly possessions in two suitcases. As with so many adolescents going off to college, I was both excited and overwhelmed by possibilities. My imagination flowed with ideas about who and what I might become, and most of those ideas centered on a hope that I could change for the better. I loved the idea of self-improvement; I was devoted to developing into a "better person." As I talked with my father, expressing my hopes in anxious tones, he listened calmly. Finally, when we arrived at the gate and it was time for me to board my plane, my father looked at me casually:

"You know, in my experience, people don't really change."

I was stunned.

From his perspective as a mature adult, using the wisdom accumulated through his life, my father told me that while people might change the things they do, the places they live, the details of their daily routine, they do not change who they are in deep and substantive ways. With youthful idealism, I firmly disagreed. I felt deeply that people could change across the life span, so much so that understanding aspects of that change became my life's work. Now, as a developmental psychologist, I've studied, read, and investigated many aspects of how people do and don't change. And in looking back, I have to admit that in ways my father was right: In certain ways, people don't change. But the story is much more complicated and wonderful than that. And that story is told through the study of life span development: the study of patterns in human thought, feelings, and behavior in relation to particular ages, with general attention to change over time.

The study of life span development makes clear that even the continuities in life—the things that do not change—take place in shifting contexts: changing social environments, changing physical capacities, changing psychological perspectives. As such, I've come to appreciate, and be fascinated by, the necessary interaction of change and continuity in people through their lives—how can people be both the same and different? That question involves inherent contradictions and inherent controversy, which suggests that the study of life span development is particularly well-suited to the nature of this book: It advances by taking conflicting perspectives on complex and important issues regarding change and continuity through life.

# History of the Study of Life Span Development

Historically, the question of how people do (or do not) change through their lives has evoked opposing perspectives. Many ancient societies assumed that people were created with a predetermined character that was destined through some supernatural power. Yet those beliefs were tempered by the realization that what people experience matters. Parents, societies, and philosophers have long negotiated between an assumption that people have an inherent developmental destiny, and the knowledge that what happens to people in the social world can alter that destiny.

While these positions have an extensive history, in academic circles they are most commonly identified with seventeenth and eighteenth century European philosophers Jean-Jacques Rousseau and John Locke. Rousseau suggested that infants were "noble savages" born with an inherent nature that is only corrupted by society. Locke, in contrast, is known for the famous claim that people come into the world as a *tabula rasa,* or blank slate, to be shaped entirely by experience. In a recent book about the history of child-rearing advice in America, Ann Hulbert argues this opposition plays itself out in many subsequent historical epochs: One group argues that people have potent natural dispositions guiding development with a strong hand, while another group asserts that people develop entirely through social experiences. The recurring nature of this opposition shows one way in which those who are concerned with life span development have always been "taking sides."

Taking a scientific, rather than philosophical or parental, approach to understanding development has only become a widespread endeavor in recent centuries. In fact, the idea of childhood as a distinct life span stage, rather than as just adulthood in miniature, may be a relatively recent invention. In a famous and controversial book titled *Centuries of Childhood,* French historian Philippe Aries argued Western societies only began treating children as different from adults in the fifteenth and sixteenth centuries, and such treatment did not become commonplace until the nineteenth and twentieth centuries. This theory has generated strong reactions, with many scholars responding to say that childhood has always been associated with distinct characteristics. Nevertheless, the idea that contemporary perspectives on childhood are historically exceptional has much support: The transition to worlds of adulthood with work and responsibility happens later than ever. Partially as a result, we now take for granted that people advance through different stages of life. Further, scholars and scientists from diverse fields of study recognize that the life span needs to be understood within the context of those stages.

So what are the stages? That question turns out to be more complicated than many people expect. While we are always talking about "children," the "youth," "middle-age," or the "elderly," the characteristics of such stages are not entirely distinct. Much of how we understand these stages depends on earlier schemes.

Perhaps the most famous such scheme was presented by Sigmund Freud. In the late nineteenth century, Freud provoked and dismayed Western society by proposing that unconscious experiences in very early childhood, often of a sexual nature, formed personality throughout the rest of the life span. Freud further asserted that the formative experiences cohered around different foci at different ages: Infants were concerned with oral gratification (being able to suck and bite), toddlers with anal functions and toilet training, young children with phallic organs (learning about gender roles), and teenagers with genital functions (experiencing puberty and a blossoming sexuality). For Freud, the way a person negotiated those foci influenced them for the rest of their lives. While there is a general consensus that Freud placed far too much emphasis on sexuality as the axis of all development, his theory contributed much. We now take for granted that early experiences shape later life, and we recognize that those experiences occur in a stagewise progression.

While Freud focused on personality development, another influential scientist working in the early and middle part of the twentieth century turned scholarly attention to stages of cognitive development: The Swiss psychologist Jean Piaget virtually founded modern developmental psychology through his recognition that the way children think progresses in orderly patterns. Piaget based his provocative insight on rigorous observations suggesting that children's cognitive functioning (the way they think) develops naturally through a series of detached steps. In a way, Piaget provided enduring support for stage models, suggesting that children's thinking is not just less sophisticated than that of adults—it is qualitatively different. Thus, when children make assumptions about toy dolls being alive, or about objects existing only when they can see them, they are not making "errors" but instead are demonstrating patterns of thought that meaningfully represent their age. Piaget's work is still the standard for much research in child development, though some of his specific claims have become controversial. As such, several issues in this book explicitly reference the work and legacy of Piaget.

A third giant in the history of the study of life span development was a student of Freud's named Erik Erikson. In the middle part of the twentieth century, Erikson took Freud's basic insights about personality, built on the increasing popularity of stage models for the life span, and outlined an influential framework for understanding life span development—a framework that guides the organization of this book. Erikson's model of the life span had two major advantages over previous models. First, in contrast to Freud, Erikson reduced the emphasis on sexuality, focusing on psychosocial challenges rather than psychosexual stages. Second, in contrast to both Freud and Piaget, Erikson asserted that developmental stages continue throughout life, rather than ending after adolescence.

Although this now seems somewhat obvious—of course adults continue to develop—for much of the twentieth century, scholars paid little attention to anything other than child development. The implicit assumption was that the life span included a period of rapid growth during childhood, a period of decline at the end of life, and was largely at stasis in the many years of adulthood. In recent decades, however, scholars have recognized that a great deal of patterned development and change occur during the long years of adulthood.

Finally, Erik Erikson was influential because he recognized the "biopsycho-social" nature of life span development. While biology, psychology, and society are often studied separately, biological factors (such as physical health, sexual maturation, and genetic predispositions) interact with psychological factors (such as personality, attitudes, and cognitive appraisals) that interact with social factors (such as schools, peer networks, the media, and cultural meaning systems) to craft our individual lives. Some of the issues addressed in this book involve all three of these types of influences, while some emphasize one or the other. Overall, however, the collection of issues as a whole represents diverse and interacting influences.

Modern advances in technology and research methods allow us to study biological, psychological, and sociological influences on the life span with increasing depth and accuracy. But the contemporary issues covered in this book still rely on some fundamental insights from history, and as such are organized by an idea shared by all the major scholars of life span development: different ages associate with meaningfully different patterns of thought and behavior. Beyond that shared idea, however, no stage model proposed by any one leading scholar is perfect: The nature and definition of the stages remain controversial. Perhaps the only thing about stages of the life span that we can say with certainty is that they are only as meaningful as the society in which they are used. Thus, it is important to consider the stages of life span in their own historical and cultural context.

## Stages of the Life Span in Context

Representations of the life span as a series of stages exist across centuries and across cultural traditions. These representations are interesting to consider both for their diversity and for their similarity. There is something universal about patterns of development, but there are also tremendous local differences in how those patterns look.

From an Eastern tradition, stages are represented in a parable about how Confucius, who lived from 551–479 BC, reflected on his life:

> At 15 I set my heart upon learning.
> At 30 I had planted my feet firmly upon the ground.
> At 40 I no longer suffered from perplexities.
> At 50 I knew what were the biddings of heaven.
> At 60 I heard them with docile ear.
> At 70 I could follow the dictates of my own heart; for what I desired no longer overstepped the boundaries of right.

From classic Western literature, Shakespeare articulated the life span in his play "As You Like It" as different ages of man:

> At first the infant, Mewling and puking in the nurse's arms.
> And then the whining school-boy, with his satchel
> And shining morning face, creeping like snail
> Unwillingly to school.

And then the lover,
Sighing like furnace, with a woeful ballad
Made to his mistress' eyebrow.
Then a soldier,
Full of strange oaths and bearded like the pard,
Jealous in honour, sudden and quick in quarrel,
Seeking the bubble reputation
Even in the cannon's mouth.
And then the justice,
In fair round belly with good capon lined,
With eyes severe and beard of formal cut,
Full of wise saws and modern instances;
And so he plays his part.
The sixth age shifts
Into the lean and slipper'd pantaloon,
With spectacles on nose and pouch on side,
His youthful hose, well saved, a world too wide
For his shrunk shank; and his big manly voice,
Turning again toward childish treble, pipes
And whistles in his sound.
Last scene of all,
That ends this strange eventful history,
Is second Childishness and mere oblivion,
Sans teeth, sans eyes, sans taste, sans everything.

From one of the great books of religion, "The Sayings of the Fathers" in the *Talmud* set out the life span as marked by specific ages:

5 years is the age for reading;
10 for Mishnah (the laws);
13 for the Commandments (moral reasoning);
15 for Gemara (Talmudic discussions—abstract reasoning);
18 for Hupa (wedding canopy);
20 for seeking a livelihood;
30 for attaining full strength;
40 for understanding;
50 for giving counsel;
60 for becoming an elder;
70 for white hair;
80 for Gevurah (new, special strength of age);
90 for being bent under the weight of the years;
100 for being as if already dead and passed away from the world

And finally modern society, beyond academia, we represent the life span in advertising and different consumer choices—as in advertisements for Farmers' Insurance suggesting that the stages of the life span focus on:

Buying a Car,
Buying a Home,
Getting Married,
Having a Baby,
Beginning Driver,

Sending a Child to College,
Starting a Business,
Planning your Retirement.

Regardless of the source or the historical period, most people find something that resonates in all of these representations. Yet history also teaches us that stages are not universal; in fact, the life span could easily be represented simply as one continuous stage. There are, however, several reasons that dividing the life span into multiple stages proves useful. For one thing, the life span is extraordinarily complex, and categorizing information into smaller groups helps make it feel more manageable and less daunting. Likewise, learning about ordered change that seems consistent across different people and groups helps to make sense of what is fundamental in development. If, for example, we find that the teen years are tumultuous and stressful in all societies, then we can reasonably suspect that there is something fundamental about development during that age.

As it turns out, in the case of adolescence, many components of development vary significantly in different societies—adolescence is not tumultuous for all teens around the world, and thus it seems that the "storm and stress" of adolescence is at least partially a social and cultural construction. In fact, even the definition of stages is not as simple as it might first appear. Adolescence, for example, was not considered a major stage of the life span until the end of the nineteenth century, when the broadening of educational opportunities created a longer transition between childhood and adulthood. In contemporary Western society, some scholars have proposed that the continuing expansion of higher education and longer transition to independent adulthood has created another "new stage" of something like "emerging adulthood." In some senses, then, the very nature of the stages in the life span is controversial.

Even placing the term "life span" in front of the word "development" generates disagreement. The notion of a life span suggests a progressive and constrained period of time that some scholars feel unfairly minimizes the disjointed and social nature of development. Thus, some people prefer the term "life-course" as more accurately representing the twists and turns of development that necessarily occur in a social world. Still others prefer the term "life-cycle" as more accurately representing the sequential process that brings people through a full circle of growth and decline.

Ultimately, despite viable alternatives, this book is organized into nine parts. The first part covers general issues in the study of life span development, and the other eight parts invoke a basic set of eight life span stages: prenatal, infancy, early childhood, middle childhood, adolescence, youth and early adulthood, middle adulthood, and later adulthood. The issues discussed in relation to these stages can, however, be considered equally topically. Although there are multiple ways of topically organizing the issues in this book, several possible examples include:

- Focusing on the topic of cognitive development and intellectual ability by combining Issue 7 (regarding symbolic representation in infants), Issue 8 (regarding the "Mozart Effect"), and Issue 17 (regarding intelligence and work success).

- Focusing on gender differences in development by combining Issue 3 (regarding innate gender differences) and Issue 12 (regarding how males and females handle adolescence).
- Focusing on biological and physiological influences on developmental outcomes by combining Issue 1 (regarding the relative influence of genes and culture upon development), Issue 4 (regarding prenatal drug use), Issue 14 (regarding medication for depression during college), and Issue 20 (regarding technological enhancement of the life span).

# Fundamental Questions

Regardless of how the issues are organized, several questions underlie the topics in this book. First is a question that runs across the social sciences, but that is particularly relevant to thinking about development: the question of nature or nurture. Is life span development more a product of natural and biological dispositions, or is development the result of nurturing experiences in the world? This question has become particularly contentious with the advent of modern technology that allows researchers to map genetic codes and produce detailed images of mental activity. It is clear that human thought, feeling, and behavior all originate in a biological organ: the brain. Yet scientists are actively debating what aspect of the brain activity that guide such thought, feeling, and behavior comes from biological programs and what comes from learned concepts. It is obvious that we are products of both nature and nurture, but the necessary balance for life span development is the subject of tremendous controversy. This question is implicit in most of the issues in this book, while being explicitly addressed in Issue 1 (regarding the relative influence of culture and genes), Issue 7 (regarding the innate ability of symbolic representation), and Issue 11 (regarding the nature of attention deficit disorder).

A second fundamental question relates to the role of culture. While cultural differences and diversity are genuine, it is not clear whether culture fundamentally alters patterns of development. Can we apply research about human development in a city in the United States to human development in rural India? Could we even apply research from urban cities to the rural United States? Could we apply knowledge equally to males and females? Implicit in many studies of life span development is the idea that there is a "best" pattern of development. But what if there is no one best pattern of development, only patterns of development that are more or less appropriate to different cultural settings and groups? Does that invalidate the effort of finding general principles of life span development? This question is fundamental to most of the issues in this book, being directly addressed in Issue 2 (regarding the influence of parents on development), Issue 6 (regarding the importance of infancy), Issue 19 (regarding diversity in "successful aging"), and Issue 12 (regarding gender and risk during adolescence).

A third fundamental question fits best with the issue raised at the start of this Introduction: Do people really change? As noted earlier, development is a process of both continuity and change. Yet, the above models of stages in the life span suggest that each stage is a discrete entity. But are they? Where does one stage begin and another end? When teaching about the life span, I often ask my traditionally college-aged undergraduate students whether they are adults—they usually are not entirely sure. They are kind of adults, kind of adolescents, kind of kids. So when do they become adults? Do they just wake up one day and there they are? Of course not; becoming an adult is a slow and gradual process. Further, the very idea that what happens to us as children has a direct impact on how we turn out in later life suggests a continuous process of development. If it were not, we wouldn't care so much about the quality of schools, parenting, and programs for children.

Yet when we step back, we can all acknowledge that there are clear differences between children and adults, and between younger adults and older adults. Those differences are not just physical; there are differences in the way people think and the contexts in which they live their lives. The question of whether it is best to conceptualize the life span as one continuous process, or as a series of discrete stages, is particularly important in our increasingly specialized society where products, services, and interactions are guided by understandings of people at specific ages. The question also influences numerous scholarly debates, and as such it orients several of the issues in this book including Issue 6 (regarding the developmental importance of infancy), Issue 9 (regarding academic skills for at-risk preschool children), and Issue 15 (regarding the preparation of college graduates for adulthood).

## The Uses of Controversy

The fundamental questions for the study of life span development continuously manifest themselves in different and specific topical controversies. While this process can be occasionally confusing and frustrating to those who want to know the "right" answers about development, controversy is how our knowledge of the life span advances. Over time, controversies spark knowledge and ideas that are central to all of our lives. There are several prominent historical examples of how this works.

One example comes from the start of the life span: What happens to newborn babies? Prior to advances in medical technology during the twentieth century, an extraordinarily high number of babies died before reaching their first birthday (sadly, this is still the case in many parts of the developing world—but that is a slightly different issue). When the germ theory of disease became prominent, doctors and scientists realized that inadequate hygiene and unnecessary exposure to germs caused many infant deaths. In a well-intentioned effort to keep babies safe and healthy, many hospitals started keeping babies in sterile conditions separate from human contact. Over time, such efforts were extended to children born to mothers who were considered deviant, such as those convicted of crimes. The logic in all these cases was that of contagion: Certain types of human contact were too risky for vulnerable infants.

Fortunately, this logic was controversial, and researchers studying the earliest stages of life began to challenge the new scientifically based practices. Studies of children removed at birth from their mothers demonstrated remarkable physical, social, and psychological deficits. Researchers began to hypothesize that something about human contact, and forming an attachment bond, was virtually essential to healthy human development. For many years, controversy raged; with one side suggesting that infants needed to be kept safely away from excessive contact, and the other suggesting that human contact was exactly what made infants safe. Eventually the evidence became overwhelming in favor of the latter position; the debate promoted scholarship demonstrating irrefutably that babies have an innate need for attachment, contact, and simple touch. Without any controversy, we would not possess that essential knowledge.

In a more contemporary example, recent decades have brought increasing attention to the role of self-esteem in life span development. Due to a confluence of historical and social conditions, the idea that feeling good about one's self is a foundation for healthy development received wisdom in the 1970s and 1980s. Numerous social service agencies, schools, activity programs, and therapists made promoting self-esteem the centerpiece of efforts to facilitate healthy development. While self-esteem is still extremely popular— as it is indeed nice to feel good about one' s self—scholars have generated controversy by raising important questions about the evidence for self-esteem as a cure for social and personal ills. Despite massive research attention, the evidence that self-esteem alone provides a direct foundation for healthy development is sorely lacking. Although a virtual industry of self-esteem promoters has resisted the challenge, the controversy continues to have important implications for schools, counselors, parents, and programs. The question of whether there is still a role for promoting self-esteem as part of healthy development is still at play (and as such is included as Issue 10 in this book), but the controversy has generated a much more nuanced and realistic perspective on how and why feeling good about one's self might matter.

In both of these examples, and in most of the issues discussed in this book, controversy provides useful knowledge when scholars and individuals combine a genuine interest in facilitating healthy life span development with a concern for tangible evidence. In the case of infant attachment and touch, both sides cared about healthy babies, and both sides deeply believed their side was right. In the case of self-esteem and positive development, both sides care about reducing social ills, and both sides believe in what they are doing. Ultimately, however, resolving these issues, and resolving other controversies in social science, requires intelligent interpretations of evidence that goes beyond taken-for-granted beliefs.

Our taken-for-granted beliefs are strong and pervasive, partially because many of the issue questions in this book relate to issues people confront in their daily lives; we are all experienced in our own process of development. As such, when considering these questions, it is natural to have instinctive reactions and beliefs. The material in this book will, however, be most useful when readers get beyond initial beliefs to carefully consider the points and the evidence. In fact, when I teach about these issues, I do not allow my students to make statements that start with "I believe. . ." or "in my opinion. . .". While I value the importance of students' beliefs and opinions, the controversies that we study must be evaluated primarily in regard to available evidence.

Evidence is the foundation of scientific understanding, even though it may contradict deeply help beliefs. But much educational value lies in the space between evidence and beliefs: I hope that both my students, and those who read this book, are able to learn what scholars know and apply that knowledge to form educated positions on issues of great importance in contemporary society.

# Conclusion

Ultimately, focusing on evidence and carefully considering intelligent positions from all viewpoints is how I have dealt with the challenge posed by my father when I was starting my own college experience: concluding that people do indeed change. While my own approach has focused on developmental psychology, the evidence and intelligent positions in this book come from diverse sources because the study of life span development takes many perspectives. A partial list of the academic disciplines that both contribute to and draw from the study of life span development might include psychology, sociology, anthropology, education, social work, biology, history, cognitive science, geriatrics, and pediatrics. Thus, the readings and positions in this book represent quality work from many fields. Clear and quality thinking about controversial issues is not limited to any particular academic approach.

As you consider the issues in this book, reflecting on the questions raised in this Introduction may facilitate your own clear and quality thinking. Ask yourself, for example, about how each issue relates to what you know or imagine from your own experience regarding each stage of the life span. Ask yourself how much nature and nurture play a role in influencing the different developmental issues. Ask yourself about the social and policy implications of taking specific positions on each issue. And keep in mind that vexing question raised by so many people starting to learn about life span development: Do people really change?

Seriously studying these issues has certainly helped me change: I've become a better scholar of life span development, and my hope is that readers will have a similar experience. I'd like for readers to experience some small level of change in their own development by earnestly confronting the different sides of these controversial issues. By keeping in mind the history of the field, the useful but historically particular nature of defining life span stages, the fundamental questions underlying most controversies, and the value of controversy for advancing knowledge, readers should indeed be able to experience change firsthand.

# *On the Internet . . .*

## Developmental Psychology

This Web site provides academic resources and links related to developmental psychology.

`http://www.psy.pdx.edu/PsiCafe/Areas/Developmental/`

## American Psychological Association

The American Psychological Association is a general resource for many of the issues most pertinent to developmental psychology and life span development.

`http://www.apa.org/`

## Nature vs. Nurture

An overview of the debate on whether nature or nurture—culture or genes—is more influential in life span development.

`http://en.wikipedia.org/wiki/Nature_versus_nurture`

## American Academy of Pediatrics

The American Academy of Pediatrics is a professional organization focused on the health of children. Their Web site provides featured articles, books, and other reference materials on children's health topics.

`http://www.aap.org/`

## Do Parents Matter?

This Web site provides extensive links related to the controversial argument that parents do not matter as much in development as most people think.

`http://home.att.net/~xchar/tna/`

## Future of Children

Future of Children is a digital journal, providing an example of developmental research aimed at promoting effective policies and programs for families and children.

`http://www.futureofchildren.org/`

# PART 1

# General Issues in the Study of Life Span Development

*A*lthough this book organizes development into a series of stages, several issues central to understanding the life span are not exclusive to one particular age. These issues relate to larger questions about the nature of development: What forces and characteristics shape us into the people we become? The issues in this section deal with this larger question and provide a foundation for thinking about specific stages by directly addressing the role of culture, genes, parents, and sex/gender in shaping the thoughts, feelings, behaviors, and experiences that make us human.

- Does Culture and Environment Influence Life Span Development More Than Our Genes?

- Are Peers More Important Than Parents During the Process of Development?

- Do Significant Innate Differences Influence the Success of Males and Females?

# ISSUE 1

## Does Culture and Environment Influence Human Development More Than Our Genes?

**YES: Paul Ehrlich and Marcus Feldman,** from "Genes and Cultures: What Creates Our Behavioral Phenome?" *Current Anthropology* (February 2003)

**NO: Gary Marcus,** from "Making the Mind: Why We've Misunderstood the Nature-Nurture Debate," *Boston Review* (December 2003/January 2004)

### ISSUE SUMMARY

**YES:** Stanford University professors of biology Paul Ehrlich and Marcus Feldman argue that human behavior exhibits such complexity that genetic programs simply can't explain the way people develop.

**NO:** Psychologist and researcher Gary Marcus asserts that research clearly demonstrates how a relatively small number of genes influence our environmental learning by "cascading" to determine the paths of our behavioral development.

Perhaps the most central question in the study of life span development is whether nature or nurture exerts more influence on our developing thoughts, feelings, and behavior. Even in daily life, we regularly wonder about people—do they act that way because of things in their experience (nurture), or is it just the way they were born (nature)? This debate takes many different forms, and it underlies many of the important topics of study within life span development.

Most reasonable people agree that both nature and nurture shape development. Thus, the debate is mostly about the relative influence of each: Does nature overwhelm nurture, or does nurture trump nature? The pendulum of popular opinion has tended to swing back and forth between trusting nature or emphasizing nurture.

In past centuries, people were assumed to come into the world with their character predetermined—often by divine forces. Thus, the work of development was simply to provide people appropriate social roles. In the early part of the twentieth century, as life span development became a viable field of study in the social sciences, experts began to claim that parents, adults, and communities could shape developmental experiences into any form—for better or worse. This type of thinking may have reached a public apex in the 1950s and 1960s when powerful psychological theories such as behaviorism and social trends such as feminism gave rise to the idea that people were infinitely malleable—nurture could even shape something as seemingly basic as the differences between men and women.

With advanced technology and research methods, the pendulum seems to have again swung in favor of nature. With the ability to identify individual genes and image activity in the brain, scientists have made regular claims about how diverse aspects of behavior and development—everything from political affiliation to sexual behavior—is controlled by innate biology.

With regard to behavior, this argument has been made particularly strongly by "evolutionary psychologists," who explore ways that biological adaptations in our evolutionary past may have programmed developmental trends. The nature argument is also supported by neuroscientists who use sophisticated research and animal models to investigate the way biology shapes our brain. These lines of research have proven simultaneously very popular and very controversial. The controversy arises because many feel that life span development is simply too diverse and complicated to ever be precisely dissected.

Evolutionary psychology, for example, depends on guesses about what life was like for our distant ancestors. This is something we can never know for certain. Likewise, much research in neuroscience depends on experiments with animals that are not possible to do with humans—yet many argue that human language, consciousness, and culture makes us a distinctive species in the animal kingdom.

In the first of the following selections, renown biologists Paul Ehrlich and Marcus Feldman argue that biological determinism does not make biological sense. Drawing from the recent mapping of the human genome, they claim there are simply too few genes and too much variation in human development. They take particular aim at claims that gender differences are biological, which has been an important part of this debate because gender differences often seem to persist despite diverse environments. Ehrlich and Feldman, however, claim that in looking at the grand scheme of history, the clear variations in behavior patterns belie a biological explanation.

In contrast, Gary Marcus claims that the dominant influence of genes on development has only become more clear in recent research. While acknowledging that genes and the environment always interact, Marcus draws on extensive research with animals demonstrating that small genetic manipulations have dramatic influences on behavior. He also responds to the claim that there are not enough genes to control complex behaviors by insisting that relationships between genes and behavior don't have to be one-to-one.

Paul Ehrlich and
Marcus Feldman

 **YES**

# Genes and Cultures: What Creates Our Behavioral Phenome?

The recent publication of the first draft of the human genome has brought to public attention the relationship between two concepts, genotype and phenotype—a relationship that had previously been discussed largely by academics. The genotype of an organism is encoded in the DNA that is held in chromosomes and other structures inside its cells. The phenotype is what we are able to observe about that organism's biochemistry, physiology, morphology, and behaviors. We will use the term "phenome" to circumscribe a set of phenotypes whose properties and variability we wish to study. Our focus will be on that part of the human phenome that is defined by behaviors and especially on the behavioral phenome's connection with the human genome.

Our understanding of human behavioral traits has evolved; explanations of the control of those traits offered 50 years ago differ from those most common today. In prewar decades genetic determinism—the idea that genes are destiny—had enormous influence on public policy in many countries: on American immigration and racial policies, Swedish sterilization programs, and, of course, Nazi laws on racial purity. Much of this public policy was built on support from biological, medical, and social scientists, but after Hitler's genocidal policies it was no longer politically correct to focus on putative hereditary differences. The fading of genetic determinism was an understandable reaction to Nazism and related racial, sexual, and religious prejudices which had long been prevalent in the United States and elsewhere. Thus, after World War II, it became the norm in American academia to consider all of human behavior as originating in the environment—in the way people were raised and the social contexts in which they lived.

Gradually, though, beginning in the 1960s, books like Robert Ardrey's *Territorial Imperative* and Desmond Morris's *The Naked Ape* began proposing explanations for human behaviors that were biologically reductionist and essentially genetic. Their extreme hereditarian bias may have been stimulated by the rapid progress at that time in understanding of the role of DNA, which spurred interest in genetics in both scientists and the public. But perhaps no publication had broader effect in reestablishing genetic credibility in the behavioral sciences than Arthur Jensen's article "How Much Can We Boost IQ?"

Although roundly criticized by quantitative geneticists and shown to be based on the fraudulent data of Sir Cyril Burt, Jensen's work established a tradition that attempts to allocate to genetics a considerable portion of the variation in such human behaviors as for whom we vote, how religious we are, how likely we are to take risks, and, of course, measured IQ and school performance. This tradition is alive and well today.

Within the normal range of human phenotypic variation, including commonly occurring diseases, the role of genetics remains a matter of controversy even as more is revealed about variation at the level of DNA. Here we would like to reexamine the issue of genetics and human behavior in light of the enormous interest in the Human Genome Project, the expansion of behavioral genetics as described above, and the recent proliferation of books emphasizing the genetic programming of every behavior from rape to the learning of grammar. The philosopher Helena Cronin and her coeditor, Oliver Curry, tell us in the introduction to Yale University Press's "Darwinism Today" series that "Darwinian ideas . . . are setting today's intellectual agenda." In the *New York Times*, Nicholas Wade has written that human genes contain the "behavioral instructions" for "instincts to slaughter or show mercy, the contexts for love and hatred, the taste for obedience or rebellion—they are the determinants of human nature."

## Genes, Cultures, and Behavior

It is incontrovertible that human beings are a product of evolution, but with respect to behavior that evolutionary process involves chance, natural selection, and, especially in the case of human beings, transmission and alteration of a body of extragenetic information called "culture." Cultural evolution, a process very different from genetic evolution by natural selection, has played a central role in producing our behaviors.

This is not to say that genes are uninvolved in human behavior. *Every* aspect of a person's phenome is a product of interaction between genome and environment. An obvious example of genetic involvement in the behavioral phenome is the degree to which most people use vision to orient themselves—in doing everything from hitting a baseball to selecting new clothes for their children. This is because we have evolved genetically to be "sight animals"—our dominant perceptual system is vision, with hearing coming in second. Had we, like dogs, evolved more sophisticated chemical detection, we might behave very differently in response to the toxic chemicals in our environment. The information in our DNA required to produce the basic morphology and physiology that make sight so important to us has clearly been molded by natural selection. And the physical increase in human brain size, which certainly involved a response to natural selection (although the precise environmental factors causing this selection remain something of a mystery, has allowed us to evolve language, a high level of tool use, the ability to plan for the future, and a wide range of other behaviors not seen in other animals.

Thus at the very least, genetic evolution both biased our ability to perceive the world and gave us the capacity to develop a vast culture. But the long-running nature-versus-nurture debate is not about sight versus smell. It is about the degree to which differences in today's human behavioral patterns from person to person, group to group, and society to society are influenced by genetic differences, that is, are traceable to differences in human genetic endowments. Do men "naturally" want to mate with as many women as possible while women "naturally" want to be more cautious in choosing their copulatory partners? Is there a "gay gene"? Are human beings "innately" aggressive? Are differences in educational achievement or income "caused" by differences in genes? And are people of all groups genetically programmed to be selfish? A critical social issue to keep in mind throughout our discussion is what the response of our society would be if we knew the answer to these questions. Two related schools of thought take the view that genetic evolution explains much of the human behavioral phenome; they are known as evolutionary psychology and behavioral genetics.

# Evolutionary Psychology

Evolutionary psychology claims that many human behaviors became universally fixed as a result of natural selection acting during the environment of evolutionary adaptation, essentially the Pleistocene. A shortcoming of this argument, as emphasized by the anthropologist Robert Foley (1995–96), lies in the nonexistence of such an environment. Our ancestors lived in a wide diversity of habitats, and the impacts of the many environmental changes (e.g., glaciations) over the past million years differed geographically among their varied surroundings. Evolutionary psychologists also postulate that natural selection produced modules ("complex structures that are functionally organized for processing information") in the brain that "tell" us such things as which individuals are likely to cheat, which mates are likely to give us the best or most offspring, and how to form the best coalitions. These brain "modules," which are assumed to be biological entities fixed in humans by evolution, also have other names often bestowed on them by the same writers, such as "computational machines," "decision-making algorithms," "specialized systems," "inference engines," and "reasoning mechanisms." The research claims of evolutionary psychology have been heavily criticized by, among others, colleagues in psychology.

Those critics are correct. There is a general tendency for evolutionary psychologists vastly to overestimate how much of human behavior is primarily traceable to biological universals that are reflected in our genes. One reason for this overestimation is the ease with which a little evolutionary story can be invented to explain almost any observed pattern of behavior. For example, it seems logical that natural selection would result in the coding of a fear of snakes and spiders into our DNA, as the evolutionary psychologist Steven Pinker thinks. But while Pinker may have genes that make him fear snakes, as the evolutionist Jared Diamond points out, such genes are clearly lacking in New Guinea natives. As Diamond says, "If there is any single place in the world where we might expect an innate fear of snakes among native peoples, it would be in New Guinea, where one-third or more of the snake species are poisonous, and certain non-poisonous constrictor snakes are sufficiently big to be dangerous." Yet there is no sign of innate fear of snakes or spiders among the indigenous people, and children regularly "capture large spiders, singe off the legs and hairs, and eat the bodies. The people there laugh at the idea of an inborn phobia about snakes, and account for the fear in Europeans as a result of their stupidity in being unable to distinguish which snakes might be dangerous." Furthermore, there is reason to believe that fear of snakes in other primates is largely learned as well.

Another example is the set of predictions advanced by Bruce Ellis about the mating behavior that would be found in a previously unknown culture. The first five characteristics that "the average woman in this culture will seek . . . in her ideal mate," he predicts, are:

1. He will be dependable, emotionally stable and mature, and kind/considerate toward her.
2. He will be generous. He may communicate a spirit of caring through a willingness to share time and whatever commodities are valued in this culture with the woman in question.
3. He will be ambitious and perceived by the woman in question as clever or intelligent.
4. He will be genuinely interested in the woman in question, and she in him. He may express his interest through displays of concern for her well-being.
5. He will have a strong social presence and be well liked and respected by others. He will possess a strong sense of efficacy, confidence, and self-respect.

Evolutionary theory does not support such predictions, even if an "average woman" could be defined. First of all, it would be no small developmental trick genetically to program detailed, different, and *independent* reproductive strategies into modules in male and female brains. Those brains, after all are minor variants of the same incredibly complex structures, and, furthermore, the degree to which they are organized into modules is far from clear. If the women in the unknown culture actually chose mates meeting Ellis's criteria, a quite sufficient alternative evolutionary explanation would be that women (simultaneously with men) have evolved big brains, are not stupid, and respond to the norms of their cultures. Scientifically, the notion that the detailed attributes of desirable mates must be engraved in our genetic makeup is without basis, especially in light of the enormous cultural differences in sexual preferences.

For any culture, Ellis's evolutionary arguments would require that in past populations of women there were DNA-based differences that made some more likely to choose in those ways and others more likely to seek mates with other characteristics. And those that chose as Ellis predicts would have to have borne and raised more children that survived to reproduce than those with other preferences. Might, for example, a woman who married a stingy male who kept her barefoot and pregnant out-reproduce the wife of a generous and considerate mate? That is the way genetic evolution changes the characteristics of populations over time: by some genetic variants' out-reproducing others. When that happens, we say that natural selection has occurred. But, unfortunately, there are no data that speak to whether there is (or was) genetic variation in human mate preferences—variation in, say, ability to evaluate specifically whether a potential mate is "ambitious"—upon which selection could be based. And there are no data for any population showing that women who seek those characteristics in their sexual partners are more successful reproductively—are represented by more children in the subsequent generation—than women who seek husbands with other characteristics. Ellis is simply confusing the preferences of women he knows in his society with evolutionary fitness. . . .

## What Does Determine the Behavioral Phenome?

Geneticists know that a large portion of the behavioral phenome must be programmed into the brain by factors in the environment, including the internal environment in which the fetus develops and, most important, the cultural environment in which human beings spend their entire lives. Behavioral scientists know, for instance, that many dramatic personality differences *must* be traced to environmental influences. Perhaps the most important reason to doubt that genetic variation accounts for a substantial portion of observed differences in human behavior is simply that we lack an extensive enough hereditary apparatus to do the job—that we have a "gene shortage." To what extent could genes control the production of these differences?

It is important to remember that behaviors are the results of charge changes that occur in our network of neurons, the specialized cells that make up our nervous system. Behaviors are ultimately under some degree of control in the brain. Neuron networks are the locus of the memories that are also important to our behavior. That genes can control some general patterns is unquestioned; they are obviously involved in the construction of our brains. They might therefore also build in the potential for experience to affect a large part of the details involved in the neural circuitry. But they cannot be controlling our individual behavioral choices.

Human beings have only three times as many genes as have fruit flies (many of those genes appear to be duplicates of those in the flies, and the biochemistry of fly nerve cells seems quite close to ours). But in addition to having sex and eating (what flies mostly do) we get married, establish charities, build hydrogen bombs, commit genocide, compose sonatas, and publish books on evolution. It is a little hard to credit all this to the determining action of those few additional genes. Those genes are, however, likely to have contributed to the increased brain size and complexity that support the vast cultural superstructure created by the interaction of our neurons and their environments. They may also contribute to the wonderful flexibility and plasticity of human behavior—the very attributes that make our behavior less rather than more genetically determined. But to understand the development of and variation in specific human behaviors such as creating charities and cheesecakes, we must invoke culture, its evolution, and its potential interaction with biology.

It might be argued that since a relative handful of genes can control our basic body plan—one's height depends on millions of the body's cells' being stacked precisely—a handful could also determine our behavioral phenome. Genes initiate a process of development that might be analogized with the way a mountain stream entering a floodplain can initiate the development of a complex delta. Why, then, couldn't just a few genes have evolved to program millions of our behaviors? In theory they might have, but in that case human behavior would be very stereotyped. Consider the problem of evolving human behavioral flexibility under such circumstances of genetic determination. Changing just one behavioral pattern—say, making women more desirous of mating with affluent men—would be somewhat analogous to changing the course of one distributary (branch in the delta) without altering the braided pattern of the rest of the delta. It would be difficult to do by just changing the flow of the mountain stream (equivalent to changing the genes) but easily accomplished by throwing big rocks in the distributary (changing the environment).

This partial analogy seems particularly apt in that it is apparently difficult for evolution to accomplish just one thing at a time. There are two principal reasons for this. The first is the complexity of interactions among alleles and phenotypic traits, especially pleiotropy and epistasis. Because there are relatively so few of them, most genes must be involved in more than one process (pleiotropy). Then if a mutation leads to better functioning of one process, it may not be selected for because the change might degrade the functioning of another process. And changes in one gene can modify the influence of another in very complex ways (epistasis). Second, because they are physically coupled to other genes on the same chromosome, the fates of genes are not independent. Selection that increases the frequency of one allele in a population will often, because of linkage, necessarily increase the frequency of another. Selection favoring a gene that made one prefer tall mates might also result in the increase of a nearby gene that produced greater susceptibility to a childhood cancer.

## The Mysteries of Environmental Control

Behavioral scientists are still, unhappily, generally unable to determine the key environmental factors that influence the behavioral phenome. For instance, in the case of the Dionne quintuplets, quite subtle environmental differences—perhaps initiated by different positions in the womb or chance interactions among young quints, their parents, and their observers—clearly led to substantially different behavioral and health outcomes in five children with identical genomes. As their story shows, we really know very little about what environmental factors can modify behavior. For example, some virtually undetectable differences in environments may be greatly amplified as developing individuals change their own environments and those of their siblings. Equally, subtle and undetected environmental factors may put individuals with the same genetic endowments on similar life courses even if they are reared apart, perhaps explaining anecdotes about the similarities of some reunited identical twins.

We also know too little about the routes through which genes may influence behavior, where again changes may be behaviorally amplified. Suppose that a study shows that identical twins, separated at birth, nonetheless show a high correlation of personality type—both members of twin pairs tend to be either introverted or extraverted. This is interpreted as a high heritability of introversion and extraversion. What really is heavily influenced by genetics, however, could be height, and tall people in that society (as in many societies) may be better treated by their peers and thus more likely to become extraverted. Genes in this case will clearly be involved in personality type but by such an indirect route as to make talk of "genes for introversion or extraversion" essentially meaningless.

And, of course, scientists *do* know that what appears to be "genetic" is often simply a function of the environment. An example suggested by the philosopher Elliott Sober illustrates this. In England before the 18th century, evolutionary psychologists (had there been any) would have assumed that males had a genetic proclivity for knitting. The knitting gene would have been assumed to reside on the Y chromosome. But by the 19th century, evolutionary psychologists would have claimed that women had that genetic proclivity, with the knitting gene on the X chromosome. With historical perspective, we can see that the change was purely culture-driven, not due to a genetic change. As it did with knitting, the environment, especially the cultural environment, seems to do a good job of fine-tuning our behavior. A major challenge for science today is to elucidate how that fine-tuning occurs.

## Would Selection Generally Favor Genetic Control of Behavior?

Would we be better off if we had more than enough genes to play a controlling role in every one of our choices and actions and those genes could operate independently? Probably not. One could imagine a Hobbesian battle in which genes would compete with each other to improve the performance of the reproducing individuals that possessed them—genes for caution being favored in one environment one day and genes for impulsiveness in another environment the next ("Look before you leap," "He who hesitates is lost"). It is difficult to imagine how *any* organism could make the grade evolutionarily if its behavior were completely genetically determined and interactions between its genes and its environments did not exist. Even single-celled organisms respond to changes in their surroundings. Without substantial environmental inputs, evolution would not occur and life could not exist.

Biological evolution has avoided that problem by allowing our behavior to be deeply influenced by the environments in which genes operate. In normal human environments, genes are heavily involved in creating a basic brain with an enormous capacity for learning—taking in information from the environment and incorporating that information into the brain's structure. It is learning that proceeds after birth as an infant's brain uses inputs such as patterns of light from the eyes to wire up the brain so that it can see, patterns of sound that wire up the brain so that it can speak one or more languages, and so on. As the brain scientist John Allman put it, "the brain is unique among the organs of the body in requiring a great deal of feedback from experience to develop its full capacities." And the situation is not so different for height. There aren't enough genes to control a child's growth rate from day to day—adding cells rapidly in favorable (e.g., food-rich) situations and slowly or not at all under starvation. And there aren't enough genes to govern the growth of each column of cells, some to regulate those in each column on the right side of the spine, some for each in the left. Instead, all growth patterns depend on environmental feedback. . . .

# Conclusions

What the recent evidence from the Human Genome Project tells us is that the interaction between genes, between the separate components of genes, and between controlling elements of these separate components must be much more complex than we ever realized. Simple additive models of gene action or of the relationship between genes and environments must be revised. They have formed the basis for our interpretation of phenotype-genotype relationships for 84 years, ever since R. A. Fisher's famous paper that for the first time related Mendelian genes to measurable phenotypes. New models and paradigms are needed to go from the genome to the phenome in any quantitative way. The simplistic approach of behavioral genetics cannot do the job. We must dig deeper into the environmental and especially cultural factors that contribute to the phenome. The ascendancy of molecular biology has, unintentionally, militated against progress in studies of cultural evolution.

Theories of culture and its evolution in the 20th century, from Boas's insistence on the particularity of cultural identities to the debates between material and cultural determinism described by Sahlins, were proudly nonquantitative. Recent discussions on the ideational or symbolic nature of the subjects of cultural evolution, while critical of attempts to construct dynamical models of cultural evolution based on individual-to-individual cultural transmission, nevertheless acknowledge the centrality of cultural evolution to human behavioral analysis. Thus, although the quantitative paradigms used in behavioral genetics do not inform evolutionary analysis, this does not mean that we cannot or should not take an evolutionary approach to the understanding and modification of human behavior. Genetically evolved features such as the dominance of our visual sense should always be kept in mind, but an evolutionary approach to changing behavior in our species must primarily focus on *cultural* evolution. In the last 40,000 years or so, the scale of that cultural evolution has produced a volume of information that dwarfs what is coded into our genes. Just consider what is now stored in human memories, libraries, photographs, films, video tapes, the Worldwide Web, blueprints, and computer data banks—in addition to what is inherent in other artifacts and human-made structures. Although there have been preliminary investigations by Cavalli-Sforza and Feldman and Boyd and Richerson, scientists have barely begun to investigate the basic processes by which that body of information changes (or remains constant for long periods)—a task that social scientists have been taking up piecemeal and largely qualitatively for a very long time. Developing a unified quantitative theory of cultural change is one of the great challenges for evolutionary and social science in the 21st century.

Identifying the basic mechanisms by which our culture evolves will be difficult; the most recent attempts using a "meme" approach appear to be a dead end. Learning how to influence that evolution is likely to be more difficult still and fraught with pitfalls. No sensible geneticist envisions a eugenic future in which people are selected to show certain behavioral traits, and most thinking people are aware of the ethical (if not technical and social) problems of trying to change our behavior by altering our genetic endowments. Society has long been mucking around in cultural evolution, despite warnings of the potential abuses of doing so. Nazi eugenic policies and Soviet, Cambodian, Chinese, and other social engineering experiments stand as monuments to the ethical dangers that must be guarded against when trying systematically to alter either genetic or cultural evolution.

Nevertheless, we are today all involved in carrying out or (with our taxes) supporting experiments designed to change behavior. This is attested to by the advertising business, Head Start programs, and the existence of institutions such as Sing Sing Prison and Stanford University. The data used by evolutionary psychologists to infer the biological antecedents of human behavior, while not telling us anything about genetic evolution, may actually be helpful in improving our grasp of cultural evolution. What seems clear today, however, is that evolutionary psychology and behavioral genetics are promoting a vast overemphasis on the part played by genetic factors (and a serious underestimation of the role of cultural evolution) in shaping our behavioral phenomes.

# NO

**Gary Marcus**

# Making the Mind: Why We've Misunderstood the Nature-Nurture Debate

**W**hat do our minds owe to our nature, and what to our nurture? The question has long been vexed, in no small part because until recently we knew relatively little about the nature of nature—how genes work and what they bring to the biological structures that underlie the mind. But now, 50 years after the discovery of the molecular structure of DNA, we are for the first time in a position to understand directly DNA's contribution to the mind. And the story is vastly different from—and vastly more interesting than—anything we had anticipated.

The emerging picture of nature's role in the formation of the mind is at odds with a conventional view, recently summarized by Louis Menand. According to Menand, "every aspect of life has a biological foundation in exactly the same sense, which is that unless it was biologically possible it wouldn't exist. After that, it's up for grabs." More particularly, some scholars have taken recent research on genes and on the brain as suggesting a profoundly limited role for nature in the formation of the mind.

Their position rests on two arguments, what Stanford anthropologist Paul Ehrlich dubbed a "gene shortage" and widespread, well-documented findings of "brain plasticity." According to the gene shortage argument, genes can't be very important to the birth of the mind because the genome contains only about 30,000 genes, simply too few to account even for the brain's complexity—with its billions of cells and tens of billions of connections between neurons—much less the mind's. "Given that ratio," Ehrlich suggested, "it would be quite a trick for genes typically to control more than the most general aspects of human behavior."

According to the brain plasticity argument, genes can't be terribly important because the developing brain is so flexible. For instance, whereas adults who lose their left hemisphere are likely to lose permanently much of their ability to talk, a child who loses a left hemisphere may very well recover the ability to speak, even in the absence of a left hemisphere. Such flexibility is pervasive, down to the level of individual cells. Rather than being fixed in their fates the instant they are born, newly formed brain cells—neurons—can sometimes shift their function, depending on their context. A cell that would ordinarily help to give us a sense of touch can (in the right circumstances) be recruited into the visual system and accept signals from the eye. With that high level of brain plasticity, some imagine that genes are left on the sidelines, as scarcely relevant onlookers.

All of this is, I think, a mistake. It is certainly true that the number of genes is tiny in comparison to the number of neurons, and that the developing brain is highly plastic. Nevertheless, nature—in the form of genes—has an enormous impact on the developing brain and mind. The general outlines of how genes build the brain are finally becoming clear, and we are also starting to see how, in forming the brain, genes make room for the environment's essential role. While vast amounts of work remain to be done, it is becoming equally clear that understanding the coordination of nature and nurture will require letting go of some long-held beliefs.

## How to Build a Brain

In the nine-month dash from conception to birth—the flurry of dividing, specializing, and migrating cells that scientists call embryogenesis—organs such as the heart and kidney unfold in a series of ever more mature stages. In contrast to a 17th century theory known as preformationism, the organs of the body cannot be found preformed in miniature in a fertilized egg; at the moment of conception there is neither a tiny heart nor a tiny brain. Instead, the fertilized egg contains information: the three billion nucleotides of DNA that make up the human genome. That information, copied into the nucleus of every newly formed cell, guides the gradual but powerful process of successive approximation that shapes each of the body's organs. The heart, for example, begins as a simple sheet of cell that gradually folds over to form a tube; the tube sprouts bulges, the bulges sprout further bulges, and every day the growing heart looks a bit more like an adult heart.

Even before the dawn of the modern genetic era, biologists understood that something similar was happening in the development of the brain—that the organ of thought and language was formed in much the same way as the rest of the body. The brain, too, develops in the first instance from a simple sheet of cells that gradually curls up into a tube that sprouts bulges, which over time differentiate into ever more complex shapes. Yet 2,000 years of thinking of the mind as independent from the body kept people from appreciating the significance of this seemingly obvious point.

The notion that the brain is drastically different from other physical systems has a long tradition; it can be seen as a modernized version of the ancient belief that the mind and body are wholly separate—but it is untenable. The brain is a physical system. Although the brain's function is different from that of other organs, the brain's capabilities, like those of other organs, emerge from its physical properties. We now know that strokes and gunshot wounds can interfere with language by destroying parts of the brain, and that Prozac and Ritalin can influence mood by altering the flow of neurotransmitters. The fundamental components of the brain—the neurons and the synapses that connect them—can be understood as physical systems, with chemical and electrical properties that follow from their composition.

Yet even as late as the 1990s, latter-day dualists might have thought that the brain developed by different principles. There were, of course, many hints that genes must be important for the brain: identical twins resemble each other more than nonidentical twins in personality as well as in physique; mental disorders such as schizophrenia and depression run in families and are shared even by twins reared apart; and animal breeders know that shaping the bodies of animals often leads to correlated changes in behavior. All of these observations provided clues of genetic effects on the brain.

But such clues are achingly indirect, and it was easy enough to pay them little heed. Even in the mid-1990s, despite all the discoveries that had been made in molecular biology, hardly anything specific was known about how the brain formed. By the end of that decade, however, revolutions in the methodology of molecular biology—techniques for studying and manipulating genes—were beginning to enter the study of the brain. Now, just a few years later, it has become clear that to an enormous extent the brain really is sculpted by the same processes as the rest of the body, not just at the macroscopic level (i.e., as a product of successive approximation) but also at the microscopic level, in terms of the mechanics of how genes are switched on and off, and even in terms of which genes are involved; a huge number of the genes that participate in the development of the brain play important (and often closely related) roles in the rest of the body. . . .

The . . . power of genes holds even for the most unusual yet most characteristic parts of neurons: the long axons that carry signals away from the cell, the tree-like dendrites that allow neurons to receive signals from other nerve cells, and the trillions of synapses that serve as connections between them. What your brain does is largely a function of how those synaptic connections are set up—alter those connections, and you alter the mind—and how they are set up is no small part a function of the genome. In the laboratory, mutant flies and mice with aberrant brain wiring have trouble with everything from motor control (one mutant mouse is named "reeler" for its almost drunken gait) to vision. And in humans, faulty brain wiring contributes to disorders such as schizophrenia and autism.

Proper neural wiring depends on the behavior of individual axons and dendrites. And this behavior once again depends on the content of the genome. For example, much of what axons do is governed by special wiggly, almost hand-like protuberances at the end of each axon known as growth cones. Growth cones (and the axonal wiring they trail behind them) are like little animals that swerve back and forth, maneuvering around obstacles, extending and retracting feelers known as filopodia (the "fingers" of a growth cone) as the cone hunts around in search of its destination—say in the auditory cortex. Rather than simply being launched like projectiles that blindly and helplessly follow whatever route they first set out on, growth cones constantly compensate and adjust, taking in new information as they find their way to their targets.

Growth cones don't just head in a particular direction and hope for the best. They "know" what they are looking for and can make new plans even if experimentally induced obstacles get in their way. In their efforts to find their destinations, growth cones use every trick they can, from "short-range" cues emanating from the surface of nearby cells to long-distance cues that broadcast their signals from millimeters away—miles and miles in the geography of an axon. For example, some proteins appear to serve as "radio beacons" that can diffuse across great distances and serve as guides to distant growth cones—provided that they are tuned to the right station. Which stations a growth cone picks up—and whether it finds a particular signal attractive or repellent—depends on the protein receptors it has on its surface, in turn a function of which genes are expressed within.

Researchers are now in a position where they can begin to understand and even manipulate those genes. In 2000, a team of researchers at the Salk Institute in San Diego took a group of thoracic (chest) motor neurons that normally extend their axons into several different places, such as axial muscles (midline muscles that play a role in posture), intercostal muscles (the muscles between the ribs), and sympathetic neurons (which, among other things, participate in the fast energy mobilization for fight-or-flight responses), and by changing their genetic labels persuaded virtually the entire group of thoracic neurons to abandon their usual targets in favor of the axial muscles. (The few exceptions were a tiny number that apparently couldn't fit into the newly crowded axial destinations and had to find other targets.)

What this all boils down to, from the perspective of psychology, is an astonishingly powerful system for wiring the mind. Instead of vaguely telling axons and dendrites to send and accept signals from their neighbors, thereby leaving all of the burden of mind development to experience, nature in effect lays down the cable: it supplies the brain's wires—axons and dendrites—with elaborate tools for finding their way on their own. Rather than waiting for experience, brains can use the complex menagerie of genes and proteins to create a rich, intricate starting point for the brain and mind.

The sheer overlap between the cellular and molecular processes by which the brain is built and the processes by which the rest of the body is built has meant that new techniques designed for the study of the one can often be readily imported into the study of the other. New techniques in staining, for instance, by which biologists trace the movements and fates of individual cells, can often be brought to bear on the study of the brain as soon as they are developed; even more important, new techniques for altering the genomes of experimental animals can often be almost immediately applied to studies of brain development. Our collective understanding of biology is growing by leaps and bounds because sauce for the goose is so often sauce for the gander.

## Nature and Nurture Redux

This seemingly simple idea—that what's good enough for the body is good enough for the brain—has important implications for how we understand the roles of nature and nurture in the development of the mind and brain.

## Beyond the Blueprint

Since the early 1960s biologists have realized that genes are neither blue-prints nor dictators; instead, as I will explain in a moment, genes are better seen as *providers of opportunity*. Yet because the brain has for so long been treated as separate from the body, the notion of genes as sources of options rather than purveyors of commands has yet to really enter into our understanding of the origins of human psychology.

Biologists have long understood that all genes have two functions. First, they serve as templates for building particular proteins. The insulin gene provides a template for insulin, the hemoglobin genes give templates for building hemoglobin, and so forth. Second, each gene contains what is called a regulatory sequence, a set of conditions that guide whether or not that gene's template gets converted into protein. Although every cell contains a complete copy of the genome, most of the genes in any given cell are silent. Your lung cells, for example, contain the recipe for insulin but they don't produce any, because in those cells the insulin gene is switched off (or "repressed"); each protein is produced only in the cells in which the relevant gene is switched on. So individual genes are like lines in a computer program. Each gene has an IF and a THEN, a precondition (IF) and an action (THEN). And here is one of the most important places where the environment can enter: the IFs of genes are responsive to the environment of the cells in which they are contained. Rather than being static entities that decide the fate of each cell in advance, genes—because of the regulatory sequence—are dynamic and can guide a cell in different ways at different times, depending on the balance of molecules in their environment.

This basic logic—which was worked out in the early 1960s by two French biologists, François Jacob and Jacques Monod, in a series of painstaking studies of the diet of a simple bacterium—applies as much to humans as to bacteria, and as much for the brain as for any other part of the body. Monod and Jacob aimed to understand how *E. coli* bacteria could switch almost instantaneously from a diet of glucose (its favorite) to a diet of lactose (an emergency backup food). What they found was that this abrupt change in diet was accomplished by a process that switched genes on and off. To metabolize lactose, the bacterium needed to build a certain set of protein-based enzymes that for simplicity I'll refer to collectively as lactase, the product of a cluster of lactase genes. Every *E. coli* had those lactase genes lying in wait, but they were only expressed—switched on—when a bit of lactose could bind (attach to) a certain spot of DNA that lay near them, and this in turn could happen only if there was no glucose around to get in the way. In essence, the simple bacterium had an IF-THEN—if lactose and not glucose, then build lactase—that is very much of a piece with the billions of IF-THENs that run the world's computer software.

The essential point is that genes are IFs rather than MUSTs. So even a single environmental cue can radically reshape the course of development. In the African butterfly *Bicyclus anynana*, for example, high temperature during development (associated with the rainy season in its native tropical climate) leads the butterfly to become brightly colored; low temperature (associated with a dry fall) leads the butterfly to become a dull brown. The growing butterfly doesn't learn (in the course of its development) how to blend in better—it will do the same thing in a lab where the temperature varies and the foliage is constant; instead it is genetically programmed to develop in two different ways in two different environments.

The lesson of the last five years of research in developmental neuro-science is that IF-THENs are as crucial and omnipresent in brain development as they are elsewhere. To take one recently worked out example: rats, mice, and other rodents devote a particular region of the cerebral cortex known as barrel fields to the problem of analyzing the stimulation of their whiskers. The exact placement of those barrel fields appears to be driven by a gene or set of genes whose IF region is responsive to the quantity of a particular molecule, Fibroblast Growth Factor 8 (FGF8). By altering the distribution of that mole-cule, researchers were able to alter barrel development: increasing the concen-tration of FGF8 led to mice with barrel fields that were unusually far forward, while decreasing the concentration led to mice with barrel fields that were unusually far back. In essence, the quantity of FGF8 serves as a beacon, guid-ing growing cells to their fate by driving the regulatory IFs of the many genes that are presumably involved in barrel-field formation.

Other IF-THENs contribute to the function of the brain throughout life, e.g., supervising the control of neurotransmitters and participating . . . in the process of laying down memory traces. Because each gene has an IF, every aspect of the brain's development is in principle linked to some aspect of the environment; chemicals such as alcohol that are ingested during pregnancy have such enormous effects because they fool the IFs that regulate genes that guide cells into dividing too much or too little, into moving too far or not far enough, and so forth. The brain is the product of the actions of its component cells, and those actions are the products of the genes they contain within, each cell guided by 30,000 IFs paired with 30,000 THENs—as many possibili-ties as there are genes. (More, really, because many genes have multiple IFs, and genes can and often do work in combination.)

## From Genes to Behavior

Whether we speak of the brain or other parts of the body, changes in even a single gene—leading to either a new IF or a new THEN—can have great conse-quences. Just as a single alteration to the hemoglobin gene can lead to a pre-disposition for sickle-cell anemia, a single change to the genes involved in the brain can lead to a language impairment or mental retardation.

And at least in animals, small differences within genomes can lead to significant differences in behavior. A Toronto team, for example, recently used genetic techniques to investigate—and ultimately modify—the foraging habits of *C. elegans* worms. Some *elegans* prefer to forage in groups, others are loners, and the Toronto group was able to tie these behavioral differences to differences in a single amino acid in the protein template (THEN) region of a particular gene known as npr-1; worms with the amino acid valine in the critical spot are "social" whereas worms with phenylalanine are loners. Armed with that knowledge and modern genetic engineering techniques, the team was able to switch a strain of loner *C. elegans* worms into social worms by altering that one gene.

Another team of researchers, at Emory University, has shown that changing the regulatory IF region of a single gene can also have a significant effect on social behavior. Building on an observation that differences in sociability in different species of voles correlated with how many vasopressin receptors they had, they transferred the regulatory IF region of sociable prairie voles' vasopressin receptor genes into the genome of a less sociable species, the mouse—and in so doing created mutant mice, more social than normal, with more vasopressin receptors. With other small genetic modifications, researchers have created strains of anxious, fearful mice, mice that progressively increase alcohol consumption under stress, mice that lack the nurturing instinct, and even mice that groom themselves constantly, pulling and tugging on their own hair to the point of baldness. Each of those studies demonstrates how behavior can be significantly changed when even a single gene is altered.

Still, complex biological structures—whether we speak of hearts or kidneys or brains—are the product of the concerted actions and interactions of many genes, not just one. A mutation in a single gene known as FOXP2 can interfere with the ability of a child to learn language; an alteration in the vasopressin gene can alter a rodent's sociability—but this doesn't mean that FOXP2 is solely responsible for language or that vasopressin is the only gene a rat needs in order to be sociable. Although individual genes can have powerful effects, no trait is the consequence of any single gene. There can no more be a single gene for language, or for the propensity for talking about the weather, than there can be for the left ventricle of a human heart. Even a single brain cell—or a single heart cell—is the product of many genes working together.

The mapping between genes and behavior is made even more complex by the fact that few if any neural circuits operate entirely autonomously. Except perhaps in the case of reflexes, most behaviors are the product of multiple interacting systems. In a complex animal like a mammal or a bird, virtually every action depends on a coming together of systems for perception, attention, motivation, and so forth. Whether or not a pigeon pecks a lever to get a pellet depends on whether it is hungry, whether it is tired, whether there is anything else more interesting around, and so forth. Furthermore, even within a single system, genes rarely participate directly "on-line," in part because they are just too slow. Genes do seem to play an active, major role in "off-line" processing, such as consolidation of long-term memory—which can even happen during sleep—but when it comes to rapid on-line decision-making, genes, which work on a time scale of seconds or minutes, turn over the reins to neurons, which act on a scale of hundredths of a second. The chief contribution of genes comes in advance, in laying down and adjusting neural circuitry, not in the moment-by-moment running of the nervous system. Genes build neural structures—not behavior.

In the assembly of the brain, as in the assembly of other organs, one of the most important ideas is that of a cascade, one gene influencing another, which influences another, which influences another, and so on. Rather than acting in absolute isolation, most genes act as parts of elaborate networks in which the expression of one gene is a precondition for the expression of the next. The THEN of one gene can satisfy the IF of another and thus induce it to turn on. Regulatory proteins are proteins (themselves the product of genes) that control the expression of other genes and thus tie the whole genetic system together. A single regulatory gene at the top of a complex network can indirectly launch a cascade of hundreds or thousands of other genes leading to, for example, the development of an eye or a limb.

In the words of Swiss biologist Walter Gehring, such genes can serve as "master control genes" and exert enormous power on a growing system. PAX6, for example, is a regulatory protein that plays a role in eye development, and Gehring has shown that artificially activating it in the right spot on a fruit fly's antenna can lead to an extra eye, right there on the antenna—thus, a simple regulatory gene leads directly and indirectly to the expression of approximately 2,500 other genes. What is true for the fly's eye is also true for its brain—and also for the human brain: by compounding and coordinating their effects, genes can exert enormous influence on biological structure.

## From a Tiny Number of Genes to a Complex Brain

The cascades in turn help us to make sense of the alleged gene shortage, the idea that the discrepancy between the number of genes and the number of neurons might somehow minimize the importance of genes when it comes to constructing brain or behavior.

Reflection on the relation between brain and body immediately vitiates the gene shortage argument: if 30,000 genes weren't enough to have significant influence on the 20 billion cells in the brain, they surely wouldn't have much impact on the trillions that are found in the body as a whole. The confusion, once again, can be traced to the mistaken idea of genome as blueprint, to the misguided expectation of a one-to-one mapping from individual genes to individual neurons; in reality, genomes describe processes for building things rather than pictures of finished products: better to think of the genome as a compression scheme than a blueprint.

Computer scientists use compression schemes when they want to store and transmit information efficiently. All compression schemes rely in one way or another on ferreting out redundancy. For instance, programs that use the GIF format look for patterns of repeated pixels (the colored dots of which digital images are made). If a whole series of pixels are of exactly the same color, the software that creates GIF files will assign a code that represents the color of those pixels, followed by a number to indicate how many pixels in a row are of the same color. Instead of having to list every blue pixel individually, the GIF format saves space by storing only two numbers: the code for blue and the number of repeated blue pixels. When you "open" a GIF file, the computer converts those codes back into the appropriate strings of identical bits; in the meantime, the computer has saved a considerable amount of memory. Computer scientists have devised dozens of different compression schemes, from JPEGs for photographs to MP3s for music, each designed to exploit a different kind of redundancy. The general procedure is always the same: some end product is converted into a compact description of how to reconstruct that end product; a "decompressor" reconstructs the desired end product from that compact description.

Biology doesn't know in advance what the end product will be; there's no StuffIt Compressor to convert a human being into a genome. But the genome is very much akin to a compression scheme, a terrifically efficient description of how to build something of great complexity—perhaps more efficient than anything yet developed in the labs of computer scientists (never mind the complexities of the brain—there are trillions of cells in the rest of the body, and they are all supervised by the same 30,000-gene genome). And although nature has no counterpart to a program that stuffs a picture into a compressed encoding, it does offer a counterpart to the program that performs decompression: the cell. Genome in, organism out. Through the logic of gene expression, cells are self-regulating factories that translate genomes into biological structure.

Cascades are at the heart of this process of decompression, because the regulatory proteins that are at the top of genetic cascades serve as shorthand that can be used over and over again, like the subroutine of a software engineer. For example, the genome of a centipede probably doesn't specify separate sets of hundreds or thousands of genes for each of the centipede's legs; instead, it appears that the leg-building "subroutine"—a cascade of perhaps hundreds or thousands of genes—gets invoked many times, once for each new pair of legs. Something similar lies behind the construction of a vertebrate's ribs. And within the last few years it has become clear that the embryonic brain relies on the same sort of genetic recycling, using the same repeated motifs—such as sets of parallel connections known as topographic maps—over and over again, to supervise the development of thousands or even millions of neurons with each use of a given genetic subroutine. There's no gene shortage, because every cascade represents the shorthand for a different reuseable subroutine, a different way of creating more from less.

## From Prewiring to Rewiring

In the final analysis, I think the most important question about the biological roots of the mind may not be the question that has preoccupied my colleagues and myself for a number of years—the extent to which genes prewire the brain—but a different question that until recently had never been seriously raised: the extent to which (and ways in which) genes make it possible for experience to *rewire* the brain. Efforts to address the nature-nurture question typically falter because of the false assumption that the two—prewiring and rewiring—are competing ideas. "Anti-nativists"—critics of the view that we might be born with significant mental structure prior to experience—often attempt to downplay the significance of genes by making what I earlier called "the argument from plasticity": they point to the brain's resilience to damage and its ability to modify itself in response to experience. Nativists sometimes seem to think that their position rests on downplaying (or demonstrating limits on) plasticity.

In reality, plasticity and innateness are almost logically separate. Innateness is about the extent to which the brain is prewired, plasticity about the extent to which it can be rewired. Some organisms may be good at one but not the other: chimpanzees, for example, may have intricate innate wiring yet, in comparison to humans, relatively few mechanisms for rewiring their brains. Other organisms may be lousy at both: *C. elegans* worms have limited initial structure, and relatively little in the way of techniques for rewiring their nervous system on the basis of experience. And some organisms, such as humans, are well-endowed in both respects, with enormously intricate initial architecture and fantastically powerful and flexible means for rewiring in the face of experience. . . .

# POSTSCRIPT

## Does Culture and Environment Influence Human Development More Than Our Genes?

The way people understand the relative influence of genes and culture on behavior has crucial implications for contemporary society. As articulated by Paul Ehrlich and Marcus Feldman, general assumptions of biological determinism have been at the root of some heinous social policies—including forced sterilization and Nazi efforts to biologically create a "master race." No legitimate contemporary scholar would endorse such policies, but many biologically oriented experts on life span would also note that such policies are not reason to discount the role of genes in crafting development. As Ehrlich and Feldman assert in their article, applying Darwin's ideas to behavior is one of the dominant trends in the contemporary study of life span development. After reading these sides of the argument, it is crucial to consider for yourself whether the popularity of applying Darwinian principles to social behavior is a good thing.

While not dealing extensively with policy implications, Gary Marcus clearly takes the position that recognizing the biological influences on our life span is an essential task in the study of life span development. While Ehrlich and Feldman suggest there are simply too few genes to craft complex behavior, Marcus argues that combinations of a few genes have potential to create nearly infinite complexity. Thus, the task of understanding this process is also increasingly complex. Marcus' rendering of the overwhelming influence of genes upon behavior and development requires facing the immense task of not only understanding the role of individual genes, but also understanding the way genes combine with one another.

Marcus also takes on an argument given less attention by Ehrlich and Feldman: the major finding in recent neuroscience that the brain maintains high levels of plasticity—the capability of shifting functions to different brain regions—through much of the life span. Some have argued that such plasticity demonstrates the dominant role of culture in shaping behavior. If our experiences can actually change our brain wiring, doesn't that suggest experience is what matters most? Marcus answers no. Of course experiences matter, but only in how they modify the initial wiring (the initial "programming") provided by biology. In other words, plasticity is not infinite. Plasticity itself is determined by our genetic material. So we are again left with the important distinction of which takes priority: the genetic programming or the experiential rewiring?

These readings also demonstrate how such questions depend heavily on animal research. Ultimately, much of the contemporary nature and nurture controversy depends on interpreting this research and on confronting the question of human uniqueness in relation to animals. What is distinctive about humans as a species? Marcus argues that denying the overwhelming influence of genes depends upon a false body-mind "dualism" that has been prominent in human thought for 2000 years—the idea that our soul or mind is distinct from the biological brain in body. Clearly the mind is the brain, and as such is a biological organ like the heart or the liver. But the human brain has several capacities not available to other species to any significant degree: the human brain has consciousness, high-level cognitive awareness of the self, and complex language. And, ultimately, the human brain has the capacity to create complex culture—systems of meanings and belief that by definition guide behavior. The question of whether this biologically endowed capacity for culture is more meaningful than the cultural influences thusly created will continue to evolve as we learn more about the origins of behavior throughout the life span.

## Suggested Readings

S. Ceci and W. Williams, *The Nature—Nurture Debate: The Essential Readings* (Blackwell Publishers, 1999).

S. Johnson, "Sociobiology and You," *The Nation* (November 18, 2002).

G. Marcus, *The Birth of the Mind: How a Tiny Number of Genes Creates the Complexity of Human Thought* (Basic Books, 2004).

L. Menand, "What Comes Naturally," *The New Yorker* (November 25, 2002).

S. Pinker, *The Blank Slate* (Viking Adult, 2002).

M. Ridley, *Nature via Nurture* (Harper Collins, 2003).

# ISSUE 2

## Are Peers More Important Than Parents During the Process of Development?

**YES: Judith Rich Harris,** from "How to Succeed in Childhood," *Wilson Quarterly* (Winter 1999)

**NO: Howard Gardner,** from "Do Parents Count?" *The New York Review of Books* (November 5, 1998)

### ISSUE SUMMARY

**YES:** Developmental psychology writer Judith Rich Harris presents a strong and provocative argument suggesting that parents do not influence child development to any significant degree, while peers and social groups have a primary influence.

**NO:** Harvard psychologist Howard Gardener reviews Harris' work and suggests her argument is overstated and misleading—parents do matter.

If you ask people about their personal development—why did you turn out the way you have?—most will tell you about their parents. In contrast, when you ask researchers and scholars about the role of parents in personal development, their answer tends to be a little more complicated. Many years' worth of research have focused on estimating and understanding the influence of parenting, but the results have not been as clear as you might expect. So if the evidence is really not very strong, then why do most people think parents matter so much?

Much of the popular perception has to do with the dominant figure in the history of psychology: Sigmund Freud. Freud's "psychoanalytic" theory posited that dynamic relationships between infants and parents shape people's experience of the world. From this standpoint, those relationships create personality patterns that endure throughout the life span (unless there is serious therapeutic intervention).

While very few people still adhere to a strict Freudian version of psychoanalytic theory, the idea that relationships with parents determine future personality remains strong. And this idea has only been enhanced by the popularity of child-rearing "experts" who write and speak about ways that parents can make sure their children turn out well. But are these experts just playing on the insecurities of parents and giving an illusion of control over how children turn out?

In fact, many scholars now feel the influence of parental "socialization" (the forming of behavior and personality by parenting behaviors) may be much less than most people think. There are two alternative explanations receiving significant research attention. One explanation is based on increased attention to biological and genetic influences on behavior, finding high levels of significance for our inherited predispositions. The other explanation is based on the role of culture and society, beyond individual parents, that shapes norms and expectations for children.

That being the case, perhaps it was inevitable that someone would turn the tables on all the parenting experts by drawing on developmental research to suggest that parents may not really matter much at all. That person turned out to be Judith Rich Harris, who had been writing textbooks about developmental psychology for years before realizing that there was very little evidence for all the emphasis on the influence of parents in development. She eventually turned this realization into a provocative and award-winning article for psychologists and a controversial book for a popular audience. Her basic argument, stated simply as "parents don't matter nearly as much as we think, and peers matter a lot more," went against both popular wisdom and academic trends. Harris' work instigated a flurry of debate.

One of the prominent psychologists to respond was Howard Gardner, most well known for his influential theory of multiple intelligences. While appreciating Harris' ability to challenge conventional wisdom, Gardner asserts that she significantly overstates her case by massaging data. Gardner is relatively certain that parents do matter, and that the problem with research is simply that personality and character are too difficult to measure. He suggests that the lack of evidence for parent's direct influence derives from an over-reliance on crude surveys, which creates an impression of development that is not true to its complex nature.

As such, this controversy has two important levels. On one level is the basic debate of whether parents matter as much as people tend to think they do. A level below is a more subtle debate about whether it is possible to turn the complex phenomenon of life span development into basic research data. It may be useful to think about these questions while reading the following selections: While most people automatically assume parents are the most significant influence on life span development, what is the tangible evidence?

# YES

**Judith Rich Harris**

## How to Succeed in Childhood

**E**very day, tell your children that you love them. Hug them at least once every 24 hours. Never hit them. If they do something wrong, don't say, "You're bad!" Say, "What you did was bad." No, wait—even that might be too harsh. Say, instead, "What you did made me unhappy."

The people who are in the business of giving out this sort of advice are very angry at me, and with good reason. I'm the author of *The Nurture Assumption*—the book that allegedly claims that "parents don't matter." Though that's not what the book actually says, the advice givers are nonetheless justified in their anger. I don't pull punches, and I'm not impressed by their air of benevolent omniscience. Their advice is based not on scientific evidence but on prevailing cultural myths.

The advice isn't wrong; it's just ineffective. Whether parents do or don't follow it has no measurable effect on how their children turn out. There is a great deal of evidence that the differences in how parents rear their children are not responsible for the differences among the children. I've reviewed this evidence in my book; I will not do it again here.

Let me, however, bring one thing to your attention: the advice given to parents in the early part of this century was almost the mirror image of the advice that is given today. In the early part of this century, parents were not warned against damaging their children's self-esteem; they were warned against "spoiling" them. Too much attention and affection were thought to be bad for kids. In those days, spanking was considered not just the parents' right but their duty.

Partly as a result of the major retoolings in the advice industry, child-rearing styles have changed drastically over the course of this century. Although abusive parents have always existed, run-of-the-mill parents—the large majority of the population—administer more hugs and fewer spankings than they used to.

Now ask yourself this: Are children turning out better? Are they happier and better adjusted than they were in the earlier part of the century? Less aggressive? Less anxious? Nicer?

It was Sigmund Freud who gave us the idea that parents are the be-all and end-all of the child's world. According to Freudian theory, children learn right from wrong—that is, they learn to behave in ways their parents and their society deem acceptable—by identifying with their parents. In the calm after the storm of the oedipal crisis, or the reduced-for-quick-sale female version of the oedipal crisis, the child supposedly identifies with the parent of the same sex.

Freud's name is no longer heard much in academic departments of psychology, but the theory that children learn how to behave by identifying with their parents is still accepted. Every textbook in developmental psychology (including, I confess, the one I co-authored) has its obligatory photo of a father shaving and a little boy pretending to shave. Little boys imitate their fathers, little girls imitate their mothers, and, according to the theory, that's how children learn to be grownups. It takes them a while, of course, to perfect the act.

It's a theory that could have been thought up only by a grownup. From the child's point of view, it makes no sense at all. What happens when children try to behave like grownups is that, more often than not, it gets them into trouble. Consider this story, told by Selma Fraiberg, a child psychologist whose book *The Magic Years* was popular in the 1960s:

> Thirty-month-old Julia finds herself alone in the kitchen while her mother is on the telephone. A bowl of eggs is on the table. An urge is experienced by Julia to make scrambled eggs. . . . When Julia's mother returns to the kitchen, she finds her daughter cheerfully plopping eggs on the linoleum and scolding herself sharply for each plop, "NoNoNo. Mustn't dood it! NoNoNo. Mustn't dood it!"

Fraiberg attributed Julia's lapse to the fact that she had not yet acquired a superego, presumably because she had not yet identified with her mother. But look at what was Julia doing when her mother came back and caught her egg-handed: she was imitating her mother! And yet Mother was not pleased.

ᴄ⋖⊙⋗ᴏ

Children cannot learn how to behave appropriately by imitating their parents. Parents do all sorts of things that children are not allowed to do—I don't have to list them, do I?—and many of them look like fun to people who are not allowed to do them. Such prohibitions are found not only in our own society but everywhere, and involve not only activities such as making scrambled eggs but patterns of social behavior as well. Around the world, children who behave too much like grownups are considered impertinent.

Sure, children sometimes pretend to be adults. They also pretend to be horses and monsters and babies, but that doesn't mean they aspire to be horses or monsters or babies. Freud jumped to the wrong conclusions, and so did several generations of developmental psychologists. A child's goal is not to become an adult; a child's goal is to be a successful child.

What does it take to be a successful child? The child's first job is to learn how to get along with her parents and siblings and to do the things that are expected of her at home. This is a very important job—no question about it.

But it is only the first of the child's jobs, and in the long run it is over-shadowed in importance by the child's second job: to learn how to get along with the members of her own generation and to do the things that are expected of her outside the home.

Almost every psychologist, Freudian or not, believes that what the child learns (or doesn't learn) in job 1 helps her to succeed (or fail) in job 2. But this belief is based on an obsolete idea of how the child's mind works, and there is good evidence that it is wrong.

Consider the experiments of developmental psychologist Carolyn Rovee-Collier. A young baby lies on its back in a crib. A mobile with dangling doo-dads hangs overhead. A ribbon runs from the baby's right ankle to the mobile in such a way that whenever the baby kicks its right leg, the doodads jiggle. Babies are delighted to discover that they can make something happen; they quickly learn how to make the mobile move. Two weeks later, if you show them the mobile again, they will immediately start kicking that right leg.

But only if you haven't changed anything. If the doodads hanging from the mobile are blue instead of red, or if the liner surrounding the crib has a pattern of squares instead of circles, or if the crib is placed in a different room, they will gape at the mobile cluelessly, as if they've never seen such a thing in their lives.

⋅⊰◉⊱⋅

It's not that they're stupid. Babies enter the world with a mind designed for learning and they start using it right away. But the learning device comes with a warning label: what you learn in one situation might not work in another. Babies do not assume that what they learned about the mobile with the red doodads will work for the mobile with the blue doodads. They do not assume that what worked in the bedroom will work in the den. And they do not assume that what worked with their mother will work with their father or the babysitter or their jealous big sister or the kids at the daycare center.

Fortunately, the child's mind is equipped with plenty of storage capacity. As the cognitive scientist Steven Pinker put it in his foreword to my book, "Relationships with parents, with siblings, with peers, and with strangers could not be more different, and the trillion-synapse human brain is hardly short of the computational power it would take to keep each one in a separate mental account."

That's exactly what the child does: keeps each one in a separate mental account. Studies have shown that a baby with a depressed mother behaves in a subdued fashion in the presence of its mother, but behaves normally with a caregiver who is not depressed. A toddler taught by his mother to play elabo-rate fantasy games does not play these games when he's with his playmates—he and his playmates devise their own games. A preschooler who has per-fected the delicate art of getting along with a bossy older sibling is no more likely than a first-born to allow her peers in nursery school to dominate her. A school-age child who says she hates her younger brother—they fight like cats and dogs, their mother complains—is as likely as any other child to have warm and serene peer relationships. Most telling, the child who follows the rules at home, even when no one is watching, may lie or cheat in the schoolroom or on the playground, and vice versa.

Children learn separately how to behave at home and how to behave outside the home, and parents can influence only the way they behave at home. Children behave differently in different social settings because different behaviors are required. Displays of emotion that are acceptable at home are not acceptable outside the home. A clever remark that would be rewarded with a laugh at home will land a child in the principal's office at school. Parents are often surprised to discover that the child they see at home is not the child the teacher sees. I imagine teachers get tired of hearing parents exclaim, "Really? Are you sure you're talking about *my* child?"

The compartmentalized world of childhood is vividly illustrated by the child of immigrant parents. When immigrants settle in a neighborhood of native-born Americans, their children become bicultural, at least for a while. At home they practice their parents' culture and language, outside the home they adopt the culture and language of their peers. But though their two worlds are separate, they are not equal. Little by little, the outside world takes precedence: the children adopt the language and culture of their peers and bring that language and culture home. Their parents go on addressing them in Russian or Korean or Portuguese, but the children reply in English. What the children of immigrants end up with is not a compromise, not a blend. They end up, pure and simple, with the language and culture of their peers. The only aspects of their parents' culture they retain are things that are carried out at home, such as cooking.

❧

Late-20th-century native-born Americans of European descent are as ethnocentric as the members of any other culture. They think there is only one way to raise children—the way they do it. But that is not the way children are reared in the kinds of cultures studied by anthropologists and ethologists. The German ethologist Irenäus Eibl-Eibesfeldt has described what childhood is like in the hunter-gatherer and tribal societies he spent many years observing.

In traditional cultures, the baby is coddled for two or three years—carried about by its mother and nursed whenever it whimpers. Then, when the next baby comes along, the child is sent off to play in the local play group, usually in the care of an older sibling. In his 1989 book *Human Ethology,* Eibl-Eibesfeldt describes how children are socialized in these societies:

> Three-year-old children are able to join in a play group, and it is in such play groups that children are truly raised. The older ones explain the rules of play and will admonish those who do not adhere to them, such as by taking something away from another or otherwise being aggressive. Thus the child's socialization occurs mainly within the play group. . . . By playing together in the children's group the members learn what aggravates others and which rules they must obey. This occurs in most cultures in which people live in small communities.

Once their tenure in their mothers' arms has ended, children in traditional cultures become members of a group. This is the way human children were designed to be reared. They were designed by evolution to become members of a group, because that's the way our ancestors lived for millions of years. Throughout the evolution of our species, the individual's survival depended upon the survival of his or her group, and the one who became a valued member of that group had an edge over the one who was merely tolerated.

Human groups started out small: in a hunter-gatherer band, everyone knows everyone else and most are blood relatives. But once agriculture began to provide our ancestors with a more or less dependable supply of food, groups got bigger. Eventually they became large enough that not everyone in them knew everyone else. As long ago as 1500 B.C. they were sometimes that large. There is a story in the Old Testament about a conversation Joshua had with a stranger, shortly before the Battle of Jericho. They met outside the walls of the beleaguered town, and Joshua's first question to the stranger was, "Are you for us or for our adversaries?"

Are you one of *us* or one of *them*? The group had become an idea, a concept, and the concept was defined as much by what you weren't as by what you were. And the answer to the question could be a matter of life or death. When the walls came tumbling down, Joshua and his troops killed every man, woman, and child in Jericho. Even in Joshua's time, genocide was not a novelty: fighting between groups, and wholesale slaughter of the losers, had been going on for ages. According to the evolutionary biologist Jared Diamond, it is "part of our human and prehuman heritage."

Are you one of *us* or one of *them*? It was the question African Americans asked of Colin Powell. It was the question deaf people asked of a Miss America who couldn't hear very well but who preferred to communicate in a spoken language. I once saw a six-year-old go up to a 14-year-old and ask him, "Are you a kid or a grownup?"

The human mind likes to categorize. It is not deterred by the fact that nature often fails to arrange things in convenient clumps but instead provides a continuum. We have no difficulty splitting up continua. Night and day are as different as, well, night and day, even though you can't tell where one leaves off and the other begins. The mind constructs categories for people—male or female, kid or grownup, white or black, deaf or hearing—and does not hesitate to draw the lines, even if it's sometimes hard to decide whether a particular individual goes on one side or the other.

Babies only a few months old can categorize. By the time they reach their first birthday, they are capable of dividing up the members of their social world into categories based on age and sex: they distinguish between men and women, between adults and children. A preference for the members of their own social category also shows up early. One-year-olds are wary of strange adults but are attracted to other children, even ones they've never met before. By the age of two, children are beginning to show a preference for members of their own sex. This preference grows steadily stronger over the next few years. School-age girls and boys will play together in places where there aren't many children, but when they have a choice of playmates, they tend to form all-girl and all-boy groups. This is true the world around.

∙◦❀◦∙

The brain we won in the evolutionary lottery gave us the ability to categorize, and we use that skill on people as well as things. Our long evolutionary history of fighting with other groups predisposes us to identify with one social category, to like our own category best, and to feel wary of (or hostile toward) members of other categories. The emotions and motivations that were originally applied to real physical groups are now applied to groups that are only concepts: "Americans" or "Democrats" or "the class of 2001." You don't have to like the other members of your group in order to consider yourself one of them; you don't even have to know who they are. The British social psychologist Henri Tajfel asked his subjects—a bunch of Bristol schoolboys—to estimate the number of dots flashed on a screen. Then half the boys were privately told that they were "over-estimators," the others that they were "underestimators." That was all it took to make them favor their own group. They didn't even know which of their schoolmates were in their group and which were in the other.

∙◦❀◦∙

The most famous experiment in social psychology is the Robber's Cave study. Muzafer Sherif and his colleagues started with 22 eleven-year-old boys, carefully selected to be as alike as possible, and divided them into two equal groups. The groups—the "Rattlers" and the "Eagles"—were separately transported to the Robber's Cave summer camp in a wilderness area of Oklahoma. For a while, neither group knew of the other's existence. But the first time the Rattlers heard the Eagles playing in the distance, they reacted with hostility. They wanted to "run them off." When the boys were brought together in games arranged by researchers disguised as camp counselors, push quickly came to shove. Before long, the two groups were raiding each other's cabins and filling socks with stones in preparation for retaliatory raids.

When people are divided (or divide themselves) into two groups, hostility is one common result. The other, which happens more reliably though it is less well known, is called the "group contrast effect." The mere division into two groups tends to make each group see the other as different from itself in an unfavorable way, and that makes its members *want* to be different from the other group. The result is that any pre-existing differences between the groups tend to widen, and if there aren't any differences to begin with, the members create them. Groups develop contrasting norms, contrasting images of themselves.

In the Robber's Cave study, it happened very quickly. Within a few days of their first encounter, the Eagles had decided that the Rattlers used too many "cuss-words" and resolved to give up cussing; they began to say a prayer before every game. The Rattlers, who saw themselves as tough and manly, continued to favor scatology over eschatology. If an Eagle turned an ankle or skinned a knee, it was all right for him to cry. A Rattler who sustained a similar injury might cuss a bit, but he would bear up stoically.

❧❦☙

The idea for group socialization theory came to me while I was reading an article on juvenile delinquency. The article reported that breaking the law is highly common among adolescents, even among those who were well behaved as children and who are destined to turn into law-abiding adults. This unendearing foible was attributed to the frustration teenagers experience at not being adults: they are longing for the power and privilege of adulthood.

"Wait a minute," I thought. "That's not right. If teenagers really wanted to be adults, they wouldn't be spraying graffiti on overpasses or swiping nail polish from drugstores. If they really wanted to emulate adults they would be doing boring adult things, like sorting the laundry or figuring out their taxes. Teenagers aren't trying to be like adults; they are trying to *contrast* themselves with adults! They are showing their loyalty to their own group and their disdain for adults' rules!"

I don't know what put the idea into my head; at the time, I didn't know beans about social psychology. It took eight months of reading to fill the gaps in my education. What I learned in those eight months was that there is a lot of good evidence to back up my hunch, and that it applies not only to teenagers but to young children as well.

Sociologist William Corsaro has spent many years observing nursery school children in the United States and Italy. Here is his description of four-year-olds in an Italian *scuola materna*, a government-sponsored nursery school:

> In the process of resisting adult rules, the children develop a sense of community and a group identity. [I would have put it the other way around: I think group identity leads to the resistance.] The children's resistance to adult rules can be seen as a routine because it is a daily occurrence in the nursery school and is produced in a style that is easily recognizable to members of the peer culture. Such activity is often highly exaggerated (for instance, making faces behind the teacher's back or running around) or is prefaced by "calls for the attention" of other children (such as, "look what I got" in reference to possession of a forbidden object, or "look what I'm doing" to call attention to a restricted activity.

Group contrast effects show up most clearly when "groupness"—Henri Tajfel's term—is salient. Children see adults as serious and sedentary, so when the social categories *kids* and *grownups* are salient—as they might be, for instance, when the teacher is being particularly bossy—the children become sillier and more active. They demonstrate their fealty to their own age group by making faces and running around.

This has nothing to do with whether they like their teachers personally. You can like people even if they're members of a different group and even if you don't much like that group—a conflict of interests summed up in the saying, "Some of my best friends are Jews." When groupness is salient, even young children contrast themselves with adults and collude with each other in defying them. And yet some of their best friends are grownups.

❧

Learning how to behave properly is complicated, because proper behavior depends on which social category you're in. In every society, the rules of behavior depend on whether you're a grownup or a kid, a female or a male, a prince or a peon. Children first have to figure out the social categories that are relevant in their society, and then decide which category they belong in, then tailor their behavior to the other members of their category.

That brief description seems to imply that socialization makes children more alike, and so it does, in some ways. But groups also work to create or exaggerate differences among their members—differences in personality. Even identical twins reared in the same home do not have identical personalities. When groupness is not salient—when there is no other group around to serve as a foil—a group tends to fall apart into individuals, and differences among them emerge or increase. In boys' groups, for example, there is usually a dominance hierarchy, or "pecking order." I have found evidence that dominant boys develop different personalities from those at the bottom of the ladder.

Groups also typecast their members, pinning labels on them—joker, nerd, brain—that can have lifelong repercussions. And children find out about themselves by comparing themselves with their group mates. They come to think well or poorly of themselves by judging how they compare with the other members of their own group. It doesn't matter if they don't measure up to the standards of another group. A third-grade boy can think of himself as smart if he knows more than most of his fellow third-graders. He doesn't have to know more than a fourth-grader.

❧

According to my theory, the culture acts upon children not through their parents but through the peer group. Children's groups have their own cultures, loosely based on the adult culture. They can pick and choose from the adult culture, and it's impossible to predict what they'll include. Anything that's common to the majority of the kids in the group may be incorporated into the children's culture, whether they learned it from their parents or from the television set. If most of the children learned to say "please" and "thank you" at home, they will probably continue to do so when they're with their peers. The child whose parents failed to teach her that custom will pick it up from the other children: it will be transmitted to her, via the peer group, from the parents of her peers. Similarly, if most of the children watch a particular

TV show, the behaviors and attitudes depicted in the show may be incorporated into the norms of their group. The child whose parents do not permit him to watch that show will nonetheless be exposed to those behaviors and attitudes. They are transmitted to him via the peer group.

Thus, even though individual parents may have no lasting effects on their children's behavior, the larger culture does have an effect. Child-rearing practices common to most of the people in a culture, such as teaching children to say "please" and "thank you," can have an effect. And the media can have an effect.

In the hunter-gatherer or tribal society, there was no privacy: everybody knew what everybody else was doing. Nowadays children can't ordinarily watch their neighbors making love, having babies, fighting, and dying, but they can watch these things happening on the television screen. Television has become their window on society, their village square. They take what they see on the screen to be an indication of what life is like—what life is supposed to be—and they incorporate it into their children's cultures.

—◦◉◦—

One of my goals in writing *The Nurture Assumption* was to lighten some of the burdens of modern parenthood. Back in the 1940s, when I was young, the parents of a troublesome child—my parents, for instance—got sympathy, not blame. Nowadays parents are likely to be held culpable for anything that goes wrong with their child, even if they've done their best. The evidence I've assembled in my book indicates that there is a limit to what parents can do: how their child turns out is largely out of their hands. Their major contribution occurs at the moment of conception. This doesn't mean it's mostly genetic; it means that the environment that shapes the child's personality and social behavior is outside the home.

I am not advocating irresponsibility. Parents are in charge of how their children behave at home. They can decide where their children will grow up and, at least in the early years, who their peers will be. They are the chief determiners of whether their children's life at home will be happy or miserable, and they have a moral obligation to keep it from being miserable. My theory does not grant people the license to treat children in a cruel or negligent way.

Although individual parents have little power to influence the culture of children's peer groups, larger numbers of parents acting together have a great deal of power, and so does the society as a whole. Through the prevailing methods of child rearing it fosters, and through influences—especially the media—that act directly on peer-group norms and values, a society shapes the adults of the future. Are we shaping them the way we ought to?

 **NO**

# Do Parents Count?

## 1.

We all want to know how and why we got to be who we are. Parents have a special interest in answering the "how" and "why" questions with respect to their own children. In addressing the mysteries of human growth, traditional societies have invoked God, the gods, the fates, with luck sometimes thrown in. Shakespeare called our attention to the struggle between "nature and nurture."

In our own time the natural sciences and the social sciences have been supplying a bewildering variety of answers. Those with biological leanings look to heredity—the gene complexes of each parent and the ways in which their melded sets of genes express themselves in the offspring. The traits and capacities of the biological parents are seen as in large part determining the characteristics of offspring. Those with a psychological or sociological perspective point to the factors beyond the child's physiology. Psychoanalysts emphasize the pivotal role of parents, and especially the young child's relationship to his or her mother. Behaviorists look at the contingencies of reward and punishment in the child's experience; the character of the child depends on the qualities that are "reinforced," with those in control of reinforcement in early life having an especially significant influence.

Recently, three new candidates have been proposed to explain "socialization"—i.e., how children grow up within a society and absorb its norms. Impressed and alarmed by the powers of new means of communication, particularly television, students of culture like Marie Winn and Neil Postman have described a generation raised by the electronic media. The historian of science Frank Sulloway has brought new attention to the once discounted factor of "birth order": on his account, first-borns embrace the status quo, while later-borns are far more likely to support scientific, political, or religious revolutions. And now, in a much publicized new work, Judith Rich Harris suggests that all of these authorities have got it wrong. On her account, the most potent "socializers" are the child's peers, with parents having little or no effect.

Harris's work has many things going for it. For a start, she has an arresting hypothesis, one that should strike especially responsive chords in adults who feel they are inadequately involved in the formation of the post-baby boom Generation X and the generations to come. She has an appealing personal story. Kicked out of graduate school in psychology in the early 1960s and a victim of a lupus-like disease, she has hitherto led the life of a semi-invalid, making her living coauthoring textbooks in psychology. One day in 1994, after reading a scholarly article about juvenile delinquency, she was struck by the idea that the role of peers in socialization had largely been ignored while the influence of parents had been much overestimated. She succeeded in publishing a theoretical statement of her view in *Psychological Review*, the most prestigious journal of psychological theory. She soon gained recognition among scholars and, in a delicious irony, won a prestigious award named after George Miller, the very professor who had signed her letter of expulsion from Harvard almost four decades ago. Harris's book is well-written, toughly argued, filled with telling anecdotes and biting wit. It has endorsements from some of the most prestigious names in the field. Already it has been widely—and mostly favorably—reported on and reviewed in the popular press.

However, in my view, Harris's thesis is overstated, misleading, and potentially harmful. Overstated in the sense that she highlights evidence consistent with her thesis and understates evidence that undermines it. Misleading because she treats as "natural" and "universal" what, in my view, is really a characterization of contemporary American culture (and those societies influenced by America). Potentially harmful in that it may, if inadvertently, discourage parents from promoting their own beliefs and values, and from becoming models of behavior, at a time when such values and models should be clearly and continually conveyed to children.

## 2.

Harris begins by outlining familiar positions in psychology. On her account, Freud's view of the Oedipal period is quaint and unsupported, while the behaviorists have been widely discredited, both by the cognitivists (who put the mind back into psychology) and the biologists (who reminded us that we are as much a product of our genes as of our experiences). She then turns her keen critical skills to an attack on the branch of empirical psychology that attempts to document important contributions of parents to their children's personality and character. (Harris uses both terms.)

For over half a century, psychologists and anthropologists have observed parents and children in different settings; they have filled out checklists in which they record predominant kinds of behavior and action, and they have administered questionnaires to the parents and children themselves. These researchers, according to Harris, began with the "nurture assumption"; they presupposed that the most important force in the child's environment is the child's parents and then collected evidence to support that assumption. Moreover, while scholars themselves are often guarded in their conclusions, some "pop" psychologists have no inhibitions whatever. They stress the role of parents over all other forces, thus making parents feel guilty if they fail (according to their own criteria), and full of pride when they succeed.

As Harris shrewdly points out, there are two problems with the nurture assumption. First, when viewed with a critical eye, the empirical evidence about parental influences on their children is weak, and often equivocal. After hundreds of studies, many with individually suggestive findings, it is still difficult to pinpoint the strong effects that parents have on their children. Even the effects of the most extreme experiences—divorce, adoption, and abuse—prove elusive to capture. Harris cites Eleanor Maccoby, one of the leading researchers in the field, who concluded that "in a study of nearly four hundred families, few connections were found between parental child-rearing practices (as reported by parents in detailed interviews) and independent assessments of children's personality characteristics—so few, indeed, that virtually nothing was published relating the two sets of data.

The second problem with the nurture assumption is potentially more devastating. Harris draws heavily on recent results from behavioral genetics to argue that, even in those cases where children resemble their parents, the presence and actions of parents have little to do with that resemblance. The argument she makes from behavioral genetics runs as follows. Studies of siblings, fraternal twins, identical twins reared together, and identical twins reared apart all point to the same conclusion: about half of one's intellect and personality results from one's genes. That is, in any group of people drawn from a particular "population" (e.g., middle-class white youngsters living in the United States), about one half of the variations in an observed trait (for instance, IQ or aggressiveness) is owing to one's parents' genetic contribution. The other half is, of course, the result of one's environment.

For those who assume that the behavior of parents and the models they offer make up a major part of the child's environment, the results of studies in behavioral genetics are surprising. According to those studies, when we examine any population of children and try to account for the nongenetic variations among them, we find that remarkably few variations can be attributed to their "shared environment"—i.e., when parents treat all of their children the same way, for example, being equally punitive to each child.

In fact, according to the behavioral geneticists, nearly all of the variation is due to what is called the "nonshared environment"—i.e., the variety of other influences, including instances where children are treated differently by the parents (e.g., a brother is punished more than his sister, or differently). In the case of any particular child, we simply do not know with any accuracy what makes up the nonshared environment. We can guess that it consists of siblings, printed matter, radio and television, other adults, school, luck, accident, the different (as opposed to the common or "shared") ways in which each parent responds to each child, and—if Judith Rich Harris is correct— most especially, a child's peers.

❧◈❧

So much for Harris's demolition of the importance of parents—except genetically—to the behavior and psyche of the child. Harris adduces evidence from a wide variety of sources, moreover, to stress the important contribution of peers. She goes back to the studies of nonhuman primates to indicate the importance of peer groups in child-rearing—pointing out that monkeys can be successfully reared by peers alone but not by their mothers alone. (It's not known whether this would be true in "higher" primates.) She cites observations of children in different cultures who play together as much and as early as possible, and routinely gang up on the adults (teachers, parents, masters). She searches in the experimental literature for cases where peers exert an appreciable influence upon one another—for example, adolescents who have the same friends turn out to resemble one another. And she places great emphasis on the human tendency to form groups—and particularly "in-groups" with which one strongly identifies.

Harris also provides many telling anecdotes from her own experiences, and from the press and television, about how adults are ignored and peers admired. British boys who rarely see their parents successfully absorb social values at boarding school. Secretary of Labor Robert Reich quit the Cabinet to be with his sons in Cambridge and found that they would rather hang out "in the Square." Touchingly she indicates how she and her husband tried to deal with their wayward adopted daughter but finally realized that the peers had more influence. No such problems existed with their biological daughter, who simply followed her biological destiny; the model provided by her parents was no more than an unnecessary bonus.

Harris describes recurrent situations where youngsters overlook the evident models of their parents in favor of those provided by peers. Deaf children of speaking parents ignore their parents' attempts to teach them to read lips and instead begin to invent gestural signs to communicate with other deaf children and seek opportunities to learn formal signing. The hearing children of deaf parents, Harris points out, learn to speak normally in the absence of a parental model. Analogously, children raised by parents with foreign accents soon begin to speak like their peers, without an accent; like the deaf children, they ignore the models at home and turn, as if magnetized, to the most available set of peers. Arguments like these convince Harris, and apparently many readers (both lay and professional), that young human beings are wired to attend to people of similar age, rather than to those large and obvious authority figures who give them birth and early shelter.

## 3.

Harris has collected an impressive set of examples and findings to fortify a position that is indeed novel in empirical investigations of "human socialization." I have sought to do justice to her arguments, though I cannot convey her passion, her missionary sense of having seen the light. Yet I do not find her "peer hypothesis" convincing, partly because I read the literature on the subject differently. My deeper reservations come from my belief that Harris has misconstrued the problem of socialization and, in doing so, has put forth a position that harbors its own dangers.

When we consider the empirical part of Harris's argument, we find it is indeed true that the research on parent-child socialization is not what we would hope for. However, this says less about parents and children and more about the state of psychological research, particularly with reference to "softer variables" such as affection and ambition. While psychologists have made genuine progress in the study of visual perception and measurable progress in the study of cognition, we do not really know what to look for or how to measure human personality traits, individual emotions, and motivations, let alone character.

Consider, as an example, the categories that the respondents must use when they describe themselves or others on the Personal Attributes Questionnaire, a test used to obtain data about a person's self-esteem and gender-linked traits. Drawing on a list reminiscent of the Boy Scout oath, those who answer the questionnaire are asked whether they would describe themselves as Gentle, Helpful, Active, Competitive, and Worldly. These terms are not easy to define and people are certainly prone to apply them favorably to their own case. Or consider the list of acts from which observers can choose to characterize children from different cultures—Offers Help, Acts Sociably, Assaults Sociably, Seeks Dominance. Even if we could agree on what kinds of physical behavior merit these labels, we don't know with any confidence what these acts mean to children, adolescents, and adults in diverse cultures—let alone to the observers from a distant university. What does a raised fist or a frown mean to a three-year-old or to the thirty-year-old who observes it? The same question could be asked about a wink or an imitated curtsy. We are not measuring chemical bonds or electrical voltage in such cases. We are seeking to quantify the most subtle human characteristics—the sentiments described so finely by Henry James. And therefore it is not surprising when studies—whether by empirical psychologists or behavioral geneticists—do not yield strong results.

I do not want to elevate psychoanalytic theory or practice over other kinds of inquiry, but at least the Freudians were grappling with the deeper aspects of human character and personality—our urgent longings, our innermost fears and anxieties, our wrenching conflicts. We might perhaps find evidence for these complex feelings—and their putative causes—through long narratives, or projective testing (where the subjects respond to ambiguous photographs or inkblots), or by analyzing a series of sessions on the couch. We won't reach them through questionnaires or checklists; yet Harris relies on many studies that use them.

As social scientists we have been frustrated by our own clumsy efforts to understand personality and character, and even relatively measurable skills, like intelligence or the capacity for problem-solving. And perhaps that is why so many talented psychologists—including the ones quoted on the jacket of *The Nurture Assumption*—have become drawn to evolutionary psychology and behavioral genetics. Here, at last, is the chance to put psychology and social science (and even squishy inquiries into personality, temperament, and character) on what seems a "real" scientific footing. Physics envy has been replaced by biological bias.

But things are not as clear-cut in the biobehavioral world as outsiders may imagine. Because of the possibility of controlled experiments, sociobiology has made genuine progress in explaining the social life of insects; but its account of human behavior remains controversial. The speculations of evolutionary psychology are just that; as commentators such as Stephen Jay Gould and Steve

Jones have pointed out . . . , it is difficult to know how to disprove a hypothesis in evolutionary psychology. (For example, what evidence can help us decide whether genes, or humans, are really selfish, or really altruistic, or really both?—in which case we are back where we started.)

❧

And what of behavioral genetics? Certainly the opportunity to study twins who have been separated early in life gives us an additional advantage in understanding the heritability of various traits. And Judith Harris rightly calls attention to two enigmas: the fact that identical twins reared apart are almost as alike as those that are reared together; and the fact that identical twins still turn out to be quite different from one another.

But this subject is also dogged by difficulties. We cannot really do experiments in human behavioral genetics; we have to wait until events happen (as when twins are separated early in life) and then study the effects retrospectively. But this approach leaves too many puzzles unaddressed. First of all, for at least nine crucial months, the twins share the same environment—the womb of the birth mother—and we still know very little about the shared chemical and other effects of gestation on their neurological systems. Then, too, they may or may not have been separated right at birth. (And under what extraordinary circumstances does such separation occur?) They may or may not have been raised for a while by family members. The children are not randomly placed; in nearly all cases, they are raised within the same culture and very often in the same community, with similar social settings. Also, infants who look the same and behave the same are likely to elicit similar responses from adults, while those who are raised in the same house may try all the harder to distinguish themselves from one another. Or they may not.

When you add together the uncertainties (and I have only suggested a few of them here) of human behavioral genetics, and the imprecision of the measures used to describe personality and character, it is no wonder that we find little reliable evidence of parental influence. It would be reassuring if we did—but it is not surprising that we do not.

Which brings me to the alternative picture that Harris attempts to construct. She argues that "peers" are the real instrument of socialization. She may be right; but she does not have the evidence to show this. Her assertions depend almost entirely on what she thinks could one day be shown. Indeed, I find it extremely telling that she relies very heavily on the arguments about language—language-learning among the deaf, and the loss of foreign accents. Neither of these has to do with personality, character, or temperament, her supposed topics. In the case of accents, I assume that we are dealing with an unconscious (and presumably innate) process in which the growing child generalizes from his encounters with many of the adults and children he meets outside the home and through television, the movies, and other media. In the case of deafness, the enormous difference between child and parents forces youngsters to make use of resources outside the home—ranging from adult teachers to television and other visual media.

Indeed, despite some imaginative suggestions by Harris, it is very difficult to envision how one could test her hypothesis. For, after all, who are peers? Do they include siblings? Are they the children in the neighborhood? The children in class? The children in after-school activities or in Sunday school? The children on television? In the movies? At some remote spot on the Internet? Who decides? What happens when peers change because the family moves, or one child switches schools, or leaves (or is kicked out of) one group and then enters another? Most important, who selects peers? At least with parents, we researchers stand on fairly firm ground; and with siblings as well. But for all Ms. Harris's anecdotes, when it comes to peers, we're afloat.

Undoubtedly, psychological researchers inspired by Harris's book will seek evidence bearing on her thesis. We will learn from these studies; and some of us who have taken skeptical positions in this debate may have to acknowledge influences we hadn't sufficiently recognized. Meanwhile, I want to suggest an entirely different approach to the problem, one that might be called "the culture assumption."

# 4.

What is socialization about? It is about becoming a certain kind of person—gaining specific knowledge, skills, manners, attitudes, and habits. Animals have little culture; human beings revel in it. Yet what is striking in Harris's book is that the words "disciplines," "civilization," and "culture" (in the sense of civilization) are largely absent from the text and from her thinking. Socialization is reduced to having, or not having, certain personality traits—traits that are measured by rather coarsely conceived and applied tests.

The work of the much-maligned Freud remains the best point of departure for a treatment of these issues. In his *Civilization and Its Discontents*, Freud defined culture: "the sum of the achievements and institutions which differentiate our lives from those of our animal forebears, namely that of protecting humanity against nature and of regulating the relations of human beings among themselves." He concentrates particularly on "the one feature of culture which characterizes it better than any other, and that is the value that it sets upon the higher mental activities—intellectual, scientific, and aesthetic achievement." And he speculates that culture (or civilization) rests upon the human superego—the sense of guilt—which develops (or fails to develop) during the child's early interactions with his parents. Guilt keeps us from murdering our fellow citizens; guilt prompts us to delay gratification, to sublimate our primordial passions in favor of loftier pursuits.

Whether one examines the least developed preliterate culture or the most advanced technological society, the question remains the same: What structures and practices will enable children to assume their places in that culture and ultimately aid in transmitting it to the generations to come?

Children will have some say in this process, and it is to Harris's credit (and that of the authorities whom she cites) that she has called attention to this fact. But children are not born just into a family or into a peer group.

They are born into an entire culture, whose assumptions begin when the parents say, happily or with a twinge of regret, "It's a girl," and continues to exert its influence in nearly every interaction and experience until the funerary rites, burial, cremation, or ascent to heaven takes place.

Earlier, I referred to Eleanor Maccoby's pessimistic conclusions about documenting parental influence, and I mentioned some of the studies of it that both Maccoby and Harris seem to have had in mind. But let me reconsider the most ambitious of these studies in a different light. In the 1950s and 1960s, John Whiting, Beatrice Whiting, and their colleagues studied childrearing in six cultures, ranging from a small New England town to agricultural settings in Kenya, India, Mexico, the Philippines, and Okinawa. What emerges from that study is that childrearing practices are distinctly different around the globe: different in treatment of infants, in parental sleeping patterns, in how children do chores, in their helping or not helping in rearing younger siblings, in initiation rites, in ways of handling aggression, and in dozens of other variables. So differently are children reared in these cultures that no one would confuse an adult New Englander with an adult Gusii of Kenya or an adult Taira of Okinawa—whether in their knowledge, skills, manners, habits, personality, or temperament.

For the social scientist, the analytic problem is to find the source of these differences. Parents behave differently in these cultures, but so do siblings, peers, other adults, and even visiting anthropologists. And of course the adult roles, natural resources, technology, and means of communication (primitive or modern) differ as well. In all probability, each of these factors makes its contribution to the child's "personality and character." But how to tell them apart? Harris chooses to minimize these other factors and zooms in on the peers, but her confident choice is not justified.

# 5.

Harris takes little note of a crucial fact: all but a few of the studies that she reviews, including several of the most influential behavioral genetic ones, were carried out in the United States. The United States is not a country without culture; it has many subcultures and a more general "national" culture as well. Harris and most of the authorities that she cites are not studying child-rearing in general; indeed, they are studying child-rearing largely in the white, middle-class United States during the last half-century.

From the time of Alexis de Tocqueville's visit to the United States in the early 1830s, observers have noted the relative importance in this country of peers, friends, or fellow workers of the same age, the members of one's own community. Tocqueville commented, "In America the family, in the Roman and aristocratic signification of the word, does not exist. All that remains are a few vestiges in the first years of childhood. . . ." As a sociologist might put it, America is a more horizontal, "peer-oriented" society than most others, and particularly more so than most traditional societies.

When empirical social science began in this country, these unusual cultural patterns were noted as well. Studying the America of the 1940s, the sociologist

David Riesman and his coauthors called attention to the decline of tradition-centered and "inner-directed" families, where the parental models were powerful; and to the concomitant rise of the "other-directed families" that made up "the Lonely Crowd." In this increasingly common family constellation, much socialization occurred at the behest of the peer group, whether for adults or for children. Riesman wrote, "The American peer group, too, cannot be matched for power throughout the middle-class world."

Examining the America of the 1950s and 1960s, the psychologist Urie Bronfrenbrenner noted that children spend more time with peers than with parents and reached the same conclusion: "Whether in comparison to other contemporary cultures, or to itself over time, American society emerges as one that gives decreasing prominence to the family as a socializing agency. . . . We are coming to live in a society that is exaggerated not only by race and class, but also by age." Thus not only has the peer group had an important part in American society from the first; but in recent decades this trend has accelerated.

But there are many possible peer groups. To which ones are children drawn and why? Here I believe (and Harris concedes this) that parents have a decisive role—by the friendships they encourage or discourage, by the schools they select or avoid, by the after-school activities they encourage and summer camps they approve of, parents contribute substantially to the choice of possible peer groups. I would go one step further. Children themselves select—and are selected for—various peer groups according to parental predilections. The work of the social psychologist Mihaly Csikszentmihalyi on "talented teens" strongly suggests that the values exhibited at home—integrity vs. dishonesty, hard work vs. laziness, artistic interests vs. philistinism—imprint themselves on children and in turn serve as major determinants of the peer groups to which children are attracted and, not incidentally, the ones where they are welcomed or spurned.

# 6.

It seems that in every passing decade—perhaps in every passing selection of fall books—we are told of a new approach to bringing up children or of a new, villainous influence on family life. Certainly, we do not have the feeling of a steady scientific march toward truth. It is more as if we are on a roller-coaster, with each new hypothesis tending to invalidate the previous one.

Still, it would be defeatist simply to embrace the opposite perspective, to declare that each of the various factors—mother, father, grandparents, same-sex siblings, different-sex peers, television, etc.—is important and be done with it. As a scientific community, we can do better than this. To do so, we should be undertaking two activities.

First, even as we welcome the clarifications provided by evolution and genetics, we cannot lose sight of the different cultural settings in which research is carried out and the different meanings attached to seemingly similar traits and actions. Parents and peers have different meanings in Japan, Brazil, and the United States; what we learn from the Whitings, and from much other sociological and anthropological research, is that these "independent variables" cannot simply be equated in designing research or in interpreting findings. In fact, a father may be treated more like a sibling in one society, and an older sibling more like a father in another; parents may encourage children to associate with peers in one culture and to steer clear of them in another and, in yet another, to combat their influence in every way they can.

Second, even as we discover genes or gene clusters that appear to influence important social or psychological variables, we must not assume that we have "solved" the problem of socialization. We still don't know the physical mechanisms by which genes actually affect the brain and cause people to make one choice or another. What triggers (or fails to trigger) genes will vary across cultural settings; and how their expression is understood will also vary. Young men, for example, may have a proclivity to imitate other young men of similar size and power, but that proclivity can be manipulated, depending upon whom the child is exposed to and which rewards and punishments are contingent upon imitation or non-imitation.

Each of the numerous influences on a child's personality I have mentioned can surely have an effect, but the effect will vary among different children, families, and cultures. As science progresses, we may someday be able to predict the relative importance of each across these different factors. My reading of the research suggests that, on the average, parents and peers will turn out to have complementary roles: parents are more important when it comes to education, discipline, responsibility, orderliness, charitableness, and ways of interacting with authority figures. Peers are more important for learning cooperation, for finding the road to popularity, for inventing styles of interaction among people of the same age. Youngsters may find their peers more interesting, but they will look to their parents when contemplating their own futures.

Parental attitudes and efforts will determine to a significant extent how a child resolves the conflicting messages of the home and the wider community as well as the kind of parent the child one day becomes. I would give much weight to the hundreds of studies pointing toward parental influence and to the folk wisdom accumulated by hundreds of societies over thousands of years. And I would, accordingly, be skeptical of a perspective, such as Ms. Harris's, that relies too heavily on heritability statistics and manages to reanalyze numerous studies and practices so that they all somehow point to the peer group.

To gain attention, an author often states a finding or hypothesis very strongly. (I've been guilty of this myself.) In Harris's case, this has led to a belittling of the roles of parents in child-rearing and to a stronger endorsement of the role of peers than the current data allow. I do not question Harris's motives but I do question her judgment, which might have been better guided by the old medical oath "first, do no harm."

It is all to the good if parents do not become crushed with anxiety when they have problems with their children or when their children turn out differently than they would like. Guilt is not always productive. But to suggest, with little foundation, that parents are not important in socialization borders on the irresponsible. Perhaps, on the average, those of us who are parents are not particularly successful in encouraging the personality traits we would hope to see in our children, whether because we do not know how to get their attention, or because they are "primed" to pay attention to their peers and we are not aware of how long and how hard we must work to counter these proclivities.

But children would not—could not—grow to be members of a civilized culture if they were simply left to the examples of their peers. Indeed, parents are especially important when children's peers set strong and destructive examples. In the absence of credible parents and other adults, most children will not be able to deal effectively with life. A social science—or a layman's guide—that largely left out parents after birth would be absurd. So would a society.

Whether on the scene, or behind the scenes, parents have jointly created the institutions that train and inspire children: apprenticeships, schools, works of art and literature, religious classes, playing fields, and even forms of resistance and rebellion. These institutions, and the adults who run them, sustain civilization and provide the disciplines—however fragile they may seem—that keep our societies from reverting to barbarism.

Sad to say, these most important parts of life—which make life satisfying and fascinating—are largely absent from *The Nurture Assumption*. They are absent as well from most of the work emanating from the biotropic pole of contemporary social science. Until their importance is realized, and the biological and cultural perspectives are somehow deeply integrated with one another, scientific claims about children and family life are bound to remain barren.

# POSTSCRIPT

## Are Peers More Important Than Parents During the Process of Development?

**B**efore reading about this controversy, most people take for granted that parents are the most important influence on life span development. Many express a sincere belief that their parents made them into the men or women they are today. But after reading about this controversy, students of life span development often take pause when thinking about the influence of parents. Whether or not you ultimately agree with Judith Rich Harris, she does raise powerful and provocative questions about the role of parents in life span development.

Harris' most general point is that the scientific evidence for parental influence in the process of socialization is simply lacking. Despite extensive research attention, she suggests that there is little convincing evidence for the influence of parents. Thus, her strongest claim can be paraphrased as: You could take the children in a given community, switch around their parents, and find the same developmental outcomes. In response, Howard Gardner provides a critique allowing us to maintain our faith in the importance of parents. Gardner provides an intelligent review of the ways Harris' argument relies on limited types of data, and asserts that parents matter in the deep and complex ways that we can only appreciate through respecting the expansiveness of socialization experiences.

While Gardner focuses on the content of Harris' argument, some scholars of life span development have challenged Harris because of her lack of a formal academic position—she never finished the Harvard Ph.D. that she began, instead turning to a life as a housewife and textbook author. Yet Harris' initial academic article questioning the role of parents was awarded a prestigious annual prize for scientific work given by the American Psychological Association (an award, ironically, named for the former chairman of Harvard's psychology department who was responsible for telling Harris she did not have the potential to do meaningful work and should not continue with her Ph.D. studies).

The implication of criticizing Harris' lack of a formal academic position is that she is not really able to engage a scientific approach to understanding life span development. Ultimately, this is the root of most critiques of her thesis that parents don't matter. Her thesis is provocative, her argument is logical, and she raises important concerns about the state of research on developmental influences. But does it hold up to science? Gardner asserts that the answer is no, but he also acknowledges that science does not yet clearly delineate the key influences on development.

Many scholars continue to maintain and investigate ways that parents matter most. But in fine scientific form, others pursue different directions, some asserting that culture overwhelms any other influence on the lifespan, some focusing on genes, some focusing on peers, some focusing on the media. Perhaps the only certainty here is that what matters most for development will continue to be controversial.

## Suggested Readings

N. Barber, *Why Parents Matter: Parental Investment and Child Outcomes* (Greenwood Publishing Group, 2000).

W.A. Collins, E.E. Maccoby, L. Steinberg, E.M. Hetherington, and M.H. Bornstein, "Contemporary Research on Parenting: The Case for Nature and Nurture," *American Psychologist* (February 2002).

J. Rich Harris, *The Nurture Assumption: Why Children Turn Out the Way They Do* (The Free Press, 1998).

J. Rich Harris and J. Kagan, "Slate Dialogues: E-mail Debates of Newsworthy Topics—The Nature of Nurture: Parents or Peers?" http://slate.msn.com/id/5853/ (November 1998).

M. Spett, "Is It True That Parenting Has No Influence on Children's Adult Personalities?" *NJ-ACT Newsletter* (March 1999).

D.L. Vandell and J.R. Harris, "Genes, Parents, and Peers: An Invited Exchange of Views," *Developmental Psychology* (November 2000).

W. Williams, "Do Parents Matter? Scholars Need to Explain What Research Really Shows," *The Chronicle of Higher Education* (December 11, 1998).

# ISSUE 3

## Do Significant Innate Differences Influence the Success of Males and Females?

**YES: Steven Pinker,** from "Sex Ed: The Science of Difference," *The New Republic* (February 14, 2005)

**NO: Cynthia Russett,** from "All About Eve: What Men Have Thought about Women Thinking," *The American Scholar* (vol. 74, 2005)

### ISSUE SUMMARY

**YES:** Cognitive psychologist and author Steven Pinker considers the loud response to the suggestion of Harvard president Lawrence Summers that differences between the numbers of men and women in science might be partly related to innate abilities. Pinker asserts that this possibility is well grounded in research, but provokes reactions based on flawed assumptions of gender equality.

**NO:** Cynthia Russett, a professor at Yale, argues that harmful assumptions of innate deficiencies in woman have a long, and significantly flawed, historical precedent without basis in fact.

In 2004, the president of Harvard University Lawrence Summers stirred an energetic controversy about the origin of differences between males and females in fields such as science and math. While making comments at a conference of elite academics and scientists, he provocatively suggested that one of the reasons (and, it is important to note, Summers clearly identified other social forces as influential) for the differences could be innate mental capacity. Immediately after making the comments, a prominent female scientist attending the talk left the room appalled by the suggestion, and a popular uproar ensued. Newspaper editorial pages everywhere were filled with comment and controversy.

The notion of innate differences in mental functioning between men and women is foundational to the popular contemporary study of evolutionary psychology. Applying Darwinian evolutionary principles to the study of human behavior, evolutionary psychologists have devoted extensive attention to sex differences. For these researchers, sex differences are a ripe area for study because of two basic facts: Many differences between males and females are evident across diverse cultural settings—suggesting that there is something universal about gender differences, and there are clear natural differences in factors influencing the reproductive success of men and women—suggesting that psychological predispositions may have evolved differently by gender.

In diverse cultural (and historical) settings, women are, on average, generally found to take primary responsibility for child rearing and caring for a family. Men, in contrast, on average are generally tasked with providing resources to sustain families and communities. This has led to a general conception of women as more caring and family oriented, while men are often characterized as more independent and achievement oriented. The challenge, however, is that these conceptions fit well with what are clearly social stereotypes; there are many exceptions to both of these broad generalizations.

Nevertheless, when average differences are found across diverse settings, evolutionary psychologists tend to investigate. The evolutionary pressures for men and women contain clear and obvious differences. From this perspective, a general need to insure that one's genetic material is passed on to future generations guides human behavior. For women, passing on one's genetic material usually requires a significant investment of time and energy. Men, in contrast, are able to pass on their genetic material with a much less significant investment of time.

So what does all of this have to do with adult success? In recent social science research and writing, it has been common to suggest that evolution designed the male and female brain for slightly different adaptive tasks. Steven Pinker, contextualizing Summers' remarks in relation to such research, has been a prominent proponent of the idea that our minds have clear innate predispositions. As one of the most prodigious academic psychologists of recent decades, Pinker argues forcefully that the idea that the mind is originally a "blank slate"—is highly improbable. He is familiar with extensive research showing that cognitive development in areas as diverse as language and spatial reasoning seems subject to diverse evolutionary pressures. Such research was the foundation for Lawrence Summers' controversial suggestion that biology may be one of the reasons for differing levels of success in certain academic fields. De-contextualized, it seems Summers was simply claiming women are less able than men. We all know too many personal examples of women's achievement to believe this to be the case.

And, in fact, as Cynthia Russett observes in arguing against innate gender differences, the tendency to attribute male and female differences in cognitive abilities to innate biological capacities has been a comically repetitive historical endeavor. From the ancient Greeks to twentieth-century pseudo-scientists, there seems to be an impulse to explain gender differences (implicitly acknowledged to be a consistent feature of most human societies) as biological. Russett points out a clear irony, however, in the fact that the types of gender differences addressed change pending socio-historical context. Ultimately then, Russett challenges us to consider whether the innate human tendency is not aptitude, but a compulsion to falsely attribute gender differences to biology.

# YES

**Steven Pinker**

## Sex Ed: The Science of Difference

**W**hen I was an undergraduate in the early 1970s, I was assigned a classic paper published in *Scientific American* that began: "There is an experiment in psychology that you can perform easily in your home. . . . Buy two presents for your wife, choosing things . . . she will find equally attractive." Just ten years after those words were written, the author's blithe assumption that his readers were male struck me as comically archaic. By the early '70s, women in science were no longer an oddity or a joke but a given. Today, in my own field, the study of language development in children, a majority of the scientists are women. Even in scientific fields with a higher proportion of men, the contributions of women are so indispensable that any talk of turning back the clock would be morally heinous and scientifically ruinous.

Yet to hear the reaction to Harvard President Lawrence Summers's remarks at a conference on gender imbalances in science, in which he raised the possibility of innate sex differences, one might guess that he had proposed exactly that. Nancy Hopkins, the eminent MIT biologist and advocate for women in science, stormed out of the room to avoid, she said, passing out from shock. An engineering dean called his remarks "an intellectual tsunami," and, with equal tastelessness, a *Boston Globe* columnist compared him to people who utter racial epithets or wear swastikas. Alumnae threatened to withhold donations, and the National Organization of Women called for his resignation. Summers was raked in a letter signed by more than 100 Harvard faculty members and shamed into issuing serial apologies.

Summers did not, of course, say that women are "natively inferior," that "they just can't cut it," that they suffer "an inherent cognitive deficit in the sciences," or that men have "a monopoly on basic math ability," as many academics and journalists assumed. Only a madman could believe such things. Summers's analysis of why there might be fewer women in mathematics and science is commonplace among economists who study gender disparities in employment, though it is rarely mentioned in the press or in academia when it comes to discussions of the gender gap in science and engineering. The fact that women make up only 20 percent of the workforce in science, engineering, and technology development has at least three possible (and not mutually exclusive) explanations. One is the persistence of discrimination, discouragement, and other barriers. In popular discussions of gender imbalances in the

---

workforce, this is the explanation most mentioned. Although no one can deny that women in science still face these injustices, there are reasons to doubt they are the only explanation. A second possibility is that gender disparities can arise in the absence of discrimination as long as men and women differ, on average, in their mixture of talents, temperaments, and interests—whether this difference is the result of biology, socialization, or an interaction of the two. A third explanation is that child-rearing, still disproportionately shouldered by women, does not easily co-exist with professions that demand Herculean commitments of time. These considerations speak against the reflex of attributing every gender disparity to gender discrimination and call for research aimed at evaluating the explanations.

❦

The analysis should have been unexceptionable. Anyone who has fled a cluster of men at a party debating the fine points of flat-screen televisions can appreciate that fewer women than men might choose engineering, even in the absence of arbitrary barriers. (As one female social scientist noted in *Science Magazine*, "Reinventing the curriculum will not make me more interested in learning how my dishwasher works.") To what degree these and other differences originate in biology must be determined by research, not fatwa. History tells us that how much we want to believe a proposition is not a reliable guide as to whether it is true.

Nor is a better understanding of the causes of gender disparities inconsequential. Overestimating the extent of sex discrimination is not without costs. Unprejudiced people of both sexes who are responsible for hiring and promotion decisions may be falsely charged with sexism. Young women may be pressured into choosing lines of work they don't enjoy. Some proposed cures may do more harm than good; for example, gender quotas for grants could put deserving grantees under a cloud of suspicion, and forcing women onto all university committees would drag them from their labs into endless meetings. An exclusive focus on overt discrimination also diverts attention from policies that penalize women inadvertently because of the fact that, as the legal theorist Susan Estrich has put it, "Waiting for the connection between gender and parenting to be broken is waiting for Godot." A tenure clock that conflicts with women's biological clocks, and family-unfriendly demands like evening seminars and weekend retreats, are obvious examples. The regrettably low proportion of women who have received tenured job offers from Harvard during Summers's presidency may be an unintended consequence of his policy of granting tenure to scholars early in their careers, when women are more likely to be bearing the full burdens of parenthood.

Conservative columnists have had a field day pointing to the Harvard hullabaloo as a sign of runaway political correctness at elite universities. Indeed, the quality of discussion among the nation's leading scholars and pundits is not a pretty sight. Summers's critics have repeatedly mangled his suggestion that innate differences might be one cause of gender disparities (a suggestion that he drew partly from a literature review in my book, *The Blank Slate*) into the claim that they must be the only cause. And they have converted his suggestion that the statistical distributions of men's and women's abilities are not identical to the claim that all men are talented and all women are not—as if someone heard that women typically live longer than men and concluded that every woman lives longer than every man. Just as depressing is an apparent unfamiliarity with the rationale behind political equality, as when Hopkins sarcastically remarked that, if Summers were right, Harvard should amend its admissions policy, presumably to accept fewer women. This is a classic confusion between the factual claim that men and women are not indistinguishable and the moral claim that we ought to judge people by their individual merits rather than the statistics of their group.

Many of Summers's critics believe that talk of innate gender differences is a relic of Victorian pseudoscience, such as the old theory that cogitation harms women by diverting blood from their ovaries to their brains. In fact, much of the scientific literature has reported numerous statistical differences between men and women. As I noted in *The Blank Slate*, for instance, men are, on average, better at mental rotation and mathematical word problems; women are better at remembering locations and at mathematical calculation. Women match shapes more quickly, are better at reading faces, are better spellers, retrieve words more fluently, and have a better memory for verbal material. Men take greater risks and place a higher premium on status; women are more solicitous to their children.

Of course, just because men and women are different does not mean that the differences are triggered by genes. People develop their talents and personalities in response to their social milieu, which can change rapidly. So some of today's sex differences in cognition could be as culturally determined as sex differences in hair and clothing. But the belief, still popular among some academics (particularly outside the biological sciences), that children are born unisex and are molded into male and female roles by their parents and society is becoming less credible. Many sex differences are universal across cultures (the twentieth-century belief in sex-reversed tribes is as specious as the nineteenth-century belief in blood-deprived ovaries), and some are found in other primates. Men's and women's brains vary in numerous ways, including the receptors for sex hormones. Variations in these hormones, especially before birth, can exaggerate or minimize the typical male and female patterns in cognition and personality. Boys with defective genitals who are surgically feminized and raised as girls have been known to report feeling like they are trapped in the wrong body and to show characteristically male attitudes and interests. And a meta- analysis of 172 studies by psychologists Hugh Lytton and David Romney in 1991 found virtually no consistent difference in the way contemporary Americans socialize their sons and daughters. Regardless of whether it explains the gender disparity in science, the idea that some sex differences have biological roots cannot be dismissed as Neanderthal ignorance.

Since most sex differences are small and many favor women, they don't necessarily give an advantage to men in school or on the job. But Summers invoked yet another difference that may be more consequential. In many traits, men show greater variance than women, and are disproportionately found at both the low and high ends of the distribution. Boys are more likely to be learning disabled or retarded but also more likely to reach the top percentiles in assessments of mathematical ability, even though boys and girls are similar in the bulk of the bell curve. The pattern is readily explained by evolutionary biology. Since a male can have more offspring than a female—but also has a greater chance of being childless (the victims of other males who impregnate the available females)—natural selection favors a slightly more conservative and reliable baby-building process for females and a slightly more ambitious and error-prone process for males. That is because the advantage of an exceptional daughter (who still can have only as many children as a female can bear and nurse in a lifetime) would be canceled out by her unexceptional sisters, whereas an exceptional son who might sire several dozen grandchildren can more than make up for his dull childless brothers. One doesn't have to accept the evolutionary explanation to appreciate how greater male variability could explain, in part, why more men end up with extreme levels of achievement.

❧

What are we to make of the breakdown of standards of intellectual discourse in this affair—the statistical innumeracy, the confusion of fairness with sameness, the refusal to glance at the scientific literature? It is not a disease of tenured radicals; comparable lapses can be found among the political right (just look at its treatment of evolution). Instead, we may be seeing the operation of a fascinating bit of human psychology.

The psychologist Philip Tetlock has argued that the mentality of taboo—the belief that certain ideas are so dangerous that it is sinful even to think them—is not a quirk of Polynesian culture or religious superstition but is ingrained into our moral sense. In 2000, he reported asking university students their opinions of unpopular but defensible proposals, such as allowing people to buy and sell organs or auctioning adoption licenses to the highest-bidding parents. He found that most of his respondents did not even try to refute the proposals but expressed shock and outrage at having been asked to entertain them. They refused to consider positive arguments for the proposals and sought to cleanse themselves by volunteering for campaigns to oppose them. Sound familiar?

The psychology of taboo is not completely irrational. In maintaining our most precious relationships, it is not enough to say and do the right thing. We have to show that our heart is in the right place and that we don't weigh the costs and benefits of selling out those who trust us. If someone offers to buy your child or your spouse or your vote, the appropriate response is not to think it over or to ask how much. The appropriate response is to refuse even to consider the possibility. Anything less emphatic would betray the awful truth that you don't understand what it means to be a genuine parent or spouse or citizen. (The logic of taboo underlies the horrific fascination of plots whose protagonists are agonized by unthinkable thoughts, such as *Indecent Proposal* and *Sophie's Choice*.) Sacred and tabooed beliefs also work as membership badges in coalitions. To believe something with a perfect faith, to be incapable of apostasy, is a sign of fidelity to the group and loyalty to the cause. Unfortunately, the psychology of taboo is incompatible with the ideal of scholarship, which is that any idea is worth thinking about, if only to determine whether it is wrong.

At some point in the history of the modern women's movement, the belief that men and women are psychologically indistinguishable became sacred. The reasons are understandable: Women really had been held back by bogus claims of essential differences. Now anyone who so much as raises the question of innate sex differences is seen as "not getting it" when it comes to equality between the sexes. The tragedy is that this mentality of taboo needlessly puts a laudable cause on a collision course with the findings of science and the spirit of free inquiry.

# All About Eve: What Men Have Thought about Women Thinking

**H**as there ever been a time when people did not speculate about the differences between men and women? Probably not, since men and women are alike in so many obvious ways, and yet different enough to invite endless commentary. When President Lawrence Summers of Harvard recently ventured to suggest that women's lesser success as scientists might result from lesser innate ability, he placed himself in a long line of philosophers, theologians, scientists, and social and political theorists, stretching back to ancient times, who attempted to differentiate between the sexes by focusing on their mental capacities.

The most obvious differences in men and women are of course found in the anatomy and physiology of the human body, and early philosophers tended to concentrate on what could be learned from studying physical characteristics, often extrapolating from bodies to minds. Plato was a notable exception; he was no empiricist, and his ideas about women did not depend on their bodily form. But Plato's ideas are confusing, since they do not cohere, and are fragmentary and sometimes contradictory. His dialogues contain many derogatory comments about women and "womanish" traits. Women are overly emotional; they weep and lack self-control. They are less courageous than men. Plato makes a radical distinction between bodies and souls. The noble individual possesses a soul able to rise above the body to contemplate the Forms. But women are less likely to transcend their bodies, and cowardly men are likely to return in a later incarnation as women. Plato certainly did not see men and women as equals. Women are weaker in body, and perhaps in mind. Men's accomplishments outshine women's.

It is worth remembering, though, that Plato lived in a period when equality between men and women was almost inconceivable, and certainly not practiced in the city of Athens. The women he saw around him—uneducated, confined to their homes, unable to participate in philosophical dialogues or in the public life of the polis—were without doubt underdeveloped socially and intellectually. It is remarkable, therefore, that Plato's *Republic* offers a vision of an ideal society very different from that of Athens, one in which both men and women are members of the Guardians, or rulers. In the *Republic,* Plato makes the case for choosing individuals for certain positions on the basis not of their sex but of their abilities. He offers the analogy of two cobblers, one bald and one with abundant hair. You would not suppose that the hairy one had a particular aptitude for cobbling while the bald one did not. So also for the procreative differences between women and men: they are no more significant for channeling the two sexes into different occupations than are variations in hirsuteness. Thus, based on their capacities, women as well as men could be part of a social and political elite. To be sure, women who were educated and trained just like men would have to put aside a normal home life and the rearing of their children, but the inference is clear that they could be as rational in the service of the state as their male colleagues. What is notable about Plato, compared to Aristotle, is that he was not an essentialist: the male model was the ideal, but at least in utopia women could successfully approximate the male soul.

Plato's pupil Aristotle finds no ambiguity whatsoever. In his writings, women are definitely inferior: "We must look upon the female character as being a sort of natural deficiency," Aristotle writes in *Generation of Animals*. Woman's defectiveness lies in her lack of bodily heat and consequent inability to concoct matter—that is, to cause it to develop. Thus, even in reproduction women play a lesser role, since the male provides the form of the fetus, while the female only provides the matter. Men take the active and creative role in conception, women the passive and receptive role. Furthermore, the male child represents the fullness of procreation, while the female child results from a defect in development.

Since, unlike Plato, Aristotle was something of an empiricist, he tried to support his views with observations. He suggested, for instance, that women conceive males (or have males conceived on them) when in the prime of life, while only very young or aging women conceive females. He also asserted that the male fetus moves in the womb earlier than the female fetus, indicating greater activity and greater perfection.

Thus Aristotle placed much greater emphasis on women's biological inferiority than Plato did. When he turned to the intangible dimension of the soul, however, Aristotle resembles Plato in holding that women's rationality lacks sufficient strength to keep the irrational soul and its desires in check. Unable to control the irrational part of the soul, women let their appetites run away with them, doing as they please rather than as reason ordains. Since women lack internal governance, they require constant governance by men. But unlike Plato, Aristotle made the divide between male and female essentially unbridgeable. There would be no female Guardians in an Aristotelian utopia.

In the Middle Ages the theologian Thomas Aquinas continued the Aristotelian paradigm of generation in his *Summa Theologica,* a work that had profound influence on Catholic philosophers and theologians for centuries. Aquinas believed women to be biologically "accidental," that is, unintended in the natural order, though not in God's cosmic order. For Aquinas, the male seed always intends to create another male, but weakness in the seed or in the female material, or some exterior circumstance such as a south wind that brings greater atmospheric humidity, may result in the creation of a female. More important, Aquinas, like Aristotle, believed women to be intellectually as well as physically inferior to men: "Woman is naturally subject to man because in man the discretion of reason predominates," he wrote. The male is more ordered to "intellectual operation" than the female.

Throughout the Middle Ages and the early modern period, disparagement of women's intellect was commonplace in Western civilization. Here and there, however, a voice of dissent arose. Probably the best known of these protests was that of the 15th-century poet Christine de Pisan. Struggling with the sense of inferiority engendered by male misogyny, Christine opens her *Book of the City of Ladies* with a visitation from three allegorical goddesses, Reason, Rectitude, and Justice. These three were carefully chosen to refute men's charges of feminine irrationality, feeble moral sense, and inability to understand abstract concepts of law. Her book inaugurated the "querelle des femmes," a roughly three-century European debate over women's virtues and vices.

Nature continued to explain the differences between the sexes during the Enlightenment of the 18th century. Perhaps the most influential of all the philosophical disquisitions on the nature and role of women was that of Jean-Jacques Rousseau. In his manual of education, *Emile*, Rousseau notes that women have special qualities of mind like "quick wit, taste, [and] grace," but they do not have the ability to be creative or to reason abstractly. They are good at details, bad at the principles underlying them. They do not possess genius. Their education, dictated by their functions as females, should fit them for a domestic life, directed not at drawing out their capacities but at instilling the virtues needed to become loving wives and mothers.

For Rousseau there was no question that nature had determined the very different mental and physical characteristics of men and women, but his views did not go unchallenged. Other philosophes, like Helvetius and Baron d'Holbach, argued that environment and schooling shaped the female qualities that Rousseau took to be innate. D'Holbach wrote in *Systeme Social* (1733): "From the way in which [women] are brought up, it seems that it is only intended to turn them into beings who retain the frivolity, fickleness, caprices and lack of reason of childhood, throughout their lives."

Such was also the central argument of Mary Wollstonecraft's *Vindication of the Rights of Women* (1792), a work that is generally acknowledged to be the founding document of European and American feminism. Outraged at Rousseau's doctrine of women's natural inferiority and his prescription for their education, Wollstonecraft, who otherwise admired him greatly, took it upon herself to write a heated response. Never denying that many women in their current condition lacked true morality and virtue, she insisted that nature had nothing to do with it. Women were what society had made them by encouraging their frivolous pursuits and denying them a serious education. What was needed was to provide little girls with the same education as that of their brothers: "Women must be allowed to found their virtue on knowledge, which is scarcely possible unless they have been educated by the same pursuits as men." The nature/nurture debate on mental endowments was well under way.

The discussion of sex differences took a new turn in the early 19th century, when the science of phrenology proposed to present concrete empirical evidence of mental functioning in men and women. Enormously popular in Europe and America in the middle of the century, phrenology asserted that the contours of the skull, its prominences and depressions, revealed the mental qualities and character traits of the individual. The brain had many faculties, each located in a specific place on the brain mass that determined a particular exterior conformation. Careful examination of the head could thus provide information about the person's mind and character.

Phrenology did not disturb the conventional wisdom of the time: in men, intellect predominated over feeling; in women, the reverse. "It is almost an axiom that women are guided by feelings, whilst men are superior in intellectual concentration," wrote J. G. Spurzheim in *Phrenology, or the Doctrine of Mental Phenomena* (1833). Yet despite such pronouncements, phrenology on both sides of the Atlantic seems to have been cordial to the aspirations of women, apparently because it managed the considerable feat of positing both that mental endowments were constitutionally determined and that they were malleable. Weak faculties could be strengthened by exercise, overly powerful ones curbed. This reformist optimism gave at least one Scottish feminist grounds for proclaiming that "phrenologists had proved . . . that women's brains were capable of being improved to a degree which would make them equal and even excel the men in all the better accomplishments of our common nature, and give them power to break the chains of the tyrant and the oppressor, and set them completely free."

Always under challenge from the major authorities in psychology and physiology, phrenology saw its claim to scientific status dim even during the years of its greatest popularity. Though phrenology purported to be based on empirical evidence, its pioneering attempt to localize cerebral functions did not, in fact, rest on experimental work. Yet its conception of mental phenomena as biologically based and susceptible to empirical study shaped the future of research in psychology and physical anthropology during the remainder of the 19th century.

Physical anthropology, above all, used skull measurement as the sure path to unlocking the secrets of the mind. Its characteristic and crowning achievement was craniology, the study of the skull and brain. Measuring skulls, it was believed, could disclose the size of the brain, with the understanding that bigger was better. "Other things being equal," wrote the eminent French anthropologist Paul Broca in 1861, "there is a remarkable relationship between the development of intelligence and the volume of the brain." In examining the brains of men and women, scientists in Europe and America shared a unanimous conclusion: women's brains were smaller than those of men. In this finding they were correct: women's brains *are* smaller than men's. But it does not follow from this (though many drew the conclusion) that women are less intelligent than men, since their body weight is also less, and less brain mass is required to move it around and maintain motor function. Skull measurement did not, as it happened, prove a reliable indicator of brain weight. Craniologists needed to weigh actual brains. These were in short supply, but enough were found to confirm that women's brains weighed less than men's. To the educated English-speaking public, the gender disparity in brain weights became familiar as "the missing five ounces of female brain," from a phrase in the widely read and reprinted article "Mental Differences Between Men and Women" (1887) by the Darwinian psychologist George John Romanes.

Faced with discouraging results from the crude correlation of brain weight with intelligence (in 1894, Havelock Ellis found that the heaviest brain weights yet recorded were those of "a totally undistinguished individual, an imbecile, the Russia novelist Turgenev, an ordinary workman, a bricklayer, and the French zoologist Cuvier"), physical anthropologists resorted to increasingly sophisticated examinations of brains, analyzing the complexity of their fissures and recesses. Smooth brains indicated low intellect; highly convoluted brains bespoke excellence. Shape mattered too. Despite the collapse of phrenology, scientists still maintained the belief that intelligence was seated in the forefront of the brain. Thus massive foreheads promised intellectual power.

By the turn of the 20th century, the correlation of brain measurements, and even of more advanced indices like brain topography, began to be abandoned under the attack of further neuroanatomical research. Scientists interested in the study of the mind had, up until this point, had little recourse but to use somatic analysis; there were, after all, no intelligence tests and indeed no psychological tests of any kind. The endeavor to learn about the mind itself from its physical manifestation, the brain, was reasonable, however much the interpretations drawn from this enterprise were shaped by preconceptions. But now the turn away from somaticism left a void. New analytical instruments would have to be devised. In this country, a graduate student at the University of Chicago, Helen Bradford Thompson, tried to fill the breach with a series of word associations, puzzles, and general-information examinations administered to university undergraduates. Her dissertation, published as *The Mental Traits of Sex*, pioneered what we might consider to be the empirical study of mental differences between the sexes. It was shortly rendered obsolete, however, by the advent of IQ tests and their popularization after World War I.

Gradually, in the years after 1918, a consensus grew that IQ tests showed very little difference between the intelligence of men and women. The British psychologist Charles Spearman, referring to the search for such difference, wrote, "The pack of investigators can be called off. . . . They are following a false scent." Yet the idea of sexual difference lingered on. Defeated in one guise, it emerged renewed in another. Probably the most popular new form was the variability hypothesis, the idea that on a bell-shaped curve of intelligence, women cluster around the average, while men are more scattered. At the extremes of genius and idiocy, men predominate.

Another new development in the study of intelligence was a more precise understanding that it was not one capacity but many. Thus a person might excel in languages but do poorly in mathematics. The growing use of Scholastic Aptitude Tests beginning in the 1930s helped to cement this notion and to establish the common wisdom that males do better at mathematics than females. Male variability appeared to be reinforced by the figures for mathematical ability, which show males doing both very badly and very well. At the upper end, male mathematical prodigies have been found to outnumber female prodigies by a large margin. It was on the basis of this kind of information (though these issues are far from conclusively settled) that President Summers made his remarks about the reason for the scarcity of women in scientific careers.

Can anything be learned from this lengthy and not always edifying story? One conclusion, at least, seems plausible. Nowhere in the work of these 19th- and 20th-century scientists has mention been made of the influence of the environment on the mental functioning of an individual of either sex. That is because environment was routinely dismissed by them. Nature, not nurture, was what counted. "If a man is gifted with vast intellectual ability, eagerness to work, and power of working," wrote Francis Galton, the father of eugenics, "I cannot comprehend how such a man should be repressed." Hardheaded physician Henry Maudsley sniffed, "Village Hampdens, mute inglorious Miltons, and bloodless Cromwells do *not* sleep in the graves of the rude forefathers of the hamlet." As for gifted women, they "suffered no other hindrance to the exercise and evolution of their brains and their intellect than those that are derived from their constitution and their faculties of development." No obstacles hindered, no customs entrapped them.

Not a single psychologist or social theorist alive would hold such a position, when examples of its falsity come daily to mind. Nor does Summers fail to acknowledge the importance of culture in his analysis. He is, however, skeptical about its explanatory power, asserting that "the human mind has a tendency to grab to the socialization hypothesis when you can see it, and it often turns out not to be true." He would prefer to place emphasis on women's comparative unwillingness to accept the long hours and intense commitment demanded by "high-powered" careers like science (without ever asking whether these conditions are desirable). He also prefers to emphasize differences in innate ability. "It does appear," he writes, "that on many, many different human attributes . . . there is relatively clear evidence that whatever the difference means—which can be debated—there is a difference in the standard deviation, and variability of a male and a female population." At the high end, Summers continues, that means about five males are found for every one female. Fewer females on the rarified heights of scientific intellect results in fewer females in scientific careers.

Even if we were to agree that the variability hypothesis was proven, we might suggest that, while science does indeed require a high level of intelligence, most scientific work is not done by geniuses (who do not come along every day). Scientists are no doubt very bright, but an individual does not have to be at the extreme high end of mathematical ability to do well in science. And motivation, of course, counts for much.

Lawrence Summers has rekindled a debate that has simmered for centuries, and good will likely come of it, since universities will probably feel the need to work harder at diversifying their science faculties because of the attention the debate has received. It is also likely that research into sex differences in mind and brain will continue. Meanwhile, the wisest statement on this matter might well have been made more than 140 years ago by the British political theorist John Stuart Mill: "I deny that any one knows or can know, the nature of the two sexes, as long as they have only been seen in their present relation to one another. . . . What is now called the nature of women is an eminently artificial thing—the result of forced repression in some directions, unnatural stimulation in others." Any differences that might be found between the sexes, Mill believed, could only be judged natural if they could not possibly be artificial, the effects of education or socialization.

We do not live in the Victorian era; the artificialities of women's lives have diminished. Can anyone say that they have been altogether eliminated?

# POSTSCRIPT

## Do Significant Innate Differences Influence the Success of Males and Females?

**S**teven Pinker concludes his article by noting that one of the most limiting factors in genuinely learning whether innate sex differences influence developmental outcomes is the general social taboo surrounding discussion of the issue. He notes that science and progress in understanding derives from being able to openly and freely debate legitimate research perspectives. If you are reading this book, hopefully you agree that genuinely addressing different sides of a controversy is a positive way to develop better understandings. Thus, impulsively reacting against Summers' suggestion of innate differences may be as counterproductive as accepting his suggestions in the first place.

While it is easy to oversimplify claims of innate gender differences, legitimate scholars assert only that there may be some small average differences between groups—which is not useful information for assessing individual differences. Further, in regard to cognitive abilities, the data suggest that gender differences occur primarily in the distribution of abilities across men and across women. The suggestion is that more men than women are at the extremes of cognitive ability: both very high and very low. Further, no legitimate scholar is claiming that innate differences alone create different developmental outcomes. Any innate differences clearly and inevitably interact with experiences in the social world.

Yet, as Pinker points out, when researchers look at large groups of people and carefully examine the data, the average gender differences persist. Pinker finds it improbable that the accumulating research evidence about innate gender differences could be entirely due to a misguided search for support of social stereotypes. Instead, Pinker argues that the topic should be open for discussion.

In contrast, one strength of Russett's position is that she clearly identifies ways that the social world seems to look for and accentuate potential differences between men and women. Identifying gender is common, easy, and tempting. The first question we ask of new parents, for example, is whether they have had a boy or a girl. From the start of daycare and schooling, children are regularly put in lines or otherwise divided by gender. The message that gender differences exist does not take long to sink in (research suggests that children are already aware of significant gender stereotypes by age two). Russett provides provocative examples of how this has played out historically, including such strange ideas as ascribing social differences to differences in head size.

We now know that differences between people in the size and shape of the head has virtually nothing to do with the effective functioning of our brain cells, but Russett implies that a similar logic drives explanations of gender differences in achievement. She suggests that the predominance of men in top-level scientific positions has as little to do with the evolutionary distribution of cognitive skills as it has to do with the size and shape of their heads. In fact, common sense tells us that the simple fact of male dominance in high-level scientific positions produces a self-fulfilling inequity; men have more role models, more clear expectations, and more existing places in the opportunity structure.

Further, many commentators have responded to Summers' remarks by noting the clear gains made by women in science and technical fields in recent decades. A century ago, high-level science was almost exclusively a male domain. Today we have innumerable examples of essential contributions made by women in important scientific posts. The notion that improving the opportunities for women in science, and in the world of work more generally, has led to tremendous gains for society is not particularly controversial. The question, rather, is what will happen next?

## Suggested Readings

A. Fausto-Sterling, "Beyond Differences: A Biologist's Perspective," *Journal of Social Issues* (vol. 53, no. 2, 1997).

D. Geary, "Evolution and Developmental Sex Differences," *Current Directions in Psychological Science* (August 4, 1999).

S. Glazer, "Gender and Learning: Are There Innate Differences Between the Sexes?" *The CQ Researcher* (May 20, 2005).

C. Leaper, "The Social Construction and Socialization of Gender During Development," *Toward a Feminist Developmental Psychology* (Routledge, 2000).

R. Monastersky, "Women and Science: The Debate Goes On," *The Chronicle of Higher Education* (March 4, 2005).

A. Ripley, N. Mustafa, D. van Dyk, and U. Plon, "Who Says a Woman Can't be Einstein?" *Time* (March 7, 2005).

## Baby Center

This Web site provides information and resources related to pregnancy and prenatal development.

        http://www.babycenter.com/

## Birthing Naturally

This site is focused on how to make natural childbirth a healthy and successful experience.

        http://www.birthingnaturally.net/

## Pregnancy and Baby

A general portal related to pregnancy, this site offers resources related to practical aspects of very early development.

        http://pregnancyandbaby.com/

## Safe Fetus

This Web site is an extensive reference for checking the influence of various substances on a fetus during pregnancy.

        http://www.safefetus.com

# PART 2

# Prenatal Development

*T*he period of our most rapid and astonishing change is the approximately nine months prior to birth within our mothers' wombs. This is a unique period in development because we do not experience human social interaction. Prenatal development is primarily physical and biological. Yet, society and scholars pay great attention to prenatal development because of a valid sense that it provides a crucial foundation for the rest of our lives. This section considers issues focused on two aspects of prenatal development: the exposure of a fetus to external agents, and the method chosen for being born into the social world.

- Does Prenatal Exposure to Drugs Such as Cocaine Create "Crack Babies" With Special Developmental Concerns?

- Is a Natural Childbirth, Without Pain Medication, Best for Development?

# ISSUE 4

## Does Prenatal Exposure to Drugs Such as Cocaine Create "Crack Babies" with Special Developmental Concerns?

**YES: Sherri McCarthy and Thomas Franklin Waters,** from "A Crack Kid Grows Up: A Clinical Case Report," *Journal of Offender Rehabilitation* (vol. 37, 2003)

**NO: Mariah Blake,** from "Crack Babies Talk Back," *Columbia Journalism Review* (September/October 2004)

### ISSUE SUMMARY

**YES:** Sherri McCarthy and Thomas Franklin Waters, educational psychology and criminal justice professors at Northern Arizona University, review the research on "crack babies," suggesting a link between prenatal cocaine exposure and serious physical, socioemotional, and cognitive effects requiring special care and attention.

**NO:** Journalist and editor Mariah Blake contends that the idea of "crack babies" with special needs is more a media creation than a medical fact; her investigation does not support the popular idea that prenatal exposure to cocaine determines permanent negative developmental effects.

$\mathbf{M}$ost people are familiar enough with the idea of "crack babies" to be somewhat surprised in learning there is a scientific controversy about the validity of that label. While no scientist would ever endorse using crack cocaine, or any illicit drug, during pregnancy, many scientists have raised questions about whether research evidence warrants the powerfully negative stigma of labeling "crack babies."

Any external agent that causes malformation of organs and tissue during prenatal development is called a teratogen. Common teratogens include alcohol, tobacco, and narcotics. Fetal exposure to these drugs, most often through use by the mother, has varying degrees of detrimental influence on prenatal development. While the generally negative influence of exposure to teratogens is clear and accepted, the controversy comes with regard to the relative influence of particular quantities and types of exposure.

Because crack cocaine is illegal, it is associated with a much more negative social taboo than alcohol or cigarettes. Yet research about prenatal development suggests that, aside from social appropriateness, the actual biological effects of alcohol and cigarette smoking are at least as harmful to a fetus as the biological effects of narcotics such as cocaine. In fact, according to ratings by the FDA, a drug like aspirin has more established negative biological effects on a fetus than cocaine. These biological effects, however, cannot necessarily be removed from their social context—the direct effects of drug use are almost always compounded by other health and parenting behaviors of a mother and father. A great deal of research on cocaine exposure in utero suggests that any prenatal effects are at least compounded by problems that may exist in the postnatal environment.

So can a good postnatal environment make up for significant exposure to teratogens in a bad prenatal environment? And should people interested in life span development focus more on the ability of a healthy postnatal environment to allow for normal development, or the fact that a crack cocaine epidemic in the 1980s that created a large number of babies challenged by an environment that started with prenatal crack exposure? This is the crux of the controversy, which questions key life span development issues such as prenatal environment, plasticity, and evidence.

With regard to evidence, note that while McCarthy and Waters focus on the negative outcomes of "crack kids" by citing a variety of research studies, they also note that some of the research results are contradictory and few are firmly established. But, based on some knowledge of the influence of the prenatal environment on later outcomes, does that necessarily mean crack exposure is not as bad as it seems? They also point out that the effects of crack specifically are difficult to disentangle from other potential developmental influences that are either prenatal (such as alcohol or tobacco exposure) or postnatal (such as malnutrition or lack of parental warmth). Yet, using a case study to illustrate their argument, they feel that a category of "crack kids" is still warranted.

In contrast, Blake suggests the inability of research to disentangle the effects of crack from other developmental influences provides strong evidence that the category of "crack babies" is based on moralistic stereotypes and the tendency of the media to want to craft good stories regardless of science. In fact, she explains, the original fear of an epidemic of "crack babies" was based on the media exaggerating the results of a very limited research study, using a small sample, that has since been brought into much question. She also notes examples of children who were exposed to cocaine in utero, but suffered more from the label than from an inherent biological deficiency.

Finally, Blake notes that this controversy is as relevant as ever because it echoes in new concerns about the use of methamphetamine creating a generation of "meth babies." Thus, it is helpful to consider whether being exposed to drugs in utero, even though not absolutely determining a negative outcome of development, is still a significant enough developmental influence to warrant a labeled category.

Sherri McCarthy and
Thomas Franklin Waters

 **YES**

# A Crack Kid Grows Up: A Clinical Case Report

"Crack baby" is a term commonly utilized in the U.S. to describe infants born to mothers who ingested rock cocaine while pregnant. Early research, often exaggerated or misrepresented by the popular media, heightened social concern to epidemic proportions resulting in a moral crusade to "save" infants from the addicted caregivers. A public fervor to prosecute and jail mothers who abused drugs during pregnancy developed, along with a despair that public education would be destroyed when these babies entered school. Biogenics, class politics and stereotypes of the "evil mother" shadowed the debates. The fervor has now faded, replaced by more thoughtful but often contradictory or confounded research on the developmental effects of in utero exposure to cocaine.

In 1987, it was estimated that as many as 375,000 infants born in the U.S. each year had been exposed to crack cocaine by maternal use. Although many consider this estimate high, and there are probably no reliable national estimates of prenatal cocaine exposure, there are doubtless many adolescents and young adults today who were exposed to rock cocaine during gestation. Little information is available on how these maturing "crack kids" fare as they enter the passage to adulthood. It is our purpose to offer some insight into this passage. . . .

## Background Research

### Physical Effects

Women who abuse cocaine during pregnancy may experience a variety of complications, including spontaneous abortions, stillbirths, ruptured placentas and premature delivery. Because cocaine crosses the blood/brain barrier after passing through the placenta during pregnancy, it also potentially effects the developing fetal brain as well as other organs and tissues. Since the fetal liver is not fully developed and cannot quickly eliminate the drug, it also has a far longer half-life in a fetus than in an adult. Documented consequences of exposure include impaired fetal growth, low birth weight and

From *Journal of Offender Rehabilitation,* vol. 37, 2003, pp. 201–207, 210–216. Copyright © 2003 by Haworth Press. Reprinted by permission.

small head circumference. Respiratory and urinary tract difficulties also appear more common among cocaine-exposed infants. Some studies also report birth defects of the kidneys, arms and heart; however, these studies may not have accounted for synergistic effects of other teratogens used during pregnancy, such as alcohol. Cocaine also appears to be linked to the likelihood of Sudden Infant Death Syndrome (SIDS), although this relationship is uncertain due to the difficulty of separating out the multiple effects of poverty, cigarette smoking, alcohol use, poor nutrition and inadequate prenatal care from cocaine use. Thus, studies do not agree regarding the increase of incidence of SIDS and other health problems among cocaine-exposed infants and are often difficult to interpret due to other risks present such as use of other teratogens and poor prenatal care. Regardless, there appears to be sufficient evidence to assume that "crack babies" are likely to be less healthy than other infants. Some researchers have claimed that difficulties seem to disappear as early as three years of age and others have noted that nutrition and environment after birth may account for either continued poor health or improvement. However, if crack exposure during infancy does have long-term effects on physical health, "crack kids" may be less healthy, overall, than their non-exposed peers during adolescence and early adulthood and may require more frequent medical care.

## Socioemotional Effects

Because cocaine is a powerful central nervous system stimulant with lasting neurobehavioral effects, it can potentially retard social and emotional development. Mayes notes that potential manifestations include excessive crying, heightened reactivity to light and touch, delays in language development and lower intelligence. It has been difficult to demonstrate long-term behavioral, cognitive and language problems in children who were exposed prenatally to cocaine. Because prenatal cocaine exposure was not widely recognized or researched until the mid-1980s, the study of neurological impairment related to use has a brief history and continued study is necessary to confirm or refute general clinical impressions. Documented clinical impressions of crack-exposed infants include sleep dysfunction, irregularities in response to stimuli, excessive crying and fussiness. Most studies suggest these infants are more easily aroused but others have found cocaine-exposed infants to be more difficult to stimulate. Lester suggests this can be accounted for by the fact that the easily aroused infants are experiencing the effects of recent maternal cocaine use while the others are displaying the effect of chronic use on infant growth and development.

Studies employing tools such as the Brazelton Neonatal Behavioral Assessment Scale (NBAS) or the Bayley Scales of Infant Development (BSID) have mixed results. Dow-Edwards found that newborns exposed to crack had decreased interactive skills, short attention spans, comparatively depressed performance in psychomotor development and oversensitivity to stimulation, coping with stimulus by either frantic wails or sleep. Bateman reported brief tremors for the first 24 hours after birth. Mayes, Bornstein, Chawarska and Granger found evidence that visual information processing demonstrated increased arousal to stimuli which may exceed optimal levels for sustaining attention or processing information. Chasnoff, Griffith, Macgregor, Dirkes and Burns found that cocaine-exposed infants demonstrated poorer state regulation, orientation and motor performance than controls and presented more abnormal reflexes. Richardson, Hamel, Goldschmidt and Day, in a carefully controlled study, found maternal cocaine use was significantly related to poorer autonomic stability, poorer motor maturity and tone and increased abnormal reflexes 2 days after birth. They suggest that infants exposed to cocaine may be more vulnerable to the stress of birth and exhibit a delayed recovery from that stress. Mentis and Lundgren suggest that explicit conclusions are difficult to reach from this data because measures used may not be sufficiently sensitive to identify other potential problems which may not manifest until later stages of development.

In a study of toddlers who had been exposed to crack cocaine while in utero, Howard, Beckwith, Rodning and Kropenske found that, compared to controls, subjects were emotionally and socially underdeveloped and had difficulty learning. Drug-exposed children did not show strong feelings of pleasure, anger or distress and appeared to be less purposeful and organized when playing. They also appeared unattached to their primary caregivers. During infancy, development of empathy is fostered by the affective relationship that develops between infant and caregiver. Later, empathy develops when caregivers provide opportunities for children to experience a variety of emotions and encourage them to attend to the emotional experiences of others. Lack of attachment combined with poor attention span may make it difficult for "crack kids" to develop empathy. Similarly, avoidant or ambivalent attachment appears to foster an external locus of control. Individuals with highly external loci of control assume that they have no control over their own actions or circumstances. From the perspective of these individuals, fate or destiny, those in power or other criteria determine the outcome of events. They do not see their own behavior or effort as having any effect on the events in their lives.

Implications of this research for later development of "crack kids" suggests lack of empathy and a highly external locus of control as defined by Rotter may be common characteristics as they mature. The current profile for Attention Deficit Hyperactivity Disorder (ADHD), a condition which has been increasingly common in recent years, also sounds strikingly consistent with this early research on "crack babies." Leichtman notes that parent/child attachment, internal representation of the world, empathy, self-soothing, self-regulation, self-esteem, values and competencies, learning and organizational strategies, social skills, responsibility and problem-solving are all difficulties encountered in a child with ADHD personality development. Martinez and Bournival note that ADHD children exhibit low cortical arousal as infants. Rapoport and Castellanos found evidence that ADHD children had significantly smaller right frontal brain regions and right striatum than controls. These findings seem consistent with the physiological and neurological data gathered on crack-exposed newborns and suggest that ADD or ADHD may be yet another manifestation of in utero crack exposure as children mature. This is not to suggest that ADD or ADHD is indicative of maternal cocaine use, as a variety of other factors may also contribute to the condition. However, one precursor to the condition may, indeed, be exposure to teratogens in utero, making it far more likely that "crack kids" will suffer from this condition than others.

## Cognitive Effects

An ADD or ADHD profile markedly effects learning, cognition and educational success. Other cognitive developmental influences of cocaine exposure include delays in the acquisition of language skills, literacy and memory. In a study of 35 crack-exposed infants and 35 matched controls, van Baar and Graaff concluded that drug-exposed children tended to score lower on all general intelligence and language measures than controls and were functioning at a lower cognitive level as preschoolers. Similar studies by Mentis and Lundgren and Nulman provided similar results. However, cognitive assessments using general cognitive, verbal performance, quantitative and memory scales given by Hawley, Halle, Drasin and Thomas did not reveal significant differences between drug-exposed and non-drug-exposed children. Barone studied 26 cocaine-exposed children from 1 to 7 years of age who were placed in stable foster homes. She reported there were some noticeable delays but, overall, literacy patterns were developing in a manner similar to non-exposed children. It appears adverse cognitive effects may be mediated to some degree by a stable home environment and exacerbated by an unstable environment. Mayes suggested that a number of neurobehavioral differences between crack-exposed and non-exposed infants may disappear by 6 months of age, noting that the plasticity of the brain, combined with adequate caretaking, may compensate for some or all of the neurological insult. Zuckerman concurs. However, it seems to be evident that prenatal cocaine exposure does effect neurological functioning and is manifested by inappropriate response to stimulus, attentional impairments, language difficulties and learning problems. Such data suggests that difficulty in school, difficulty holding jobs and relatively low verbal intelligence scores may be characteristic of "crack kids" during adolescence and early adulthood.

## Summary

No comparative studies of adolescents and young adults who were exposed to crack cocaine in utero are presently available. Based on the data gathered on cocaine-exposed infants and children, however, several likely characteristics can be extrapolated. Adolescents and young adults exhibiting several of these characteristics may have difficulty completing their schooling, holding jobs and functioning in society. Homelessness and incarceration may be likely potential outcomes for many members of this cohort unless intensive early intervention is continued throughout adolescence and early adulthood. Given the characteristics likely to present themselves during adolescence and early adulthood such as a strong desire to "fit in" with peers, low impulse control, low self-esteem and poor self-monitoring ability, prison is a likely future outcome for this group, but not necessarily a useful one. The case study presented here supports this conclusion.

# Methodology

## Subject

The subject of this case study is a young American male of Scottish and German heritage. He was born in January 1979, in southern California. His father was a college-educated U.S. Naval officer; his mother had also attended college but, according to interview data gathered from the subject, the subject's father and his maternal grandmother, his mother was addicted to crack cocaine and smoked it regularly throughout her pregnancy. Despite this, the subject was delivered normally, only two weeks prior to full term. He was healthy and weighed approximately 6.5 lbs. at birth. He is currently 6 3 tall, slim and muscular.

At the age of 2, he reportedly ingested a rock of crack cocaine from his mother's "stash" and was hospitalized for several days. His parents subsequently divorced, ostensibly because of his mother's addiction. His father remarried and acquired custody when the subject was 4 years of age. The subject attended elementary school at a Department of Defense school in Japan, where his father was stationed. He was retained in second grade. He next attended middle school in the Washington, D.C., area, where he was diagnosed as ADHD. He moved to a small city in the southwestern U.S. in early adolescence where he remained until being sent to prison at the age of 21.

The subject was unable to finish high school, but obtained a G.E.D. at the age of 20. He reports being close to his stepmother who "tried hard to be a Mom but had problems of her own." He has two half-brothers, over ten years younger than he is. He reports that he enjoys spending time with them and says he "loves my brothers really a lot–kids are so cool!" He viewed his childhood as normal, although he reports his father was "very strict, had a lot of rules and got mad at me a lot." He reports still admiring and loving his father and reports that "I understand why he doesn't like me. I wish I hadn't disappointed him so much but I guess I just can't help it." The subject has had no contact with his birth mother (now dead) for the last eighteen years. His stepmother died of a heroin overdose when he was 17 years of age. His father kicked him out of the house on his eighteenth birthday, telling him it was "time he became a man." He was homeless and lived on the street for approximately one month before being invited to participate in this study. He and his father had no contact for approximately one year after that time. They now have a limited but civil relationship. He reported to his probation officer on one occasion that "I think I need a lot of counseling because of all that stuff, but as long as I have my friends, I'll be okay."

The subject reported his long-range goals at the time the study began as "I want to get a job I like, maybe doing something with science where I can take things apart and mix chemicals or in a hospital . . . and to marry and have a family." . . .

## Physical Effects

As noted earlier, it may be expected that early physical and neurological stress imposed by cocaine exposure can impair health. The subject's diagnosis as ADHD may well be related to early exposure. In addition, compared to other young adults with similar lifestyles, he appeared far more prone to colds, pneumonia, accidents and infections, and made frequent visits to medical facilities for these conditions. Early evidence of respiratory and urinary difficulty and of poor motor coordination appears, in this case, to be long lasting. He reported, on several occasions "I get sick a lot," and "I have a lot of accidents and I'd like to play sports but I've never been very good at running or catching things."

The subject appears to have a rapid metabolism. He consumes large quantities of food, yet remains lean and reports being constantly hungry. His preferences are for healthy food. Fruits, vegetables, juices and pasta were preferred menu choices. He sleeps comparatively little, having difficulty sleeping at night and generally remaining awake until 2 or 3 a.m. He was generally awake by 7 a.m. each morning during the years observed and occasionally took short afternoon naps. Sleep dysfunction, apparently, also was a lasting effect of inutero exposure in this case. It should be noted, however, that the subject did not view his health or his sleep patterns as problematic or different from others.

## Socioemotional Effects

The subject exhibited delays in social development. He gravitated toward peers who were much younger, chronologically. In fact, he often reported viewing the first author's son, nearly four years his junior, as "like a big brother to me." That son also noted that the subject "sure seems a lot younger than me." The subject seemed to relate best to friends between the ages of 11 and 14 (early adolescence) even at the age of 21. His preferred pastimes included music, video games, activities with large, mixed-sex peer groups, disassembling mechanical objects, creating strange chemical compounds to "kill bugs," and riding a bicycle. These behavior patterns are characteristic of early, not late, adolescence.

Observations indicated the subject was frequently preoccupied with justice and fairness and had a very literal view of the world and of good and evil. He perceived himself as evil. He demonstrated tremendous concern for and loyalty to friends and family and especially enjoyed participating in family meals and outings. He reported "macaroni and cheese with tomatoes is my favorite food because that's what my (step)mom used to make when things were going good and she was trying to be a mom." He also loved caring for and spending time with his younger brothers and considered his peer group "my best family." He often demonstrated sensitivity to others. He saw himself as a peaceloving flower child who "would only fight if I absolutely had to, because I think it is wrong." He did, however, report that he had, on occasion, needed to fight to establish himself in new neighborhoods or to "stand up for myself against gangs and stuff" and according to peer accounts, motor coordination aside, he was a good "street-fighter" who was "safe to be around 'cuz gang kids leave us alone if he's there." He liked "taking care of his friends and of people that are good to me." He reported that "playing music is the best thing in the world for me. It really helps me cope and calms me down." He always appeared relatively calm, demonstrating either good emotional control or relatively flat effect. He displayed a ready smile, good sense of humor, interesting perspective on many issues and generally sunny disposition.

He often noted that "I really want to get married and have a family and take good care of them." During the course of the study, he had only one serious romantic relationship. It lasted for approximately six months before the girl, four years younger than he and equally troubled, albeit for different reasons, broke it off. He reported "I'll still always love her and take care of her." She later became a teen, unwed mother (the father was a friend of the subject's, now also in prison). The subject remained helpful and supportive, often caring for her child, trying to "cheer her up" and in other ways supporting her. He still writes to her frequently from prison. Although she has yet to return a letter, he states "she's the only one for me." He is almost chivalrous in his general treatment of women.

The subject demonstrates strong contradictory urges "to fit in and earn respect" and to "stand out and be really unique." This is not inconsistent with early adolescent development. In his peer group, he is more a follower than a leader in activities even though he associates with younger peers.

He admittedly "is really a stoner and need my pot." He also frequently used hallucinogens and drank alcohol. He is adamantly opposed to any other illegal drug use, however. "I've seen what that stuff does to people—no way! If one of my friends was doing meth or smoking crack, I'd take it away and flush it or even turn them in."

Based on the data collected, he did not seem to demonstrate major problems with attachment. He attributed many events to "luck" or "karma," demonstrating a more external locus of control, but often accepted responsibility for his actions. He did not seem particularly aggressive, violent, antisocial or insensitive, although cruelty to animals was observed on more than one occasion. Other destructive tendencies noted were a penchant for "killing bugs" and a habit of disassembling mechanical objects.

## Cognitive Effects

Disorganization was apparent. Care for personal property was chaotic; the subject consistently forgot even such simple tasks as closing doors and turning out lights, although he responded well to a structured behavior-management program using social praise and token reinforcement. He seemed to respond well to highly structured situations and short, specific orders but had difficulty with complex directions. Although friendly, he was not highly verbal and, although he had a unique way of expressing his feelings, he often had difficulty doing so. He had been retained in elementary school and was a "fifth-year senior" in high school when he was first displaced from his home. Due to several events (described in Outcomes, below) he was unable to finish high school, although he was very motivated to do so. His teachers reported that "he tries really hard," "he likes and needs a lot of attention," and "he can learn; in fact he's pretty good at science compared to some kids, but he has a hard time studying and doing homework."

He was persistent with his studies, and seemed almost oblivious to his difficulties. "Oh, don't worry, I can help you with your homework," he eagerly told a friend who was complaining about his Freshman Algebra class on one occasion. "I've already taken that class 3 times, so I know the stuff really good by now!" Standardized testing done during his senior year of high school indicated he was reading at approximately a ninth-grade level and his math skills were at approximately the eighth-grade level. He scored at approximately the 25th percentile, overall, compared to his chronological peers. He was eventually able to pass the exam for a General Education Diploma (G.E.D.) after approximately six months of tutoring and preparation.

## Vocational and Life Skills Implications

The subject had difficulty functioning in the workplace. He maintained a job at a fast-food restaurant for approximately one month. He was fired, according to his supervisor, "because of constant illness and because he seemed to get flustered when things got busy. During rush hours, he couldn't count change correctly if he was at the cash register and he couldn't produce food quickly enough when he was in the kitchen. He did okay during training or when things were slow. He was a nice kid and he tried really hard, but it just didn't work out." He next worked as a taxi driver but, after two accidents in his first week of work, was again dismissed. He worked on construction sights, first mixing concrete. "He was so clumsy," reported his supervisor. "He tripped over things and spilled things all the time. He was a hazard on the worksite and probably cost us $1000.00 in broken equipment and wasted supplies." He also apprenticed briefly as a drywall finisher. "I could train him if I had enough time," reported his supervisor. "He had a good eye and he had the height, strength and speed necessary. He needed a lot of direction, though." The job he held the longest was in a warehouse, loading crates of fertilizer and other chemicals for delivery. He eventually quit because "being around all that stuff all the time was making me sick. My skin stung and I couldn't breathe." Currently, in prison, he is employed cleaning bathrooms. "I think I'm pretty good at it, but it doesn't pay very well," he reported in a letter to a friend.

He was always willing to help with household tasks, especially when structured chore lists and operant behavior management strategies were used. He was best at simple tasks, however, and needed constant direction and step-by-step instructions to complete assigned chores. His attention deficits were noticeable; even when playing music, which he loved, it was rare for him to be able to finish a song without stopping in the middle. His memory for events, however, seemed good. He often demonstrated novel, creative problem-solving skills, especially in social situations and enjoyed disassembling various household items and reassembling the parts together into "new machines." . . .

## Present Outcomes

When the subject was 16, he was involved in a break-in. According to his own report and the report of several peers, his involvement was not intentional. "It was one of those times when his Dad had kicked him out of the house because he forgot to feed the dog or something," reported one source. "It was kinda late and he was tired and didn't have anywhere to go and he ran into this kid who said 'Hey, come with me, I have a place.' He was supposedly watching these people's trailer for them or something. He went and there was a big party going on. He pretty much just slept on the couch. But they really trashed the place while he was asleep and the cops came and when they got there it was just him and a couple of little kids that they caught inside 'cuz everybody else ran out the back. He got blamed for it 'cuz he was the oldest and the whole thing was on film, too. His Dad said to the cops he probably did it 'cuz he was no good."

The subject was not charged with the crime until after his eighteenth birthday. Despite the fact that it had occurred nearly two years earlier, he was tried as an adult. He was arrested and locked up until his trial less than a month from his projected high school graduation date. His absences from school made it impossible for him to finish his educational goal. Undaunted, he reported "jail wasn't that bad," and began studying for his G.E.D. As a result of his trial, he was sentenced to intensive probation and required to pay over $60,000.00 in restitution over the course of his life. After serving over two-and-one-half years on probation successfully, he was issued a violation by a newly assigned probation officer when a urine screen tested positive for marijuana use. He was sentenced to 5 years in prison, where he currently resides. His initial response was characteristically sunny and concrete—"You know what they say; if you're gonna do the crime than you gotta do the time." He advises his friends in letters from jail to "stay out of trouble; you don't want to go the route I've gone. Stupidity is why I'm here. I rebelled against the system and look where I'm at. I have learned from my mistakes." His letters have remained generally upbeat; he has access to a guitar and has formed a band with other inmates. He reports that they may have a CD made soon. He reads frequently, is happy that he has a job cleaning toilets and is "making lots of new friends."

Other indicators in letters, however, suggest that these "new friends," combined with his high influenceability and the desire to fit in documented elsewhere, may be part of a process that obliterates any chance for a normal, prosocial life for this young man when he is released. He is learning how to make "homemade acid" and getting tattoos. He is learning "I have to fight to stand up for myself." His formerly sunny disposition is being replaced by bouts with depression. "I feel so alone, confined to my own hell," he writes in a letter to a friend. "I'm left to rot in my own depressions and hatreds of life, locked in a closet. I sit here and do the same shit everyday. My young life has grown old. I wish I could take a step forward into the good side. Sometimes I want to die and be free from my terrors and fears, but one thing keeps me here alive and that is the thought of being able to be with you and all the others I care about that also care for me again some day."

# Discussion

## Social Implications

There may be a strong underlying relationship between the current plethora of ADD- and ADHD-diagnosed students in American public schools and maternal drug use that bears further investigation. It is worth noting that the subject described here was not in any way reminiscent of the "crack kids" portrayed in the media. He was not Black or Hispanic. He was not born to a single, uneducated mother in the inner city and was not raised in poverty. Overall, despite obvious deficits, he experienced good parenting in a stable, structured home throughout most of his childhood. He had adequate nutrition, good medical care and education.

This case supports the hypothesis that much of the early "crack data" was politically motivated, reflecting racial bias, gender bias and classism. There are undoubtedly many other cases like this young man—crack kids born to white, middle and upper class homes who were missed in all of the early hype when data was collected primarily in treatment centers and public health facilities. A large cohort of "hidden" cases may exist, suggesting estimates should be higher, rather than lower, for incidence of maternal drug use.

It is also worth noting that many characteristics noted in "crack babies" seemed to have lasting effects on this subject. Developmental delays, poor health and coordination and cognitive deficits seemed lasting. On the other hand, the more labile emotional traits such as failure to attach, inability to bond, aggressiveness and lack of control were lacking. Perhaps this suggests that a nurturing environment more easily ameliorates social outcomes than physical and cognitive outcomes. As Zuckerman and Frank note, intervention focused on parenting is well worth pursuing and very effective.

Lasting physical and cognitive outcomes may be problematic for the social welfare system, especially as homelessness may be a particular problem for this group. Additional vocational counseling and jobs skills training may be needed to help this generation of "crack babies" as they enter adulthood. These services should perhaps also be coordinated with criminal justice organizations, where many of this group may find themselves. . . .

**Mariah Blake**  **NO**

# The Damage Done: Crack Babies Talk Back

Antwaun Garcia was a shy boy whose tattered clothes reeked of cat piss. Everyone knew his father peddled drugs and his mother smoked rock, so they called him a "crack baby."

It started in fourth grade when his teacher asked him to read aloud. Antwaun stammered, then went silent. "He can't read because he's a crack baby," jeered a classmate. In the cafeteria that day no one would sit near him. The kids pointed and chanted, "crack baby, crack baby." Antwaun sat sipping his milk and staring down at his tray. After that, the taunting never stopped. Unable to take it, Antwaun quit school and started hanging out at a local drug dealer's apartment, where at age nine he learned to cut cocaine and scoop it into little glass vials. "*Crack baby*," he says. "Those two words almost cost me my education."

Antwaun finally returned to school and began learning to read a year later, after he was plucked from his parents' home and placed in foster care. Now twenty, he's studying journalism at LaGuardia Community College in New York City and writing for *Represent*, a magazine for and by foster children. In a recent special issue he and other young writers, many of them born to crack addicts, took aim at a media myth built on wobbly, outdated science: crack babies. Their words are helping expose the myth and the damage it has done.

Crack hit the streets in 1984, and by 1987 the press had run more than 1,000 stories about it, many focusing on the plight of so-called crack babies. The handwringing over these children started in September 1985, when the media got hold of Dr. Ira Chasnoff's *New England Journal of Medicine* article suggesting that prenatal cocaine exposure could have a devastating effect on infants. Only twenty-three cocaine-using women participated in the study, and Chasnoff warned in the report that more research was needed. But the media paid no heed. Within days of the first story, CBS News found a social worker who claimed that an eighteen-month-old crack-exposed baby she was treating would grow up to have "an IQ of perhaps fifty" and be "barely able to dress herself."

Soon, images of the crack epidemic's "tiniest victims"—scrawny, trembling infants—were flooding television screens. Stories about their bleak future abounded. One psychologist told *The New York Times* that crack was "interfering with the central core of what it is to be human." Charles Krauthammer, a columnist for the *The Washington Post,* wrote that crack babies were doomed to "a life of certain suffering, of probable deviance, of permanent inferiority." The public braced for the day when this "biological underclass" would cripple our schools, fill our jails, and drain our social programs.

But the day never came. Crack babies, it turns out, were a media myth, not a medical reality. This is not to say that crack is harmless. Infants exposed to cocaine in the womb, including the crystallized version known as crack, weigh an average of 200 grams below normal at birth, according to a massive, ongoing National Institutes of Health study. "For a healthy, ten-pound Gerber baby this is no big deal," explains Barry Lester, the principal investigator. But it can make things worse for small, sickly infants.

Lester has also found that the IQs of cocaine-exposed seven-year-olds are four and a half points lower on average, and some researchers have documented other subtle problems. Perhaps more damaging than being exposed to cocaine itself is growing up with addicts, who are often incapable of providing a stable, nurturing home. But so-called crack babies are by no means ruined. Most fare far better, in fact, than children whose mothers drink heavily while pregnant.

Nevertheless, in the midst of the drug-war hysteria, crack babies became an emblem of the havoc drugs wreak and a pretext for draconian drug laws. Hospitals began secretly testing pregnant women for cocaine, and jailing them or taking their children. Tens of thousands of kids were swept into foster care, where many languish to this day.

*Represent* magazine was founded at the height of the crack epidemic to give voice to the swelling ranks of children trapped in the foster-care system. Its editors knew that many of their writers were born to addicts. But it wasn't until late last year, when a handful expressed interest in writing about how crack ravaged their families, that the picture snapped into focus. "I remember hearing about crack babies and how they were doomed,'" says editor Kendra Hurley. "I suddenly realized these were those kids."

Hurley and her co-editor, Nora McCarthy, had worked with many of the writers for years, and had nudged and coddled most through the process of writing about agonizing personal experiences. But nothing compared to the shame their young scribes expressed when discussing their mothers' crack use. Even the most talented believed it had left them "slow" "retarded" or "damaged" The editors decided to publish a special crack issue to help break the stigma and asked the writers to appear on the cover, under the headline 'CRACK BABIES'—ALL GROWN UP. Initially, only Antwaun agreed. He eventually convinced three others to join him. "I said, 'Why shouldn't we stand up and show our faces?" he recalls. "We rose above the labels. I wanted to reach other kids who had been labeled and let them know it doesn't mean you can't succeed."

As it happens, when the crack issue went to press, a group of doctors and scientists was already lobbying *The New York Times* to drop terms like "crack baby" from its pages. The group included the majority of American researchers investigating the effects of prenatal cocaine exposure or drug addiction. They were spurred to action by the paper's coverage of a New Jersey couple found to be starving their four foster children in late 2003. For years the couple had explained the children's stunted growth to neighbors and friends by saying, among other things, that they were "crack babies." The *Times* not only failed to inform readers that crack babies don't exist, but reinforced the myth by reporting, without attribution, that "the youngest [of the children] was born a crack baby."

Assistant Managing Editor Allan Siegal refused to meet with the researchers, saying via e-mail that the paper simply couldn't open a dialogue with all the "advocacy groups who wish to influence terminology." After some haggling, he did agree to publish a short letter to the editor from the researchers. While the paper hasn't used "crack baby" in the last several months, it has referred to babies being "addicted" to crack, which, as the researchers told the editors, is scientifically inaccurate, since babies cannot be born addicted to cocaine.

The researchers later circulated a more general letter urging all media to drop the term "crack baby." But the phrase continues to turn up. Of the more than 100 news stories that have used it in the last year, some thirty were published after the letter was distributed in late February.

*Represent*'s writers made a more resounding splash. National Public Radio and AP both featured them in stories on crack's legacy. Inspired by their words, the columnist E.R. Shipp called on New York *Daily News* readers to consider the damage the crack-baby myth has done. A July *Newsday* op-ed made a similar plea, and also urged readers to avoid rushing to judgment on the growing number of babies being born to mothers who use methamphetamines.

Still, a number of recent "meth baby" stories echo the early crack-baby coverage. A July AP article cautioned, for instance, that an "epidemic" of meth-exposed children in Iowa is stunting infants' growth, damaging their brains, and leaving them predisposed to delinquency. In May, one Fox News station warned that meth babies "could make the crack baby look like a walk in the nursery." Research is stacking up against such claims. But, then, scientific evidence isn't always enough to kill a good story.

# POSTSCRIPT

## Does Prenatal Exposure to Drugs Such as Cocaine Create "Crack Babies" with Special Developmental Concerns?

**W**hile most people have heard at least passing references to the idea of "crack babies," these articles should help make you aware that the label is much more complicated than such passing references suggest. McCarthy and Waters review the extensive research attention put toward understanding the influence of the crack epidemic on development. While they conclude that the evidence overwhelmingly supports particular concern about prenatal exposure to crack cocaine, they are qualified in how conclusive the research proves to be. In one sense, they agree with Blake that many diverse influences determine the outcomes of prenatal drug use. Blake, however, looks at the other side and shows that the label of "crack babies" can be more harmful than helpful. She emphasizes the fact that the evidence is inconclusive, and gives persuasive examples as to how such labels can simply be wrong.

Overall, both of the articles agree that the initial popular response to the crack epidemic was guided by social responses. There is little controversy about the intensity of the stereotypes regarding crack cocaine—unfairly attributed as entirely a problem for the poor in the inner city. But that unfair attribution does not necessarily mean that a label of "crack babies" is unwarranted.

Labels are important developmental influences. As noted by Blake, some "crack babies" struggled throughout their school years with the altered expectations of assumed deficiency. While the case examples she cites were able to overcome those labels, the case example cited by McCarthy and Waters ended up in jail partially due to an inability—despite environmental intervention—to overcome early developmental problems.

Even more generally, after reading these articles it is important to consider why we have labels for babies born to narcotics users, but not babies exposed to other teratogens. Why do we not talk about "aspirin babies" or "cigarette babies" when those substances can be just as harmful biologically? Part of the answer is that those substances do not carry the same social connotation as narcotics.

In engaging the issue, it becomes clear that labels do not only influence the children themselves. They also influence public responses to those children. If we take for granted that crack has an irrefutable biological influence on prenatal development, then there is little reason to intervene after birth with hopes of the child turning out to be "normal." If, on the other hand, we assume that the influence of crack and other narcotic drugs does not biologically determine negative outcomes, then we create an incentive to facilitate positive postnatal developmental environments that can allow children to thrive.

Ultimately then, there are two different sides that derive from one point of agreement: The problems attributed to prenatal drug use are beyond simple biology. If "crack babies" are disadvantaged more by their environment and stigma, then prenatal drug use influences development primarily as part of a larger social web. So we might, as Blake suggests, best devote our developmental attention to that larger social web. Or we might, as McCarthy and Waters suggest, best devote our developmental attention to the individual children limited by their parents' prenatal drug use. Any of these possibilities, however, depends upon central concerns to the study of life span development: the interaction of biological and social influences, the importance of strong research evidence, and the role of the prenatal environment in shaping later life.

# Suggested Readings

L. Berger and J. Waldfogel, "Prenatal Cocaine Exposure: Long-Run Effects and Policy Implications," *Social Science Review* (March 2000).

W. Chavkin, "Cocaine and Pregnancy—Time to Look at the Evidence," *Journal of the American Medical Association* (March 28, 2001).

D. Frank, M. Augustyn, W. Grant Knight, T. Pell, and B. Zuckerman, "Growth, Development, and Behavior in Early Childhood Following Prenatal Cocaine Exposure," *Journal of the American Medical Association* (March 28, 2001).

K. Greider, "What About the "Drug Babies"? Crackpot Ideas," *Mother Jones* (July/August, 1995).

S. Hans, "Studies of Prenatal Exposure to Drugs Focusing on Prenatal Care of Children," *Neurotoxicology and Teratology* (2002).

J. Harvey, "Cocaine Effects on the Developing Brain: Current Status," *Neuroscience and Biobehavioral Reviews* (2004).

J. Jackson, "The Myth of the 'Crack Baby'," *Extra! The Magazine of FAIR* (September/October 1998).

B. Lester, "Is Day Care Worse Than Cocaine?" *Brown University News Service* (2001).

B. Lester, "No Simple Answer to 'Crack Baby' Debate," *Alcoholism & Drug Abuse Weekly* (September 20, 2004).

B. Lester and L. LaGasse, "Cocaine Exposure and Children: The Meaning of Subtle Effects," *Science* (October 23, 1998).

L. Marcellus, "Critical Social and Medical Constructions of Perinatal Substance Misuse: Truth in the Making," *Journal of Family Nursing* (November 2003).

D. Messinger and B. Lester, "Prenatal Substance Exposure and Human Development," *Human Development in the 21st Century* (Council on Human Development, February 12, 2005).

L. Singer, R. Arendt, S. Minnes, K. Farkas, A. Salvator, H. Kirchner, and R. Kleigman, "Cognitive and Motor Outcomes of Cocaine-Exposed Infants," *Journal of the American Medical Association* (April 17, 2002).

T. Van Beveren, B. Little, and M. Spence, "Effects of Prenatal Cocaine Exposure and Postnatal Environment on Child Development," *American Journal of Human Biology* (2000).

B. Zuckerman, D. Frank, and L. Mayes, "Cocaine-Exposed Infants and Developmental Outcomes," *Journal of the American Medical Association* (April 17, 2002).

# ISSUE 5

## Is a Natural Childbirth, Without Pain Medication, Best for Development?

**YES: Lennart Righard,** from "Making Childbirth a Normal Process," *Birth* (March 2001)

**NO: Gilbert J. Grant,** from *Enjoy Your Labor: A New Approach to Pain Relief for Childbirth* (Russell Hasting Press, 2005)

### ISSUE SUMMARY

**YES:** Pediatrician and professor Lennart Righard draws from research and from his experience attending to natural childbirth in Sweden to assert that natural childbirth is vastly preferable to the artificial interventions of medical technology.

**NO:** Obstetric anesthesiologist Dr. Gilbert Grant asserts that social pressure toward natural childbirth and misplaced anxiety about risks to the baby lead many pregnant women to unnecessarily suffer through childbirth.

**W**hen thinking about giving birth, most women confront a consistent opposition between the "natural" and the technological. This opposition presents itself in controversies about artificial fertility methods, increasing rates of cesarean section births, and the use of pain-management drugs during the process of birth itself. In each case, there is an alternative that is seen as more "natural" and an alternative that is seen as "unnatural." Simultaneously, however, some argue that the alternatives can be described as either more safe or less safe.

"Natural" childbirth has not always been associated with purity and positive outcomes. Prior to the advent of modern medicine, bearing children was often a dangerous and risky proposition. While humans are incredibly well-designed for the process of reproducing, giving birth itself is an event that challenges our capacities. In past centuries, it was not at all uncommon for children and mothers to suffer serious ill-health and death from the process of childbearing. Just over the course of the twentieth century, the rate of infant mortality in the United

States (the number of babies who die within a year of birth) has declined from approximately 150 deaths per 1000 live births to approximately 10 deaths per 1000 live births.

In this way, twentieth-century medical science has made tremendous advances in ways to protect the health of mothers and their babies. These advances were idealized for a time because they provided a completely hygienic, sanitary, and safe birth process in hospital settings where all variables could be controlled. At points in the twentieth century, hospitals prioritized cold technology over warm natural processes. Gradually, however, it has become clear that the ultimate birthing technology is embedded in the human body. We know, for example, that newborn babies thrive most when given the opportunity to touch, feel, and hear their parents early in life so as to develop an attachment bond. Healthy development depends upon some level of "natural" connection between mother and child during and around birth. The question is where to draw the line.

Two perspectives influence the decision of whether natural childbirth without pain medication is best for development. One perspective is biology. On the one hand, birth can be a complicated biological process, and ignoring modern technology can put both mother and child at risk. On the other hand, there is some evidence that pain-management medication can cross the placental barrier, enter a baby's system, and cause some short-term damage. Another perspective is social. On the one hand, why should woman be forced to suffer unnecessary pain simply for the sake of maintaining a veneer of "naturalness"? On the other hand, why should women submit themselves to the whims of a medical system that is often more focused on efficiency and minimizing risk than on the overall quality of a birthing experience?

In the selections that follow, Lennart Righard, a pediatrician who has both delivered babies and taught future doctors about delivering babies, takes the position that epidural pain management (such as pitocin) and modern technologies (such as those that allow us to artificially break a pregnant woman's water—phrased by Righard as "rupturing the membranes") are overused. Note particularly the argument that our reliance on modern medicine has caused us to ignore traditional methods for managing labor pain—relaxation, nutrition, exercise, breathing, social support, etc. In the process of discussing the overwhelming popularity of using epidurals, Righard raises an important question about whether we always need to accept medical science as an advance.

In contrast, Gilbert J. Grant suggests that the argument against using pain-management drugs relies upon a detrimental reverence for suffering. In his experience as delivering anesthesia and delivering babies he has observed women to suffer more from the stigma of using pain-management medication than from anything else. He thus raises another simple but important question: Why should women have to suffer? Is there really something wrong when a women, as Grant titles his book, enjoys her labor?

Lennart Righard

 **YES**

# Making Childbirth a Normal Process

**I**t is an exhausting experience for a baby to be born, especially if interventions or complications occur during birth. Do birth attendants consider the possibility that the interventions of modern birth technology could affect the baby in the womb?

Consider some examples. Rupturing the membranes artificially instantly produces much higher pressure on the baby's head than if they are left to rupture spontaneously in a natural birth, when the bag of water protecting the baby's head is usually intact until the cervix is almost fully open. The artificial use of Pitocin in an intravenous drip makes the contractions stronger and more frequent than in a natural birth, in which oxytocin is released in spurts with an interval in between. In a drip Pitocin is given more continuously and at a higher level than in a natural birth, and the frequent contractions often make the pause between them too short for the baby to rest and recover sufficiently.

The strong and frequent contractions make it difficult for a woman to cope. Therefore, she is often given epidural analgesia, an intervention that does not help the baby, because the woman will need still more Pitocin in her drip. The baby in the womb cannot escape the stress of the strong and frequent contractions. Moreover, an epidural increases the likelihood of a forceps or vacuum extraction, which in turn, hurts the baby's head.

Cutting the cord at once, as is a routine in many places, adds to the stress on the infant. The baby needs oxygen, and the mother breathes for her baby through the cord as long as it is intact and pulsating.

At birth the baby experiences a huge change of environment and life conditions. Immediately after the birth he or she needs time to recover. It feels good for the baby to be on the mother's abdomen skin-to-skin or in a bath. The experience of being naked on the mother's warm soft skin, safe and secure, and feeling her caressing hands is soothing and comforting for the baby. Being in warm water, listening to the mother's voice, is also very relaxing. Indeed, everything that resembles life in the womb is helpful to the baby's transition to the outside world.

From *Birth*, vol. 28, issue 1, 2001, pp. 1–4. Copyright © 2001 by Blackwell Publishing, Ltd. Reprinted by permission.

My definition of natural childbirth is a birth without medical intervention. How can health caregivers make this possible? In the first stage of labor, the woman could move about and adopt the positions she finds comfortable. If she is given a peaceful atmosphere with minimal disturbances, she will be able to tune in to herself and find the rhythm of her contractions. The woman in labor should be treated with respect. Other people in the birthing room should avoid unnecessary chatting about trivial matters. Soft voices and dimmed lighting could help her tune in and relax. With good relaxation throughout the first stage and between the pushes in the second stage, drugs are unnecessary for a natural birth.

In the second stage, birth is easier if the woman is allowed to push by herself when she feels an urge to push. In a squatting or some other upright position, the force of gravity will help the woman and make birth easier for her and her baby.

In many countries Pitocin is often given immediately at birth to speed up the delivery of the placenta. In Sweden, it is not given routinely, however, and consequently there is no stress to expel the placenta. The practitioner may wait for at least 4 to 5 minutes before cutting the cord or until the pulsations have ceased, resulting in about 100 mL of extra blood for the baby. The most natural thing is to leave the cord intact until the placenta has been expelled, which occurs with the instinctual behavior of mammals and some indigenous peoples.

Breastfeeding will be facilitated if the newborn baby is allowed to search and touch, smell and lick, and finally latch on to the breast by his or her own efforts. In this way the baby's own reflexes come into play. The baby should be allowed to nurse until he or she is satisfied. Early breastfeeding behavior can be disturbed by labor analgesia.

When the mother is relaxed and trustful and everything works smoothly, childbirth seems so easy. Maternity care practitioners complicate this biological process by using many interventions, and as a result, most of the magical happiness is lost. Within minutes, a woman who has experienced natural birth is extremely engaged with her baby, talks to the baby, tries to make eye contact, and feels a happiness that she has not experienced before. Where are the emotional elation and euphoria in medicated births? What makes this difference?

If a woman experiences spontaneous physiological birth without medication or an epidural, the beta-endorphin rises to high levels in her body. Endorphin opiates increase tolerance to pain and suppress irritability and anxiety in laboring women. Prolactin, beta-endorphin, oxytocin, and other substances influence moods and feelings, caregiving behavior, mother-infant bonding, and breastfeeding. The placenta is full of beta-endorphins and other substances, and the practice of promptly cutting the umbilical cord deprives newborn infants of these substances designed to induce bonding between the mother-infant couple. Beta-endorphin levels fall in response to epidural anesthesia.

Swedish investigators have conducted retrospective studies on heroin addicts, and found that they were more often born to women exposed to drugs in labor than to women not so exposed. Because drugs pass over the placenta and affect the baby, the authors speculated that this exposure may give human infants an increased susceptibility to drugs later in life.

Research has also shown that the presence of a doula, a relative, or a close friend during labor can decrease the intervention and complication rates significantly. This labor companion should be a calm and experienced person who is there to support the mother-to-be.

Why do most births take place in large hospitals when small hospitals, birth centers, and even homes are statistically speaking equally safe places to give birth? In England expectant couples are given a pamphlet entitled *Informed Choice—Hospital or Home*. This pamphlet is supported by the Royal Colleges of Midwives, General Practitioners, Obstetricians and Gynaecologists and informs prospective parents that home birth is safe in uncomplicated pregnancies. The corresponding pamphlet for professionals about the place of birth lists 58 references. In England home birth is gaining recognition as a viable alternative for interested couples.

It is my belief that the difficulty of changing routines at hospitals will continue as long as doctors attend uncomplicated births, because they want to be in control of what is happening. For example, they want to control labor by having the woman lie down in a bed, they sometimes start labor by induction, and in a cesarean delivery their control is complete. Contractions and the baby's heartbeats are followed by use of electronic monitoring on a screen or a strip. Although this practice is neither safer nor results in a healthier baby than by just observing the woman and listening to the baby's heartbeat at intervals with Doppler ultrasound, the monitoring is usually done routinely and gives the practitioner a feeling of better control. Twelve randomized controlled studies compared electronic monitoring with intermittent auscultation of the fetal heart rate and reported an increase in both operative vaginal and cesarean delivery rates. The extra cesareans associated with electronic fetal monitoring did not lead to substantive benefits for the baby. A reduction in neonatal seizures was reported to be associated with continuous monitoring of the fetal heart and fetal acid-base estimation in one trial, but no differences in infant health at 1-year follow-up were found.

The contractions are often controlled by giving the woman a Pitocin drip, and the woman's pain is controlled by pain-killers and epidurals. In the last stage, when the baby is about to be born, the practitioner tries to control the pushing. If the woman has not received an epidural or a drip, the pushing urge is a very strong force that the woman can just follow. Instead, the doctor, midwife, or nurse often takes command, forcing the woman to push. On the other hand, if they try to avoid telling the woman when to push and just let her push when she feels the urge, the birth will be entirely different—much calmer and more relaxed. It will be a good experience, not only for the woman and the baby but also for the practitioner.

In the third stage practitioners control the delivery of the placenta by giving Pitocin and pulling the cord. Finally, and immediately, they cut the cord to examine the newborn, and thus mother and baby are separated.

If birth is seen from the woman's perspective, however, everything she has heard or read about birth, the films she has seen, and the hospital setting in which she gives birth will make her either more or less anxious. If she does not trust the signals from her own body and is given little support, she is likely to have problems. If she has low self-esteem and is not assertive, the doctor, midwife, and other hospital staff will take charge. She is more likely to lie down passively on a bed. Once on the bed, the pain will be worse and the woman will need help. The doctor, midwife, and nurse are there to help her. Now she has become a patient. Sooner or later she might be asked, "Do you want a pain-killer?" or "Do you want an epidural?" How often do doctors ask, "Do you want a natural birth?"or even "Do you want a bath?" A pain-killer or an epidural makes the woman even more passive, and it is much easier to have her under control than if she is walking around or kneeling on the floor or relaxing in a bath. Her anxiety or feelings of intimidation will make it easier to accept the suggestion of a pain-killer or an epidural, even though she may not really want it.

Recently, in a large London hospital, I entered a birthing room in which an anesthetist was about to set up an epidural. I could see that the woman was frightened, so I went up to her and asked, "Do you want this epidural?" "No," she said, "I want a normal birth. Could you help me?" "We can try," I said, and asked her husband who was sitting in a corner of the room to come forward. I showed him how to give his wife back massage, and when the next contraction came, I was sitting in front of the woman looking into her eyes and we were together breathing through the contraction. "Ah, this feels good," she said, "I will try it." The anesthetist left the room with all his equipment, and the woman had a spontaneous birth with no drugs. Her acceptance of an epidural had simply been a submission to the doctor's authority, and with just a little help she had a normal birth. From this experience and those in other hospitals, I conclude that maternity care practitioners can help more women have a natural birth when they and the women have a positive attitude.

If the doctor, midwife, or nurse asks every woman, "Do you want a normal birth?" they will learn what she wants. Another question, "Do you want a bath or shower?" is also important. In most cases where an epidural is proposed, a bath or a shower is an alternative. It is very relaxing and the cervix will most often open up; it is also distracting, time passes by, and the moment of birth draws nearer.

Some hospitals around the world have a policy of accommodating the concerns of ordinary people and their interest in natural childbirth. They use invasive methods restrictively and are open to alternative birth methods. Until more hospitals change their routines, women who would like a more natural approach to birth could choose small units or their own homes. At large hospitals women in labor tend to be strictly controlled, and they have few opportunities to decide for themselves. At small hospitals women are still controlled but to a lesser extent. At a birth center or in her own home, however, a woman is most likely to be listened to and respected by her caregivers.

Today, medical interventions are performed in almost all situations in Western hospitals. Perhaps we need an educational and psychological revolution in maternity care! Childbirth should become a normal process as it used to be and still is in all mammals. Let doctors help in cases where something has gone wrong, but let midwives be responsible for normal births. In Lund, the city in Sweden where I live, we have around 3500 births a year and just two obstetricians for complicated cases. Midwives are in charge of all normal births in Sweden, and the country has one of the world's lowest neonatal mortality rates. If every practitioner that a woman meets during pregnancy and in the birthing room looked on birth as a normal physiological process, as part of life, natural birth would be the norm and a birth with medical intervention the exception.

# NO

Gilbert J. Grant

# Enjoy Your Labor: A New Approach to Pain Relief for Childbirth

**A**s an anesthesiologist, I have been caring for women during labor and delivery for 20 years. I specialize in relieving the pain of childbirth using the most effective and reliable means available—epidurals and spinals. In my experience, I've noticed that many mothers-to-be are concerned about the safety of these pain relief techniques. The thought of receiving an epidural, which involves inserting a needle into the lower back, can be very unsettling. The mere mention of the term "spinal" may cause even more fear, often compounded by having heard a frightening story about anesthesia. A woman's double-edged fear, of both labor pain and the techniques commonly used to treat it, can cause anxiety for months before delivery.

Women attending childbirth education classes, who are predominantly first-time mothers-to-be, report that some instructors put a negative spin on epidurals and spinals, dismissing them as "unnatural" or even harmful interventions. Social pressures may needlessly dissuade women from choosing an epidural or spinal if they feel that a request for pain relief will be interpreted as a sign of weakness. Women also refrain from asking for pain medication out of concern that it will harm their babies—an unnecessary fear, mixed with guilt.

Beyond these issues, I came to realize that the leading cause of misunderstandings about modern pain relief techniques is simply a lack of accurate and up-to-date information. Browsing through the books my wife read during her first pregnancy, I found that although many of them discussed a variety of ways to manage the pain of childbirth, none presented the full picture of epidurals and spinals, even though these methods are used by most women who give birth in the United States. Worse still, I found that some books were filled with erroneous information about these techniques.

In 1996, to better inform and educate patients about epidurals and spinals, I began offering a monthly seminar at New York University Medical Center, where I work and teach. The success of this program persuaded me to extend its reach by writing this book. *Enjoy Your Labor* is based on the questions that expectant mothers have asked me over the years. . . .

Once women have a thorough understanding of what's involved, I have found that they are much less anxious about receiving pain relief, and perhaps about the process of delivery itself.

In addition to presenting incomplete and inaccurate information about epidurals and spinals, however, there is something else missing from other books: not one describes the "new" approach to labor pain relief that I recommend. My philosophy is quite simple. It is based on common sense: if you choose to have the best pain relief possible for labor and delivery (an epidural and/or a spinal), you should receive it *before* severe pain begins, assuming it has been established that you are in labor. Unfortunately, most women today receive the epidural *after* their labor pain becomes unbearable. Although my approach seems obvious and logical, many people oppose it, perhaps because it is so radically different from the way childbirth pain has been handled for so long. After reading this book, you'll understand why it makes sense to get the epidural as soon as it is clear that you are truly in labor, and before the pain becomes intolerable.

I chose the title *Enjoy Your Labor* because that is what I tell my patients after I give them their epidural. You *can* enjoy your labor, by educating yourself about the types of pain relief you may choose, and by taking advantage of what modern medicine has to offer. . . .

A clear understanding of the process of labor pain relief will reduce your fears about your upcoming delivery. Empower yourself with knowledge so that you can make an informed choice. Furthermore, knowing what to expect in terms of pain management will help to focus your thoughts on the one that is most important: the anticipation of your new baby.

# Perceptions of Childbirth Pain Relief

## The Double Standard

Imagine this: you are being wheeled in to have your appendix removed when a member of the surgical team peers down from above his mask and says, "Tell you what we'll do. Bear up as best you can without anesthesia, and if it gets too rough we'll give you something for the pain." Sounds crazy, right? No man would be asked to submit to an appendectomy, which can be performed in 24 minutes, without anesthesia. Yet the severe pain of labor, which can persist for more than 24 hours, is somehow viewed as a condition that women should simply endure, since childbirth is a natural process—as if "natural" pain is any less intense than that induced by a surgeon's scalpel. In fact, the pain of childbirth is the worst pain that most women will experience in their entire lives.

So why is there so much prejudice against epidurals and spinals? Part of the explanation is that women are often treated as second-class citizens. How else can one explain why pain relief for labor is still considered an option or a luxury? Menstrual cramps, which pale in comparison to labor contractions, are routinely treated with pain relievers. So why does anyone question whether labor pain merits treatment? As more than a few women have observed, if men had labor pain, its relief would probably be viewed quite differently.

The Huichol Indians of north-central Mexico sought to make childbirth a more equitable experience. Their interesting birthing practice intimately involved the father-to-be in the process. "According to Huichol tradition, when a woman had her first child, the husband squatted in the rafters of the house, or in the branches of a tree, directly above her, with ropes attached to his scrotum. As she went into labor pain, the wife pulled vigorously on the ropes, so that her husband shared in the painful, but ultimately joyous, experience of childbirth."

## Natural or Unnatural?

The term "natural" implies that a birth in which the mother receives pain medication is somehow "unnatural." Who would ever chose an "unnatural" childbirth? However, the term "unnatural" sounds plain silly when applied to, for example, pneumonia, for which you could choose the "unnatural" approach and take penicillin, or do it the "natural" way and die. Granted, these two situations are not identical: unlike untreated pneumonia, the pain of labor and delivery will not kill anyone. However, I attach no less importance to the suffering of a woman in labor than to the suffering of a patient with pneumonia: both situations deserve treatment if the individual who is suffering desires it.

I vividly recall a conversation with a physician who told me that, in his practice, laboring women are informed that the pain they are experiencing is a natural part of childbirth, and that once they understand this, the pain is much more bearable. Interesting, I thought. If someone told me the severe pain I was experiencing was natural, I do not think it would hurt any less: I would want relief, and quickly!

Natural childbirth preparation may be a set-up for feeling inadequate. This is because some childbirth educators teach that if you learn the breathing and focusing techniques and practice them properly, you'll be able to avoid pain medication. For many mothers-to-be, this approach is doomed to fail because in reality, breathing and focusing cannot eliminate the pain. So when the woman in labor breathes and focuses but still experiences pain, she may think that it is all her fault: "If only I had paid more attention in class and learned how to do the breathing better, it wouldn't hurt now." If she ends up asking for and receiving an epidural, she may feel even more of a failure.

---

## EPIDURAL EPISODES: BIRTH PANGS AND PANGS OF CONSCIENCE

F.S. was a first-time mother-to-be who was convinced that she did not want any type of pain medication for labor. She was highly motivated, and had dutifully attended a childbirth education course. Her labor pains gradually became more intense and ultimately much more severe than she had imagined they would be. She did her breathing and focusing that she had learned, but found that the intensity of her labor pain was no match for the techniques she was using to cope with them. But she was determined to avoid an epidural. It was only after six agonizing hours that she finally tired of her pain, and pleaded for an epidural. We immediately gave her one, which worked as it was intended to, relieving all of her pain within 15 minutes. I thought that she would be pleased, now that we had ended her agony, but I was mistaken. When I visited her room half-an-hour later she was crying uncontrollably—out of guilt for having taken the epidural. What a scene: she was completely comfortable, no longer feeling her contractions but she thought she had failed her "test." This dramatically demonstrates the problem with "natural" approaches: a woman is made to feel a failure if she asks for pain relief.

## Feelings of Guilt

Mothers-to-be are often made to feel guilty for asking for pain relief. This attitude is inappropriate, especially in light of the recent advances that have been made in obstetric anesthesia, and improvements in epidural and spinal techniques. Nevertheless, this thinking persists in our culture, along with numerous myths and misconceptions about modern techniques for relieving childbirth pain. One example of this is the belief that modern anesthesia is an "easy way out" that compromises the safety of both mother and child. As you will see after reading this book, not only are epidurals and spinals safe for the overwhelming majority of mothers and their babies, mothers who do not use them may be exposing themselves to unnecessary risks. . . .

## Only You Can Judge

Pain is a completely subjective sensation, so no one else can judge how much or how little you are experiencing. Individuals not in labor (doctors, midwives, nurses and coaches) tend to underestimate the intensity of the woman's pain and suffering; yet these are the people who often advise her whether she should take something for the pain. This process begins long before labor: childbirth educators often mislead women about the severity of the pain that they will experience during labor and delivery. In discussing how some individuals downplay the severity of the pain, Dr. Peter Brownridge, an Australian anesthesiologist, wrote: "To pretend, therefore, that natural childbirth is other than very painful for most women can only be described as a cruel and callous deception." Learn about what to expect during labor and delivery, and find out what options are available, so that you can make an informed decision about what type of pain relief, if any, you want.

### KEY CONCEPTS TO CARRY AWAY

Although many women are made to feel guilty for wanting to relieve the pain of childbirth, most end up requesting and receiving epidurals and/or spinals. Don't let anyone else make the decision for you. Empower yourself by obtaining the knowledge that you need to decide what type of pain relief, if any, will be best for you when you deliver your baby.

# POSTSCRIPT

## Is a Natural Childbirth, Without Pain Medication, Best for Development?

In recent decades, according to some estimates, 75 to 90 percent of births in the United States take place with epidural intervention and pain management. The simple fact that most children develop into healthy adults suggests that such interventions do not determine negative outcomes. Yet, controversy continues because we want to do everything possible during prenatal development to not only avoid negative outcomes, but actually enhance positive outcomes. So the question remains: Do we best enhance positive outcomes by allowing natural processes to run their course, or by taking advantage of modern medical technology?

Righard's assertion that natural childbirth is best for everyone involved builds upon one self-evident fact: Women have been giving birth for as long as humans have been a species. For generations, the birth process occurred without the interventions of modern medical science. A woman's body is beautifully able to go through the birth process and produce healthy children.

While Grant would not dispute that idea, he suggests that we should not revere something positioned as "natural" when that something is pain that can be easily managed by modern technology. The process of science is one of progress. Grant's argument relies on the logic of progress: If we have the ability to manage pain with minimal risk, why not use it?

One reason to be wary of medical technology is subtly referenced by Righard: Revering technology gives excess power to those, such as doctors, who are specialists with the technology. Both authors would agree that women should be able to make well-informed choices about how their birth process can be most successful for them. But many would argue that such a choice is not possible once a woman enters the foreign world of a hospital and submits to the expertise of medical professionals.

Partially for that reason, there is an increasing trend toward using people other than medical doctors to facilitate birthing. Righard, for example, notes that most births in his part of Sweden are attended by midwives who are presumably more prone to allow natural processes to run their course. Righard also discusses doulas, specialists in the psychosocial aspects of birth who work throughout a pregnancy with families to insure the birth process is both physically and psychologically healthy. Doulas are rapidly increasing in popularity in the United States.

Yet, the dilemma remains both for women giving birth and for those interested in the study of life span development. Ironically, the dilemma itself may be part of the problem because it creates an anxiety during pregnancy that is already full of pressures real and imagined. While the tension between the "natural" and the "unnatural" seems to be an inevitable challenge for development, the anxiety deriving from that tension may be at least partially relieved through better understanding.

## Suggested Readings

J. DeLee, "The Push Against Vaginal Birth," *Birth* (September 2003).

J. Dozer and S. Baruth, "Epidural Epidemic—Drugs in Labor: Are They Really Necessary . . . or Even Safe?" *Mothering* (July/August 1999).

N. Griffin, "The Epidural Express: Reasons Not to Jump On Board," *Mothering* (Spring 1997).

J. Hanff Korelitz, "Cut Me Open!" *Salon* (August 2, 1999).

R. Newman, "Toward a New Era of Childbirth Education" *Journal of Prenatal and Perinatal Psychology and Health* (Summer 2004).

T. Quan, "The Cult of Nature-Worship," *The Human Quest* (September/October 2004).

N. Shapiro, "Give Me Drugs! What's So Feminist About a Painful Childbirth?" *Salon* (August 3, 1999).

## Infant Development

This site provides links to various resources related to physical, cognitive, language, and social development in infants.

http://www.mhhe.com/socscience/devel/
common/infant.htm

## Infant Capacity

This site provides information about the capacities of infants at various months of development.

http://www.envisagedesign.com/ohbaby/develop.html

## Healthy Infant Development

Part of a larger site for pediatricians, this site provides information about healthy infant development.

http://www.keepkidshealthy.com/infant/
infantdevelopment.html

## Child Development

A site with extensive links to information about many aspects of child development.

http://www.childdevelopmentinfo.com/

## Rutgers Infant Development

This research lab provides an example of how scholars study infant development.

http://babylab.rutgers.edu/

## Jean Piaget

This site provides a good overview of the work of Jean Piaget, who started the discussion of infant symbolic representation.

http://www.ship.edu/~cgboeree/genpsypiaget.html

## James S. McDonnell Foundation

The James S. McDonnell Foundation funds research related to brain development, and is headed by the author of "The Myth of the First Three Years."

http://www.jsmf.org/

# PART 3

# Infancy

*I*nfants are fascinating because they represent both great potential and a certain level of helplessness. They also happen to usually be incredibly cute—a fact some researchers cite as an innate quality that insures they receive attention and care. But such an explanation is only speculation: Because infants do not have a capacity for language, they are a particular challenge to study and understand. This section raises two issues that confront this challenge by asking whether there really is something special about a human infant.

- Is There a "Myth of the First Three Years"?

- Are Infants Born With an Innate Ability to Make Symbolic Mental Representations of Objects?

# ISSUE 6

# Is There a "Myth of the First Three Years"?

**YES: Gwen J. Broude,** from "Scatterbrained Child Rearing," *Reason Magazine* (December 2000)

**NO: Zero to Three: National Center For Infants, Toddlers and Families,** from *Zero to Three Response to the Myth of the First Three Years,* http://www.zerotothree.org/no-myth.html.

## ISSUE SUMMARY

**YES:** Gwen J. Broude, who teaches developmental psychology and cognitive science at Vassar College, reviews, supports, and augments John Bruer's idea that a "myth of the first three years" has falsely used neuroscience to claim that infancy is the only critical developmental period.

**NO:** Zero to Three, a national organization devoted to promoting healthy infant development, contradicts Bruer's idea by asserting that a great deal of diverse research supports the idea that the first three years are critical to development and success in adulthood.

**A**dvances in technology and research methods have allowed developmental scientists to establish that there is a massive amount of complex brain activity going on during the infant years. In fact, the explosion of changing neuronal and synaptic activity (neurons being brain cells and synapses being the connections between brain cells) during infancy may be unmatched at any other point in the lifespan. After infancy it seems that much of brain development and cognitive functioning depends upon synaptic pruning—the process of shaping and organizing the way brain cells communicate with each other. The implications of these basic findings, however, are subject to much controversy.

The elaborate developments of the brain during infancy include the foundation of several fundamental cognitive skills, such as language and mature sensory perception. Famous research with animals (such as studies of cats not exposed to a visual environment during infancy), and famous case studies of children raised in extreme deprivation (such as abused children who are not exposed to language until teen years), have demonstrated that infancy is a "critical period" for certain basic brain functions such as vision and language. While there is no question that critical periods exist for certain basic cognitive skills, there is significant debate as to whether all of infant cognitive development can be considered a critical period.

If infancy should generally be considered a critical period in brain development, does that mean infants need special attention and expertly enriched environments? One strain of popular wisdom suggests yes; many parents feel extremely anxious about the need to provide careful attention and stimulation to ensure their infants develop well, and will buy videos, games, music, and toys that claim to be specially designed for proper brain stimulation. Most developmental scientists would agree that this extreme anxiety is unnecessary—infants for generations and across cultures have developed successfully in natural environments without scientific intervention. But does that mean that we are wrong to consider the first three years of life as special? Does that create a harmful "myth of the first three years?"

Gwen J. Broude writes that, indeed, the first three years are only crucially important to sensationalist journalism, misguided child advocates, and misinformed anxious parents. In discussing ideas from a well publicized book titled *The Myth of the First Three Years* by John T. Bruer, Broude substantiates the idea that misinterpretations of neuroscience and developmental ideas, such as critical periods, have created the mistaken impression that infancy is a developmental stage that requires extra attention to brain development. For Broude the problem is not that we fail to provide enough attention and stimulation to infants, but that we fail to appreciate the amazing ability of a brain to develop in its own time in its own normal environment.

In contrast, Zero to Three, a national parenting organization, fears that the real danger lies in promoting the idea that the importance of the first three years is a "myth". They acknowledge that some findings related to cognitive development have been mis-interpreted, but assert strongly that the first three years of life are a distinct and crucial developmental period. Thus, from this perspective, while the direct influence of brain stimulation may be overplayed by some sources, the first three years provide an essential foundation for whatever development will occur later in life.

Both readings are addressing the provocative argument made by John T. Bruer in his book *The Myth of the First Three Years*. This book was divisive to those interested in life span development. While many people found the ideas in that book an important anecdote to contemporary attitudes trying to exaggerate the need for control of infancy, others found the ideas dangerous in their potential for allowing people to ignore the need for special attention to infants. Either position depends upon fundamental questions for life span development about the distinctiveness of infancy as a stage often considered to have more influence than any other.

**Gwen J. Broude**

 **YES**

# Scatterbrained Child Rearing

**W**hen it comes to raising children, there is no such thing as too much good advice. So when accounts of neuroscientific advances in our understanding of child development began to appear in the popular press a couple of years ago, it sure sounded like good news. Parents could now raise their children in line with the hard facts about the relationship between human growth and brain development.

Don't rejoice just yet. . . . Education expert John T. Bruer warn(s) us not to believe what we have been hearing about the new neuroscience of child rearing. [He points] out that the media's version of brain-based child development bears little resemblance to the real thing. Even worse, those same wrongheaded theories have landed on the desks of policy makers. The result, as Bruer describe(s) in grim detail, is policy initiatives that can be very dangerous to children.

The mangled accounts of brain science that Bruer . . . want[s] to debunk begin with the assumption that brain development is crucial to child development. So far, so good. It is the more detailed claims, or "myths," as Bruer calls them, about the relationship between brain maturation and a child's maturation that can lead to trouble. *The Myth of the First Three Years* focuses on three such myths, which will doubtless sound familiar to most readers-though most Americans would probably consider them rock-solid facts about how the brain works. Although Bruer is not himself a neuroscientist, his discussion of where and how popular brain science has gone wrong accurately reflects the current neuroscientific literature.

Bruer's three myths are that learning is limited to "windows of opportunity," or critical periods; that these windows of opportunity occur only as long as there is a significant growth of connections, or synapses, between brain cells; and that children require enriched environments for optimal learning to take place during these windows of opportunity. As there is substantial evidence of an explosion in synaptic connections during the first three years of a child's life, the conclusion from popular neuroscience is that development is basically over by the end of the third birthday.

Many recent public policy initiatives have been based on the "vital first three years" vision of brain development. For instance, the frantic push toward universal preschool from the Clinton administration follows logically

From *Reason,* vol. 32, issue 7, December 2000. Copyright © 2000 by Reason Foundation. Reprinted by permission. *Gwen J. Broude* (broude@vassar.edu) teaches developmental psychology and cognitive science at Vassar College.

from that vision, as does the loony notion from Georgia Gov. Zell Miller that state legislators should distribute CDs of classical music to newborns to give them an intellectual head start. This notion causes many parents to believe that the early experiences of their children will seal their fates forever, and to worry that a single parenting mistake will doom their youngsters for life. Bruer argues that all those ideas are based on fantasy.

The myth that learning is limited to the first years of life is based on the finding that the density of connections among brain cells increases very rapidly during the second and third years of life. After that, the number of connections begins to stabilize or to actually decrease. This is a correct description of brain maturation. But as Bruer explains, it's not correct to assume that the brain is gaining connections during the first years of life because children are cramming their skulls with learning.

The "Mythmakers" of popular neuroscience, as Bruer calls them, suppose that brain growth means that learning is happening, and that the subsequent decrease in synaptic density must mean that learning is no longer happening. While that sounds logical, no neuroscientist believes this is an accurate description of the relationship between brain maturation and development. Indeed, it would be more nearly correct to posit the opposite relationship between children's learning and what the brain is doing.

The consensus among neuroscientists is that the explosion of connections among neurons that we see in early life merely sets the stage for the acquisition of knowledge. It is as if nature is preparing the canvas on which the world subsequently paints. The decrease, or pruning, of connections is what seems to coincide with actual learning. Ironically, then, the brain is most prepared to begin learning at just the point when popular brain science says it is too late for learning to take place. After the synaptic explosion happens, children become newly capable of learning things that they could not learn before.

The idea that there are critical periods is similarly wrongheaded as a general theory of how children develop. There are certain skills that are most easily learned early in life—for instance, seeing or talking. But as Bruer points out, we are dealing here with abilities that all normal human beings acquire. Psychologists call these "experience-expectant traits" to underscore the plain fact that the kinds of experience required for their proper development are so basic that virtually no child can help but be exposed to them. It is as if the neurophysiology underlying the trait "expects" to meet up with the needed experience. And indeed, the number of children who are not exposed to language, or light, is vanishingly small. Experience-expectant traits, Bruer observes, are acquired "easily, automatically, and unconsciously."

Not all traits are experience-expectant. My brain did not expect to meet up with algebra in the environment. Nor did it expect to encounter writing. Or the piano. But the skills of math or reading or playing music are just the sorts of skills for which there are no critical periods. They are experience-dependent traits that can be learned at any point in life. These, ironically, are also the very sorts of skills on which popular versions of brain science focus when they warn us about critical periods. Children in our culture do tend to learn particular skills, such as reading or adding, at predictable ages. But "we should not confuse this kind of learning with the existence of critical periods for those skills," Bruer writes. "What is culturally normal is not biologically determined."

Bruer also debunks the idea that enriched environments are required for optimal development. This notion originates from a misunderstanding of decades-old rat studies in which the learning of rats placed in a so—called enriched environment was superior to that of rats placed in less enriched environments. From this we are to conclude that human children should be exposed to as much stimulation as possible. This is in spite of the fact that the rats in the original experiment were adults and that their enriched environments were still deprived in comparison with what any rat would experience in the wild.

Bruer assures us that all kids need for normal development is exposure to very basic experiences, like ambient light to see, a language to hear, gravity with which to interact, and so on. Thus, his advice is that parents should make sure that their children's sensory systems are in good working order—not too tough a challenge.

Indeed, there is good reason to believe that children can't make use of all the enrichment we offer them, as they tend to develop according to their own timetables regardless of our ambitions. Try to correct the grammar of a young child who is not ready to learn the lesson. Janie comes home bursting with excitement. "My teacher brought a rabbit to school and I holded it," she gushes. "You held the rabbit?" you say. "Yes, I holded it." "Did you say you held it tightly?" you ask. "No, I holded it loosely," she responds. Janie will learn about irregular verbs on her schedule, not on yours.

Contrary to the almost blatant idiocy of the "first three years" myth–clearly, most useful human learning happens long after age 3–brains are always changing, which is another way of saying that people are always learning, regardless of their age. The greatest surprises from the laboratories of neuroscientists come in the form of evidence that the brain is far more plastic than we used to think. Since the 1980s neuroscientists have demonstrated that adult brains are extremely malleable, so much so that areas of the adult primate brain originally responsible for one function can change jobs. For instance, adult primate brain cells once receiving input from the animal's arm will subsequently reorganize to receive input from the chin and jaw if connections from the arm to the brain are interrupted. If adult brains seem stable, that's only because their experiences have been stable.

This isn't just of interest to academic neuropsychologists. Bruer's Myth-makers have a message that can hurt kids: that we should try to cram all of life's lessons into the first three years of development and then call it quits. This would clearly be fatal to any child's development, as anyone familiar with how brains—or children—actually function will plainly see. If we followed the advice implied by this version of brain development, we would be trying to teach children at exactly the time in their lives when their brains are not yet ready to learn and then stop teaching them at precisely the time that their brains do become ready. Bruer tells us that public policy is in fact heading in this direction. For instance, state legislatures are already considering bills that would decrease or eliminate support for later child interventions to invest those funds in birth–to–3 programs in the belief that this is the only time during which brains are capable of learning.

. . . As Bruer tells us, children respond to the environment at their own pace. Some psychologists have begun to suggest that this allows youngsters to fine-tune basic competencies before taking up the challenge of developing more sophisticated ones. We see this self–pacing in the way that children naturally regulate the amount of stimulation to which they will respond. Babies turn their heads away if you try to get in their faces. When there is too much going on around them, infants will go to sleep on you. Basically, children tune out stimulation for which they are not ready.

. . . Bruer's robust child [is] illustrated in his example from rural Guatemala, where children spend the first 18 months of life in circumstances that we would call severely deprived. Nevertheless, these kids perform at the same cognitive level as middle-class American children by the time they reach adolescence. Neuroscientist Steve Peterson, quoted by Bruer, captures the meaning of this anecdote when he observes that "development really wants to happen. It takes very impoverished environments to interfere with development because the biological system has evolved so that the environment alone stimulates development." How does this translate into advice for parents? "Don't raise your children in a closet, starve them, or hit them in the head with a frying pan."

. . . *The Myth of the First Three Years* is a fine rebuttal to the claim that children are fragile and a vindication for those of us who have always suspected that we were still capable of growing and learning even though we were well past 3 years old.

# Zero to Three: Response to *the Myth of the First Three Years*

*T*he Myth of the First Three Years, by John Bruer, is an attempt to redress some popular misconceptions about the importance to brain development of a child's earliest experiences. The book is an extension of "Education and the Brain: A Bridge Too Far," a scholarly article by Bruer that appeared in the November 1997 issue of *Educational Researcher*. Bruer, who is president of the James S. McDonnell Foundation, which awards $18 million annually for biomedical, educational, and international projects, has no formal training in either neuroscience or child development. But his "Bridge Too Far" article provided an astute examination of the ways in which recent findings in neuroscience have been blown out of proportion and used to imply that we know how to increase the neural connections in a child's brain and ultimately, the child's intelligence. Take the so-called "Mozart effect," for example, the notion that playing classical music, especially Mozart, will boost a child's IQ. This idea was popularized in the press and capitalized on by entrepreneurs selling Mozart CDs for babies and parents, but it has no clear foundation in science.

However, in *The Myth of the First Three Years,* a book written for a popular, mass audience, Bruer crosses his own bridge and then burns it, taking his correct observation that the neuroscience of early childhood is, in a sense, in its own infancy, and leaping to the extreme conclusion that what happens to a child in the early years is of little consequence to subsequent intellectual development. He also suggests that intervening in the lives of very young children at risk for poor outcomes in school and adulthood will have little or no effect. Nothing could be further from the truth.

We are particularly concerned that readers will come away from this book confused about what babies need and what parents can do to encourage development, and that policymakers will see Bruer's argument as an excuse to ignore the growing interest and demand for policies and services that support babies, toddlers, and their families.

## The Myth of Boosting Baby's Brain

Zero to three agrees with some of Bruer's assertions. He is right that science has just begun to sort out how the trillions of nerve cells in a child's brain are organized during the first three years of life to allow a child to learn to talk, read, and reason. The application of these new and exciting findings has sometimes been exaggerated, particularly by the media, or used inappropriately to make claims about what parents, educators, and policymakers should or should not be doing.

Much of the confusion centers on the notion that the first three years are a "critical period," defined as a window of opportunity for laying down circuits in a child's brain or learning a particular set of skills that closes irrevocably after a set amount of time. What we know from early research is that critical periods exist in children only for some very basic capacities, such as vision, and to a lesser extent for learning language. For example, it has been well-documented that young children can learn a second language much more easily—and often with better pronunciation and grammar—than can adolescents or adults.

We agree with Bruer that a child's brain is not even close to being completely wired when the third candle on the birthday cake has been blown out. In fact, brain research suggests the opposite conclusion: Important parts of the brain are not fully developed until well past puberty, and the brain, unlike any other organ, changes throughout life. The human brain is capable of learning and laying down new circuitry until old age. But this does not mean that the first three years are unimportant.

# Why the Early Years Are So Important

While scientists have so far only confirmed a few "critical periods" in the development of the human brain, there is no doubt that the first three years of life are critical to the growth of intelligence and to later success in adulthood. We know from rigorous psychological and sociological research, and from compelling clinical experience, that early childhood is a time when infants and toddlers acquire many of the motivations and skills needed to become productive, happy adults. Curiously, Bruer turns a blind eye to the immense and crucial social and emotional development that begins during a child's first three years, which provides a foundation for continued later intellectual development. *The importance of the first three years is no myth, and parents and policymakers must not be misled by Bruer's book.*

Following are a few examples that underscore why and how a child's intellectual development rests on social and emotional skills learned in the early years:

## 1. Development of Trust

Every person needs to learn to trust other human beings in order to function successfully in society. It is crucial that this sense of trust begins to grow during the earliest years. While it is certainly possible to learn this later, it becomes much more difficult the older a child gets. Years of living in an interpersonal environment that is unresponsive, untrustworthy, or unreliable is difficult to undo in later relationships.

Trust grows in infancy in the everyday, ordinary interactions between the child and the significant caregivers. A baby learns to trust through the routine experiences of being fed when she is hungry, and held when she is upset or frightened. The child learns that her needs will be met, that she matters, that someone will comfort her, feed her, and keep her warm and safe. She feels good about herself and about others.

Children whose basic needs are not met in infancy and early childhood often lack that sense of trust, and have difficulty learning to believe in themselves or in others. We know this from a multitude of scientific studies, including the research of Alan Sroufe and Byron Egeland, at the University of Minnesota. In a long-term study that followed infants through toddlerhood and into adulthood, Sroufe and his colleagues found that when children were reared within relationships they could count on, they had fewer behavior problems in school, had more confidence, and were emotionally more capable of positive social relationships.

## 2. Development of Self-Control

From the time a child begins to walk, we can see the progress she is making in mastering an important skill: self-control. Babies do not come into the world knowing that nobody likes it when they bite and hit, or grab toys and food from them; they need help from adults to understand that these impulses are not socially acceptable. John Gottman, of the University of Washington, among others, has demonstrated that children who get no help monitoring or regulating their behavior during the early years, especially before the age of three, have a greater chance of being anxious, frightened, impulsive, and behaviorally disorganized when they reach school. Further, these children are more likely to rely on more violent or other intimidating means to resolve conflicts than their peers who have successfully begun the long process of learning self-control.

## 3. The Source of Motivation

Another pillar of intellectual development and success in school is motivation. Infants and toddlers develop this through day-to-day interactions with responsive caregivers. Responding to the needs of the child is a powerful process that builds confidence and an inner sense of curiosity. This motivates the child to learn and has direct effects on success in school. The more confident a child is, the more likely she is to take on new challenges with enthusiasm.

# The Emotional Foundations of Learning

Trust, self-control, and motivation form the bedrock of a child's intellectual development. Intelligence and achievement in school do not depend solely on a young child's fund of factual knowledge, ability to read or recite the alphabet, or familiarity with numbers or colors. Rather, in addition to such knowledge and skills, success rests on children, of whatever background, coming to school curious, confident, and aware of what behavior is expected. Successful children are comfortable seeking assistance, able to get along with others, and interested in using their knowledge and experience to master new challenges.

Bruer is right that there is no magic bullet for making kids smart. *But by erroneously focusing exclusively on intellectual achievement, he fails to recognize that all aspects of development affect one another, and that children cannot learn or display their intelligence as well if they have not developed emotionally and socially.* The task for parents and other caregivers who want their children to succeed in school is not to force development. Rather, it is to try to ensure that the moment-to-moment events of daily life give babies and toddlers the sense of security, encouragement, and confidence that are the foundation of emotional health. It is this that will ultimately allow them to learn at home, in school and throughout life.

## Dangers of the Book

We are concerned that readers will draw the wrong conclusions. Many **parents** are likely to be confused by Bruer's message, which contradicts what they may know instinctively about the importance of the first three years. The book may let other parents off the hook—particularly those parents who aren't willing or able to devote the time and attention that is needed to provide a nurturing environment for babies and toddlers.

Moreover, some parents will be offended by Bruer's assertion that "mothers who behave in acceptable American middle-class fashion tend to have securely attached children. The challenge is to get more non-complying, mostly minority and disadvantaged, mothers to act in this way." We know that there are plenty of poor, minority parents doing a marvelous job of raising their children in securely attached relationships. Whether by design or accident, Bruer stigmatizes minority racial and ethnic groups by defining them as the exception to the rule. And just what is "acceptable American middle-class" parenting? We know of no such thing as a homogeneous approach to parenting and attachment.

**Policymakers** may come away from Bruer's book with the misconception that efforts to help young children are a waste of money and time. Indeed, it appears that this may be Bruer's intent. For example, he attacks the very modest funding provided for such programs as Early Head Start, a desperately needed initiative that is a drop in the bucket relative to other government programs. Early Head Start was conceived on the basis of ample evidence for the value of early intervention—evidence that was gathered long before the hoopla began over neuroscience, but that Bruer conveniently omits from his book.

Pioneering work done in the 1970s by Sally Provence, at the Child Study Center at Yale University provides just one example. Over a period of several years, Provence studied two groups of families with young children who were at risk for poor outcomes in school and adulthood. One group was offered free medical care and high quality day care, which included help in learning to be more responsive parents. The other group received no assistance. Provence found that when the children of both groups reached school age, those who received help missed far less school than the others, were able to learn and retain information more easily, and were more motivated. Their families had fewer children and the births were spaced farther apart.

*Efforts to help all children achieve the basic skills of trust, motivation, and self-control needed for later intellectual and emotional development should not be aimed at creating super-babies, or giving anxious parents one more thing to worry about, or overambitious parents one more reason to push their children. Our aim should be to ensure that all children reach school age with a solid foundation for learning and relating to others, and that all parents know what they can do to help their children develop. In the last decade, the United States has made important progress in recognizing the needs of young children. Businesses have made efforts to create family-friendly policies. Government has made efforts to provide services to families. Parents are increasingly interested in how best to encourage and prepare their children. Taking to heart many of the negative messages of* The Myth of the First Three Years *can only set back those efforts. Our nation's youngest citizens deserve better.*

# POSTSCRIPT

## Is There a "Myth of the First Three Years"?

There is no controversy about the fact that contemporary parents are overwhelmed with advice and products intended to facilitate infant development. Clever marketers and well-meaning experts both have combined to create a sense that without the "correct" intervention an infant will not develop to their full potential. There is, however, an obvious irony in recognizing that geniuses of the past such as Einstein and Mozart experienced nothing in their infancy such as the "Baby Einstein" DVD's and "Baby Mozart" CD's that are so popular amongst contemporary parents.

A common attitude is that while science may not fully support the notion of essential intervention in infancy, treating infancy as a special stage can do no harm. It may not do any good, but it can't hurt. But even that notion is not as simple as it appears. There are at least two levels at which exaggerating the importance of infancy for development can be detrimental. At a more general level, it creates a tremendous pressure and anxiety for parents to treat their infant in the "right" way. Assuming that infants need special and expert intervention takes away the value of parental instinct and a trust in the natural bonding that parents and children experience. At a more specific level, there is some speculation that over-stimulation of infants can be as harmful as under-stimulation. In recent years there have been several accounts of infants who have become nearly addicted to videos and music intended to facilitate brain development. Some also suggest that the proliferation of childhood problems with attention deficits may arise from being conditioned in infancy to excessive and constant environmental stimulation.

Broude points out ways that our scientific understanding of early brain development is easily misinterpreted by a culture interested in "building better brains". This cultural mentality is not universal. Many cultures do not compel parents towards intense stimulation of infants, and yet development happens. Likewise, throughout history infants have grown up to be successful adults without the benefits of intensive expert intervention during infancy. Infants are indeed the most incredible learning machines found in the world; they develop more complex capacities in less time than any other beings. This development is part of our innate capacities. Yet we want more; we want to believe that we can enhance development by virtue of how we stimulate infants.

It is important to note, therefore, that Zero to Three does not focus on brain stimulation as the reason infancy is special. They acknowledge that citing findings regarding critical periods as a basis for using products to enhance brain development is misguided. But they assert that because some neuroscience has been exaggerated does not mean we should take the opposite extreme and assume the first three years of life don't matter. Zero to Three makes a crucial distinction between cognitive development and socio-emotional development; they accept that cognitive development during infancy proceeds reasonably well with normal stimulation, but they assert strongly that socio-emotional development requires particular attention and provides a foundation for cognitive development. Citing widely accepted attachment literature, Zero to Three points out that children who do not develop a socio-emotional bond in early life may have long-term problems in their social relationships and other aspects of life.

Ultimately, cognitive and socio-emotional aspects of development constantly interact. Separating out how we think from the environment and feelings through which we think is necessary for tightly controlled research, but it is not always practical. A child's intelligence depends upon what is necessary to function in a particular social world. So finally we are left with a controversy about nothing less than what matters for making sure people have the general ability to succeed in their lives. Do they simply need normalcy? Or do they need special care? What is necessary to ensure infants fulfill their full human potential?

## Suggested Readings

J. Bruer, "Education and the Brain: A Bridge Too Far," *Educational Researcher* (November 1997).

J. Bruer, *The Myth of the First Three Years: A New Understanding of Early Brain Development and Lifelong Learning* (Free Press, 1999).

L. Eliot, *What's Going on in There?* (Bantam Books 2000).

S. Gerhardt, "Why Love Matters: How Affection Shapes a Baby's Brain" (Brunner-Routledge 2004).

H. Guldberg, "The Myth of 'Infant Determinism'," www.spiked-online.com (October 2004).

K. Hirsh-Pasek and R.M. Golinkoff with D. Eyer, *Einstein Never Used Flash Cards* (Rodale 2003).

# ISSUE 7

# Are Very Young Infants Born with an Innate Ability to Make Symbolic Representations of Objects?

**YES: Elizabeth S. Spelke,** from "Core Knowledge," *American Psychologist* (November 2000)

**NO: Bruce Hood,** from "When Do Infants Know About Objects?" *Perception* (vol. 30, 2001)

## ISSUE SUMMARY

**YES:** Harvard professor Elizabeth Spelke draws on a large quantity of infant research to suggest infants have an innate understanding of the properties of objects, which is part of what she considers core knowledge systems that are the foundation of thought.

**NO:** Developmental psychologist Bruce Hood points out that the type of research Spelke relies upon is controversial—learning what infants are thinking requires potentially unfair assumptions.

The most famous name in the study of child development is that of the twentieth-century Swiss psychologist Jean Piaget. Piaget virtually founded the study of cognitive development, and his decades-old developmental theory is the standard by which all others are judged. In the classic scholarly tradition, however, this level of notoriety brings inevitable challenges. Perhaps the most fundamental challenge to Piaget's theory of development relates to his assertion that infants prior to approximately one and a half years of age have virtually no ability to "think" beyond relatively automatic physical experiences with the world.

The question of whether very young infants can "think" has profound implications. If humans are born with the ability to think, it supports that notion that biology programs much of who we are as people. It means that our distinct ability to think is not exclusively a product of our human environment, but rather it is a product of our evolutionary history. While any intentional effort to facilitate child development is based on an implicit assumption that the complexity of human thought is a product of our experiences with the

115

world, if infants are born with the ability to think, then our experiences with the world may matter much less than we often assume.

The first significant challenges to Piaget's timetable for the gradual development of complex thought came in the 1980s when researchers found that, contrary to Piaget's assertions, young infants had some concept of "object permanence." That is, young infants had the ability to recognize that objects continue to exist when out of sight. This research took advantage of new methodological techniques that involved measuring how long infants looked at possible and impossible events. In one famous example, researchers tested whether infants would look longer at a car moving down a track if led to believe the track were blocked by a solid object. Reliably, very young infants are surprised to see a toy car continue rolling down a track when they have seen a solid object blocking the way.

Such research has led to a spate of studies using infant looking time as a marker of thinking. These studies have become the dominant paradigm for investigating cognition in infants, and have led to many seemingly incredible claims about the "intelligence" of babies. The popular media have even latched onto scientific headlines claiming provocative findings such as the innate ability of infants to do math and physics problems.

Elizabeth Spelke, a distinguished developmental psychologist and infant researcher at Harvard, recognizes that there are limits to the abilities of infants but firmly asserts that research shows they have core knowledge about objects. She describes a variety of studies about infant cognition, arguing that each demonstrates thought and knowledge that indicates a complexity to the infant brain beyond previous imagination. For Spelke, when infants imitate an adult's facial expression or stare at an impossible event, they are using powerful inborn, natural capacities for thinking about the world.

Bruce Hood, an experimental psychologist, is not so ready as Spelke to dismiss Piaget's assertion about the limits of infant cognition. Hood's explicit critique of Spelke is methodological—he notes that infant research depends on assumptions about what is happening in an infant's mind when making visual discrimination. Hood asserts that the simple ability to discriminate between possible and impossible events does not necessarily represent complex thought (I can instinctively discriminate between two similar faces without any conscious knowledge of why those faces are different). But Hood also raises important implicit questions about the assumptions researchers are making with regard to the infant mind. Is it fair to assume simple gazes from an infant represent the foundation of complex thought, or is that a projection of researchers wanting to explain the human mind?

As you read these articles, note the two levels of this controversy. On one level is the methodological issue regarding the study of research participants without the facility of language. Is it valid to assume that looking time tells us about thinking? On another level is the conceptual issue regarding these types of thinking that makes our brains so powerful. Do we come into the world with the foundations of abstract thought, or does human intelligence come from the developmental interaction of our brain and our experienced world?

# YES

**Elizabeth S. Spelke**

# Core Knowledge

## Core Knowledge of Objects

Twenty years of research provides evidence that infants build representations of objects as complete, connected, solid bodies that persist over occlusion and maintain their identity through time (e.g., Baillargeon, 1993; Spelke & Van de Walle, 1993). One of the situations that reveal this ability was devised by Karen Wynn (1992). Wynn's studies used a preferential looking–expectancy violation method, based on the assumption that infants would look longer at an unexpected event than at an otherwise similar but expected one. In one experiment, 5-month-old infants saw a single toy animal placed on a stage, a screen was lowered to occlude the toy, a second, featurally identical toy was introduced in view of the child, and then that toy was placed behind the screen. Finally, the screen was removed to reveal either one or two toys on alternating trials. If infants failed to keep track of these objects over occlusion, then they might be expected to look longer at the display of two toys, because only one toy ever had been visible at a time. If infants kept track of each object as it moved behind the occluder and maintained distinct representations of the two objects, then the display containing just one toy would have been unexpected, eliciting longer looking. The latter looking preference was obtained. In subsequent studies, moreover, infants presented with the task of adding one object to another looked longer at three objects than at two objects, indicating that their representation of two objects was exact, and infants presented first with an array of two objects and then with the removal of one object from behind the occluder successfully computed the subtraction of two minus one to yield one object rather than two (Wynn, 1992).

Wynn's (1992) exciting findings generated many replications and extensions. In particular, Simon, Hespos, and Rochat (1995) found that infants responded appropriately to the number of objects in Wynn's task even when the features of those objects changed behind the occluder (e.g., when an Elmo puppet was replaced by an Ernie puppet), indicating that infants truly were representing the number of objects and not the amount of some property common to the objects such as their coloring or detailed shape. Moreover, Koechlin, Dehaene, and Mehler (1998) found that infants responded to number in Wynn's task even when the occluded objects moved on a turntable, so

From *American Psychologist,* November 2000, pp. excerpts from 1233–1240. Copyright © 2000 by Elizabeth S. Spelke. Reprinted by permission.

that their locations were variable and unpredictable, indicating that infants responded to object number rather than to object locations. As Wynn (1992) observed, infants' looking preferences in these experiments provided evidence for three kinds of representations: representations of objects as enduring bodies over occlusion, representations of number—of the distinction between one, two, and three objects, and representations of the operations of addition and subtraction of one object.

All of the previously discussed studies used a preferential looking method, and so one may ask whether the competencies they reveal are specific to that method. This question is difficult to answer for 5-month-old infants, because their action systems are so limited, but further studies, focusing on 8- to 12-month-old infants, provide evidence for the same abilities using two quite different response systems: manual search and locomotion. In the box search task, Van de Walle, Carey, and Prevor (in press) presented Wynn's (1992) one-plus-one event by successively hiding two objects in a box, surreptitiously removing one object from the box, allowing infants to retrieve the one remaining object and then taking it away, and observing infants' further exploration of the box. Relative to infants who originally saw just one object hidden in the box, infants who had seen the one-plus-one event searched the box longer and more persistently, as if they expected to find a second object. In the locomotor choice task, Feigenson, Carey, and Hauser (2000) presented infants with two boxes into which they placed different numbers of cookies, one at a time. After two cookies were placed in one box and three cookies in the other box, the boxes were widely separated, and infants were allowed to crawl toward them. Infants selectively approached the box with the three cookies, suggesting that they represented the numbers of cookies in the boxes.

Three tasks using different response systems and different objects therefore provide evidence that human infants keep track of objects that become occluded and construct, from a pattern of successive occlusion, a representation of the precise number of objects in the array. Further studies reveal, however, two interesting limits to infants' abilities. First, infants fail to represent number when presented with entities that do not behave as objects do. For example, Huntley-Fenner and Carey (2000) repeated Wynn's ( 1992) studies using nonsolid, noncohesive sandpiles instead of objects, and they found no consistent response to the number of sandpiles. As a second example, Chiang and Wynn (in press) conducted experiments similar to Wynn's using collections of objects: a pile of blocks. Except in cases where the collections could be represented as separate, individual objects, infants failed to track the collections over occlusion. These findings provide evidence that the system of representation at work in this family of experiments is domain specific: It operates on objects but not on other detectable entities.

The second limitation to infants' object representations in Wynn's task appears as the number of objects is increased. Infants succeed in representing objects over occlusion as long as the total number of objects behind an occluder is small—up to about three—but they fail with larger numbers. For example, Feigenson et al.'s (2000) participants in the locomotor search experiments successfully approached a box containing two cookies rather than one or three cookies rather than two, but they failed to approach a box containing eight cookies rather than four. Although infants can keep track of multiple objects over occlusion, this ability appears to break down as the number of objects increases beyond about three.

In summary, diverse findings provide evidence that infants have a system for representing objects that allows them to keep track of multiple objects simultaneously. The system is domain specific (it applies to objects but not to other perceptible entities such as sandpiles), it is subject to a set size limit (it allows infants to keep track of about three objects but not more), and it survives changes in a number of object properties, including color, detailed shape, and spatial location. . . .

# Core Knowledge of Numerosity

I turn now to a second core knowledge system that serves to represent approximate numerical magnitudes. Many studies of number representation, both in infants and in adults, have been plagued by a tricky methodological problem: Whenever two displays differ in numerosity, they differ on other, continuous dimensions as well. For example, if two sets with different numbers of objects present objects of the same sizes and colors, then the more numerous set also will present a larger colored surface area. And if the sets present objects that appear at equal densities, then the more numerous set will cover a larger region of the display. Recent experiments by Fei Xu, Jennifer Lipton, and Hilary Barth nevertheless have circumvented these problems and provide a test of infants' and adults' representations of large numerosities.

Xu's experiments used a different preferential looking method, focusing on infants' tendency to look longer at novel arrays than at more familiar ones. In Xu and Spelke (2000b), 6-month-old infants were presented with a succession of arrays of dots on a series of familiarization trials. From trial to trial, the positions and sizes of the dots changed, but the number of dots remained the same: 8 dots for half the participants and 16 dots for the rest. Moreover, the arrays of 8 and 16 dots were equated for overall size (and therefore differed in density) and for overall brightness and covered surface area (and therefore differed in average element size). After looking time to the array sequence had declined, all the infants were presented with test arrays of 8 versus 16 dots on alternating trials. For the test, arrays at the two numerosities were equated for density and element size and differed, therefore, in overall size, brightness, and total filled surface area. These stimulus controls effectively disentangled responses to number from responses to correlated continuous variables: If infants failed to respond to number and instead responded to variables like density or brightness, then the infants in the two groups would have looked equally at the two test displays.

In this experiment, infants looked longer at the display presenting the novel numerosity, providing evidence that they discriminated between the 8- and 16-dot arrays on the basis of their numerosity. Xu and Spelke (2000a) replicated this effect with larger numerosities: Six-month-old infants successfully discriminated 16 from 32 dots. In contrast, infants in Xu and Spelke's (2000a,

2000b) experiments failed to discriminate 8 from 12 or 16 from 24 dots when tested by the same method, just as infants in an earlier experiment by Starkey and Cooper (1980), tested with a similar method although without the same stimulus controls, failed to discriminate 4 from 6 dots. These findings suggest that infants' large-number discriminations are imprecise and depend on the ratio of the set sizes to be discriminated: Infants succeed with set sizes in a 2:1 ratio such as 8 versus 16 or 16 versus 32, but they fail with set sizes in a 3:2 ratio such as 8 versus 12 or 4 versus 6. . . .

Putting all these findings together, I suggest that two core knowledge systems are at work in these experiments. One is the system for representing objects and their persisting identity over time, as already described. The other is a system for representing sets and their approximate numerical values. These systems are domain specific (one applies to objects, the other to sets), task specific (one allows for addition of one, the other allows for comparisons of sets), and independent (the situations that evoke one are different from the situations that evoke the other). . . .

What role do these systems play in the development of complex cognitive skills? To approach this question, I consider how children develop the number concepts that are at the heart of the elementary school curriculum: concepts of the natural numbers and of simple arithmetic.

# Learning of Number Words and the Counting Routine

Research by many investigators provides evidence that before most children get to school, they have a basic understanding of the natural numbers (Butterworth, 1999, Gelman & Gallistel, 1978). Children understand, for example, that numbers form a progression that starts with one and continues by successive additions of one with no upper bound. They also understand that two sets can be added or subtracted to yield a third and that counting forward or backward provides a way to assess the numerical values of these sets. How do children gain this understanding?

Comparing the young schoolchild's number concepts to the core knowledge systems of infants suggests how far children have to go. For infants, small numbers and large numbers are represented differently; for schoolchildren, all natural numbers have the same general properties. Moreover, infants' small-number representations are limited in set size, and their large-number representations are limited in precision, but the schoolchild's number representations show neither limit: The number of individuals in a set can be represented precisely, in principle, and with no upper bound. Finally, infants can perform addition and subtraction on small numbers of objects and they can compare the cardinal values of large sets, but they cannot add or subtract large sets or compare the cardinal values of small numbers of objects; schoolchildren, in contrast, perform additions and numerical comparisons with all set sizes. Studies of infants should lead us to predict, therefore, that developing an understanding of counting and the natural numbers will be difficult for children, and research shows that it is.

Studies by Fuson (1988), Wynn (1990), Griffin and Case (1996), and others reveal that when children first begin to engage in the counting routine, pointing to objects in succession while running through the count list, they have little understanding of what they are doing. For example, Wynn (1990) assessed 2- to 4-year-old children's understanding of the words in their own count lists through a simple task in which she presented a pile of objects and asked children to give her (e.g.) "two fish." The youngest counters correctly gave her one object when asked for one, but they performed at chance, grabbing a handful, when asked for other numbers. (Interestingly, children never gave her just one object when asked for a higher number, suggesting that they understood that the other number words picked out sets larger than one.) About 9 months later, children mastered the meaning of the word *two:* They correctly produced one or two objects when asked for "one fish" or "two fish," respectively, and they grabbed a pile containing more than two objects when asked for any other number. Some 3 months later, on average, children mastered the meaning of the word *three* while continuing to respond at chance for higher numbers. Finally, some time after the acquisition of *three,* children appeared to figure out the workings of the counting routine and the meanings of all the number words. From that point on, children who were asked for any number of objects within their count list would attempt to produce that specific number and would use counting to do so.

The developmental progression observed in preschool children makes sense in the light of the capacities of infants. At the earliest point in the development of number words and counting, I suggest, children learn to relate the word *one* to their core system for representing objects: They learn that *one* applies just in case there's an object in the scene, and it is roughly synonomous with the determiner *a*. About the same time, children learn to relate the other number words to their core system for representing numerosities: They learn that the other number words apply just in case there's a set in the scene, and those words are all roughly synonomous with *some* (see also Bloom and Wynn, 1997). The next and very difficult step requires that children bring their representations of objects and numerosities together. They have to learn that *two* applies just in case there's a set composed of an object and another object. When *two* is mastered, children must learn that *three* also applies to a combination of object and numerosity representations: to a set composed of an object, an object, and an object.

Once this learning is complete, children are in a position to make two general inductions. First, they can discover that the progression from *two* to *three* involves adding one object to the set of objects. Second, they can generalize this discovery to all the number words and infer that each word picks out a set containing one more object than the preceding word. The behavior of number words in natural language syntax, as well as their behavior within the counting routine, may support this generalization (Bloom & Wynn, 1997). The language of number words and the counting routine allow young children to combine their representations of objects as enduring individuals with their representations of numerosities to construct a new system of knowledge of number, in which each distinct number picks out a set of individuals with a distinct cardinal value.

On the view I'm recommending, therefore, children construct the natural number concepts by combining representations from two core systems: the system for representing objects as persisting individuals and the system for representing approximate numerical magnitudes. More specifically, the object system is the source of the child's understanding that number applies to discrete individuals and that numbers can be changed by adding one, and the approximate numerosity system is the source of the child's understanding that number applies to sets and that sets can be compared according to their cardinal values. Number words, the counting routine, and natural language syntax all may support this combination. Children's understanding of the natural number concepts, of the counting routine, and of the counting-based operations of arithmetic may follow from it. . . .

## Conclusion

My excursion through studies of human infants, nonhuman primates, [and] children learning counting, . . . centers on one specific and one more general proposal. The specific proposal is that the cognitive functioning of all these disparate groups can be understood, in part, in terms of the same systems of core knowledge. These systems serve to construct abstract representations of basic features of the world, including objects and numerosities, but they are limited in three respects: They are domain specific, task specific, and largely independent of one another. I have focused on one core system for representing objects and a second core system for representing approximate numerical magnitudes. These systems appear to exist both in human infants and in adult monkeys, to dominate young children's earliest attempts to understand number words and the counting routine, and to persist into human adulthood. Moreover, these systems appear to serve as the building blocks for later developing numerical concepts and calculation skills, which children construct and adults deploy by combining representations from the two core systems.

Behind these specific suggestions is a more general proposal. When cognitive and educational psychologists attempt to understand humans' most complex cognitive skills, we should take a broad view and study not only adults who have mastered the skills and children who are acquiring them but also human infants and other animals. Although no young child or nonhuman animal possesses these skills, both exhibit many of the cognitive systems that serve as their building blocks. The architecture of these systems may be especially amenable to study in infants, where they appear in relatively pure form, and in nonhuman animals, where they can be studied through a rich array of behavioral and physiological methods.

Many of adults' richest and most complex cognitive skills may be assembled from core knowledge systems. For example, our uniquely human patterns of prolific tool use and tool construction may depend on the orchestration of two core systems found in infants: the system for representing objects that I have discussed in this address and a system for representing persons and their goal-directed, intentional actions that has been found both in human infants (e.g., Woodward, 1998) and in nonhuman primates (e.g., Cheney & Seyfarth, 1990). By combining representations from these systems, children may come to view artifacts both as bearers of mechanical properties and as products of human intentions: representations that become well established during the preschool years (Bloom, 1996; Kelemen, 1999). . . .

In these cases and others, human children and adults may gain new abilities not by creating those abilities out of whole cloth, but by bringing together building-block representational systems that have existed in us since infancy. By shedding light on those systems, studies of human infants may contribute to understanding of some of the highest achievements of human adults.

# References

Baillargeon, R. (1993). The object concept revisited: New directions in the investigation of infants' physical knowledge. In C. E. Granrud (Ed.), *Carnegie-Mellon Symposia on Cognition: Vol. 23. Visual perception and cognition in infancy* (pp. 265–315). Hillsdale, NJ: Erlbaum.

Bloom, P., & Wynn, K. (1997). Linguistic cues in the acquisition of number words. *Journal of Child Language, 24,* 511–533.

Butterworth, B. (1999). *What counts: How every brain is hardwired for math.* New York: Free Press.

Cheney, D., & Seyfarth, R. (1990). *How monkeys see the world.* Chicago: University of Chicago Press.

Chiang, W.-C., & Wynn, K. (in press). Infants' tracking of objects and collections. *Cognition.*

Feigenson, L., Carey, S., & Hauser, M. (2000). *Ten- and 12-month-old infants' ordinal representation of number.* Poster presented at International Conference on Infant Studies, Brighton, England.

Fuson, K. C. (1988). *Children's counting and concepts of number.* New York: Springer-Verlag.

Gelman, R., & Gallistel, C. R. (1978). *The child's understanding of counting.* Cambridge, MA: Harvard University Press.

Griffin, S., & Case, R. (1996). Evaluating the breadth and depth of training effects, when central conceptual structures are taught. *Monographs of the Society for Research in Child Development, 61* (1/2, Serial No. 246), 83–102.

Huntley-Fenner, G., & Carey, S. (2000). *Infant representations of objects and non-cohesive substances.* Manuscript submitted for publication.

Koechlin, E., Dehaene, S., & Mehler, J. (1998). Numerical transformations in five-month-old human infants. *Mathematical Cognition, 3,* 89–104.

Simon, T. J., Hespos, S. J., & Rochat, P. (1995). Do infants understand simple arithmetic? A replication of Wynn (1992). *Cognitive Development, 10,* 253–269.

Spelke, E. S., & Van de Walle, G. (1993). Perceiving and reasoning about objects: Insights from infants. In N. Eilan, R. McCarthy, & W. Brewer (Eds.), *Spatial representation* (pp. 132–161). Oxford, England: Basil Blackwell.

Starkey, P., & Cooper, R. (1980). Perception of numbers by human infants. *Science, 210,* 1033–1035.

Van de Walle, G., Carey, S., & Prevor, M. (in press). The use of kind distinctions for object individuation: Evidence from manual search. *Journal of Cognition and Development.*

Woodward, A. L. (1998). Infants selectively encode the goal object of an actor's reach. *Cognition, 69,* 1–34.

Wynn, K. (1990). Children's understanding of counting. *Cognition, 36,* 155–193.

Wynn, K. (1992). Addition and subtraction by human infants. *Nature, 358,* 749–750.

Xu, F., & Spelke, E. S. (2000a, July). *Large number discrimination in infants: Evidence for analog magnitude representations.* Paper presented at the International Conference on Infant Studies, Brighton, England.

Xu, F., & Spelke, E. S. (2000b). Large number discrimination in 6-month-old infants. *Cognition, 74,* B1–B11.

# NO

**Bruce Hood**

# When Do Infants Know About Objects?

It may seem obvious to researchers in adult perception that discrimination and knowledge are not the same thing. One can detect that two perceptual patterns differ without necessarily knowing why they differ. That is, in the absence of explicit understanding and awareness. Sometimes differences are not available to explicit scrutiny or, if they are, not fully appreciated. There are many examples of phenomena where individuals discriminate events that do not achieve explicit awareness. This seems fairly unremarkable for sensory events where stimulation does not evoke explicit awareness. As Weiskrantz (1988) points out, there are more bodily processes that we are unaware of than those to which we are able to provide a commentary.

But, even when we can provide a commentary, it may be incomplete, misguided, or completely wrong. One of my favourite examples published in this journal is Peter Thompson's "Thatcher Illusion" (Thompson 1980). Here we have a case where two inverted faces appear similar and yet different. Close inspection allows us to detect that the individual features of the eyes and mouth are in a different orientation, but that discrimination cannot compare with the radically explicit perception that occurs when the configurational information is provided by turning the face into the correct upright orientation. However, this explicit awareness is lost when the faces are inverted, again providing a dramatic example of how configurational information plays a role in face perception. Face perception provides a number of examples of dissociation between implicit and explicit processing. We can distinguish mirror-image faces from normal asymmetrical faces without being aware of the basis for the discrimination. We can tell that someone looks different after a trip to the hairdressers without being aware of the haircut. The point is that detecting that there is a difference is not the same as being explicitly aware of what that difference is.

So readers of *Perception* may be surprised to hear that discrimination is proving to be an extremely thorny issue in the world of infancy research, because telling that there is a difference and knowing what that difference is have become confused. Traditionally, discrimination measures have been the

From *Perception*, vol. 30, 2001, pp. 1281–1284. Copyright © 2001 by Pion Ltd. Reprinted by permission.

bedrock of perceptual-development studies. One of the earliest measures of infant discrimination, pioneered by Robert Fantz in the late 1950s and early 1960s, was the technique of preferential looking. By measuring the amount of time spent looking at different stimuli, Fantz (1961) demonstrated that, contrary to the wisdom of the day, not only were very young infants capable of seeing, but they also preferred to look at certain types of visual patterns in comparison to others. In later years, a refinement was made to the preferential-looking technique by adding an initial habituation phase (Caron and Caron 1968). Preferences could be experimentally induced by habituating the infant to one stimulus until his or her interest dropped back to some predefined baseline, and then presenting a novel stimulus to invoke a recovery of interest. If this novel stimulus produced a significant increase in duration of looking, the experimenter could be reasonably sure that the infant could discriminate the first habituated stimulus from the second novel one. This enabled researchers to investigate infant discrimination of stimuli for which there may be no inherent preferences. Although there have been subsequent further refinements concerned with how the habituation criterion is defined, the habituation-recovery technique has remained relatively the same for the past 30 years and is used to investigate infant perception in every modality.

In recent years, developmental psychologists have used the habituation-recovery technique to investigate infants' understanding of the physical world. This focus of interest arises from Piaget's theorising on the origins of knowledge (Piaget 1954). For Piaget, cognitive development began with the first interactions of the infant within his or her world. Initially, world knowledge was confined to sensory stimulation derived from the relatively limited repertoire of the reflexes. However, from these simple beginnings, knowledge in the form of sensorimotor representations emerged as a consequence of the child's interaction with the world, and therefore was strictly tied to the infant's ability to act on the world. Piaget constructed his theory around the central issue of action, and used examples of the infant's behaviour to illustrate his main stages of development. In particular, he described manual retrieval of objects on search tasks, or more often the failure to do so, as indicative of the infant's limited ability to form representations of the object during the hiding sequence.

However, as pointed out by his critics, infant's manual search is constrained by a number of factors other than the ability to form a mental picture of the hidden object. To begin, young infants are motorically immature and so search is likely to underestimate their true capacity to retrieve the object. Likewise, search requires planning behaviour in order to anticipate the sequence of actions necessary for recovering the object. Again, failure does not necessarily reflect an absent or inaccurate representation of the hidden object; rather, it could be due to a number of performance limitations. With these problems in mind, a new paradigm based on the habituation-recovery technique was developed to investigate infants' representations of objects (Baillargeon et al 1985). Like the early Fantz studies, this paradigm used changes in looking time as an index of discrimination; but, instead of showing infants simple stimuli, these experimenters measured whether infants could discriminate between sequences of events involving objects that were either consistent or inconsistent with the object's physical attributes. Initially, these sequences addressed the issue whether infants understood that objects continued to exist when out of sight, as this had been one of Piaget's initial milestones on the road to representation. However, sequences in which objects moved and interacted with other objects enabled experimenters to study the infant's appreciation of a number of object properties, including numerosity, animacy, transformations, and so on.

The logic of using looking time to study object knowledge is based on the principle of the magic trick. Magic tricks are appealing because the magician creates an illusion that violates our belief systems. Magicians make objects vanish, materialise, transform, jump across space and time, and so on. Because these sorts of events contravene the rules of the physical world that we appreciate as adults, our expectations are violated and we gasp, stare in disbelief, applaud, and so on. Likewise, infants have been shown to look significantly longer at event sequences that violate physical laws, in comparison to control sequences that do not. (There is little evidence that they show any discriminating behaviour other than increased fixation.) For example, if a ball is dropped behind an occluder from which protrudes a previously seen shelf, 4-month-old infants will look longer— once the occluder is removed—at the outcome of the ball *under* the shelf, compared to the ball on top (Spelke et al 1992). This visual preference is measured against a series of control conditions, to ensure that the difference only emerges when there is an apparent violation. This, and many other studies, has been interpreted as evidence for an early appreciation of the physical constraints operating on objects. In this regard, these findings go beyond the simple issue whether infants can form a mental picture of an invisible object but, rather, address the nature of invisible objects and how they should behave in a Newtonian world. Indeed, the methodology is no longer referred to as the preferential-looking technique, but more commonly known as the violation-of-expectancy paradigm; a title which reflects the I cognitive baggage believed to accompany longer looking.

Findings from these studies are not universally accepted, and there are many criticisms which can be categorised into methodological, statistical, procedural, and interpretation issues (Haith 1998). However, there is now a substantial weight of evidence from replication studies that strongly support that infants look longer at impossible events. As indicated by the opening gambit, this editorial will concentrate on the interpretation issue. The habituation-recovery technique is a powerful methodology so long as the central question is: "Are X and Y different?" Problems arise when habituation-recovery technique is used to tackle a different type of question: "Why are X and Y different?" The first question requires a yes/no discrimination, whereas the second requires yes/no plus an explicit formulation for that distinction. If we accept that discrimination is taking place in these experiments, then we must accept that this discrimination is on the basis of violation of physics. In one sense, the 4-month-old knows something about shelves and balls. But can we say that this knowledge is the same as that of an older child, or adult, as some of the theorists using the new paradigm would argue? How can we ever measure this? I don't think we can, so long as the infants are unable to provide a commentary for what they have just witnessed. We cannot make the inference that infants look longer because their expectations have been violated.

A simple example demonstrates the flaw. Many adults and most children hold misconceptions about object motion (McCloskey 1983) but can detect that motions that conform to their naïve theories are in fact anomalous (Proffitt and Gilden 1989). Do they have an understanding about object motion, or not? Their commentaries based on naïve theories would suggest not, but their reports and looking behaviour on viewing impossible trajectories may indicate the contrary. Consider a thought experiment. Imagine that these same adults were infants in a looking-time experiment and that they looked longer at the impossible motion relative to the possible motion. How could one interpret their longer looking at impossible object motions? Clearly, it would not be due to a violation of their expectancy, as their expectancy based on their beliefs was otherwise. This example points out the danger of inferring knowledge states in the absence of a commentary.

In their haste to abandon Piaget, developmental psychologists may be forced to return to his fold. Clearly, infants are never going to provide a commentary related to their knowledge. The word derives from the Latin (ins—without; fari—past part; 'to speak'). But actions speak louder than words, and—before the advent of language—actions would have to had reflected world knowledge in an adaptive way, or otherwise the individual would have been selected against. In spite of the problems of limited ability to execute actions, they may still provide a useful channel to investigate the developing knowledge of the physical world. What kinds of action reflect world knowledge? There is not an immediate answer for this, but infant cognitive development may need to find new ways of thinking about measuring action rather than abandoning it in favour of looking time. Supporters of looking-time experiments could retaliate that looking is an action; but, as noted earlier, this only reflects discrimination between two event sequences.

When the criticisms of Piaget's action-based paradigms were voiced, the limitations of the action system were considered impediments to demonstrating object knowledge. The violation of expectancy was seen as a means for avoiding these impediments—but, in turn, has generated its own controversy, about what looking time truly reflects. It seems to me that both search and looking-time studies reflect knowledge of sorts. It is up to the field of cognitive development to decide what is the acceptable criterion for determining when the child knows something.

# References

Baillargeon R, Spelke E S, Wasserman S, 1985 "Object permanence in five-month-old infants" *Cognition* **20** 191–208

Caron R F, Caron A J, 1968 "The effect of repeated exposure and stimulus complexity on visual fixation in infants" *Psychonomic Science* **10** 207–208

Fantz R L, 1961 "The origin of form perception" *Scientific American* **204** 66–72

Haith M H, 1998 "Who put the cog in cognition? Is rich interpretation too costly?" *Infant Behavior* & *Development* **21** 167–179

Piaget J, 1954 *The Construction of Reality in the Child* (New York: Basic Books)

McCloskey M, 1983 "Intuitive physics" *Scientific American* **284** 122–130

Proffitt D R, Gilden D L, 1989 "Understanding natural dynamics" *Journal of Experimental Psychology* **15** 384–393

Spelke E S, Breinlinger K, Macomber J, Jacobson K, 1992 "Origins of knowledge" *Psychological Review* **99** 605–632

Thompson P, 1980 "Margaret Thatcher: A new illusion?" *Perception* **9** 483–484

Weiskrantz L, 1988 "Some contributions of neuropsychology of vision and memory to the problem of consciousness," in *Consciousness in Contemporary Science* Eds A J Marcel, E Bisiach (Oxford: Oxford Science Publications) pp 183–199

# POSTSCRIPT

## Are Very Young Infants Born with an Innate Ability to Make Symbolic Representations of Objects?

**A**re humans unique among animals? This seemingly simple question has been the root of tremendous controversy in academic circles. The question of whether infants have a capacity for symbolic representation has a surprisingly large role in responding to this question. On the one hand, if we come into the world able to represent abstract objects, then we have a significant start on the mental complexity that distinguishes humans from other animals. On the other hand, we are animals, and as such, our mental capacities have been shaped by the same forces that bring us into the world with functional eyes, lungs, kidneys, and toes.

Yet we do develop unparalleled mental complexity—as developmental psychologist Paul Bloom suggests, we become "mindreaders" with the distinctive ability to understand that other people have beliefs, desires, and minds that match our own. Being endowed with the capacity to make complex symbolic mental representations means being endowed with significant levels of consciousness. Other animals don't have this capacity. Dogs and cats, no matter how empathic they may seem after a long day, have no capacity to actually recognize what you are thinking. They can respond to your behavioral cues, your body language, your tone of voice, but they cannot read your mind. Many developmental psychologists are convinced that babies can.

Hood, however, raises important questions about this certainty. He agrees that infants seem able to discriminate between possible and impossible events. But making the leap from discrimination to symbolic thought, to knowing that infants have conscious mental expectations to be violated, requires inferences that cannot be substantiated. It is common for people to discriminate between events and things (such as the example of two different faces), knowing they differ without knowing why. In fact, your pets, those same dogs and cats that seem empathic after a long day, may be able to discriminate subtle differences between your moods. But few psychologists would argue that ability to discriminate is a sign of significant cognition—or an ability to be "mindreaders."

Beyond the implications for questions of innate human uniqueness, the question of symbolic thought in infancy is important for those interested in the study of life span development because it can be so provocative. The popular media are quick to latch onto sensational claims about the miraculous abilities of infants—to claim that infants can do math and physics has the shock value journalists love. But the attraction to such claims is not just for shock value; we also live in a society that treats infants as being born ready to function. There is a complex cultural ambivalence that wants to see people as simultaneously formed by biology, and also ready to be trained and socialized from the moment of birth. The controversy around infant symbolic thought captures this ambivalence; it challenges us to consider the wonders of infant development as biologically determined, while also allowing us to feel as though we adults can start to manage and influence those wonders at an earlier and earlier age. How different would our attitudes toward infants be if we were sure they could already engage in the type of complex thought that we often work so hard to teach?

## Suggested Readings

R. Baillargeon, "Infants' Reasoning About Hidden Objects: Evidence for Event-General and Event-Specific Expectations," *Developmental Science* (September 2004).

P. Bloom, *Descartes' Baby: How the Science of Child Development Explains What Makes Us Human* (Basic Books, 2004).

B. Bower, "Babies' Ballyhooed Counting Skills Add Up to Controversy," *Science News Online* (June 22, 2002).

L. Cohen, "Can Infants Really Add and Subtract?" *International Conference on Infant Studies* (2002).

L. Cohen and K. Marks, "How Infants Process Addition and Subtraction Events," *Developmental Science* (2002).

B. Hood, "Is Looking Good Enough or Does It Beggar Belief?" *Developmental Science* (September 2004).

J. Mandler, "Seeing Is Not the Same as Thinking: Commentary on 'Making Sense of Infant Categorization'," *ScienceDirect* (November 1998).

A. Wakeley, S. Rivera, and J. Langer, "Can Young Infants Add and Subtract?" *Child Development* (December 2000).

K. Wynn, "Do Infants Have Numerical Expectations or Just Perceptual Preferences?" *Developmental Science* (2002).

K. Wynn, "Findings of Addition and Subtraction in Infants Are Robust and Consistent: Reply to Wakeley, Rivera, and Langer," *Child Development* (December 2000).

# On the Internet . . .

## Kid Source

This site provides links and information about parenting, with a particular emphasis on early childhood.

http://www.kidsource.com

## National Association for the Education of Young Children

Official site for the National Association for the Education of Young Children, an organization focused on preschool and other forms of early childhood education.

http://www.naeyc.org/

## Association for Childhood Education International

The Association for Childhood Education International is a group focused on the optimal education and development of children.

http://www.acei.org/

## Early Childhood

This site is a resource for teacher and parents. It focuses on activities and curriculum for early childhood.

http://www.earlychildhood.com/

## Don Campbell

This site is primarily related to the commercial endeavors of Don Campbell, who sells a variety of produces based on music and child development.

http://www.mozarteffect.com/

## Mozart Effect

This page provides information explaining how scholars consider the "Mozart Effect" to be a myth.

http://skepdic.com/mozart.html

# PART 4

# Early Childhood

*E*arly childhood, or toddlerhood, generally encompasses the years between 2 and 6. This period is fascinating and important because it is when we first develop our distinctly human capacities for language and self-recognition. Early childhood also marks the beginning of a particularly intense phase of socialization into the cultures in which we will experience most of our lives. Much of this early socialization occurs within a family: Parents often feel particular pressure during early childhood to insure kids develop well. Increasingly, children also spend parts of early childhood outside the home in daycare and preschool settings. The issues in this section focus on how experiences during these years might influence later outcomes.

- Does Exposure to Music, Including Mozart, During Early Childhood Have a Special Capacity to Enhance Development?

- Does Emphasizing Academic Skills Help At-Risk Preschool Children?

# ISSUE 8

## Does Exposure to Music, Including Mozart, During Early Childhood Have a Special Capacity to Enhance Development?

**YES: Gordon L. Shaw,** from *Keeping Mozart in Mind* (Academic Press, 2004)

**NO: Michael Linton,** from "The Mozart Effect," *First Things: The Journal of Religion, Culture, and Public Life* (March 1999)

### ISSUE SUMMARY

**YES:** Neuroscientist Gordon L. Shaw, acknowledges that the effect of Mozart on infants is not yet known but argues that the generally positive effect of music on spatial-temporaral reasoning supports efforts to endorse music for children.

**NO:** Michael Linton, professor of music at Middle Tennessee State University, asserts that the idea of music having special brain-enhancing powers has been recycled historically and consistently proven an inaccurate myth.

**W**hen we look at small children, we see beings who seem to simply absorb everything around them, and we want to do everything we can to enhance that process. In the last few decades, one popular idea for enhancing early childhood development has involved the so-called Mozart effect, where listening to particular types of music is promoted as an enhancement to brain functioning. While most researchers would agree that much of the "Mozart effect" is simply marketing without scientific basis, there is disagreement about the general role of music and stimulation as potential aids to early development.

Throughout much of history, music as been associated with advanced human functioning. As both authors note, music held a special place in ancient Greek society as a tool for both sophisticated philosophy and a general enhancement of life. In more contemporary times, many intellectuals acknowledge a deep affinity for music. Thus, the idea of music serving some special function in the life span has a strong foundation in conventional wisdom. Speculation about a special role for music in brain development, however, did not arise until scientific advances in recent decades allowed researchers to understand and explore the details of how the brain works.

Researchers from the University of California at Irvine seized that stage in the early 1990s by publishing a now famous paper in the prestigious scientific journal *Nature* reporting that listening to Mozart before performing cognitive tasks produced improved performance. The popular media latched onto the story enthusiastically, ignoring most of the details of the research to simply proclaim that Mozart music was a magic elixir for the brain, enhancing neural functioning and actually making people smarter. Almost inevitably, an entrepreneur with a background in music (but no background in brain science) took the opportunity to trademark the "Mozart effect" and produce a line products that made grand claims about enhancing life span development. Eventually, this all coalesced into a popular understanding that for children to get the most of their brains, they needed early and frequent exposure to music.

Unfortunately, the popular media rarely attended to the details of the original research published in *Nature*. The study involved college students, not children, and merely showed a short-term enhancement in abilities on a cognitive task (involving visualizing the way a piece of paper would look when folded—a relatively common test of visual-spatial reasoning and cognitive ability). No long-term developmental effects were documented.

When researchers began the process of evaluating the original research, there was much to critique. While several attempts to replicate the "Mozart effect" research have failed, and much scientific criticism has been levied at the popularization of the concept, several scientists have continued to work on understanding the influence of music on the brain and have documented some beneficial effects for children, adults, and even rats.

One of those scientists, Gordon L. Shaw has developed an extensive program of research about music and the brain and argues in the following selection that all indicators suggest music, and Mozart music specifically, does indeed have the potential to enhance cognitive development. While he stresses that the "Mozart effect" itself has been exploited for profit, he argues that the science is promising enough to recommend special efforts to play music for children.

In contrast, Michael Linton, a professor of music who believes strongly in the general value of music in society, asserts that Shaw's position is just the latest iteration in a long history of false claims about the power of music. Partially because music has a prominent place in the social world, Linton suggests it has been easy to use anecdotal evidence to suggest that music serves a special function for individual development. Yet science provides no convincing support for that suggestion.

As you read the selections, note that much of the controversy centers around what really counts as good evidence. Both authors agree there is not enough evidence to conclusively prove that a "Mozart effect" exists, but they differ in how they speculate from the preliminary suggestive evidence. Likewise, both authors note that music has a long historical association with intelligence and genius, but they again differ in how they interpret those anecdotal associations.

Gordon L. Shaw

 **YES**

# History, Anecdotes, Correlations, and Interviews

## General Remarks

On October 15, 1993, the front page of the Tokyo edition of the *International Herald Tribune* reported on our *Nature* findings: Students who listened to the Mozart Sonata for Two Pianos in D Major (K. 448) as performed by Murray Perahia and Radu Lupu did better on reasoning tasks than after listening to a relaxation tape or silence. This result, coined the "Mozart effect" by the media, was widely reported around the world, and continues to receive extensive attention. The particular recording we used sold out immediately in Boston (where many universities are located, including Harvard and MIT).

Why did this huge reaction occur, particularly since a connection between music and math had been discussed for perhaps thousands of years? Somehow the idea that just listening to Mozart made you smarter, even if only for 10–15 minutes, captured the imagination of people around the world. *It was as if you got something for free.* Previously, **anecdotal** and **correlational** connections had been made: persons good or exceptional at math might be good or exceptional at music. Our experiment was the first to present evidence for a cause and effect relationship: music could causally enhance reasoning, if even temporarily.

It is of great importance for the nonscientist to understand this distinction between correlation and causation and the distinction between anecdotal studies and controlled studies. For example, important, controlled correlational studies by Marianne Hassler showed higher scholastic performance in students who had years of music training. However, these results might be due to some selection process by parents rather than the music training. Anecdotally, it seems that scientists and mathematicians have an above average interest in classical music. However, I know of no published results on this matter that controlled for possible bias in the sampling. For example, in my gathering of data, I have more everyday contact with scientists than with politicians.

This chapter presents anecdotal and correlational stories relating music and other higher brain functions, since they can be very interesting and enlightening. Also, . . . the study of truly exceptional talented individuals can give insights of enormous value if the right questions are addressed.

The relationships and similarities among such higher brain functions as the creativity involved in music, mathematics, and chess have been known for millennia. The ancient Greek Pythagoreans considered music as one of the four branches of mathematics; some of the mathematical relations in music were discovered by the Babylonians and introduced into Greece.

For example, take the ratio of two quantities $a$ and $b$ or $a$ divided by $b$ ($a/b$) and the ratio of two other quantities $c$ and $d$ or $c/d$. Proportional math, which the majority of school children have difficulty learning, relates these two ratios $a/b$ to $c/d$. (When you are at the supermarket comparing the cost per ounce—price divided by weight—of a big can of corn to a little one, you are doing **proportional math**.)

One of the most important proportions to Pythagoras, the philosopher and mathematician who lived in the sixth century B.C., and the mathematicians under him was called the harmonical proportion since it included those in music concerning harmony and melody. Thus, is it any surprise that learning to play a musical instrument might enhance one's ability to learn ratios and proportions? This is precisely what we were able to prove in our most recent dramatic study with second grade students. . . .

Original results have been created before the age of puberty by Mozart and Rossini in music, by Gauss in mathematics, and by Capablanca and Reshevsky in chess. A high percentage of gifted individuals are proficient or highly interested in more than one of these skills. Perhaps one of the most familiar is Albert Einstein, who played the violin. Einstein is undoubtedly the most famous scientist of the twentieth century; his genius as a physicist is universally recognized. He was moved by Mozart's music into an awareness of the mathematical structure of music (the playing of Mozart by his talented pianist mother was one of the few distractions that could draw Albert away from his books).

Einstein explained that music was in some ways an extension of his thinking processes, a method of allowing the subconscious to solve tricky problems. "Whenever he felt that he had come to the end of the road or into a difficult situation in his work," his eldest son has said, "he would take refuge in music, and that would usually resolve all his difficulties." Einstein himself once remarked that "Music has no effect on research work, but both are born of the same source and complement each other through the satisfaction they bestow." The theme of this book is that this connection goes much deeper—that music and mathematics are causally linked through the built-in, innate ability of the brain to recognize symmetries and use them to see how patterns develop in space and time. The transformation and development of spatial patterns is the central theme in the startling masterpieces of the brilliant artist M. C. Escher.

Some research studies in child development have shown correlations between music training (and music ability) and measures of spatial reasoning ability. Our structured trion model of cortex provided a *causative* basis for such relations. The first series of experiments that we performed demonstrated that music enhances spatial-temporal reasoning used in the higher brain functions of math and chess.

It is worthwhile to look for clues to understanding higher brain function from as many points of view as possible, in particular, from glimpses of recognized geniuses. Relevant anecdotes are informative as well as enjoyable to note. It would be remiss not to recount a few:

*Mozart:* As judged by biographer Davenport:

> He [God] planted in Wolfgang Mozart what is probably the purest, sheerest genius ever born in man. . . . Until just before his sixth birthday, then, Wolferl [*sic*] led a happy and not too burdened life. . . . He learned his lessons, whatever they were, easily and quickly. His mind was usurped by music until he discovered the rudiments of arithmetic. Suddenly the house erupted with figures scribbled on every bit of space—walls, floors, tables and chairs. This passion for mathematics is plainly in close alliance with his great contrapuntal facility. Music, however, was his only real interest.

Mozart is this magic genius (as defined below) whose music will live forever, and I predict become even more widely listened to. In contrast, the magic genius in math, Srinivasa Ramanujan, is barely known, except to mathematicians. However, I believe it is enormously important to try to understand the origin of Ramanujan's staggering abilities. If a theory of higher brain function is eventually established, it must be able to explain the magic genius of both Mozart and Ramanujan.

*Ramanujan:* As noted by biographer Kanigel, this relatively untaught mathematician is recognized as

> "so great that his name transcends jealousies, the one superlatively great mathematician whom India has produced in the last thousand years." His leaps of intuition confound mathematicians even today, seven decades after his death. His papers are still plumbed for their secrets. . . . Ramanujan, in the language of the . . . [renowned] mathematician Mark Kac, was a "magical genius" rather than an "ordinary genius." [According to Kac], "An ordinary genius is a fellow that you and I would be just as good as, if we were only many times better. There is no mystery as to how his mind works. Once we understand what he has done, we feel certain that we, too, could have done it. It is different with the magical genius. They are, to use mathematical jargon, in the orthogonal [no overlap] complement of where we are and the working of their minds is for all intents and purposes incomprehensible. Even after we understand what they have done, the process by which they have done it is completely dark."

The "discovery" of the unknown, not formally trained Ramanujan is a fascinating story. On his own, Ramanujan worked out many problems in mathematics texts, and then after some calculations made simply enormous leaps to write down without proof amazing relationships never before imagined. From his home in Madras, India, he sent several notebooks full of these to the renowned British mathematician G. H. Hardy. The world had the good fortune that Hardy worked through some of these examples and recognized the genius of Ramanujan, and then invited him to come work with him in England. How many more potential math geniuses (with even a *small* fraction of Ramanujan's abilities) are out there waiting to be found and nurtured? . . .

A recently compiled list of India's top mathematicians and scientists indicates that Southern India has produced a remarkably high proportion of them, including Ramanujan. It is noted that

> Carnatic music may have been another contributing factor. Being so very precise and mathematical in its structure, it apparently imparted a sense of highly precise, mathematical cadences to the mind . . . thereby somehow "programming" it for scientific thought. . . . Now in the South there has been a strong and very special Carnatic music tradition that has flourished over the centuries. The strength of this tradition lies in the fact that . . . it has had genuine mass following, drawing people from all social, economic and age groups.

Thus, perhaps for fun, I might apply Mark Kac's subjective distinction between the ordinary genius and the magic genius and assign Einstein to the category of "ordinary" genius and Mozart along with Ramanujan to the very rarefied category of magic genius. Although Einstein's contributions to physics were monumental, his reasoning process can be understood. Mozart was composing at the age of four, and it was stated that he would sometimes write down an entire composition without changing a note. When Rauscher and I designed our listening experiments, it was obvious that we should choose Mozart. I will share our reasoning with you later.

## Spatial-Temporal Reasoning in Chess

There are two complementary ways that we reason: spatial-temporal and language-analytic: Language-analytic reasoning is more involved when we solve equations and obtain a quantitative result. Spatial-temporal reasoning is used in chess when we have to think ahead several moves, developing and evaluating patterns in space and time totally in our mind.

An important paper by Chase and Simon presents very insightful results on understanding the bases of chess-playing skill. Their experiments with groups of chess Masters, class A players, and beginners extend the pioneering work of de Groot to go beyond the recall of chess positions to analyze the nature of finding good chess moves.

They show that the amazing recall by the chess Master of a middle game position takes place through the use of "local clusters of pieces." When the pieces are randomly arranged at the first trial presentation, the Master's recall ability is reduced to that of the beginner and class A player and actually falls below them for subsequent trials! Their conclusions as to the Master's strategy in choosing a next move in a middle game is fascinating:

> As we have shown, the board is organized into smaller units representing more local clusters of pieces. Since some of these patterns have plausible moves associated with them in long-term memory, the Master will start his search by taking one of these moves and analyzing its consequences. Since some of the recognizable patterns will be relevant, and some irrelevant, to his analysis, we hypothesize that he constructs a more concrete internal

representation of the relevant patterns in the mind's eye, and then modifies these patterns to reflect the consequences of making the evoked move. The information processes needed . . . are akin to the mental rotation processes . . . and the mental processes for solving . . . cube-cutting puzzles. . . . When the move is made in the mind's eye—that is, when the internal representation of the position is updated—the result is then passed back through the pattern perception system and new patterns are perceived. These patterns in turn will suggest new moves, and the search continues.

It is clear that the ability of the chess Master to think several moves ahead is a truly amazing feat of spatial-temporal reasoning. It is amusing how structured the chess ratings are: There is no luck or bad referee mistakes that allow chess players to gather the points to improve their ratings. They get their ratings the old-fashioned way, they earn them. A sophisticated formula (you can find it on the official website of the U.S. Chess Federation determines the number of points a chess player earns when she beats another player depending on the rating of the opponent and the nature of the match or tournament. Rating classifications are Senior Master, above 2399; Master, 2200–2399; Expert, 2000–2199; and Class A, 1800–1999. There are also super levels of Grand Master and International Grand Master, as well as nine levels below Class A.

As a chess player with very modest abilities, I had always been very impressed with the spectacular genius of Bobby Fisher, arguably the most exciting chess genius of all time. It is evident that digital computers work on a totally different principle, and only by linking hundreds of such computers together, each being millions of times faster than the computational time of the human brain, was IBM's "Deep Blue" barely able to defeat the present world champion Garry Kasparov. The number of possibilities when looking ahead 6–8 moves in many situations is just staggering! It becomes impossible for the computer to go through the possibilities that far ahead, whereas a Grand Master like Kasparov is able to see particular sequences of potentially winning possibilities involving that many moves. Deep Blue excels in examining all possibilities when looking ahead "only" perhaps 4–5 moves in complicated situations. Just imagine the technological impact of a computer that could perform spatial-temporal reasoning like a chess Grand Master. One day this will surely happen!

We have a lot to learn about higher brain function from studying our best and brightest scientists, musicians, chess players, mathematicians, engineers, artists, and athletes, all of whom use spatial-temporal reasoning at its highest levels. I will show a connection among these abilities and demonstrate that, unlike the influential model of seven separate intelligences proposed by Howard Gardner, strong evidence exists that they are not separate: *any higher level brain function must make use of many of the same cortical areas.*

# Interviews with Research Mathematicians

With the foregoing belief that we can learn much from our best and brightest thinkers, Wendy Boettcher, Sabrina Hahn, and I designed and carried out in-depth interviews with 14 research mathematicians at the University of

California at Irvine. In addition to information about each mathematician's research area and math and music background, we were particularly interested in the mixing of the two fields of math and music. One question asked the researcher's opinion about a possible relationship between mathematics and music. Another question asked whether the researcher could listen to music while doing math. We hypothesized that if these activities make use of the same cognitive processes, music should interfere with mathematical operations. The most frequent response to listening to music while doing math was negative, either as a general rule or in particular when doing serious research. Five of the respondents mentioned that Baroque or classical music was particularly distracting.

Maren Longhurst followed up with a more focused interview and a more quantitative measure of the ability of 28 math (including a few physicists) researchers, at U.C. Irvine and the Mathematical Sciences Research Institute at U.C. Berkeley, to listen to a specific piece of music [the Mozart Sonata (K. 448)] while reading an article from a math journal on their desk. These interesting results confirmed that "spatial-temporal reasoning is used extensively by math researchers in their work." Further, "there was no average 'background level' at which the Sonata could be heard that would not interfere with most of the researchers."

Maren had the math researchers listen to a one-minute selection of the Mozart Sonata and recorded the average power (using a gadget built for us by Jim Kelley) going to the headphones. The first trial measured a comfortable listening level, and the second trial used the highest level at which the subject could still maintain concentration while reading a journal article in their specialty (as well as a third trial to determine the threshold hearing level for each researcher). The spread of listening power levels while reading the journal was a surprisingly large factor! This result is quite important, since it would argue *strongly against playing background music to a group of students in order to enhance reasoning during an exam*. . . . The use of music in this way is thought to be *highly* individual.

A qualitative remark is the often stated one that we know many mathematicians who say that they are respectable musicians, but there are relatively few musicians who say that they are good at math. I suggest that perhaps these musicians are referring to poor performance in language-analytic math reasoning rather than spatial-temporal math reasoning. It is music and spatial-temporal math that are intertwined in our brain. . . .

# Child Development

Music indeed plays a very special role in child development. Recent studies have demonstrated that sophisticated cognitive abilities are present in children as young as 5 months old. Similarly, musical abilities are evident in infants and neonates. Xiao Leng and I proposed that music may serve as a "pre-language" (with centers distinct from language centers in the cortex), available at an early age, which can access the inherent cortical spatial-temporal firing patterns and enhance the ability to perform spatial-temporal reasoning. It seems likely that well-designed experiments will be able to test whether the Mozart effect is present even for very young children. Whether there will be long-term enhancements is the big question. The crucial ingredient in such experiments is the ability to test enhanced spatial-temporal reasoning. . . .

It is crucial to conduct these experiments, since state programs in Georgia and Florida are encouraging parents to have their very young children listen to classical music in order to improve their thinking abilities. State officials say that their programs are based on our research, yet they have never spoken with me! *Currently, there is no directly relevant research.* In several media interviews after these state programs were begun, I stated that the relevant scientific studies must be done. . . .

*◦❀◦*

# Role of Music in Child Brain Development

I conclude with how music might enhance child brain development, since it is perhaps the most important area in which science can make a positive impact. If I controlled science spending,

> *I would put 10 billion dollars into a 10-year program to improve our understanding of infant brain development and to learn how to optimize the child's neural hardware for thinking and reasoning. These children will determine the world's future. Let's give them the opportunity to reach their potential.*

This high level of funding would ensure that the best and brightest scientists would strongly consider devoting their energies to this enormously important field. I hope that this book has convinced you that it is not enough to simply know that the infant brain is complex and develops rapidly. The newborn infant brain is *not* a blank slate. We must learn what active inputs at each developmental stage will generate the most effective enhancement of brain function.

Clearly, the role of music in the spatial-temporal reasoning of infants and primates deserves much more study. . . .

I have a special interest in this because of the many commercial and political distortions of the Mozart effect that are being aimed at eager parents. As mentioned earlier, one of the reasons that I wrote this book was to counteract the numerous misuses of our research. I discussed these cases in the Prologue. It is wrong to sell or even give away CDs and tapes of Mozart or Beethoven when stating that listening to the music will make your infant smarter or more creative. Our Mozart effect studies were with adults and focused on the Mozart Sonata (K. 448). There is *no* information about other classical pieces of music, and there is *no* relevant research on the Mozart effect in young children. However, you can make your own informed decision. I suggest that reading this . . . has made you informed.

As a neuroscientist and grandparent, I encourage my daughter Karen to play Mozart to her two young sons even though the relevant research on young children has not been conducted. Our research has shown that piano keyboard training for three-year-olds enhances their spatial-temporal reasoning. One of my goals is to do research on whether the reasoning abilities of infants are enhanced by listening to different kinds of music. This research should begin soon. A possible pilot study of the effects of having children listen to Mozart starting at birth and continuing for several years is now being discussed with a parent group in Moberly, Missouri, who have just contacted me. . . .

*Caution:* My main concerns are that the commercial exploitation of the Mozart effect will take advantage of the concerned parent's desire to improve their infant's reasoning abilities. There is no directly relevant research with infants. On the other hand, as a parent, you can observe your infant and check that there are no bad side effects from listening to classical music *in moderation.* In fact, you will probably see your child relax or become calm or go to sleep. However, I do not recommend the long-term playing of music to your fetus. . . . To summarize these cautions: I urge restraint in trying to influence the fetus's development through, for example, constant music input applied to the mother's stomach. No one knows the effects of such a program. It is possible that the common sequential time development of movement patterns of the fetus, as observed by Heinz Prechtl, could be disrupted by premature overstimulation through the auditory system. *I strongly doubt that this is the case, but I advise moderation.* I am fond of saying that there are no known bad side effects of listening to Mozart, but caution must be applied with the human fetus. My colleague Fran Rauscher advised me to add the same cautions for premature infants.

## My Dream

I suspect that all of my dreams about music enhancing learning and the crucial role of symmetry in higher brain function will come true. Whether it will take 5–10 years or 20–30 years for these dreams to be fulfilled is unknown. I hope it is the shorter period, so that I can see the results. It would be wonderful if all children could begin to fully utilize their innate spatial-temporal abilities to think, reason, and create.

 **NO**

# The Mozart Effect

**I**t can cure backache. And asthma. And obesity, writer's block, alcoholism, schizophrenia, prejudice, heart disease, drug addiction, headaches, and AIDS. It makes bread rise better and improves the taste of beer. It can even make you smarter—so smart that in Florida it's now the law that all child-care facilities receiving state aid include at least half an hour of it every day. The governors of both Tennessee and Georgia give newborns in their states examples of it along with cards reminding their parents of their tykes' immunization needs. At a community college in New York, administrators have set aside a room in their library for it. Across the nation, professional educators pelt school boards with demands for its inclusion in the curriculum. An Indiana obstetrician even markets a device that administers it in utero.

What is this philosopher's stone that can so dramatically change the world? It's music. Or better, Mozart's music, or so says Don Campbell in his best-selling *The Mozart Effect: Tapping the Power of Music to Heal the Body, Strengthen the Mind, and Unlock the Creative Spirit* (Avon Books, 1997). In high demand as a speaker, Campbell addresses a different conference almost weekly, hopscotching across the nation from his base in Boulder, Colorado. Trademarking the name "Mozart Effect," Campbell has even gone cable with infomercials for his book and its accompanying compact discs and cassettes. In the great tradition of P. T. Barnum and the "Veg-O-Matic," Mozart has now hit the mainstream of American life.

❧

The impetus for this remarkable turn of events was a modest letter by Frances Rauscher, Gordon Shaw, and Katherine Ky published under "scientific correspondence" in the October 14, 1993 issue of *Nature*. In their barely three-column report, these University of California at Irvine researchers summarized the findings of an experiment conducted upon thirty-six UCI students. After ten minutes spent either listening to Mozart's *Sonata in D major for Two Pianos,* K488, to a "relaxation tape," or simply sitting in silence, the students were given a paper folding and cutting test. (A piece of paper is

From *First Things*, March 1999, pp. 10–13. Copyright © 1999 by Institute on Religion and Public Life. Reprinted by permission.

folded over several times and then cut. You have to mentally unfold it and choose the right shape from five examples.) The students who listened to the Mozart sonata showed a 8–9 point increase in their IQ scores over their scores when they took the test after either a period of silence or listening to the relaxation tape. The bump in IQ was temporary, not lasting beyond the time required to sit through the experiment.

The researchers were testing the suspicion that there might be a kind of "music box" analogous to Chomsky's famous yet-undiscovered "language box." Might the symmetries and patterns characteristic of music be fundamentally connected to the symmetries and patterns researchers were tracking in brain waves? If so, might not music really be tapping into a structure inherent in the brain itself? And if this were true, ultimately might music be a kind of fundamental, or pre-linguistic—or even supra-linguistic—speech? The researchers tested Mozart's music because they thought that if anyone was "tapping into this inherent structure for patterns," it was Mozart. Who else was composing music so early and so well?

Although the researchers were professionally circumspect with their conclusions, the media that reported them were not. The story that "Mozart makes you smarter" made network news, and the wire services carried it to newspapers and magazines across the country. The Mozart Effect was born, and began its trek from the lab to the publishing house to the legislature.

Well, not born really. Reincarnated, let's say. And it wasn't so much a trek as a march along a well-worn path. The notion that music has properties and powers that can sharpen the mind and transform the soul is ancient. Such ideas formed the basis of Confucian civilization in China. In the West, they are attributed to Pythagoras and his followers and played a central role in Plato's ideal state.

Greek intellectuals generally had little patience with the gods of mythology, preferring to view the world in more abstract ways. At an early date, they observed that the basic condition of their world was change (we grow old, rivers flow, winter becomes spring, etc.), and reasonably concluded that if so, the basic condition of divinity (or otherworldliness) would be the opposite of it— or changelessness. This changelessness they considered perfection. Such divine perfection they couldn't see in the world around them, but they could observe it in the stars, in arithmetic, and in geometry. They credited Pythagoras with discovering that such divinity could also be encountered in music.

Pythagoras argued that music was divine because it was constructed of musical intervals that could be defined by mathematical ratios. Take a string and pluck it and you get a note. Divide it exactly in half, pluck it, and you get the same pitch an octave above it. Take that same string, divide it in thirds, hold down that string at a point two-thirds along its length, pluck the longer side, and you get a pitch a perfect fifth above the note you get plucking the whole string undampened. In a similar way each interval can be described by number. The octave by 2:1. The fifth by 3:2. The fourth by 4:3. The major second by 9:8. The major third by 81:64. And so on and so forth, every interval being described by an unchanging ratio. Because one, two, three, and four added together equal the Pythagorean perfect number ten, the intervals defined by these numbers are themselves also perfect (which is why we still refer to the octave, fourth, and fifth as the "perfect").

The Pythagoreans believed that number was the core to the universe and that because numbers do not change they were of divine origin. Since musical intervals were an expression of number, they too were divine. But the Pythagoreans themselves had little or no use for real music—that is if by "music" we mean musical compositions, or actual musicians for that matter. At least according to Aristides Quintilianus, an early Pythagorean, listening to actual music just got in the way. Best just to stick to thinking about the ratios.

In spite of this warning, tales developed of music's supernatural abilities. Orpheus charms Hades by his singing. Terpender of Methymna is credited with calming a revolt by his music. The mighty Alexander the Great is driven to murder—and remorse—by the playing of a servant. Even David's soothing of Saul's rages is probably rooted in a notion of music's supernatural nature being able to restore equilibrium. But no one makes music more central to his thought than does Plato. In the *Timeaus'* creation myth, he makes music the essential stuff of the cosmos. In *The Republic,* Plato develops it into the notion of the "doctrine of ethos."

Plato's purpose in writing *The Republic* is to describe the ideal state. Since an ideal state cannot be made up of un-ideal people; a good deal of his discussion concerns how to educate boys into the kind of men who would lead such a society. Briefly put, he thinks that this could best be accomplished by stressing two things in elementary education: gymnastics and music. The ways in which gymnastics would train the body are pretty clear; similarly, music was supposed to mold the spirit.

◦◦◦◦◦

Plato held that music does not merely depict qualities and emotional states but embodies them (this is the "doctrine of ethos"). A performer singing about the rage of Achilles, for instance, would not only be depicting the emotional states of anger and violence and the personal qualities of Homer's hero but would be experiencing those things himself. And not only the performer—so too would the listeners. Plato believed that music encodes ethical qualities already found in human conduct and that music feeds those qualities back into the soul of the performer and his listeners. Thus certain sorts of music would educate boys into living highly ethical lives while other sorts could educate them into baseness.

Plato forbids music in the Mixolydian and intense Lydian modes for his boys (they are "useless even for women if they are to be decent") as well as the music in the Ionian and lax Lydian modes (which are "soft, lazy, and fit for drunkenness"). Boys should be allowed to hear music only in the Dorian and Phrygian modes. In this way they might imitate the actions of a brave man "defending himself against fortune steadily with endurance."

Plato's ideal state was never established in antiquity. But his musical ideas weren't forgotten. In 1570, as France was being torn by the wars of religion, Charles IX's Catholic intelligentsia prodded him into creating the Académie de Poésie et de Musique. In the *lettres patents* which created the academy, the king declared that "it is of great importance for the morals of the citizens of a town that the music current in the country should be kept under certain laws, all the more so because men conform themselves to music and regulate their behavior accordingly, so that whenever music is disordered, morals are also depraved, and whenever it is well ordered, men are well tutored."

❦

It was the king's hope that proper music-making would restore order to his land, ending the bloodshed between Catholic and Protestant, or, if not ending it, at least making the Protestants take their humiliations a little more quietly. Here we have the "Mozart effect" roughly two hundred years before Mozart's birth.

Problem is, it didn't work. French Protestants and Catholics did not lay down their arms and embrace each other upon hearing the strain of fifes playing music in the Dorian mode. Plato's educational theories—on this point at least—are sheer nonsense. Do we really believe that training in ballet (which is really the union of gymnastics and music that Plato is talking about) is the best preparation for politics? Should Winston Churchill have spent more time in a tutu? The idea that requiring boys to listen to music in a particular mode will make them act with courage is perhaps the stupidest notion a great mind has ever come up with. Play whatever music you like for them—boys will be boys. And Pythagoras was wrong. The perfect fifth is not the temporal manifestation of supra-cosmic divinity sent to illuminate the land with transcendence. Moses did not come down the mountain with a tuning fork (nor, for that matter, did Muhammad or Jesus or Joseph Smith).

And the "Mozart Effect" is no effect at all. Soon after the original Irvine project, researchers at the University of Auckland tried to replicate Rauscher's results. They were unsuccessful, and concluded that listening to Mozart had no effect upon short-term IQ. Although Rauscher has replicated her original findings in a subsequent project, the conflicts between the studies have yet to be resolved. In any case, the parameters of the study weaken under scrutiny. Did the students really listen to the Mozart, or were they just in the room while the music was going on? Did the students who listened with care—in other words, listened to the music as it is supposed to be listened to (following the change of themes, the modulations, noting the surprise deceptive cadence near the close)—perform differently than those who just sat back and let the music wash over them?

❦

The researchers seemed surprisingly unaware of the music itself. When they suggested parameters for further investigation, they hypothesized that "[music] which is repetitive may interfere with, rather than enhance, abstract reasoning." Yet the movements of the sonata they selected are themselves highly repetitive. And the choice of work is regrettable, since the second movement is probably one of the silliest things Mozart ever wrote. The very best thing that could be said of their experiment—were it completely uncontested—would be that listening to bad Mozart enhances short-term IQ.

Prof. Rauscher has since joined the faculty of the University of Wisconsin at Oshkosh, where she is now studying the effects of music upon rodents. While her and her colleagues' findings remain controversial, these folks are insightful scientists and did not exaggerate their findings. Don Campbell knows no similar inhibitions. Using Rauscher's research as his base, Campbell has legally laid claim to The Mozart Effect™ and launched a commercial enterprise independent of the scientists whose curiosity initiated the investigation.

The claims that Campbell makes for music are of an almost rococo flamboyance. And like the rococo, just about as substantive. The ailments that head this article are part of a list of nearly fifty problems Campbell suggests that music corrects. His evidence is usually anecdotal, and even this he misinterprets. Some things he gets completely wrong. For instance, Campbell cites Georgie Stehli's famous cure from autism as an example of music's therapeutic effects. But in her autism, music, and indeed almost all sound, was a source of tremendous pain to little Georgie, not comfort. Her therapy was successful because it desensitized her to sound.

◦◦◉◦◦

And the whole structure of his argument collapses under simple common sense. If Mozart's music were able to improve health, why was Mozart himself so frequently sick? If listening to Mozart's music increases intelligence and encourages spirituality, why aren't the world's smartest and most spiritual people Mozart specialists? According to the argument in Campbell's book, the world's intellectual and spiritual center, populated with our civilization's most generous and healthful beings, ought to be where Mozart is most revered, studied, and performed; in other words, some place like the Metropolitan Opera's canteen during the intermission of *Così fan tutte*. It isn't.

The world's greatest orchestras have a good number of people in them who passionately hate each other. (The principal oboe and flute of one of our major orchestras so detested each other that no one remembered a time when they spoke.) And far from being healthy, orchestral musicians are beset by ailments. Carpal-tunnel syndrome, back problems, high blood pressure, exhaustion, diabetes, depression; look down from the balcony on the orchestra and you're looking on a group of men and women poised on the brink of physical collapse.

Music academics are no better. The annual meeting of the American Musicological Society is full of displays of one-upmanship, conceit, and subtle and not-so-subtle public back-stabbing and professional murder. And our greatest musicians, the star virtuosi, are more than infrequently notorious for their cruelty, faithlessness, arrogance, selfishness, and stupidity. And in all of these areas, Mozart's music only makes matters worse. His work is so technically demanding and his textures so lean that little less than a perfect performance will do. Almost any musician would prefer the gymnastics of Rachmaninoff to the delicacy of Mozart since with Mozart you always perform without a net.

In short, musicians—the ones who know Mozart best—are cantankerous, egotistical, selfish, stupid, cowardly, generous, even-tempered, compassionate, intelligent, humble, and kind in about the same proportion as Teamsters—who, for the most part, hardly know any Mozart at all.

•◆◆•

Music can do many things. A work song can coordinate physical labor. A march can keep an army in step. A bugle call can signal retreat and a melodic phrase can assist in the memorization of Torah. And art music, or that music which is intended to be primarily listened to for its aesthetic content, can be a powerful means for emotional self-reflection, self-illumination, and expression. But the one thing that music most certainly cannot do is overcome the will.

Music is not a drug that incapacitates the listener and produces a predictable result. A whole lifetime spent listening to Bach will not automatically make a woman love God. And—despite the warning of two generations of moralists—a lifetime listening to the Rolling Stones will not make a man fornicate. Particular kinds of music may express things that appeal to the listener, and the listener may select a particular kind of music because he finds that it resonates with his own—pre-musical—emotional condition, but the music itself can never cause the listener to act. Action is a function always of the will, and while music may prod, and it may suggest, it cannot force. We must indeed pay the piper, but we always choose the tune and decide whether or not to dance.

Poor Mozart. Where is he in all of this? Lost. Mozart's magnificent dances, the terrifying thunder of *Don Giovanni,* the bliss of *The Magic Flute,* the harmonic intricacies of his symphonies, and the transcendence of the final works: the "Ave verum corpus," *La Clemenza di Tito,* and the Requiem— all of this is lost in the rabble of Campbell's traveling snake-oil show barker's sales pitch. Mozart's greatest music isn't about being intelligent, or acquiring power. It's about becoming a human being and living, as he signed his scores, *in nomine Domini*. That is what the Mozart effect is supposed to be.

# POSTSCRIPT

## Does Exposure to Music, Including Mozart, During Early Childhood Have a Special Capacity to Enhance Development?

The idea of a "Mozart effect" that enhances child development is familiar to many people and most parents. Therefore, many people are surprised to learn that the "Mozart effect" is not nearly as certain as popularly imagined. As the readings make clear, conclusive research evidence for the effect is lacking. Building from this fact, however, it is possible to take at least two distinct positions on the role of music in development.

On one side, Gordon Shaw thinks the lack of evidence is likely to be rectified over time. While he acknowledges the media and commercial interests have made more of the existing research than science actually merits, he argues there are simply too many indications that music and Mozart facilitate cognitive development. Note, however, that Shaw suggests any effect is likely to be particular to spatial-temporal abilities rather than to a general cognitive enhancement. In fact, at its most basic level, Shaw is merely asserting that specific experiences in early childhood, such as exposure to music, can influence the brain. So is music really special?

Michael Linton claims that it is not. From his perspective, music is a wonderful part of human culture. Perhaps partially because so many people love music, Linton observes that there has been a clear historical pattern of falsely attributing miraculous capabilities to music that simply do not exist. He points out ways that historical claims about the wonders of music fall apart upon closer observation, and he thinks that the "Mozart effect" is no different. When we take the time to look at the original research, it becomes clear that the scientific base for music's special powers is weak.

So what is it about music that makes people continuously and historically ascribe magical powers? Clearly music has a special place in the human heart that allows it to occasionally overwhelm the mind. In many ways, the popularity of the idea of a "Mozart effect" provides a poignant example of how biased our understandings of development often may be. There are many popular ideas in child development that we feel strongly about; the academic study of lifespan development is often negotiating between those ideas and the cold data that occasionally tell us otherwise. And that may not always be a bad thing. As Shaw emphasizes—why not try music? Simply because the evidence is not yet conclusive does not mean we should not be looking for ways to improve child development.

The challenge, however, comes when popular understandings of the life span and misinterpretations of science confuse people—and even the government. As noted by Linton, the former governor of Georgia, Zell Miller, initiated a program at tax payers expense to distribute Mozart CDs to all newborns in his state. The package exclaimed that parents could enhance their babies' brains through Mozart, vaguely citing developmental research. Likewise, the legislature of Florida proposed 30 minutes of classical music for all its preschool children. While most would agree these efforts went too far, the question remains as to whether and how we should turn our concern for the preciousness of young children into action and stimulation?

## Suggested Readings

A. Bangerter and C. Heath, "The Mozart Effect: Tracking the Evolution of a Scientific Legend," *British Journal of Social Psychology* (2004).

D. Campbell, *The Mozart Effect: Tapping the Power of Music to Heal the Body, Strengthen the Mind, and Unlock the Creative Spirit* (Harper, 2001).

M. Krakovsky, "Dubious 'Mozart Effect' Remains Music to Many American Ears," *Stanford Report* (February 2, 2005).

K. Nantais and E. Schellenberg, "The Mozart Effect: An Artifact of Preference," *Psychological Science* (July 1999).

F. Rauscher, "What Educators Must Learn from Science: The Case for Music in Schools," *WMEA Convention* (February 1996).

S. Spinks, "The 'First Years' Fallacy: Mozart, Mobiles, and the Myth of Critical Windows," *Frontline* (May 12, 2005).

K. Steele, K. Bass, and M. Crook, "The Mystery of the Mozart Effect: Failure to Replicate," *Psychological Science* (July 1999).

C. Tavris, "Mozart Isn't the Answer," *The New York Times* (May 12, 2005).

N. Weinberger, "'The Mozart Effect': A Small Part of the Big Picture," *MUSICA Research Notes* (Winter 2000).

M. West, A. King, and M. Goldstein, "Singing, Socializing, and the Music Effect," in P. Marler, H. Slabbekoorn, & S. Hope (eds.), *Nature's Music: The Science of Bird Song* (Academic Press, 2004).

# ISSUE 9

## Does Emphasizing Academic Skills Help At-Risk Preschool Children?

**YES: U.S. Department of Health and Human Services,** from *Strengthening Head Start: What the Evidence Shows* (June 2003)

**NO: C. Cybele Raver and Edward F. Zigler,** from "Another Step Back? Assessing Readiness in Head Start," *Young Children* (January 2004)

### ISSUE SUMMARY

**YES:** The U.S. Department of Health and Human Services, which is responsible for Head Start—a preschool program for at-risk children—argues that preschool programs can most help young children by emphasizing academic and cognitive skills.

**NO:** Professors C. Cybele Raver and Edward F. Zigler (a founder of Head Start in the 1960s) respond by arguing that overemphasizing academic and cognitive skills at the expense of social, emotional, and physical well-being is a mistake dependent on misguided efforts to make the entire educational system focused on concrete assessment.

$\mathbf{A}$ hallmark of early childhood is the start of educational experiences outside the home. For many children, this means formal preschool. Many people take for granted that a quality preschool experience is essential to future success. You may have heard stories about exclusive New York preschools that are as competitive for admission as Ivy League colleges—and as expensive to match.

On the other side of the spectrum, many children raised by families mired in poverty lack the opportunity for quality preschool. These children often start primary school behind their more well-off peers and have difficulty breaking the cycle of poverty.

The most famous and intensive North American effort to facilitate early childhood development for children from poor families is the Head Start program. Started in the 1960s as part of President Lyndon Johnson's "War on Poverty," Head Start was a collaborative effort between the government and scholars to provide an educational environment that would allow children living in poverty to succeed. Head Start preschools are now a fixture in poverty-stricken communities from the rural South to blighted inner-cities to Native American reservations.

One of the foundational ideas upon which Head Start was built is that early childhood development progresses as an integration of distinct components of children's well-being. Thus, rather than focusing exclusively on academic skills, Head Start has attempted to provide diverse services that attend to academic, social, emotional, cognitive, and physical aspects of development.

While participants in Head Start have historically identified themselves as well satisfied with the program and the way it facilitates early childhood development, longitudinal research following children years after Head Start has shown mixed results. Research on IQ, for example, shows that Head Start does provide an early bump in IQ scores that lasts several years. The positive impact, however, dissipates over time until Head Start children end up returning to IQ levels consistent with other poor individuals who did not experience Head Start. Other evidence, however, suggests that Head Start children are less likely to be held back later in school, less likely to be labeled with learning disabilities, and more likely to stay with their education.

Nevertheless, as you read the following selections, you will note that both sides agree Head Start has not done enough to eliminate the gaps between the success of children from poor and rich families. The controversy is about what needs to change. Can we separate out the different aspects of development, or do they all work in integrated ways?

The U.S. government's Department of Health and Human Services under the George W. Bush administration declares that to break the cycle of poverty, the most important developmental aspect of early childhood is cognitive skills. They assert that Head Start needs to focus more on cognitive and academic skills such as pre-math (e.g., recognizing numbers) and pre-literacy (e.g., recognizing letters and words). The idea is to test these specific cognitive capacities and hold teachers and administrators accountable if they do not give young children from poor families the cognitive skills necessary for later school success.

C. Cybele Raver and Edward F. Zigler point out that focusing exclusively on cognitive skills runs counter to the way most developmental scholars understand the importance of early childhood. These authors offer a convincing historical perspective, partially because Edward Zigler was one of the scholars involved in the founding of Head Start and has been perhaps the most important academic through the program's history. He notes that children from poor families do not simply have a cognitive disadvantage, but they have an integrated set of developmental needs. Head Start, from Raver and Zigler's viewpoint, has always been successful at facilitating social competence, emotional development, connections with families and services, and other outcomes that are difficult to empirically test.

Ultimately, identifying the developmental needs of children is the central issue for this controversy. What do young children need from schools and societies in order to develop well?

# Strengthening Head Start: What the Evidence Shows

## Introduction

The period from birth through age 5 is a critical time for children to develop the physical, emotional, social, and cognitive skills they will need to be successful in school and the rest of their lives. Children from poor families, on average, enter school behind children from more privileged families. Targeting preschoolers in low-income families, the Head Start program was created in 1965 to promote school readiness to enable each child to develop to his or her fullest potential. Research shows that acquiring specific pre-reading, language, and social skills strongly predict future success in school.

As our knowledge about the importance of high quality early education has advanced dramatically since 1965, so have data on the outcomes for children and families served by Head Start. The knowledge and skill levels of low-income children are far below national averages upon entering the program. When the school readiness of the nation's poor children is assessed, it becomes clear that Head Start is not eliminating the gap in educational skills and knowledge needed for school. Head Start is not fully achieving its stated purpose of "promot[ing] school readiness by enhancing the social and cognitive development of low-income children." Head Start children show some progress in cognitive skills and social and emotional development. However, these low-income children continue to perform significantly below their more advantaged peers once they enter school in areas essential to school readiness, such as reading and mathematics.

States and the federal government fund a wide variety of programs that are either intended to enhance children's educational development or that could, with some adjustments, do a better job of preparing children for school. Head Start is one of many federal and state programs that together provide approximately $23 billion in funding for child-care and preschool education. Because these programs have developed independently, they are not easily coordinated to best serve the children and families who need them. In programs other than Head Start, states have the responsibility and the authority through planning, training, and the regulatory process to have

From U.S. Department of Health and Human Services, June 2003.

a substantial impact on the type and quality of services provided, and are held accountable for the delivery of high quality programs. However, Head Start funding goes directly from the federal level to local organizations, and thus states do not have the authority to integrate or align Head Start programs with other early childhood programs provided by the states.

The single most important goal of the Head Start reauthorization should be to improve Head Start and other preschool programs to ensure children are prepared to succeed in school. This paper describes the limited educational progress for children in Head Start and the problems resulting from a fragmented approach to early childhood programs and services. The paper also presents evidence from early childhood research and documents state efforts that have successfully addressed these problems. Finally, the paper explains the President's proposal for Head Start reauthorization, which builds on the evidence to strengthen the program and, through coordination, improve preschool programs in general to help ensure that children are prepared to succeed in school.

## Children in Head Start Are Not Getting What They Need to Succeed in School

Certain knowledge, skills, and experiences are strong markers of school readiness. For example, we know that children who recognize their letters, who are read to at least three times a week, who recognize basic numbers and shapes, and who demonstrate an understanding of the mathematical concept of relative size as they entered kindergarten have significantly higher reading skills in the spring of first grade than children who do not have this background. In fact, the difference between children who do and do not have this knowledge upon entering kindergarten is approximately one year's worth of reading development at the end of first grade. This is true regardless of family income and race or ethnicity.

Head Start is a comprehensive early childhood development program designed to provide education, health, and social services to low-income children, ages 3 to 5, and their families. Last reauthorized in FY 1998, Head Start is scheduled for reauthorization in FY 2003. Federal grants to operate Head Start programs are awarded directly to the local organizations that implement the program, including public agencies, private non-profit and for-profit organizations, Indian Tribes, and school systems. Since it began in 1965, Head Start has enrolled over 20 million children.

However, while making some progress, Head Start is not doing enough to enhance the language, pre-reading, and pre-mathematics knowledge and skills that we know are important for school readiness. The knowledge and skill levels of young children entering Head Start are far below national averages. Children graduating from Head Start remain far behind the typical U.S. child. We know also that all disadvantaged children who need high quality early educational instruction are not in Head Start. Some are in pre-kindergarten programs, others are in child-care settings, and still others are at home with parents.

## Most Children Enter and Leave Head Start with Below-Average Skill and Knowledge Levels

Currently, the primary source of information on outcomes for children and families served by Head Start comes from the Family and Child Experiences Survey (FACES). . . . These data are from the class of children who entered the program in 1997. The percentile scores show how Head Start children perform compared with the average performer. On a percentile scale, an average performer would be at the 50th percentile, meaning that half of children who take the test score above the average performer and half score below the 50% mark. Head Start children as a group fall far below the 50th percentile in all areas of achievement. Though children are making some progress, clearly few children perform as poorly as children who enter and leave the Head Start program. . . .

Both higher achieving and lower achieving Head Start children have low scores overall and show limited progress. Children who were in the upper 25% of their Head Start class when they entered Head Start in 1997 showed no gains on any measure of cognitive ability over the course of the Head Start program year, and actually experienced losses on some measures in comparison to national norms. Gains over the Head Start year were limited to children who were in the bottom 25% of their class. However, even these gains fell far short of bringing children to levels of skill necessary for school success. For example, children in the bottom 25% of their Head Start class left Head Start with language skill scores at the 5th percentile, meaning that only 5% of all children who take the test score lower than these Head Start children do. Findings for mathematics showed a similar pattern.

The more recent 2000 FACES data show modest improvement in results for children, but overall progress is still too limited. Children continue to lag behind national norms when they exit Head Start. Data from Head Start FACES 2000 shows that:

- The level of children's achievement in **letter-recognition** for the 2000 Head Start year is far below the majority of U.S. children who know all letters of the alphabet upon entering kindergarten, according to the Early Childhood Longitudinal Study of the Kindergarten class of 1998.

  Spanish-speaking children in Head Start did not gain at all in **letter recognition** skills in 2000.
- Although **writing** scores increased 2 points during the 2000 Head Start year, this was a drop from children who entered Head Start in 1997 who increased 3.8 points in writing during the 1997 Head Start year.
- Children entered Head Start in 2000 with scores at about the 16th percentile in **vocabulary**, or about 34 percentile points below the average. Children entering Head Start scored at about the 31st percentile in **letter recognition** and at about the 21st percentile in early **mathematics.**
- Children who entered Head Start in 2000 made progress in early **mathematics** during the Head Start year that was statistically significant; however the difference was small (from 87.9 to 89.0 on a scale for which 100 is the average). [This] 1.2-point difference is not a substantial

gain toward national averages. Moreover, this amount of progress was no greater than that found for children who attended Head Start from Fall to Spring in 1997.

- Children who entered the program in 2000 with overall lower levels of knowledge and skill showed larger gains during the program year compared to children who entered with higher levels of knowledge. However, they still lagged far behind national averages.
- Head Start children did not start kindergarten with the same social skill levels as their more socio-economically advantaged peers, and they continued to have more emotional and conduct problems.
- A follow-up study of children enrolled in Head Start in 1997 showed that children who attend Head Start make less progress than the average kindergartener. Thirty-four percent of Head Start children showed proficiency in knowing the ending sounds of words, 53% in knowing the beginning sounds of words, and 83% in letter recognition. Data from a nationally representative sample of all first-time kindergartners shows that fifty-two percent demonstrated proficiency in knowing the ending sounds of words, 72% in knowing the beginning sounds of words, and 94% in letter recognition.

. . . Head Start children have made some progress in some areas. A more detailed looks shows that:

- In 2000, the mean standard score for vocabulary increased 3.8 points, from 85.3 to 89.1 on a scale for which the average is 100. This result is similar to the data for 1997 that showed Head Start children scored about 85 at the beginning of the year and gained about 4 points by the end of the year.
- In 2000, the mean standard score for writing increased by 2 points, from 85.1 to 87.1.
- In 2000, children showed gains in book knowledge and print conventions (that is, they can show an adult the front of a storybook and open it to where the adult should start reading). This progress is statistically greater than for the 1997 Head Start year during which no progress was made in this area.
- In 2000, Spanish-speaking children in Head Start showed significant gains in English vocabulary skills without declines in their Spanish vocabulary.
- In 2000, children showed growth in social skills and reduction in hyperactive behavior during the Head Start year. Even children with the highest levels (scoring in the top quarter) of shy, aggressive, or hyperactive behavior showed significant reductions in these problem behaviors. Teachers rated children's classroom behavior as more cooperative at the end of the Head Start year than when children first entered the program.
- In 2000, children who received higher cooperative behavior ratings and lower problem behavior ratings from Head Start teachers scored better on cognitive assessments at the end of kindergarten, even after controlling for their scores on cognitive tests taken while in Head Start.
- Children who entered Head Start in 1997 showed significant gains in their social skills, such as following directions, joining in activities,

and waiting turns in games, and gains in cooperative behaviors, according to ratings by teachers and parents. The quality of children's social relationships, including relating to peers and social problem solving, also improved.

Head Start program and teacher characteristics show some positive relationships to educational and social outcomes for children. Examples include:

- Teachers' educational credentials are linked to greater gains in early writing skills. Children taught by Head Start teachers with bachelors' degrees or associates' degrees showed gains toward national averages in an assessment of early writing skills, whereas children taught by teachers with lesser credentials merely held their own against national norms.
- Provision of preschool services for a longer period each day is linked to greater cognitive gains. Children in full-day classes in Head Start showed larger fall to spring gains in letter recognition and early writing skills than did children in part-day classes.

Head Start has other positive qualities:

- In 1997, the program received very high ratings of satisfaction from parents, and for the roughly 16% of children in Head Start with a suspected or diagnosed disability, 80% of parents reported that Head Start had helped them obtain special needs resources for the child.
- A follow up study of children who attended Head Start in 1997 showed that children were capable of making some progress during their kindergarten year in vocabulary, writing, and early mathematics, though performance remained significantly below national norms.

How do eligible children fare when they do not receive Head Start services? The FACES study is not designed to answer this question; there is no control group. Eligible children who do not receive services could be falling further behind or could be making gains similar to or greater than those for children in the program. The national Head Start Impact Study was launched in 2002 and is using a randomized design to answer this question. Additional experimental studies are being conducted to assess the effectiveness of specific quality improvement strategies.

A national study of Early Head Start, which is part of the Head Start program serving low-income pregnant women and children from birth through three, was recently conducted using a randomized experimental design. Results show that children receiving Early Head Start have scores that are statistically higher than their peers who did not receive Early Head Start on measures of cognitive, language, and social and emotional competency. Fewer Early Head Start children scored in the "at-risk" range of functioning in both language and cognitive functioning. However, Early Head Start children continue to perform below the national average.

In summary, there is more work to do. Despite the positive qualities of Head Start programs, children in Head Start are making only very modest progress in only some areas of knowledge and skill, and children in Head Start are leaving the program far behind their peers. More progress must be made and can be made to put Head Start children on par with others by the time they enter kindergarten.

## Disadvantaged Children Lag Behind Throughout the School Years

Effective early childhood intervention is important because disadvantaged children are at great risk for poor educational outcomes throughout the school years. Data from the National Center for Education Statistics' (NCES) Early Childhood Longitudinal Study—Kindergarten Cohort (ECLS-K) and National Assessment of Educational Progress (NAEP) are reviewed below.

### Children with Multiple Risks Suffer the Greatest Educational Disadvantage

Achievement differences in school are greatest for children who suffer the greatest disadvantage, in particular for children whose families have **multiple risk factors** or **receive welfare.** While many of the children we are trying to reach in early childhood are in Head Start and federal and state pre-kindergarten programs, others are in child-care and home-settings.

A key set of **risk factors** has been repeatedly associated with educational outcomes, such as low achievement test scores, grade repetition, suspension or expulsion, and dropping out of high school. These risk factors include: (a) having parents who have not completed high school, (b) coming from a low-income or welfare-dependent family, (c) living in a single-parent family, and (d) having parents who speak a language other than English in the home. Children who have one or more of these characteristics are more likely to be educationally disadvantaged or have difficulty in school.

These same risk factors are linked to achievement disparities in reading and mathematics skills at the point of kindergarten entry. Research emphasizes that achievement difficulties children experience in school "cannot be attributed solely to bad schools; many children are already behind when they open the classroom door."

- Children with **two or more risk factors** are about three times as likely as those with no risk factors to score in the bottom 25% in reading.
- Children from families with **3 or more risk factors** typically do not know their letters and cannot count to 20. Fifty-six percent could not identify letters of the alphabet compared with 25% in the no risk group. They are about one-third as likely to be able to associate letters with sounds at the end of words.
- Children with even **one risk factor** are twice as likely to have reading scores that fall into the lowest 25% of children studied compared to children with no risk factors. They are half as likely to be able to associate letters with sounds at the ends of words. Some children with one risk factor have good reading scores, but far too few. They are half as likely to score in the top quartile as children with no risk factors (16% vs. 33%).

- In mathematics, 38% of the multiple risk group could count beyond 10 or make judgments of relative length compared with 68% in the no risk group. They were one-third as likely to be able to recognize 2-digit numerals or identify the ordinal position of an object in a series.
- Forty-four percent of children with multiple risk factors rarely paid attention, compared to 28% of children with no risk factors.

Children are at risk for poor educational outcomes when their families receive **welfare** (defined as receiving welfare or having received welfare in the past). These children were significantly less competent in reading, mathematics, and social skills compared to children who had never received welfare.

- In reading, children of welfare recipients are less likely to show pre-reading competencies that include letter recognition, recognition of beginning and ending sounds, and print familiarity. Forty-nine percent of these children scored in the lowest quartile, compared to 22% of children whose families were not welfare recipients.
- In mathematics, half of children whose families received welfare scored in the lowest quartile for mathematics, compared to 22% of children whose families had never received welfare. Twenty-three percent of children of welfare recipients scored in the top half for reading, compared to 53% of children whose families had never received welfare.
- Children from welfare families also are under-represented in the higher performing category: Fifty-three percent of children who had never received welfare scored in the top half for reading, compared to only 24% of children whose families were welfare recipients.
- Children of welfare recipients are also at risk for poor social skills. Kindergarten teachers rated these children as having more difficulty with forming friendships and interacting with peers compared to children whose families were not welfare recipients.

### The Achievement Gap for Disadvantaged
### Children Widens During Kindergarten

Children who start behind are likely to stay behind and get further behind. Research shows that the achievement gap between advantaged and disadvantaged groups of children widens from Fall to Spring. Global reading and mathematics scores show gains for all children in reading and mathematics scores during the kindergarten year. But a closer look shows that achievement disparities between disadvantaged and more advantaged children depend on the particular knowledge and skills assessed.

By Spring, children from homes with at least one risk factor begin to close gaps in basic skills, such as recognizing letters, counting beyond 10, or comparing the size of objects. But because their more advantaged classmates move on to acquire more complex skills, these children are even further behind by Spring in reading and mathematics skills, such as reading words or solving simple addition and subtraction problems. Moreover, despite improvements in basic reading and mathematics skills during the kindergarten year, the disparity between advantaged and disadvantaged children was not eliminated.

*The Achievement Gap Persists into Elementary and High School*
Poor children eligible for the National School Lunch Program do not perform as well as more advantaged children who are ineligible for the program. Average scores for reading, mathematics and writing achievement are statistically lower for children who are eligible for the school lunch program compared to ineligible children. This achievement gap continues throughout the school years. . . .

# Research Evidence Shows We Can Do Better in Helping Children Achieve

## Research Has Identified What Children Need to Succeed in School

Before children can read, write or calculate, research shows that children must acquire foundational knowledge, skills, and behaviors that are stepping stones toward mastery of more advanced and complex skills.

*Children Are Better Off If They Enter Kindergarten*
*with Cognitive Resources*
Children who bring certain knowledge and skills with them to kindergarten are likely to be at an advantage in classroom learning compared to their peers who do not possess these resources. A Department of Education report described the predictive power of having specific cognitive and health "resources" on children's reading and mathematics achievement. These resources included:

- possessing specific basic literacy knowledge and skills;
- being read to at least three times a week at kindergarten entry;
- being proficient in recognizing numbers and shapes at kindergarten entry;
- showing productive approaches to learning, such as an eagerness to learn, task persistence and ability to pay attention; and
- possessing good to excellent health.

Each of these was a key predictor of children's reading and mathematics achievement in the Spring of kindergarten and in first grade, even after controlling for children's race, ethnicity and poverty status. These data confirm that we must ensure that *all* children, regardless of background, are physically healthy *and* have the same basic literacy, mathematics, and cognitive experiences and skills needed to succeed in school.

*Child Development Research Shows Which*
*Areas of Competency to Target*
Research experts and practitioners in fields relating to early childhood recommend that children make progress in each of the following areas to help ensure they are developing school readiness knowledge and skills.

- In the area of **pre-reading,** children should develop: phonological processing skills (hearing and playing with sounds in words, for example, through rhyming games), letter knowledge (knowing the names and sounds of letters), print awareness (knowing how to hold a book, that we read in English from left to right and usages of print), writing, and interest in and appreciation of books, reading, and writing.
- In the area of **language,** children should develop receptive and expressive vocabulary skills (ability to name things and use words to describe things and actions); narrative understanding (ability to understand and produce simple and complex stories, descriptions of events, and instructions); phonology (ability to distinguish and produce the different sounds of language); syntactic or grammatical knowledge (knowing how to put words together in order to communicate with meaning); and oral communication and conversational skills (knowing how to use words in appropriate contexts for a variety of purposes, such as knowing when and how to ask a teacher for more information, or understanding how to take turns in a conversation).
- Children should develop **pre-mathematics** knowledge and skills that include number concepts (recognizing written numerals, counting with an understanding of quantity, knowing quantitative relationships such as "more" and "less"), number operations (such as adding and subtracting); geometry concepts (such as recognizing shapes); space, patterns, and measurement concepts and skills (such as measuring length using their hands or measuring using conventional units such as inches).
- Children should develop **cognitive skills** that include the ability to plan and problem-solve, the ability to pay attention and persist on challenging tasks, intellectual curiosity and task engagement, and achievement motivation and mastery.
- Children need **social and emotional competencies** important for school success and a constructive learning environment. These include the ability to relate to teachers and peers in positive ways, the ability to manage feelings of anger, frustration and distress in age-appropriate ways, and the ability to inhibit negative behaviors with teachers and peers, for example, aggression, impulsiveness, noncompliance, and constant attention-seeking.

## The Right Programs and Training Can Improve Children's School Readiness

Research, though limited, clearly demonstrates the value of providing comprehensive interventions with strong language and pre-academic components that develop the knowledge and skills necessary for kindergarten and the early grades and for closing the achievement gap. Though more research is needed, a few approaches that have been evaluated using rigorous designs show that comprehensive and language and literacy-rich early childhood programs can reduce achievement gaps for disadvantaged children. Here are highlights of major studies.

*The Chicago Child-Parent Center (CPC) Program*

This program for low-income minority children in high-poverty neighborhoods in innercity Chicago, funded in part by the Department of Education, includes half-day preschool for one or two years, full or part-day kindergarten, continuing support services in linked elementary schools, and a parent education program. The Chicago CPC program provides educational and health and nutrition services, such as hearing screening, speech therapy and nursing services, to children ages 3 to 9 years. The intervention emphasizes the acquisition of basic knowledge and skills in language arts and mathematics through relatively structured but diverse learning experiences. An intensive parent program includes volunteering in the classroom, attending school events and field trips, and completing high school. Teachers are required to have bachelor's degrees, are paid at the level of teachers in public school, and participate in regular staff development activities. Child-to-staff ratios are low (17:2).

A longitudinal study funded by the National Institutes of Health and other funders compared participant children to a non-experimental comparison group of children with similar demographics. Findings include:

**Reading and mathematics achievement.**    At the end of the program in third grade, CPC graduates surpassed their comparison group counterparts by 4 to 6 points in reading and mathematics achievement, as measured by the Iowa Test of Basic Skills.

*Preschool participation.*    One or two years of CPC preschool participation was associated with statistically significant advantages of 5.5 and 4.2 points in standard scores for reading achievements for ages 14 and 15. This corresponds to about a 4- to 5-month change. Likewise, preschool participation was significantly associated with a 4.4-point increase in standard scores in math achievement at age 14 and a 3.3-point advantage at age 15, above and beyond gender, environmental risk factors, and participation in follow-on interventions. This translates into a 3- to 4-month performance advantage over the comparison group. These effect sizes are considered moderate; however the effects persist up to 10 years after children leave the program, which is unique among early interventions and almost all social programs.

*Follow-on participation.*    Because the early childhood program is linked to the kindergarten and elementary schools, children may participate in the program from 1 to 6 years. Each year of participation was associated with an increase of 1.3 to 1.6 points in the standard score for reading. Years in the follow-on intervention were significantly associated with reading achievement at ages 14 and 15 and went beyond that attributable to preschool participation. The most dramatic effect occurring after 4 years of intervention: Five or six years of participation resulted in the best performance, with children performing at or above the Chicago averages in reading and mathematics. (Even 6 years of participation, however, did not elevate the performance of the maximum intervention group to the national average.) A similar pattern occurred for mathematics achievement, though the size of the effect was smaller. The findings showed that the relationship between years of participation and school achievement is not strictly linear—greater advantages accrue as the length of the intervention increases.

**Other outcomes.**   Preschool participation was associated with lower rates of grade retention (23% vs. 38.4%) and special education placement (14.4% vs. 24.6%). Preschoolers who participated in the intervention spent an average of 0.7 years in special education compared with 1.4 years for non-participants. Children who participated in the preschool intervention for 1 or 2 years had a higher rate of high school completion (49.7% vs. 38.5%), more years of completed education (10.6 vs. 10.2), and lower rates of juvenile arrests (16.9% vs. 25.1%). Boys benefited from preschool participation more than girls, especially in reducing the school dropout rate.

**Cost-benefit analyses.**   With an average cost per child of $6,692 for 1.5 years of participation, the preschool program generates a total return to society at large of $47,759 per participant. These benefits are the result of participants' increased earnings capacity due to educational attainment, criminal justice system savings, reduced school remedial services, and averted tangible costs to crime victims. Benefits realized in each of these areas exceed the cost of just one year of the preschool program, which is $4,400. Overall, every dollar invested in the preschool program returns $7.14 in individual, educational, social welfare and socioeconomic benefits.

### The Abecedarian Project

The Abecedarian Project was a carefully controlled study in which 57 infants from low-income families living in a small North Carolina town were randomly assigned to receive early intervention in a high quality child care setting and 54 were in a non-treated control group. The treated children received full-time educational intervention in a high quality child care setting from infancy through age five, which included cognitive development activities with a particular emphasis on language, and activities focusing on social and emotional development. Teachers were required to have bachelor's degrees and were paid at the level of teachers in public school.

Starting at age 18 months, and through follow-ups at ages 12 and 15, the treatment children had significantly higher scores on cognitive assessments. Treated children scored significantly higher on tests of reading and math from the primary grades through age 21 (though scores did not reach national averages).

At age 21, those in the treatment group were significantly more likely to still be in school and more likely to have attended a four-year college. Employment rates were higher for the treatment group than for the control group, although the trend was not statistically significant.

### The Perry Preschool Study

This pioneering study begun in the 1960s was one of the first to identify lasting effects of high quality preschool programs on children's outcomes. One hundred twenty-three poor African American 3- and 4-year-olds were randomly assigned either to attend a high quality preschool program or to no preschool. The two groups began the study with equivalent IQ scores and socioeconomic status. Children attended $2^1/_2$ hour classes and teachers conducted weekly 1.5-hour home-visits.

Results showed positive impacts on several intellectual and language tests prior to school entry and up to age 7, showing that the program enhanced children's school readiness. At age 14, participants outperformed non-participants on a school achievement test in reading, language, and mathematics. At age 19, participants' general literacy skills were better than non-participants. At age 27, participants had higher earnings and economic status, higher education and achievement levels in adolescence and young adulthood, as well as fewer arrests.

Benefit-cost analyses show that by the time participants were 27 years old, the program showed a sound economic investment, with significant savings from settlement costs for victims of crimes never committed, reduced justice system costs, increased taxes paid due to higher earnings, reduced need for special education services, and reduced welfare costs. . . .

## Conclusions

Research shows that children in Head Start are falling behind and too often are not ready for school. In particular, those children who are the poorest and have the most risk factors do not enter kindergarten with the intellectual resources they need to succeed. Some of these children are being served by Head Start, but others are in state pre-kindergarten, childcare, and home-settings. From basic science on learning and development and from intervention studies we know a great deal about how to narrow the achievement gap for Head Start and other disadvantaged children before they enter kindergarten. Research tells us the knowledge and skills children need in language, pre-reading, and pre-mathematics, and the social and emotional competencies they must have to succeed in school. The President believes that the Head Start program must be strengthened and provide more emphasis on pre-reading, language, pre-mathematics and other cognitive skills, while continuing to promote children's health and social and emotional competence as part of school readiness. Research tells us that early childhood education implemented with qualified and well-trained teachers can make a significant and meaningful impact on the development of children's knowledge and skills, their achievement in school, and success in life. . . .

C. Cybele Raver and
Edward F. Zigler

 **NO**

# Another Step Back?
# Assessing Readiness in Head Start

**S**ince its founding in 1965, Head Start's goal has been to help children who live in poverty prepare for school. Over the last three and a half decades, Head Start has maintained a staunch commitment to the provision of genuinely comprehensive services. While impressive in its breadth, this wide range of services has made it difficult for researchers to benchmark children's progress in the program. One solution has been to rely on strictly cognitive measures as a means to assess the benefits of Head Start. We criticized this approach in an earlier paper entitled "Three Steps Forward, Two Steps Back." In that article, we pointed out that sole reliance on children's cognitive outcomes was neither in keeping with the goals of Head Start nor with many definitions of what it means to be ready to succeed in early elementary school.

Recently Head Start has been subjected to major policy changes at the federal administrative and legislative levels. In particular, the Bush Administration instituted a new set of accountability measures that will be used to test Head Start children twice a year on language, literacy, and pre-math skills. This policy is swiftly being put into place with full implementation plans announced in both April and June 2003. The assessment system, under the National Reporting System that is part of the current law but left to the Secretary to determine, has been controversial. The measures were quickly developed by Westat, Inc., and the national assessment process is now underway. This fall, all four- and five-year-old children in Head Start (who are eligible to enroll in kindergarten next year) will undergo the first of two annual assessments. This quick pace of change proceeded despite a letter to administrators signed by some 300 professionals questioning the psychometric properties of the measures.

⌘

The spring of 2003 was also the time Congress began work on reauthorizing Head Start's funding. The House version of the reauthorization bill (HR 2210) proposed substantial changes to the 38-year-old program. Most controversial was a plan to devolve Head Start to the states, but the bill also raised the issue of assessment. The bill (as introduced) emphasized children's knowledge and skills in the areas of language, literacy, and pre-math and deleted the current law's references to children's social competence, emotional development, and cultural diversity. Why did the Bush Administration move so sharply away from Head Start's emphasis on school readiness in broadly defined terms, and toward a narrow emphasis on cognitive development as the critical factor in preparing for school?

Perhaps these moves are driven by well-meaning intentions on the part of policy makers to improve the educational chances of our nation's most disadvantaged young children. The evidence shows that while Head Start children make significant gains in preschool, they still score well below the national average on vocabulary, pre-reading, writing, and early math skills. Secretary of Health and Human Services Tommy Thompson argues that poor children deserve a better start to their educational trajectories. Lawmakers on both sides of the political spectrum began to focus the debate on what it means to close the achievement gap of Head Start children with their middle-class peers. However, their pathways to that goal were quite different, as were their expectations of closing that gap merely by adding a stronger focus on literacy and math skills.

On the face of it, there is some logic to the idea that if children are less knowledgeable regarding early academics like letters and numbers, strengthening these skills should help them when they begin school. And perhaps lawmakers were persuaded by a small number of studies that suggest that some programs (but not others) have shown limited short-term improvements in older children's educational achievement when "high-stakes" achievement tests are used to increase school monitoring and accountability. In our view, however, these intentions are misguided. As we will argue, the application of a strictly cognitive focus to assessments of school readiness runs counter to what the best developmental research tells us and what past policy experience has shown. A narrow focus on benchmarking Head Start's programmatic success on early cognitive gains to the exclusion of children's emotional and social development has been tried in the past and has backfired. In this article, we briefly review these past rounds of policy debate, and consider scientific evidence regarding what disadvantaged preschoolers need to be ready for school. We then offer three concrete policy recommendations for alternatives to the steps that are in the works for Head Start accountability.

## What Does Past Policy Experience Tell Us?

This is not the first time that policy makers and research scientists have tried to peg evidence of Head Start's success to children's cognitive gains. During Head Start's early years, evaluators commonly found substantial gains in children's IQ scores after even brief periods of intervention. These gains were publicized as striking evidence that the programs worked. However, when the IQ benefits were found apparently to dissipate as children progressed through elementary school, intervention efforts were quickly deemed a failure not worthy of public support.

⋅◦✦◦⋅

When Head Start and other early interventions failed to show permanent gains in children's cognitive scores (as assessed by IQ), policy makers had two choices: either to capitulate to the skeptical view that early intervention is not effective, or to question whether IQ gains were the appropriate metric to have used in the first place and whether the programs were improperly evaluated. Workers in a variety of disciplines eventually convinced policy makers that intelligence alone does not guarantee academic success—that even a very bright child will do poorly in school if he or she suffers physical health or emotional problems, has trouble staying motivated, or does not interact well with teachers or peers. Consequently, researchers, policy professionals, and practitioners in the field of early childhood education seemingly resolved this issue by establishing that Head Start must continue to encompass a broader mission of school readiness that includes physical and mental health, social and emotional needs, and academic skills. This emphasis on both cognitive and social-emotional development was validated by specific language in the 1998 Head Start reauthorization act. Further verifying policy makers' acceptance, data on children's social and emotional development (though in limited form) began to be collected in large-scale national surveys including the Family and Child Experiences Survey (FACES, Department of Health and Human Services), the Early Childhood Longitudinal Study (ECLS-K, Department of Education), and the Head Start National Impact Study (U.S. Department of Health and Human Services). Suddenly, however, the current administration decided to reverse course.

In part, we suspect that this reversal is due to consensus that there is an unacceptably large "achievement gap" between economically disadvantaged children and their more advantaged counterparts, and that it is our responsibility as a nation to do something to reduce that gap. Yet there is major disagreement regarding the best remedies to take. Similar to ongoing debate in educational research and policy, one view is that early interventions such as Head Start are not doing a good job teaching disadvantaged preschoolers. From an economic and partisan perspective, the argument is that Head Start programs (like public schools) are monopolies that are inefficient and have few incentives to improve because of the lack of competition. More strictly defined standards of child performance are seen as a way to impose accountability. Literacy and math skills can be tested, and test scores can yield information about school performance to consumers (e.g., parents, government funding agencies, etc.). The hope is that market-based systems will weed out bad performers and reward higher performers, that providers will strive to improve, and that children will benefit.

The opposing view, held by many early childhood educators and advocates, sees this emphasis on accountability as a way for fiscally conservative policy makers to avoid paying for the relatively expensive solutions that are needed to enact real gains in poor children's educational attainment. This group contends that high-quality early education and care can advance disadvantaged children's learning but that it is not cheap to provide. Advocates and educators in early childhood suggest that if policy makers really wanted to close the education gap, they would make the kind of fiscal investments that are needed to provide children with the things that we know work: comprehensive, full-day services with highly trained, well-paid staff, with fewer children in each classroom, and with more time and resources to devote to learning, literacy, and social and emotional development. They further argue that changes at the preschool level will not be enough. For Head Start children to maintain the gains they make in preschool, fiscal resources will be needed to improve the elementary schools they attend and—even more daunting—to alleviate home and community stressors that are likely to impede their future academic performance.

Our point is not to take one side of this debate or the other, but to suggest that a strictly cognitive approach to early education and assessment is likely to backfire, regardless of the position taken on best remedies for the "achievement gap" between affluent and poor preschoolers. For the sake of argument, let us consider the highly touted Texas prekindergarten program that Secretary of Health and Human Services Thompson uses as a model of success and as a purportedly strong contrast to Head Start. Using a nonexperimental research design (where investigators can inflate program effects by assigning better-performing schools to the treatment group), the evaluation of the program revealed moderate impacts on children's language scores for *less than half* of the participating sites. At best, this translates to modest success in narrowing the educational gap between low-income Texas preschoolers and their more affluent counterparts. But, even if we believe that the Texas program included the strongest of teaching efforts tied to the best curricular choices, it could just as easily be argued that the program did not meaningfully close the gap between poor and wealthier children. Using such narrow, cognitively oriented definitions of success, not only will programs be viewed as failures but poor children will be viewed as impervious to help.

To avoid this likely scenario, policy makers must understand that vocabulary, pre-reading, and pre-math tests only provide a rough approximation of where preschoolers stand in relation to their agemates, or where they stand relative to their own prior performance. But these tests do not capture the value of a program in supporting the multiple facets of development and learning that are undoubtedly taking place, both in those Texas classrooms and in Head Start classrooms across the country. For example, while IQ gains children make in preschool arguably fade out, graduates of quality intervention programs (including Head Start) are less likely to be retained in grade or placed in special education than similar children without good preschool experience. Clearly a wealth of learning experiences and benefits were accrued during intervention and carried through later schooling, but these were not tapped by cognitive measures. Thus a focus on cognitive outcomes without an understanding of the multiple processes that lead to school success runs the risk of disenfranchising children from learning, disenfranchising good teachers from teaching disadvantaged preschoolers, and disenfranchising voters from the view that investments in young children pay off.

## What Does Early Educational Research Tell Us?

Policy makers must also understand that sole reliance on cognitively oriented measures is unsupported by the best scientific evidence we have about ways to support early learning. There is a bounty of scientific literature indicating that children's social and emotional skills are predictive of early achievement, with children's thinking skills *and* self-regulation likely to play important roles in early learning.

One might ask: What does self-regulation have to do with learning the basics such as preliteracy and early math? Children must be able to handle their emotions when sharing instructional materials, taking turns holding or choosing a book for story time, or getting in line. They must be able to focus their attention away from distracting sights and sounds outside the classroom window and toward the task at hand. They must be able to organize their activities and listen to and heed teachers' instructions. Emotionally supportive preschool classrooms foster children's motivation, their development of enthusiasm about school as a good place to be, and positive views of themselves as learners capable of tackling new problems and challenges. Children who are less distractible and more emotionally positive are viewed by teachers as more "teachable." In fact, a majority of teachers surveyed suggested that curiosity, enthusiasm, and ability to follow directions play a potent role in their judgment of children's "readiness" to learn.

*≈◉≈*

Recent research in both areas of cognitive and emotional development has highlighted the ways in which children differ from each other in terms of "executive functioning" or "behavioral self-control." That is, while some children are good at planning, staying organized and focused when given a difficult task, and remaining attentive and calm in a classroom setting, other children have problems regulating their emotions and their attention. Decades of research suggest that (1) Children with emotional and behavioral difficulties are at greater risk for long-term academic problems, and (2) poverty-related stressors impose additional psychological strain on young children that may interfere with their ability to concentrate, pay attention, and control their feelings of sadness and frustration. Prevalence estimates suggest that between

7 percent and 25 percent of low-income children enrolled in early educational settings exhibit elevated behavioral problems. Children exposed to high levels of community and family violence also are more likely to be sad and withdrawn, with symptoms of inattentiveness and difficulty interacting prosocially with teachers and peers. In short, these problems are likely to have serious ramifications for learning. Low-income preschoolers' acquisition of preliteracy and other cognitive skills is likely to be *suppressed* unless the social and emotional domains of learning and development are recognized and supported.

In addition, research suggests that preschool-age children learn more and are more motivated when they are in emotionally supportive, "child-centered" classrooms, as compared to classrooms that emphasize drills, worksheets, seat-work, and "basic skills." In the recent U.S. Department of Health and Human Services report critiquing Head Start, the authors recognize the importance of teaching pre-academic content "without compromising social and emotional development." In the model Texas program that the report endorses, the evaluation included assessments of children's readiness in both cognitive and socioemotional domains. It is therefore baffling that some leaders want to eradicate social and emotional assessments from Head Start's planned evaluation efforts.

Plans to abandon assessment of children's social and emotional competencies in Head Start represent a grave loss of opportunity for social scientists and educators. With the emotional and behavioral data from the FACES and Head Start Impact Study, we can address questions of how changes in particular noncognitive domains are associated with changes in learning. Without the data that these assessments will provide, researchers will be unable to test the very hypotheses that may lead to teaching and curricula innovations. Finally, if measures of social and emotional development are struck from national evaluations, policy makers will be making a statement that these features are unrelated to learning and are therefore unimportant. A slew of developmental evidence, and a modicum of common sense, should tell them otherwise.

## Cautions and Recommendations

What will the impact of national testing of Head Start's preschoolers be? We can imagine a range of scenarios that might result from the plan to use cognitively oriented tests to assess Head Start children. One benefit might be that training and technical assistance could be targeted to centers that need the help the most. On the other hand, classrooms in areas with high levels of community and family violence are likely to have children who are less able to weather the behavioral challenges involved in test-taking, so programs serving our nation's most vulnerable families will receive the greatest share of blame and the least amount of help for children's compromised performance. In short, we may repeat past policy mistakes, with Head Start and poor children blamed for their supposed educational failures rather than rewarded and supported for their successes in the face of substantial income and educational inequality. Without being able to predict the outcome, and without being able to forestall the implementation of cognitively oriented assessments, we offer a set of cautions and recommendations.

1. First, we remind readers that there is no single cognitive "magic bullet" to the problems of poverty or to the achievement gap between economically disadvantaged children and their more affluent classmates. Good curriculum and hard work on the part of teachers may partially remedy that gap, and programs, teachers, parents, and children themselves are to be lauded when such successes are achieved. Certainly, comprehensive services that address families' economic self-sufficiency, housing, health, and welfare are also needed, and we know that those services are expensive. If policy makers genuinely wish to see Head Start and low-income children succeed, they must match their interest in cognitive assessment with a substantially increased investment in families, programs, and teachers so that desired gains can be realized.

2. Second, we caution readers that there is not clear consensus of the predictive value of cognitive assessments in guaranteeing later school performance. School success likely rests on an integrated foundation, with physical health, cognitive features, and behavioral/emotional adjustment all playing key facilitative roles in children developing positive orientations toward learning. Children's beliefs in themselves as capable learners, their skills in working with teachers and peers in prosocial ways, their ability to stay focused and on task, and their capacity to maintain emotional and behavioral self-control may offer important advantages in learning. We will not know the relative importance of these abilities if we do not collect the data. Thus, we urge that the twin foci on both learning and socioemotional outcomes be maintained in all Head Start evaluation and research efforts.

3. Third, we recommend that current teacher-rated assessments of emotional and social development be continued. But we also recommend that better methods and measures be used to provide more direct assessments. The task is possible. Emotionally and behaviorally oriented direct assessments were developed and successfully implemented in the national evaluation of Early Head Start that included thousands of toddlers. Researchers have adequate empirical background on which to develop a comprehensive battery, through "consensus conference" on what measures provide most specificity and predictive validity on measurable change in children's emotional and behavioral adjustment. In short, researchers could standardize and validate a short set of age-appropriate measures that could be included in future years of Head Start assessments. Without such direct measurements, children's emotional and behavioral development will always be more vaguely defined and less vigorously measured than their cognitive development.

# POSTSCRIPT

## Does Emphasizing Academic Skills Help At-Risk Preschool Children?

The subtext of both of these readings is that after 40 years of intense effort at breaking cycles of poverty by intervening with young children, huge gaps remain. The children who attended the early years of Head Start have generally faired little better than other children from poor families who face lifelong challenges when trying to climb the socioeconomic ladder. Why?

Both of these readings seem to largely accept that early intervention is important, but they differ on how early intervention should look. Perhaps, some have suggested, we need to intervene even earlier. There is, in fact, a program for "early Head Start" to try and facilitate the development of children even before preschool age. Perhaps, the Bush administrations suggests, we need to shift the focus of early intervention to emphasize specific and measurable cognitive skills. These programs are now in place, and Head Start children undergo twice yearly testing on their pre-math and pre-literacy skills. Perhaps, the traditional Head Start proponents have suggested, we just need to make sure that the model designed by developmental psychologists (with an understanding that different aspects of development overlap) has better implementation. Most do agree that better qualified teachers and the availability of quality resources (including nutrition and health services) make a difference for children.

Is it possible, however, that early intervention alone is simply not enough? Head Start has been a popular program despite its limited empirical support partially because it is hard to look in the innocent eyes of a three- or four-year-old child and feel like that child does not deserve a chance. And certainly, we know that early childhood is a crucial developmental stage. But is it *the* crucial stage? Is it reasonable to expect that simple intervention during early childhood will produce a lifetime of change?

In addition to the larger developmental question about early intervention, there is also a question about the interaction of various developmental domains: the cognitive, the social, the emotional, the physical, etc. Is development best facilitated by considering these diverse domains as they relate to each other? Or can we pick specific domains that are more important toward specific ends? Can we isolate cognitive development as the single key for interventions leading to later success?

The U.S. government takes the latter position, stressing that cognitive testing is the only sure way to insure children from poor families get a reasonable chance. The government also notes that most parents agree, identifying academic skills as their priority for preschool. C. Cybele Raver and Edward F. Zigler take the former position, asserting that different aspects of

173

development overlap and only together do they allow children to thrive. Why does government and popular opinion contrast so sharply with the opinion of scholars and academics? Does considering all the various aspects of development simply muddy the waters—overwhelming basic needs during early childhood? Is it possible that good intentions have done nothing more than overcomplicate early childhood development?

## Suggested Readings

S. Barnett and J. Huestedt, "Head Start's Lasting Benefits," *Infants & Young Children* (January–March 2005).

C. Bordignon and T. Lam, "The Early Assessment Conundrum: Lessons from the Past, Implications for the Future," *Psychology in the Schools* (September 2004).

R. Fewell, "Assessment of Young Children with Special Needs: Foundations for Tomorrow," *Topics in Early Childhood Special Education* (2000).

K. Keafer, "A Head Start for Poor Children?" *Backgrounder* (May 4, 2004).

S. Meisels, "Testing Culture Invades Lives of Young Children," *FairTest Examiner* (Spring 2005).

J. Neisworth and S. Bagnato, "The Case Against Intelligence Testing in Early Intervention," *Topics in Early Childhood Special Education* (Spring 1992).

J. Neisworth and S. Bagnato, "The Mismeasure of Young Children: The Authentic Assessment Alternative," *Infants and Young Children* (2004).

S. Olfman, "All Work and No Play: How Educational Reforms Are Hurting Our Preschoolers," *Rethinking Schools Online* (Winter 2004/2005).

A. Papero, "Is Early, High-Quality Daycare an Asset for the Children of Low-Income, Depressed Mother," *Developmental Review* (2005).

R. Stahlman, "Standardized Tests: A Teacher's Perspective," *Childhood Education* (Summer 2005).

P. Williamson, E. Bondy, L. Langley, and D. Mayne, "Meeting the Challenge of High-Stakes Testing While Remaining Child-Centered," *Childhood Education* (Summer 2005).

## Character and Education

The character and education partnership is a coalition trying to promote character education as a way of shaping children to be good citizens.

http://www.character.org/

## Partnership for Learning

This group produces publications focused on successful child development.

http://www.partnershipforlearning.org/

## Attention Deficit Disorder Association

Official site for the Attention Deficit Disorder Association, which is one of the largest international clearinghouses of information about AD/HD.

http://www.add.org/

## National Association for Self-Esteem

The National Association for Self-Esteem is an organization promoting the value of self-esteem for society in general.

http://www.self-esteem-nase.org/

## Self-Esteem

This page is an entry in a psychology-oriented encyclopedia. It lays out some of the research controversy regarding the value of self-esteem.

http://www.enpsychlopedia.com/psypsych/
Self-esteem

# PART 5

# Middle Childhood

*M*iddle childhood generally refers to the early school years, between the ages of 5 or 6 to 11 or 12. During this period, most children experience a change in their social world, moving from a world of family to a world of peers, school, and activities outside the home. Children during these ages also begin to develop complex abstract thinking. This leads to intense social comparison and to an improved recognition of rules in one's society and community. The two issues in this section deal with self-esteem and behavior regulation, which are two implications of these changing points of focus during middle childhood.

- Has Promoting Self-Esteem Failed to Improve the Education of School-Age Children?

- Is Attention Deficit Disorder (ADD/ADHD) a Legitimate Medical Condition That Affects Childhood Behavior?

# ISSUE 10

## Has Promoting Self-Esteem Failed to Improve the Education of School-Age Children?

**YES: Roy F. Baumeister, Jennifer D. Campbell, Joachim I. Krueger, and Kathleen D. Vohs,** from "Does High Self-Esteem Cause Better Performance, Interpersonal Success, Happiness, or Healthier Lifestyles?" *Psychological Science in the Public Interest* (May 2003)

**NO: Neil Humphrey,** from "The Death of the Feel-Good Factor? Self-Esteem in the Educational Context," *School Psychology International* (vol. 25, 2004)

### ISSUE SUMMARY

**YES:** Social psychologist Roy F. Baumeister and his colleagues engaged in an extensive review of research on the popular idea that self-esteem produces academic achievement and conclude that it does nothing of the sort.

**NO:** Educational psychologist Neil Humphrey asserts that reviews concluding self-esteem does not contribute to achievement are not definitive because they ignore the contextual nature of self-esteem and its importance in creating a generally healthy learning environment.

$\mathbf{S}$elf-esteem feels good. It is pleasant to offer praise, and to be able to evaluate oneself positively. Because that simple idea is beyond dispute, it is often surprising to learn that the implications of self-esteem for development have become intensely debated. While promoting self-esteem as a benefit to many aspects of child development has been a popular endeavor, years of accumulated research evidence has begun to raise important questions about the exact role feeling good about oneself plays in growing up.

Self-esteem has become such a popular concept in recent decades that many commentators have come to refer to the "self-esteem movement" as a prominent historical phenomenon. The increasing profile of self-esteem came along with an increasingly popular profile for the role of psychology in contemporary life. The relative affluence and high levels of education in post–World War II North America accompanied a trend toward abstract concerns like self-reflection and self-actualization. Self-esteem fit perfectly with the shifting socio-cultural milieu: The idea of feeling good about oneself as a foundation for success meshed with feelings of empowerment allowing one to live one's life and pursue happiness.

This attitude took particular hold among parents and child development experts who proclaimed self-esteem to be the key concern of childhood. The idea was that children should be praised and reinforced constantly as a way of producing happy, eager, and productive youth. Likewise, these attitudes were accompanied by a sense that problems and social ills were caused by low self-esteem and an absence of feeling worthy. This may have reached its apex in the 1980s when the California state legislature put together a commission using tax payer dollars to promote self-esteem with the intention of facilitating the development of a generation of youth.

The California commission to promote self-esteem has become frequently cited—and mocked—by scholars who have collected evidence from years of self-esteem research. In general, the huge volume of research on self-esteem has found limited effects that do not match the popular claims of the self-esteem movement. Most researchers now agree that if self-esteem has a positive impact on development, it is indirect and likely somewhat small. Among some academics, opinion has even gone to the opposite end of the spectrum, arguing that self-esteem has actually caused developmental problems by creating a generation of youth that has been indulged regardless of their achievements.

In response to this ongoing controversy, prominent social psychologist and self-esteem researcher Roy F. Baumeister and his colleagues engaged in an extensive evaluation of what research tells us about self-esteem. While their review deals with a variety of popular ideas about self-esteem (such as its role in mental health and interpersonal success), they note that ideas about the positive impact of self-esteem have been particularly influential in relation to school and education. Many teachers, parents, and administrators have taken for granted that high self-esteem produces improved performance for school-age children. Baumeister and colleagues find virtually no research support for this position, and assert that the relationship between school performance and self-esteem is much more a popular myth than an empirical reality.

In response, Neil Humphrey, a professor who works on educational support and inclusion, acknowledges that the direct effects of self-esteem do not generally show up in research studies, but suggests there are still reasons to promote self-esteem as a facilitator of education. He notes several challenges in accurately assessing the role of self-esteem, and argues that the indirect effects of self-esteem in creating a generally positive learning environment warrant continuing attention.

Roy F. Baumeister et al.  **YES**

# Does High Self-Esteem Cause Better Performance, Interpersonal Success, Happiness, or Healthier Lifestyles?

**M**ost people feel that self-esteem is important. It is difficult, if not impossible, for people to remain indifferent to information that bears on their own self-esteem, such as being told that they are incompetent, attractive, untrustworthy, or lovable. Increases and decreases in self-esteem generally brings strong emotional reactions. Moreover, these fluctuations are often coincident with major successes and failures in life. Subjective experience creates the impression that self-esteem rises when one wins a contest, garners an award, solves a problem, or gains acceptance to a social group, and that it falls with corresponding failures. This pervasive correlation may well strengthen the impression that one's level of self-esteem is not just the outcome, but indeed the cause, of life's major successes and failures.

But is self-esteem a cause of important consequences in life? In this monograph, we report the results of a survey of major research findings bearing on this question. Our mission was to conduct a thorough review of empirical findings—emphasizing the most methodologically rigorous research studies—to ascertain whether high self-esteem is in fact a cause of positive or negative outcomes. We anticipated we would find that self-esteem has positive value for bringing about some hypothesized benefits, but not others. Such a pattern would presumably allow an accurate and nuanced understanding of just what high self-esteem is good for. This would be beneficial both for theory (in that it would promote a better understanding of self-esteem as well as the outcomes it predicts) and for practical applications—and even for determining whether efforts at boosting self-esteem are worth undertaking in order to solve particular social problems.

Self-esteem is literally defined by how much value people place on themselves. It is the evaluative component of self-knowledge. High self-esteem refers to a highly favorable global evaluation of the self. Low self-esteem, by definition, refers to an unfavorable definition of the self. (Whether this signifies an absolutely unfavorable or relatively unfavorable evaluation is a problematic distinction, which we discuss later in connection with the distribution of

From *Psychological Science*, vol. 4, no. 1, May 2003, pp. 1–5, 10–14, 38–39. Copyright © 2003 by Blackwell Publishing, Ltd. Reprinted by permission.

self-esteem scores.) Self-esteem does not carry any definitional requirement of accuracy whatsoever. Thus, high self-esteem may refer to an accurate, justified, balanced appreciation of one's worth as a person and one's successes and competencies, but it can also refer to an inflated, arrogant, grandiose, unwarranted sense of conceited superiority over others. By the same token, low self-esteem can be either an accurate, well-founded understanding of one's shortcomings as a person or a distorted, even pathological sense of insecurity and inferiority.

Self-esteem is thus perception rather than reality. It refers to a person's belief about whether he or she is intelligent and attractive, for example, and it does not necessarily say anything about whether the person actually is intelligent and attractive. To show that self-esteem is itself important, then, research would have to demonstrate that people's beliefs about themselves have important consequences regardless of what the underlying realities are. Put more simply, there would have to be benefits that derive from believing that one is intelligent, regardless of whether one actually is intelligent. To say this is not to dismiss self-esteem as trivial. People's beliefs shape their actions in many important ways, and these actions in turn shape their social reality and the social realities of the people around them. The classic study *Pygmalion in the Classroom,* by Rosenthal and Jacobson, showed that teachers' false, unfounded beliefs about their students later became objective, verifiable realities in the performance of those students. In the same way, it is quite plausible that either high or low self-esteem, even if initially false, may generate a self-fulfilling prophecy and bring about changes in the objective reality of the self and its world.

Then again, self-esteem might not bring about such changes. Many researchers, clinicians, teachers, parents, and pundits have taken it as an article of faith that high self-esteem will bring about positive outcomes. Such an assumption was perhaps reasonable several decades ago, given the lack of firm data either way and the anecdotal impression and theoretical bases for assuming that self-esteem has strong effects. It is particularly understandable that practitioners would accept this assumption without proof, because they cannot generally afford to admonish their suffering clients to hang on for a few decades until needed research is conducted. They must use the best evidence available at the time to design their interventions.

By now, however, the excuse of inadequate data is beginning to wear thin. The fascination with self-esteem that began to spread during the 1970s infected researchers too, and in the past couple of decades, a number of methodologically rigorous, large-scale investigations on the possible effects of self-esteem have been conducted. We do not think all the final answers are in, but many of them are taking shape. There is no longer any justification for simply relying on anecdotes, impressions, and untested assumptions about the value of self-esteem.

## Why Study Self-Esteem?

In the heady days of the 1970s, it might have seemed possible to assert that self-esteem has a causal effect on every aspect of human life, and by the 1980s, the California legislature might well have been persuaded that funding a task force to increase the self-esteem of Californians would ultimately produce a huge financial return because reducing welfare dependency, unwanted pregnancy, school failure, crime, drug addiction, and other problems would save large amounts of taxpayers' money. However, as Karl Marx, Sigmund Freud, and other grand thinkers could assert if they were alive today, even the most elaborate and persuasive theories about human behavior do not generally receive empirical support in all aspects. Thus, we note at the outset that we did not expect all the extravagant claims of the self-esteem movement to be supported.

Even if the self-esteem movement was wrong in crucial respects, its positive aspects and contributions deserve to be recognized and celebrated. The self-esteem movement showed that the American public was willing to listen to psychologists and to change its institutional practices on the basis of what psychology had to teach. It would not be in psychology's best interest to chastise the American public for accepting the advice of psychologists. If errors were committed, perhaps psychologists should reduce their own self-esteem a bit and humbly resolve that next time they will wait for a more thorough and solid empirical basis before making policy recommendations to the American public. Regardless of the outcome of the self-esteem movement, it showed that there is a voice for psychology in public policy and discourse. If psychology uses that voice judiciously, it may still be able to make a major contribution to the well-being of society.

## The Appeal of Self-Esteem

As self-aware and self-reflective creatures, many people intuitively recognize the importance of self-esteem. Not surprisingly, a great deal of psychological theorizing has focused on the motivation to protect and, if possible, enhance self-esteem. Research is showing that even psychodynamic defense mechanisms, which Freud originally understood as ways of keeping threatening sexual and aggressive impulses at bay, serve as strategies to bolster self-esteem.

But the desire to feel good about oneself is certainly not the only self-related motive at play. Having to cope with reality, people are also motivated to perceive themselves accurately and admit awareness of their undesirable characteristic. Nevertheless, people would rather learn positive things about themselves than negative things. Although they may want to know whether they are good or not, they much prefer to learn that they are good.

Over the past few decades, the need for high self-esteem has risen from an individual to a societal concern. North American society in particular has come to embrace the idea that high self-esteem is not only desirable in its own right, but also the central psychological source from which all manner of positive behaviors and outcomes spring. This strong psychological claim has begun to permeate popular beliefs. Its corollary, the idea that low self-esteem lies at the root of individual and thus societal problems and dysfunctions, has obvious implications for interventions on both the individual and the societal level. The hope that such interventions might work has sustained an ambitious social movement. Nathaniel Branden, a leading figure in the self-esteem movement, stated categorically that "self-esteem has profound consequences for every aspect of our existence," and, more pointedly, that he "cannot think of a single psychological problem—from anxiety and depression, to fear of intimacy or of success, to spouse battery or child molestation—that is not traceable to the problem of low self-esteem." Other advocates of the movement have endorsed this sentiment. Andrew Mecca, for example, is cited as saying that "virtually every social problem can be traced to people's lack of self-love."

Academic and professional psychologists have been more hesitant to endorse strong categorical claims. Eminent clinical psychologist Albert Ellis, for example, is convinced that "self-esteem is the greatest sickness known to man or woman because it's conditional." According to Ellis, people would be better off if they stopped trying to convince themselves that they are worthy. Others believe that concerns about self-esteem are a peculiar feature of Western individualist cultures. According to this perspective, the search for high self-esteem is not a universal human motive, but a cultural or ideological artifact. Indeed, such a motive is difficult to detect in collectivist cultures, and especially in Japan. Even in Western culture, the need for high self-esteem seems to be a rather recent development. The Judeo-Christian tradition has long considered modesty and humility as virtues conducive to spiritual growth. In this tradition, high self-esteem is suspect because it opens the door to sentiments of self-importance. Medieval theologians considered pride or vainglory to be particularly satanic and thus a deadly sin. To combat it, religious devotees cultivated an unattractive appearance (e.g., shorn hair, no makeup, unfashionable clothes, no jewelry), spoke with self-effacement, and submitted to degrading exercises (e.g., begging, prostrations, self-flagellations).

Such practices are but a faint memory in contemporary popular culture, in which high self-esteem seems to reign supreme. Prodded by Assemblyman John Vasconcellos, the then governor of California George Deukmeijian agreed in 1986 to fund a Task Force on Self-Esteem and Personal and Social Responsibility with a budget of $245,000 per annum for several years. Vasconcellos argued that raising self-esteem would help solve many of the state's problems, including crime, teen pregnancy, drug abuse, school underachievement, and pollution. At one point he expressed the hope that raising self-esteem would help balance the state's budget because people with high self-esteem earn more money than people with low self-esteem and therefore pay more taxes. It is easy to dismiss and satirize such claims. However, Vasconcellos and the task force also speculated astutely about the possibility that self-esteem might protect people from being overwhelmed by life's challenges and thus reduce failures and misbehaviors, much as a vaccine protects against disease.

Concurrent with its activities in the field, which included creating self-esteem committees in many California counties, the task force assembled a team of scholars to survey the relevant literature. The results were presented in an edited volume. Echoing Branden, Smelser prefaced the report by stating that "many, if not most, of the major problems plaguing society have roots in the low self-esteem of many of the people who make up society." But the findings did not validate the high hopes of the task force, and Smelser had to acknowledge that "one of the disappointing aspects of *every* [italics added] chapter in this volume . . . is how low the associations between self-esteem and its [presumed] consequences are in research to date." Given that the correlations were so low, the question of whether low self-esteem in fact caused the societal problems did not even arise.

The lack of supportive data created a dilemma. Should a notion as attractive as self-esteem be abandoned and replaced with more promising concepts, or should the validity of the evidence be questioned? The editors and the authors opted for a mix of these two strategies. Some re- treated to a defense of self-esteem on a priori grounds. Undeterred, Smelser maintained that

> diminished self-esteem stands as a powerful *independent variable* (condition, cause, factor) in the genesis of major social problems. We all know this to be true, and it is really not necessary to create a special California task force on the subject to convince us. The real problem we must address—and which the contributors to this volume address—is how we can determine that it is scientifically true.

Others, however, acknowledged the limitations of the findings and called for additional study, or tried to fit more complex theoretical models of self-knowledge to the data. Our report is focused primarily on studies conducted since the review by the California task force. Instead of examining the merits of the more complex models of self, we have retained the hypothesis that global self-esteem causes desirable, adaptive, and beneficial behaviors. There is a certain beauty to this hypothesis because it is simple, clear, and testable. There have also been sufficient methodological advances in study design and statistical analysis that warrant a fresh look at the evidence.

Meanwhile, the self-esteem movement was not deterred by the disappointing findings of the task force. After it was disbanded in 1995, the National Council for Self-Esteem inherited its mandate, which was subsequently taken on by the National Association for Self-Esteem, or NASE. Vasconcellos (now a member of the California Senate) and Jack Canfield (*Chicken Soup for the Soul*) are on NASE's advisory board, and such media personalities as Anthony Robbins (*Unlimited Power*), Bernie Siegel (*Love, Medicine, and Miracles*), and Gloria Steinem (*A Revolution From Within: A Book of Self-Esteem*) are members of a "Masters Coalition," created by NASE. The mission statement of NASE minces no words about the presumed benefits of self-esteem. Its goal is to "promote awareness of and provide vision, leadership and advocacy for improving the human condition through the enhancement of self-esteem." The goal of the Masters Coalition is no less ambitious. "It is hoped that the Master Coalition can, in a meaningful way, facilitate the actualization of society and lead to the amelioration, if not elimination, of various negative influences which have operated in part to trivialize and demean the human condition."

It is hard not to conclude that the self-esteem movement has ignored its own major scholarly document. In the quest for enhanced self-esteem, any tool in the psychological—and pseudopsychological—box is thrown into the fray, including

> disparate psychological models that have given rise to such popular notions as the "inner child"; the "self-image"; principles of proper griev- ing; "super learning"; "community networking"; "relaxation techniques" and their effects on overall mental and physical well-being; the principles of "neuro-linguistic programming"; and the well-founded scientific basis for the connection between the body and the mind and the effect of this interface on overall wellness.

Even a contributor to the volume edited by Mecca et al. (1989) argued that self-esteem must be enhanced, although its causal role is far from established. "To abandon the search for esteem-related solutions . . . is to admit defeat before exploring all our options."

Was it reasonable to start boosting self-esteem before all the data were in? Perhaps. We recognize that many practitioners and applied psychologists must deal with problems before all the relevant research can be conducted. Still, by now there are ample data on self-esteem. Our task in this monograph is to take a fresh look and provide an integrative summary.

## An Epidemic of Low Self-Esteem?

A key assumption of the self-esteem movement is that too many people have low self-esteem. Under this assumption, raising self-esteem becomes a mean- ingful goal. But what does "too many" mean? Self-esteem scales are designed to capture valid individual differences that exist in a population. Thus, a good measure will yield a distribution of scores from low to high. However, unlike some other measurement instruments, such as IQ tests, that are con- structed to yield symmetrical distributions centered around an arbitrary mean (e.g., 100), self-esteem scales allow skewed distributions to emerge. The average score typically lies far above the midpoint of the scale, often by more than a standard deviation (Baumeister, Tice, & Hutton, 1989). The fact that most people score toward the high end of self-esteem measures casts serious doubt on the notion that American society is suffering from widespread low self-esteem. If anything, self-esteem in America is high. The average person regards himself or herself as above average.

The skewed distribution of self-esteem scores raises two methodologi- cal issues. First, when researchers split samples at the median to distinguish between respondents with high versus low self-esteem, the range of scores among respondents classified as having low self-esteem is much greater than the range of scores among respondents classified as having high self-esteem. A good number of respondents in the low self-esteem category have scores above the midpoint of the scale. In other words, the classification of a person as someone with low self-esteem has no longer an absolute, but only a relative meaning. Second, correlations involving variables with skewed distributions tend to be smaller than correlations involving variables with symmetric distri- butions. Moreover, when self-esteem is raised selectively for those respondents with the lowest initial values, correlations between self-esteem and relevant outcome variables shrink further, not necessarily because the elevation of self-esteem had the desired causal effect, but simply because of the restriction in the range of scores. It is always necessary to ask whether relevant outcomes also changed in the desired direction.

The standard finding that most self-esteem scores are high raises the possibility that at least some scores are affected by deliberate or unwitting self-enhancement. Brown, for example, found that people high in self-esteem were also most likely to rate themselves more positively than they rated other people. Because self-enhancement may involve invalid and undesirable distortions of the self-concept, it is unwarranted to rush to boost everyone's self-esteem.

In short, we find no evidence that modern Western societies are suffering from an epidemic of low self-esteem. If anything, self-esteem seems generally high in most North American samples. Regardless of their race, gender, or socioeconomic status, Americans already appear to live in a "culture of self-worth." Indeed, levels of self-esteem increased at a time when the self-esteem movement bemoaned the lack of self-love. Disturbingly, academic performance decreased at the same time. . . .

# School Performance

The self-esteem movement has been especially influential in American schools, and part of the reason for this is the assumption that raising self-esteem will lead to improvements in children's academic performance. There are plausible reasons for thinking that high self-esteem will lead to good schoolwork. People with high self-esteem may set higher aspirations than people with low self-esteem. They may be more willing to persist in the face of initial failure and less likely to succumb to paralyzing feelings of incompetence and self-doubt. Learning, by definition, involves acquiring information and skills that one does not initially have, and high self-esteem may help prevent the recognition of one's initial incapability from producing a sense that the cause is hopeless. High self-esteem may foster the confidence to tackle difficult problems and enable people to derive satisfaction from progress and success.

## Correlational Findings

Many studies have found that self-esteem is positively correlated with academic performance. In an early review, Wylie concluded that the correlation between self-esteem and students' grade point averages was about .30. She added that similar or slightly stronger relationships had been reported between self-esteem and scores on various achievement tests. Creativity, however, was not consistently related to any form of self-regard.

The most definitive compilation was Hansford and Hattie's meta-analysis of 128 studies involving more than 200,000 participants. These studies explored a variety of measures of self-regard (mostly self-esteem) and a variety of objective performance measures, most of which were achievement tests. The correlations reported varied widely, from –.77 to +.96, and averaged between +.21 and +.26 (depending on how the average was computed, how studies were weighted, etc.).

Hansford and Hattie concluded that overall there is a significant positive relationship between self-esteem and academic performance, with self-esteem accounting for between 4 and 7% of the variance in academic performance.

More recent studies have yielded similar conclusions. Using standard achievement tests, Davies and Brember found significant though weak positive relationships between self-esteem and academic performance in a large ($N = 3,001$) British sample. The correlations ranged from .10 to .13, and averaged .12. A somewhat stronger relationship was found by Bowles (1999), who showed that self-esteem correlated at .29 with students' most recent semester grades in mathematics and English. Kugle, Clements, and Powell found that scores on a reading achievement test correlated .18 with level of self-esteem. However, when these authors controlled for ethnicity, the effect of self-esteem was no longer significant. Thus, these recent studies also indicate that self-esteem goes with doing well in school, although the relationship is weaker than one might have expected in a society that values doing well in school.

As already noted, people with high self-esteem report their intelligence to be high, although there is no relationship between self-esteem and scores on objective IQ tests. Simon and Simon found scores on self-esteem to be correlated significantly ($r = .33$) with scores on academic achievement tests and also with IQ test scores (thus contradicting the null result obtained by Gabriel et al.). In general, though, there is very little evidence that self-esteem correlates with IQ or other academic abilities.

Self-esteem also predicts performance in minority and at-risk samples. Ortiz and Volloff found significant correlations between self-esteem and tests of IQ and school abilities, using a limited sample of Hispanic students in grades 3 to 6 who had been nominated for testing as candidates for gifted classes. Howerton, Enger, and Cobbs studied at-risk Black male students, and found that self-esteem predicted grades and school achievement. Although Howerton et al. used objective measures (school records) of achievement, a drawback of the study is that the sample was very small ($N = 42$).

Different authors have drawn very different conclusions from correlations between self-esteem and school performance. Among the most optimistic was that of Zimmerman, Copeland, Shope, and Dielman: "Efforts either to prevent and stabilize decreasing self-esteem or to build self-esteem may have vital effects on . . . outcomes for youth." In their own study, Zimmerman et al. measured performance by asking students for general ratings of their grades (e.g., "Are your grades mostly A's, mostly A's and B's . . . ?"), so their results were vulnerable to subjective bias. In addition, the correlations with self-esteem were very weak. Their results do not seem to support their confidence that high self-esteem leads to better grades.

Other authors have inferred that significant correlations between self-esteem and school performance support the opposite causal conclusion, namely, that good work in school leads to high self-esteem. Bowles specifically measured self-esteem after the semester for which he obtained school grades, so the positive correlation he found seems most consistent with the view that self-esteem is a result, not a cause, of doing well in school. This conclusion was further supported by path analysis (a statistical technique for testing theories about complex chains of causes), which indicated that there was no direct causal path from self-esteem to achievement.

Still other researchers have concluded that the correlations between self-esteem and school performance, albeit significant, are so small as to be not worth pursuing. Rubin, Dorle, and Sandidge found that self-esteem was significantly correlated with all their measures of achievement, as well as with teachers' ratings of students' behavior and performance. Yet statistical analysis showed that taking self-esteem into account barely improved the accuracy of predictions of achievement that were based on socioeconomic status and intelligence (IQ) alone. Rubin et al. wrote, "While these increases were significant, their practical significance is negligible," and they concluded that the links between self-esteem and academic performance are based on "common underlying factors such as ability and background."

These and other findings generally point to a positive but weak and ambiguous relationship between self-esteem and school performance. Students with high self-esteem generally have done somewhat better in school and on school achievement tests than students with low self-esteem. The correlational findings do not indicate whether self-esteem is a cause or a result of school performance. They do, however, furnish one possible explanation for the continuing belief that self-esteem may be beneficial for school performance. Teachers, parents, and others may observe that high self-esteem and good school performance go together and infer that self-esteem plays a causal role. Unfortunately, impressions—even when backed up by significant correlations—do not justify causal conclusions. We now turn to studies that have investigated whether there is a causal relationship between self-esteem and academic performance.

## Investigating Causality

Several studies have investigated the time course of the positive relation between self-esteem and academic performance, as a way of establishing causal priority. Some of these studies have also investigated whether third variables, such as socioeconomic status or intelligence (IQ), could be responsible for the correlations between self-esteem and academic performance.

An early and still well respected study by Bachman and O'Malley used data from a nationwide longitudinal study that tracked more than 1,600 young men from 1966, when they were in 10th grade, up through 1974. All participants in this study completed a modified version of the Rosenberg self-esteem scale at several points during this period. Although Bachman and O'Malley found that self-esteem correlated with school performance, their more sophisticated statistical tests (i.e., path analyses) did not point to any causal role for self-esteem. Instead, they concluded that shared prior causes, including family background, ability, and early school performance, affect self-esteem and later educational attainment and were responsible for the correlation between the two. They also concluded that occupational success caused self-esteem to rise, whereas obtaining higher education had a negligible impact on self-esteem. Of all their findings, the one that gives the most credence to the view that self-esteem is an important cause of successful outcomes is that self-esteem in high school predicted eventual level of educational attainment (final degree earned), but in their path analysis the direct link from high school self-esteem to later educational attainment was only .072. Its link to eventual occupational status was similar, at .061. These numbers indicate that the relationship is extremely weak, if it exists at all. Neither link was significant.

The findings of Bachman and O'Malley are important for several reasons. First, these researchers were perhaps the first to conduct such a thorough and sophisticated study of the impact of self-esteem. Second, they plainly had hoped to find that self-esteem played a causal role, and they favored this hypothesis in their initial exposition. Indeed, they proposed that high self-esteem fosters high aspirations and persistence, which lead ultimately to better academic performance and career success. Third, most subsequent work has generally confirmed their conclusions that self-esteem is a result rather than a cause, and that any correlations between self-esteem and achievement are likely to be due to third variables such as family background.

Another milestone study was conducted by Maruyama, Rubin, and Kingsbury. This research is an important complement to Bachman and O'Malley's study because it focused on a much younger age: Maruyama et al. followed a final sample of more than 700 students from age 4 to age 15. Achievement was measured using academic achievement tests, including the Stanford Achievement Test and, later, the Wide Range Achievement Test, which emphasizes spelling, vocabulary, and arithmetic. Like Bachman and O'Malley, Maruyama et al. found that self-esteem and academic achievement are correlated, but concluded that there is no causal relationship between those variables. Instead, they argued that ability (IQ) and social class are the underlying causal factors that affect the levels of both self-esteem and academic achievement.

A follow-up by Bachman and O'Malley confirmed their previous findings. In this follow-up, they sought to improve their methodological rigor in several ways. One of these was to confine analyses to White males in White-majority schools. Although the exclusion of minorities is not considered methodologically desirable today, Bachman and O'Malley had quite persuasive reasons for deciding that such inclusion might have weakened the chance for self-esteem to emerge as causally significant. Specifically, in their original sample, African American students scored lower than White students on achievement and ability tests but higher on self-esteem. Combining data from White and African American students could therefore obscure a positive relationship between self-esteem and achievement. The authors also acknowledged that the low achievement scores of African American students might indicate some lack of validity of those measures for such a sample. Any lack of validity would make self-esteem look less effective than it actually is.

Despite their effort to increase the potential for their study to demonstrate effects of self-esteem, Bachman and O'Malley found that global self-esteem had a negligible relationship to eventual educational attainment. Family background (socioeconomic status), ability (IQ), and early school grades predicted eventual level of educational attainment, and self-esteem added little to the accuracy of prediction. Self-esteem was correlated with actual ability, although self-rated ability was consistently inflated: People thought they were smarter than they actual were. In short, these findings support the role of illusion in self-esteem, but they contradict the view that self-esteem causes long-term educational success.

An article titled "Is There a Causal Relation Between Self-Concept and Academic Achievement?" was published by Pottebaum, Keith, and Ehly. Their answer was a rather blunt negative: "The results suggest that there is no significant causal relation between self-concept and academic achievement [in either direction], but rather that the observed relation is the result of one or more uncontrolled and unknown third variables." A great deal of methodologically sophisticated work went into producing that conclusion. Pottebaum et al. used a sophisticated research design, testing a very large sample of high school students (more than 23,000) in the 10th grade and again in the 12th grade. Self-esteem in 10th grade predicted academic achievement in 12th grade quite weakly ($r = .11$). Conversely, academic achievement in 10th grade predicted self-esteem in 12th grade only trivially better ($r = .12$). The authors noted that a reciprocal causal relationship between self-esteem and academic performance could produce the pattern of findings they obtained—but only if the two variables cause each other with about the same amount of power, which seemed a priori implausible. Hence, Pottebaum et al. concluded it is more likely that self-esteem and academic performance are both the result of a third variable (or set of variables). This conclusion is clearly consistent with what Bachman and O'Malley and Maruyama et al. found, despite different methods and somewhat different numerical results.

A slightly different conclusion was reached by Rosenberg, Schooler, and Schoenbach. They analyzed data from the Youth in Transition longitudinal study that was also the basis for Bachman and O'Malley's work. They used the 10th- and 12th-grade data for nearly 1,900 boys, including measurements of achievement that relied on having the students report their grade point average in school. This sort of measure is in the middle of the span of methodological rigor that we have outlined: It is not fully objective, but it is somewhat specific and verifiable. A slight tendency of people with high self-esteem to furnish self-flattering reports is to be expected, although the scope for such inflation may be more limited than if respondents are asked a general self-rating question, such as "How good are you at school?"

Rosenberg et al. did find significantly positive, although weak, correlations between self-esteem and self-reported grades, $r = .24$ in 10th grade and $r = .25$ in 12th grade. Of greater interest were the findings across time. These supported the conclusion that self-esteem is the result of grades, rather than the cause. There was a modest causal relationship (.15) leading from grades to self-esteem, but the causal relationship leading from self-esteem to grades was only .08, which was not significantly different from zero. In other words, there was no solid evidence that self-esteem had any effect on grades, despite the fact that even a weak relationship would likely have been significant because Rosenberg et al. tested so many people.

The view that self-esteem is an outcome rather than a cause of good school performance was further supported in another large and sophisticated study, by Skaalvik and Hagtvet. Their sample consisted of 600 Norwegian schoolchildren in two cohorts, one in third grade (about age 9) and the other in sixth grade at the start of the study. A second set of data was obtained a year and a half later. Achievement was measured by teachers' ratings, which furnish a good measure although erroneous perceptions by the teacher could affect a student's self-esteem (e.g., if the teacher treats the student as a genius or dullard). Skaalvik and Hagtvet found evidence that doing well in school one year led to higher self-esteem the next year, whereas high self-esteem did not lead to performing well in school. In fact, high global self-esteem in grade 6 predicted lower academic achievement in grade 7.

Skaalvik and Hagtvet also measured students' self-concept of their academic ability. Although our focus is not on domain-specific measures of self-esteem in this review, the findings are of interest. These researchers concluded that self-concept of ability mediates the relation between academic performance and global self-esteem. Specifically, doing well in school leads to thinking of oneself as good at schoolwork, which in turn can boost global self-esteem. There was also some evidence for a causal influence of academic self-concept on school performance, which is thus one finding that suggests thinking well of oneself can lead to better schoolwork (although this relationship involves thinking of oneself as good at schoolwork rather than as good overall). This causal influence was found in some analyses but not others and was not strong. Still, the fact that it was demonstrated at all helps dispel worries that some kind of methodological or measurement problem renders it impossible to verify causal effects of self-concept. This in turn lends further credence to the conclusion that global self-esteem is not a cause of school performance.

## Interventions

We found relatively little evidence on how self-esteem programs or other interventions affect self-esteem. Such interventions are practiced in many schools and other places, but it is common for them to target not only self-esteem but also study skills, citizenship, conflict reduction, and other variables. Obviously, if a program that attempts to boost self-esteem and improve study skills ends up producing an improvement in grades, it is hardly safe to conclude that self-esteem is responsible for the improvement. Furthermore, given that the studies investigating causality have not demonstrated that self-esteem has an impact on academic achievement, it seems likely that any attempt to collect solid data on the impact of boosting self-esteem would end up with null results, and the evaluators would not be anxious to publish their results even if they could.

An impressive review of research on such programs was published by Scheirer and Kraut. The title, "Increased Educational Achievement via Self-Concept Change," sounds promising with respect to the benefits of self-esteem, but the findings were not. Scheirer and Kraut covered evidence from both published and unpublished evaluations of school-based interventions and programs, including Head Start, the Early Training Project, and Upward Bound. By and large, the evaluations of these studies "generally failed to find an association between self-concept change and academic achievement." When there was an association, it tended to be temporary (i.e., it was not maintained beyond the end of the program), or it indicated that self-esteem was the result of academic achievement rather than the cause. Programs that targeted factors other than self-esteem (such as by encouraging parents to become involved in their children's school-work) seemed to get better results.

Scheirer and Kraut carefully considered a variety of factors that could have led to the general pattern of null results, including poor measurement, methodological problems, and failure to implement interventions properly, among others. Yet as far as they could tell, these factors were not sufficient to explain the broad pattern of results. For example, they noted that some intervention that did not target self-esteem had produced measurable gains in academic performance. Hence they concluded that the most likely explanation of the disappointing results was that the basic theoretical hypothesis—namely, that improving self-esteem will lead to better academic performance—was wrong. They said that self-esteem may be an outcome of academic achievement, but it does not appear to be a cause or a mediating variable.

A nicely controlled field experiment by Forsyth and Kerr provided converging evidence using an adult (college student) sample. This investigation was conducted in connection with a regular course. Students who received a C, D, or F on the first examination were targeted to receive weekly e-mail messages from the professor. Each message contained a review question pertaining to that week's assignment. In the control condition, the review question was all that was included in the e-mail. Students who were randomly assigned to two other groups, however, received either a message aimed at boosting their sense of personal control and responsibility for their own performance or a message aimed at boosting and maintaining their positive sense of self-worth. These manipulations had no effect on the C students, but the D and F students who received the self-esteem boost performed significantly worse on subsequent tests than the D and F students in the other conditions.

Forsyth and Kerr's study is of interest because it involved full random assignment and because it found significant differences as a function of treatments aimed at self-esteem. Unfortunately for the self-esteem movement, the findings suggest that the intervention aimed at boosting self-esteem was counterproductive in its impact on academic performance. We have already noted some evidence linking high self-esteem to subsequently poorer performance, although the preponderance of findings suggests that self-esteem is positively linked to academic achievement. Still, Forsyth and Kerr used an intervention rather than simple measurement of current self-esteem, and they aimed their intervention specifically at low-performing students. Their results are consistent with the view that self-esteem is an important reinforcer for good academic performance and that supplying the reward indiscriminately (i.e., not linking it to good performance) may deflate its reward value. In plainer terms, students may ordinarily work hard in order to be permitted to feel good about themselves, and an intervention that encourages them to feel good about themselves regardless of work may remove the reason to work hard—resulting in poorer performance.

# Conclusion

The impact of self-esteem on school performance has been studied more carefully and thoroughly than any other outcome we discuss in this review. We were able to find studies that used longitudinal designs and other methods that can address causation, used objective methods rather than relying on self-report, and attempted to untangle self-esteem from other variables.

The results do not support the view that self-esteem has a strong causal effect on school achievement. Indeed, most of the evidence suggests that self-esteem has no impact on subsequent academic achievement. The few studies suggesting any positive causal impact of self-esteem generally found only tiny effects. Some findings even point (again weakly) in the opposite direction, suggesting that high or artificially boosted self-esteem may detract from subsequent performance.

There were in fact some reasons to hope that self-esteem would be more potent. On a theoretical basis, self-esteem seemed likely to enhance academic strivings and persistence. Early empirical findings may also have encouraged the belief that self-esteem is helpful, because simple correlations between self-esteem and academic performance have often been positive and significant. Unfortunately, those correlations appear to be due to processes other than self-esteem causing good performance. First, good performance in school may sometimes lead to higher self-esteem, instead of the reverse. (Even that tendency is disappointingly weak, however.) Second, self-esteem overlaps with other variables, and when these are controlled in the statistical analyses, the proportion of variance in performance accounted for by self-esteem dwindles rapidly. . . .

# Concluding Reflections

Our views on the merits of boosting self-esteem have gone through multiple changes, and were further revised during the process of compiling this review. We conclude by offering our current view, with frank acknowledgment that it should be regarded more as informed expert opinion than as an unassailable summary of proven facts.

In some ways, the grandfather of the self-esteem movement was Carl Rogers, who promoted the idea of "unconditional positive regard" as a way of helping children avoid the feeling that their parents might stop loving them if they failed to perform up to high standards. Sadly, over time unconditional positive regard has taken the form of suggesting that parents and teachers should never criticize children and indeed should praise children even for mediocre or trivial accomplishments, or just for being themselves. Always praising and never criticizing may feel good to everyone concerned, but the data we have reviewed do not show that such an approach will produce desirable outcomes.

We have already indicated what the data do show. They suggest that the benefits of high self-esteem are far fewer and weaker than proponents of self-esteem had hoped. Still, there are some benefits, and the costs to the individual do not outweigh them. The possible costs to society, such as from having some people regard themselves as superior to others and hence entitled to exploit their fellows or demand preferential treatment, may be another matter. Even so, these costs are associated with only particular subcategories of high self-esteem.

The heterogeneity of high self-esteem is central to our thinking, and it suggests that self-esteem per se is the wrong focus. There are many ways to think well of oneself, and some of these produce more desirable outcomes than others. Even such leaders of the self-esteem movement as Nathaniel Branden have begun to speak of the need for self-esteem to be linked in particular ways to other aspects of life (such as moral virtue or legitimate achievement). To them, perhaps, this strategy is a matter of cultivating genuine self-esteem instead of other forms. To us, all favorable views of self may be genuine self-esteem, and so self-esteem is inherently too broad a focus.

Thus, we recommend that instead of trying to find the right "kind" of self-esteem and perhaps dismissing other kinds as unreal, policymakers and practitioners should seek the right usage of self-esteem. High self-esteem feels good and fosters initiative. It may still prove a useful tool to promote success and virtue, but it should be clearly and explicitly linked to desirable behavior. After all, Hitler had very high self-esteem and plenty of initiative, too, but those were hardly guarantees of ethical behavior. He attracted followers by offering them self-esteem that was not tied to achievement or ethical behavior—rather, he told them that they were superior beings simply by virtue of being themselves, members of the so-called Master Race, an idea that undoubtedly had a broad, seductive appeal. We have found no data to indicate that indiscriminately promoting self-esteem in today's children or adults, just for being themselves, has any benefits beyond that seductive pleasure.

Hence, we think self-esteem should be used in a limited way as one of a cluster of factors to promote positive outcomes. It should not be an end in itself. Raising self-esteem will not by itself make young people perform better in school, obey the law, stay out of trouble, get along better with their fellows, or respect the rights of others, among many other desirable outcomes. However, it does seem appropriate to try to boost people's self-esteem as a reward for ethical behavior and worthy achievements. Although that may sound banal, we think it will require a basic change in many self-esteem programs, which now seek to boost everyone's self-esteem without demanding appropriate behavior first.

Using self-esteem as a reward rather than an entitlement seems most appropriate to us. To be sure, there may still be a place for unconditional positive regard, such as when a parent shows love for a child independent of achievement. But when achievement or virtue is involved, self-esteem should be conditional upon it. A favorable view of self should be promoted on the basis of performing well and behaving morally. By the same token, we think it appropriate and even essential to criticize harmful or unethical behavior and lazy or deficient performance, without worrying that someone's self-esteem might be reduced.

In particular, we think that success in modern society depends on lifelong learning and improvement—academically, socially, culturally, and occupationally.

We encourage linking self-esteem to learning and improvement. Learning is most effective when one receives both praise and criticism, contingent on current performance. The praise-only regimen of the self-esteem movement is ultimately no more effective for learning than the criticism-only regimen of the previous era (although praise-only may feel much more pleasant for all concerned). Praise that bolsters self-esteem in recognition of good performance can be a useful tool to facilitate learning and further improve performance in the future. Praising all the children just for being themselves, in contrast, simply devalues praise and confuses the young people as to what the legitimate standards are. In the long run, if such indiscriminate praise has any effect on self-esteem, it seems more likely to contribute to narcissism or other forms of inflated self-esteem than to the kind of self-esteem that will be best for the individual and for society.

A focus on improvement, in particular, allows people to compare themselves against themselves so that they do not have to boost themselves at the expense of others. Improvement strikes us as the ideal condition for boosting self-esteem: As the person performs or behaves better, self-esteem is encouraged to rise, and the net effect will be to reinforce both good behavior and improvement. Those outcomes are conducive to both the happiness of the individual and the betterment of society.

**Neil Humphrey**

 **NO**

# The Death of the Feel-Good Factor? Self-Esteem in the Educational Context

## Introduction

The ability to self-reflect is a uniquely human attribute, and research on 'the self' has a long, prolific history in psychology and the social sciences. Interest in self-esteem, the evaluative component of the self, peaked in the latter two decades of the 20th century, with the emergence and subsequent decline of the so-called 'self-esteem movement.' A central dispute in what became one the most fascinating debates in the history of psychology was over the role of self-esteem in educational outcomes. Many educators believed that boosting students' self-esteem was the key to increasing academic achievement (and reducing society's social problems, such as teen pregnancy and substance abuse), and as such, millions of dollars were spent in the US alone on the development of self-esteem programs. However, in a recent large scale review of articles published on the subject, Baumeister et al. reach two conclusions that make worrying reading for the self-esteem lobbyists. Firstly, they state that 'most of the evidence suggests that self-esteem has no impact on subsequent academic achievement.' Secondly, they found 'relatively little evidence of how self-esteem programs or other interventions affect self-esteem.' Does this mark the death of the feel-good factor in education? In this article I aim to examine the key issues and research findings in this important debate, and hope to provide some insight as to the role of self-esteem in the facilitation of inclusive schooling. Prior to addressing such points, however, I begin with a definition and overview of the key concepts under scrutiny.

## What Is Self-Esteem, and What Influences Its Development?

These two questions need to be answered for two reasons, the first of which is clarity. As Smelser observed, 'We have a fairly firm grasp of what is meant by self-esteem, as revealed by our own introspection and observation of the

From *School Psychology International,* vol. 25, no. 3, 2004, pp. 247–35. Copyright © 2004 by Sage Publications, Ltd. Reprinted by permission.

behaviour of others. But it is hard to put that understanding into precise words.' The second reason relates to our understanding and interpretation of research findings in this area; that is, if we are aware of exactly what self-esteem is and what influences its development, we are better prepared to interpret those studies that have sought to examine or modify it. Terms such as 'self-concept,' 'self-esteem,' 'self-image,' 'self-perceptions' and 'self-worth' are used in reference to an individual's cognitions and feelings about the self. Indeed, in the psychology literature, these terms are often used interchangeably. In this article I will refer in the main to self esteem, one of three constructs that contribute to our overall 'sense of self.' The first of these, *self-concept,* is used to describe an individual's perceived competencies, and is therefore descriptive in nature. The second, *ideal self,* is used in reference to an individual's pretensions (how they would like to be) and is aspirational in nature. Finally, *self-esteem* is an evaluation of personal worth based on the difference between one's ideal-self and one's self-concept. These are in line with widely accepted theory on the self. Although the focus of this article is primarily on self-esteem, it is important that the other two constructs are defined, given the mutual interdependence between the three (that is, one cannot arrive at an acceptable definition of self-esteem without mentioning self-concept and ideal self).

Research on the self has suggested that it is far from a unitary construct, and it is generally accepted that 'individuals can have a high opinion of their competence in some domains (e.g. athletics) and a low opinion of their competence in other domains (e.g. academics).' The multidimensional and hierarchical models of self that have been proposed therefore refer to such domains as *academic* self-esteem and *physical appearance* self-esteem in addition to *global* self-esteem. These distinctions are particularly pertinent in light of research evidence that suggests that an individual's notions of the *importance* of each domain affects the strength with which perceived competencies affect global self-worth. For example, two individuals can have similar perceived competencies in the various domains, but their levels of self-esteem may differ because they attach different levels of importance to them. Such ideas will also be relevant when we examine research evidence on the role of self-esteem in academic performance.

Self-representations during childhood follow a developmental path that is generally reflective of development of underlying (i.e. linguistic and cognitive) skills. In very early childhood, children's statements about themselves tend to focus on concrete, observable characteristics, which are often unrealistically positive. In early to middle childhood, the child's self picture becomes more elaborate, but is still often characterized by unrealistic positivity and 'uni-dimensional' (all-or-nothing) thinking is evident. At this stage, children focus on: temporal comparisons (how I am performing now compared to when I was younger), along with rudimentary social comparisons (although it should be noted that such social comparisons do not yet contribute to the child's self-evaluations). During middle to late childhood, trait labels that focus on abilities and interpersonal characteristics begin to appear, and social comparisons are used for the purpose of self-evaluation. As a result, the unrealistic positivity that characterizes earlier stages reduces, as more accurate evaluations are made. At this age, children also begin to internalize the opinions and standards of others, particularly so in reference to scholastic competence. During adolescence, use of trait labels describing personality characteristics, emotional control and values become evident, and the focus on scholastic abilities continues to develop.

What, then, are the most important influences on the development of self-esteem? It should be clear from the brief normative development sketch outlined above that the social context is extremely important in shaping the child's sense of self. However, certain individuals, known as 'significant others,' seem to be more influential than others, and it is worth considering who they are. Emler has suggested that the most influential significant others are the child's parents, and indeed that parental behaviour (such as the amount of acceptance, approval and affection shown) is perhaps the strongest source of individual differences in self-esteem. Other authors have argued that teachers and peers are also extremely influential, especially (but not exclusively) in the context of academic self-esteem. With regard to the former, Humphrey has argued that teachers strongly influence the self-esteem of their pupils because they are perceived as experts and authority figures, and also because they are one of two primary sources of feedback about scholastic competence (the other being the child's peer group). In the case of the latter, peer groups not only provide an important source of comparison in self-evaluations, but also transmit cultural values, standards and expectations, which give the child a sense of how well he or she fits into society.

## The Relationship Between Self-Esteem and Academic Achievement

As intimated in the introductory section of this article, the role of self-esteem in academic achievement has been an extremely contentious issue over the last two decades, and as such there has been a great deal of research in this area. However, a comprehensive review of this research is not the aim of this section; rather, I will describe some indicative studies as a prelude to examining some of the key issues that surround research in this area.

Davies and Brember report a study that typifies the kind of research conducted in this area. They found significant but very weak positive relationships (averaging 0.12) between self-esteem and academic achievement in a sample of 3000 children. Similar findings have been reported by a number of authors. In longitudinal studies that have investigated causal priority, weak and often non-significant links have been found between self-esteem scores and subsequent academic performance. For example tracked a group of 1600 adolescents for eight years and performed path analyses on self-esteem ratings and academic test scores at different time points, finding a (non-significant) link of only 0.072. Taken in Sum, these types of studies have led many to suggest that there is no meaningful relationship between self-esteem and academic performance. Others have suggested that self-esteem is actually more likely to be a consequence, rather than a cause of academic achievement.

In examining research on the relationship between self-esteem and academic achievement we have to be cautious, for a number of reasons. Firstly, the majority of studies in this area have examined the relationship between *global* as opposed to *academic* self-esteem (or self-concept) and achievement. As already noted, there is a great deal of evidence to suggest that self-esteem is far from a unitary construct, with evaluations of worth from several different domains contributing to our overall sense of worth. Given this, it is perhaps unreasonable to expect global self-esteem to be strongly related to academic achievement, since academic competence is the only one of between five and eight domains of the self which is likely to have any bearing on academic achievement (for instance, it is unlikely that evaluations of worth concerning physical appearance will be related to maths or English grades). It is perhaps unsurprising, therefore, that those studies which have specifically examined the academic domain of the self, much stronger relationships with academic achievement have been reported.

Secondly, many of the myriad studies that have been conducted are correlational in nature, meaning that causality in either direction (self-esteem influencing achievement, achievement influencing self-esteem) cannot be implied. Further, even in those studies whose design allows estimations about casual priority, dismissing results because of the lack of a strong relationship is somewhat naive. After all, as Emler has pointed out, 'the most important direct determinant of educational attainment is ability.' Thus, it is not logical to expect self-esteem scores to account for a large proportion of the variance of subsequent achievement scores (especially so given the fact that most of these studies have only measured global self-esteem). Rather, self-esteem should be seen as a construct that mediates *between* ability and achievement, providing some form of explanation as to why, for instance, some children fail to achieve what might be expected based on their ability. In this context, self-esteem could influence subsequent achievement, and achievement could influence subsequent levels of self-esteem (which highlights another problem with much of the research and theory in this area—it has been assumed that a *single causal relationship* must be found). This notion has received an increasing amount of empirical support in recent years.

A final consideration in examining the relationship between self-esteem and academic achievement is the notion of perceived importance of the different domains of self. As already mentioned, authors such as Harter have suggested that in order to accurately assess self-esteem, one has to take into account how important competence in a particular domain is to an individual's feelings of worth. Indeed, the notion of such 'contingent' self-esteem has gained considerable theoretical and empirical support recently. This is particularly relevant in the context of the self-esteem/achievement debate since it is all too often assumed that contingencies in the developing self are homogeneous across different groups of children (that is, all children consider the same things as being important in order to feel worthy). However, there is emerging evidence that this is not the case, particularly in the context of academic achievement. For instance, Humphrey et al. found significant differences between high- and low-achieving pupils on ratings of the importance of scholastic competence in determining self-worth. It has been suggested that differences such as these are the result of changes in the developing self that occur primarily to protect global self-esteem. Students may deal with the threat posed by low academic achievement by reorganizing their domain-specific evaluations, so that investment is reduced in those areas that represent a threat to self-esteem (i.e. scholastic competence), and is increased in other areas that are potentially more rewarding (such as social acceptance). This interesting and potentially important idea warrants future research.

## The Bigger Picture: Self-Esteem and Inclusive Education

It is clear that there are no easy answers in unravelling the complex relationship that exists between self-esteem and achievement in school. At this point, however, I would like to change direction slightly, and return to one of the questions posed in the introductory section of this article. Let us assume for the moment that self-esteem, whether global or domain specific, is *not* related to academic achievement. Does this mean that active facilitation of self-esteem no longer has a place in our education system? Several authors have answered with a resounding 'No!', and with some justification. Firstly, there are benefits of positive self-esteem independent of academic achievement, as Mruk points out: 'this vital human phenomenon is often understood in relation to positive mental health and general psychological well-being.' This comment mirrors the opinions of several influential authors, who have suggested that a positive sense of self is critical to personal and social adjustment, and the adaptive functioning and everyday happiness of the individual. Within the educational context, however, positive self-esteem may have a more immediate role, in the push for inclusive education.

The goals of the self-esteem movement and those of the inclusive education movement overlap significantly. In a recent book on self-esteem, Mruk suggests that the facilitation of a positive sense of self can be achieved through providing individuals with experiences of: (a) personal achievements or successes; (b) acceptance or being valued; (c) evidence of influence or power and (d) virtue or acting on beliefs (doing the 'right thing'). This is in line with the views of other eminent figures in the field, such as Branden and Harter. In relation to *personal achievements or successes,* Booth and Ainscow have suggested that one of the key principles of inclusive education is 'emphasising the role of schools . . . in increasing achievemet.' It is suggested that assessment should take into account the skills, knowledge and experiences of all students, including those with different learning styles and access needs. Thus, students are actively rewarded for all their successes, whether these are in traditional academic subjects (with traditional assessment techniques) or not. Key to this strategy, though, is instilling a belief system in both teachers and students that *all* successes should be valued. For instance, brushing one's teeth is not a particularly significant act for many of us, but it may be a great personal achievement for an intellectually or physically challenged individual. Thus, whilst what counts as a success for one person may not be deemed a success for another, it is still worthy of celebration, as Harris describes:

> One of the things that characterise these exceptional classrooms is the attitude students adopt toward the slow learners among them. Instead of making fun of them, they cheer them on. There was a boy with reading problems in one of Rodriguez's classes and when he started making progress the whole class celebrated.

Within this framework, therefore, teacher and pupil knowledge of individual contingencies of self-worth (i.e. what is important to the individual in order to feel worthy) are of paramount importance in promoting an inclusive school culture.

Another important source of self-esteem, experience of *acceptance or being valued*, is also one of the fundamental features of inclusive schooling. Indeed, Booth and Ainscow suggest that making students feel valued and welcome is the crucial underpinning to building a sense of community within schools, without which positive change at practice level is difficult. Humphrey has suggested that the key to making children feel accepted and valued lies with changing the role of teachers and peers. In particular, teachers should be encouraged to develop their existing counselling skills so that they become more accepting, genuine and empathetic towards their students. This is in line with the views of McKissock, who suggests that counselling skills can be adopted into teaching roles at a general level, in which a change in perspective (rather than extensive training) could bring about the counselling qualities inherent in all people: 'teachers retain their right to give instructions, information, advice, feedback, alongside counsellors' roles of nonjudgemental support, 'clarification and guidance.' In terms of peers, it has been suggested by several authors that feelings of acceptance and being valued can be achieved through the development of peer support systems that encourage a sense of community within school. Thus, students are actively encouraged to seek help from each other and to offer help when it is needed, to share rather than compete for friends, and to act as advocates for those who they feel have been treated unfairly. Such practices, alongside an over-arching humanistic school climate which is characterized by preference for democratic procedures, high degrees of interaction, and a respect for individual dignity, have been shown to foster positive self-perceptions in students.

The third and fourth of Mruk's four sources of self-esteem, *evidence of influence or power* and *virtue and acting on beliefs*, whilst not necessarily central to the inclusion movement, are clearly part of the wider push for increasing student 'voice' in education matters (for the former), as well as the increasing emphasis on citizenship in the primary and secondary sectors (for the latter). By allowing students to contribute ideas about the way their school develops, we are not only fostering their self-esteem, but also helping them to acquire democratic value systems (this is, of course, directly in line with the aforementioned notion of the 'humanistic' school climate). Further, by promoting citizenship across the Key Stages, we are not only helping students to become socially and morally responsible individuals, but also instilling feelings of worthiness that are contingent on *doing the right thing*. This may go some way to combating the mounting evidence that suggests marginalized students are turning to antisocial behaviour as a source of self-esteem.

It is clear that the self-esteem and inclusive education movements share many goals, if not being entirely mutually interdependent. Given this, it may even be suggested that the self-esteem of pupils (and teachers) can provide an indicator of the relative success of inclusive practices within schools. For instance, several studies have examined the role of educational placement in self-development for pupils with special educational needs (SEN), and found that SEN pupils in mainstream education had lower levels of self-esteem than their counterparts in segregated environments. The indication from such studies is that SEN pupils in mainstream environments exhibited low levels of self-esteem because although they were 'included' in locational and functional terms, they did not feel included socially and psychologically. . . .

In conclusion, I suggest that despite the continuing controversy surrounding the relationship between self-esteem and academic achievement, it would be unwise for the educational community to discard efforts to facilitate self-development in pupils. Whilst the main focus of educators is (and will continue to be) on raising achievement, we have a responsibility to provide children with a school environment that promotes effective as well as academic growth (although we must be careful about how this is achieved in practice). This is particularly pertinent given the close links between the principles of the inclusive education movement and what research has suggested are the main sources of self-esteem. In an education system that values its pupils and encourages them to value themselves, we can realistically expect excellence for all.

# POSTSCRIPT

## Has Promoting Self-Esteem Failed to Improve the Education of School-Age Children?

The rhetoric of self-esteem is a constant presence in the contemporary world of childhood. Sports programs claim to raise self-esteem, televisions shows give advice about dealing with low self-esteem, and parents go to great lengths to ensure their children feel good about themselves. The popularity of self-esteem as an idea has translated into the world of research about life span development; self-esteem is one of the most intensively researched topics in all of developmental scholarship. Perhaps a backlash was inevitable?

The shear quantity of available research made an extensive review, such as that provided by Baumeister et al., both challenging and important. It was challenging because there are many contingencies to consider and many types of research. As just one example, it is extraordinarily difficult to disentangle the specific influence of self-esteem from many other factors. If, for example, a researcher wants to investigate the influence of self-esteem on academic achievement, that researcher has to have a way to control for the realistic possibility that academic achievement would influence self-esteem.

The extensiveness of the self-esteem literature does, however, mean that we can draw on a great deal of data in evaluating this controversy. Baumeister et al., along with several other prominent developmental scholars including William Damon and Martin Seligman, have examined the data on self-esteem and come away unconvinced as to its merit. Instead of improving individual developmental outcomes, such scholars argue, emphasizing self-esteem seems more like part of a larger change in our societal focus from tangible achievement to self-gratification.

This is really a controversy about the indirect effects of self-esteem; both sides of the scholarly debate (though not the popular debate) generally agree that the promise of self-esteem creating direct developmental outcomes has not come to fruition. But where those arguing that we should avoid emphasizing self-esteem suggest indirect effects can actually be negative (producing qualities such as narcissism and self-indulgence, and problematic cultural shifts), scholars like Humphrey stress that the indirect effects of self-esteem are positive and justify its emphasis in the life of children. From this viewpoint, self-esteem creates a positive atmosphere where children are able to do the hard practical work of improving their skills and abilities. Of course, Humphrey argues, research does not demonstrate immediate individual impact on outcomes such as grades or IQ scores. Those developmental outcomes are primarily determined by basic abilities. But basic abilities must come from an inclusive and positive environment that stresses self-esteem.

In the broader scope of thinking about life span development, the prominence of self-esteem is a relatively recent phenomena. It is only in the last few decades that teachers, scholars, and parents took on the positive self-evaluations of children as central to healthy development in middle childhood. The accumulation of a solid research base regarding the actual effects of self-esteem, and the surprising lack of direct effects, suggests the "self-esteem movement" may be past its peak of influence. But it is unlikely that self-esteem will go away. It simply has too much popular appeal, and too much of a foothold in the way we think about childhood. Ultimately, then, thinking about the appropriate place and role of self-esteem in middle childhood—as a cause, effect, facilitator, or by-product—will likely continue to play a role in the contribution that the study of life span development makes to the way we think about middle childhood.

# Suggested Readings

R. Baumeister, J. Campbell, J. Krueger, and K. Vohs, "Exploding the Self-Esteem Myth," *Scientific American* (January 2005).

R. F. Baumeister, "Should Schools Try to Boost Self-Esteem?" *American Educator* (Summer 1996).

J. Crocker and L. Park, "The Costly Pursuit of Self-Esteem," *Psychological Bulletin* (2004).

D. DuBois and B. Flay, "The Healthy Pursuit of Self-Esteem: Comment on and Alternative to the Crocker and Park (2004) Formulation," *Psychological Bulletin* (2004).

D.L. Dubois and H.D. Tevendale, "Self-Esteem in Childhood and Adolescence: Vaccine or Epiphcnonmenon?" *Applied & Preventative Psychology* (1999).

Carol S. Dweck, "Caution—Praise Can Be Dangerous," *American Educator* (Spring 1999).

A. Kohn, "Five Reasons to Stop Saying 'Good Job'," *Young Children* (September 2001).

D. Michaels, "The Trouble with Self-Esteem," *The New York Times Magazine* (February 3, 2002).

S. Rubin, "Self Esteem and Your Child," *Pull-Through Network News* http://www.pullthrough.org/ptnn8.html (accessed October 2005).

R. Sylvester, "The Neurobiology of Self-Esteem and Aggression," *Educational Leadership* (February 1997).

# ISSUE 11

## Is Attention Deficit Disorder (ADD/ADHD) a Legitimate Medical Condition That Affects Childhood Behavior?

**YES: Michael Fumento,** from "Trick Question," *The New Republic* (February 3, 2003)

**NO: Jonathan Leo,** from "Attention Deficit Disorder: Good Science or Good Marketing?" *Skeptic* (vol. 8, no. 1, 2000)

### ISSUE SUMMARY

**YES:** Science journalist and writer Michael Fumento suggests that despite the extensive political controversy, it is clear that attention deficit hyperactivity disorder (ADHD) is a legitimate medical condition disrupting childhood.

**NO:** Professor of medicine Jonathan Leo suggests that there is no good science to support ADHD; rather, pharmaceutical advertising has taken advantage of the often extreme behavior of school-aged children.

Middle childhood is often a period of changing behavior. As children move from primarily spending time with their parents and family to primarily spending time with peers and at school, they often establish new habits and attitudes. While most children adapt to the changes well, there are inevitably some children who struggle. In these cases, many children become disruptive, hyperactive, and deviant. The question, which has been extremely controversial in recent years, is whether extreme behavior constitutes a medical disorder or a radical variation on normal childhood created by social forces.

A primary reason this question has become controversial in recent years is the success of the drug Ritalin in modifying the behavior of children. Individuals who were previously out of control and unable to concentrate have used Ritalin to control their attention and behavior. Ritalin has allowed parents to manage unruly children and schools to educate difficult students. The debate, therefore, is not about Ritalin, but rather about whether the efficacy of Ritalin proves the existence of ADHD as a disorder.

Ritalin, like any psychoactive drug, alters brain chemistry. Our brain chemistry guides our behavior through physiologically influencing all of our behavioral functioning: our concentration, mood, attention, excitement, energy, etc. As such, a drug that alters brain chemistry has the potential to both rectify disordered behavior and manage normal behavior.

Beyond the fact that Ritalin works to influence children's brains, statistics about ADHD stir further controversy. First, ADHD is a relatively recent disorder—the diagnosis did not exist until the last few decades. To some, this suggests that ADHD is not an organic, or biological, disorder but an artifact of changing social norms. To others, this demonstrates the advances made in medical science. Second, the overwhelming majority of cases of ADHD are diagnosed in North America. To some, this suggests that ADHD reflects part of our culture that refuses to accept responsibility for the challenges of middle childhood. To others, this shows the advanced progress of our system for managing children with serious problems. Third, ADHD is much more commonly diagnosed in boys than in girls. To some, this means that ADHD is linked to male biology (like many other disorders that tend to be more common in one gender or the other). To others, this suggests that the tendency of boys to be more aggressive and assertive is more than contemporary parents and teachers can handle.

All of these arguments are addressed in the following readings, and provided alternative interpretations. Michael Fumento asserts that any argument against the reality of ADHD is misguided. He points out that the efficacy of Ritalin in changing behavior should be considered positive, rather than negative. Children diagnosed with ADHD are different, and it is not just because of parenting. Ritalin helps them function effectively but it does not, contrary to popular opinion, create zombies. Fumento challenges what he considers to be common myths related to ADHD and concludes that denying its reality does a disservice to struggling children and families in contemporary society.

Jonathan Leo, professor of anatomy, argues strongly that science does not support ADHD. Yes, he agrees, Ritalin works. But researchers, despite great effort, have not been able to identify a clear organic disorder. Instead, marketers have capitalized on the efficacy of Ritalin along with the challenges of contemporary child rearing to overmedicate children. We would, Leo suggests, be much better off focusing on behavioral techniques for managing the challenges inherent in middle childhood. The alternative is to repress distinct personalities and force children to submit themselves to the sedate existence achieved with Ritalin use.

From the perspective of life span development, this issue encapsulates several crucial issues. First, is our development dictated by biological factors to such a degree that behavioral challenges should be dealt with through psychiatric interventions? Second, and more broadly, is there such a thing as "normal" development? Are children who deviate from obedient and compliant behavioral expectations troubled or simply challenging? Third, how much can parents, communities, teachers, and schools change the behavior of difficult children?

# YES

**Michael Fumento**

# Trick Question

**I**t's both right-wing and vast, but it's not a conspiracy. Actually, it's more of an anti-conspiracy. The subject is Attention Deficit Disorder (ADD) and Attention Deficit Hyperactivity Disorder (ADHD), closely related ailments (henceforth referred to in this article simply as ADHD). Rush Limbaugh declares it "may all be a hoax." Francis Fukuyama devotes much of one chapter in his latest book, *Our Posthuman Future,* to attacking Ritalin, the top-selling drug used to treat ADHD. Columnist Thomas Sowell writes, "The motto used to be: 'Boys will be boys.' Today, the motto seems to be: 'Boys will be medicated.'" And Phyllis Schlafly explains, "The old excuse of 'my dog ate my homework' has been replaced by 'I got an ADHD diagnosis.'" A March 2002 article in *The Weekly Standard* summed up the conservative line on ADHD with this rhetorical question: "Are we really prepared to redefine childhood as an ailment, and medicate it until it goes away?"

Many conservative writers, myself included, have criticized the growing tendency to pathologize every undesirable behavior—especially where children are concerned. But, when it comes to ADHD, this skepticism is misplaced. As even a cursory examination of the existing literature or, for that matter, simply talking to the parents and teachers of children with ADHD reveals, the condition is real, and it is treatable. And, if you don't believe me, you can ask conservatives who've come face to face with it themselves.

## Myth: ADHD Isn't a Real Disorder

The most common argument against ADHD on the right is also the simplest: It doesn't exist. Conservative columnist Jonah Goldberg thus reduces ADHD to "ants in the pants." Sowell equates it with "being bored and restless." Fukuyama protests, "No one has been able to identify a cause of ADD/ADHD. It is a pathology recognized only by its symptoms." And a conservative columnist approvingly quotes Thomas Armstrong, Ritalin opponent and author, when he declares, "ADD is a disorder that cannot be authoritatively identified in the same way as polio, heart disease or other legitimate illnesses."

The Armstrong and Fukuyama observations are as correct as they are worthless. "Half of all medical disorders are diagnosed without benefit of a lab

From *The New Republic,* February 3, 2003, pp. 18–21. © 2003 by The New Republic, LLC. Reprinted by permission.

procedure," notes Dr. Russell Barkley, professor of psychology at the College of Health Professionals at the Medical University of South Carolina. "Where are the lab tests for headaches and multiple sclerosis and Alzheimer's?" he asks. "Such a standard would virtually eliminate all mental disorders."

Often the best diagnostic test for an ailment is how it responds to treatment. And, by that standard, it doesn't get much more real than ADHD. The beneficial effects of administering stimulants to treat the disorder were first reported in 1937. And today medication for the disorder is reported to be 75 to 90 percent successful. "In our trials it was close to ninety percent," says Dr. Judith Rapoport, director of the National Institute of Mental Health's Child Psychiatry Branch, who has published about 100 papers on ADHD. "This means there was a significant difference in the children's ability to function in the classroom or at home."

Additionally, epidemiological evidence indicates that ADHD has a powerful genetic component. University of Colorado researchers have found that a child whose identical twin has the disorder is between eleven and 18 times more likely to also have it than is a non-twin sibling. For these reasons, the American Psychiatric Association (APA), American Medical Association, American Academy of Pediatrics, American Academy of Child Adolescent Psychiatry, the surgeon general's office, and other major medical bodies all acknowledge ADHD as both real and treatable.

# Myth: ADHD Is Part of a Feminist Conspiracy to Make Little Boys More Like Little Girls

Many conservatives observe that boys receive ADHD diagnoses in much higher numbers than girls and find in this evidence of a feminist conspiracy. (This, despite the fact that genetic diseases are often heavily weighted more toward one gender or the other.) Sowell refers to "a growing tendency to treat boyhood as a pathological condition that requires a new three R's—repression, re-education and Ritalin." Fukuyama claims Prozac is being used to give women "more of the alpha-male feeling," while Ritalin is making boys act more like girls. "Together, the two sexes are gently nudged toward that androgynous median personality . . . that is the current politically correct outcome in American society." George Will, while acknowledging that Ritalin can be helpful, nonetheless writes of the "androgyny agenda" of "drugging children because they are behaving like children, especially boy children." Anti-Ritalin conservatives frequently invoke Christina Hoff Sommers's best-selling 2000 book, *The War Against Boys*. You'd never know that the drug isn't mentioned in her book—or why.

"Originally I was going to have a chapter on it," Sommers tells me. "It seemed to fit the thesis." What stopped her was both her survey of the medical literature and her own empirical findings. Of one child she personally came to know she says, "He was utterly miserable, as was everybody around him. The drugs saved his life."

## Myth: ADHD Is Part of the Public School System's Efforts to Warehouse Kids Rather Than to Discipline and Teach Them

"No doubt life is easier for teachers when everyone sits around quietly," writes Sowell. Use of ADHD drugs is "in the school's interest to deal with behavioral and discipline problems [because] it's so easy to use Ritalin to make kids compliant: to get them to sit down, shut up, and do what they're told," declares Schlafly. The word "zombies" to describe children under the effects of Ritalin is tossed around more than in a B-grade voodoo movie.

Kerri Houston, national field director for the American Conservative Union and the mother of two ADHD children on medication, agrees with much of the criticism of public schools. "But don't blame ADHD on crummy curricula and lazy teachers," she says. "If you've worked with these children, you know they have a serious neurological problem." In any case, Ritalin, when taken as prescribed, hardly stupefies children. To the extent the medicine works, it simply turns ADHD children into normal children. "ADHD is like having thirty televisions on at one time, and the medicine turns off twenty-nine so you can concentrate on the one," Houston describes. "This zombie stuff drives me nuts! My kids are both as lively and as fun as can be."

## Myth: Parents Who Give Their Kids Anti-ADHD Drugs Are Merely Doping Up Problem Children

Limbaugh calls ADHD "the perfect way to explain the inattention, incompetence, and inability of adults to control their kids." Addressing parents directly, he lectures, "It helped you mask your own failings by doping up your children to calm them down."

Such charges blast the parents of ADHD kids into high orbit. That includes my Hudson Institute colleague (and fellow conservative) Mona Charen, the mother of an eleven-year-old with the disorder. "I have two non-ADHD children, so it's not a matter of parenting technique," says Charen. "People without such children have no idea what it's like. I can tell the difference between boyish high spirits and pathological hyperactivity. . . . These kids bounce off the walls. Their lives are chaos; their rooms are chaos. And nothing replaces the drugs."

Barkley and Rapoport say research backs her up. Randomized, controlled studies in both the United States and Sweden have tried combining medication with behavioral interventions and then dropped either one or the other. For those trying to go on without medicine, "the behavioral interventions maintained nothing," Barkley says. Rapoport concurs: "Unfortunately, behavior modification doesn't seem to help with ADHD." (Both doctors are quick to add that ADHD is often accompanied by other disorders that are treatable through behavior modification in tandem with medicine.)

# Myth: Ritalin Is "Kiddie Cocaine"

One of the paradoxes of conservative attacks on Ritalin is that the drug is alternately accused of turning children into brain-dead zombies and of making them Mach-speed cocaine junkies. Indeed, Ritalin is widely disparaged as "kiddie cocaine." Writers who have sought to lump the two drugs together include Schlafly, talk-show host and columnist Armstrong Williams, and others whom I hesitate to name because of my long-standing personal relationships with them.

Mary Eberstadt wrote the "authoritative" Ritalin-cocaine piece for the April 1999 issue of *Policy Review,* then owned by the Heritage Foundation. The article, "Why Ritalin Rules," employs the word "cocaine" no fewer than twelve times. Eberstadt quotes from a 1995 Drug Enforcement Agency (DEA) background paper declaring methylphenidate, the active ingredient in Ritalin, "a central nervous system (CNS) stimulant [that] shares many of the pharmacological effects of amphetamine, methamphetamine, and cocaine." Further, it "produces behavioral, psychological, subjective, and reinforcing effects similar to those of d-amphetamine including increases in rating of euphoria, drug liking and activity, and decreases in sedation." Add to this the fact that the Controlled Substances Act lists it as a Schedule II drug, imposing on it the same tight prescription controls as morphine, and Ritalin starts to sound spooky indeed.

What Eberstadt fails to tell readers is that the DEA description concerns methylphenidate *abuse.* It's tautological to say abuse is harmful. According to the DEA, the drugs in question are comparable when "administered the same way at comparable does." But ADHD stimulants, when taken as prescribed, are neither administered in the same way as cocaine nor at comparable doses. "What really counts," says Barkley, "is the speed with which the drugs enter and clear the brain. With cocaine, because it's snorted, this happens tremendously quickly, giving users the characteristic addictive high." (Ever seen anyone pop a cocaine tablet?) Further, he says, "There's no evidence anywhere in literature of [Ritalin's] addictiveness when taken as prescribed." As to the Schedule II listing, again this is because of the potential for it to fall into the hands of abusers, not because of its effects on persons for whom it is prescribed. Ritalin and the other anti-ADHD drugs, says Barkley, "are the safest drugs in all of psychiatry." (And they may be getting even safer: A new medicine just released called Strattera represents the first true non-stimulant ADHD treatment.)

Indeed, a study just released in the journal *Pediatrics* found that children who take Ritalin or other stimulants to control ADHD cut their risk of future substance abuse by 50 percent compared with untreated ADHD children. The lead author speculated that "by treating ADHD you're reducing the demoralization that accompanies this disorder, and you're improving the academic functioning and well-being of adolescents and young adults during the critical times when substance abuse starts."

# Myth: Ritalin Is Overprescribed Across the Country

Some call it "the Ritalin craze." In *The Weekly Standard,* Melana Zyla Vickers informs us that "Ritalin use has exploded," while Eberstadt writes that "Ritalin use more than doubled in the first half of the decade alone, [and] the number of schoolchildren taking the drug may now, by some estimates, be approaching the *4 million mark."*

A report in the January 2003 issue of *Archives of Pediatrics and Adolescent Medicine* did find a large increase in the use of ADHD medicines from 1987 to 1996, an increase that doesn't appear to be slowing. Yet nobody thinks it's a problem that routine screening for high blood pressure has produced a big increase in the use of hypertension medicine. "Today, children suffering from ADHD are simply less likely to slip through the cracks," says Dr. Sally Satel, a psychiatrist, AEI fellow, and author of *PC, M.D.: How Political Correctness Is Corrupting Medicine.*

Satel agrees that some community studies, by the standards laid down in the APA's *Diagnostic and Statistical Manual of Mental Disorders (DSM),* indicate that ADHD may often be over-diagnosed. On the other hand, she says, additional evidence shows that in some communities ADHD is *under-*diagnosed and *under-*treated. "I'm quite concerned with children who need the medication and aren't getting it," she says.

There *are* tremendous disparities in the percentage of children taking ADHD drugs when comparing small geographical areas. Psychologist Gretchen LeFever, for example, has compared the number of prescriptions in mostly white Virginia Beach, Virginia, with other, more heavily African American areas in the southeastern part of the state. Conservatives have latched onto her higher numbers—20 percent of white fifth-grade boys in Virginia Beach are being treated for ADHD—as evidence that something is horribly wrong. But others, such as Barkley, worry about the lower numbers. According to LeFever's study, black children are only half as likely to get medication as white children. "Black people don't get the care of white people; children of well-off parents get far better care than those of poorer parents," says Barkley.

# Myth: States Should Pass Laws That Restrict Schools from Recommending Ritalin

Conservative writers have expressed delight that several states, led by Connecticut, have passed or are considering laws ostensibly protecting students from schools that allegedly pass out Ritalin like candy. Representative Lenny Winkler, lead sponsor of the Connecticut measure, told *Reuters Health,* "If the diagnosis is made, and it's an appropriate diagnosis that Ritalin be used, that's fine. But I have also heard of many families approached by the school system [who are told] that their child cannot attend school if they're not put on Ritalin."

Two attorneys I interviewed who specialize in child-disability issues, including one from the liberal Bazelon Center for Mental Health Law in Washington, D.C., acknowledge that school personnel have in some cases stepped over the line. But legislation can go too far in the other direction by declaring, as Connecticut's law does, that "any school personnel [shall be prohibited] from recommending the use of psychotropic drugs for any child." The law appears to offer an exemption by declaring, "The provisions of this section shall not prohibit *school medical staff* from recommending that a child be evaluated by an appropriate medical practitioner, or prohibit school personnel from consulting with such practitioner, with the consent of the parent or guardian of such child." [Emphasis added.] But of course many, if not most schools have perhaps one nurse on regular "staff." That nurse will have limited contact with children in the classroom situations where ADHD is likely to be most evident. And, given the wording of the statute, a teacher who believed a student was suffering from ADHD would arguably be prohibited from referring that student to the nurse. Such ambiguity is sure to have a chilling effect on any form of intervention or recommendation by school personnel. Moreover, 20-year special-education veteran Sandra Rief said in an interview with the National Education Association that "recommending medical intervention for a student's behavior could lead to personal liability issues." Teachers, in other words, could be forced to choose between what they think is best for the health of their students and the possible risk of losing not only their jobs but their personal assets as well.

"Certainly it's not within the purview of a school to say kids can't attend if they don't take drugs," says Houston. "On the other hand, certainly teachers should be able to advise parents as to problems and potential solutions. . . . [T]hey may see things parents don't. My own son is an angel at home but was a demon at school."

If the real worry is "take the medicine or take a hike" ultimatums, legislation can be narrowly tailored to prevent them; broad-based gag orders, such as Connecticut's, are a solution that's worse than the problem.

## The Conservative Case for ADHD Drugs

There are kernels of truth to every conservative suspicion about ADHD. Who among us has not had lapses of attention? And isn't hyperactivity a normal condition of childhood when compared with deskbound adults? Certainly there are lazy teachers, warehousing schools, androgyny-pushing feminists, and far too many parents unwilling or unable to expend the time and effort to raise their children properly, even by their own standards. Where conservatives go wrong is in making ADHD a scapegoat for frustration over what we perceive as a breakdown in the order of society and family. In a column in *The Boston Herald*, Boston University Chancellor John Silber rails that Ritalin is "a classic example of a cheap fix: low-cost, simple and purely superficial."

Exactly. Like most headaches, ADHD is a neurological problem that can usually be successfully treated with a chemical. Those who recommend or prescribe ADHD medicines do not, as *The Weekly Standard* put it, see them as "discipline in pill-form." They see them as pills.

In fact, it can be argued that the use of those pills, far from being liable for or symptomatic of the Decline of the West, reflects and reinforces conservative values. For one thing, they increase personal responsibility by removing an excuse that children (and their parents) can fall back on to explain misbehavior and poor performance. "Too many psychologists and psychiatrists focus on allowing patients to justify to themselves their troubling behavior," says Satel. "But something like Ritalin actually encourages greater autonomy because you're treating a compulsion to behave in a certain way. Also, by treating ADHD, you remove an opportunity to explain away bad behavior."

Moreover, unlike liberals, who tend to downplay differences between the sexes, conservatives are inclined to believe that there are substantial physiological differences—differences such as boys' greater tendency to suffer ADHD. "Conservatives celebrate the physiological differences between boys and girls and eschew the radical-feminist notion that gender differences are created by societal pressures," says Houston regarding the fuss over the boy-girl disparity among ADHD diagnoses. "ADHD is no exception."

But, however compatible conservatism may be with taking ADHD seriously, the truth is that most conservatives remain skeptics. "I'm sure I would have been one of those smug conservatives saying it's a made-up disease," admits Charen, "if I hadn't found out the hard way." Here's hoping other conservatives find an easier route to accepting the truth.

Jonathan Leo

 **NO**

# Attention Deficit Disorder: Good Science or Good Marketing?

**I**n the 1960s, Americans discovered illegal mind-altering drugs for themselves. In the 1990s, Americans discovered a legal mind-altering drug for their children. Although it is illegal drugs that draw the attention of the media and law enforcement agencies, over the past decade there has been a meteoric rise in the number of children, under the guidance of a physician, taking mind-altering drugs.

The drug? Ritalin. The most recent estimate is that somewhere between three to five million children in this country are taking Ritalin or a similar type of drug. Furthermore, American children consume 90% of all the Ritalin produced worldwide, making this a unique aspect of American culture. Ritalin is the drug of choice for children who have been diagnosed with Attention Deficit Hyperactivity Disorder or ADHD. It has now become acceptable to give children a drug to alter their personality and behavioral patterns in a specific situation, usually school. The acceptance of this practice, however, has more to do with marketing than science. In the past 10 years, millions of dollars have been spent by scientists to investigate the biological basis of ADHD. Likewise, millions of dollars have been spent by the marketing departments of pharmaceutical companies to promote the use of drugs such as Ritalin.

By comparing the success rate of the scientists on one hand and the marketing departments on the other, it is clear why medicating children has more to do with marketing than science. The scientific basis of ADHD is on shaky ground and very little progress has been made in the last decade. It is hard to pin down the ADHD experts on what they think is the most convincing scientific proof of this disorder. Instead of one very good study that proves their case, there are numerous marginal studies that individually have little significance. However, when these little pieces are piled high it appears to some that significant understanding is at hand.

The phrase "this is one of the most studied pediatric conditions" appears frequently in the ADHD literature, but the major scientific evidence for ADHD is that hyperactive children can be helped, at least in the short run, by taking Ritalin, a pill that increases a neurotransmitter called dopamine. So, the argument goes, if we know that Ritalin both increases dopamine levels and

From *Skeptic,* vol. 8, no. 1, 2000, pp. 63–69. Copyright © 2000 by Skeptic. Reprinted by permission.

subdues hyperactive children, then the original hyperactivity must have been due to a dearth of dopamine. This line of reasoning is flawed. We do not use a parallel argument to explain the effects of other drugs such as aspirin. Aspirin relieves headaches but that doesn't mean that a shortage of aspirin caused the headache. ADHD may be one of the most extensively studied pediatric conditions, yet there is still no proof of any underlying neuropathology.

Ask a psychiatrist to explain ADHD and Ritalin, and he will most likely recite the diabetes analogy, which goes something like this: ADHD is like diabetes in that both are due to a shortage of a chemical in the body. Diabetics are short of insulin, a condition that causes their blood sugar level to increase. This condition is helped by administering insulin, which brings the blood sugar level down. The child with ADHD has a shortage of dopamine, which leads to impulsive behavior. By administering Ritalin we can increase the dopamine levels and normalize the child.

The problem with this analogy is that, while for diabetes a blood test can be implemented to detect abnormal glucose levels, for ADHD no such biological test exists to detect decreased dopamine levels. For diabetes, too, insulin can be administered, the blood test repeated, and the effect of the drug measured. We cannot measure the effect of Ritalin in this way. Recently, parents who have been concerned with Ritalin affecting their child's growth have withheld the drug on vacations and during summer holidays. This is even referred to as a "drug holiday." Clearly, there is no room in the diabetes analogy for a drug holiday, because diabetics cannot stop taking their insulin whenever they feel like it. Any scientist with a modicum of critical thinking skills can see that the diabetes analogy is not valid.

Psychiatrists frequently use the diabetes analogy to explain any mental illness. The ADHD proponents also have their own unique analogy—eyeglasses. According to the National Institutes of Mental Health, "Parents and teachers can help children view their medication in a positive way: Compare the pills to eyeglasses. Explain that their medicine is simply a tool to help them focus and pay attention." The problem with the eyeglass analogy is that comparing Ritalin to eyeglasses is like comparing a lightning bolt to a flashlight.

## Brain Scans or Scams?

The Holy Grail for ADHD research is to find a diagnostic test that a physician could use to determine if a patient actually has ADHD. For years scientists have sought a legitimate biological marker to lend credence to the ADHD diagnosis. The current trend is to use PET (Positron Emission Tomography) scans to compare the brains of ADHD children with the brains of normal children. Dr. Alan Zametkin, a leader in the effort to show some biological abnormality in the brains of ADHD children, is often cited in Ritalin advertising literature. He has conducted two major brain scan studies in which he compares ADHD patients to controls. The first study was in 1990 when he examined adult brains. This study received considerable press attention because, in the words of Zametkin himself, "Zametkin et al. published a study showing, for the first time, definite and quantifiable central neurophysiological differences between ADHD adults and normal adults." One problem with the Zametkin study was that, while there was an 8% difference in glucose metabolism, there was no difference in outcome on a continuous performance test.

The other (and major) problem is that Zametkin's study included both females and males, but when ADHD males are compared to control males there is no significant difference. The only way to get a statistically significant difference is to group the males and females together. In a subsequent study independent researchers analyzed Zametkin's data and compared the male controls to the female controls and found that there was a significant difference between normal males and normal females. Based on Zametkin's logic that a difference in metabolism leads to medication, then either the normal males or normal females should be medicated. Again, just because there is a difference does not mean there is a disease. Based on the "success" of his first study, Zametkin published a second in 1993 that compared ADHD adolescents to control adolescents. In this study, however, he found no differences in global brain metabolism.

In a review article Zametkin discusses these results: "Several reasons could have accounted for the overall lack of brain metabolism difference between ADHD and normal teenagers. First, the adolescent control group was not as pure as the control group used in the adult study, because 63% of the normal adolescents had a first-degree relative with ADHD, in contrast to the absence of ADHD pathology in families of normal adults. Second, 75% of the adolescents with ADHD had been previously exposed to treatment with stimulants, compared to no history of stimulant treatment in the ADHD adults. Third, an age effect in the development of brain abnormalities in ADHD individuals cannot be ruled out." One of the possibilities that Zametkin seems to ignore is that his findings actually show that there is no biological difference between ADHD and control brains.

It is astonishing that he does not even consider this possibility (at least in print). Despite the negative findings of this second study, the ADHD marketing forces have taken the PET scan research and presented it to the general public as if there were evidence of a neurobiological disorder. CHADD (Children and Adults with Attention Deficit Disorders) is a national organization that promotes the concept that ADHD is a neurobiological disorder, and it has received close to a million dollars from the drug companies that manufacture Ritalin. . . . To the non-scientist it seems as if the brain scan research has revealed some underlying biological deficit. But this is misleading. The advertisement could also be used to describe the difference between the sexes.

The brain scan literature is probably the best example of the very weak science but the very strong marketing forces behind the push to medicate children. Compare two publications. If literature on ADHD is requested from the National Institute of Mental Health, they will send a pamphlet entitled *Attention Deficit Hyperactivity Disorder* (NIMH publication No. 94-3572). This pamphlet is clearly designed for parents who is considering putting their child on Ritalin. Under the causes of ADHD there is the following statement:

> "They are finding more and more evidence that ADHD does not stem from the home environment, but from biological causes. When you think about it there is no clear relationship between home life and ADHD. Not all children from unstable or dysfunctional homes have ADHD."

The ADHD marketing literature is filled with statements like this, but the ADHD professional literature is considerably more equivocating. In 1998, for example, there was a NIMH consensus conference on ADHD. Its final report contained these cautionary statements: "We don't have an independent valid test for ADHD; further research is necessary to firmly establish ADHD as a brain disorder; existing studies come to conflicting conclusions as to whether the use of psychostimulants increases or decreases the risk of abuse; and finally after years of clinical research and experience with ADHD, our knowledge about the cause or causes of ADHD remain largely speculative." How many parents who are considering putting their children on Ritalin have seen this paper? I suspect the answer is close to zero.

## Show Me the Evidence

The superficiality of the scientific evidence for ADHD is most obvious in the writings of the ADHD experts themselves. As an example, consider Russell Barkley, who wrote a major review article in *Scientific American* entitled "Attention Deficit Hyperactivity Disorder." One would think that a review article in such a highly regarded popular journal of science would present the most powerful data available, yet Barkley's evidence in support of a biological link to ADHD is minimal. In fact, the author admits: "No one knows the direct and immediate causes of the difficulties experienced by children with ADHD, although advances in neurological imaging techniques and genetics promise to clarify this issue over the next five years." We are still waiting.

Barkley's statement sums up both the science and the philosophy of the ADHD movement, and should be quoted on the front of every NIMH brochure describing ADHD. Here is a bald admission that we do not understand the scientific basis for this so-called disease. It is also interesting that Barkley is one of the biggest proponents of Ritalin. His resolution to this paradox is to speculate that science will catch up with the drug. Peter Breggin, a doctor and author who does not believe in medicating children with Ritalin, has been accused by Barkley of violating the Hippocratic oath. The fact that a leader of the push to medicate children, who admits we do not understand this disease, accuses a skeptical doctor of ethical impropriety says more about the Ritalin movement than Barkley's review article.

In the past 10 years, while scientists have made very little progress in understanding ADHD, their partners down the hall in the marketing department have been extremely successful. The ADHD marketing forces have taken the decision to medicate children out of the ethical arena, and reshaped the decision to medicate based on three flawed beliefs: (1) Diagnosis equals disease;

(2) ADHD is due to biology and not the environment; and (3) a disease can be treated with a pill.

1. *Does Diagnosis Equal Disease?* Every human trait falls into a range of values. Some people are tall, some are short, some are dark skinned, some are light skinned, some are outgoing, and some are shy. With height, for example, if we measure the general population we see a bell-shaped curve with the very tall and very short at either end of the spectrum. Regardless of a person's height, or what factors cause a person to be tall or short, we do not label the people in the upper 10% as diseased. We recognize these people as merely being at the upper end of normal biological variability. They don't have faulty genes, just different genes.

    The ADHD experts have convinced the American public that the description of a personality trait is actually a disease. This is perhaps the biggest flaw and mistake of the ADHD proponents. They do not understand normal human variation. Where do you draw the line on the scale of children's activity level that demarcates normal children from ADHD children? Even the ADHD experts cannot agree. Some estimate that from 3 to 4% of American children have ADHD, while others go as high as 10, 17, or even 20%. Since there is no diagnostic test to determine if a child has this condition, such percentages are arbitrary. Dr. Lawerence Diller addresses the problems of diagnosis in a book chapter titled, "Attention Deficit Disorder: In the Eye of the Beholder." Dr. Diller points out that if we adhere to Dr. Joseph Biederman's estimates that 10% of American Children have ADD, and that we take into account that it is four to five times more common in males than females, then approximately one out of every six boys between the ages of five and twelve years old would be diagnosed with ADHD.

    The problem is that in one school, family, or doctor's office these children would have a disease but in another school, family, or doctor's office these children would not have a disease. Of all the variables that go into making a diagnosis of ADHD, "science" is the least important. It should strike the skeptical reader as odd that 5–10% of American children have ADHD, whereas in England only 0.03% of their children have the disease. This discrepancy highlights the shortcomings of the science of ADHD.

    Even if scientists are successful in developing a diagnostic test that shows 10% of the children in this country have a different biochemical makeup, or different activity levels in the brain, or even a genetic difference, how do we as a society respond to this? Do we say that they have a disease or do we change the environment? ADHD proponents opt for the former and prescribe Ritalin as a treatment.

2. *Genes or Environment?* In the past decade research on ADHD has leaned toward a possible genetic component. One hears in the media talk of finding "the gene" for ADHD. This is a grand over-simplification of the interplay between genes and the environment, but administering mind-altering drugs to children is easier to rationalize if the pill is nothing more than a way to correct neurotransmitter deficit caused by faulty genes. In Dr. Alan Zametkin's paper in the *Journal of the American Medical Association,* for example, he states: "Is there a particular gene

linked to the disorder?" To even seriously consider that ADHD is due to a single gene goes against everything that science know about genes and behavior. As Caltech geneticist Seymour Benzer has shown with fruit flies, even a behavior as simple as moving toward a light involves hundreds of genes.

A child's brain is enormously more complicated than the brain of a fruit fly, so to postulate that the ability to sit still in a classroom is due to a single gene, or even a small cohort of genes, seems preposterous. If ADHD is genetic then it must have something to do with the Y chromosome because it is much more prevalent in boys than girls. Also, if ADHD is genetically caused, why is it so much more common in this country and why does ADHD vary among states and school districts? In one school district in Virginia, for example, 20% of the children are diagnosed with ADHD. Is this due to an overabundance of ADHD genes in Virginia, or overzealous school psychiatrists?

Despite such speculations, at this point the only way to diagnose ADHD is by examining the relationship of a child to his environment. A physician does not discover ADHD at an annual check up; it is the teacher observing the child in the school environment who makes the initial diagnosis. The parent and child then go to a specialist, but in the office the child might even seem normal, so the expert then relies on the testimony of the teachers and parents. They then go through a checklist to determine if medication is appropriate. Given the level of subjective evaluation involved in such a checklist, it is not unusual for parents to walk out of the office with a prescription for Ritalin.

3. *From Diagnosis to Medication.* Whether ADHD has a predominantly genetic or environmental cause, intervention through drugs is ethically problematic. Even the proponents of Ritalin, for example, acknowledge that the drug is an easy substitute for good parenting and good schools. Consider the following statement in the *New England Journal of Medicine,* in an article titled "Treatment of Attention Deficit Hyperactivity Disorder" by Dr. Judith Rapoport. "Training and supporting parents and teachers in techniques of contingency reinforcement (e.g., the point-token reward system, 'time out,' and earning or losing privileges) has substantial beneficial effects on disruptive behavior. The value of these strategies is limited because they are labor intensive (and therefore expensive), are effective only at the time they are administered, cannot be generalized to non-targeted behavior or across settings, and are dependent on the compliance and motivation of teachers and parents."

Here Rapoport is acknowledging that the environment matters, that good parenting does have an effect on behavior, and that teachers and parents can improve their teaching and parenting skills. The problem is time, effort, and money. Ritalin is quick, easy, and cheap. But as Rapoport notes: "Behavior management combined with methylphenidate (Ritalin) is substantially more effective than behavior management alone, but usually no more effective than methylphenidate alone. However, behavior management implemented in a highly structured setting may permit the use of a lower dose of methylphenidate." In other words, there is an inverse relationship between a highly structured environment and the dose of Ritalin. Perhaps the national push to reduce class size will also result in a reduction of the number of children on Ritalin.

The difference between good science and bad science does not depend on where the grants came from but funding certainly should be taken into account. Dr. Rapoport's article was mentioned in an editorial in the *New England Journal of Medicine* as one of 19 articles that should not have been published because it violated the journal's conflict of interest policy. One of the authors (Elia) of the article received a grant from Celgene, a company that is developing a drug to treat ADHD.

## Who Cares About Science?

When you talk to the parents of children taking Ritalin they typically rave about the success of the drug. To put it simply, this stuff works. Who cares about all the scientific arguments concerning etiology, neurochemistry, and the pharmacological mechanisms of treatment? If school performance is enhanced, who cares about science? Of course, since amphetamines were first discovered it has been known that they increase performance.

The marketing of Ritalin has made it hard for physicians who do not believe in it to withhold prescriptions. What is a doctor's response to a parent, who says "My little boy is a monster without his Ritalin? We've tried everything and nothing works. Our lives are in complete disarray. He's about to get kicked out of school. I can't afford private tutors and home schooling. Our family life is in turmoil. But when we put him on Ritalin I'm telling you it is a miracle. He calms down, he does well in school, and our home life is blissful. If you don't believe in Ritalin show me what I can do to replace Ritalin and still have a relatively normal life?"

This is a very real cry of anguish and a sympathetic doctor is going to want to assist the family. But, a concerned and knowledgeable doctor also knows that: (1) parents have faced this dilemma for years; (2) a Ritalin Band-Aid would help only in the short run; (3) it would be more appropriate to recommend a family counselor for the long run; (4) in the world of managed care a pill is easier and cheaper, and (5) if the parents don't get a prescription here they will get it someplace else.

The fact that Ritalin is a uniquely American response to this dilemma raises several questions about the direction our society is going. It is very hard for an individual doctor who does not believe in medicating children to go against the grain. What needs to happen is that the American medical community needs to address a tough question: "Are we treating a disease, or are we handing out a performance enhancing pill to put a temporary patch over other problems in our society?" If we are just handing out a temporary patch then let's call it that, and not a "neurobiological deficit." This is especially problematic because we do not know the long term effects of the drug. In her review article in 1999 Judith Rapoport says, "Important questions regarding the occurrence of tics, drug doses, and the effects of long-term therapy remain unanswered." Again, Rapoport is considered one of the ADHD experts and she said this only one year ago.

There is also the dilemma for parents who do not want their children labeled with ADHD, yet are under pressure from the school district to have the children evaluated. No one disagrees that a child on Ritalin is easier to control. This is about the only fact that the ADHD scientists have proved. However, there are other ways to make it easier for teachers to control children, the most obvious being fewer children in the classroom. For instance, Dr. Howard Gardner believes that schools today are too dependent on numbers and words and need to spend more time on the arts, music, and physical education. Multiple intelligences is one answer to the ADHD dilemma: these kids are smart and creative in their own ways and those talents should be exploited, not drugged.

One of the many alternative views to medication is summed up by John Holt: "We consider it a disease because it makes it difficult to run our schools as we do, like maximum security prisons, for the comfort and convenience of the teachers and administrators who work in them. . . . Given the fact that some children are more energetic and active than others, might it not be easier, more healthy, and more humane to deal with this fact by giving them more time and scope to make use of and work off their energy? . . . Everyone is taken care of, except, of course, the child himself, who wears a label which to him reads clearly enough "freak," and who is denied from those closest to him, however much sympathy he may get, what he and all children most need-respect, faith, hope, and trust."

Most readers of Skeptic are probably familiar with Dr. Dean Edell, who openly shares the fact that he had ADHD as a child. "I had an attention disorder as a kid and consider myself to be a very successful person. It wasn't easy, but when I needed to go back to medical school, I understood that I needed to buckle down and learn the material. Because of my situation, I have led a very creative life and have found it to be very valuable." He continues, "We just can't drug all the kids who won't fit into the mold. Our culture needs people who think and act differently and there is nothing more frightening to me than looking into a classroom in America where every little kid is the same, all paying attention, all doing their homework and marching to the same drummer." What would have happened to the voice of science and reason in medicine if he had been medicated as a child?

If the medical community is not treating a disease but handing out a performance enhancing drug, then, if anything, Ritalin is underprescribed, because the drug will help almost anyone. College students, for example, have discovered that Ritalin will give them extra focus. Can we fault these students when they are seeking to improve their performance, and then turn around and use the performance enhancing aspect of the drug as the major reason for prescribing it? Clearly we have a disconnect between the science of ADHD and the art of behavioral modification with drugs.

# Berkeley or Jail?

As we approach the next presidential election, one of the issues facing our country is how to increase the number of children who go into higher education and decrease the number of children in our jails. The Democrats have one agenda and the Republicans have another, but according to Ritalin proponents the cure for society's problems can be found in a pill. ADHD expert

Dr. James Swanson summed it up this way: "Treatment can mean the difference between a kid ending up at Berkeley or ending up in prison. This is a disorder where we can really make a difference." Of course, the world would be a better place if more adolescents went to Berkeley instead to prison, but to suggest that the answer to our country's sociological problems is as easy as taking more drugs is simplistic. It shows a lack of understanding, or at least blissful ignorance, of politics, race relations, sociology, ethics, and child development in this country. America has one of the highest incarceration rates on the planet, marginal race relations, a breakdown of the family, problems with schools, and the list goes on and on. Is the answer to our social problems as easy as taking a pill?

While believing that more Ritalin will keep kids out of jail might not show a very good understanding of science and sociology it does show a good understanding of parental vulnerability. Everyone wants the best for their kids, but if there is ever a time for healthy skepticism it is when someone claims that they have a magic pill that is the difference between failure and success.

## Disease or Growing Pains?

Since there are no diagnostic tests to determine who has ADHD, the diagnosis is based on observing the child in the classroom. How do doctors tell the difference between normal childhood behavioral growing pains and actual ADHD? From what I have presented thus far it should not surprise you to learn that there is no rigorous scientific basis for ADHD diagnosis. The following case studies are from an educator's in-service training program on ADHD presented in a seminar format to teachers and other educators. The program includes overheads and a pamphlet for the presenter to use for the presentation. The pamphlet is titled, "A Comprehensive Presentation to Inform Educators about Attention Deficit Disorders," and is produced by CHADD (Children and Adults with Attention Deficit Disorder). Keep in mind this is a pamphlet that is distributed to teachers all over our country. CHADD is a strong proponent of the view that ADHD is a neurobiological disease.

*Case #1.* John, a third grade student, is often noncompliant and does not begin tasks when asked. During a two-week observation period he exhibited the following behaviors on a routine basis: John sharpened his pencil three times before sitting down and working. John fell out of his chair when given an assignment with 50 problems. He pretended to be a clown. The class laughed. After leaving his reading group, on the way back to his seat for independent work, John tripped Sally. He was sent to the corner of the room.

*Case #2.* Sally is a middle school or senior high student who never gets from class A to class B on time. Often, she doesn't have the materials necessary for the next class. Her tardiness interferes with the class routine. Sally often misses class directions because she is busy trying to make up for lost time. The class has already started working while she is looking for yesterday's homework, which she has left in her locker.

In defense of CHADD, these two case studies are presented in conjunction with behavioral management techniques which are actually very appropriate.

Medication is not at first discussed, but it is clear in CHADD's view that these two children have a neurobiological deficit. The overall theme of CHADD's presentation is that these children have a disease, and later in the presentation the wonders of medication are presented: "Medications can have a strong positive effect for a high percentage (70% or more) of children with ADHD."

Is little John a diseased child, or is he the class clown? Is little Sally sick, or is she just at one end of a spectrum of behavioral variability? Do these kids need medication or social structure and intellectual stimuli? Of course, there is in the literature no mention of PET scans, blood work, or any other diagnostic test on John and Sally, just behavioral observations. So what it comes down to is this: should these children be medicated to control their behavior? Since scientific evidence is lacking, this is a practical and ethical question.

More and more physicians and scientists have publicly questioned whether the Ritalin proponents have misused science and overlooked ethics in the marketing of ADHD. It is time for the bioethical departments of medical schools to participate in this debate. So far, the idea of "normalizing" children with medication has eluded their radar. The pro-Ritalin advocates are considering gene manipulation in the womb for children who fall in the upper 10% of activity levels, yet the bio-ethicists seem more concerned with the ethics of genetically altering tomatoes and fruit flies. They ignore this problem at their peril. We can only hope that the groundswell for a more rational view of childhood will gain ascendancy before the technology of genetically altering John, Sally and 10% of the next generation is available.

# The Future for Children with ADHD

It will be interesting to see what happens in the next millennium if we follow the Ritalin movement's philosophy and its view of child development. Continuing the diabetes analogy, currently diabetics need to take a drug, but in the future these patients will probably be treated with gene therapy. By altering diabetics' genetic makeup they will be disease-free and never need to take medication again.

If we believe that ADHD is a disease like diabetes, what will we do with the 5–10% of the children in this country who have been diagnosed with ADHD? If one agrees with the Ritalin proponents, then gene therapy for a large portion of the children in this country would be a viable option. Consider Alan Zametkin's closing remark in his previously mentioned article, in a discussion on the future of ADHD research: "Can pharmacological or gene manipulations lead to a cure?"

Contemplating gene therapy for children by people who cannot agree on how many children have the disease is alarming. Nobel laureate Sir Peter Medawar addresses the question of genetic engineering for humans: "The moral-political answer is that no such regimen of genetic improvement could be practiced within the framework of a society that respects the rights of individuals." He also notes: "It is the great glory as it is also the great threat of science that everything which is in principle possible can be done if the intention to do it is sufficiently resolute. Scientists may exult in the glory, but in the middle of the 20th century the reaction of ordinary people is more often to cower at the threat."

Even if science does show a mechanistic or a biological basis for this variable personality trait, as a society we still face an important value judgement. If our schools are like pegboards designed for round holes, and 10% of the pegs are square, then we have two choices. Either we must change the peg board (the environment), which requires time and money to accommodate more of the pegs. Or, we can chisel away at the 10% of square pegs (children with problems sitting still) so that they fit into the round holes.

In the past several years pro-Ritalin advocates have had nothing but disregard at best, and contempt at worst, for anybody who is skeptical or concerned about the rising use of Ritalin in this country. In 1996 Dr. Lawrence Stone, the head of the American Academy of Child and Adolescent Psychiatry, said, "The media in general tend to take the particular issues of drugs and also ADHD out of the domain of science and clinical judgement where it really belongs." Judith Rapoport stated, "Most of the media coverage on Ritalin has been overblown." Since these statements the use of Ritalin has been documented to exceed most people's fears, or expectations. The *Journal of American Medical Association (JAMA)* recently confirmed that Ritalin use in this country has skyrocketed (about 12 out of 1,000 preschoolers in one mid-western population). I would expect that the pro-Ritalin advocates would say that this is a step forward. After all, they have been saying for several years that 10% of our children have a neurobiological disease. I think this is a step backward and that our expectations of childhood have become distorted. I also think the majority of Americans, including many scientists, are seeing that in retrospect the media coverage has not been overblown but that the "science" has been overblown. For a drug addict the first step on the road to recovery is to admit to having a drug problem. For our country the first step on the road to recovery would be for the National Institutes of Health to acknowledge the reality of the current situation in this country—we have a drug problem. If we don't face the reality do not be surprised if 10 years from now even more of our children are taking Ritalin.

# POSTSCRIPT

## Is Attention Deficit Disorder (ADD/ADHD) a Legitimate Medical Condition That Affects Childhood Behavior?

The diagnosis of ADHD has unquestionably helped many families and children. There are true and meaningful stories about Ritalin helping families recover from the chaos of an out-of-control child and saving children from failing out of school. The individual cases of ADHD should not be taken lightly. Yet, the academic study of life span development, and social science generally, requires considering larger group patterns at stages in the life span. And for ADHD, the patterns raise difficult questions.

To start, ADHD is a relatively recent category of childhood disorder. It has only been prominent during recent decades (only being included in the *Diagnostic and Statistical Manual of Mental Disorders,* or DSM, since 1980), and rates of diagnosis increased exponentially in the 1990s. If ADHD is a "real" disorder, then wouldn't it have always existed with the same frequency? In fact, critics argue, a diagnosis of ADHD depends on a checklist of criteria—not, as Leo points out in his article, on an objective test such as a blood test or a brain scan. A controversy as to whether ADHD should be considered a legal handicap has often revolved around the risks of making behavioral criteria (rather than medical conditions) sufficient for special services.

What this critique of ADHD neglects to consider is that many psychological disorders are defined by diagnostic criteria rather than objective medical tests. Disorders ranging from depression to schizophrenia depend upon clinical judgment defining what most would agree are genuine and serious medical conditions. Nevertheless, the criteria for ADHD are fairly broad and, according to the American Psychiatric Association's *Diagnostic and Statistical Manual-IV, Text Revision (DSM-IV-TR),* approximately 3 percent to 7 percent of North American children fulfill enough of the criteria to qualify for the disorder. But those children are not evenly distributed among demographic groups. ADHD, for example, is diagnosed three times more often in boys than in girls. Further, rates of diagnosis among ethnic minorities tend to be lower.

Such statistics have led to claims similar to that of Jonathan Leo that ADHD is constructed by drug companies serving parents who see a market in parents challenged by the sometimes extreme behavior of children. Yet, as Fumento points out, Ritalin works. It makes a difference in the lives of families and children. Isn't that enough?

225

Whichever side one takes in this controversy, the issues surrounding ADHD have tremendous relevance to the way we understand middle childhood. Middle childhood is a period where behavioral norms are established. But norms are never universal. There are always differences both between and within groups. Often those differences cause stress; extremely inattentive children are indeed stressful to manage and educate. But are they disordered? That question seems certain to continue as an important controversy.

## Suggested Readings

American Academy of Pediatrics, "Clinical Practice Guideline: Treatment of the School-Aged Child with Attention-Deficit/Hyperactivity Disorder," *Pediatrics* (October 2001). Also at http://www.aap.org/policy/s0120.html.

"An Update on Attention Deficit Disorder," *Harvard Medical Health Letter* (May 2004). Also at http://www.health.harvard.edu/newsweek/An_update_on_attention_deficit_disorder.htm.

R.A. Barkley, "Psychosocial Treatments for Attention-Deficit/Hyperactivity Disorder in Children," *Journal of Clinical Psychiatry* (vol. 63, 2002).

L. Diller, "Defusing the Explosive Child," *Salon* (August 18, 2001).

D. Matthews, *Attention Deficit Disorder Sourcebook* (Omnigraphics, 2002).

M. Olfson, et al., "National Trends in the Treatment of Attention Deficit Hyperactivity Disorder," *American Journal of Psychiatry* (June 2003).

# On the Internet . . .

## About Our Kids

This Web site is sponsored by a center at New York University focused on mental health in childhood and adolescence.

http://aboutourkids.org/

## ANSWER

This site is provided by the ANSWER (Adolescents Never Suicide When Everyone Responds) Network, which focuses on serious adolescent mental health issues.

http://www.teenanswer.org/

## U.S. Centers for Disease Control

This site provides an overview of youth violence from the U.S. Centers for Disease Control.

http://www.cdc.gov/ncipc/factsheets/
yvoverview.htm

## Society for Research on Adolescence

The Society for Research on Adolescence provides information for academics, clinicians, and students.

http://www.s-r-a.org/

## Gender and Achievement Research Program

The Gender and Achievement Research Program is a large-scale research effort at the University of Michigan to understand gender and achievement throughout development.

http://www.rcgd.isr.umich.edu/garp/

# PART 6

# Adolescence

*A*dolescence is a distinctive stage in the life span because it is marked by a clear biological change: puberty. Developing adolescents cope with dramatic physical changes that often seem to combine a mature body with an immature mind. Further, because adolescence is associated with increasing independence and responsibility, adolescents seem both powerful and vulnerable. Society is compelled to provide adolescents care and opportunity, while simultaneously fearing that they will rebel. The issues in this section deal with the nature of success and failure in adolescence by asking about society's perceptions of gender differences in adolescent risk, and about the susceptibility of adolescents to media influence.

- Are Boys More At-Risk Than Girls as They Develop Through Adolescence?

- Does Violent Media Cause Teenage Aggression?

# ISSUE 12

## Are Boys More At-Risk Than Girls as They Develop Through Adolescence?

**YES: Christina Hoff Sommers,** from "The War Against Boys," *The Atlantic Monthly* (May 2000)

**NO: Michael Kimmel,** from "A War Against Boys?" *Tikkun* (November/December 2000)

### ISSUE SUMMARY

**YES:** Author and philosopher Christina Hoff Sommers asserts that feminist concern for girls has had the ironic effect of leaving boys behind. She notes that in most high schools it is boys, rather than girls, most at risk.

**NO:** Professor of sociology Michael Kimmel responds to Sommers' argument by noting that her statistics are spun so as to make a particular case, and ignore the real disadvantages faced by girls in contemporary society.

For whatever debatable progress has been made toward gender equality, there seems to be a natural tendency to pit boys against girls. From infancy, when boys and girls start wearing different colors to school, where teachers regularly set children into lines by gender for simple organizational efficiency, gender is used as a standard of comparison. And the conventional wisdom is that in such comparisons, girls fare poorly. Throughout much of Western history, men have held the majority of positions of public power. Twentieth-century feminism has reacted against that inequity, and has focused a great deal of attention on how people develop into their relative positions in society. As such, the nature of developmental gender differences is central to much larger debates about power and society.

Several developmental outcomes are central to this controversy. One is self-concept, which is a central construct to social development. There is a general conception, based on theoretical scholarly work, that adolescence tends to damage girls self-concept. This idea is easy to recognize because of its familiarity to personal experience; we probably all know some girls whose outgoing, playful, athletic personas changed after puberty to become awkward, quiet, and dependent. While such anecdotes may be familiar, the larger group data are not so clear. In the readings, note that some interpretations of the data regarding the change in girls' self-concepts may have been interpreted with particular preconceptions. Puberty and adolescence can be difficult, but they are not necessarily so for everyone and not necessarily more so for girls.

The other developmental outcome that is central to this controversy is academic achievement as measured by diverse criteria including test scores and college attendance. Each criterion tells a slightly different story. With regard to test scores, for example, overall boys do tend to have generally higher scores on tests such as the SAT, but the difference is particularly significant in math. In reading and writing-related tests, girls tend to do better. Further, the distribution of scores for males and females demonstrates significant differences; there tend to be more boys both at the very high and very low ends of score distributions—more boys do very, very well and more boys do very, very poorly. How should such differences be interpreted?

Likewise, with regard to college attendance, there has been a clear general shift for females to make up a larger percentage of the college-going population. This is a significant historical change, since just 30 years ago there was still a concern among some college administrators that females would struggle with the rigors of college. But this seemingly straightforward statistic also turns out to be complicated. At many elite colleges, including Harvard and the University of Chicago, there is still a disproportionately male population. Further, the proportion of white males and females attending college is relatively even; much of the gender imbalance is due to much higher percentages of minority females who attend college.

Thus, there is an interesting subtext to this controversy regarding what counts as a meaningful group. For Christina Hoff Sommers, the meaningful groups are simply males and females. She emphasizes these broad groups partially because her position is a general response to feminism—which traditionally has focused on the broad inequities in society between males and females. She identifies feminist scholarship suggesting girls struggle more than boys with developmental transitions through adolescence as the root of the conventional wisdom that boys have all the advantages. And she points out how she perceives this scholarship and the conventional wisdom to be wrong; by emphasizing the needs of girls, we have silently marginalized boys.

For Michael Kimmel, several other groups are significant beyond just males and females. Kimmel points out that middle-class white males, on average, continue to enjoy the advantages of relative social power and to do reasonably well. The real differences here are about class and race—poor minority adolescents of both genders continue to struggle. Further, Kimmel asserts that setting out categorical differences between males and females actually reinforces stereotypes about gender. For Kimmel, the real problem for boys during adolescence is not feminist efforts to facilitate female achievement, but artificial ideas about masculinity that oppose conventional achievement.

**Christina Hoff Sommers**  **YES**

# The War Against Boys

**I**t's a bad time to be a boy in America. The triumphant victory of the U.S. women's soccer team at the World Cup last summer has come to symbolize the spirit of American girls. The shooting at Columbine High . . . might be said to symbolize the spirit of American boys.

That boys are in disrepute is not accidental. For many years women's groups have complained that boys benefit from a school system that favors them and is biased against girls. "Schools shortchange girls," declares the American Association of University Women. Girls are "undergoing a kind of psychological foot-hinding," two prominent educational psychologists say. A stream of books and pamphlets cite research showing not only that boys are classroom favorites but also that they are given to schoolyard violence and sexual harassment.

In the view that has prevailed in American education over the past decade, boys are resented, both as the unfairly privileged sex and as obstacles on the path to gender justice for girls. This perspective is promoted in schools of education, and many a teacher now feels that girls need and deserve special indemnifying consideration. "It is really clear that boys are Number One is this society and in most of the world," says Patricia O'Reilly, a professor of education and the director of the Gender Equity Center, at the University of Cincinnati.

The idea that schools and society grind girls down has given rise to an array of laws and policies intended to curtail the advantage boys have and to redress the harm done to girls. That girls are treated as the second sex in school and consequently suffer, that boys are accorded privileges and consequently benefit—these are things everyone is presumed to know. But they are not true.

The research commonly cited to support claims of male privilege and male sinfulness is riddled with errors. Almost none of it has been published in peer-reviewed professional journals. Some of the data turn out to be mysteriously missing. A review of the facts shows boys, not girls, on the weak side of an education gender gap. The typical boy is a year and a half behind the typical girl in reading and writing; he is less committed to school and less likely to go to college. In 1997 college full-time enrollments were 45 percent male and 55 percent female. The Department of Education predicts that the proportion of boys in college classes will continue to shrink.

Data from the U.S. Department of Education and from several recent university studies show that far from being shy and demoralized, today's girls outshine boys. They get better grades. They have higher educational aspirations. They follow more-rigorous academic programs and participate in advanced-placement classes at higher rates. According to the National Center for Education Statistics, slightly more girls than boys enroll in high-level math and science courses. Girls, allegedly timorous and lacking in confidence, now outnumber boys in student government, in honor societies, on school newspapers, and in debating clubs. Only in sports are boys ahead, and women's groups are targeting the sports gap with a vengeance. Girls read more books. They outperform boys on tests for artistic and musical ability. More girls than boys study abroad. More join the Peace Corps. At the same time, more boys than girls are suspended from school. More are held back and more drop out. Boys are three times as likely to receive a diagnosis of attention-deficit hyperactivity disorder. More boys than girls are involved in crime, alcohol, and drugs. Girls attempt suicide more often than boys, but it is boys who more often succeed. In 1997, a typical year, 4,483 young people aged five to twenty-four committed suicide: 701 females and 3,782 males.

In the technical language of education experts, girls are academically more "engaged." Last year an article in *The CQ Researcher* about male and female academic achievement described a common parental observation: "Daughters want to please their teachers by spending extra time on projects, doing extra credit, making homework as neat as possible. Sons rush through homework assignments and run outside to play, unconcerned about how the teacher will regard the sloppy work."

School engagement is a critical measure of student success. The U.S. Department of Education gauges student commitment by the following criteria: "How much time do students devote to homework each night?" and "Do students come to class prepared and ready to learn? (Do they bring books and pencils? Have they completed their homework?)" According to surveys of fourth, eighth, and twelfth graders, girls consistently do more homework than boys. By the twelfth grade boys are four times as likely as girls not to do homework. Similarly, more boys than girls report that they "usually" or "often" come to school without supplies or without having done their homework.

The performance gap between boys and girls in high school leads directly to the growing gap between male and female admissions to college. The Department of Education reports that in 1996 there were 8.4 million women but only 6.7 million men enrolled in college. It predicts that women will hold on to and increase their lead well into the next decade, and that by 2007 the numbers will be 9.2 million women and 6.9 million men.

## Deconstructing the Test-Score Gap

Feminists cannot deny that girls get better grades, are more engaged academically, and are now the majority sex in higher education. They argue, however, that these advantages are hardly decisive. Boys, they point out, get higher scores than girls on almost every significant standardized test—especially the

Scholastic Assessment Test and law school, medical school, and graduate school admissions tests.

In 1996 I wrote an article for *Education Week* about the many ways in which girl students were moving ahead of boys. Seizing on the test-score data that suggest boys are doing better than girls, David Sadker, a professor of education at American University and a co-author with his wife, Myra, of *Failing at Fairness: How America's Schools Cheat Girls* (1994), wrote, "If females are soaring in school, as Christina Hoff Sommers writes, then these tests are blind to their flight." On the 1998 SAT boys were thirty-five points (out of 800) ahead of girls in math and seven points ahead in English. These results seem to run counter to all other measurements of achievement in school. In almost all other areas boys lag behind girls. Why do they test better? Is Sadker right in suggesting that this is a manifestation of boys' privileged status?

The answer is no. A careful look at the pool of students who take the SAT and similar tests shows that the girls' lower scores have little or nothing to do with bias or unfairness. Indeed, the scores do not even signify lower achievement by girls. First of all, according to *College Bound Seniors,* an annual report on standardized-test takers published by the College Board, many more "at risk" girls than "at risk" boys take the SAT—girls from lower-income homes or with parents who never graduated from high school or never attended college. "These characteristics," the report says, "are associated with lower than average SAT scores." Instead of wrongly using SAT scores as evidence of bias against girls, scholars should be concerned about the boys who never show up for the tests they need if they are to move on to higher education.

Another factor skews test results so that they appear to favor boys. Nancy Cole, the president of the Educational Testing Service, calls in the "spread" phenomenon. Scores on almost any intelligence or achievement test are more spread out for boys than for girls—boys include more prodigies and more students of marginal ability. Or, as the political scientist James Q. Wilson once put it. "There are more male geniuses and more male idiots."

Boys also dominate dropout lists, failure lists, and learning-disability lists. Students in these groups rarely take college-admissions tests. On the other hand, the exceptional boys who take school seriously show up in disproportionately high numbers for standardized tests. Gender-equity activists like Sadker ought to apply their logic consistently: if the shortage of girls at the high end of the ability distribution is evidence of unfairness to girls, then the excess of boys at the low end should be deemed evidence of unfairness to boys.

Suppose we were to turn our attention away from the highly motivated, self-selected two fifths of high school students who take the SAT and consider instead a truly representative sample of American schoolchildren. How would girls and boys then compare? Well, we have the answer. The National Assessment of Educational Progress, started in 1969 and mandated by Congress, offers the best and most comprehensive measure of achievement among students at all levels of ability. Under the NAEP program 70,000 to 100,000 students, drawn from forty-four states, are tested in reading, writing, math, and science at ages nine, thirteen, and seventeen. In 1996, seventeen-year-old boys outperformed seventeen-year-old girls by five points in math and eight points in science, whereas the girls outperformed the boys by fourteen points in reading and seventeen points in writing. In the past few years girls have been catching up in math and science while boys have continued to lag far behind in reading and writing.

In the July, 1995, issue of *Science,* Larry V. Hedges and Amy Nowell, researchers at the University of Chicago, observed that girls' deficits in math were small but not insignificant. These deficits, they noted, could adversely affect the number of women who "excel in scientific and technical occupations." Of the deficits in boys' writing skills they wrote, "The large sex differences in writing . . . are alarming. . . . The data imply that males are, on average, at a rather profound disadvantage in the performance of this basic skill." They went on to warn,

> The generally larger numbers of males who perform near the bottom of the distribution in reading comprehension and writing also have policy implications. It seems likely that individuals with such poor literacy skills will have difficulty finding employment in an increasingly information-driven economy. Thus, some intervention may be required to enable them to participate constructively.

Hedges and Nowell were describing a serious problem of national scope, but because the focus elsewhere has been on girls' deficits, few Americans know much about the problem or even suspect that it exists.

Indeed, so accepted has the myth of girls in crisis become that even teachers who work daily with male and female students tend to reflexively dismiss any challenge to the myth, or any evidence pointing to the very real crisis among boys. Three years ago Scarsdale High School, in New York, held a gender-equity workshop for faculty members. It was the standard girls-are-being-shortchanged fare, with one notable difference. A male student gave a presentation in which he pointed to evidence suggesting that girls at Scarsdale High were well ahead of boys. David Greene, a social-studies teacher, thought the student must be mistaken, but when he and some colleagues analyzed department grading patterns, they discovered that the student was right. They found little or no difference in the grades of boys and girls in advanced-placement social-studies classes. But in standard classes the girls were doing a lot better.

And Greene discovered one other thing: few wanted to hear about his startling findings. Like schools everywhere, Scarsdale High has been strongly influenced by the belief that girls are systematically deprived. That belief prevails among the school's gender-equity committee and has led the school to offer a special senior elective on gender equity. Greene has tried to broach the subject of male underperformance with his colleagues. Many of them concede that in the classes they teach, the girls seem to be doing better than the boys, but they do not see this as part of a larger pattern. After so many years of hearing about silenced, diminished girls, teachers do not take seriously the suggestion that boys are not doing as well as girls even if they see it with their own eyes in their own classrooms.

# The Incredible Shrinking Girl

How did we get to this odd place? How did we come to believe in a picture of American boys and girls that is the opposite of the truth? And why has that belief persisted, enshrined in law, encoded in governmental and school policies, despite overwhelming evidence against it? The answer has much to do with one of the American academy's most celebrated women—Carol Gilligan, Harvard University's first professor gender studies.

Gilligan first came to widespread attention in 1982, with the publication of *In a Different Voice*, which this article will discuss shortly. In 1990 Gilligan announced that America's adolescent girls were in crisis. In her words, "As the river of a girl's life flows into the sea of Western culture, she is in danger of drowning or disappearing." Gilligan offered little in the way of conventional evidence to support this alarming finding. Indeed, it is hard to imagine what sort of empirical research could establish such a large claim. But she quickly attracted powerful allies. Within a very short time the allegedly vulnerable and demoralized state of adolescent girls achieved the status of a national emergency. . . .

# "Politics Dressed Up as Science"

Gilligan's ideas about demoralized teenage girls had a special resonance with women's groups that were already committed to the proposition that our society is unsympathetic to women. The interest of the venerable and politically influential American Association of University Women, in particular, was piqued. Its officers were reported to be "intrigued and alarmed" by Gilligan's research. They wanted to know more.

In 1990 *The New York Times Sunday Magazine* published an admiring profile of Gilligan that heralded the discovery of a hidden crisis among the nation's girls. Soon after, the AAUW commissioned a study from the polling firm Greenberg-Lake. The pollsters asked 3,000 children (2,400 girls and 600 boys in grades four through ten) about their self-perceptions. In 1991 the association announced the disturbing results, in a report titled *Shortchanging Girls, Shortchanging America*. "Girls aged eight and nine are confident, assertive, and feel authoritative about themselves. Yet most emerge from adolescence with a poor self-image, constrained views of their future and their place in society, and much less confidence about themselves and their abilities." Anne Bryant, the executive director of the AAUW and an expert in public relations, organized a media campaign to spread the word that "an unacknowledged American tragedy" had been uncovered. Newspapers and magazines around the country carried reports that girls were being adversely affected by gender bias that eroded their self-esteem. Sharon Schuster, at the time the president of the AAUW, candidly explained to *The New York Times* why the association had undertaken the research in the first place; "We wanted to put some factual data behind our belief that girls are getting shortchanged in the classroom."

As the AAUW's self-esteem study was making headlines, a little-known magazine called *Science News*, which has been supplying information on scientific and technical developments to interested newspapers since 1922, reported the skeptical reaction of leading specialists on adolescent development. The late Roberta Simmons, a professor of sociology at the University of Pittsburgh (described by *Science News* as "director of the most ambitious longitudinal study of adolescent self-esteem to date"), said that her research showed nothing like the substantial gender gap described by the AAUW. According to Simmons, "Most kids come through the years from 10 to 20 without major problems and with an increasing sense of self-esteem." But the doubts of Simmons and several other prominent experts were not reported in the hundreds of news stories that the Greenberg-Lake study generated.

The AAUW quickly commissioned a second study, *How Schools Shortchange Girls*. This one, conducted by the Wellesley College Center for Research on Women and released in 1992, focused on the alleged effects of sexism on girls' school performance. It asserted that schools deflate girls' self-esteem by "systematically cheating girls of classroom attention." Such bias leads to lower aspirations and impaired academic achievement. Carol Gilligan's crisis was being transformed into a civil-right issue: girls were the victims of widespread sex discrimination. "The implications are clear," the AAUW said. "The system must change."

With great fanfare *How Schools Shortchange Girls* was released to the remarkably uncritical media. A 1992 article for *The New York Times* by Susan Chira was typical of coverage throughout the country. The headline read **"bias against girls is found rife in schools, with lasting damage."** The piece was later reproduced by the AAUW and sent out as part of a fundraising package. Chira had not interviewed a single critic of the study.

In March of last year I called Chira and asked about the way she had handled the AAUW study. I asked if she would write her article the same way today. No, she said, pointing out that we have since learned much more about boys' problems in school. Why had she not canvassed dissenting opinions? She explained that she had been traveling when the AAUW study came out, and was on a short deadline. Yes, perhaps she had relied too much on the AAUW's report. She had tried to reach Diane Ravitch, who had then been the former U.S. assistant secretary of education and was a known critic of women's-advocacy findings, but without success.

Six years after the release of *How Schools Shortchange Girls*, *The New York Times* ran a story that raised questions about its validity. This time the reporter, Tamar Lewin, did reach Diane Ravitch, who told her, "That [1992] AAUW report was just completely wrong. What was so bizarre is that it came out right at the time that girls had just overtaken boys in almost every area. It might have been the right story twenty years earlier, but coming out when it did, it was like calling a wedding a funeral. . . . There were all these special programs put in place for girls, and no one paid any attention to boys. . . .

# The Myth Unraveling

By the late 1990s the myth of the downtrodden girl was showing some signs of unraveling, and concern over boys was growing. In 1997 the Public Education Network (PEN) announced at its annual conference the results of a new teacher-student survey titled *The American Teacher 1997: Examining Gender Issues in Public Schools.* The survey was funded by the Metropolitan Life Insurance Company and conducted by Louis Harris and Associates.

During a three-month period in 1997 various questions about gender equity were asked of 1,306 students and 1,035 teachers in grades seven through twelve. The MetLife study had no doctrinal ax to grind. What it found contradicted most of the findings of the AAUW, the Sadkers, and the Wellesley College Center for Research on Women: "Contrary to the commonly held view that boys are at an advantage over girls in school, girls appear to have an advantage over boys in terms of their future plans, teachers' expectations, everyday experiences at school and interactions in the classroom."

Some other conclusions from the MetLife study: Girls are more likely than boys to see themselves as college-bound and more likely to want a good education. Furthermore, more boys (31 percent) than girls (19 percent) feel that teachers do not listen to what they have to say.

At the PEN conference, Nancy Leffert, a child psychologist then at the Search Institute, in Minneapolis, reported the results of a survey that she and colleagues had recently completed of more than 99,000 children in grades six through twelve. The children were asked about what the researchers call "developmental assets." The Search Institute has identified forty critical assets—"building blocks for healthy development." Half of these are external, such as a supportive family and adult role models, and half are internal, such as motivation to achieve, a sense of purpose in life, and interpersonal confidence. Leffert explained, somewhat apologetically, that girls were ahead of boys with respect to thirty-seven out of forty assets. By almost every significant measure of well-being girls had the better of boys: they felt closer to their families; they had higher aspirations, stronger connections to school, and even superior assertiveness skills. Leffert concluded her talk by saying that in the past she had referred to girls as fragile or vulnerable, but that the survey "tells me that girls have very powerful assets."

The Horatio Alger Association, a fifty-year-old organization devoted to promoting and affirming individual initiative and "the American dream," releases annual back-to-school surveys. Its survey for 1998 contrasted two groups of students: the "highly successful" (approximately 18 percent of American students) and the "disillusioned" (approximately 15 percent). The successful students work hard, choose challenging classes, make schoolwork a top priority, get good grades, participate in extracurricular activities, and feel that teachers and administrators care about them and listen to them. According to the association, the successful group in the 1998 survey is 63 percent female and 37 percent male. The disillusioned students are pessimistic about their future, get low grades, and have little contact with teachers. The disillusioned group could accurately be characterized as demoralized. According to the Alger Association, "Nearly seven out of ten are male."

In the spring of 1998 Judith Kleinfeld, a psychologist at the University of Alaska, published a thorough critique of the research on schoolgirls titled "The Myth That Schools Shortchange Girls: Social Science in the Service of Deception." Kleinfeld exposed a number of errors in the AAUW/Wellesley Center study, concluding that it was "politics dressed up as science." Kleinfeld's report prompted several publications, including *The New York Times* and *Education Week,* to take a second look at claims that girls were in a tragic state.

The AAUW did not adequately respond to any of Kleinfeld's substantive objections; instead its current president, Maggie Ford, complained in the *New York Times* letters column that Kleinfeld was "reducing the problems of our children to this petty 'who is worse off, boys or girls?' [which] gets us nowhere." From the leader of an organization that spent nearly a decade ceaselessly promoting the proposition that American girls are being "shortchanged," this comment is rather remarkable.

## Boys and Their Mothers

Growing evidence that the scales are tipped not against girls but against boys is beginning to inspire a quiet revisionism. Some educators will admit that boys are on the wrong side of the gender gap. In 1998 I met the president of the Board of Education of Atlanta. Who is faring better in Atlanta's schools, boys or girls? I asked. "Girls," he replied, without hesitation. In what areas? I asked. "Just about any area you mention." A high school principal from Pennsylvania says of his school. "Students who dominate the dropout list, the suspension list, the failure list, and other negative indices of nonachievement in school are males by a wide margin." . . .

Every society confronts the problem of civilizing its young males. The traditional approach is through character education: Develop the young man's sense of honor. Help him become a considerate, conscientious human being. Turn him into a gentleman. This approach respects boys' masculine nature; it is time-tested, and it works. Even today, despite several decades of moral confusion, most young men understand the term "gentleman" and approve of the ideals it connotes.

What feminists are proposing is quite different: civilize boys by diminishing their masculinity. "Raise boys like we raise girls" is Gloria Steinem's advice. This approach is deeply disrespectful of boys. It is meddlesome, abusive, and quite beyond what educators in a free society are mandated to do.

~◆~

Did anything of value come out of the manufactured crisis of diminished girls? Yes, a bit. Parents, teachers, and administrators now pay more attention to girls' deficits in math and science, and they offer more support for girls' participation in sports. But do these benefits outweigh the disservice done by promulgating the myth of the victimized girl or by presenting boys as the unfairly favored sex?

A boy today, through no fault of his own, finds himself implicated in the social crime of shortchanging girls. Yet the allegedly silenced and neglected girl sitting next to him is likely to be the superior student. She is probably more articulate, more mature, more engaged, and more well-balanced. The boy may be aware that she is more likely to go on to college. He may believe that teachers prefer to be around girls and pay more attention to them. At the same time, he is uncomfortably aware that he is considered to be a member of the favored and dominant gender.

The widening gender gap in academic achievement is real. It threatens the future of millions of American boys. Boys do not need to be rescued from their masculinity. But they are not getting the help they need. In the climate of disapproval in which boys now exist, programs designed to aid them have a very low priority. This must change. We should repudiate the partisanship that currently clouds the issues surrounding sex differences in the schools. We should call for balance, objective information, fair treatment, and a concerted national effort to get boys back on track. That means we can no longer allows the partisans of girls to shape the discussion and to write the rules.

# NO

Michael Kimmel

# A War Against Boys?

**B**y now, you've probably heard there's a "war against boys" in America. The latest heavily-hyped right-wing fusillade against feminism, led by Christina Hoff Sommers's new book of that title, claims that men are now the second sex and that boys—not girls—are the ones who are in serious trouble, the "victims" of "misguided" feminist efforts to protect and promote girls' development. At the same time, best-selling books by therapists, like William Pollack's *Real Boys* and Dan Kindlon and Michael Thompson's *Raising Cain,* also sound the same tocsin, warning of alarming levels of depression and suicide among boys, and describing boys' interior lives as an emotionally barren landscape, with all affect suppressed beneath postures of false bravado. They counsel anguished parents to "rescue" or "protect" boys—not from feminists but from a definition of masculinity that is harmful to boys, girls, and other living things.

In part, they're both right. There *is* a crisis among boys. But the right-wing jeremiads misdiagnose the cause of the crisis and thus their proposed reforms would take us even further away from enabling young boys to negotiate the difficult path to a manhood of integrity, ethical commitment, and compassion. At least the therapists get that part right. But, in part, both sides are also wrong: on most measures boys—at least the middle class white boys everyone seems concerned about—are doing just fine, taking the places in an unequal society to which they have always felt entitled.

## The Boy Crisis

Let's begin with the evidence of crisis. The signs are everywhere. Boys drop out of school, are diagnosed as emotionally disturbed, and commit suicide four times more often than girls; they get into fights twice as often; they murder ten times more frequently and are fifteen times more likely to be the victims of a violent crime. Boys are six times more likely to be diagnosed with Attention Deficit Disorder. Boys get lower grades on standardized tests of reading and writing, and have lower class rank and fewer honors than girls.

From *Tikkun,* vol. 15, no. 6, November/December 2000, pp. 57–60. Copyright © 2000 by Tikkun. Reprinted by permission.

On college campuses, women now constitute the majority of students, passing men in 1982, so that in eight years women will earn 58 percent of bachelor's degrees in U.S. colleges. Doomsayers lament that women now outnumber men in the social and behavioral sciences by about 3 to 1, and they've "invaded" such traditionally male bastions as engineering (where they now make up 20 percent of all students) and biology and business (virtually par).

Elementary schools, we hear, are "anti-boy," emphasizing reading and restricting the movements of young boys. They "feminize" boys, forcing active, healthy, and naturally rambunctious boys to conform to a regime of obedience, "pathologizing what is simply normal for boys," as one psychologist put it. Michael Gurian argues in *The Wonder of Boys* that despite the testosterone surging through their little limbs, we demand that boys sit still, raise their hands, and take naps. We're giving them the message, he says, that "boyhood is defective."

According to Christina Hoff Sommers, it's "misguided feminism" that's been spreading such calumnies about boys. It's boys, not girls, who face the much-discussed "chilly classroom climate," according to Sommers. Schools are an "inhospitable," hostile environment for boys, where their natural propensities for rough and tumble play, competition, aggression, and rambunctious violence are cast as social problems in the making.

"Misguided" feminists have ignored the natural biological differences between boys and girls, and, in their fear and loathing of all things masculine, have demeaned an entire sex. Sommers quotes a line from a speech by Gloria Steinem that "we need to raise boys like we raise girls." (In fact, she quotes it three times in her short, but repetitive book.) She vilifies William Pollack, author of *Real Boys,* and others (including myself) for our efforts to "save the males"—to rescue boys from the dangerous myths of masculinity. Boys, she argues, are simply different from girls, and efforts to transform time-tested and beneficial definitions of masculinity will run counter to nature's plan. Categorical differences are "natural, healthy, and, by implication, best left alone."

On the other hand, Sommers reserves her fiercest animus for Carol Gilligan, whose work on girls' development suggests that there is more than one moral voice which guides people in their ethical decision-making, and who has explored the ways in which girls lose their voice as they approach adolescence. In fact, Sommers is so filled with misplaced rage at Gilligan that one is tempted to speculate about her motives, accusing Gilligan of ethical impropriety in her research, duplicity, intellectual fraud, and deceptive cover-ups. (This because Gilligan won't show her raw field notes and interview transcripts to some smarmy Harvard undergraduate who did not identify himself as working for Sommers.)

But Sommers goes after Gilligan precisely because Sommers believes (based on a misreading of the work) that Gilligan posits categorically different moral voices for boys and girls. Here, Sommers offers evidence that the differences between boys and girls are minimal. When she discusses boys' aggression, those same testosterone-propelled, hard-wired, natural sex differences magically disappear. "[S]chool problems have very little to do with misogyny, patriarchy, or sex discrimination," she writes. "They have everything to do with *children's* propensity to bully and be cruel" (my italics).

So which is it? She attacks the therapists for failing to recognize the hard-wired differences between the sexes, but then excoriates Gilligan for crediting those same differences.

## Misguided Anti-Feminism as Misdiagnosis

Anyone who has kids in school today knows that some of this appears true: some boys seem defensive, morose, unfocused, taciturn, and withdrawn, while the girls in their classes seem to be sailing on towards bright and multifaceted futures, performing science experiments, playing soccer, and delivering valedictory addresses. So, what's wrong with Sommers' picture?

In addition to its internal contradictions, Sommers and the boys-as-victims crowd make several key errors. For one thing, though driven to distraction by numbers, Sommers, Gurian, and others never factor in the number zero—as in zero dollars for new public school programs, the death of school bond issues that have passed, the absence of money from which might have developed remedial programs, intervention strategies, teacher training. Money which might have prevented cutting school sports programs and after-school extracurricular activities. Money which might have enabled teachers and administrators to do more than "store" problem students in separate classes. Far larger portions of those school budgets go towards programming for boys (special education, school sports) than for girls. So much for feminization. (This mirrors apparent national priorities: we can't seem to pass any school bond issues, but we'll tax ourselves into the next millennium to build a new sports stadium.) Nor do they mention managed care health insurance, which virtually demands that school psychologists diagnose problem behavior as a treatable medical condition so that drugs may be substituted for costly, "unnecessary" therapy.

And what about the numbers of boys going to college? Well, for one thing, more *people* are going to college than ever before. In 1960, 54 percent of boys and 38 percent of girls went directly to college; today the numbers are 64 percent of boys and 70 percent of girls. And while some college presidents fret that to increase male enrollments they'll be forced to lower standards (which is, incidentally, exactly the opposite of what they worried about twenty-five years ago when they all went coeducational) no one seems to find gender disparities going the other way all that upsetting. Of the top colleges and universities in the nation, only Stanford sports a 50-50 gender balance. Harvard and Amherst enroll 56 percent men, Princeton and Chicago 54 percent men, Duke and Berkeley 52 percent and Yale 51 percent. And that doesn't even begin to approach the gender disparities at Cal Tech (65 percent male, 35 percent female) or MIT (62 percent male, 38 percent female). Not does anyone seem driven to distraction about the gender disparities in nursing, social work, or education. Did somebody say "what about the girls?" Should we lower standards to make sure they're gender balanced?

Much of the gender difference offered is actually what sociologist Cynthia Fuchs Epstein calls a "deceptive distinction," a difference that appears to be about gender but is actually about something else—in this case, class or race. Girls' vocational opportunities are far more restricted than boys' are. Their opportunities are from the service sector, with limited openings in manufacturing or construction. A college-educated woman earns about the same as a high-school educated man, $31,000 to $35,000. Note, too, that the shortage of male college students is actually a shortage of *non-white* males. The actual gender gap between college-age white males and white females is rather small, 51 percent women to 49 percent men. But only 37 percent of black college students are male compared with 63 percent female, and only 45 percent of Hispanic students are male, compared with 55 percent female.

These differences among boys—by race or class, for example—do not typically fall within the radar of the cultural critics who would rescue boys. These differences are incidental because, in their eyes, all boys are the same: aggressive, competitive, rambunctious little devils. They argue that testosterone makes boys into boys, and that our society fails by making it impossible for boys to be boys.

Now, personally, I find those words, "boys will be boys" (which, incidentally, are the final four words of Sommers' book) to be four of the most depressing words in policy circles today, because they suggest resignation, a hopeless throwing up of the hands. If boys will be boys, then there is simply nothing we can do about it.

## Rethinking Masculinity

"Masculinity is aggressive, unstable, combustible," writes Camille Paglia, whom Sommers quotes approvingly, in one of the most insulting—yes, male-bashing—definitions available. Are we hard-wired only for aggression and competition? Are we not also hard-wired for compassion, nurturance, love?

The therapists (Pollack, Kindlon, and Thompson) understand that what lies beneath boys' problems (apparent or real) is an outdated ideology of masculinity to which boys are struggling desperately to adhere, and which is applied ruthlessly and coercively by other boys.

For example, the reason it appears that boys are lagging behind in reading and languages is not because of feminist efforts to improve the lives of girls, nor even because testosterone inhibits the memorization of French syntax. It's about an ideology of masculinity.

Consider the parallel for girls. Gilligan's often moving work on adolescent girls describes how these assertive, confident, and proud youngsters "lose their voices," when they hit adolescence. At the same moment, Pollack notes, boys become *more* confident, even beyond their abilities. You might even say that boys *find* their voices, but it is the inauthentic voice of bravado, of constant posturing, of foolish risk-taking and gratuitous violence. The Boy Code teaches them that they are supposed to be in power, and thus begin to act like it. They "ruffle in a manly pose," as William Butler Yeats once put it, "for all their timid heart."

What's the cause of all this posturing and posing? It's not testosterone, but privilege. In adolescence both boys and girls get their first real dose of gender inequality: girls suppress ambition, boys inflate it.

Recent research on the gender gap in school achievement bears this out. Girls are more likely to undervalue their abilities, especially in the more traditionally "masculine" educational arenas such as math and science. Only the most able and most secure girls take such courses. Thus, their numbers tend to be few, and their grades high. Boys, however, possessed of this false voice of bravado (and many facing strong family pressure) are likely to *over value* their abilities, to remain in programs though they are less qualified and capable of succeeding.

This difference, and not some putative discrimination against boys, is the reason that girls' mean test scores in math and science are now, on average, approaching that of boys. Too many boys who over value their abilities remain in difficult math and science courses longer than they should; they pull the boys' mean scores down. By contrast, the few girls whose abilities and self-esteem are sufficient to enable them to "trespass" into a male domain skew female data upwards.

A parallel process is at work in the humanities and social sciences. Girls' test scores in English and foreign languages outpace boys not because of some "reverse discrimination," but because the boys bump up against the norms of masculinity. Boys regard English as a "feminine" subject. Pioneering research in Australia by Wayne Martino found that boys are uninterested in English because of what it might say about their (inauthentic) masculine pose. "Reading is lame, sitting down and looking at words is pathetic," commented one boy. "Most guys who like English are faggots." The traditional liberal arts curriculum is seen as feminizing; as Catharine Stimpson recently put it sarcastically, "real men don't speak French."

Boys tend to hate English and foreign languages for the same reasons that girls love it. In English, they observe, there are no hard and fast rules, but rather one expresses one's opinion about the topic and everyone's opinion is equally valued. "The answer can be a variety of things, you're never really wrong," observed one boy. "It's not like math and science where there is one set answer to everything." Another boy noted:

> I find English hard. It's because there are no set rules for reading texts. . . . . English isn't like math where you have rules on how to do things and where there are right and wrong answers. In English you have to write down how you feel and that's what I don't like.

Compare this to the comments of girls in the same study:

> I feel motivated to study English because . . . you have freedom in English— unlike subjects such as math and science—and your view isn't necessarily wrong. There is no definite right or wrong answer and you have the freedom to say what you feel is right without it being rejected as a wrong answer.

It is not the school experience that "feminizes" boys, but rather the ideology of traditional masculinity that keeps boys from wanting to succeed. "The work you do here is girls' work," one boy commented to a British researcher. "It's not real work."

Ideologies of masculinity are reinforced ruthlessly on playgrounds and in classrooms all across the country. Boys who do like school, or who don't like sports, or who dress or act "different," are often subject to a constant barrage of insults, harassment, beatings. School may become an interminable torment. Students at Columbine High School described how the jocks beat up Eric Harris every day. This isn't playful rambunctious rough and tumble play: it's harassment, and is actionable under the law. And if masculinity is so "natural" and hard-wired, why does it have to be enforced with so much constant coercion?

Efforts to improve boys' lives in school will either adequately address the cultural—not natural—equation of masculinity and anti-intellectualism or they will fail.

And that leads to the final and most telling problem with these works: They assert a false opposition between girls and boys, pretending that the educational reforms undertaken to enable girls to perform better actually hindered boys' educational development. But these reforms—new initiatives, classroom configurations, teacher training, increased attentiveness to students' processes and individual learning styles—actually enable larger numbers of boys to get a better education. As Susan McGee Bailey and Patricia Campbell point out, "gender stereotypes, particularly those related to education, hurt both girls and boys," while the challenging of those stereotypes, decreased tolerance for school violence and bullying, and increased attention to violence at home actually enables *both* girls *and* boys to feel safer at school.

Since Sommers quotes Gloria Steinem's statement no less than three times, out of context, it might be interesting to conclude with what Steinem actually did say:

> We've begun to raise our daughters more like sons—so now women are whole people. But fewer of us have the courage to raise our sons more like daughters. Yet until men raise children as much as women do—and are raised to raise children, whether or not they become fathers—they will have a far harder time developing in themselves those human qualities that are wrongly called "feminine."

Hardly a call for androgyny—she seeks to degender traits, not people—Steinem reminds us of the most vital connection between parents and children, the centrality of caring, nurturing parenting as the fulfillment of our ethical responsibilities, and suggests that the signal success of feminism has been to raise girls to become competent, confident, and strong-minded. Would that our boys could achieve those traits.

# POSTSCRIPT

## Are Boys More At-Risk Than Girls as They Develop Through Adolescence

**W**e have a general conception of adolescence as a period of challenge and crisis. In fact, one of the most famous developmental perspectives on adolescence is Erik Erikson's suggestion that successfully negotiating adolescence requires resolving an "identity crisis." Yet, in the selection above, Sommers notes that 80 to 90 percent of adolescents generally report that they are doing well. Ironically, part of the reason that Sommers' writing on boys and girls generated so much controversy was because it emphasized that many adolescents seem all right. Don't adolescents need help?

Many academics believe that adolescents, and particularly adolescents from marginalized groups including females, do need help. The Sommers article you have just read generated a series of exchanges and controversy, including a direct response from distinguished feminist psychologist Carol Gilligan, who defended her work contending that girls face particular developmental challenges in adolescence. Sommers went on to elaborate on her argument in a popular book that generated more controversy and discussion. Sommers directly critiqued many leading scholars who have produced research demonstrating gender differences that favor boys.

A good number of these researchers, including Kimmel, provided direct responses to Sommers' critiques. Such exchanges are healthy for scholarship and knowledge, as research data can allow diverse interpretations, and part of the academic process is to refine understandings through critical evaluation. Unfortunately, much of the discourse deriving from Sommers' work tended toward the political. Sommers is affiliated with several conservative political groups, while feminist scholarship is generally associated with liberal politics. For purposes of understanding life span development, it is important to try and get beyond these political associations because the facts presented by both sides, by Sommers and Kimmel, are meaningful.

There are significant group differences in developmental outcomes during adolescence. More women than men are attending college. More children from middle- and upper-class families succeed in school compared to children from lower-class families. Some students in diverse groups struggle with the transition to adolescence and lose what was previously a healthy self-concept. So what is to be done about these facts? Should we follow Sommers' advice and encourage boys to be boys and girls to be girls? Should we accept Kimmel's perspective that artificially separating genders creates more problems than it solves, especially as everyone is looking for a similar outcome: what he talks about as competence, confidence, and strong-mindedness? Or will the controversy about gender and adolescence continue regardless of the scholarship in life span development?

## Suggested Readings

G. Broude, "Boys Will Be Boys," *The Public Interest* (Summer 1999).

M. Conlin, "The New Gender Gap," *Business Week* (May 26, 2003).

M. Edmundson, "Bad Boys, Watcha Gonna Do . . ." *Nation* (November 9, 2000).

D. Geary, J. Byrd-Craven, M. Hoard, J. Vigil, and C. Numtee, "Evolution and Development of Boys' Social Behavior," *Developmental Review* (2003).

C. Hoff Sommers, *The War Against Boys* (Simon & Schuster, 2000).

B. Kamler, *Constructing Gender and Difference: Critical Research Perspectives on Early Childhood* (Hampton Press, 1999).

E. Maccoby, *The Two Sexes: Growing Up Apart, Coming Together* (Harvard University Press, 1998).

D. Sadker, "Gender Games," *The Washington Post* (July 30, 2000).

J. Udry, "Biological Limits of Gender Construction," *American Sociological Review* (June 2000).

"The War Against Boys: Carol Gilligan et al. versus Christian Hoff Sommers," *Atlantic Monthly* (August 2000).

C. Young, "Where the Boys Are," *Reason* (February, 2001).

# ISSUE 13

## Does Violent Media Cause Teenage Aggression?

**YES: Dave Grossman,** from "Teaching Kids to Kill," *National Forum* (vol. 80, 2000)

**NO: Jonathan L. Freedman,** from *Media Violence and Its Effect on Aggression: Assessing the Scientific Evidence* (University of Toronto Press, 2002)

### ISSUE SUMMARY

**YES:** Researcher, author, and former military officer Dave Grossman argues that the contemporary media teaches youth to kill in much the same way that the military prepares soldiers for war. From his perspective, both use psychological foundations to develop an appetite for aggression.

**NO:** Professor of psychology Jonathan L. Freedman argues that, despite many research efforts to demonstrate a link between media violence and teen aggression, the data do not support that case.

The spate of dramatic violence perpetrated by teenagers in recent years—from Littleton, Colorado, to Paducah, Kentucky—has garnered much attention from society and scholars. It is not hard to find an intuitive link; violent teenagers often consume violent media, and it is easy to assume the violence is connected. The killers in Littleton, for example, had a much-publicized affinity for a violent video game titled "Doom," and they may have felt as though they were enacting a similar game on the horrific day in 1999 when they murdered 15 students and teachers in cold blood. But any social scientist knows that anecdotal evidence rarely proves a causal link. Is it possible that the association between violent media and violent acts is simply an association?

The controversial nature of this issue is compounded by the power of the media in contemporary society. When the surgeon general of the United States commissioned a group of expert scholars to review youth violence for a 2000 report, a statement of connection between media violence and youth violence was submitted. For reasons unclear to the scholars, that section of the report was later omitted in favor of a more general statement regarding media violence that did not make any causal link to youth violence. While a modified version of the report with its original findings was later published by the American Psychological Society, the implication of the anecdote is that powerful interests do not want connections being made between the media and antisocial behavior (for a review of this incident, see Ceci and Bjork, 2003).

On the other hand, it is possible that the surgeon general concluded there was not enough evidence to support a definitive statement linking the media and youth violence. This is the position taken by Jonathan L. Freedman in the reading selection. He recognizes that massive amounts of attention have been devoted to researching the effects of media violence, and he knows that many scholars and scholarly groups have concluded that media causes youth violence. But Freedman does not believe that those two facts necessarily go together. In fact, he asserts, the easy intuitive assumption that media violence causes youth violence has provoked experts to draw conclusions that go well beyond the data. Freedman has done careful reviews of the psychological research about media violence, and he finds no conclusive evidence for a causal link to youth violence. It is important to note that even the studies expert scholars often rely upon often address only aggressive impulses and actions immediately after consuming violent media. There is a significant difference between feeling aggressive in the minutes immediately after watching violent media and executing vicious acts of pre-meditated violence such as that committed by the Columbine killers in Littleton, Colorado.

Nevertheless, Dave Grossman makes the case that violent youth such as those at Columbine High School could only learn the skills they display at killing from the media. Based on his experience in the military, Grossman insists that violent acts are difficult to provoke—in World War II, the U.S. military had a hard time getting soldiers to shoot to kill. But society has changed since World War II. Television has become ubiquitous, and violent television has a prominent place in the minds of children. Further, video games often train children with the same skills used in military training. From Grossman's perspective, the influence of media violence can't be anything but more violence.

Both of these authors raise important questions about what counts as evidence. For Grossman, the obvious similarities between the military's training to kill and media violence is sufficient proof. Freedman wants more. He suggests that the intuitive nature of the link between media violence and youth violence is almost too obvious. Part of the job of good science is to counter bad common sense. Yet this issue is complicated by the inherent complexities of violent behavior—adolescents rarely commit violent acts for just one reason. Youth violence can potentially derive from virtually any combination of situational opportunity, moral socialization, cultural influences, developmental limitations, interpersonal tension, family dysfunction, and more. When dealing with such a phenomena, it is helpful to think about what qualifies as good evidence. Is the connection between the media and youth violence so logical and obvious that it becomes self-evident, or does it require definitive statistical evidence showing that there are not other factors more directly involved?

# YES

**Dave Grossman**

# Teaching Kids to Kill

*Michael Carneal, the fourteen-year-old killer in the Paducah, Kentucky, school shootings, had never fired a real pistol in his life. He stole a .22 pistol, fired a few practice shots, and took it to school. He fired eight shots at a high school prayer group, hitting eight kids, five of them head shots and the other three upper torso.*

I train numerous élite military and law enforcement organizations around the world. When I tell them of this "achievement," they are stunned. Nowhere in the annals of military or law enforcement history can we find an equivalent achievement.

Where does a fourteen-year-old boy who never fired a gun before get the skill and the will to kill? Video games and media violence.

## A Virus of Violence

First we must understand the magnitude of the problem. The murder rate does not accurately represent our situation because it has been held down by the development of ever more sophisticated life-saving skills and techniques. A better indicator of the problem is the aggravated-assault rate—the rate at which human beings are attempting to kill one another. And that rate went up from around 60 per 100,000 in 1957, to over 440 per 100,000 by the mid-1990s.

Even with small downturns recently, the violent-crime rate is still at a phenomenally high level, and this is true not just in America, but also worldwide. In Canada, per-capita assaults increased almost fivefold between 1964 and 1993. According to Interpol, between 1977 and 1993 the per-capita assault rate increased nearly fivefold in Norway and Greece, and in Australia and New Zealand it increased approximately fourfold. During the same period it tripled in Sweden and approximately doubled in Belgium, Denmark, England-Wales, France, Hungary, the Netherlands, and Scotland. In India during this period the per-capita murder rate doubled. In Mexico and Brazil violent crime is also skyrocketing, and in Japan juvenile violent crime went up 30 percent in 1997 alone.

This virus of violence is occurring worldwide, and the explanation for it has to be some new factor that is occurring in all of these countries. As in heart disease, there are many factors involved in the causation of violent crime, and we must never downplay any of them. But there is only one new variable that is present in each of these nations, bearing the same fruit in every case, and that is media violence being presented as "entertainment" for children.

# Killing Unnaturally

I spent almost a quarter of a century as an Army infantry officer, a paratrooper, a Ranger, and a West Point psychology professor, learning and studying how we enable people to kill. Most soldiers have to be trained to kill.

Healthy members of most species have a powerful, natural resistance to killing their own kind. Animals with antlers and horns fight one another by butting heads while against other species they go to the side to gut and gore. Piranha turn their teeth on everything, but they fight one another with flicks of the tail. Rattlesnakes bite anything, but they wrestle one another.

When we human beings are overwhelmed with anger and fear, our thought processes become very primitive, and we slam head on into that hard-wired resistance against killing. During World War II, we discovered that only 15 to 20 percent of the individual riflemen would fire at an exposed enemy soldier (Marshall, 1998). You can observe this phenomenon in killing throughout history, as I have outlined in much greater detail in my book, *On Killing,* in my three peer-reviewed encyclopedia entries, and in my entry in the *Oxford Companion to American Military History* (all posted at www.killology.com).

That was the reality of the battlefield. Only a small percentage of soldiers were willing and able to kill. When the military became aware of this, they systematically went about the process of "fixing" this "problem." And fix it they did. By Vietnam, the firing rate rose to over 90 percent.

# The Methods in this Madness

The training methods that the military uses are brutalization, classical conditioning, operant conditioning, and role-modeling. Let us explain these and then observe how the media does the same thing to our children, but without the safeguards.

## Brutalization

Brutalization, or "values inculcation," is what happens at boot camp. Your head is shaved, you are herded together naked, and you are dressed alike, losing all vestiges of individuality. You are trained relentlessly in a total immersion environment. In the end, you embrace violence and discipline and accept it as a normal and essential survival skill in your brutal new world.

Something very similar is happening to our children through violence in the media. It begins at the age of eighteen months, when a child can begin to understand and mimic what is on television. But up until they are six or seven years old they are developmentally, psychologically, and physically unable to discern the difference between fantasy and reality. Thus, when a young child sees somebody on television being shot, stabbed, raped, brutalized, degraded, or murdered, to them it is real, and some of them embrace violence and accept it as a normal and essential survival skill in a brutal new world.

On June 10, 1992, the *Journal of the American Medical Association (JAMA)* published a definitive study on the effect of television violence. In nations, regions, or cities where television appears there is an immediate explosion of violence on the playground, and within fifteen years there is a doubling of the murder rate. Why fifteen years? That is how long it takes for a brutalized toddler to reach the "prime crime" years. That is how long it takes before you begin to reap what you sow when you traumatize and desensitize children.

*JAMA* concluded, "the introduction of television in the 1950s caused a subsequent doubling of the homicide rate, i.e., long-term childhood exposure to television is a causal factor behind approximately one-half of the homicides committed in the United States, or approximately 10,000 homicides annually." The study went on to state, "if, hypothetically, television technology had never been developed, there would today be 10,000 fewer homicides each year in the United States, 70,000 fewer rapes, and 700,000 fewer injurious assaults."

Today the data linking violence in the media to violence in society is superior to that linking cancer and tobacco. The American Psychological Association (APA), the American Medical Association (AMA), the American Academy of Pediatrics (AAP), the Surgeon General, and the Attorney General have all made definitive statements about this. When I presented a paper to the American Psychiatric Association's (APA) annual convention in May, 2000, the statement was made: "The data is irrefutable. We have reached the point where we need to treat those who try to deny it, like we would treat Holocaust deniers."

## Classical Conditioning

Classical conditioning is like Pavlov's dog in Psych 101. Remember the ringing bell, the food, and the dog that could not hear the bell without salivating?

In World War II, the Japanese would make some of their young, unblooded soldiers bayonet innocent prisoners to death. Their friends would cheer them on. Afterwards, all these soldiers were treated to the best meal they had in months, sake, and the so-called "comfort girls." The result? They learned to associate violence with pleasure.

This technique is so morally reprehensible that there are very few examples of it in modern U.S. military training. But the media is doing it to our children. Kids watch vivid images of human death and suffering, and they learn to associate it with laughter, cheers, popcorn, soda, and their girlfriend's perfume.

After the Jonesboro shootings, one of the high school teachers told me about her students' reaction when she told them that someone had shot a bunch of their little brothers, sisters, and cousins in the middle school. "They laughed," she told me with dismay, "they laughed." We have raised a generation of barbarians who have learned to associate human death and suffering with pleasure.

## Operant Conditioning

The third method the military uses is operant conditioning, a powerful procedure of stimulus-response training. We see this with pilots in flight simulators, or children in fire drills. When the fire alarm is set off, the children learn to file out in orderly fashion. One day there is a real fire and they're frightened out of their little wits, but they do exactly what they've been conditioned to do.

In World War II we taught our soldiers to fire at bullseye targets, but that training failed miserably because we had no known instances of any soldiers being attacked by bullseyes. Now soldiers learn to fire at realistic, manshaped silhouettes that pop up in their field of view. That is the stimulus. The conditioned response is to shoot the target, and then it drops. Stimulus-response, stimulus-response, repeated hundreds of times. Later, when they are in combat and somebody pops up with a gun, reflexively they will shoot and shoot to kill. Of the shooting on the modern battlefield, 75 to 80 percent is the result of this kind of training.

When children play violent video games, especially at a young age, they receive this same kind of operant conditioning in killing. In his national presidential radio address on April 24, 1999, shortly after the Littleton high school massacre, President Clinton stated, "A former lieutenant colonel and professor, David Grossman, has said that these games teach young people to kill with all the precision of a military training program, but none of the character training that goes along with it." The result is ever more homemade pseudo-sociopaths who kill reflexively and show no remorse. Our kids are learning to kill and learning to like it. The most remarkable example of this is Paducah, Kentucky. The killer who fired eight shots and got eight hits on eight different milling, scrambling, screaming kids.

Where did he get this phenomenal skill? Well, there is a $130-million law suit against the video game manufacturers in that case, working itself through the appeals system, claiming that the violent video games, the murder simulators, gave that mass murderer the skill and the will to kill.

In July 2000, at a bipartisan, bicameral Capital Hill conference in Washington, D.C., the AMA, the APA, the AAP, and the American Academy of Child and Adolescent Psychiatry (AACAP) issued a joint statement saying that "viewing entertainment violence can lead to increases in aggressive attitudes, values and behavior, particularly in children. Its effects are measurable and long lasting. Moreover, prolonged viewing of media violence can lead to emotional desensitization toward violence in real life. . . . Although less research has been done on the impact of violent interactive entertainment [such as video games] on young people, preliminary studies indicate that the negative impact may be significantly more severe than that wrought by television, movies, or music."

## Role Models

In the military your role model is your drill sergeant. He personifies violence, aggression, and discipline. The discipline, and doing it to adults, is the safeguard. The drill sergeant, and hero figures such as John Wayne, Audie Murphy,

Sergeant York and Chesty Puller, have always been used as role models to influence young, impressionable teenagers.

Today the media are providing our children with role models, not just in the lawless sociopaths in movies and in television shows, but in the transformation of these schoolyard killers into media celebrities.

In the 1970s we learned about "cluster suicides," in which television reporting of teen suicides was directly responsible for numerous copycat suicides of other teenagers. Because of this, television stations today generally do not cover teen suicides. But when the pictures of teenage killers appear on television, the effect is tragically similar. If there are children willing to kill themselves to get on television, are there also children willing to kill your child to get on television?

Thus we get the effect of copycat, cluster murders that work their way across America like a virus spread by the six o'clock local news. No matter what someone has done, if you put his or her picture on television, you have made that person a celebrity whom someone, somewhere, may emulate them. This effect is greatly magnified when the role model is a teenager, and the effect on other teens can be profound.

In Japan, Canada, and other democracies around the world it is a punishable, criminal act to place the names and images of juvenile criminals in the media because they know that it will result in other tragic deaths. The media has every right and responsibility to tell the story, but do they have a "right" to turn the killers into celebrities?

# Unlearning Violence

On the night of the Jonesboro shootings, clergy and counselors were working in small groups in the hospital waiting room, comforting the groups of relatives and friends of the fifteen shooting victims. Then they noticed one woman sitting alone.

A counselor went up to the woman and discovered that she was the mother of one of the girls who had been killed. She had no friends, no husband, no family with her as she sat in the hospital, alone. "I just came to find out how to get my little girl's body back," she said. But the body had been taken to the state capital, for an autopsy. "I just don't know how we're going to pay for the funeral. I don't know how we can afford it."

That little girl was all she had in all the world, and all she wanted to do was wrap her little girl's body in a blanket and take her home. Some people's solution to the problem of media violence is, "If you don't like it, just turn it off." If that is your only solution to this problem, then come to Jonesboro, and tell her how this would have kept her little girl safe.

All of us can keep our kids safe from this toxic, addictive substance, but it will not be enough if the neighbors are not doing the same. Perhaps the time has come to consider regulating what the violence industry is selling to kids, controlling the sale of violent, visual imagery to children, while still permitting free access to adults, just as we do with guns, pornography, alcohol, tobacco, sex, and cars.

# Fighting Back: Education, Legislation, Litigation

We must work against child abuse, racism, poverty, and children's access to guns, and toward rebuilding our families, but we must also take on the producers of media violence. The solution strategy that I submit for consideration is, "education, legislation, litigation."

Simply put, we need to work toward legislation that outlaws violent video games for children. In July 2000, the city of Indianapolis passed just such an ordinance, and every other city, county or state in the United States has the right to do the same. There is no Constitutional right to teach children to blow people's heads off at the local video arcade, And we are very close to being able to do to the media, through litigation, what is being done to the tobacco industry, hitting them in the only place they understand—their wallets.

Most of all, the American people need to be informed. Every parent must be warned of the impact of violent visual media on children, as we would warn them of some rampant carcinogen. Violence is not a game, it is not fun, it is not something that we let children do for entertainment. Violence kills.

CBS President Leslie Moonves was asked if he thought the school massacre in Littleton, Colorado, had anything to do with the media. His answer was, "Anyone who thinks the media has nothing to do with it, is an idiot." That is what the networks are selling, but we do not have to buy it. An educated and informed society can and must find its way home from the dark and lonely place to which it has traveled.

# NO

Jonathan L. Freedman

# Villain or Scapegoat? Media Violence and Aggression

**O**n 20 April 1999, at around 11:20 a.m. local time, two students wearing black trenchcoats walked into Columbine High School in Littleton, Colorado. Eric Harris, eighteen, and Dylan Klebold, seventeen, were armed with semiautomatic handguns, shotguns and explosives. They killed twelve students, one teacher, and then themselves.

On 1 December 1997, Michael Carneal killed three students at Heath High School in West Paducah, Kentucky.

On 30 April 1999 a fourteen-year-old Canadian boy walked into the W.R. Myers High School in Taber, a quiet farming community of 7,200 people two hours southeast of Calgary, Alberta. He shot and killed one seventeen-year-old student and seriously injured another eleventh-grade student.

It is difficult to imagine events more terrible than our young people deliberately killing each other. These horrifying incidents have caused almost everyone to wonder what has gone wrong with North American society. How can it be that in quiet, affluent communities in two of the richest countries on earth, children are taking guns to school and killing their classmates?

Many answers have been suggested. It was the parents' fault; it was Satanism and witchcraft; it was lack of religion in the schools and at home; it was moral breakdown; it was the availability of guns; it was the culture.

One answer proposed whenever events like this occur is that they are a result of exposure to media violence. Children who watch television and go to the movies see thousands of murders and countless other acts of violence. They see fistfights, martial arts battles, knifings, shootings, exploding cars, and bombs. These acts of violence are committed by heroes and villains, by good guys and bad guys. They are committed by live actors and animated figures; they appear in the best movies and TV programs as well as in the worst. It is almost impossible for children to avoid witnessing these violent acts time and time again. All of this has caused many people to ask whether watching violent television programs and movies causes people, especially children, to be more aggressive and to commit crimes.

Another reason some people worry about the effects of media violence is that television became available in the United States and Canada in the

From *Media Violence and Aggression* by Jonathan L. Freedman, pp. 3–4, 7–16, 19–21. Copyright © 2002 by University of Toronto Press-Scholarly Div. Reprinted by permission.

1950s and violent crime increased dramatically in both countries between 1960 and 1990. Many people see a connection. They think that watching violence on television makes children more aggressive and causes them to grow into adults who are more likely to commit violent crimes. Brandon Centerwall, a psychiatrist and epidemiologist, has even suggested that the increase in violent crime during this period was due entirely to television. As he put it, 'if, hypothetically, television technology had never been developed, there would today be 10,000 fewer homicides each year in the United States, 70,000 fewer rapes, and 700,000 fewer injurious assaults.'

The belief that media violence is harmful is widespread. In a recent poll in the United States, 10 percent of people said that TV violence is the major cause of the increase in crime. This tendency to blame media violence has been fostered by some social scientists and whipped up by politicians and lobby groups. It has led politicians to propose bills restricting access to violent movies, banning violent television programs during certain hours, forcing television companies to rate every single program in terms of violence, and requiring that all television sets be fitted with V-chips to enable parents to block out programs they find offensive. We are told that all of this will reduce crime and make children better behaved, and that if we do not deal with media violence our society will continue to experience increased violence and crime.

Some people say they don't need science to know that watching violence makes children violent. To these people it is so clear, so self-evident, that we don't need to bother with research. They point to some horrible incidents to support this view.

On 14 October 1992 the headlines in many American papers read **boy lights fire that kills sister.** Two days earlier a television program had shown young boys setting fires. The very next day, Tommy Jones (not his real name) an eight-year-old boy, set a fire that burned down the trailer in which he and his family lived. His baby sister was trapped inside and burned to death. All over the United States, newspapers, television stations, and politicians concluded that Tommy must have seen the television program and gotten the idea of playing with matches and setting a fire. Surely this was a perfect example of why children should not be allowed to watch violent programs.

In February 1993 the whole world shuddered at an awful crime committed by two young boys in England. That month a small boy who was about to turn three was taken from a shopping mall in Liverpool by two ten-year-old boys. Jamie Bulger had walked away from his mother for only a second—long enough for Jon Venables to take his hand and lead him out of the mall with his friend Robert Thompson. They took Jamie on a walk of over two-and-a-half miles, along the way stopping every now and again to torture the poor little boy, who was crying constantly for his mommy. Finally they left his beaten small body on the tracks so that a train could run him over.

Jamie's frantic mother noticed almost at once that he was missing, and a massive search began. Jon and Robert were identified from surveillance tapes in the mall. At first they denied any knowledge of Jamie, but eventually they admitted everything and led police to the dead body. Although they confessed to taking Jamie, each accused the other of doing the torturing and killing. During the trial, Jon cried a lot and looked miserable, while Robert seemed unaffected. They were convicted and sentenced to long prison terms.

The trial judge had observed the boys for many days and heard all the testimony. At the sentencing he denounced them as inhuman monsters. He also said he was convinced that one of the causes of their crime was television violence. According to the judge, shortly before the crime the boys had watched a television program, involving kidnapping and murder. They had imitated this program and the result was Jamie's kidnapping, torture, and murder. It was, he said, one more case of the harmful effects of television violence.

People think they see the effects of media violence in their daily lives. Every day, parents and teachers watch children practising martial arts at home and in schoolyards. Pass by a playground and you will see martial arts in action—slashing arms, jumps, kicks, the works. A generation ago young boys almost never used karate kicks; now they all do. And this goes along with increased violence in our schools. Again, surely television violence has caused it.

The terrible crimes related to television programs, the increase in violent crime since the introduction of television, and the ordinary occurrences of fighting in imitation of television heroes have convinced many people that television violence causes aggression, violence and crime. It seems so obvious that there is no need to worry about the scientific evidence. Why should anyone care what the research shows?

Don't be so sure. Not so terribly long ago it was obvious that the world was flat, that the sun revolved around the earth, and that the longer women stayed in bed after childbirth the healthier they would be. Scientific research has proven all of these wrong. An awful lot of people also knew that men were smarter than women, that picking babies up when they cried would only encourage them to cry more in the future, and that rewarding kids for playing games would make them like the games more. Research has proven all of these wrong too. Perhaps it will do the same for beliefs about the effects of media violence—that is why so many people have done so much research to establish whether watching violent programs really does make children more aggressive.

Anecdotes are not always very reliable. Let's look at the examples I offered above. Consider the case of the fire that killed the little girl. At first glance there seems no question what happened. The newspapers all reported that the boy was a well-behaved child who had never been in trouble before. He happened to watch the TV program about setting fires, and he imitated what he saw. What more could one ask? Clearly, this was a simple case of TV causing a tragedy.

But it wasn't. As those reporters who looked into the incident more carefully found out, the truth was quite different from the early reports. First of all, little Tommy was not a very well-behaved boy. He had been playing with matches and setting fires for some time—long before the program was aired. No one had been killed or hurt in any of the fires before this, so they did not make the news, but they were set nonetheless. Second, and more important, the TV program in question was shown only on cable, not on the regular networks. *And Tommy's family did not have cable television.* In fact, no one in the trailer park had it, and no one he knew had it. *So there was no way he could have seen the show.* The tragic incident had nothing whatsoever to do with the television program that had been shown the day before. Rather than it being a case of television causing the tragedy, it was simply one more instance of children playing with fire and someone getting hurt.

Also consider the case of the two boys who killed Jamie Bulger. The judge announced in court that he was convinced that TV played a crucial role in the crime—that the boys had watched a program about kidnapping and had imitated it. Again, an obvious case of TV violence producing violence?

Yet the judge's belief had no basis in fact. The police made it absolutely clear that the boys had not watched the program in question, that they did not watch television much, and that there was no reason to believe that TV had anything to do with the crime. The last time children of this age had been found guilty of murder in England had been several hundred years earlier. It hadn't been due to television then, so why in the world would the judge think so this time? This was a horrific crime beyond human comprehension. We have no idea how they could have committed it, but there is not the slightest bit of evidence that it was caused by television.

Yes, the rate of violent crime increased after television was introduced. But there is no reason to think the two are in any way related. [Television] was also introduced to France, Germany, Italy, and Japan at around the same time as it came to the United States and Canada. Yet crime rates did not increase in these other countries. If television violence were causing the increase, surely it should have had the same effect elsewhere. We have to remember that the availability of television in the United States and Canada coincided with vast changes in our societies. Between 1960 and 1985—the period of the increase in crime—the divorce rate more than doubled, many more single parents and women began working outside the home, the use of illegal drugs increased, the gap between rich and poor grew, and because of the postwar baby boom, there was a sharp increase in the number of young males. Almost all of the experts, including police, criminologists, and sociologists, agree that these factors played a crucial role in the increase in crime, and no one seriously blames television for these changes in society. It is an accident, a coincidence, that television ownership increased during this same period. These important social changes are certainly some of the causes of the increase in crime; television ownership may be irrelevant.

Although it may seem as if youth violence is increasing, it is actually declining. In 1999 the rate of murder by white youths in California was at a record low, 65 per cent less than in 1970, and the rates for Black, Latino, and Asian youths were also low. According to FBI records, elementary-school students are much less likely to murder today than they were in the 1960s and 1970s. And, both Black and white children feel less menaced now by violence in their schools than twenty-five years ago. True, over the past seven years there has been an increase in incidents in school in which more than one person was killed. However, the number of children killed in schools in the United States and Canada has dropped during the same period, from a high of fifty-five in the 1992–93 school year to sixteen in 1998–99. This last year included one killing in Canada, which shocked a country not used to this kind of violence in its schools, but it is the only case of its kind in this decade.

Moreover, the rates for all violent crimes have been dropping steadily and dramatically since the early 1990s. The number of homicides in the big American cities has plunged to levels not seen since the early 70s, and the numbers for other violent crimes have been falling as well. This, at a time when movies and television shows are as violent as ever. Add to this the rising popularity of rap music, with its violent language and themes; and of video games, which are just as violent and just as popular. If violence in the media causes aggression, how can real-life violence and crime be dropping?

None of this proves that television violence plays no role in aggression and violence. The point is that stories about its effects are often false and that obvious effects may be explainable in other ways. People's intuitions and observations are sometimes wrong, and may be this time. That is why we have to rely on scientific research to answer the question whether exposure to media violence really makes children more aggressive. . . .

## What about Pronouncements by Scientific Organizations?

The public has been told by panel after panel, organization after organization, that media violence causes aggression. A long list of prestigious scientific and medical organizations have said that the evidence is in and the question has been settled. The American Psychiatric Association and the Canadian Psychological Association have all weighed in on this matter. Recently, under some prodding by a congressional committee, the American Medical Association, the American Academy of Pediatrics, the American Psychological Association, and the American Academy of Child and Adolescent Psychiatry issued a joint statement. According to these groups, it is now proven that media violence causes aggression and probably causes crime. The pediatric group went so far as to urge that children under two should watch no television because it interferes with their normal development. The National Institute of Mental Health has published an extensive report on television in which it concludes that media violence causes aggression.

If all these respectable scientific organizations agree that media violence is harmful, surely it must be. Well, it isn't. Although they have all made unequivocal statements about the effects of media violence, it is almost certain that not one of these organizations conducted a thorough review of the research. They have surely not published or made available any such review. If they made these pronouncements without a scientific review, they are guilty of the worst kind of irresponsible behaviour. If they were in court as expert witnesses, they could be convicted of perjury. It is incredible that these organizations, which purport to be scientific, should act in this manner. Yet that seems to be the case.

Consider the policy statement from the American Academy of Pediatricians published in August 1999. It states: 'More than 1000 scientific studies and reviews conclude that significant exposure to media violence increases the risk of aggressive behavior in certain children and adolescents, desensitizes them to violence, and makes them believe that the world is a "meaner and scarier" place than it is.' Apparently not satisfied, in its November 2001 Policy Statement on Media Violence the AAP stated: 'More than 3500 research studies have examined the association between media violence and violent behavior [and] all but 18 have shown a positive relationship.' That sounds pretty impressive. After all, if over 3500 scientific studies reached this conclusion, who could doubt it? The only problem is that this is not true. There have not been over 3500 or even 1000 scientific studies on this topic. This vastly exaggerates the amount of work that has been done. That the pediatricians give such an inflated figure is only one indication that they do not know the research. Imagine the response if an organization of economists asserted that there were serious economic problems in over 150 American states. No one would bother asking for their statistics, since if they were so sloppy as to think there were that many states, who could possibly trust the rest of their statement? In the same way, since the pediatricians say that they are basing their statement on over 3500 scientific studies, it must be clear that they have not read the research because there are not anywhere near that many studies.

To make matters worse, the studies that do exist do not all reach the conclusion that media violence has any of the effects listed by the AAP. Indeed, . . . most of the studies show no ill effects of exposure to media violence. And there is virtually no research showing that media violence desensitizes people to violence. Why do these presumably well-meaning pediatricians make these unsupported and inaccurate statements? Who knows.

To cap it off, the policy goes on to 'urge parents to avoid television viewing for children under the age of 2 years.' It supports this extreme recommendation by saying that 'research on early brain development shows that babies and toddlers have a critical need for direct interactions with parents . . . for healthy brain growth and the development of appropriate social, emotional and cognitive skills.' I am not a neuroscientist and I have not reviewed the relevant research. However, an article in the *New York Times* quotes neuroscientists at Rockefeller University, the University of Minnesota, and the Washington University Medical School, as saying that there is no evidence to support the pediatricians' advice. 'There is no data like that at all,' according to Charles Nelson. The author of the *Times* article goes on to say that the person who wrote the pediatric academy's report agreed that there was no evidence but that they had 'extrapolated' from other data.

This is incredible. This organization is giving advice to medical doctors who deal directly with millions of American parents and children. And it is telling these doctors to urge their patients (i.e., the parents of their patients) to keep children under two away from television—not just limit their exposure but to keep them away from television entirely. Given the role that television plays in the lives of most families, following this advice would be a major undertaking. In the first place, it would be very difficult for the parents to manage it. Television keeps children occupied, stimulates them, entertains them, and educates them. Even if it did none of these things, imagine how difficult it would be for parents who like to watch television themselves or have older children who like to watch. Would they have to turn off the television whenever the under-two children are in the room? Or are they supposed to keep the young children out of the room with the television? Be serious.

Yet the pediatricians are supposed to tell parents that watching television will harm their children by preventing them from developing normally. This is quite a threat. Many parents will presumably take it to heart, worry about doing damage to their children, and try to follow the advice. This is not a matter of reducing fat intake a little or giving them enough milk—this is telling them to alter the social environment in their home, supposedly on the basis of hard, scary, scientific facts. Do *this* or your child will not grow up normally.

But there is no scientific evidence that television harms children under two—nothing at all to support this recommendation. It is junk science; pop psychology of the worst sort based on nothing but some vague extrapolations from research that is not cited and may not exist. This is truly irresponsible. Fortunately, I think we can trust most pediatricians to ignore this nonsensical policy and not give the advice; and if they do give it, we can probably trust most sensible parents to ignore it. . . .

# POSTSCRIPT

## Does Violent Media Cause Teenage Aggression?

The prominence of the media in the lives of children, adolescence, and society is beyond dispute. The advent of television during the twentieth century, and the prominence of computers at the turn of the twenty-first century, has changed the way society functions. But has it changed human nature?

Grossman is among a large group of scholars and experts who believe that the media has changed us in fundamental ways. Children who grow up watching violent television and playing violent video games are exposed to levels of violence and aggression that were likely beyond the imagination of prior generations of adolescents. Our Western attitudes toward violence have changed; we are extremely aware of the potential for youth violence, and we have come to understand the world as a violent place.

It is possible, however, that such awareness is what leads us to assume that the media causes acts of violence. In other words, while some youth and adolescents have always had violent and aggressive tendencies, in prior generations we were rarely made aware of those tendencies in dramatic ways. We did not have 24-hour news coverage to investigate every detail of violent acts, to learn what games young killers liked to play. And, in fact, while dramatic incidents such as Columbine suggest a rising rate of violence, when looking at large samples of teens, there is some evidence that rates of violence and violent crime is going down.

Freedman emphasizes this tendency for the media to create intuitive associations that may not be true to reality. In fact, Freedman even acknowledges that violent media may contribute some to violent crime. But he insists that it is not the major cause we popularly assume. There are simply too many other factors that explain violence and aggression; the increasing prominence of the media in the lives of youth has corresponded with many other significant changes in family structure and the experience of adolescence.

This demonstrates an important principle in the study of life span development: Most developmental phenomenon are determined by multiple causes. Development, like youth violence, is complicated. Adolescents act the way they do because of physical changes that influence their interests and instincts, psychological perceptions of the world, social forces that put them in particular roles and situations, interactions between these, and more. Yet people have a need to understand. Whether youth violence is going up, down, or staying the same, any quantity of violence is too much for most of us. Trying to understand the causes is time well spent.

The controversy surrounding whether the media is one of the most significant causes is particularly important because it is one that people perceive as possible to control. The media does not have to include gratuitous violence to provide information and entertainment, nor do children and adolescents need to have access to violent shows, movies, and games. There is much public debate about rating systems and restrictions on media production that is important as a political issue regarding free speech, and as a developmental issue regarding what matters in the minds of children. But many, including Freedman, would assert that the media provides entertainment—the data provide no conclusive link between that entertainment and widespread violence and aggression. After reading about this controversy, hopefully you can decide for yourself how the media and adolescents should mix.

## Suggested Readings

B. Bushman and C. Anderson, "Media Violence and the American Public: Scientific Facts Versus Media Misinformation," *American Psychologist* (June/July 2001).

C. Olson, "Media Violence Research and Youth Violence Data: Why Do They Conflict?" *Academic Psychiatry* (2004).

S. Ceci and R. Bjork, "Science, Politics, and Violence in the Media," *Psychological Science in the Public Interest* (December 2003).

C. Anderson, L. Berkowitz, E. Donnerstein, L. Huesmann, J. Johnson, D. Linz, N. Malamuth, and E. Wartella, "The Influence of Media Violence on Youth," *Psychological Science in the Public Interest* (December 2003).

M. Cutler, "Whodunit—The Media?" *Nation* (March 26, 2001).

D. Grossman, "We Are Training Our Kids to Kill," *The Saturday Evening Post* (September/October 1999).

J. Garbarino and E. deLara, "On the Anniversary of Columbine: Ten Lessons Learning and Forgotten," *Family Life Development Center, Cornell University* (2001). Available at `http://www.news.cornell.edu/releases/April01/Columbine.lessons.html`.

G. Kleck, "There Are No Lessons to Be Learned from Littleton," *Criminal Justice Ethics* (1999).

R. Long, "Hollywood, Littleton, and Us," *National Review* (July 26, 1999).

J. Wenner, "Guns and Violence," *Rolling Stone* (June 10, 1999).

# On the Internet . . .

## Adolescence and Adulthood

An academic's Web site about a life span stage between adolescence and adulthood.

http://www.hs.ttu.edu/hd3317/emerging.htm

## National Mental Health Association

The National Mental Health Association is a larger national organization dealing with all aspects of mental health and mental illness.

http://www.nmha.org/

## College Women

This site provides health information, with an emphasis on addressing women during their college years.

http://www.4collegewomen.org/

## Future of Work

"The Future of Work" is an example of an organization looking at the changing nature of work, the workforce, and the workplace.

http://thefutureofwork.net/

## Dr. Mel Levine

A page on the Web site of Dr. Mel Levine's "All Kinds of Minds" organization, this is a summary of his book about "work-life unreadiness."

http://www.allkindsofminds.org/product/
Summary_ReadyOrNot.aspx

## Anti-Depressant Drugs

A site with extensive references about anti-depressant drugs.

http://www.antidepressantsfacts.com/

# PART 7

# Youth and Early Adulthood

*W*hile we often talk about "youth" in everyday conversation, it is an ill-defined concept as a stage of the life span. Generally, "youth" refers to a period when a person is developing the characteristics of adulthood but does not yet have adult responsibilities (such as a career and marriage). In contemporary society, this period of life seems longer and more intense because of increasing educational expectations and later average ages for starting a family. Thus, youth and early adulthood are primarily times where people gradually make the transition to fully adult roles. That transition involves both psychological and practical challenges, two of which are dealt with in the issues covered in this section.

- Should We Use Medication to Deal with the Angst of College and Young Adulthood.

- Are College Graduates Unprepared for Adulthood and the World of Work?

# ISSUE 14

## Should We Use Medication to Deal with the Angst of College and Young Adulthood?

**YES: Harold S. Koplewicz,** from *The Big Bump: College* (G.P. Putnam's Sons, 2002)

**NO: Joli Jensen,** from "Let's Not Medicate Away Student Angst," *The Chronicle of Higher Education* (June 13, 2003)

### ISSUE SUMMARY

**YES:** Psychiatrist Harold S. Koplewicz asserts that antidepressants have a major role to play in reducing genuine distress in college students and young adults.

**NO:** Communications professor Joli Jensen argues that medicating young adults when they are facing the inevitable challenges of young adulthood primarily serves to diminish valuable developmental experiences.

**I**f you are reading this book as part of a college course, you are likely aware of the challenges that youth face during the transition to higher education. After 12 years of strict required education, most often while living at home with a family who has a vested stake in your success, many young people arrive at college confronted by a dramatic new independence. There is pressure to make choices with direct relevance to a career and the rest of your working life. There are new social groups to enter and exit. The world is suddenly full of unscripted challenges and opportunities. This has been true for youth in industrialized society for many generations. But the current generation is distinctive in having access to sophisticated medicines, such as antidepressants, that hold the promise of limiting the stresses associated with independent youth.

The most prominent antidepressants are in a class commonly referred to as selective serotonin reuptake inhibitors (SSRIs). These drugs, including commonly known brand names such as Prozac and Zoloft, influence the transmission of serotonin, a neurotransmitter that plays a key role in moods in the brain. Although antidepressant drugs have existed for many decades, it was only in the 1980s and 1990s that effective SSRIs with limited side effects became widely available. The rates of use to manage depression and other mood disorders have subsequently exploded at all stages of the life span.

Early adulthood is a particularly rich stage during which to consider the controversy surrounding the use of medication to deal with angst and distress. The transition to adulthood is a time traditionally marked by precisely the types of changes and disruptions SSRIs treat. While puberty produces major physical changes, early adulthood in contemporary society produces major environmental changes. While childhood is not always easy, it is a period where people are usually free from the stressful responsibilities and decisions made by adults. Likewise, while early adulthood is not always hard, it is a period where many people are suddenly thrust into new roles, choices, and tasks.

This distinctive sociohistorical moment, when the availability of relatively safe drugs coincides with the intense pressure on youth in modern society, has generated controversy about the role of stress and chemistry during life span transitions. While numerous books have informed and provoked the general debate about antidepressant drugs, Harold S. Koplewicz's book about adolescent depression provides a focused consideration of these drugs in the context of making the transition to adulthood. Having written other books about childhood depression, Koplewicz explains that he always gets tremendous response about the particulars of adolescence and early adulthood—people want to know whether the stereotypes of adolescent "storm and stress" is a necessary part of growing up. In his selection, Koplewicz answers a thoughtful "no." He notes that while the transition to adulthood might always have challenges, in previous generations the people least able to cope with those challenges were often lost to society and to themselves. He strongly endorses the somewhat controversial notion that major depressive disorder (MDD) is a medical disease and that treating it with medication helps young adults in desperate need.

In contrast, Joli Jensen deals with college students in her daily teaching and represents a much more concerned perspective on medicating youth. For Jensen, college and the transition to adulthood are times of necessary angst and challenge. For generations, people have used early adulthood as a stage of the life span in which it is reasonable to struggle with big questions and develop a meaningful philosophy of life. If we dismiss these struggles as pathological medical conditions, we risk failing today's young adults as we prepare them for the big questions they will face through the rest of their life span.

One reason this issue generates controversy is because it requires a mix of biological and social forces. To genuinely understand the challenges of early adulthood requires understanding both the physical properties of the mind as it enters maturity, and the social properties of a society that makes youth a major environmental transition. As you read the selections, consider the interaction of these factors. Since mood is always both social and biological, can we ever separate our developmental experiences and their chemical effects? Does using medication create more stresses and challenges than it solves, introducing another environmental problem for the newly independent person? And who is really in a position to judge?

**Harold S. Koplewicz**

 **YES**

# The Big Bump: College

**W**hen I was young, I had a friend named Scott. We were close through most of high school, and though we drifted apart a bit as graduation approached, we both wound up going to the University of Maryland. During freshman year, whenever I saw Scott he seemed downcast. He would walk staring at the ground, oblivious to all the energy of our expansive college campus. Pretty girls didn't turn his head, and he was almost invisible to the kids who walked past him.

We drove home together on spring break, and he talked about how he felt it wasn't worth staying in college. This was 1971, and the Vietnam War was still going, so it was definitely worth staying in college. But Scott was unhappy—pretty much with everything. He didn't like his courses, the professors were stupid, he hated his roommate, his girlfriend was three states away. Apparently, he had no friends at school, and he didn't seem all that interested in making any. This was startling to me. Scott had always been one of the friendliest guys I knew, and an extremely engaged student. But now it sounded like he might actually flunk out of college.

When we returned to school after spring break, Scott stopped going to classes. Every time I called his dormitory room, he was sleeping. He didn't make it through freshman year. Adrift, he quit and went home. His parents were shattered. It seemed all their dreams for their only son were evaporating. Their immediate concern was that he would be drafted, but fortunately, he got a high lottery number. His parents persuaded him to try going to the local community college, but that didn't work either. Floundering, he got a job as an editorial aide at a newspaper where his father's friend was an editor. But he couldn't get motivated enough to go to work after the first week.

I didn't see Scott again until three years later, when he came to my house while I was home at Thanksgiving during my first year in medical school. "Is there a disease that causes you to lose your motivation?" he asked me. The last few years had been lost ones for Scott. He had lived at home, working occasionally in jobs he hated. His parents had tried everything. They bought him weights, hoping the exercise would get him going. Scott promised to use them. But they sat in his room, in pristine condition. His parents redecorated his tiny room in bright blue—blue walls, blue carpet, blue bedding. They were that desperate. That Thanksgiving was the last time I saw Scott. He didn't show up at

From *The Brown University Child and Adolescent Behavior Letter*, vol. 18, issue 12, December 2002. Copyright © 2002 by John Wiley & Sons. Reprinted by permission.

either our tenth or twentieth high school reunions. I heard later that he worked in a supermarket and had never married.

When I was young, someone like Scott was often said to be "finding himself." A generation later he might be called a slacker. But although nobody seemed to realize it at the time, Scott was in all likelihood depressed. Looking back, there were signs of it in high school, but it really emerged during that freshman year in college, when he was both overwhelmed by a big school with huge classes and lonely without his girlfriend. Drugs might have helped precipitate the depression—marijuana doesn't do much for motivation—or it might have been the other way around, depression leading to drug use. But one thing is for sure: Scott was far from the only student at the University of Maryland, or at any college in the country, who found himself in a depression at that point in his life. And he was not the only student who didn't get help and never really came back.

College is tricky terrain for mental health. During the course of working on this book, many people told me about periods of stifling depression that they experienced during those years. One colleague remembered feeling very down in the weeks before leaving home for the first time in his life and starting college in another part of the country. That was "anticipatory anxiety," and it evolved into depression after he arrived at school. Fortunately, the depression eventually lifted on its own, and he was able to get back on track. As any number of cases I've described demonstrate, what happens during a depression can have huge long-term consequences for a young person. A 40-year-old who has already reached at least some of his goals might have a terrible period while depressed, but he can recover and return to where he was. Younger people have a much harder time catching up.

Reams of statistics cross my desk in the course of a year, but some of the most sobering I've seen come from the National College Health Assessment, a survey conducted in the spring of 2000 by the American College Health Association. The survey asked some 16,000 students, from 28 public and private universities, questions about drinking, sex, nutrition, and mental health issues. Here's what they asked and how students responded (percentages are rounded):

- How many times in the past academic year have you felt intense hopelessness? Only 38 percent said never. Nearly 10 percent said more than 11 times.
- How many times have you felt overwhelming sadness and were so depressed that you couldn't function? More than 15 percent said at least five times, including nearly 7 percent who said more than 11 times.
- Have you ever been diagnosed with depression? Ten percent said yes. Of these, about a quarter said they had been diagnosed in the past year. Twenty-one percent of those diagnosed were currently taking medication.
- In the past school year, how many times have you seriously contemplated suicide? A total of 9.5 percent said at least once, including 1 percent who said 11 or more times.
- In the past school year, how many times have you attempted suicide? A total of 1.6 percent said at least once.

Even accounting for the possibility that some who took the survey were overstating the case, the results indicate that a significant percentage of American college students feel very bad a good deal of the time. What may be most striking is that the *majority* of college students apparently feel "intense hopelessness" at least occasionally, and some feel this way quite often. The results also indicate that most of them are not getting help. If they were, the percentage who said they had been diagnosed with depression would no doubt be much higher than ten.

&#x2766;

Adolescence always reflects society—and vice versa. In the 1950s, teenagers were the picture of Eisenhower-era innocence, but a decade later it seemed that they were angry, confused, and rebelling against authority. Today, adolescents reflect the pressured, overtechnological world of the new millennium. But while styles, attitudes, events, and other societal forces change, some basic things stay the same. Whatever the era, adolescence can be broken down into three stages—early, middle, and late—that roughly correlate with age. The late phase starts as a teenager is preparing to graduate from high school and extends until he or she is 21 or 22. This is a generality, of course. For some, adolescence continues until the midtwenties or even later. (Note that 25 is often the minimum age for renting a car.) Just as puberty is a key marker in depression in early adolescence—more so than strict chronological age—college is another milestone. The difference is that puberty is a biological factor. College is environmental.

As complicated and difficult as early and middle adolescence can seem at the time, in many ways the college years are a much bigger challenge. These are the key years for reaching career goals and forming a social network. There is more sexual activity and more access to diversions such as drugs and alcohol that can alter brain chemistry and either trigger depression or worsen it. The big issue in all of this, especially for kids who go away to school, is independence: Mom and Dad are no longer on the scene, watching over them. They're no longer in a position to see Jason or Jennifer every day and notice changes in their behavior and habits that might signal trouble. Now it's largely up to the kids themselves to acknowledge changes in their own moods and take steps to ease their stress and get help if they need it. Realistically, this may be too much to ask. Likewise, the parents' jobs change. First, they have to be alert to the special challenges and risks of depression at this unique time of life. Then they have to figure out how to stay engaged in their child's life from a distance. And, potentially most important, especially for parents of kids who are vulnerable to depression, they need to be ready and able to swoop in and get their children the help they need.

The college years as a whole present unique challenges, but within these four years are distinct phases. The trials of freshman year are different from those of senior year. And a student's response to those stressors will be different. An adolescent is not the same person when he's leaving college as when he arrived.

## Freshman Year

Though he won't think of it exactly in these terms, what the college freshman faces is all those developmental tasks of adolescence coming to a head all at once: separating from parents, figuring out what he wants to do with his life, forming intimate and social relationships, developing his personal ethics. High school was just a prelude; now the pressure is really on, and without the cocoon of home. It's fair to say that among the four undergraduate classes at any university, it's the freshmen who have the most challenges and the least maturity to handle them.

Of all the stressful adjustments confronting college freshmen who go away to school, the most difficult is separating from parents. Sure, they're thrilled to be out of the house and on their own, but just beneath the surface—or maybe right out in the open—is the frightening realization that being on their own doesn't just mean glorious freedom. It also means real *responsibility*. Not responsibilities like taking out the garbage or doing well on a test, but personal accountability. They are now responsible for their own well-being.

One of the big, unspoken tasks for many college freshman is reconciling fantasy and reality. To begin with, think about what most teenagers base their choice of college on: maybe a few pages in a college guide, perhaps a visit to campus and a tour conducted by a student who made the place sound like heaven. Maybe they just liked that the school has a great basketball team. They may soon realize that the place is something other than what they envisioned. Or that they really hadn't thought about how hard it would be to live with strangers they had little in common with. A student from a small town may be overwhelmed by the size of a major university, struck by a feeling of insignificance. Some freshmen fantasize about the opportunity college offers to reinvent themselves. They've left behind everyone they know. People they saw every day for 12 years are nowhere in sight. Time to start fresh. Some can pull this off, but no matter what stage of life we're in, most of us find ourselves still dealing with the same assets and flaws we've always had.

As mundane as it may sound, sleep deprivation is a big problem for college students. Teenagers are likely to be night owls to begin with, and now they have all those temptations: hanging out with roommates and friends, drinking, drugs, sex. Yet there are responsibilities in the morning. A student with bipolar disorder has to pay special attention to getting adequate sleep. In this case, it might be necessary to request a single room, if the only alternative is a roommate who stays up late and plays music.

All these are stressors that can trip the switch on a depressive episode, especially for a teenager who is vulnerable—one who either has risk factors (such as family history) or who has already had depression. So a parent who sends a susceptible adolescent off to college has to make sure the student is prepared, should she become depressed. This is where psychoeducation is important. A vulnerable individual has to understand the illness, the same way a diabetic knows that she will go into a coma if she doesn't watch her diet. If depression is an issue arrangements should be made ahead of time with a psychiatrist on or off campus who can meet with the student before school starts and monitor her medication. It's not enough to send your child off to school with a bottle of pills and casual plans for her to check in with her psychiatrist at home when she comes home for Thanksgiving. Your child lives at school; she needs a doctor there. Facilitate this in advance.

Those with children who already have depression aren't the only parents who need to think about mental health. While it's not necessary to have the name of a psychiatrist at college posted on the refrigerator, every parent should make sure his or her child knows how to get help, if it becomes necessary, from the college health service. It's no different from knowing where to go if you get the flu.

## The Middle Years

Having survived the myriad adjustments of freshman year, students will find academics and career goals their primary stressor in their sophomore and junior years. They are forced to focus on where they are headed. They have to declare a major, and realize that it should have something to do with what they're going to do after they graduate. They know that how well they do in these years will have more long-term consequences than their performance in high school did. There is something seemingly irrevocable about these choices, and yet it's an unusually clear-thinking and resolute 20-year-old who knows exactly what he's going to do in life.

Pressures may also be mounting on the social front. To be sure, some students find it easy to hook up romantically with others. Their stressor may be the fallout of a breakup. Others are less comfortable and less adept with the rituals of dating. They can take a pass as a freshman—boys say that freshmen girls want to go out with upperclassmen, and girls feel they just haven't met the right guy—but by their sophomore year, they are likely to be putting pressure on themselves to start a relationship. It doesn't help if their roommate is sleeping with someone in the next bed. Certainly, sexual orientation issues also become prominent.

## Senior Year

Ironically, as uncomfortable and nervous as she may have been as a freshman, a student can be almost *too* comfortable as a senior. This has become her home. She has close friends with whom she has a strong emotional bond, roommates she's chosen rather than had assigned to her. They've shared experiences and spent many late nights talking about life. She feels safe here. But now what lies ahead is not only the separation from these friends, but something much bigger: the great unknown.

It's different from the transition between high school and college. In an article in *The New York Times* about the emotional stress of senior year, Lewis Fortner, an associate dean of students at the University of Chicago, observed: "After all, it isn't just the end of four years. It's the end of 16 or 17 years of education, which is a highly artificial form of existence. At that time in their lives, students can hardly remember a time when they were not in school, so they usually feel some trepidation about this extraordinary change. The abyss of freedom yawns." Most students get through this transition just fine, but it can be stressful—and a potential depression trigger—for even the healthiest person. So students and parents should be aware and open to getting help if symptoms of depression emerge. Again, young people at risk, and their parents, should be especially vigilant.

⋄⟨◉⟩⋄

Given that the whole college experience could be viewed as one stress after another, it's remarkable how well the overwhelming majority of students do. A week after my son went to college, he called—just to chat. Frankly, I was stunned. We had left Josh in a state of barely controlled tension. But now, all those daunting challenges he had been anxious about, and that were so worrisome to my wife and me, had somehow become *fun* for him. He was enjoying taking care of himself. He felt liberated. This is not to say that the next four years would be a cakewalk. I thought again of my old friend Scott, whose undiagnosed depression had caused him to suffer through a torturous freshman year before he flunked out and spent the next years floundering.

Curious to find out what mental health services there had been at our university back then, I called the current director of the student health service, Dr. Maggie Bridwell. She told me that mental health services at the University of Maryland in the early 1970s consisted of a couple of psychiatrists who came in for a few hours each once a week. Students were generally referred to these doctors when they were seen as being "too hippie," she said. Dr. Bridwell became medical director in 1975. That year, there was a rash of suicides on campus, and she responded by hiring psychiatrists who helped primary-care physicians recognize and treat minor depression symptoms. But those psychiatrists were from the Freudian school, and their traditional 50-minute sessions of psycho-analysis were not designed specifically to treat depression, the way today's SSRI medications and cognitive behavioral therapy are.

I asked Dr. Bridwell how a student like my friend Scott would have been treated back then. No one would have paid him much attention, she said. "The older and more conservative physicians would write notes excusing students who were missing classes and then tell them, 'Straighten up and you'll be fine,' instead of addressing their problems and recognizing depression."

Since the 1980s, Dr. Bridwell has overseen a student health service that recognizes mental health as one of its most important components. There is a fully staffed counseling center that refers the most seriously ill students to the main health center that employs three psychiatrists (two full-time) and several clinical social workers. During the 2000–2001 academic year, some 1,400 students came to the health center for psychiatric help, nearly half of them because of depression. But treating depression that comes on during college is only part of the story. Dr. Bridwell, like many of her peers, believes that some students would never even make it to college if not for the help they received in their early teen years. Thanks to the development of SSRIs and more effective treatments for depression, as well as better identification and diagnosis of bipolar disorder, many bright young people whose debilitating mental illnesses might have kept them from attending school in earlier eras are now enrolling and succeeding. This is one of the reasons why college health services today are seeing a greater number of patients with depression: more students arrive at college already diagnosed and under treatment.

The increased incidence and awareness of depression at the University of Maryland is mirrored at just about every other major university in the United States. A survey conducted during the 2001–2002 academic year by *The New York Times* found that demand for campus mental health services had exploded across the country, at both intensely demanding private schools and at less competitive public colleges. For instance, Columbia University saw a 40 percent increase in the use of its counseling service between 1994 and 2001. At a nearby public university, the State University of New York (SUNY) at Purchase, meanwhile, there was a 48 percent jump in just three years. And at the Massachusetts Institute of Technology—which has had the highest student suicide rate in the country—50 percent more students were using the mental health service in 2000 than in 1995. There was also a huge jump, 69 percent, in the number of students who were hospitalized for psychiatric illnesses during that period. Nationally, about 8 percent of the general population uses mental health services. Among college students, the figure is 13 percent.

College health centers have traditionally not been set up to provide for the chronically ill, whether it's a physical or mental illness. The psychiatrists or psychologists on staff have been there mainly to help students adjust to college life and to try to intervene in a crisis, rather than to care for a serious, ongoing mental illness. But the increasing demand has led many major universities to expand their mental health services on campus. Depression leads to dropping out, and colleges are interested in retaining their students. So it's in everybody's interest to provide students with access to mental health services. The University of Michigan, for instance, has opened its Comprehensive Depression Center, both to conduct research into depression for all age groups and to treat students. And at the University of Maryland, resident assistants in dormitories are given mental health education as part of their training, which includes talks on recognizing the warning signs of depression. Freshman orientation includes a program of weekly discussions about mental health issues. Dr. Bridwell noted that the last suicide on campus was in 1980, though there are a number of attempts each year. The heightened awareness of depression on campus is also a factor in increased numbers of freshmen making it through that first year instead of dropping out. Only 77 percent of Maryland freshmen completed the year in 1977. In 2000, 91 percent did. The steepest increase occurred since the 1990s, around the time that SSRI antidepressants came into wide use.

## Annie Gets Help

Annie was 3,000 miles from home, but that didn't stop her mother in California from taking the first step to get her some help. Annie's mom was in the entertainment industry, an assertive woman who was used to picking up the phone and making arrangements. I met her while on vacation in California, and soon after I returned home, I found her on the phone. She wanted to make an appointment for her 19-year-old daughter, who had become depressed during her sophomore year in college.

When Annie came to my office one day in spring, she was initially a bit guarded, but soon she became more attentive and engaged. Unlike some young patients I see, she knew she had a problem, and she really wanted help. She had been depressed since the past fall, she said, and felt as though she was "wallowing." She wasn't sleeping well, and felt she had way too much time on her hands. She looked straight at me and said, "I can't fix it." As she said this, tears formed in her bright blue eyes and began to trickle down her cheeks. Annie had a sweet, open face and an engaging manner—she wasn't one of those just-leave-me-alone-I'm-not-depressed sort of kids.

I handed her a tissue and asked her to take me back to the beginning. Annie told me a big turning point in her life had come when she was eight and her parents divorced. "They were fighting like cats and dogs, so when they split up it was much better," she said. "At least it was quieter. But I got really sad about it, and I don't think I was easy to be around. I've always been a sensitive person."

"Sensitive in what way?" I asked.

"News affects me in a big way. It can be anything. If a friend is sick. Divorce, definitely. So I reacted badly to my parents' divorce. I was fighting with my friends all the time."

Life settled down by high school. However, when I asked her if she'd ever felt the same way she did now, she told me that at one point when she was 16 she had fallen into a period of extreme lethargy. It had been diagnosed as chronic fatigue syndrome, a controversial and poorly defined condition that often mimics the symptoms of depression. By her senior year, Annie was looking forward to going off on her own. "I wanted to get out of California," she said. She went about as far as possible, across the country to New York. "But my freshman year here was horrible. I got depressed, and it took me about four months to get out of it. I couldn't concentrate, and my grades were miserable."

"How was your social life?"

"Not good. I had a single dorm room so I felt like I wasn't connecting with people."

"So how do you compare that to the way you feel now? Or to the way you felt when you had chronic fatigue in high school?"

"This feels a lot worse than that," Annie said softly. "It's hard to sleep. I wake up at five in the morning. My mind wanders a lot, which never happened before. I've felt exhausted since last fall and I think it's getting worse. I just feel so terrible."

Annie admitted that she had been drinking a lot—it made her numb, she said—and she had used cocaine and Ecstasy. The drugs made her feel good, but the people she was doing them with scared her.

It was also clear that Annie had a lot of anxieties. Some were reasonable: though she had come from privileged circumstances, she had worked since high school; but now she wasn't working, and she worried that she was being lazy, wasting her time. Other anxieties were less rational. She feared, for instance, that her father, who was not sick, might soon die. (Significantly, she also said that her father and brother had some kind of depression in their histories, though she wasn't sure about the specifics).

Annie seemed to have a prime example of the kind of depression that comes on during the college years. And since this wasn't the first episode, I thought she was a good candidate for medication. I wanted to talk to her mother first, and I asked Annie if that would be okay. She nodded yes.

Later that day, I called Annie's mother in California and told her that Annie had described two previous episodes, one in high school and the other last year, during her freshman year. I thought both were probably bouts of depression. This would make three. "Oh, she's definitely had three episodes," her mother said. "And I'm worried she's going to become an alcoholic. I know she drinks when she gets depressed."

I asked her how she felt about putting Annie on Prozac. She chuckled. "Where I come from it's hard to find someone who's *not* on Prozac."

Annie was not so glib about taking the medicine. She wanted to know about side effects and, more important, whether it would change "who I am," frequently asked and reasonable questions. She decided to give the medicine a try, and it lifted her. In fact, she blossomed. She cut down on her drinking and became an academic standout, getting straight As, much better than her performance in high school. She became socially much more at ease as well. She had always had a great sense of humor and an unusual ability to enjoy and relate to people of all ages, but now she had a new-found confidence as well. She joined a swing dance class, and made friends there. "That made a big difference," she said. And with renewed energy and motivation, Annie got an afternoon job working for a photographer. She used what she earned to travel during vacations. She had a new sense of independence. Part of it was maturity, and part of it was her renewed ability to draw from her own inner resources. Without depression, the barriers were down. By her junior year, Annie had decided that she wanted to go on to film school when she graduated, and would spend her senior year making a short film that was the main part of the application.

After Annie had been taking Prozac for a year, we talked about gradually lowering her dosage and then stopping it. To some extent this was a test. With depression, the more episodes a person has, the greater the risk for additional ones. The rule of thumb with SSRI medications is that a patient can stop taking them if he or she has had six months to a year without symptoms after the first depressive episode. But if it recurs, it's advisable to stay on medication for two years. If there is a recurrence after that, it might be a lifelong proposition. The issue with Annie was whether she had been in a depression during high school, rather than having chronic fatigue syndrome. But she had been doing well for a year, and she was anxious to stop taking Prozac. We waited until October, so that if she had a quick relapse, it wouldn't be during the stressful part of the beginning of her senior year.

Annie was fine throughout that year, and I looked forward to our monthly visits. She would talk excitedly about her student film project, about a boyfriend she had been seeing, about her job. But one day in spring she called and said she was depressed again. She hadn't been accepted into film school. "I didn't even get an interview," she said dejectedly. I didn't want her to leap right back to Prozac, just in case this turned out to be a brief and understandable down period from which she would recover. But after several more weeks in a funk, it was clear this was a relapse. She went back on Prozac. Within three weeks, she had fully stabilized.

Annie was remarkable for her maturity and astuteness about her illness. Her father had it, her brother had it, and she took ownership of it as well. She was never pleased to be taking medicine, questioning it all the time and wondering if she would have to take it the rest of her life. But she sensed it would be hard for her to have a fulfilling life without it.

In June, I received an invitation to Annie's graduation and to a party afterward. I was honored and touched, but felt slightly awkward on her behalf. A cancer survivor might invite her oncologist, but did Annie really want her psychiatrist attending a small family party? As unfortunate as it is, I do recognize the stigma of having a mental illness. I told Annie I'd feel more comfortable just attending the graduation. I went, planning to sit anonymously in an aisle seat so she would see me during the procession into the field house. Afterward I would slip out. But at the door I found Annie's mother waiting for me. She had saved a seat with the family, and happily introduced me to her ex-husband, whom I'd never met. "Oh, I've heard so much about you," he said with a big smile and hearty handshake. Afterward, Annie hugged me and thanked me. But I told her she did it herself. So many people have illnesses they do nothing about. But Annie's ability to confront her illness was remarkable.

She still had her share of problems, like anyone else. She struggled with her weight and continued to search for the right boyfriend. After graduation, she was still upset about not getting into film school. She was living back in California and feeling like a failure. Like many people her age, she was in what might be called extended adolescence, that passage to true independence and adulthood. For some people it's a short bridge, but for others it's a long, dark tunnel. Annie found herself in tears just about every day those first few weeks. But she realized that it's possible to be unhappy without being depressed.

Her mother helped get her a job as a television production assistant and set her up in a small apartment. But that didn't help much. Annie hated the job. And she was as lonely as could be. She tried reconnecting with friends from high school and tried making friends with people from work, but she still found herself alone on Saturday nights. "I go to yoga every day at six-thirty, and nobody talks," she told me over the phone. She had huge phone bills. She called her friends in New York almost obsessively.

Annie's mother was impatient. "I don't understand why you're not happy," she told her. She thought Annie was going through some sort of postcollege letdown. Annie was still on Prozac, and her psychiatrist in California raised the dosage and augmented it with Wellbutrin, an "atypical" antidepressant that doesn't affect serotonin but increases two other neurochemicals, norepinephrine and dopamine. (That approach may be more effective than simply increasing the dosage of the SSRI.) And slowly, Annie emerged—and then she had the motivation for a job change. She began working as an assistant for an entertainment lawyer, and loved the job. Her boss was appreciative and thanked her every day for her work. Meanwhile, she looked forward to reapplying to film school.

There had been a very good chance that Annie would have dropped out of college if she hadn't sought and received help, the same kind of help that my friend Scott never got. Though she went off Prozac again after going another six months without symptoms, Annie knows that keeping depression at bay may well be a lifelong struggle for her—but a struggle she can win.

# NO

Joli Jensen

# Let's Not Medicate Away
# Student Angst

**M**y student told me that she was having trouble in my class because her doctor hadn't yet found the "right" mood medication for her. I had known something was up because she hadn't been the delightfully contentious student I had met the year before. This semester she seemed distracted and subdued, and she had been missing class. A few weeks after talking with me, she returned to attending class regularly, but mostly to listen while others spoke. The "right" medication for her, apparently, was one that made her no longer want to argue in class.

A surprising number of my best students are on antidepressant or anti-anxiety medication. Both the student health center and their own physicians prescribe the drugs in response to complaints that seem to me to be normal, even necessary, aspects of young-adult life. None of these students previously felt themselves to be at risk; none were behaving in self-destructive ways. Many were initially surprised by their diagnosis of "clinical depression" or "social anxiety disorder." Yes, they were feeling self-doubt, uncertainty, insecurity, melancholy, as my best students always have, and as do I, still. But they accept the diagnosis because they find that the medications help them succeed in college, and they are grateful for their newfound calm.

I'm not so sure. Are the characteristics of late adolescence—and of life—being mistaken for evidence of pathology? Do our best and brightest students now believe that they need drugs to handle class? And, in taking prescription mood medication, do they avoid, even stifle, the emotionality and zeal that feed intellectual growth and make the life of the mind worth living?

Good students use college as a time to explore and experiment, to try on different perspectives, and to become different selves. Strong emotions, shifting commitments, and difficult relationships help all of us sort out who we are and what we believe. Emotional upheaval helps us figure out what matters and what doesn't. But for students focused on productivity, those developmental struggles stand in the way of what they define as academic success. It's hard to write good papers, study assigned material, join clubs, be a leader, do community service, and build a compelling résumé if you are experiencing doubt

From *Chronicle of Higher Education,* vol. 49, issue 40, June 13, 2003, pp. 214–226, 229–233.

about what it all means. Existential angst makes it more difficult to do the kinds of things that supposedly get you ahead in the world.

My students have been told that their feelings of sadness or worry or fear are due to a chemical imbalance in their brain, and that the imbalance can be corrected by drugs like Prozac or Celexa or Paxil. A *Newsweek* cover story last fall featured a sad-eyed adolescent girl holding a teddy bear, and described an "epidemic" of undiagnosed mood disorders among teenagers. The article quoted a professor of child psychiatry warning parents that moodiness, oppositionality, and irritability aren't normal teenage traits and should be treated as symptoms of an underlying disorder.

But those traits don't seem all that abnormal to me, particularly in academe. Frustration, hostility, anger, and resentment, as well as feelings of hopelessness and insecurity, have long been features of our common life. Oppositionality is our stock in trade. Another supposed symptom of mood disorder is absorption in particular activities (research? writing?) to the exclusion of an active social life. All the introverts, eccentrics, and productive intellectuals I know have those "symptoms," as do many lively, interesting teenagers and young adults. Does that mean we are all diseased and need medication? Or that, whether or not we are dysfunctional, we would benefit from taking mood-altering medication?

Much is still not known about the biochemistry of emotion. The neuroscientist Elliot Valenstein notes in *Blaming the Brain* that there are surprisingly few long-term studies on mood-altering drugs, but quite a few troubling side effects, and even scary suggestions about permanent changes the medications may cause. Nonetheless, drug-company advertisements offer glowing images of confident, restored selves, implying that drugs bring the brain back to a naturally happy state.

Does this matter? What my students (and increasing numbers of my colleagues) tell me is that they don't really care how *their* drug works, just that it allows them to function more normally. But who is defining normal? And for what purposes?

Academic life is indeed stressful. There are many good reasons to be moody and irritable. Others may imagine a relaxed and contemplative work environment; we know a demanding, all-too-corporate existence, replete with competition, status anxiety, politics, and chicanery. There is a risk, I believe, in seeking ways to thrive cheerfully, no matter how toxic our situation. If the pills work, we can believe that we, not circumstances, create "the problem." If the pills work, we may give up the chance to learn from our persistent or recurring melancholy and discontent. If the pills work, we won't have to think about our collective beliefs that we should publish or perish, or lecture at alienated students, or train graduate students for nonexistent jobs, or be at peak performance all the time.

For our students, in particular, who are in a period of life when they have both the energy and the mandate to question and transform, pills can be a tragic deflection. Not only do the students lose the chance to struggle with what is true and right for them as individuals, but they also quench the discontent that fuels the desire to make a difference in the world. Discontent is volatile, but it is also a necessary catalyst. Our students are being told that their unhappiness is about their brain chemistry, not their situation, and that they should address their unhappiness with medication, not action.

In my media-studies classes, we read social critics who warn about the ways mass culture deflects social change by semi-satisfying the discontents that modernity creates. Many cultural critics contend that we keep going back to popular culture or shopping or work, seeking but never finding what we really need. As Theodor Adorno and Max Horkheimer put it, we are being given the menu, but never the meal. What is especially worrisome is that we don't even realize the switch has been made; we keep expecting the menu to feed us.

Adorno and Horkheimer's claim that we are being duped into meeting capitalism's needs rather than our own usually hits home with at least a few of my most contentious students. They understand that what pleases them right now may not be what is best for them in the long run. Such students can often get their classmates to see how easy it is to fall for stories that serve the interests of those who are doing the telling. This semester, however, the class consensus seems to be "so what if we're being duped, as long as we're happy." Few students argue for the value of "seeing through" myths in order to challenge them and come up with something better. Why make yourself unhappy for no reason?

I've always felt a little uncomfortable with my pedagogical role as the skeleton at the feast. Much of my professorial energy is spent getting my students to at least consider the possibility that the very things that give them solace and pleasure—like television and shopping—may not be giving them what they need to lead a meaningful life. Part of my obligation as a professor is to demonstrate the nature and worth of being an intellectual. And I assume that the value of the life of the mind is that it takes nothing for granted without interrogating it for consequences.

So I think that it is our responsibility to help our students become more alert, more contentious, and yes, more troubled. I'm not arguing that medication is never appropriate. Just that it may be given too easily, and taken too unthinkingly. I want students to be motivated to recognize what is absent or being hidden in contemporary culture, and to become familiar with alternatives from the past, and from points of view other than their own. In the end, I want them to seek ways to imagine themselves more as citizens than as consumers.

Unfortunately, many of my students (and colleagues) subscribe to what I'm starting to call "psychic Taylorism." They are willing—even eager—to trade messy, inefficient doubt and worry for neat, effective productivity and cheer. Just as Frederick W. Taylor, the father of "scientific management," found ways to eliminate the idiosyncratic movements of individual workers so that they could perform their repetitive jobs more efficiently, my students and colleagues are willing to eliminate their idiosyncratic emotional responses in order to become more resilient and productive workers. But messy, inefficient, troubling angst is the very stuff of creative, productive, challenging intellectual life. It wakes us up. It shouldn't be medicated away.

# POSTSCRIPT

## Should We Use Medication to Deal with the Angst of College and Young Adulthood?

There is no controversy as to whether antidepressant drugs, and drug treatments for other psychological problems, have made a positive difference in people's lives. They have. For some people so depressed as to consider suicide, antidepressants can save lives. As Koplewicz notes, he has personally treated a number of people who may not have made it without antidepressants. Students with psychological disorders who would have previously been lost to society are now able to finish school and excel. As Koplewicz notes, college retention rates have gone up—students who in past generations dropped out have been able to complete their educations. Overall, in cases of serious mental illness, no reasonable person would argue that medications are a bad choice. The controversy then centers on the issue of what classifies as serious mental illness and what classifies as normal stress and strain at a difficult point in the life span.

Society has an ambivalent relationship with the challenges of youth and early adulthood. People often look back at their college years as the best times of their lives. Part of that fondness derives from an appreciation for the distinctive opportunities to wrestle with new challenges and big questions that inevitably arise when trying to make one's way in the world. As Joli Jensen notes in the above selection, "existential angst" can provide a distinctive opportunity to think through the meaning of life—and the meaning of life span development. By definition, college is supposed to be about challenging the mind. If we never confronted challenges, we would never learn. Jensen is concerned that the contemporary tendency to medicate any form of discontent takes away these challenges.

Jensen is also concerned that the trend toward medicating discontent sends a problematic message to young adults about what matters. She notes experiences with students who excuse problems or failures by suggesting "it's not me, it's my brain chemistry." Implicit in this attitude is a false mind-body dualism that has pervaded Western thought for generations: Any scientific account must accept that our mind is never independent of the biological influence of our body. Likewise, in the process of life span development, our biology is always working together with our thinking and our social environment to craft behavior and change. Does medication cause young adults to ignore this basic fact?

On the other hand, the fact that our body and mind are one entity could support the widespread use of medication during the stressful transition to adulthood. Because our development is inextricably linked to our biology, why not use our knowledge of biology to facilitate development? Medications allow us to manage developmental changes that make the transition to adulthood particularly difficult for individuals who genuinely do have functionally different brain chemistry. In the reading, Koplewicz is not arguing that everyone should use medication, but simply that we should respect the positive role of medication in allowing people to cope.

This controversy vividly highlights both the social challenges that are inevitable during the life span and the biological functions that orient our development. With technological advances, it is likely that we will continue to gain both understanding and potential biochemical control over our psychological experience of development. Undoubtedly, such control will be controversial in its potential for both good and bad.

# Suggested Readings

K. Alishio and J. Hersh, "Working with Students in the Medical Era: Do We All Have to Know How to Diagnose and Treat Mental Conditions?" *About Campus* (March–April 2005).

C. Bailey, "Is It Really Our Chemicals that Need Balancing?" *Journal of American College Health* (July 2002).

L. Burdette Williams, "My Medicated Students," *About Campus* (March–April 2005).

L. Diller, *Should I Medicate My Child? Sane Solutions for Troubled Kids With—and Without—Psychiatric Drugs* (Basic Books, 2002).

R. Dworkin, "The Medicalization of Unhappiness," *The Public Interest* (Summer 2001).

H. Estroff Marano, "Up Against the Ivy Wall in 2004," *Psychology Today* (2004).

S. Fried, "Sex, Meds and Teens," *Rolling Stone* (May 11, 2000).

J. Jensen, "Emotional Choices: What Story You Choose to Believe About Antidepressants Reveals a Deeper Truth About Who You Are," *Reason* (April 2004).

R. Kadison, "The Mental-Health Crisis: What Colleges Must Do," *The Chronicle of Higher Education* (December 10, 2004).

R. Kadison and T. DiGeronimo, *College of the Overwhelmed: The Campus Mental Health Crisis and What to Do About It* (Jossey-Bass, 2004).

G. Marino, "Altered States: Pills Alone Won't Cure the Blues," *Commonweal* (May 21, 2004).

K. Painter, "Colleges Throw Lifeline to Students," *USA Today* (March 3, 2004).

P. Raeburn, "The Pill Paradox: Are Antidepressants Killing Teens, or Saving Their Lives? A Father Searches for Answers," *Psychology Today* (September–October 2004).

# ISSUE 15

# Are College Graduates Unprepared for Adulthood and the World of Work?

**YES: Mel Levine,** from "College Graduates Aren't Ready for the Real World," *The Chronicle of Higher Education* (February 18, 2005)

**NO: Frank F. Furstenberg, Jr., et al.,** from "Growing Up Is Harder to Do," *Contexts* (Summer 2004)

### ISSUE SUMMARY

**YES:** Professor of pediatrics, author, and child-rearing expert Mel Levine argues that contemporary colleges are producing a generation of young adults who are psychologically "unready" for entering adulthood and the world of work.

**NO:** Distinguished sociologist Frank Furstenberg and his research colleagues assert that major social changes have extended the transition to adulthood, and college graduates are the group most apt to cope with these social changes.

T here seems to be something attractive about idealizing previous generations. In each successive cohort, there is a group of people who are convinced that the "youth today" are just not as able as those of previous decades. It's possible that even at the founding of the United States, adults were worried about the "youth today." The persistence of this perception suggests there are indeed some significant differences between successive generations of young adults. The controversy comes in assessing whether those differences are necessarily bad.

Regardless of historical context, Dr. Mel Levine thinks the current generation of youth, particularly recent college graduates, are unprepared and unready to be productive members of society. In researching a book, Levine undertook interviews with employers and young adults, and persistently found that college graduates were not ready for the world of work. In the following selection, Levine lays out a series of explanations for this problem—blaming colleges, parents, and the culture at large for allowing young adults to expect that fun and gratification should be easy and without rigorous dedication.

In contrast, Frank Furstenberg and his colleagues emphasize that young adulthood today cannot be understood outside of its historical context. In fact, they suggest, what is distinctive about the current generation of youth is that they face unprecedented expectations and challenges in making the transition to adulthood. Rather than being able to seamlessly move into career and family patterns that will provide stable lives, today's young adults face the expensive and challenging task of preparing themselves to enter a stunningly complex world. From Furstenberg et al.'s perspective, college graduates are the most able to take on that task.

While both Levine and Furstenberg et al. are directly addressing the nature of contemporary young adulthood, they end up on different sides of this issue because they emphasize different perspectives on what matters in life span development. For Levine, what matters are the daily psychological experiences that people have in their community, with their family, and in their schools. For Furstenberg and colleagues, what matters are the demands placed on people embedded in complex modern society.

In essence, this means that Levine believes college graduates today are "less developed" than those in past generations, whereas Furstenberg and colleagues say young adults are developing in a different way with different needs. Depending on one's level of analysis, in the perspective of Furstenberg et al., it is not reasonable to compare the qualities of today's generation with the youth in previous generations—that would be like comparing apples and oranges. But for Levine, today's college graduates, if classified according to the fruit metaphor, are mostly just rotten.

There is no question that the nature of early adulthood, and the expectations of college, have changed. Just one century ago, only elite youth graduated from high school. It wasn't until the 1920s that adolescents became more likely to attend high school than immediately transition to work, apprenticeships, or family responsibilities out of childhood. It wasn't until after World War II, when the GI bill paying college tuition for returning soldiers created a massive growth in the system of higher education, that college education became broadly accessible. Now, the proportion of youth who attend college is at an all-time high.

Considering that, can we say that college graduates are reasonably well prepared for the challenges of the contemporary world of work? Or has the changing historical context accompanied reduced expectations and dysfunctional attitudes among those in early adulthood? If you are reading this as a college student, it will be important to not get defensive; note that neither author is talking about particular college students as individuals. Instead, both are concerned with what they consider to be dominant trends affecting college students as a group.

Mel Levine

 **YES**

# College Graduates Aren't Ready for the Real World

**W**e are witnessing a pandemic of What I call "worklife unreadiness," and colleges face a daunting challenge in immunizing students against it.

Swarms of start-up adults, mostly in their 20s, lack the traction needed to engage the work side of their lives. Some can't make up their minds where to go and what to do, while others find themselves stranded along a career trail about which they are grievously naïve and for which they lack broad preparation. Whether they spent their undergraduate or graduate years focused on a discrete pursuit—say, engineering, law, or medicine—or whether their college education was unbound from any stated career intentions, many are unprepared to choose an appropriate form of work and manage their first job experience.

In conducting interviews for my new book, *Ready or Not, Here Life Comes,* I heard repeatedly from employers that their current crop of novice employees appear unable to delay gratification and think long term. They have trouble starting at the bottom rung of a career ladder and handling the unexciting detail, the grunt work, and the political setbacks they have to bear. In fact, many contemporary college and graduate students fail to identify at all with the world of adults.

A variety of unforeseen hazards can cause an unsuccessful crossover from higher education to the workplace. Start-up adults may often not even sense that they are failing to show initiative or otherwise please their superiors. Some early-career pitfalls are unique to our times; some derive from the characteristics of individual students themselves; some are side effects of modern parenting; and others result from an educational system that has not kept pace with the era we live in. All have policy implications for higher-education leaders.

The problems start early. While many of today's young adults were growing up, their role models were each other. Kids today don't know or take an interest in grown-ups, apart from their parents, their teachers, and entertainers. That stands in contrast to previous generations, when young people "studied" and valued older people in the community.

Thus, a lot of contemporary college students are insatiable in their quest for social acceptance and close identification with an esteemed gaggle of

From *The Chronicle of Higher Education,* vol. 51, issue 24, February 18, 2005, pp. B11. Copyright © 2005 by Mel Levine. Reprinted by permission.

peers. The commercialization of adolescence has further fueled a desire to be "cool" and accepted and respected within a kid culture. Some young adults become the victims of their own popularity, experiencing surges and spasms of immense yet highly brittle ego inflation. But that bubble is likely to burst in early career life, when their supervisors are not all that impressed by how well they play shortstop, how they express their taste through their earrings, or the direction in which they orient the brim of their baseball caps.

Life in the dormitory or the fraternity or sorority house no doubt perpetuates and even intensifies that pattern of overreliance on peer approval. It may also serve to cultivate an overwhelming preoccupation with body image and sexual and chemical bodily excitation—at times to the detriment of intellectual development and reality-based reflection on the future. We live in a period of college education in which the body may be the mind's No.1 rival. While that tension has always existed, our culture stresses more than ever bodily perfection, self-marketing through appearance, and physical fitness over cognitive strength. Unbridled athletic fervor may reinforce such a somatically bent collegiate culture.

Meanwhile, many college students carry with them an extensive history of being overprogrammed by their parents and their middle schools and high schools—soccer practice Monday through Saturday, bassoon lessons on Tuesday evening, square dancing on Wednesday, kung fu on Saturday afternoon, on and on. That may make it hard for them to work independently, engage in original thought processes, and show initiative.

Other students were the golden girls and boys of their high schools—popular, attractive, athletic, and sometimes scholarly insofar as they were talented test takers. Yet many never had to engage in active analytic thinking, brainstorming, creative activity, or the defense of their opinions. In quite a few instances, their parents settled all their disputes with teachers, guided (or did) their homework, and filled out their college applications. As a result, such students may have trouble charting and navigating their own course in college and beyond.

Not uncommonly, start-up adults believe that everything they engage in is supposed to generate praise and fun, as opposed perhaps to being interesting or valuable. The quest for effusive verbal feedback has been a prime motivator throughout their lives, as they have sought approval from parents, teachers, and coaches. Unbridled and sometimes unearned praise may, in fact, fuel the pressure for grade inflation in college.

Similarly, students' favorite professors may well be those whose lectures are the funniest. But what if, eight years later, their bosses have no sense of humor, and their work pales in comparison to the visual and motor ecstasy of computer games and the instantaneous satisfaction of their social and sexual conquests? They might then find themselves mentally out of shape, lacking in the capacity for hard cognitive work, and unable to engage successfully in any extended mind toil that they don't feel like doing.

On top of that, some college students are afflicted with significant underlying developmental problems that have never been properly diagnosed and managed. Examples abound, including difficulties in processing language or communicating verbally (both speaking and writing), an inability to focus attention or reason, quantitatively, and a serious lack of problem-solving skills. We are currently encountering far more students with learning difficulties, for a multitude or reasons. Many young adults are growing up in a nonverbal culture that makes few, if any, demands on language skills, active information processing, pattern recognition, and original thinking.

The most common learning disorder among undergraduates is incomplete comprehension. Affected students have difficulty understanding concepts, terminology, issues, and procedures. Many of them succeeded admirably in high school through the exclusive use of rote memory and procedural mimicry (known in mathematics as the "extreme algorithmic approach"). So a student may have received an A in trigonometry by knowing how to manipulate cosines and tangents yet without really understanding what they represent. Such underlying deficiencies return to haunt start-up adults striving for success and recognition on the job. A young adult may be selling a product without fully understanding it, or preparing a legal brief without perceiving its ramifications.

Trouble handling the workload is an equally prevalent, and lingering, form of collegiate dysfunction that follows students into their careers. Some college students are abysmally disorganized and have serious trouble managing materials and time, prioritizing, and handling activities with multiple components that must be integrated—like writing a term paper, applying to graduate schools or prospective employers, and preparing for a final examination. Such difficulties can manifest themselves for the first time at any academic stage in a student's life, including during law, business, or medical school. The students who are burdened with them are vulnerable to dropping out, mental-health problems, and a drastic loss of motivation.

Certainly many students leave college well prepared and well informed for careers, and not every college is affected by such negative cultural forces. But work-life unreadiness is increasingly prevalent and merits the attention of faculty members and administrators. The deterrents that I have mentioned may or may not ignite implosions of grade-point averages, but they can become crippling influences in the work lives of young adults.

Although colleges can't be expected to suture all the gaps in the culture of kids, some changes merit consideration if students are to succeed after graduation. Too many start-up adults harbor serious discrepancies between what they would like to do and what they are truly capable of doing. Often they are interested in pursuits they are not good at or wired for. They opt for the wrong careers because they are unaware of their personal and intellectual strengths and weaknesses, as well as woefully uninformed about the specific job demands of their chosen trades. That combination is a time bomb set to detonate early in a career.

Therefore, colleges should re-examine the adequacy of their career-placement or career-advisory services. Those services should be able to interview students in depth, administer vocational-interest inventories, and make use of sophisticated neuropsychological tests to help floundering students formulate career aims that fit their particular skills and yield personal gratification.

Colleges can also lessen undergraduate naïveté through formal education. Within a core curriculum, perhaps offered by the psychology department, colleges should help students get to know themselves and to think about the relationship between who they are and what they think they might do with their lives. They should provide, and possibly require, courses like "Career Studies," in which undergraduates analyze case studies and biographies to explore the psychological and political nuances of beginning a career.

Students need to anticipate the challenges and agonies of work life at the bottom rungs of a tall and steep ladder. They should be taught generic career-related skills—like how to collaborate, organize and manage projects, write proposals, and decrypt unwritten and unspoken on-the-job expectations. Colleges should also offer classes that cover topics like entrepreneurialism and leadership. Further, students should also receive formal instruction, including case studies, in the pros and cons of alternative career pathways within their areas of concentration (e.g., medical practice versus health-care administration, or teaching about real estate versus pursuing a money chase in land investment).

To elucidate the specific learning problems of students who are not succeeding, colleges need to offer up-to-date diagnostic services. Those include tests to pinpoint problems with memory, attention, concept formation, and other key brain processes that will cause a career to implode whether or not a student makes it through her undergraduate years.

Faculty members should change not only what they teach but *how* they teach, to help students make a better transition to the adult world. They should receive formal training in the latest research about brain development and the learning processes that occur during late adolescence—including such key areas as higher-language functioning, frontal-lobe performance (like planning, pacing, and self-monitoring), nonverbal thought processes, memory use, and selective attention.

Professors also should base their pedagogy on some awareness of the mechanisms underlying optimal learning and mastery of their subject matter. Chemistry professors should understand and make use of the cognition of chemistry mastery, while foreign-language instructors and those conducting political-science seminars should be aware of the brain functions they are tapping and strengthening through their coursework. Current students face complex decision-making and problem-solving career challenges, but many have been groomed in high school to rely solely on rote memory—an entirely useless approach in a meaningful career.

At the same time, professors must have keen insight into the differences in learning among the students who take their courses. They should seek to offer alternative ways in which students can display their knowledge and skills. They might discover, for instance, that their tests should de-emphasize rote recall and the spewing out of knowledge without any interpretation on the part of the student.

In short, faculty members must learn about teaching. It should not be assumed that a learned person understands how people learn.

What's more, colleges should offer opportunities for scholarly research into the cognitive abilities, political strategies, and skills needed for career fulfillment in various fields. The study of success and failure should be thought of as a topic worthy of rigorous investigation at all higher-education institutions.

Finally, every college should also strive to promulgate a campus intellectual life that can hold its own against social, sexual, and athletics virtuosity. Varsity debating teams should receive vigorous alumni support and status, as should literary magazines, guest lectureships, concerts, and art exhibitions. Undergraduate institutions reveal themselves by what gets tacked up on campus bulletin boards—which often are notices of keg parties, fraternity and sorority rush events, and intramural schedules. Colleges can work to change that culture.

Our colleges open their doors to kids who have grown up in an era that infiltrates them with unfettered pleasure, heavy layers of overprotection, and heaps of questionably justified positive feedback. As a result, childhood and adolescence may become nearly impossible acts to follow.

Higher education has to avoid hitching itself to that pleasure-packed bandwagon. Otherwise, students will view the academic side of college as not much more than a credentialing process to put up with while they are having a ball for four years. Colleges must never cease to ask themselves, "What roles can and should these young adults play in the world of our times? And what must we do to prepare them?"

# NO

### Frank F. Furstenberg, Jr., et al.

# Growing Up Is Harder to Do

*In the past several decades, a new life stage has emerged: early adulthood. No longer adolescents, but not yet ready to assume the full responsibilities of an adult, many young people are caught between needing to learn advanced job skills and depending on their family to support them during the transition.*

In the years after World War II, Americans typically assumed the full responsibilities of adulthood by their late teens or early 20s. Most young men had completed school and were working full-time, and most young women were married and raising children. People who grew up in this era of growing affluence—many of today's grandparents—were economically self-sufficient and able to care for others by the time they had weathered adolescence. Today, adulthood no longer begins when adolescence ends. Ask someone in their early 20s whether they consider themselves to be an adult, and you might get a laugh, a quizzical look, a shrug of the shoulders, or a response like that of a 24-year-old Californian: "Maybe next year. When I'm 25."

Social scientists are beginning to recognize a new phase of life: early adulthood. Some features of this stage resemble coming of age during the late 19th and early 20th centuries, when youth lingered in a state of semi-autonomy, waiting until they were sufficiently well-off to marry, have children and establish an independent household. However, there are important differences in how young people today define and achieve adulthood from those of both the recent and the more distant past.

This new stage is not merely an extension of adolescence, as has been maintained in the mass media. Young adults are physically mature and often possess impressive intellectual, social and psychological skills. Nor are young people today reluctant to accept adult responsibilities. Instead, they are busy building up their educational credentials and practical skills in an ever more demanding labor market. Most are working or studying or both, and are developing romantic relationships. Yet, many have not become fully adult—traditionally defined as finishing school, landing a job with benefits, marrying and parenting—because they are not ready, or perhaps not permitted, to do so. For a growing number, this will not happen until their late 20s or even early 30s. In response, American society will have to revise upward the "normal" age of full adulthood, and develop ways to assist young people through the ever-lengthening transition.

Among the most privileged young adults—those who receive ample support from their parents—this is a time of unparalleled freedom from family responsibilities and an opportunity for self-exploration and development. For the less advantaged, early adulthood is a time of struggle to gain the skills and credentials required for a job that can support the family they wish to start (or perhaps have already started), and a struggle to feel in control of their lives. A 30-year-old single mother from Iowa laughed when asked whether she considered herself an adult: "I don't know if I'm an adult yet. I still don't feel quite grown up. Being an adult kind of sounds like having things, everything is kind of in a routine and on track, and I don't feel like I'm quite on track."

## Changing Notions of Adulthood

Traditionally, the transition to adulthood involves establishing emotional and economic independence from parents or, as historian John Modell described it, "coming into one's own." The life events that make up the transition to adulthood are accompanied by a sense of commitment, purpose and identity. Although we lack systematic evidence on how adulthood was defined in the past, it appears that marriage and parenthood represented important benchmarks. Nineteenth-century American popular fiction, journalism, sermons and self-help guides rarely referred to finishing school or getting a job, and only occasionally to leaving home or starting one's own household as the critical turning point. On the other hand, they often referred to marriage, suggesting that marriage was considered, at least by middle-class writers, as the critical touchstone of reaching adulthood.

By the 1950s and 1960s, most Americans viewed family roles and adult responsibilities as nearly synonymous. In that era, most women married before they were 21 and had at least one child before they were 23. For men, having the means to marry and support a family was the defining characteristic of adulthood, while for women, merely getting married and becoming a mother conferred adult status. As Alice Rossi explained in 1968: "On the level of cultural values, men have no freedom of choice where work is concerned: they must work to secure their status as adult men. The equivalent for women has been maternity. There is considerable pressure upon the growing girl and young woman to consider maternity necessary for a woman's fulfillment as an individual and to secure her status as an adult."

Research conducted during the late 1950s and early 1960s demonstrated widespread antipathy in America toward people who remained unmarried and toward couples who were childless by choice. However, these views began to shift in the late 1960s, rendering the transition to adulthood more ambiguous. Psychologists Joseph Veroff, Elizabeth Douvan, and Richard Kulka found that more than half of Americans interviewed in 1957 viewed someone who did not want to get married as selfish, immature, peculiar or morally flawed. By 1976, fewer than one-third of a similar sample held such views. A 1962 study found that 85 percent of mothers believed that married couples should have children. Nearly 20 years later, just 40 percent of those women still agreed, and in 1993 only 1 in 5 of their daughters agreed. Arland Thornton and Linda Young-Demarco, who have studied attitudes toward family roles during the latter half of the 20th century, conclude that "Americans increasingly value freedom and equality in their personal and family lives while at the same time maintaining their commitment to the ideals of marriage, family, and children." While still personally committed to family, Americans increasingly tolerate alternative life choices.

To understand how Americans today define adulthood, we developed a set of questions for the 2002 General Social Survey (GSS), an opinion poll administered to a nationally representative sample of Americans every two years by the National Opinion Research Center. The survey asked nearly 1,400 Americans aged 18 and older how important each of the following traditional benchmarks was to being an adult: leaving home, finishing school, getting a full-time job, becoming financially independent from one's parents, being able to support a family, marrying and becoming a parent.

The definition of adulthood that emerges today does not necessarily include marriage and parenthood. [The] most important milestones are completing school, establishing an independent household and being employed full-time—concrete steps associated with the ability to support a family. Ninety-five percent of Americans surveyed consider education, employment, financial independence and the ability to support a family to be key steps on the path to adulthood. Nonetheless, almost half of GSS respondents do not believe that it is necessary to actually marry or to have children to be considered an adult. As a young mother from San Diego explained, having a child did not make her an adult; instead she began to feel like an adult when she realized that "all of us make mistakes, but you can fix them and if you keep yourself on track, everything will come out fine." Compared with their parents and grandparents, for whom marriage and parenthood were virtually a prerequisite for becoming an adult, young people today more often view these as life choices, not requirements.

## The Lengthening Road to Adulthood

Not only are the defining characteristics of adulthood changing, so is the time it takes to achieve them. To map the changing transitions to adulthood, we also examined several national surveys that contain information on young adults both in this country and abroad. Using U.S. Census data collected as far back as 1900, we compared the lives of young adults over time. We also conducted about 500 in-depth interviews with young adults living in different parts of the United States, including many in recent immigrant groups.

Our findings, as well as the work of other scholars, confirm that it takes much longer to make the transition to adulthood today than decades ago, and arguably longer than it has at any time in America's history. [Based] on the 1960 and 2000 U.S. censuses, [there is a] large decline in the percentage of young adults who, by age 20 or 30, have completed all of the traditionally-defined major adult transitions (leaving home, finishing school, becoming financially independent, getting married and having a child). We define financial independence for both men and women as being in the labor force; however, because women in 1960 rarely combined work and motherhood, married full-time mothers are also counted as financially independent in both years. In 2000, just 46 percent of women and 31 percent of men aged 30 had completed all five transitions, compared with 77 percent of women and 65 percent of men at the same age in 1960.

Women—who have traditionally formed families at ages younger than men—show the most dramatic changes at early ages. Although almost 30 percent of 20-year-old women in 1960 had completed these transitions, just 6 percent had done so in 2000. Among 25-year-olds (not shown), the decrease is even more dramatic: 70 percent of 25-year-old women in 1960 had attained traditional adult status, in 2000 just 25 percent had done so. Yet, in 2000, even as they delayed traditional adulthood, 25-year-old women greatly increased their participation in the labor force to levels approaching those of 25-year old men. The corresponding declines for men in the attainment of traditional adult status are less striking but nonetheless significant. For both men and women, these changes can largely be explained by the increasing proportion who go to college and graduate school, and also by the postponement of marriage and childbearing.

If we use the more contemporary definition of adulthood. . . —one that excludes marriage and parenthood—then the contrasts are not as dramatic. In 2000, 70 percent of men aged 30 had left home, were financially independent, and had completed their schooling, just 12 points lower than was true of 30-year-old men in 1960. Nearly 75 percent of 30-year-old women in 2000 met this standard, compared to nearly 85 percent of women in 1960. Nonetheless, even these changes are historically substantial, and we are not even taking into account how many of these independent, working, highly educated young people still feel that they are not yet capable of supporting a family.

The reasons for this lengthening path to adulthood, John Modell has shown, range from shifting social policies to changing economic forces. The swift transition to adulthood typical after World War II was substantially assisted by the government. The GI Bill helped veterans return to school and subsidized the expansion of education. Similarly, government subsidies for affordable housing encouraged starting families earlier. At the same time, because Social Security was extended to cover more of the elderly, young people were no longer compelled to support their parents. The disappearance or reduction of such subsidies during the past few decades may help to explain the prolongation of adult transitions for some Americans. The growing cost of college and housing forces many youth into a state of semi-autonomy, accepting some support from their parents while they establish themselves economically. When a job ends or they need additional schooling or a relationship dissolves, they increasingly turn to their family for assistance. Thus, the sequencing of adult transitions has become increasingly complicated and more reversible.

However, the primary reason for a prolonged early adulthood is that it now takes much longer to secure a full-time job that pays enough to support a family. Economists Timothy Smeeding and Katherin Ross Phillips found in the mid-1990s that just 70 percent of American men aged 24 to 28 earned enough to support themselves, while fewer than half earned enough to support a family of three. Attaining a decent standard of living today usually requires a college education, if not a professional degree. To enter or remain in the middle class, it is almost imperative to make an educational commitment that spans at least they early 20s. Not only are more Americans attending college than ever before, it takes longer to complete a degree than in years past. Census data reveal that from 1960 to 2000, the percentage of Americans aged 20, 25, and 30 who were enrolled in school more than doubled. Unlike during the 1960s, these educational and work investments are now required of women as well as men. It is little wonder then that many young people linger in early adulthood, delaying marriage and parenthood until their late 20s and early 30s.

Those who do not linger are likely those who cannot afford to and, perhaps as a result, views on how long it takes to achieve adulthood differ markedly by social class. Less-educated and less-affluent respondents—those, who did not attend college and those at the bottom one-third of the income ladder—have an earlier expected timetable for leaving home, completing school, obtaining full-time employment, marriage and parenthood. Around 40 percent of the less well-off in the GSS sample said that young adults should marry before they turn 25, and one-third said they should have children by this age, Far fewer of the better-off respondents pointed to the early 20s, and about one-third of them said that these events could be delayed until the 30s. These social class differences probably stem from the reality that young people with more limited means do not have the luxury of investing in school or experimenting with complex career paths.

## New Demands on Families, Schools and Governments

The growing demands on young Americans to invest in the future have come at a time of curtailed government support, placing heavy demands on families. Growing inequality shapes very different futures for young Americans with more and less privileged parents.

Early adulthood is when people figure out what they want to do and how best to realize their goals. If they are lucky enough to have a family that can help out, they may proceed directly through college, travel or work for a few years, or perhaps participate in community service, and then enter graduate or professional school. However, relatively few Americans have this good fortune. Youth from less well-off families must shuttle back and forth between work and school or combine both while they gradually gain their credentials. In the meantime, they feel unprepared for marriage or parenting. If they do marry or parent during these years, they often find themselves trying to juggle too many responsibilities and unable to adequately invest in their future. Like the mother from Iowa, they do not feel "on track" or in control of their lives.

More than at any time in recent history, parents are being called on to provide financial assistance (either college tuition, living expenses or other assistance) to their young adult children. Robert Schoeni and Karen Ross conservatively estimate that nearly one-quarter of the entire cost of raising children is incurred after they reach 17. Nearly two-thirds of young adults in their early 20s receive economic support from parents, while about 40 percent still receive some assistance in their late 20s.

A century ago, it was the other way around: young adults typically helped their parents when they first went to work, if (as was common) they still lived with their parents. Now, many young adults continue to receive support from their parents even after they begin working. The exceptions seem to be in immigrant families; there, young people more often help support their parents. A 27-year-old Chinese American from New York explained why he continued to live with his parents despite wanting to move out, saying that his parents "want me [to stay] and they need me. Financially, they need me to take care of them, pay the bills, stuff like that, which is fine."

As young people and their families struggle with the new reality that it takes longer to attain adulthood, Americans must recognize weaknesses in the primary institutions that facilitate this transition—schools and the military. For the fortunate few who achieve bachelor's degrees and perhaps go on to professional or graduate training, residential colleges and universities seem well designed. They offer everything from housing to health care while training young adults. Likewise, the military provides a similar milieu for those from less-privileged families. However, only about one in four young adults attend primarily residential colleges or join the military after high school. The other three-quarters look to their families for room and board while they attend school and enter the job market. Many of these youth enter community colleges or local universities that provide much less in the way of services and support.

The least privileged come from families that cannot offer much assistance. This vulnerable population—consisting of 10 to 15 percent of young adults—may come out of the foster care system, graduate from special education programs, or exit jails and prisons. These youth typically lack job skills and need help to secure a foothold in society. Efforts to increase educational opportunities, establish school-to-career paths, and help students who cannot afford post-secondary education must be given higher priority, even in a time of budget constraints. The United States, once a world leader in providing higher education to its citizens, now lags behind several other nations in the proportion of the population that completes college.

Expanding military and alternative national service programs also can help provide a bridge from secondary school to higher education or the labor force by providing financial credit to those who serve their country. Such programs also offer health insurance to young adults, who are often cut off from insurance by arbitrary age limits. Finally, programs for the vulnerable populations of youth coming out of foster care, special education, and mental health services must not assume that young people are fully able to become economically independent at age 18 or even 21. The timetable of the 1950s is no longer applicable. It is high time for policy makers and legislators to address the realities of the longer and more demanding transition to adulthood.

# POSTSCRIPT

## Are College Graduates Unprepared for Adulthood and the World of Work?

**A**ssuming that most people reading this are college students, how do you feel about some of the strong claims made by Mel Levine? Are you and your peers disinterested in adults outside your immediate sphere of influence? Do you and your peers prioritize physical beauty and activity over qualities of mind? Are you and your peers thinking about and preparing for the world of adulthood? If you agree with Levine, then it is important to consider why. Do you agree with the factors he identifies: excessive praise during childhood, a culture saturated with short-term gratification, a failure of colleges to make their curriculum relevant to what is needed by both youth and society? And if you don't agree with Levine, then it is important to consider why his perspective is prominent in our culture: Why is there a widespread perception that college-going youth are at risk of not making successful transitions to adulthood?

Furstenberg and his colleagues offer a strong sociohistorical argument as to why college-aged youths may be inaccurately perceived as irresponsible and ill-prepared: The transition to adulthood has changed and become more demanding. From this perspective, college graduates are as ready for adulthood as they can be considering the increasing complexity of society and of the work world. The population of youth going to college is at an all-time high, and it is likely to continue to rise—not necessarily because youth are intentionally delaying entry to adulthood, but because expectations of them have changed.

One of the main points made by Furstenberg et al. is that these changes have actually created a new developmental stage between adolescence and adulthood. While Furstenberg et al. prefer to call this stage early adulthood, it is common to hear other researchers use the term "emerging adulthood." Regardless of the terminology, however, the idea that the transition to adulthood has changed in distinctive ways creating new life span challenges has attained wide acceptance. Rather than marking adulthood with specific tangible accomplishments, such as developing a career or starting a family, people in contemporary society tend to mark adulthood with abstract qualities such as feeling independent. Yet that still leaves a question of whether such a change demonstrates that youth are not successfully transitioning to adulthood, or whether they are making the transition in a different way.

Clearly, societal changes do influence life span development. As society's structures change, so have psychosocial developmental influences. In other words, as the world of work and family changes, the attitudes and behavioral norms within families have changed. There is, for example, some truth to the idea that parents, schools, and organizations have shifted toward putting more emphasis on praise and positive feedback. In many ways this is good—there is research to suggest that people learn better from positive feedback than from punishment. But the relationship is not simple—feedback still needs to be substantive, and students still need to learn that positive outcomes come from positive achievements. Many colleges and universities, for example, are confronting controversies about grade inflation, which is often attributed to exactly this misplaced emphasis on unconditional praise. Colleges and universities thus end up facing diverse expectations from students, employers, and society with regard to successful transitions to adulthood. Perhaps the only constant is that in this, and many other ways, the experience of life span development is changing. The controversy will continue as we try to firmly establish what that change entails for the transition to adulthood.

## Suggested Readings

T. Apter, *The Myth of Maturity: What Teenagers Need from Parents to Become Adults* (W. W. Norton & Company, 2001).

J.J. Arnett, *Emerging Adulthood: The Winding Road from the Late Teens Through the Twenties* (Oxford University Press, 2004).

J.E. Cote, *Arrested Adulthood: The Changing Nature of Maturity and Identity* (New York University Press, 2000).

Institute for Research on Higher Education, "Understanding Employers' Perceptions of College Graduates," *Change* (May/June 1998).

M. Levine, *Ready or Not, Here Life Comes* (Simon & Schuster, 2005).

R.A. Settersten, F.F. Furstenberg, and R.G. Rumbaut, *On the Frontier of Adulthood: Theory, Research, and Public Policy* (MacArthur Foundation Series) (University of Chicago Press, 2005).

J. Studley, "Are Liberal Arts Dead? Far From It," *Careers and Colleges* (September–October 2003).

## American Psychological Association

This Web site provides information from Division 20 of the American Psychological Association, the division focused on adult development and aging.

http://apadiv20.phhp.ufl.edu/apadiv20.htm

## Society for Research on Adult Development

The Society for Research on Adult Development brings together researchers interested in positive adult development.

http://www.adultdevelopment.org/

## Population Council

The Population Council is an international, nonprofit, nongovernmental organization that conducts public health and social science research, some of which focuses on characteristics of adulthood.

http://www.popcouncil.org/

## Alternatives to Marriage Project

The Alternatives to Marriage Project advocates for diversity in adult relationships.

http://www.unmarried.org/

## Institute for American Values

The "Institute for American Values" promotes, among other things, marriage and traditional families.

http://americanvalues.org/

## Religion in Society

This Web site provides access to an encyclopedia about the role or religion in society.

http://hirr.hartsem.edu/ency/index.html

## PACE

The Yale Center for the Psychology of Abilities, Competencies, and Expertise (PACE) is a major research center investigating types of intelligence and their influence on success.

http://www.yale.edu/pace/

# PART 8

# Middle Adulthood

*I*n conventional terms, middle adulthood is often the most productive portion of the life span. During middle adulthood, most people deeply engage with families, the world of work, and communities. As such, some versions of the life span present middle adulthood (generally conceptualized as being between the mid-30s and the mid-60s) as the peak of development. But middle adulthood also produces significant challenges and new expectations. This section focuses on the relationship between healthy development and three challenges and expectations confronted by most adults in contemporary society: marriage, careers, and religion.

- Are Contemporary Adults Overlooking the Importance of Marriage as Part of Successful Development?

- Is One General Intelligence Factor Responsible for Career Success?

- Is Religion a Pure Good in Facilitating Well-Being During Adulthood?

# ISSUE 16

## Are Contemporary Adults Overlooking the Importance of Marriage as Part of Successful Development?

**YES: Linda J. Waite,** from "The Importance of Marriage Is Being Overlooked," *USA Today Magazine* (January 1999)

**NO: Dorian Solot and Marshall Miller,** from "Unmarried Bliss: Living Happily Ever After Doesn't Necessarily Require a Marriage License," *Providence Phoenix* (January 7–14, 1999)

### ISSUE SUMMARY

**YES:** Sociologist Linda J. Waite presents extensive data to suggest that marriage provides innumerable benefits to adults that belie its declining popularity.

**NO:** Dorian Solot and Marshall Miller, directors of the Alternatives to Marriage Project, assert that the push to promote marriage does not make sense when adults find satisfaction in having the choice to pursue alternative lifestyles.

**M**arriage is one of the most significant markers of the adult life span. Both historically and cross-culturally, adulthood is often defined by getting married and starting a family. In contemporary society, this norm is gradually changing. While there have always been a diversity of family types, the general expectation that a person will get married immediately upon becoming an adult has waned. It is much more likely for people to wait to get married or to not get married at all. This trend has generated tremendous controversy among those interested in considering the relationship between marriage and life span development.

Some of the controversy derives from divorce rates that are astonishingly high. It is common to hear that half of all marriages in the United States end in divorce—although that figure is generally used more as a high-end estimate rather than the probability of any particular marriage working out. For example, by some estimates, college-educated people are half as likely to get a divorce than the less educated. Likewise, people who marry at a young age are significantly more likely to get divorced. While such statistics can be manipulated to serve varying agendas, it is true that divorce is a common outcome of contemporary marriage. And divorce is hard on people—the couple getting divorced and any children who may be involved. While the long-term impact of divorce is another controversial area of study, few people would argue divorce is a good outcome.

One public response to much publicized high divorce rates has been to generate a renewed emphasis on "family values" and marriage. There is some indication that divorce rates are in fact declining, or at least leveling off. In addition, extensive research efforts have been devoted to analyzing the benefits of marriage. The benefits seem significant. As Linda J. Waite points out in the following reading selection, married individuals tend to demonstrate better levels of health, wealth, and general well-being than nonmarried individuals.

Findings such as those presented by Waite have been seized upon by politicians and others hoping to find new ways to serve society. Different levels of government and social service agencies are trying to administer what *The New Yorker* magazine referred to as "the marriage cure." The idea is to counsel and support people living in poverty, or who are otherwise socially marginalized, toward marriage as a way to raise their socioeconomic status. Such policies have also provoked controversy, and reaction from people who feel the push toward conventional marriage is a closed-minded way of imposing one model of successful adulthood.

Such a perspective is represented in the reading by Dorian Solot and Marshall Miller. A committed, but unmarried, heterosexual couple, Solot and Miller lead the Alternatives to Marriage Project, which is "a national nonprofit organization advocating for equality and fairness for unmarried people, including people who choose not to marry, cannot marry, or live together before marriage." From their perspective, contemporary adults do not overlook the importance of marriage; rather, they are engaging in new and healthy types of relationships that are appropriate to the diversity of contemporary society.

Diversity is another challenging topic in contemporary society. As such, it is interesting to consider why some people endorse the idea that one specific type of family structure is best for adults, while others endorse a diversity of family structures. As you read the selections, consider the evidence presented that implicitly addresses this issue of perspectives on diversity. Solot and Miller also tie the idea of diverse family types to the controversy about gay and lesbian marriage. Despite a significant and well-intentioned push toward marriage from people promoting family values, a majority of voters in recent elections have rejected the idea of allowing homosexual couples the right to legal marriage. If marriage is good for adults, should we not allow all adults the opportunity to marry? Or would that change the nature of marriage to such a degree that it would no longer maintain its traditional value? These types of questions demonstrate the way this controversial issue itself encapsulates various perspectives and interests, from psychologists and sociologists to politicians and activists to men and women of all types who engage in committed relationships during adulthood.

Linda J. Waite

 **YES**

# The Importance of Marriage Is Being Overlooked

**M**arriage seems to be less popular with Americans now than in the past. Men and women are marrying for the first time at much older ages than their parents did. They are divorcing more and living together more often and for longer periods. Perhaps most troubling, they are becoming unmarried parents at record rates.

What are the implications, for individuals, of these increases in non-marriage? If marriage is thought of as an insurance policy—which the institution is, in some respects—does it matter if more people are uninsured or are insured with a term rather than a whole-life policy?

It does matter, because marriage typically provides important and substantial benefits, to individuals as well as society. Marriage improves the health and longevity of men and women; gives them access to a more active and satisfying sex life; increases wealth and assets; boosts children's chances for success; and enhances men's performance at work and their earnings.

A quick look at marriage patterns today compared to, say, 1950 illustrates the extent of recent changes. Figures from the Census Bureau show that, at the height of the baby boom, about one-third of adult whites were not married. Some were waiting to marry for the first time; others were divorced or widowed and not remarried. Nevertheless, most Americans married at least once at some point in their lives, generally in their early 20s.

In 1950, the proportion of black adults not married was approximately equal to that among whites, but since that time, marriage behavior of blacks and whites has diverged dramatically. By 1993, 61% of black women and 58% of black men were not married, compared to 38% of white men and 41% of white women. In contrast to 1950, when slightly over one black adult in three was not married, a majority of black adults are unmarried today. Insofar as marriage "matters," black men and women are much less likely than whites to share in the benefits than they were even a generation ago.

The decline in marriage intimately is connected to the rise in cohabitation—living with someone in a sexual relationship without being married. Although Americans are less likely to be wed today than they were several decades ago, if both marriage and cohabitation are counted, they are about as likely to be "coupled." If cohabitation provides the same benefits to individuals marriage does, then is it necessary to be concerned about this shift? Yes, because a valuable social institution arguably is being replaced by one that demands and offers less.

Perhaps the most disturbing change in marriage appears in its relationship to parenthood. Today, a third of all births occur to women who are not married, with huge, but shrinking, differences between blacks and whites in this behavior. One-fifth of births to white mothers and two-thirds of births to blacks currently take place outside marriage. Although about a quarter of the white unmarried mothers are living with someone when they give birth, so that their children are born into two-parent—if unmarried—families, very few black children born to unwed mothers live with their fathers, too.

These changes in marriage behavior are a cause for concern because, on a number of important dimensions, married men and women do better than those who are unmarried. The evidence suggests that is *because* they are married.

**Healthy behaviors.** Married people tend to lead healthier lives than otherwise similar men and women who are not. For example, a 1997 national survey about problem drinking during the past year compared the prevalence of this unhealthy behavior among divorced, widowed, and married men and women. Problem drinking was defined as drinking more than subjects planned to, failing to do things they should have done because of drinking, and/or drinking to the point of hurting their health. Responses showed much lower rates of problem drinking for married than for unmarried men and extremely low reports of this condition for married or unmarried women. Excessive drinking seems to be a particularly male pattern of social pathology, one that females generally manage to avoid.

However, unmarried women report higher levels of other unhealthy acts than married women, in particular "risk-taking behavior." Risk taking reflects accidents around the house, while in the car, or on the job caused by carelessness; taking chances by driving too fast or doing things that might endanger others; and/or having serious arguments or fights at home or outside the home. Males and females reveal similar levels of risk taking on national surveys, but married men and women reflect much lower levels than those who are divorced.

University of Texas sociologist Debra Umberson examined a series of negative health behaviors in addition to those discussed here, such as marijuana use, drinking and driving, substance abuse, and failure to maintain an orderly lifestyle. She concludes that divorced and widowed men and women are more likely than their married counterparts to engage in unhealthy behaviors and less likely to lead an orderly and healthy life.

How does marriage affect healthy behaviors? It provides individuals—especially men—with someone who monitors their health and health-related behaviors and encourages them to drink and smoke less, eat a healthier diet, get enough sleep, and generally, take care of their health. In addition, husbands and wives offer each other moral support that helps in dealing with stressful situations. Married men especially seem to be motivated to avoid risky behaviors and take care of their health by the sense of meaning that marriage gives to their lives and the sense of obligation to others that it brings.

**Mortality.**    Married men and women appear to live healthier lives. Perhaps as a result, they face lower risks of dying at any point than those who never have married or whose previous marriage has ended.

With RAND Corporation economist Lee Lillard, I used a large national survey—the Panel Study of Income Dynamics—to follow men and women over a 20-year period. We watched them get married, get divorced, and remarry. We observed the death of spouses and of the individuals themselves. When we compared deaths of married men and women to those who were not married, we found that, once other factors were taken into account, the former show the lowest chances of dying. Widowed women were much better off than divorced women or those who never have married, although they still were disadvantaged when compared with married women. *All* men who were not married currently faced higher risks of dying than married men, regardless of their marital history. Other researchers have found similar differentials in death rates for unmarried adults in a number of countries besides the U.S.

How does marriage reduce the risk of dying and lengthen life? First, it appears to reduce risky and unhealthy behaviors. Second, it increases material well-being—income, assets, and wealth. These can be used to purchase better medical care, a healthier diet, and safer surroundings, all of which lengthen life. This material improvement seems to be especially important for women. Third, marriage provides individuals with a network of help and support, with others who rely on them and on whom they can rely. This seems to be especially important for men. Marriage also provides adults with an on-site, readily available sex partner.

# Sexual Satisfaction

In 1991, a national survey research organization conducted the National Health and Social Life Survey on a probability sample of 3,432 adults. It asked, among other things, how often they had sex with a partner. Married respondents reported levels of sexual activity about twice as high as singles. Married men cited a mean frequency of sexual activity of 6.8 times and single men 3.6 times per month over the last year. Married women indicated a mean of 6.1 times and single women 3.2 times per month over the last year. Cohabiting men and women also reported higher rates of sexual activity— 7.4 and 7.2 times per month, respectively, over the past year—suggesting that, as far as sexual activity, cohabitation surpasses marriage in its benefits to the individuals involved.

I also examined levels of physical satisfaction people cited from sex with their husband or wife, their cohabiting partner, or the primary partner identified by singles and found that married men more often said that sex with their wives was extremely pleasurable than cohabiting men or single men indicated that sex with their partners was. The high level of married men's physical satisfaction with their sex lives contradicts the popular view that sexual newness or variety improves sex for men. Physical satisfaction with sex is about the same for married women, cohabiting women, and single women with sex partners.

In addition to reporting more active sex lives than singles, married men and women say they are more emotionally satisfied with their sex lives than do those who are single or cohabiting. Although cohabitors report levels of sexual activity slightly higher than married people, both cohabiting men and women cite lower levels of satisfaction with their sex lives. In all comparisons where there is a difference, the married are more satisfied than the unmarried.

How does marriage improve one's sex life? Marriage and cohabitation provide individuals with a readily available sexual partner with whom they have an established, ongoing sexual relationship. Since married couples expect to carry on their sex lives for many years, and since most married couples are monogamous, husbands and wives have strong incentives to learn what pleases their partner in bed and to become good at it. Then, sex with a partner who knows what one likes and how to provide it becomes more satisfying than sex with a partner who lacks such skills. The emotional ties that exist in marriage increase sexual activity and satisfaction with it as well.

**Assets and wealth.**   In addition to having more sex, married couples have more money. Household wealth—one comprehensive measure of financial well-being—includes pension plans and Social Security, real and financial assets, and the value of the primary residence. According to RAND economist James Smith, married men and women age 51–60 had median wealth in 1992 of about $66,000, compared to $42,000 for the widowed, $35,000 for those who never had married, $34,000 among those who were divorced, and $7,600 for those who were separated. Although married couples have higher incomes than others, this fact accounts for just about a quarter of their greater wealth.

Married couples can share many household goods and services, such as a television set and heat, so the cost to each individual is lower than if each one purchased and used the same items individually. Thus, they spend less than they would for the same style of life if they lived separately. Second, married people produce more than the same individuals would if they were single. Each spouse can develop some skills and neglect others, because he or she can count on the other to take responsibility for some of the household work. The resulting specialization increases efficiency and, as will be shown, leads to higher wages for men. Moreover, married couples seem to save more at the same level of income than singles.

**Children's well-being.**   To this point, we have focused on the consequences of marriage for adults—the men and women who choose to marry (and stay married) or not—but these choices have consequences for the children borne by these adults as well. Sociologists Sara McLanahan and Gary Sandefur compared children raised in intact, two-parent families with those raised in one-parent families, resulting either from disruption of a marriage or from unmarried childbearing. They found that approximately twice as many teenagers raised in one-parent families drop out of high school without finishing. Children raised in one-parent families are more likely to become mothers or fathers while teenagers and to be "idle"—both out of school and out of the labor force—as young adults.

Youngsters living outside an intact marriage are more likely to be poor. McLanahan and Sandefur calculated poverty rates for children in two-parent families—including stepfamilies—and for single-parent families. They found very high rates of poverty for single-parent families, especially among blacks. Donald Hernandez, chief of marriage and family statistics at the Census Bureau, estimates that the rise in mother-only families since 1959 is an important cause of increases in poverty among children. Clearly, poverty, in and of itself, is a bad outcome for kids.

In addition, McLanahan and Sandefur estimate that the lower incomes of single-parent families account for about half of the worse outcomes of youngsters in these families, including higher dropout rates and unmarried childbearing. The other half comes from children's access—or lack of access—to the time and attention of two adults in two-parent families. Presence of two parents potentially means more parental supervision, more parental time helping with homework, and another parental shoulder to cry on after a hard day. Youngsters in one-parent families not only spend less time with their fathers (not surprising, given that most don't live with them), but less time with their mothers than those in two-parent families.

Single-parent families and stepfamilies move much more frequently than two-parent families. These moves are extremely difficult for kids, both academically and socially. Finally, individuals who spent part of their childhood in a single-parent family, either because they were born to an unmarried mother or because their parents divorced, report substantially lower-quality relationships with their parents as adults and have less frequent contact with them, according to University of Washington demographer Diane Lye.

**Labor force and career.**     Wharton School economist Kermit Daniel has examined the difference in the wages of young men and women who are single, cohabiting, and married, once one takes into account other characteristics that might affect salaries, and labels the remaining difference a "wage premium" for marriage. He finds that both black and white men receive a wage premium if they are married: 4.5% for blacks and 6.3% for whites. Black women receive a marriage premium of almost three percent. White women, however, pay a marriage penalty, in hourly wages, of more than four percent. Men appear to receive some of the benefit of marriage if they cohabitate, but women do not.

For women, Daniel finds that marriage and presence of children *together* seem to affect wages, and the effects depend on the woman's race. Childless black women earn substantially more money if they are married, but the marriage premium drops with each kid they have. Among white women, just the childless receive a marriage premium. Once white women become mothers, marriage decreases their earnings compared to remaining single (without children), with very large negative effects of marriage on females' earnings for those with two offspring or more. White married women often choose to reduce hours of work when they have children. They make less per hour than either unmarried mothers or childless wives.

Why should being married increase men's wages? Some researchers think that it makes men more productive at work, leading to higher wages. Wives may assist husbands directly with their work, offer advice or support, or take over household tasks, freeing their spouses' time and energy for work. As mentioned earlier, being married reduces drinking, substance abuse, and other unhealthy behaviors that may affect men's job performance. Finally, marriage increases men's incentives to perform well at work, so as to meet obligations to family members.

To this point, all the consequences of marriage for the individuals involved have been unambiguously positive—better health, longer life, more sex and more satisfaction with it, more wealth, and higher earnings. However, the effects of marriage and children on white women's wages are mixed, at best. Marriage and cohabitation increase women's time spent on housework; married motherhood reduces their time in the labor force and lowers their wages. Although the family as a whole might be better off with this allocation of females' time, women generally share their husbands' market earnings only while they are married. Financial well-being declines dramatically for women and their offspring after divorce or widowhood. Women whose marriages have ended often are quite disadvantaged financially by their investment in their husbands and children, rather than in their own earning power. Recent changes in law that make divorce easier seem to have exacerbated this situation, even while increases in women's education and work experience have moderated it.

## Is Marriage Responsible?

The obvious question, when one looks at all these benefits of marriage, is whether marriage is responsible for the differences. If all, or almost all, arise because those who enjoy better health, live longer lives, or earn higher wages *anyway* are more likely to marry, then marriage is not "causing" any changes in these outcomes. Social scientists vigorously and often acrimoniously debate the extent to which marriage is responsible for these better outcomes.

When politicians point to the high social costs and taxpayer burdens imposed by disintegrating "family values," they overlook the fact that individuals do not make the decisions that lead to unwed parenthood, marriage, or divorce on the basis of what is good for society. They weigh the costs and benefits of each of these choices to themselves—and sometimes their children.

Social scientists have a responsibility to measure the evidence on the consequences of social behaviors in the same way as medical researchers evaluate the evidence on the consequences of, say, cigarette smoking or exercise. As evidence accumulates and is communicated to the public, *some* people will change their behavior as a result. Some will make different choices than they otherwise would have because of their understanding of the costs and benefits, to them, of the options involved.

To continue with the example of medical issues such as smoking or exercise, behaviors have been seen to change substantially because research findings have been communicated to the public. In addition, there have been changes in attitudes toward behaviors shown to have negative consequences, especially when those consequences affect others, as in the case of smoking. These attitude changes then raise the social cost of newly stigmatized behaviors. HMOs and religious organizations develop programs to help people achieve the desired behavior, and support groups spring up.

In addition, society can pull some policy levers to encourage or discourage behaviors. Public policies that include asset tests (Medicaid is a good example) act to exclude the married, as do Aid to Families with Dependent Children programs in most states. The "marriage penalty" in the tax code is another example. In Illinois, young women under the age of 18 who already have become mothers must have their parents' permission to marry. Sometimes, this leads to a situation in which young couples are able to have children, but can not marry, even if they want to do so. These and other public policies can reinforce or undermine the institution of marriage.

If, as I have argued, marriage as a social institution produces individuals who drink, smoke, and abuse substances less, live longer, earn more, are wealthier, and have children who do better, society needs to give more thought and effort to supporting marriage through public policies.

# NO  

Dorian Solot and
Marshall Miller

## Unmarried Bliss: Living Happily Ever After Doesn't Necessarily Require a Marriage License

**D**uncan Smith remembers when, not so long ago, hotel check-in clerks requested evidence that he was married to his wife. Back then, he says, "If you wanted to be with someone, you had to be married."

Times have changed. Today, Smith, now divorced, lives with Lydia Breckon in the Edgewood neighborhood of Cranston with their three dogs and a cat. For 11 years, they've shared their lives, their cooking and cleaning, and their vacations. People sometimes assume they are married. But they have never taken a trip down the aisle together.

They describe themselves as pragmatists, not radicals. "I don't have a banner or a flag. I don't march around saying [being unmarried] is the right way to live. But on the other hand, I feel totally comfortable," Breckon says.

Living together without marriage, once unheard of, has become commonplace in America today. Parents often advise children to delay marriage and live with a partner to test the relationship, and growing numbers are forgoing marriage altogether. Unlike gay and lesbian couples, whose fight to legalize, same-sex marriage has dominated recent headlines, those who choose not to marry receive little attention for their unique situation.

According to the US Census, 12,000 partners like Smith and Breckon live together in Rhode Island without being married. Nationally, there are 5.6 million, a fivefold increase since 1970. "Today, the 'Ozzie and Harriet' family only constitutes about 10 percent of all families. Family diversity is now the norm," says Los Angeles attorney Thomas Coleman, an expert on family diversity and marital status discrimination.

Coleman attributes the change to a list of factors, including women in the workforce, changing religious attitudes, no-fault divorce laws, and greater visibility of gay, lesbian, bisexual, and transgendered people. Yet many unmarried people say that government and private industry have been slow to keep up with the times by implementing laws and workplace policies that recognize the new structures of families.

Most cohabiting couples will marry eventually. For many, living together is a logical way to experience a relationship without making a lifelong commitment. Ken Heskestad of Providence says, "[Living together without marriage] makes me more conscious of what I have and makes me devote more of my energies to the relationship." Living together saves money as well, another common reason people decide to move in with a sweetheart.

Significant numbers of people, however, decide to stay together long-term without a formal exchange of "I do's." Their reasons vary. Some, like Jane Fronek, Heskestad's partner, say the choice not to marry allows her a freedom from assumed roles. "Once you are considered someone's wife, people treat you in a certain way, and that is something that really scares me," says Fronek.

Television talk shows label unmarried couples "commitment phobic," but many say that their level of commitment to a relationship has nothing to do with its legal status. In California, Amy Lesen's parents divorced when she was a child, and her father went on to have a successful 20-years-and-counting relationship without being married.

Today, Amy says she does not want to marry her partner. "I saw one marriage break up, and I saw two people who did not get married stay together for the rest of my life. I think that it drove a point home to me that [marriage] does not really matter," she says.

Some people find the institution of marriage too bound to religion. Some have experienced painful or expensive divorces and have sworn never to involve the legal system in their relationships again. Growing numbers of senior citizens find that they would lose a significant amount of the pension they receive from a deceased spouse if they were to wed again. So while college students may have been the first ones to thumb their noses at societal mores by moving in with a lover, today even some grandparents decide it's the way to go.

# Close to Home

As a couple who long ago decided not to marry, this issue is a personal one for us. As children, neither of us dreamed of getting married when we grew up, possibly the legacy of our "you can do anything" feminist mothers. Our relationship was strong and felt stable and complete. We also didn't feel comfortable taking advantage of a privilege that wasn't available to many of our friends in same-sex relationships. Not getting married was an easy decision. Or so we thought.

After we'd been living together for a few years, an occasional family member would ask if we were considering marriage. One of our employers refused to give us the type of family health insurance policy for which married couples are eligible.

Then, in 1997 there was a news story about a Rhode Island man who wanted to legally adopt the biological son of his female domestic partner, a child he'd been parenting for years and considered his son. But a Family Court judge told the man that until he married the boy's mother, he would not consider the case.

Although the story was followed closely in the Rhode Island media, there was no public outrage—no letters to the editor or courthouse protests—as there had been in similar cases affecting transracial, gay, and single-parent adoptions. It was becoming clear to us that, in spite of our large and growing numbers, unmarried people didn't see themselves as a constituency, a group that could speak out and demand equal rights.

In case we weren't convinced yet, a few months later a potential landlord suggested he would not rent to us as an unmarried couple (breaking Massachusetts state law). A month later, a tenants' insurance company informed us we would have to buy separate policies, paying double what a married couple would. Finally, we got angry enough to do what we'd been talking about for years.

We decided to found a national organization to provide resources, advocacy and support for people who choose not to marry, are unable to marry, or are in the process of deciding whether marriage is right for them. The Alternatives to Marriage Project was born, and with it the beginning of a national community where none had existed before.

The conversations about what it's like to live without a ring, the challenges and the joys, are just beginning. Unmarried couples may not be harassed by hotel clerks now, but many say they still experience pressure to marry. Breckon remembers the day a newly-married friend of hers told her, "You've got to do this! Why are you holding out this back door in your relationship?"

But without marriage, Breckon says, there is a constant need to confirm her commitment to Smith. She told her friend, "There isn't a back door. The back door isn't open. Just because we're not married doesn't mean there's an escape path."

Things often get stickiest when unmarried couples decide to have children. Relatives turn up the heat, and for many, there is internal pressure to formalize the relationship. Marie Davis, who lives in Vermont and has participated in our Alternatives to Marriage Project, hasn't decided yet whether she wants to marry her partner of three years. But she says it's hard to know whether she could resist the pressure to marry if they decided to have children.

"A friend of mine recently got pregnant," Davis says. "She was married within three or four days of telling her parents. They flew out and did this clandestine little marriage ceremony, and now they're having a big wedding. And it kind of blew me away, like whoooah, those forces are strong!"

But even this last bastion of societal expectation is slowly shifting. Studies find that about one in 10 cohabitors give birth to a child while they live together, and an additional quarter bring children from a previous relationship to the current cohabiting relationship. The newest generation of children of unmarried parents, like Arthur Prokosch, a Brown University student, say it doesn't much matter.

"It never seemed to me to be that big of a deal that my parents weren't married," he says. "I was just a kid. My parents were there. And so I never really thought about it that much."

At a time when it is common for an elementary-school classroom to include children with single, divorced, foster or adoptive, and gay and lesbian parents, children raised with two unmarried parents usually don't see fitting in as a problem. Most say the issue would come up only occasionally, in insignificant ways.

Searching his mind for a way in which his parents' lack of a marriage license affected his life, Prokosch remembers, "Every so often, [a friend] would come over and say, Can I have another glass of milk, Mrs. Prokosch?" And his mother would then have to decide whether to explain that she had a different last name than Arthur and his dad and that they weren't married.

Hillary Gross, a 19-year-old from New Jersey, says she and her college friends sometimes joke about families today. "We would tease somebody 'cause their parents are still married—Oh, their parents are married! To each other? How weird!'"

## Not Just for Heterosexuals

When one thinks of gays and lesbians and marriage, images of the recent and ongoing high-profile cases to win the right to marry often come to mind. But while many same-sex couples eagerly await their chance to buy a plane ticket to whatever state first allows them to marry, others see themselves on the forefront of a movement pushing for a new definition of what constitutes a family.

"In my conception, what the gay and lesbian movement has been about has been tolerance of diversity," says Duncan A. Smith of Providence. Although he thinks same-sex couples should be allowed to marry, he says, "It just doesn't seem like marriage really works effectively for the majority of those who decide to marry."

Paula Ettelbrick, a New York attorney, law professor, and activist in the field of "family recognition," points out that since gay and lesbian couples haven't historically had the option of marrying, they have been forced to re-think the very notion of what a family is. "Through our success in creating different kinds of families, we have shown that groups of people can constitute a family without being heterosexual, biologically related, married, or functioning under a male head-of-household," she says, Ettelbrick says LGBT people would be better off continuing to expand how family is defined "rather than confin[ing] ourselves to marriage."

For some in the LGBT community, marriage is even more complicated. Julie Waters of Providence, a pre-operative male-to-female transsexual, is in a relationship with a woman. And right now, she can't afford the expensive surgery involved in the medical transition process.

Since she is still considered a man legally, she points out, "If I could get married to someone whose health insurance happened to cover conditions related to transsexualism, I could get the insurance through them, go through the [sex change] process, and then, in most places, the marriage would be considered null and void after the process." Situations like this demonstrate how the notion of debating whether marriage should be limited to "one man and one woman" may be missing the point.

# Employment Inclusion

In many ways, American society is warming to the idea that families come in many shapes and sizes. A concrete example of this is the trend toward domestic-partner benefits, an option many employers have implemented to update human-resource definitions of "family" for employees of all sexual orientations.

The most common type of discrimination unmarried people face relates to equal pay for equal work. While most employers offer health insurance to the spouse and children of an employee, it's less common for policies to be available to unmarried partners. Still, the number of companies, colleges, nonprofit organizations, and municipalities offering domestic-partner benefits to their employees is on the rise.

According to a recent poll, 6 percent of large employers now offer domestic-partner benefits, and another 29 percent say they are considering offering them. Although details vary, the plans usually require that couples have lived together for a certain amount of time and that they are jointly responsible for living expenses and are in a caring, committed relationship.

In Rhode Island, two of the top 20 largest employers offer domestic-partner benefits: Brown University and BankBoston. Brown implemented the benefits first, in 1994, and in addition to getting a positive response from staff, the benefits have improved the university's ability to recruit and retain employees, says Brown spokesman Mark Nickel.

As of today, Brown's definition of domestic partners is limited to same-sex partners, because the policy was developed in response to staff requests, says Nickel. "Same-sex domestic partners have almost no avenue open to them, since same-sex marriage is not legal in Rhode Island or any other state," he explains. "At least opposite-sex domestic partners have some options open to them."

But as a result of this same-sex-only policy, Breckon and Smith, a Brown employee, had to weigh their options. At one point, Breckon was in danger of being without health insurance, and Smith says they were frustrated by the fact that, if Breckon had been a same-sex partner, she could have been added to his benefits plan.

Instead, Breckon says, "Briefly, on one Thursday, we considered getting married in a hurry." Breckon, however, was able to get a job quickly, so they ultimately avoided this newest kind of shotgun wedding.

Other employers are moving in the direction of offering domestic-partner benefits that are more inclusive, defining partners without regard for gender or sexual orientation. BankBoston's plan, which took effect just this summer, is an example. Employees now have the option of adding a spouse, dependent children, a domestic partner of any sex, or another adult dependent who meets certain criteria. "We wanted to expand eligibility with the goal to include as much of the diverse workforce as we could," says Martha Muldoon, a senior worklife consultant at BankBoston.

Los Angeles attorney Thomas Coleman is an advocate of broad-based benefits plans like BankBoston's. "I don't see why it is a legitimate business concern to an employer as to whether an opposite-sex couple chooses to be registered domestic partners rather than become legally married," he says. "If the opposite-sex couple is willing to sign the same affidavit and assume the same obligations as the employer has same-sex couples sign, then why should they not be able to do so and get the same employment benefits?"

Despite the "family values" rallying cry of politicos, the trend away from marriage and toward less traditional families is unlikely to change anytime soon. Coleman says, "Theoretically, the Constitution protects freedom of choice in certain highly personal decisions, such as those involving marriage, family, procreation, and child-rearing." And he hopes people's freedom to choose how they will structure their families will be increasingly respected by lawmakers, courts, and businesses.

Sometimes the freedom to choose results in some unusual benefits. Prokosch, son of unmarried parents, says that when telemarketers called and asked for "Mrs. Prokosch," he could tell them honestly, "There's no one here by that name.

"That was quite convenient," he laughs.

## Note

1. To learn more about the Alternatives to Marriage Project, see www. unmarried.org.

# POSTSCRIPT

## Are Contemporary Adults Overlooking the Importance of Marriage as Part of Successful Development?

In his famous work about the challenges faced during the life span, developmental psychologist Erik Erikson posited that the primary challenge in the first part of adulthood is establishing intimacy. He warned that the failure to establish healthy intimacy could lead to isolation, hindering the developmental trajectory of people throughout the remainder of their lives. In the popular imagination, marriage is the most obvious way to demonstrate that one has successfully negotiated the developmental challenge of early adulthood—to demonstrate that one has the capacity for intimacy. Erikson, however, presented his theory in the 1950s, and times have unquestionably changed.

The changing public attitudes toward marriage have provoked diverse responses, of which two poles play out in the readings. One reaction to a lessening of conventional attitudes toward marriage is to lament the change and work to correct it. In other words, problems with marriage in society can be rectified by promoting the conventional version of marriage as a public and individual good. This is the tactic taken by Linda Waite in her article, and she is supported by persuasive data. Research shows that married people demonstrate better health, more financial well-being, and many other tangibly positive outcomes. Waite, building off the data presented in her article, went on to collaborate with a journalist and write a popular book titled *The Case for Marriage,* promoting marriage as an essential facet of well-being in adulthood. Waite argues that by eschewing conventional marriage, adults are putting themselves and contemporary society at risk.

Another reaction to the lessening of conventional attitudes toward marriage is to embrace the change and endeavor to make new definitions of committed relationships, and intimacy, work for both individuals and society. This is the intention of Solot and Miller with their Alternatives to Marriage Project. This side takes the position that rather than denying the changes—and the diversifying—of contemporary society, we need to be pragmatic and accepting. Logically, it seems feasible that not one type of committed relationship would be healthy for many different types of people. But, as with all controversies in the study of life span development, positions should come down to evidence in addition to logic.

In regard to the evidence, note that while Solot and Miller do not directly respond in this article to the statistics presented by Waite, Waite herself recognizes the controversy inherent in claiming that finding a correlation between various markers of well-being and marriage does not necessarily imply causality. This is the classic research problem of "correlation not equaling causation." In other words, simply because married people are more likely than unmarried people to have good health, wealth, and general well-being does not mean marriage caused the positive developmental outcomes. It seems feasible that, for example, the relationship might work in the opposite direction: People who are healthy, wealthy, and have high well-being may be more apt to marry. Or it is possible that other variables are responsible for both marriage and well-being. Possibly people with dynamic personalities are able to both marry and maintain well-being better than others.

The challenge in sorting out this controversy is that as we gather better data and research to address such questions of causality, society continues to change and redefine the age-graded expectations for development in adulthood. If, for example, cohabitation became the norm rather than the exception, would it still be considered a negative developmental outcome? The best we can do at this point is to evaluate the available arguments, make reasonable hypotheses, and recognize the importance of this issue for every young adult facing the challenge of establishing healthy intimacy as part of his or her trek through the life span.

## Suggested Readings

K. Boo, "The Marriage Cure," *The New Yorker* (August 18, 2003).

A. Cherlin, "Should the Government Promote Marriage?" *Contexts* (Fall 2003).

P. England, "The Case for Marriage: Why Married People Are Happier, Healthier, and Better Off Financially," *Contemporary Sociology* (November 2001).

M. Gallagher, "The Latest War Against Marriage," *Crisis* (February 2001).

T. Huston and H. Meiz, "The Case of (Promoting) Marriage: The Devil Is in the Details," *Journal of Marriage and the Family* (November 2004).

S. Jeffrey, "The Need to Abolish Marriage," *Feminism & Psychology* (May 2004).

D. Solot and M. Miller, *Unmarried to Each Other: The Essential Guide to Living Together as an Unmarried Couple* (Marlowe & Co. 2002).

L. Waite, D. Browning, W. Dohert, M. Gallagher, Y. Luo, and S. Stanley, "Does Divorce Make People Happy? Findings from a Study of Unhappy Marriages," *Institute of American Values* (2002).

L. Waite and M. Gallagher, *The Case for Marriage: Why Married People Are Happier, Healthier, and Better Off Financially* (Doubleday, 2000).

# ISSUE 17

## Is One General Intelligence Factor Responsible for Career Success?

**YES: Linda S. Gottfredson,** from "Where and Why *g* Matters: Not a Mystery," *Human Performance* (vol. 15, 2002)

**NO: Robert J. Sternberg and Jennifer Hedlund,** from "Practical Intelligence, *g*, and Work Psychology," *Human Performance* (vol. 15, 2002)

### ISSUE SUMMARY

**YES:** Psychologist Linda S. Gottfredson asserts that one core intelligence factor akin to IQ—called *g*—is primarily responsible for being successful in the world of work.

**NO:** Professors of psychology and criminal justice Robert J. Sternberg and Jennifer Hedlund argue that efforts to establish one general intelligence factor as the cause of success are misguided because many different types of practical intelligence determine how well one does at work.

Intelligence is an interesting topic to consider at any stage of the life span because we implicitly assume that higher intelligence means more success. Whether trying to evaluate the intelligence of very young children or adolescents, we want to know about intelligence in order to know about a person's potential for achievement. While there is a great deal of research (and controversy) about intelligence during childhood, the literature about the relationship between intelligence and adult career success provides the most direct setting to consider whether and how intelligence matters.

While most people agree that intelligence does matter, the subject of intelligence generates a great deal of controversy because it turns out to be surprisingly difficult to define. It is common to use an IQ score as synonymous with intelligence. Yet the first IQ tests were actually devised specifically to measure aptitude for school, and refined to measure aptitude for tasks such as military service. As predictors of performance in specific areas, IQ scores have been somewhat useful, but they are not necessarily intended to be general markers of how well a person can think.

To discuss general intelligence with regard to how well a person can think, scholars regularly refer to the concept of general cognitive ability, or $g$. $g$ is a difficult concept to understand because it is not one tangible entity—there are no direct tests of $g$. Instead, $g$ is a theoretical construct that is generally understood to exist despite our inability to see or measure it. In other words, people are assumed to have a particular level of general cognitive ability, which something like an IQ test might approximate, but general cognitive ability is simply too complex to measure precisely. It is too difficult to precisely delineate something as complex as intelligent thought.

Yet according to scholars including Linda S. Gottfredson, a psychologist who has written extensively about intelligence, $g$ is the most important factor in adult success. In her selection, Gottfredson asserts that $g$ is the best way of understanding the relationship between intelligence and success: To do well at specific tasks, people need to have a general ability to think well.

Nevertheless, because $g$ exists only in concept, many scholars feel that it is important to have other ways of understanding intelligence. If intelligence is one's ability to operate effectively in the world, then some would argue that there are multiple types of intelligence. Such thinking has been formalized by prominent psychologist Howard Gardner in his theory of "multiple intelligences." In this scheme, there are at least eight different intelligences, including artistic intelligence, verbal intelligence, interpersonal intelligence, and kinesthetic (or bodily) intelligence. In other words, a person who is a great athlete or artist, but is not good in school, is still considered to have certain forms of intelligence that can predict success.

Another prominent conception of multiple intelligences is the "triarchic" theory of intelligence proposed by Robert J. Sternberg, one of the authors of the second reading. Based on many years studying the psychology of intelligence through a research center at Yale, Sternberg has concluded that $g$ is not what most matters for success. Instead, he argues that work success relies on practical intelligence and an implicit knowledge required for specific tasks that goes beyond just general cognitive ability.

These perspectives on multiple intelligences are popular partially because they better allow for diversity—by suggesting that different ways of thinking can be equally defined as intelligent, we allow for and encourage different ways of thinking. For Gottfredson, however, this is exactly the problem. She argues that conceptualizing multiple intelligences, including Sternberg's "practical intelligence," is merely a by-product of an overzealous emphasis on diversity in the workplace. Gottfredson believes that general cognitive ability is all that really matters, but she recognizes that it is not evenly distributed across demographic groups. Thus, in order to diversify a workplace, it is necessary to either accept less-intelligent employees, or to re-define intelligence so that employees are not conceptualized as less intelligent, but rather as being intelligent in different ways.

As you read the selections, think about this key issue: Does the complexity of intellectual diversity get in the way of more simply job success? And note that there is an implicit question of how to define success in adulthood. For research purposes, most scholars focus on success as it can be measured—who has a higher status job, or who makes more money. But perhaps part of the reason this issue is controversial is because success in adulthood is not always something easy to quantify and measure.

# YES

Linda S. Gottfredson

# Where and Why *g* Matters: Not a Mystery

The general mental ability factor—*g*—is the best single predictor of job performance. It is probably the best measured and most studied human trait in all of psychology. Much is known about its meaning, distribution, and origins thanks to research across a wide variety of disciplines. Many questions about *g* remain unanswered, including its exact nature, but *g* is hardly the mystery that some people suggest. The totality—the pattern—of evidence on *g* tells us a lot about where and why it is important in the real world. Theoretical obtuseness about *g* is too often used to justify so–called technical advances in personnel selection that minimize, for sociopolitical purposes, the use of *g* in hiring.

## The *g* Factor Among People

Our knowledge of the mental skills that are prototypical of *g*, of the aspects of tasks that call forth *g*, and of the factors that increase or decrease its impact on performance together sketch a picture of where and why *g* is useful in daily affairs, including paid work. They show *g*'s predictable gradients of effect. I begin here with the common thread—the *g* factor—that runs through the panoply of people's mental abilities.

### Generality and Stability of the *g* Factor

One of the simplest facts about mental abilities provides one of the most important clues to the nature of *g*. People who do well on one kind of mental test tend to do well on all others. When the scores on a large, diverse battery of mental ability tests are factor analyzed, they yield a large common factor, labeled *g*. Pick any test of mental aptitude or achievement—say, verbal aptitude, spatial visualization, the SAT, a standardized test of academic achievement in 8th grade, or the Block Design or Memory for Sentences subtests of the Stanford–Binet intelligence test—and you will find that it measures mostly *g*. All efforts to build meaningful mental tests that do not measure *g* have failed.

Thus, try as we might to design them otherwise, all our mental tests measure mostly the same thing, no matter how different their manifest content is. This means that *g* must be a highly general ability or property

From *Human Performance*, vol. 15, 2002, pp. 25–29, 36–43. Copyright © 2002 by Lawrence Erlbaum Associates. Reprinted by permission.

of the mind. It is not bound to any particular kind of task content, such as words, numbers, or shapes. Very different kinds of test content can be used to measure $g$ well—or badly.

This dimension of human difference in intellect—the $g$ factor—does not seem bound to particular cultures, either, because virtually identical $g$ factors have been extracted from test batteries administered to people of different ages, sexes, races, and national groups. In contrast, no general factor emerges from personality inventories, which shows that general factors are not a necessary outcome of factor analysis.

$g$'s high generality is also demonstrated by the predictive validities of mental tests. It is the $g$ component of mental tests that accounts almost totally for their predictive validity. Indeed, whole batteries of tests do little better than $g$ alone in predicting school and job performance. The more $g$-loaded a test is (the better it correlates with $g$), the better it predicts performance, including school performance, job performance, and income. There are many different abilities, of course, as is confirmed by the same factor analyses that confirm the dominance of the general factor among them. Because $g$ is more general in nature than the narrower group factors (such as verbal aptitude, spatial visualization, and memory), it is, not surprisingly, also broader in applicability. The clerical (i.e., non-$g$) component of clerical tests, for instance, enhances performance somewhat in clerical jobs (beyond that afforded by higher $g$), but $g$ enhances performance in all domains of work.

The $g$ factor shows up in nonpsychometric tests as well, providing more evidence for both its reality and generality. Exceedingly simple reaction time and inspection time tasks, which measure speed of reaction in milliseconds, also yield a strong information processing factor that coincides with psychometric $g$.

In short, the $g$ continuum is a reliable, stable phenomenon in human populations. Individual differences along that continuum are also a reliable, stable phenomenon. IQ tests are good measures of individual variation in $g$, and people's IQ scores become quite stable by adolescence. Large changes in IQ from year to year are rare even in childhood, and efforts to link them to particular causes have failed. Indeed, mental tests would not have the pervasive and high predictive validities that they do, and often over long stretches of the life span, if people's rankings in IQ level were unstable.

Theorists have long debated the definition of "intelligence," but that verbal exercise is now moot. $g$ has become the working definition of intelligence for most researchers, because it is a stable, replicable phenomenon that—unlike the IQ score—is independent of the "vehicles" (tests) for measuring it. Researchers are far from fully understanding the physiology and genetics of intelligence, but they can be confident that, whatever its nature, they are studying the same phenomenon when they study $g$. That was never the case with IQ scores, which fed the unproductive wrangling to "define intelligence." The task is no longer to define intelligence, but to understand $g$.

## Meaning of $g$ as a Construct

Understanding $g$ as a construct—its substantive meaning as an ability—is essential for understanding why and where $g$ enhances performance of everyday tasks. Some sense of its practical meaning can be gleaned from the overt behaviors and mental skills that are prototypical of $g$—that is, those that best distinguish people with high $g$ levels from those with low $g$. Intelligence tests are intended to measure a variety of higher order thinking skills, such as reasoning, abstract thinking, and problem solving, which experts and laypeople alike consider crucial aspects of intelligence. $g$ does indeed correlate highly with specific tests of such aptitudes. These higher order skills are context- and content-independent mental skills of high general applicability. The need to reason, learn, and solve problems is ubiquitous and lifelong, so we begin to get an intuitive grasp of why $g$ has such pervasive value and is more than mere "book smarts."

We can get closer to the meaning of $g$, however, by looking beyond the close correlates of $g$ in the domain of human abilities and instead inspect the nature of the tasks that call it forth. For this, we must analyze data on tasks, not people. Recall that the very definition of an ability is rooted in the tasks that people can perform. To abbreviate Carroll's meticulously-crafted definition, an *ability* is an attribute of individuals revealed by differences in the levels of task difficulty on a defined class of tasks that individuals perform successfully when conditions for maximal performance are favorable. Superficial inspection of $g$-loaded tests and tasks shows immediately what they are not, but are often mistakenly assumed to be—curriculum or domain dependent. Thus, the distinguishing attributes of $g$-loaded tasks must cut across all content domains.

Comparisons of mental tests and items reveal that the more $g$-loaded ones are more complex, whatever their manifest content. They require more complex processing of information. The hypothetical IQ test items in Figure 1 illustrate the point. Items in the second column are considerably more complex than those in the first column, regardless of item type and regardless of whether they might seem "academic." To illustrate, the first item in the first row requires only simple computation. In contrast, the second item in that row requires exactly the same computation, but the person must figure out which computation to make. The similarities items in the third row differ in abstractness in the similarities involved. The more difficult block design item uses more blocks and a less regular pattern, and so on.

Task complexity has been studied systematically in various contexts, some psychometric and some not. Researchers in the fields of information processing, decision making, and goal setting stress the importance of the number, variety, variability, ambiguity, and interrelatedness of information that must be processed to evaluate alternatives and make a decision. Wood, for example, discussed three dimensions of task complexity: component complexity (e.g., number of cues to attend to and integrate, redundancy of demands), coordinative complexity (e.g., timing or sequencing of tasks, length of sequences), and changes in cause–effect chains or means–ends relations. More complex items require more mental manipulation for people to learn something or solve a problem—seeing connections, drawing distinctions, filling in gaps, recalling and applying relevant information, discerning cause and effect relations, interpreting more bits of information, and so forth.

*Figure 1*

**Hypothetical Examples of Simple Versus More Complex IQ Test Items.**

| Directions | Simple item | Complex item |
|---|---|---|
| 1. Compute | .50 x 6 = 3.00 | Apples cost 50 cents apiece and Susan bought 6. How much did she spend? |
| 2. Define | Table | Ponder |
| 3. State one similarity | Pear — Apple | Seed — Egg |
| 4. Give the next 2 numbers | 2, 4, 6, 8, __, __ | 11, 10, 9, 10, 9, 8, __, __ |
| 5. Reproduce pattern with blocks whose sides are □ ■ ◩ | Use 4 blocks: | Use 9 blocks:  |
| 6. Complete the pattern | 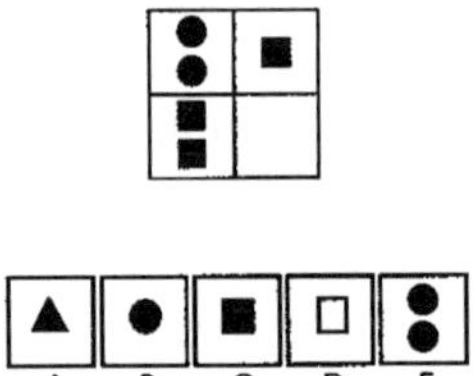 | 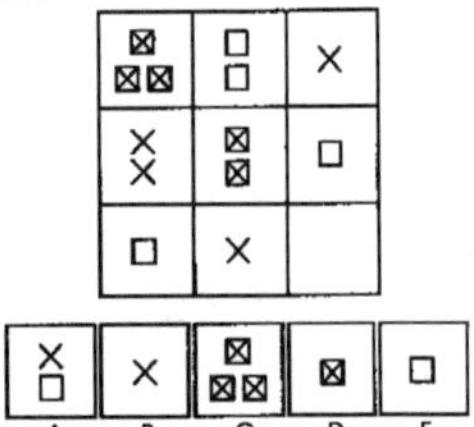 |

In a detailed analysis of items on the U.S. Department of Education's National Adult Literacy Survey (NALS), Kirsch and Mosenthal discovered that the relative difficulty of the items in all three NALS scales (prose, document, quantitative) originated entirely in the same "process complexity": type of match (literalness), plausibility of distractors (relevance), and type of information (abstractness). The active ingredient in the test items was the complexity, not content, of the information processing they required. Later research showed, not surprisingly, that the three scales represent one general factor and virtually nothing else.

One useful working definition of *g* for understanding everyday competence is therefore the ability to deal with complexity. This definition can be translated into two others that have also been offered to clarify *g*'s real-world applications—the ability to learn moderately complex material quickly and efficiently and the ability to avoid cognitive errors. Most globally, then, *g* is the ability to process information. It is not the amount of knowledge per se that people have accumulated. High *g* people tend to possess a lot of knowledge, but its accumulation is a by-product of their ability to understand better and learn faster.

They fare better with many daily tasks for the same reason. Although literacy researchers eschew the concept of intelligence, they have nonetheless confirmed *g*'s importance in highly practical daily affairs. They have concluded, with some surprise, that differences in functional literacy (using

maps, menus, order forms, and bank deposit slips; understanding news articles and insurance options; and the like) and health literacy (understanding
doctors' instructions and medicine labels, taking medication correctly, and so
on) reflect, at heart, differences in a general ability to process information.

Clearly, there is much yet to be learned about the nature of $g$, especially
as a biological construct. We know enough about its manifest nature already,
however, to dispel the fog of mystery about why it might be so useful. It is a
generic, infinitely adaptable tool for processing any sort of information,
whether on the job or off, in training or after. . . .

# Relative Importance of $g$ for Job Performance

The I/O [industrial/organizational psychology] literature has been especially
useful in documenting the value of other predictors, such as personality traits
and job experience, in forecasting various dimensions of performance. It thus
illuminates the ways in which $g$'s predictive validities can be moderated by
the performance criteria and other predictors considered. These relations,
too, are lawful. They must be understood to appreciate where, and to what
degree, higher levels of $g$ actually have functional value on the job. I/O
research has shown, for instance, how $g$'s absolute and relative levels of predictive validity both vary according to the kind of performance criterion used.
A failure to understand these gradients of effect sustains the mistaken view that
$g$'s impact on performance is capricious or highly specific across different
settings and samples. . . .

An especially important aspect of $g$'s topography is that the functional
value of $g$ increases, both in absolute and relative terms, as performance criteria focus more on the core technical aspects of performance rather than on
worker citizenship (helping coworkers, representing the profession well, and
so on). The reverse is generally true for the noncognitive "will do" predictors,
such as temperaments and interests: They predict the noncore elements best.
Another important regularity is that, although the predictive validities of $g$
rise with job complexity, the opposite is true for two other major predictors
of performance—length of experience and psychomotor abilities. The latter's
predictive validities are sometimes high, but they tend to be highest in the
simplest work.

Another regularity is that "have done" factors sometimes rival $g$ in
predicting complex performance, but they are highly job specific. Take job
experience—long experience as a carpenter does not enhance performance as a
bank teller. The same is true of job sample or tacit knowledge tests, which
assess workers' developed competence in a particular job: Potential bank tellers
cannot be screened with a sample of carpentry work. In any case, these "have
done" predictors can be used to select only among experienced applicants.
Measures of $g$ (or personality) pose no such constraints. $g$ is generalizable, but
experience is not.

As for $g$, there are also consistent gradients of effect for job experience.
The value of longer experience relative to one's peers fades with time on the

job, but the advantages of higher *g* do not. Experience is therefore not a substitute for *g*. After controlling for differences in experience, *g*'s validities are revealed to be stable and substantial over many years of experience. Large relative differences in experience among workers with low absolute levels of experience can obscure the advantages of higher *g*. The reason is that a little experience provides a big advantage when other workers still have little or none. The advantage is only temporary, however. As all workers gain experience, the brighter ones will glean relatively more from their experience and, as research shows, soon surpass the performance of more experienced but less able peers. Research that ignores large relative differences in experience fuels mistaken conceptions about *g*. Such research is often cited to support the view that everyday competence depends more on a separate "practical intelligence" than on *g*—for example, that we need to posit a practical intelligence to explain why inexperienced college students cannot pack boxes in a factory as efficiently as do experienced workers who have little education.

The foregoing gradients of *g*'s impact, when appreciated, can be used to guide personnel selection practice. They confirm that selection batteries should select for more than *g*, if the goal is to maximize aggregate performance, but that *g* should be a progressively more important part of the mix for increasingly complex jobs (unless applicants have somehow already been winnowed by *g*). Many kinds of mental tests will work well for screening people yet to be trained, *if* the tests are highly *g*-loaded. Their validity derives from their ability to assess the operation of critical thinking skills, either on the spot ("fluid" *g*) or in past endeavors ("crystallized" *g*). Their validity does not depend on their manifest content or "fidelity"—that is, whether they "look like" the job. Face validity is useful for gaining acceptance of a test, but it has no relation to the test's ability to measure key cognitive skills. Cognitive tests that look like the job can measure *g* well (as do tests of mathematical reasoning) or poorly (as do tests of arithmetic computation).

Tests of noncognitive traits are useful supplements to *g*-loaded tests in a selection battery, but they cannot substitute for tests of *g*. The reason is that noncognitive traits cannot substitute for the information-processing skills that *g* provides. Noncognitive traits also cannot be considered as useful as *g* even when they have the same predictive validity (say, .3) against a multidimensional criterion (say, supervisor ratings), because they predict different aspects of job performance. The former predict primarily citizenship and the latter primarily core performance. You get what you select for, and the wise organization will never forego selecting for core performance.

There are circumstances where one might want to trade away some *g* to gain higher levels of experience. The magnitude of the appropriate trade-off, if any, would depend on the sensitivity of job performance to higher levels of *g* (the complexity of the work), the importance of short-term performance relative to long-term performance (probable tenure), and the feasibility and cost of training brighter recruits rather than hiring more experienced ones (more complex jobs require longer, more complex training). . . .

# The Flight from $g$

Sociopolitical goals for racial parity in hiring and the strong legal pressure to attain it, regardless of large racial disparities in $g$, invite a facade of mystery and doubt about $g$'s functional impact on performance, because the facade releases practitioners from the constraints of evidence in defending untenable selection practices. The facade promotes the false belief that the impact of $g$ is small, unpredictable, or ill-understood. It thereby encourages the false hope that cognitive tests, if properly formed and used, need not routinely have much, if any, disparate impact—or even that they could be eliminated altogether. Practitioners can reduce disparate impact in ways that flout the evidence on $g$, but they, and their clients, cannot escape the relentless reality of $g$. To see why, it is useful to review the most troublesome racial gap in $g$—that between Blacks and Whites. Like $g$, its effects in selection are highly predictable.

## The Predictable Impact of Racial Disparities in $g$

The roughly one standard deviation IQ difference between American Blacks and Whites (about 15 points) is well known. It is not due to bias in mental tests, but reflects disparities in the information-processing capabilities that $g$ embodies. Figure 2 shows the IQ bell curves for the two populations against the backdrop of the job complexity continuum. The point to be made with them—specifically, that patterns of disparate impact are predictable from group differences in $g$—applies to other racial–ethnic comparisons as well. The IQ bell curves for Hispanic and Native American groups in the United States are generally centered about midway between those for Blacks and Whites. The disparate impact of mental tests is therefore predictably smaller for them than for Blacks when $g$ matters in selection. The bell curves for other groups (Asian Americans and Jewish Americans) cluster above those for Whites, so their members can usually be expected to be overrepresented when selection is $g$ loaded. The higher the groups' IQ bell curves, the greater their overrepresentation relative to their proportion in the general population. It is the Black–White gap, however, that drives the flight from $g$ in selection and thus merits closest attention.

The bell curves in Figure 2 are for representative samples of American Blacks and Whites. Racial disparities can differ somewhat from one setting to another for a host of reasons, so that the Black–White differences will sometimes be larger or smaller than those shown here. However, Figure 2 illuminates the big picture—namely, both populations in the context of the American economy. Specifically, it shows the two bell curves against the backdrop of the job complexity factor, which is arrayed along the "normal" range of the IQ continuum (from the threshold for borderline mental retardation to that for giftedness). Common occupations are arrayed along this continuum according to the IQ ranges from which they draw most of their incumbents. Those ranges therefore define the IQ ranges that make a person competitive for such work. Typical modes of training that are possible (at the higher ranges of IQ) or required (at the lower ranges) at different IQ levels are also shown.

The cumulative percentages of American Blacks and Whites at each IQ level are shown at the bottom of Figure 2. The ratios in the last row represent

*Figure 2*

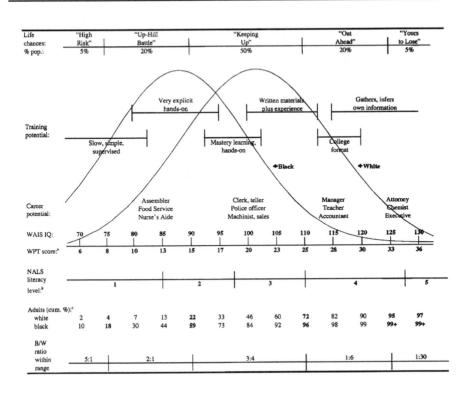

Adapted from Figure 3 in Gottfredson, L. S. (1997). Why *g* matters: The complexity of everyday life. *Intelligence, 24, 79 132,* with permission from Elsevier Science. [a]WPT = Wonderlic Personnel Test. [b]NALS = National Adult Literacy Survey. See Gottfredson (1997) for translation of NALS scores into IQ equivalents. [c]WAIS = Wechsler Adult Intelligence Scale. [d]See Gottfredson (1997) for calculation of percentiles.

the proportion of all Blacks to the proportion of all Whites within five different broad ranges of IQ. Blacks are overrepresented (5:1) in the lowest range (below IQ 75, labeled here as the "high risk" zone) and extremely underrepresented (1:30) in the highest (above IQ 125, the range where "success is yours to lose"). These ratios represent racial differences in the per capita availability of applicants who will be competitive for different levels of work, and they portend a clear trend in disparate impact. Under race–neutral hiring, disparate impact will generally be high enough to fail the 80% rule (which triggers the presumption of racial discrimination under federal guidelines) in hiring for all but the simplest jobs.

When Black and White applicants are drawn from the same IQ ranges, disparate impact will therefore be the rule, not the exception, even in jobs of modest complexity. It will get progressively worse at successively higher levels of education, training, and employment, and it will be extremely high in the most desirable jobs. Cognitive tests cannot meet the 80% rule with these two populations until the threshold for consideration falls to about IQ 77 to 78. This low estimate is consistent with other research showing that mental tests have to be virtually eliminated from test batteries to satisfy the 80% rule under typical conditions. The estimate also falls below the minimum mental standard (about IQ 80) that federal law sets for inducting recruits into the military.

To take some more specific examples, about 22% of Whites and 59% of Blacks have IQs below 90, which makes considerably fewer Blacks competitive for mid-level jobs, such as firefighting, the skilled trades, and many clerical jobs. The average IQ of incumbents in such jobs is nearer IQ 100, one standard deviation above the Black average of roughly IQ 85. IQ 80 seems to be the threshold for competitiveness in even the lowest level jobs, and four times as many Blacks (30%) as Whites (7%) fall below that threshold. Looking toward the other tail of the IQ distribution, IQ 125 is about average for professionals (e.g., lawyers, physicians, engineers, professors) and high-level executives. The Black–White ratio of availability is only 1:30 at this level. Disparate impact, and therefore political and legal tension, is thus particularly acute in the most complex, most socially desirable jobs.

Actual employment ratios are not as extreme as the per capital availability ratios shown here (other factors matter in hiring), but they follow the same systematic decline up the job complexity continuum. There is considerable IQ variability among incumbents in any occupation, of course, the standard deviation among incumbents generally averaging about 8 IQ points. The average Black–White difference is twice that large, however, which guarantees that Blacks will often cluster at the lowest levels of performance when workers are hired randomly by *g* or with race-norming.

## Minimizing Selection for *g* to Minimize Disparate Impact

The hope in personnel selection for a long time was that personnel psychologists could reduce disparate impact by developing technically better cognitive tests. If anything, improvements only worsened the disparate impact challenge because they resulted in more accurate measurement of *g*. Because good measurement has not provided the solution, it now tends to be treated as part of the problem, hence the popularity of test score banding in some quarters (it treats all scores within a specified range as equal), which reduces the reliability of measurement. Hence, also, the turning away from proven mental tests in major selection projects in favor of unproven "innovative" cognitive tests that substitute fidelity for validity and outside help for standardized conditions in taking the test. The suggestions that noncognitive tests can substitute for cognitive ones, or contextual performance for core performance, also promise to reduce the role of *g* in selecting workers. Such changes will do nothing, of course, to nullify the impact of lower *g* levels once workers are actually on the job.

One suggestion during the "Millennial Debate on *g*" at the Society for Industrial/Organizational Psychology convention in 2000 was that the value of good worker performance itself has been overemphasized, that we have overstated its utility. Such suggestions reflect the impact-driven claim, growing even in I/O circles, that a racially-balanced workforce is at least as important as a competent one; or that racial parity might even be a prerequisite to productivity. Going further along this line of argument, one panelist warned that Blacks simply will not put up with disparate impact, implying that balance should be our primary concern. No one at the debate argued that *g* was unimportant. Nonetheless, the cumulative message from its doubters, implicit but persistent, was that (without the option to race-norm) progressive practice requires cutting back on the use of *g* in selection.

Some of the arguments for doing so were implicit appeals to discredited theories. For instance, the claim that we ought to be more reluctant to use mental tests because Blacks suffer from stereotype threat when taking tests amounts to a claim that highly cognitive tests are biased against Blacks. We already know this claim to be false. The typical cognitive test has been exonerated of bias against low-scoring minorities. Indeed, personnel psychologists know that mental tests overpredict performance when they are used in a race-neutral manner. Another untenable claim, still offered frequently and flush with promise, is that we can create equally valid cognitive tests with considerably reduced disparate impact. Any claim to have succeeded is suspect. "Innovative" formats, item types, and scoring procedures for tests have all been offered with fanfare in recent years, but to the extent that they reduce disparate impact, we must suspect that they have degraded selection for mental skills. The same is true for any impact-driven switch in performance criteria. The vexing fact, which no tinkering with measurement can eliminate, is that Blacks and Whites differ most, on the average, on the most important predictor of job performance.

Some panelists also retreated into the unsubstantiated claim that there are multiple forms of intelligence, independent of *g*, that could predict job performance with less disparate impact. However, even the strongest body of evidence—that for so-called practical intelligence and its associated triarchic theory of intelligence—provides only scant and contradictory bits of evidence for such a claim. Coming from a mere six studies (four of which remain unpublished) of five occupations, those data provide no support whatsoever for Sternberg et al.'s assertion that "practical intelligence is a construct that is distinct from general intelligence and . . . is at least as good a predictor of future success as is the academic form of intelligence [*g*]".

Reducing disparate impact is a worthy goal to which probably all selection professionals subscribe. What is troubling are the new means being promulgated: minimizing or eliminating the best overall predictor of job performance. They amount to a call for reducing test validity and thereby violating personnel psychology's primary testing standard. Reducing the role of *g* in selection may be legally and politically expedient in the short term, but it delays more effective responses to the huge racial gaps in job-relevant skills, abilities, and knowledges.

# NO

**Robert J. Sternberg and Jennifer Hedlund**

# Practical Intelligence, *g*, and Work Psychology

The concept of intelligence traditionally has been viewed as integral to successful performance because it represents the ability to adapt effectively to the environment and to learn from experience. *g* is the most widely studied and validated predictor of performance in employment and educational settings. It has been suggested that *g* becomes even more important to job performance as the nature of work becomes increasingly complex and unpredictable. The important controversy surrounding *g* stems not from the evidence regarding its validity, but from the fact that there are different views about what intelligence is and how it should be measured. Rather than rehashing the familiar arguments surrounding *g*, we briefly summarize the main points before presenting an alternative approach to conceptualizing and measuring intelligence.

The traditional view is that many of the competencies needed for success can be viewed as originating with one latent factor—general intelligence (or ability). Sometimes *g* is studied in its own right, and other times as a construct at the top of a hierarchy of ability construct. So-called general cognitive ability (*g*) is considered by many to be the best single basis for selecting individuals because it is well established as a valid predictor of performance and learning across a variety of jobs. It is by far the most widely studied predictor used in personnel decisions.

Although *g* may be a valid predictor of performance in many jobs, there are several limitations and controversies surrounding *g* that warrant further efforts to understand job performance and how to predict it. First, validity estimates for so-called general mental ability (i.e., intelligence or *g*) indicate that (after correction for attenuation and restriction of range) *g* accounts for 20% to 25% of the variance in performance, leaving as much as 75% to 80% unexplained. Second, intelligence tests often exhibit differences of more than one standard deviation between various subgroups, most notably, between blacks and whites. Third, questions on intelligence tests often have little to do with the problems individuals encounter in real life. Therefore, intelligence tests may not accurately reflect all that an individual is capable of doing on the job. Fourth, intelligence tests are based on the assumption that *g* is a relatively

From *Human Performance*, vol. 15, 2002, pp. 143–153. Copyright © 2002 by Lawrence Erlbaum Associates. Reprinted by permission.

stable trait that predicts performance fairly consistently over time and across domains. However, there is increasing evidence that performance on intelligence tests varies across contexts and can be modified. Finally, Schmidt and Hunter argued that $g$ has the strongest theoretical foundation and the clearest meaning of any predictor. Other researchers have argued, however, that there is no clear agreement on what intelligence tests measure psychologically or even on what $g$ represents at a psychological level.

Many people—researchers and laypersons alike—agree that there is more to intelligent performance than what is measured by a standard IQ test. Recent theories reflect those views, identifying concepts such as interpersonal and intrapersonal intelligence, emotional intelligence, and creative and practical intelligence. These broader conceptualizations of intelligence recognize that individuals have different strengths and that these strengths may not be identified through traditional approaches to measuring intelligence. Practical intelligence provides the basis for one such approach.

*Practical intelligence* is defined as the ability that individuals use to find a more optimal fit between themselves and the demands of the environment through adapting to the environment, shaping (or modifying) the environment, or selecting a new environment in the pursuit of personally-valued goals. It can be characterized as "street smarts" or "common sense" and can be contrasted with academic intelligence or "book smarts." Practical intelligence encompasses the abilities one needs to succeed in everyday life, including in one's job or one's career. In this article, we review theoretical and empirical support for the construct of practical intelligence and consider its implications for work psychology.

# Practical Intelligence and Tacit Knowledge

Sternberg and his colleagues have taken a knowledge-based approach to understanding practical intelligence. Individuals draw on a broad base of knowledge in solving practical problems, some of which is acquired through formal training and some of which is derived from personal experience. Much of the knowledge associated with successful problem solving can be characterized as tacit. It is knowledge that typically is not openly expressed or stated—it is acquired largely through personal experience and guides action without being readily articulated.

The term *tacit knowledge* has roots in works on the philosophy of science, ecological psychology, and organizational behavior and has been used to characterize the knowledge gained from everyday experience that has an implicit, unarticulated quality. Such notions about the tacit quality of the knowledge associated with everyday problem solving also are reflected in the common language of the workplace as people attribute successful performance to "learning by doing: and to "professional intuition" or "instinct."

Research on expert knowledge is consistent with this conceptualization. Experts draw on a well-developed repertoire of knowledge in responding to problems in their respective domains. This knowledge tends to be procedural in nature and to operate outside of focal awareness. It also reflects the structure of the situation more closely than it does the structure of formal, disciplinary knowledge.

Sternberg and his colleagues view tacit knowledge as an important aspect of practical intelligence that enables individuals to adapt to, select, and shape real-world environments. It is knowledge that reflects the practical ability to learn from experience and to apply that knowledge in pursuit of personally valued goals. Research by Sternberg and his colleagues showed that tacit knowledge has relevance for understanding successful performance in a variety of domains. The conceptualization and measurement of tacit knowledge are described later, followed by a review of the relevant research on tacit knowledge and practical intelligence.

## The Conceptualization of Tacit Knowledge

Tacit knowledge is conceptualized by Sternberg and his colleagues according to three main features, which correspond to the conditions under which it is acquired, its structural representation, and the conditions of its use.

First, tacit knowledge is viewed as knowledge that generally is acquired with little support from other people or resources. In other words, the individual is not directly instructed as to what he or she should learn, but rather must extract the important lesson from the experience even when learning is not the primary objective. Formal training environments facilitate certain knowledge-acquisition processes. These processes include selective encoding (sorting relevant from irrelevant information in the environment), selective combination (integrating information into a meaningful interpretation of the situation), and selective comparison (relating new information to existing knowledge. When these processes are not well supported, as often is the case in learning from everyday experiences, the likelihood increases that some individuals will fail to acquire the knowledge. It also means that the knowledge will tend to remain unspoken, underemphasized, and poorly conveyed relative to its importance.

Second, tacit knowledge is viewed as procedural in nature. It is knowledge about how to perform various tasks in various situations. Drawing on Anderson's distinction between procedural and declarative knowledge, tacit knowledge can be considered a subset of procedural knowledge that is drawn from personal experience. And as is the case with much procedural knowledge, it tends to guide action without being easily articulated. Part of the difficulty in articulating tacit knowledge is that it typically reflects a set of complex, multicondition rules (production systems) for how to pursue particular goals in particular situations (e.g., rules about how to judge people accurately for a variety of purposes and under a variety of circumstances). These complex rules can be represented in the form of condition–action pairings. For example, knowledge about confronting one's superior might be represented in a form with a compound condition:

IF <you are in a public forum>
  AND
  IF <the boss says something or does something that you perceive is wrong or inappropriate>
  AND

IF <the boss does not ask for questions or comments>
THEN <speak directly to the point of contention and do not make evaluative statements about your boss>
BECAUSE <this saves the boss from embarrassment and preserves your relationship with him.>

In other words, tacit knowledge is more than a set of abstract procedural rules. It is context-specific knowledge about what to do in a given situation or class of situations. As discussed later, this representation serves as the basis of our approach to measuring tacit knowledge.

The third characteristic feature of tacit knowledge is that it has direct relevance to the individual's goals. Knowledge that is based on one's own practical experience will likely be more instrumental to achieving one's goals than will be knowledge that is based on someone else's experience or that is overly generic. For example, leaders may be instructed on what leadership approach (e.g., authoritative vs. participative) is supposed to be most appropriate in a given situation, but they may learn from their own experiences that some other approach is more effective in that situation.

In describing tacit knowledge, it is also helpful to clarify that we do not equate tacit knowledge with job knowledge. Rather, we view the two as overlapping concepts. Job knowledge includes both declarative and procedural knowledge, and only some procedural knowledge can be characterized as tacit. Tacit knowledge represents a component of procedural knowledge that is used to solve practical, everyday problems, but that is not readily articulated or openly conveyed.

## The Measurement of Tacit Knowledge

Because people often find it difficult to articulate their tacit knowledge, we measure tacit knowledge in the responses individuals provide to practical situations or problems, particularly those situations in which experience-based tacit knowledge is expected to provide an advantage. The measurement instruments used to assess tacit knowledge typically consist of a series of situations and associated response options, which have been characterized in the literature as situational judgment tests (SJTs). These types of tests generally are used to measure interpersonal and problem-solving skills or behavioral intentions. In a SJT or tacit-knowledge (TK) test, each question presents a problem relevant to the domain of interest (e.g., a manager intervening in a dispute between two subordinates) followed by a set of options (i.e., strategies) for solving the problem (e.g., meet with the two subordinates individually to find out their perspective on the problem; hold a meeting with both subordinates and have them air their grievances). Respondents are asked either to choose the best and worst alternatives from among a few options, or to rate on a Likert-type scale the quality or appropriateness of several potential responses to the situation.

The development of TK tests, like many SJTs, begins with the identification of critical incidents in the workplace. Individuals are asked to provide accounts of incidents from which they learned an important lesson about how to perform their job that was not something they had been taught in school or about which they had read in a textbook or manual. In other words, situations in which tacit knowledge is relevant are those for which the best response cannot be drawn from knowledge of explicit procedural rules. In fact, the best response may even contradict formal, explicit knowledge. The stories and the lessons learned from them are used to develop situational descriptions along with a set of possible responses. A TK test may consist of several situational descriptions, each followed by multiple response options, which vary in their appropriateness. . . .

TK tests have been scored in one of four ways: (a) by correlating participants' ratings with an index of group membership (i.e., expert, intermediate, novice), (b) by judging the degree to which participants' responses conform to professional "rules of thumb," (c) by computing a profile match or difference score between participants' ratings and an expert prototype, or (d) on a theory-determined basis. Scores on TK tests have been evaluated relative to various indicators of performance, measures of $g$, experience, and other predictors (e.g., personality).

# Research on Tacit Knowledge

Sternberg and his colleagues have used TK tests to study academic psychologists, salespersons, high school and college students, civilian managers, and military leaders, among people in other occupations. As yet unpublished research has also looked at elementary school teachers, principals, and individuals in roughly 50 varied occupations in the United States and Spain. We summarize here some of the findings from the research to date in regard to the relation of tacit knowledge with experience, $g$, personality, and performance.

## Tacit Knowledge and Experience

The common phrase "experience is the best teacher" reflects the view that experience provides opportunities to develop important knowledge and skills related to performance. Several meta-analytic reviews indicate that the estimated mean population correlation between experience and job performance falls in the range of .18 to .32. Additional research suggests that this relation is mediated largely by the direct effect of experience on the acquisition of job knowledge.

Consistent with this research, Sternberg and his colleagues have found that tacit knowledge generally increases with experience. Wagner and Sternberg found a significant correlation between tacit knowledge scores of 54 business managers and the manager's level within the company, $r(54) = .34$, $p < .05$, and years of schooling, $r(54) = .41$, $p < .01$. In a follow-up study with 49 business professionals, Wagner found significant correlations between tacit knowledge scores and years of management experience, $r(49) = .30$, $p < .05$. He also found mean differences in tacit knowledge scores for groups of business managers, business graduate students, and general undergraduates, with the managers exhibiting the highest mean score. Comparable results were found for a TK test for academic psychologists when comparing psychology professors, psychology graduate students, and undergraduates.

In another study involving managers, Grigorenka and Sternberg studied predictors of adult physical and mental health among adults in Russia. In particular, they looked at the predictor power of analytical and practical intelligence. They found that, although both analytical and practical intelligence were predictive of both physical and mental health, practical intelligence was the better predictor. In a study with salespeople, however, tacit knowledge scores correlated significantly both with the number of years of sales experience, $r(45) = .31, p < .01$, and the number of years with the company, $r(45) = .37, p < .01$. Finally, research with three levels of military leaders found that tacit knowledge scores did not correlate with the number of months leaders had served in their current positions, but did correlate significantly with leadership rank for two versions of the TK test for military leaders, $r(42) = .44, p < .01$, and $r(37) = .41, p < .05$, with leaders at higher levels of command exhibiting better scores than those at lower ranks. These findings suggest that rank may be a better indicator of experience than the time spent in any given position. In fact, a number of researchers have begun to question the value of purely quantitative measures of experience. What matters is not so much experience, but rather what one learns from that experience.

The research evidence to date generally supports the claim that tacit knowledge is related to experience. The correlations, however, tend to be moderate, falling in the range of .20 to .40, and suggest that although tacit knowledge has some basis in experience, it is not simply a proxy for experience.

## Tacit Knowledge and $g$

$g$ is considered by many to be the best single predictor of job performance. The relation between $g$ and performance is attributed largely to the direct influence of $g$ on the acquisition of job-related knowledge. Many job-knowledge tests, however, assess primarily declarative knowledge of facts and rules. They consist of abstract, well-defined problems that are similar to the types of problems found on traditional intelligence tests, thus explaining the observed correlations between measures of job knowledge and cognitive ability tests. TK tests, however, consist of problems that are poorly defined and context-rich. We consider performance on these tests to be a function of practical rather than abstract, general intelligence.

In the research reviewed here, TK tests exhibit trivial to moderate correlations with measures of $g$. In a sample of undergraduate students, scores on a test of verbal reasoning correlated nonsignificantly with scores on TK tests for academic psychologists, $r(29) = .04, p > .05$, and a TK test for managers, $r(22) = .16, p > .05$. Similarly, in a sample of business executives, scores on a TK test for managers exhibited a nonsignificant correlation, $r(45) = .14, p > .05$, with scores on a verbal reasoning test. Scores on the verbal reasoning test also did not correlate with scores on a TK test for sales in samples of undergraduates and salespeople. Further support comes from a study by Eddy, in which the Armed Services Vocational Aptitude Battery (ASVAB) was administered along with a TK test for managers to a sample of 631 Air Force recruits. Scores on the TK test exhibited near-zero correlations (.00 to .10) with four factors on the

ASVAB (vocational–technical information, clerical and speed, verbal ability, and mathematics).

Some studies have found significant correlations between $g$ and tacit knowledge, but these relations are not always in the positive direction. In research with military leaders, leaders at three levels of command completed Terman's Concept Mastery Test along with a TK test for their respective level. Tacit knowledge scores exhibited correlations ranging from trivial and nonsignificant, $r(344) = .02$, $p > .05$, to moderate and significant, $r(157) = .25$, $p < .01$, with verbal reasoning ability. However, in one study conducted in Kenya, tacit knowledge scores actually correlated negatively with scores on tests of $g$, suggesting that, in certain environments, development of practical skills may be emphasized at the expense of development of academic skills. Such environments are not limited to rural Kenya: Artists, musicians, athletes, and craftsmen all may decide that development of skills other than those taught in school may hold more value to them than do the more academic skills.

Over several studies, the evidence suggests that TK tests measure abilities that are distinct from those assessed by traditional intelligence tests. Even when significant correlations are observed, they tend only to be moderate. Additional research, which we discuss later, shows that TK tests measure something unique beyond $g$.

## Tacit Knowledge and Criteria

In general, job knowledge tests have been found to predict performance fairly consistently, with an average corrected validity of .48. As indicated earlier, much of this prediction is attributed to the relation between job knowledge and $g$. In other words, people with high $g$ are expected to gain more knowledge and thus perform more effectively. TK tests also are expected to predict performance. Simply put, individuals who learn the important lessons of experience are more likely to be successful. However, because tacit knowledge is a form of practical intelligence, it is expected to explain aspects of performance that are not accounted for by tests of $g$.

TK tests have been found to predict performance in a number of domains and using a number of criteria. In studies with business managers, tacit knowledge scores correlated with criteria such as salary, $r(54) = .46$, $p < .01$, and whether the manager worked for a company at the top of the Fortune 500 list, $r(54) = .34$, $p < .05$. These correlations, unlike those reported by Schmidt and Hunter, are uncorrected for either attenuation or restriction of range. In a study with bank managers, Wagner and Sternberg obtained significant correlations between tacit knowledge scores and average percentage of merit-based salary increase, $r(22) = .48$, $p < .05$., and average performance rating for the category of generating new business for the bank, $r(13) = .56$, $p < .05$. We are not the only ones to have found correlations between practical intelligence and measure of job success. A study in Brazil yielded similar findings. Colonia-Willner administered the Tacit Knowledge Inventory for Managers (TKIM) to bank managers along with measures of psychometric and verbal reasoning. She found that scores on the TKIM significantly predicted an index of managerial skill, whereas psychometric and verbal reasoning did not.

Although much of the tacit knowledge research has involved business managers, there is evidence that tacit knowledge explains performance in other domains. In the field of academic psychology, correlations were found between tacit knowledge scores and criterion measures such as citation rate, $r(59) = .44, p < .01$; number of publications, $r(59) = .28, p < .05$; and quality of department, $r(77) = .48, p < .01$. Sternberg, Wagner, and Okagaki found that the tacit knowledge of salespeople correlated with criteria such as sales volume, $r(39) = .28, p < .05$, and sales awards received, $r(45) = .32, p < .01$. In parallel studies conducted in the United States and Spain using a single measure of general tacit knowledge for people in roughly 50 diverse occupations, correlations with various ratings of job performance were at the .2 level in Spain ($N = 227$) and at the .4 level in the United States ($N = 230$).

Two studies showed the incremental validity of TK tests over traditional intelligence tests in predicting performance. In a study with business executives attending a Leadership Development Program at the Center for Creative Leadership, Wagner and Sternberg found that scores on a TK test for managers correlated significantly with performance on a managerial simulation, $r(45) = .61, p < .01$. Furthermore, tacit knowledge scores explained 32% of the variance in performance beyond scores on a traditional IQ test and also explained variance beyond measures of personality and cognitive style. In a study with military leaders, scores on a TK test for military leaders correlated significantly with ratings of leadership effectiveness made by subordinates, peers, or superiors. The correlations ranged from $r(353) = .14, p < .05$, for platoon leaders; to $r(163) = .19, p < .05$, for company commanders; to $r(31) = .42, p < .05$, for battalion commanders. More important, tacit knowledge scores accounted for small (4%–6%) but significant variance in leadership effectiveness beyond scores on tests of general verbal intelligence and tacit knowledge for managers. These studies provide evidence that tacit knowledge accounts for variance in performance that is not accounted for by traditional tests of abstract, academic intelligence.

There is fairly strong evidence to suggest that TK tests not only explain individual differences in performance, but also measure an aspect of performance that is not explained by measures of general intelligence. We consider that aspect to represent practical intelligence.

## Additional Findings Regarding Tacit Knowledge

Research on tacit knowledge has also addressed the relation between tacit knowledge and personality, the relations among different tests of tacit knowledge, differences in tacit knowledge scores across cultures, and differences in tacit knowledge scores across gender and racial groups. We briefly address those findings here.

First, Wagner and Sternberg found that tacit knowledge scores generally exhibited nonsignificant correlations with several personality-type tests, including the California Psychological Inventory, the Myers-Briggs Type Indicator, and the Fundamental Interpersonal Relations Orientation–Behavior (FIRO–B) given to a sample of business executives. The exceptions were that tacit knowledge scores correlated with the Social Presence factor of the California

Psychological Inventory, $r(45) = .29$, $p < .05$, and the Control Expressed factor of the FIRO–B, $r(45) = .25$, $p < .05$. In hierarchical regression analyses, tacit knowledge scores consistently accounted for significant increments in variance beyond the personality measures. These findings suggest that measures of tacit knowledge are distinct from personality measures.

Second, tacit knowledge measures tend to correlate among themselves and to show a general factor among themselves that is distinct from the general factor of tests of general ability. In one study, 60 undergraduates completed both a TK test for academic psychologists and a TK test for business managers; their scores on the two tests correlated .58.

Third, tacit knowledge measures have been found, in at least one instance, to yield similar results across cultures. Patterns of preferences for the quality of responses to a tacit knowledge measure for the workplace were compared between workers in the United States and Spain. The correlation between the mean profiles for the two groups across 240 responses was .91.

Finally, traditional intelligence tests often are found to exhibit group differences in scores as a function of gender and race. TK tests, because they are not restricted to knowledge or abilities developed in school, may be less susceptible to these differences. In Eddy's study of Air Force recruits, comparable levels of performance on the TK test were found among majority and minority group members and among men and women as indicated by nonsignificant correlations between tacit knowledge and dummy coded variables representing race (.03) and gender (.02). Significant correlations were found between scores on the ASVAB subtests and dummy variables for race and gender, ranging from .2 to .4. Therefore, there is some indication that TK tests do not exhibit the same group differences found on traditional intelligence tests.

The research reviewed earlier spans more than 15 years and lends support to several assertions regarding tacit knowledge. First, tacit knowledge generally increases with experience. Second, tacit knowledge is distinct from general intelligence and personality traits. Third, TK tests predict performance in several domains and do so beyond tests of general intelligence. Fourth, practical intelligence may have a substantial amount of generality that is distinct from the generality of psychometric $g$. Finally, scores on TK tests appear to be comparable across racial and gender groups. Thus, TK tests have the potential to contribute to our understanding of the competencies needed for real-world success and to address some of the limitations associated with traditional intelligence tests. . . .

# POSTSCRIPT

## Is One General Intelligence Factor Responsible for Career Success?

**W**e all know people who seem to succeed not because they are smart in the conventional "school smarts" way, but because they have something akin to "street smarts"—what Sternberg and Hedlund call practical intelligence. This is the person you know who might fail a math test, yet be able to repair a car engine in no time at all; or the person who cannot make sense of big words in the newspaper, but is able to coordinate groups using his or her gift for relating with people. How should we think about these people as we try to understand patterns in life span development?

For Linda Gottfredson, such anecdotal evidence would not be convincing. She demonstrates that in large samples of people, there seems to be a general cognitive factor at the root of adult success. Thus, someone with practical intelligence either uses general cognitive ability to derive that practical intelligence or is not doing work of sufficient complexity. Note that an important aspect of Gottfredson's claim is that *g* becomes more important to success as the complexity of a job increases. Thus, as the requirements of work in an increasingly technological society become more complex generally, we might expect general cognitive ability to become more important.

Sternberg and Hedlund agree that general cognitive ability matters, but they do not necessarily see it overwhelming practical intelligence. In their scheme, the increasing complexity of work requirements might also be met with improving people's tacit knowledge and their ability to deal with the specific tasks relevant to their chosen work. In fact, in many ways, this seems to be the more likely scenario; as the work world becomes more complex, adult's skills become more specialized so as to deal with particular demands.

The question of preparing adults for increasingly complex work roles demonstrates the importance of understanding this controversy. If we side with Gottfredson, then schools and employers should focus on selecting and training general cognitive ability, assuming that the specific skills necessary for work will develop over time. If we side with Sternberg and Hedlund, then schools and employers should devote significant attention to the practical abilities necessary for particular work tasks.

Beyond this specific question of work, however, this controversy raises significant questions about adult development more generally. What makes a successful adult? Is a successful adult a person who has the general intelligence and ability to adapt to whatever challenges he or she confronts? Or is a successful adult a person who is practical in planning and focusing his or her life according to specific situations? In the study of life span development, research and theory often take an implicit position on just this question: Does adulthood inevitably involve learning new challenges, or is adulthood a culmination of specific developmental patterns?

## Suggested Readings

C. Alderfer, "The Science and Nonscience of Psychologists' Responses to *The Bell Curve*," *Professional Psychology* (2003).

D. Fergusson, L. Howard, and E. Ridder, "Show Me the Child at Seven II: Childhood Intelligence and Later Outcomes in Adolescence and Young Adulthood," *Journal of Child Psychology and Psychiatry* (2005).

L. Gottfredson, "Intelligence: Is It the Epidemiologists' Elusive 'Fundamental Cause' of Social Class Inequalities in Health?" *Journal of Personality & Social Psychology* (January 2004).

W. Lichten, "On the Law of Intelligence," *Developmental Review* (2004).

H. Schlinger, "The Myth of Intelligence," *Psychological Record* (Winter 2003).

R. Sternberg, "Raising the Achievement of All Students: Teaching for Successful Intelligence," *Educational Psychology Review* (December 2002).

R. Sternberg, J. Lautrey, and T. Lubart, "Models of Intelligence: International Perspectives," *American Psychological Association* (2003).

# ISSUE 18

## Is Religion a Pure Good in Facilitating Well-Being During Adulthood?

**YES: David G. Myers,** from "Wanting More in an Age of Plenty," *Christianity Today* (April 2000)

**NO: Julie Juola Exline,** from "Stumbling Blocks on the Religious Road: Fractured Relationships, Nagging Vices, and the Inner Struggle to Believe," *Psychological Inquiry* (vol. 13, 2002)

### ISSUE SUMMARY

**YES:** Psychologist and author David G. Myers asserts that religion is an anecdote to the discontent many adults feel despite incredible relative material wealth.

**NO:** Professor of psychology Julia Juola Exline asserts that research suggesting religion to be a pure good for adult development neglects to account for the fact that it can also be a source of significant sadness, stress, and confusion.

The role of religion in lifespan development presents a challenging dilemma for social scientists: Religion is clearly a huge influence on people's lives, yet by nature that influence is difficult to quantify and measure. Further, many people simply prefer to keep their religious and spiritual lives separate from efforts to define and study the specific characteristics of the life span. Something about academic study often (though not always) seems to detract from the mystical power of religion. Yet, basic demographic statistics show that over 60 percent of Americans are active in a faith group, over 70 percent identify with an organized religion, and more than that consider themselves very interested in spirituality. While there is some popular trend to bemoan the loss of religion in modern society, many scholars would note that only traditionally organized religions are in decline, while American interest in spirituality may be at an all-time high.

Inevitably, despite some avoidance and trepidations, life span development scholars have investigated the role of religion in the life span. Generally steering clear of abstract spiritual questions, such as those about the nature and role of God, scholars of the life span tend to focus on aspects of religion that can be analyzed and measured using the methods of social science. One of those aspects is well-being in adulthood. After negotiating the challenges of childhood and youth, and settling into work and family roles, adults often find themselves addressing larger questions of meaning, purpose, and spirituality.

In Erik Erikson's famous schematic diagram of the life span, the primary challenge of middle adulthood is developing "generativity"—or the sense of generating something meaningful for the next generation. In the selection by David G. Myers, a prolific psychologist who has written several prominent textbooks and several other scholarly books about topics ranging from happiness to spirituality, versions of generativity are discussed in relation to religion. Myers asserts that contemporary society is incredibly well-off by structural measures such as income and material well-being. Yet, in his reckoning, what he calls "the American paradox" (our material well-being raises our psychological well-being) is in decline. The statistics that he cites are powerful and suggest that at a large-scale level, it does seem that religion and spirituality correlate with improved well-being and generativity in the form of charity, altruistic work, and communal endeavor.

Myers is also reasonable enough to concede that religion has not always been a positive social force; history presents clear examples of religious intolerance. Note, however, that for Myers, these negative uses of religion are always about religion as an institution that can negatively influence society—not about the personal experience of religion. In Myers' viewpoint, the personal experience of religion is an overall good that can develop individuals who will improve society.

In contrast, Julie Juola Exline points out four very specific ways in which religion can provide individual developmental challenges. While Exline is interested in religion partially because of its powerful potential to create meaningful psychological experiences, she is wary of understanding religion as a panacea. She notes, in concordance with Myers, that significant amounts of data suggest religion and spirituality can have significant positive benefits through the life span. But she asserts such findings should not be oversimplified. Personal experiences of religion involve interpersonal challenges, asking hard questions about faith in the face of hardship, facing intellectual and emotional inconsistencies, and dealing with the very real potential for disappointment in adulthood.

While both of these selections focus on religion and spirituality primarily in relation to a Christian tradition, the issue of religion in the adult life span transcends one particular faith. All the major religious traditions share a social function of focusing communities of individuals toward mutual goals and a personal function of addressing the spiritual needs of individuals. It may therefore be useful to think about the arguments presented by Myers and Exline in relation to religious and spiritual practices outside of Christianity—is there a universal role of religion in adult development? Likewise, is there something special about religion generally in the life span? Is religion best thought of as a broad social practice, similar to school and work, that should be analyzed for its practical contribution to development? Or is religion something more?

David G. Myers  **YES**

# Wanting More in an Age of Plenty

The Paradox of Our Time in History is that
we spend more, but have less;
we buy more, but enjoy it less.

We have bigger houses and smaller families;
more conveniences, but less time;
more medicine, but less wellness.

We read too little, watch TV too much, and pray too seldom.

We have multiplied our possessions, but reduced our values.

These are the times of tall men, and short character;
steep profits, and shallow relationships.

These are the days of two incomes, but more divorce;
of fancier houses, but broken homes.

We've learned how to make a living, but not a life;
we've added years to life, not life to years;
we've cleaned up the air, but polluted the soul.

*—Excerpted from a 1999 Internet chain mailing,
usually attributed to an unknown source.*

The past four decades have produced dramatic cultural changes. Since 1960 we have been soaring economically and, until recently, sinking socially. To paraphrase Ronald Reagan's famous question, "Are we better off than we were 40 years ago?" Our honest answer would be: materially yes, morally no. Therein lies the American paradox.

There is much to celebrate. We now have, as average Americans, doubled real incomes and doubled what money buys. We own twice as many cars per person, eat out two and a half times as often, and pay less than ever before (in real dollars and minutes worked) for our cars, air travel, and hamburgers. We have espresso coffee, the World Wide Web, sport utility vehicles, and caller ID.

Democracy is thriving. Military budgets are shrinking. Joblessness and welfare rolls have subsided. Inflation is down. The annual national deficit has become a surplus. The rights of women and various minorities are better protected than ever before. New drugs are shrinking our tumors, lengthening our lives, and enlarging our sexual potency. These are the best of times.

Yet by the early 1990s these had also become the worst of times. During most of the post-1960 years, America was sliding into a deepening social, and moral recession that dwarfed the comparatively milder and briefer economic recessions. Had you fallen asleep in 1960 and awakened today (even after the recent uptick in several indicators of societal health) would you feel pleased at the cultural shift? You would be awakening to a:

- Doubled divorce rate.
- Tripled teen suicide rate.
- Quadrupled rate of reported violent crime.
- Quintupled prison population.
- Sextupled (no pun intended) percent of babies born to unmarried parents.
- Sevenfold increase in cohabitation (a predictor of future divorce).
- Soaring rate of depression—to ten times the pre–World War II level by one estimate.

The National Commission on Civic Renewal combined social trends such as these in creating its 1998 "Index of National Civic Health"—which plunged southward from 1960 until the early 1990s. Bertrand Russell once said that the mark of a civilized human is the capacity to read a column of numbers and weep. Can we weep for the social recession's casualties—for the crushed lives behind these numbers?

## Spiritual Hunger in an Age of Plenty

It is hard to argue with Al Gore: "The accumulation of material goods is at an all-time high, but so is the number of people who feel an emptiness in their lives." Moreover, he explained in declaring his presidential candidacy, "Most Americans are hungry for a deeper connection between politics and moral values; many would say 'spiritual values.'" There is indeed "a spiritual vacuum at the heart of American society," agreed the late Lee Atwater, George Bush's 1988 campaign manager. Having solved the question of how to make a living, having surrounded ourselves with once unthinkable luxuries—air-conditioned comfort, CD-quality sound, and fresh fruit year round—we are left to wonder why we live. Why run this rat race? What's the point? Why care about anything or anyone beyond myself?

Ronald Inglehart, a University of Michigan social scientist who follows values surveys across the Western world, discerns the beginnings of a subsiding of materialist values. Not only in Eastern Europe, where materialist Marxism is licking its wounds, but in the West one sees signs of a new generation maturing with decreasing concern for economic growth and strong defense, and with increasing concern for personal relationships, the integrity of nature, and the meaning-of life. At the peak of her fortune and fame, with 146 tennis championships behind her and married to John Lloyd, Chris Evert reflected, "We get into a rut. We play tennis, we go to a movie, we watch TV, but I keep saying, 'John, there has to be more.'"

Materialism and individualism still ride strong. For America's entering collegians, "becoming very well off financially" is still the top-rated life goal among 19 goals on an annual UCLA/American Council on Education survey; it is said to be "very important or essential" by 74 percent in 1998—nearly double the 39 percent saying the same in 1970. Yet Inglehart discerns "a renewed concern for spiritual values."

Pollster George Gallup Jr. detects the same: "One of two dominant trends in society today [along with a search for deeper, more meaningful relationships] is the search for spiritual moorings. . . . Surveys document the movement of people who are searching for meaning in life with a new intensity, and want their religious faith to grow." From 1994 to late 1998, reported Gallup, the percent of Americans feeling a need to "experience spiritual growth" rose from 54 to 82 percent. Although people in surveys exaggerate their church attendance, as they do voting, religious interests seem on an upswing. Since hitting its modern low in 1993, Gallup's "Religion in America" index has been heading upward.

This spiritual hunger is manifest all about us: in a million people annually besieging Catholic retreat centers or seeking spiritual formation guided by spiritual directors; in the NFL, where once-rare chapel services have become universal and after-touchdown kneels are almost as common as struts; in the recent surge of movies with spiritual emphases (*Dead Man Walking, The Prince of Egypt, Seven Years in Tibet*) and in television's *Touched By an Angel* reaching ratings heaven; in New Age bookstore sections devoted to angels, near-death experiences, reincarnation, astrology, and other paranormal claims; in the surge of new publications, conferences, and magazine articles on religion and science and health; in the reopening of school curricula to religion's place in history and literature; and on the Internet, where AltaVista finds "God" on 3.6 million Web pages.

## The New American Dream

For Christians—people who experience spirituality in biblically-rooted faith communities—some aspects of contemporary do-it-yourself spirituality may seem gaseous, individualistic, and self-focused. Nevertheless, the essential facts are striking: while we have been surging materially and technologically we have paradoxically undergone a social and moral recession and experienced a deepening spiritual hunger. In many ways these are the best of times, yet in other ways these have been the worst of times. While enjoying the benefits of today's economic and social individualism, we are suffering the costs.

To counter radical individualism, an inclusive social renewal movement is emerging—one that affirms liberals' indictment of the demoralizing effects of poverty and conservatives indictment of toxic media models;

one that welcomes liberals' support for family-friendly workplaces and conservatives' support for committed relationships; one that agrees with liberals' advocacy for children in all sorts of families and conservatives' support for marriage and coparenting.

Do we not—whether self-described liberals or conservative—share a vision of a better world? As the slumbering public consciousness awakens, something akin to the earlier civil rights, feminist, and environmental movements seems to be germinating. "Anyone who tunes in politics even for background music can tell you how the sound has changed," observes feminist columnist Ellen Goodman. Yesterday's shouting match over family values has become today's choir, she adds. When singing about children growing up without fathers, "Politicians on the right, left and center may not be hitting exactly the same notes, but like sopranos, tenors and baritones, they're pretty much in harmony." We are recognizing that liberals' risk factors (poverty, inequality, hopelessness) and conservatives' risk factors (early sexualization, unwed parenthood, family fragmentation) all come in the same package.

Whatever our differences, most of us wish for a culture that:

- Welcomes children into families with mothers and fathers who love them, and into an environment that nurtures families.
- Rewards initiative and restrains exploitative greed, thus building a strong economy that shrinks the underclass.
- Balances individual liberties with communal well-being.
- Encourages close relationships within extended families and with supportive neighbors and caring friends, people who celebrate when you're born, care about you as you live, and miss you when you're gone.
- Values our diversity while finding unity in shared ideals.
- Develops children's capacities for empathy, self-discipline, and honesty.
- Provides media that offer social scripts of kindness, civility, attachment, and fidelity.
- Regards relationships as covenants and sexuality not as mere recreation but as life-uniting and love-renewing.
- Takes care of the soul by developing a deeper spiritual awareness of a reality greater than self and of life's resulting meaning, purpose, and hope.

Thanks partly to the emerging renewal movement, several indicators of social pathology have recently shown encouraging turns. Although still at historically high levels, teen sex, pregnancy, and violence, for example, have all subsided somewhat from their peaks around 1993.

Further progress toward the new American dream requires more than expanding our social ambulance services at the base of the social cliffs. It also requires that we identify the forces that are pushing people over the cliffs. And it requires our building new guard rails at the top—by making our business and economics more family-friendly, by reforming our media, by renewing character education in our schools, and by better balancing me-thinking with we-thinking.

Are there credible grounds for adding spiritual renewal to this list? Are George W. Bush and Al Gore both right to trumpet the potential of "faith-based" reforms and social services? Or can skeptical Oxford professor Richard Dawkins more easily find evidence for seeing faith as "one of the world's great evils, comparable to the smallpox virus, but harder to eradicate"? Sifting the evidence won't decide the bigger issue of the truth of Christian claims, but it should indicate whether faith more often uplifts or debilitates.

We now have massive evidence that people active in faith communities are happier and healthier than their unchurched peers. (Recent epidemiological studies—tracking thousands of lives through years of time—reveal they even outlive their unchurched peers by several years.) Is an active faith similarly associated with social health?

## God and Goodness

Asked by Gallup, "Can a person be a good and ethical person if he or she does not believe in God?," three in four Americans answered yes. Indeed, examples of honorable secularists and greedy, lustful, or bigoted believers come readily to mind. "God's will" has been used—often by those for whom religion is more a mark of group identity than of genuine piety—as justification for apartheid, for limiting women's rights, for ethnic cleansing, for gay bashing, and for war. As Madeleine L'Engle lamented, "Christians have given Christianity a bad name."

But anecdotes aside—"I can counter Jim Bakker's gold-plated bathroom fixtures with Mother Teresa, and Bible-thumping KKK members with Desmond Tutu," responds the believer—how might faith feed character? It might do so by providing a source of values. It might give us a convincing reason to behave morally when no one is looking. Lacking the ground of faith beneath our morality, cultural inertia may enable a lingering selflessness, but eventually the soil that feeds morality becomes depleted. "If there is no God, is not everything permissible?" Ivan asked in *The Brothers Karamazov*.

"The terrible danger of our time consists in the fact that ours is a cut-flower civilization," philosopher Elton Trueblood prophesied a half-century ago. "Beautiful as cut flowers may be, and much as we may use our ingenuity to keep them looking fresh for a while, they will eventually die, and they die because they are severed from their sustaining roots. We are trying to maintain the dignity of the individual apart from the deep faith that every man is made in God's image and is therefore precious in God's eyes."

Even the eighteenth-century French writer Voltaire found the influence of faith useful among the masses, even though he thought Christianity was an "infamy" that deserved crushing. "I want my attorney, my tailor, my servants, even my wife to believe in God," he wrote, because "then I shall be robbed and cuckolded less often." He once silenced a discussion about atheism until he had dismissed the servants, lest in losing their faith they might lose their morality. Although similarly skeptical of religion, biologist E. O. Wilson likewise acknowledges that "religious conviction is largely beneficent. Religion . . . nourishes love, devotion, and, above all, hope."

# Faith and Character

Are Voltaire and Wilson right to presume that godliness tethers self-interest and feeds character? Seeking answers, researchers have studied not just what causes crime, but what predicts virtue. Having two committed parents, a stable neighborhood, prosocial media, and schools that teach character—all of these help. So, too, does a spiritual sense, contends Stanford psychologist William Damon. Children are "openly receptive to spiritual ideas and long for transcendent truth that can nourish their sense of purpose and provide them with a moral mission in life," he believes. "Children will not thrive . . . unless they acquire a living sense of what some religious traditions have called transcendence: a faith in and devotion to concerns that are considered larger than the self." Faith, he reports, "has clear benefits for children . . . enabling some children to adapt to stressful and burdensome life events."

The bipartisan National Commission on Children has concurred that religious faith strengthens children. "Through participation in a religious community—in communal worship, religious education, and social-action programs—children learn and assimilate the values of their faith. For many children, religion is a major force in their moral development; for some it is the chief determinant of moral behavior." Studies confirm that religious adolescents (those who say their faith is important or who attend church) differ from those who are irreligious. They are much less likely to become delinquent, to engage in promiscuous sex, and to abuse drugs and alcohol.

After analyzing data from several national studies, Vanderbilt University criminologist Byron Johnson reported that "Most delinquent acts were committed by juveniles who had low levels of religious commitment. Those juveniles whose religiosity levels were in the middle to high levels committed very few delinquent acts." Even when controlling for other factors, such as socioeconomic level, neighborhood, and peer influences, churchgoing kids rarely were delinquent.

The faith-morality relationship extends to adulthood. In their studies of Jews in Israel, Catholics in Spain, Calvinists in the Netherlands, the Orthodox in Greece, and Lutherans and Catholics in West Germany, sociologists Shalom Schwartz and Sipke Huismans consistently found that people of faith tended to be less hedonistic and self-oriented. Consistent with this observation, sociologist Seymour Martin Lipset notes that charitable giving and voluntarism are higher in America than in less religious countries.

In a 1981 U.S. Values Survey, frequent worship attendance predicted lower scores on a dishonesty scale that assessed, for example, self-serving lies, tax cheating, and failing to report damaging a parked car. Moreover, cities with high churchgoing rates tend to be cities with low crime rates. In Provo, Utah, where more than nine in ten people are church members, you can more readily leave your car unlocked than in Seattle, where fewer than a third are. Voltaire, it seems, was on to something.

Many people sense this faith-morality correlation. If your car broke down in a crime-ridden area and some strapping teenage boys approached you, asks Los Angeles Rabbi Dennis Prager, wouldn't "you feel better to know they had just come from a Bible study?"

# Faith and Altruism

So, people of faith (mostly Christians in studies to date) are, for whatever reasons, somewhat more traditionally moral—more honest and law-abiding and less hedonistic. But are they more actively compassionate? Do they really walk the love talk? Or are they mostly self-righteous hypocrites?

People often wonder about Christianity, which has a curious history of links with both love and hate. On one side are Bible-thumping slave owners, Ku Klux Klanners, and apartheid defenders. On the other are the religious roots of the antislavery movement, the clergy's leadership of the American and South African civil-rights movements, and the church's establishment of universities and Third World medical care.

A mid-century profusion of studies of religion and prejudice revealed a similarly mixed picture. On the one hand, American church members expressed more racial prejudice than nonmembers, and those with conservative Christian beliefs expressed more than those who were less conservative. For many, religion seemed a cultural habit, a part of their community tradition, which also happened to include racial segregation.

Yet the most faithful church attenders expressed less prejudice than occasional attenders. Clergy expressed more tolerance and civil-rights support than lay people. And those for whom religion was an end ("My religious beliefs are what really lie behind my whole approach to life") were less prejudiced than those for whom religion was a means ("A primary reason for my interest in religion is that my church is a congenial social activity"). Thus among church members, the devout expressed less prejudice than those who gave religion lip service. "We have just enough religion to make us hate," said the English satirist Jonathan Swift, "but not enough to make us love one another."

"Faith-based" compassion becomes even clearer when we look at who gives most generously of time and money. Fortune reports that America's top 25 philanthropists share several characteristics. They are mostly self-made, they have been givers all their lives, and "they're religious: Jewish, Mormon, Protestant, and Catholic. And most attribute their philanthropic urges, at least in part, to their religious backgrounds."

The same appears true of the rest of us. In a 1987 Gallup survey, Americans who said they never attended church or synagogue reported giving away 1.1 percent of their incomes. Weekly attenders were two and a half times as generous. This 24 percent of the population gave 48 percent of all charitable contributions. The other three-quarters of Americans give the remaining half. Followup Gallup surveys in 1990, 1992, 1994, and 1999 replicated this pattern. An estate-planning attorney at one of western Michigan's largest law firms told me that people in her highly churched area of the state are much more likely to assign part of their estate to charity than are people on the state's less religious eastern side. Much of this annual and legacy giving is not to churches. Two thirds of money given to secular charities comes from contributors who also give to religious organizations.

And of the billions given to congregations, nearly half gets donated to other organizations or allocated to nonreligious programming (and that doesn't count donations of food, clothing, and shelter by most congregations).

The faith-generosity effect extends to the giving of time:

- Among the 12 percent of Americans whom Gallup classified as "highly spiritually committed," 46 percent said they were presently working among the poor, the infirm, or the elderly—many more than the 22 percent among those "highly uncommitted."
- In a followup Gallup survey, charitable and social service volunteering was reported by 28 percent of those who rated religion "not very important" in their lives and by 50 percent of those who rated it "very important."
- In the 1992 Gallup survey, those not attending church volunteered 1.4 hours a week while those attending weekly volunteered 3.2 hours. The follow-up survey in 1994 found the same pattern, as have university-based studies.
- In yet another Gallup survey, 37 percent of those rarely if ever attending church, and 76 percent of those attending weekly, reported thinking at least a "fair amount" about "your responsibility to the poor."
- Among one notable self-giving population—adoptive parents—religious commitment is commonplace. Among a national sample, 63 percent reported attending a worship service often.

So, tell me about the generosity of someone's spirit, and you will also give me a clue to the centrality of their faith. Tell me whether their faith is peripheral or pivotal, and I will estimate their generosity.

Religious consciousness, it appears, shapes a larger agenda than advancing one's own private world. It cultivates the idea that my wealth and talents are gifts of which I am the steward. Spirituality promotes a "bond of care for others," notes Boston College sociologist Paul Schervish. Such altruism, research psychologists Dennis Krebs and Frank Van Hesteren contend, is "selfless, stemming from agape, an ethic of responsible universal love, service, and sacrifice that is extended to others without regard for merit." The religious idea of a reality and purpose beyond self would seem foundational to such "universal self-sacrificial love."

Faith-based altruism is at work here in Holland, Michigan, where the Head Start Day Care program was envisioned by a prayer group at the church where it still operates. The thriving Boys and Girls Club was spawned by the Interparish Council. Habitat for Humanity construction is mostly done by church volunteers. Our community's two main nongovernmental agencies for supporting the poor—the Community Action House and the Good Samaritan Center—were begun by churches, which continue to contribute operating funds. The local theological seminary houses the community soup kitchen. Churches fund the community's homeless shelter. Annually, more than 2,000 townspeople, sponsored by thousands more—nearly all from churches—gather for a world hunger relief walk.

If the churches of my community (and likely yours) shut down, along with all the charitable action they foster, we would see a sharp drop in beds for the homeless, food for the hungry, and services to children. Partners for Sacred

Places, a nondenominational group dedicated to preserving old religious buildings, reports that nine of ten city congregations with pre-1940 buildings provide space for community programming such as food pantries, clothing closets, soup kitchens, childcare centers, recreation programs, AA meetings, and afterschool activities.

Thus, mountains of data and anecdotes make it hard to dispute Frank Emerson Andrews' conclusion that "religion is the mother of philanthropy."

To be sure, religion is a mixed bag. It has been used to support the Crusades and enslavement. But it was also Christians who built hospitals, helped the mentally ill, staffed orphanages, brought hope to prisoners, established universities, and spread literacy. It was Christians who abolished the slave trade, led civil-rights marches, and challenged totalitarianism. It was 5,000 Christians who in Le Chambon, France, sheltered Jews while French collaborators elsewhere were delivering Jews to the Nazis. The villagers, mostly descendants of a persecuted Protestant group, had been taught by their pastors to "resist whenever our adversaries will demand of us obedience contrary to the orders of the gospel." Ordered to reveal the sheltered Jews, the pastor refused, saying, "I don't know of Jews, I only know of human beings."

As the debate over government support of faith-based social services emerges—fueled by success stories such as the Rev. Eugene Rivers III's work with Boston teens, Prison Fellowship's work with inmates, and Michigan's program of connecting social-service clients with church-support groups—the church will also need to retain its prophetic voice. In Britain, which is entering a parallel national debate over "the moral and spiritual decline of the nation," the Archbishop of Canterbury, Dr. George Carey, opened "an unprecedented debate on morality" in the House of Lords in 1996 by decrying the decline of moral order and spiritual purpose and the tendency to view moral judgments as mere private taste.

Jonathan Sacks, England's Chief Rabbi, supported his compatriot:

> The power of the Judeo-Christian tradition is that it charts a moral reality larger than private inclination. . . . It suggests that not all choices are equal: some lead on to blessing, others to lives of quiet despair.

> It may be that religious leaders can no longer endorse, but instead must challenge the prevailing consensus—the role of the prophet through the ages. In which case the scene is set for a genuine debate between two conflicting visions—between those who see the individual as a bundle of impulses to be gratified and those who see humanity in the image of God; between those who see society as a series of private gardens of desire and those who make space for public parts which we do not own but which we jointly maintain for the sake of others and the future. No debate could be more fundamental, and its outcome will shape the social contours of the twenty-first century.

# NO

Julie Juola Exline

# Stumbling Blocks on the Religious Road: Fractured Relationships, Nagging Vices, and the Inner Struggle to Believe

Tossing and turning in bed, Jim finds that his mind keeps drifting to the television segment he saw on the 11:00 news. This is the third news piece that he has seen in the past year suggesting that religious involvement has benefits for health and well-being. Raised nominally Christian, Jim stopped attending church years ago. He is not even sure that he believes in God anymore, but he has been feeling troubled lately, between his arthritis flare-ups and recurring bouts of anxiety. After mulling over the pros and cons, Jim decides to give religion another try. He asks a colleague for a church recommendation and begins attending regularly. He also commits to reading his Bible each night before bed so that he can get a deeper understanding of the Christian faith. Jim does an admirable job on following through with these religious commitments. However, 6 months later, he is overcome with frustration and disappointment regarding his religious involvement. His dissatisfaction is so strong, in fact, that he decides to abandon his religious quest altogether. What could have happened? Why did Jim end up turning away from religion when he had solid reasons to pursue this coping resource? This article addresses these questions by suggesting some psychological and social stumbling blocks associated with religious belief and involvement.

## Can Religion Be Good and Still Be a Locus of Strain?

Within the past decade, a wealth of evidence has accumulated to suggest positive associations between religion, physical health, and mental health. Based on these findings, scientists, scholars, and mental health professionals are beginning to take a more positive view of the role that religious belief and involvement can play in personal and social life. It is especially noteworthy

From *Psychological Inquiry*, vol. 13, no. 3, 2002, pp. 182–188. Copyright © 2002 by Lawrence Erlbaum Associates. Reprinted by permission.

that many of these pro-religion findings have emerged within the field of psychology, which has historically taken a negative or disinterested stance toward religion. The boom in pro-religion findings is likely to prove encouraging and exciting for religiously committed psychologists, providing greater freedom to discuss, study, and perhaps even advocate religious involvement.

However, to promote a balanced view of religion and well-being, it seems wise to consider some caveats and cautions. Consider one possible consequence of the current emphasis on religion, coping, and health: Might some individuals come to view religion primarily or exclusively as a personal coping mechanism? Having noted positive links between religiosity and well-being, some people might focus on only the comforting, self-affirming aspects of religious belief or involvement. Others might go a step further, thinking about religion only in terms of how it might personally benefit them or advance their interests. In one (admittedly extreme) metaphor, some people might view God as a sort of placid smiley face in the sky, advancing humanity's ongoing quest to "have a nice day."

Granted, religious belief and involvement can be powerful tools in coping with life's problems; however, religion is not merely a coping mechanism. Religion involves a quest for ultimate truth. It attempts to answer our deepest questions about life, death, and the purpose of existence. Religion also tends to be prescriptive, telling us how we should live our lives. Thus, religion is likely to make demands on us and to challenge our beliefs and actions in ways that are not always comfortable. Religion is likely to contain seeds of both pleasure and pain, as do other vitally important elements of life (e.g., work, romantic relationships, parenting). To acknowledge the problems associated with any of these pursuits does not negate the value of the pursuit, but because negative stimuli typically carry more psychological weight than positive stimuli, it seems imperative to point out some potential pitfalls that people may encounter in their religious lives.

I make a few clarifications before proceeding. Virtually all examples presented in this article emphasize Judeo-Christian religion. Many are based on Protestant Christianity, the tradition with which I identify and am most familiar. Although different religious systems will no doubt pose different dilemmas and solutions, particularly at the level of doctrine, I believe that the basic principles raised here should be common to many religions. I also note that the goal of this article is to present a series of ideas rather than a review of existing literature. Many of the ideas presented here reflect theoretical elaboration of empirical work that my colleagues and I have done. My thinking has also been directly influenced by the work of Pargament and Altemeyer and Hunsberger. The interested reader is directed to these sources and to other reviews of the field.

The goal of this article, then, is to suggest a number of social and psychological stumbling blocks that religious seekers may encounter. Four major types of stumbling blocks will be considered: interpersonal strains, negative attitudes toward God, inner struggles to believe, and problems associated with virtuous striving. Problems in any of these areas could conceivably turn people away from religion, discourage them from increasing their religious commitment, or create sources of strain and discontent regarding religion.

# Interpersonal Strains Associated with Religion: Disagreement, Dissonance, and Disgust

In terms of physical and mental health, one of the primary benefits of religious involvement is that it can be a powerful source of social support. The need to belong, to have close connections with other people, is a central human motivation, and being part of a religious community can help to meet this need. Religious involvement may also provide people with the chance to help others, which can be a powerful antidote for feelings of depression and helplessness; however, if we look more closely, we can see potential for problems in the social arena surrounding religion.

## Religious Disagreements

Although religious involvement can help to meet a person's need to belong, it may at the same time threaten that same need. When people choose to align themselves closely with a particular religious group or to adopt a specific set of beliefs, they increase their odds for serious disagreement with others. Such differences sometimes play out in a societal context, adding fuel to intergroup hostility and conflict, but disagreements often arise closer to home, in the circle of the believer's close relationships. If one's parents, spouse, or close friends do not share one's religious convictions, painful rifts may result.

Interfaith marriage provides one example. Although interfaith marriage has become increasingly common, up from 9% in 1965 to 52% in the late 1980s, couples in such marriages are more likely to divorce than those who share the same religious faith. Even when both partners are of the same faith, problems might arise because of differences in religious commitment levels. For example, a woman whose top priority is to love God may elicit feelings of jealousy and resentment from her husband, who now views God as an unwanted third party in the relationship. How can people cope with these religious differences in close relationships? Some may simply agree to disagree, but many religiously committed people may not be satisfied with this option. Because relationship maintenance requires sacrifice and compromise, it may seem viable to convert the unbelieving spouse or to compromise by choosing some third, "neutral ground." However, problems arise with these options as well: Many committed believers will be reluctant to shift their ideas or affiliations, and conversions to please one's romantic partner prove superficial in many cases.

Interpersonal strain may also center on specific religious doctrines, such as those regarding afterlife beliefs. Exline and Yali asked college students what percentage of people they believed were destined for heaven versus hell. To the extent that the students believed that many people were destined for hell, they reported greater social strain associated with religion. These strains included being teased about religious beliefs and behaviors, being the target of religious prejudice or discrimination, and feeling sad or anxious because friends or family members did not share their beliefs. Although preliminary, these data suggest that when disturbing beliefs about the afterlife are part of one's religious system, such beliefs may not only be personally troubling, but they may also be a locus for interpersonal strain. When religious persons believe that the high stakes of eternal destiny are involved, they may find it difficult simply to agree to disagree, especially when they care deeply about the other person.

Attempts to communicate about hell with close others will often be fraught with difficulties. Even with the best of intentions, believers are likely to offend others by insinuating that they are destined for eternal punishment. Another potential problem stems from the fact that images of hell are likely to prompt high levels of fear. Studies have suggested that extremely high levels of fear, rather than prompting behavior change, often lead to emotion-focused coping efforts as people try to defend themselves from the psychological threat. Thus, a believer who confronts another person with fiery images of hell might find that the solution backfires, as the would-be convert calms himself by avoiding all thoughts of the threatening subject.

Interpersonal strains should also surround other doctrines that take a dim view of human nature or are otherwise discordant with the climate of the broader culture. For example, modern evangelical Protestantism has often been linked with conservative political views ("the Religious Right") and with intolerance of homosexuality and abortion. In an era in which tolerance is highly valued, it will prove socially divisive to confront behaviors that are gaining social acceptance. How are believers to respond when their beliefs are socially unpopular? As suggested in the literature on outgroup behavior and prejudice in religion, one response may be to derogate and distance the self from those who do not hold the beliefs of one's group. Another option is to be open about one's views and risk offending others. A more socially comfortable option would be to focus only on points of agreement, perhaps even taking the extra step of softening one's position on controversial issues. The risk, of course, is that when people soften their position on issues central to their faith, they may compromise or misrepresent what they believe to be the truth.

# Distaste Toward Religious Groups or Persons

For nonbelievers or even for persons who are privately religious or spiritual, another type of interpersonal barrier could prevent them from wanting to affiliate with religious groups: They may look at the behavior of religious persons and not like what they see. Such distaste could stem from many sources. Vivid acts of terrorism and violence, ranging from racial discrimination and abortion clinic bombings to wartime atrocities, have been committed in the name of religion. Many people have observed religious hypocrisy, in which religious individuals claim to uphold high moral standards but fail to do so in their everyday lives. When high-profile religious evangelists are caught in sexual affairs, for example, people may turn to such incidents as evidence that religious people are hypocrites and fakes. Individuals who yield to religious authority (e.g., God, scripture, the Pope, other church leaders) may be viewed as ignorant by those who place higher value on other forms of persuasion, such as empirical evidence or private, common-sense philosophies of life. Religious people may also be viewed as judgmental, prudish, intolerant, and unable to have fun in life—particularly, perhaps, by persons who want to continue pleasurable habits that the religious group views as vices (e.g., sexual promiscuity, gambling, heavy alcohol use).

In short, one probable reason that people do not join religious groups is because they hold negative attitudes toward the groups. Some people might even develop stronger responses such as disgust, in which they recoil from any contact with the group. As with a food aversion, disgust might even spread to taint a person's global impressions of religion: "If that's how religious people behave, I don't want any part of it." Because feelings of disgust are often moralized, people could easily translate their disgust toward religious persons into moral disapproval. In other words, they might come to view religious people not only as unlikable but also as wrong—perhaps even as evil. By crossing the line to moral disapproval, people who dislike religious groups have a ready rationale for derogating them.

## Summary

Religion, at least in its organized forms, is intimately tied with human relationships. At its best, it can be a major source of social support and a driving force behind prosocial behavior. However, the social aspect of religion can breed problems for believers and nonbelievers alike. Some people may have to overcome feelings of distaste to even consider affiliating with a religious group. Can they separate their religious ideals from the inevitable flaws that they observe among the all-too-human religious persons that they encounter? When they do make religious commitments, people may find themselves at odds with other important people in their social network who do not share their beliefs. For them, one major challenge is to participate meaningfully in their religious community without resorting to either of two extremes: outgroup derogation or watering down their beliefs.

# Disappointment, Anger, and Mistrust Toward God

Another major benefit of religious commitment is feeling close to God and the comfort that comes with the belief that an omnipotent being is watching over, protecting, and caring for the self. For many believers, the cultivation of an intimate relationship with God is a cornerstone of religious life. Some scholars have taken this idea a step further, conceptualizing religion as an attachment process. However, as in human relationships, a lot can go wrong in people's relationships with God. For example, some studies suggest that if people have conflicted relationships with their own fathers, they often develop negative or ambivalent feelings toward God as well. As another example, well-meaning religious parents sometimes use references to God or the Bible as self-regulation cues. For example, a parent might try to thwart a child's attempt to steal candy at the grocery store by saying "God is watching you" or quoting a Bible verse such as "Thou shalt not steal." If such statements are often used to curb misbehavior and if not tempered with positive statements about God, a child might come to see God as an oppressor primarily responsible for creating rules and policing people.

As alluded to in the previous section, both children and adults might find some aspects of God's behavior or character distasteful as they read religious texts or hear religious stories. For example, those reading the Bible may wonder this: Does God endorse killing? Why would God allow children to suffer for what their parents had done? How could a loving God send people to eternal punishment after death? For other people, the aspects of the Christian God that embody mercy and grace might be unappealing. A person who values toughness, pride, and retributive justice might be repelled by Christ's advocacy of virtues such as mercy and meekness—not to mention His own humiliating and painful death, which He accepted without protest or complaint.

Negative attitudes toward God could also stem from much more personal, intense hurts, and disappointments. In the wake of negative life events such as bereavement, illness, accidents, failures, or natural disasters, one potential response is to blame God. If God is held responsible for the act, intense feelings of mistrust, frustration, and anger can result, any of which can cause the wounded person to turn away or withdraw from God. Such pains might be especially sharp if the individual had placed hope in God, perhaps praying and trusting God for a specific outcome, only to be disappointed. We might think of such situations as parallel to those in which we feel betrayed, let down, or offended by another person, and in this case, the one who allowed our suffering could have prevented it—a thought that could fuel anger, hurt, and deep-seated grudges against God. Feelings of anger toward God have been linked with depression and anxiety and with poor coping outcomes. Some people might even decide to abandon belief altogether as a result of such incidents—a possibility that we are examining in our current research.

On the brighter side, preliminary evidence suggests that people often resolve feelings of anger toward God, and an ability to do so is associated with better mental health. How do people avoid or reduce feelings of anger at God? Although people often forgive perpetrators when they apologize or admit wrongdoing, they cannot expect such responses from God. Instead, they may have to draw on cognitive strategies. Drawing on research on interpersonal forgiveness, we might suggest that people will feel less angry toward God if they do not believe that God caused the event, if they view God's intentions as positive, or if they can see some good outcome from the incident. Also, because commitment increases the motivation to forgive, people who already feel close to God should be less likely to become angry. We are testing these hypotheses in our current research.

Another distinction made in the forgiveness literature may illuminate other problems in people's relationships with God: the distinction between *forgiveness*, which requires turning away from bitter, vengeful feelings, and *reconciliation*, which requires trust. Regardless of whether people feel angry with

God, they may find it difficult to trust God. Within evangelical Christianity, for example, there is a heavy emphasis on coming to God through Christ, confessing one's sins, receiving forgiveness, and surrendering one's life to God. For some people, the prospect of admitting one's weakness and dependence on God could be intensely shaming, and regardless of whether they trust God, many individuals are likely to balk at the notion of having to come under the authority of God (and, in some cases, under the authority of religious institutions as well). For the person who takes great pride in self-reliance, personal control, and autonomy—all of which are highly valued in our Western culture—such concerns could be a substantial barrier to deepened religious commitment.

## Summary

Individuals sometimes feel angry, mistrustful, or rebellious toward God. When having a close bond with God is the cornerstone of a person's religious commitment, it becomes crucial to resolve negative feelings or attitudes toward God before they undermine the relationship. People may develop negative attitudes or feelings about God in many ways, ranging from negative childhood associations to personal hurts and disappointments. Suffering persons may find it difficult to resolve anger toward God because God will not apologize to them or admit wrongdoing. To avoid holding a grudge against God, suffering persons might need to reframe hurtful events in positive ways or to remind themselves of their prior commitment to God.

# The Inner Struggle to Believe: Intellectual Barriers and Dissonance

Religious beliefs help people to make sense of the world and to find a sense of meaning or purpose in existence. In fact, this meaning-making aspect of religion seems to be one of the major mediators of the association between religion and health. However, for some individuals, the answers provided by religion are not satisfactory at an intellectual or emotional level. The result might be to turn a person away from religion or, at the very least, to create cognitive dissonance about perceived inconsistencies.

## Problems Faced by Nonbelievers

Studies have suggested that individuals with no childhood foundation in religion are unlikely to embrace it later in life. Young children are likely to trust what their parents tell them, and they can build worldviews consistent with their early religious learning. However, for an adult with no religious background, considering a new religious view of the world may require exceptional cognitive work. Over time, a nonbeliever will build a cognitive model of how the world works without including God in the picture, and all of these ideas may need to be revisited and challenged in order to incorporate new, God-centered ideas. Many people may not want to expend this level of effort.

Nonbelievers may also be reluctant to discard or revise their own ideas because the issues at hand are so fundamental: the purpose of life, what happens after death, who (or what) is in charge of the universe, and whether there is any reality beyond what our senses experience. Religious doctrines on these topics, faithfully accepted by believers, may not seem plausible to the nonbeliever. A religious seeker is likely to encounter many doctrines that do not offer logically consistent, coherent answers to life's difficult questions—something that a critical mind may insist on before being willing to believe.

Because many adults may find it difficult to accept religion through a purely intellectual search, we might predict that emotional pathways could serve as a shortcut to belief. For example, nonbelieving adults might be swayed by a mystical or miraculous experience by reaching a point of desperation in which they seek God's help or by finding a powerful sense of belonging within a religious group. Such emotionally charged events might provide people with a fresh incentive to adopt a particular faith, even if they have not resolved all of the intellectual fine points. Consistent with this reasoning, Altemeyer and Hunsberger found that among people with no childhood background in religion, those who embrace religion as adults often do so by means of potent social and emotional experiences. Although mainstream religions often address emotional needs, other social groups—such as cults—can also tap into emotional pathways. For a person eagerly seeking guidance, relief, or companionship, virtually any social group that promised to meet these needs could become a persuasive influence—particularly for those who are willing to suspend logic and personal judgment in the service of emotional goals.

## Problems Faced by Believers

Even for individuals with some commitment to religious belief, logical stumbling points and troubling doctrines within one's religious system could be a source of cognitive dissonance. For example, many people who read the Bible (some of whom would identify themselves as Jews or Christians) are troubled by the seeming harshness and unfairness of the Old Testament world: the wars, sacrifices, punishments, and plagues that were presented as being part of God's plan for His "chosen people." Many individuals, whether Judeo-Christian or not, may find such material disturbing and inconsistent with their personal views of God. Gender-related issues often prompt dissent, as do doctrines about sexual behavior, and as mentioned earlier, our own research has suggested that Christian doctrines about hell can be a source of fear and emotional turmoil for some believers.

When people have some commitment to religion but are disturbed by specific doctrines, what are their options? For someone who already holds strongly to a religious belief system, it may be possible to tolerate some inconsistencies in religious doctrine while retaining the core beliefs of the religion and continuing to identify oneself as part of the religious group. A person within the system may be willing to suspend reasoning to some degree as an exercise of faith. Other responses might involve changing one's beliefs to reduce dissonance while still providing the benefits of religious or spiritual involvement. For example, a conservative Christian might choose to believe in heaven but not in hell. A Catholic woman may decide to go on birth control or to have an abortion, both privately and publicly disagreeing with the church's stand on these issues but still strongly identify herself as a Catholic. Such practices might be aptly described by a term such as *cafeteria-style religion*, as they involve choosing aspects of existing religious systems that seem logical or comfortable for the self and ignoring or disbelieving those that are not. A person engaging in cafeteria-style religion might make all of his or her choices from within one religion or might choose elements from a variety of different religions. For example, a religious seeker might decide to retain a belief in Christ as an important historical figure while incorporating elements of Eastern or Native American religion into his belief system.

Another dissonance-reducing alternative to orthodox religiosity might be termed *do-it-yourself spirituality*, in which people shape spiritual beliefs and practices based on their own preferences, logic, intuition, and experience. As individualized forms of belief, both cafeteria-style religion and do-it-yourself spirituality draw people away from religious orthodoxy. More orthodox believers would thus argue that they constitute forms of self-deception, as they represent an attempt to hide the truth from oneself. However, both cafeteria-style religion and do-it-yourself spirituality would seem to be popular choices within Western culture's current postmodern ethos with its valuing of tolerance, personal freedom, subjectivity, and relativism.

## Summary

When people search for answers within religion, some of them will encounter intellectual or emotional strains surrounding the belief systems themselves. Some people may simply move on, looking for another religious system that better suits them. Others will abandon the religious search altogether. Some believers, viewing apparent inconsistencies as tests of faith, learn to tolerate the resulting confusion. Another alternative is to reduce dissonance through subtle shifts of belief, undercutting orthodoxy in an attempt to create a more personally satisfying or sensible theology.

# Cultivating Virtue and Confronting One's Imperfections

Another major benefit of religious involvement is that religion often encourages people to behave in virtuous ways. For example, religious beliefs can promote physical health by discouraging smoking, excessive drinking, and use of illegal drugs. Religion often encourages specific prosocial behaviors, such as forgiveness and generosity. It may also foster habits such as patience and perseverance that help people achieve their goals and regulate their emotions. Virtuous strivings are not specific to religious frameworks, of course. Anyone working toward self-improvement or following an abstract moral code could be seen as pursuing virtue. However, religion often does encourage people to reflect on their behavior and to improve it, and it is possible that virtues endorsed by religion might carry additional weight for many people because they have the backing of authority behind them.

Given that virtuous striving is an important part of religious life, what factors block the pursuit of virtue? Some barriers are motivational, in which people may not be certain that they want to cultivate certain characteristics. As evidenced by Christian virtues such as humility, meekness, gentleness, patience, and forgiveness, religious values often go against the grain of the larger culture. Because all of the virtues just listed involve some degree of self-transcendence or self-sacrifice, they may seem foolhardy to many. How are such behaviors going to fit within modern Western culture, with its emphasis on individual rights, immediate gratification, and materialism? Self-transcendent or self-sacrificing behaviors seem to invite abuse by others who are playing by a more self-serving set of rules. The pursuit of virtue may also entail giving up some favorite indulgences, which might range from overeating and sleeping in on Sundays to darker pleasures, such as revenge fantasies and slanderous gossip. Many people would prefer to follow their appetites than to pursue their virtuous counterparts, especially once deeply pleasurable (but now forbidden) habits have been established.

Even for those who earnestly desire to cultivate virtue and to improve their behavior, some degree of failure is inevitable. Virtuous behavior requires self-control, and humans are limited in their capacity for self-control. For example, consider a man who is trying to stop having thoughts of lust toward women. He is likely to face constant temptations in his environment to indulge in lust, whether by seeing scantily clad women on television and on billboards or by hearing his coworkers tell sexual jokes. He may have to fight a long-standing habit of engaging in sexual fantasies during idle moments, and in a cruel twist, research on ironic processes suggests that his very efforts to keep lusty thoughts out of his mind may make those very thoughts more likely to intrude. In a weak moment, this man is likely to give in and indulge in thoughts of lust.

As the prior example illustrates, individuals trying to control their thoughts and behaviors will often fail. Therefore, unless we are very adept at self-enhancement and self-justification, one consequence of trying to cultivate virtue is that we will be continually reminded of our shortcomings. With increased devotion and commitment to a religious system, people are likely to find more and more areas of their lives that are imperfect. Depending on how such failures are attributed, they might prompt negative outcomes such as self-condemnation, hopelessness, or perceptions of God as punitive or unforgiving toward the self. Another possibility is offered by research on abstinence violation effects: Seeing that the standard of perfection has been violated, people who fail to live up to idealistic standards may give up and indulge in more extreme misbehaviors.

Ideally, religious systems will help people to make sense of their imperfections and to use them in a positive way. Within Protestant Christianity, for example, seeing one's sins and limitations is the first step toward seeing a need for God's forgiveness and direction. Salvation is viewed as a free gift based on the God's grace and Christ's atoning sacrifice for sin, not something earned through good behavior. Virtue, rather than being seen as a cause of salvation, is viewed as a result of salvation and a person's subsequent cooperation with The Holy Spirit's ongoing work. All of these doctrines—the reality of human imperfection, the free gift of salvation, and the help of the Holy Spirit in fostering virtue—will ideally provide believers with a sense of safety and security while encouraging the further development of virtue. In reality, however, many Christians continue to dismiss their shortcomings or, at the other extreme, to condemn themselves for their mistakes.

## Summary

Religion often encourages the development of virtue, which can benefit both individuals and society. However, both personal and social resistance may accompany the pursuit of virtue. Virtuous striving requires us to overcome immediate impulses to gratify or protect the self, and when people do attempt to live virtuously, failures may quickly become apparent. The ideal goal would seem to be to value virtue and to cultivate it, but without insisting on perfection.

# Conclusion

Religious life is not always characterized by sunny skies. As outlined previously here, people may encounter a number of intellectual, emotional, behavioral, and social problems associated with religious commitment In spite of these problems, however, the broader picture is anything but bleak. There remains a wealth of data suggesting that religion can be a substantial positive force in personal and social life. If the problems raised in this article can be anticipated, understood, and addressed, consider some of the potential gains.

Clearly, the social world surrounding religion is far from perfect—but when people are able to unite successfully with others as part of a religious community, the sharing of values and goals may yield a sense of support, direction, and grounding that few other social ties can provide. People do experience rifts in their relationships with God, but if they can resolve their negative feelings and work to restore the relationship, a stronger bond and a more mature faith might result. Intellectual and emotional barriers may create inner conflicts about belief, but the result might be a "thinking person's faith" rather than a more passive, mindless form of devotion. Striving after virtue is difficult, especially when it confronts people with the painful reality of their imperfections, but virtuous striving might yield a more commendable life, coupled with a humble, nondefensive attitude that could serve the person well in personal, social, and spiritual contexts.

From the perspective of research and theory, an important goal for the future will be to develop empirically testable models that can help to explain when and why strain arises in religious life and how various forms of strain can best be overcome. Models of strain in religious life should complement existing frameworks on related topics such as religious coping and conversion. Some of the psychological concepts raised in this article may assist in building such frameworks. For example, future research might examine the role of self-deception in religious belief, the contrast of human relationships with relationships between humans and God, or the study of virtue and vice in a self-regulation context. Ideally, as suggested by Hill, such pursuits will not only inform the psychology of religion. Research on these religious topics may also provide fundamental insights into human nature, insights that will advance general psychological knowledge.

# POSTSCRIPT

## Is Religion a Pure Good in Facilitating Well-Being During Adulthood?

**A**fter reading David G. Myers' position on the various merits of religion, you may find yourself agreeing with the contemporary popularity of trying to use religion as part of policies oriented to the public good—so-called faith-based initiatives. After reading Julia Juola Exline's position on the various challenges inherent in religion, you may find yourself questioning the wisdom of pressuring people toward faith. In either case, the powerful role that religion plays for most adults is clear.

Myers presents impressive statistics about the relationship between religious participation and healthy developmental behaviors. He associates religion with well-being, values, morals, altruism, and a general fulfillment for people finding that material success alone may lack meaning. Even relationships that can seem negative, such as that between religious belief and racial prejudice, seem to disappear upon closer examination: Myers demonstrates that racial prejudice is really only associated with people who seem not fully committed to religion. The implication is that any harm done by religion derives from those who are not fully devoted; from this perspective, even religious problems could be fixed by more religion.

But the orientation of Myers' article is toward the big picture of religion in adulthood, not toward the daily process of individual interaction with religious life. Exline demonstrates ways in which that process can challenge adult development. In a general sense, Exline reveals that looking at religion in relation to large-scale statistics fails to address the essence of religious experience—which is often an intense engagement with our spiritual nature. And that intense engagement is not easy. Exline even points out ways that the challenges of religion can influence other major developmental tasks in adulthood—sometimes creating conflict within a marriage or within interfaith families, sometimes challenging inconsistencies in one's philosophy of life.

There are several additional critiques that could be made of both arguments, and it is worth thinking about how they come to their respective conclusions. For example, Myers notes a number of rich statistical correlations, such as that between religion and health, but such an association is not necessarily causal. Simply because religious people seem to be more healthy than non-religious people does not necessarily mean religion causes better health. Likewise, Myers points out that a renewed commitment to religious life in the United States during the 1990s correlated with decreases in rates of teen sexual activity, teenage pregnancy, and violent crime. Yet those decreases are not necessarily a product of more religion—in fact, the decline in many negative social indicators during the 1990s is the subject of a much broader controversy, with explanations ranging from the impact of the economy to demographic changes resulting from legalized abortion. Nevertheless, it is possible that religious activity played some significant role.

On the other hand, Exline's position is based largely on a synthesis of other research ideas and theoretical possibilities based on a general experience of religion. It is important to ask whether the types of challenges she outlines are exceptions to the rule. In this regard, it may be useful to think about personal experiences with religion in relation to adulthood; beyond faith, have you observed any clear pattern to the way religion influences adult development? Do those patterns relate to other aspects of adult development? In thinking about such questions, it becomes clear that while we do not all share specific religious experiences, religion does play a prominent role in any understanding of contemporary life span development.

# Suggested Readings

S. Barkan and S. Greenwood, "Religious Attendance and Subjective Well-Being Among Older Americans," *Review of Religious Research* (December 2003).

M. Hayes and H. Cowie, "Psychology and Religion: Mapping the Relationship," *Mental Health, Religion & Culture* (March 2005).

A. James and A. Wells, "Religion and Mental Health: Towards a Cognitive-Behavioral Framework," *British Journal of Health Psychology* (September 2003).

N. Krause, "God-Medicated Control and Psychological Well-Being in Late Life," *Research on Aging* (March 2005).

D. Myers, *The American Paradox: Spiritual Hunger in the Age of Plenty* (Yale University Press, 2000).

K. Pargament, "The Bitter and the Sweet: An Evaluation of the Costs and Benefits of Religiousness," *Psychological Inquiry* (2002).

L. Waite and E. Lehrer, "The Benefits from Marriage and Religion in the United States: A Comparative Analysis," *Population & Development Review* (June 2003).

## Social Gerontology

An academic's site with references to information about "social gerontology" or the study of sociological aspects of old age.

`http://www.trinity.edu/~mkearl/geron.html`

## Biology of Aging

A Web site with links to information about research into mostly biological aspects of aging.

`http://www.senescence.info/`

## American Geriatric Society

The American Geriatric Society Foundation for Health in Aging works to connect aging research and practice.

`http://www.healthinaging.org/`

## Healthy Living

This Web site presents health topics, reviews, and articles addressing healthier living in later adulthood.

`http://www.healthandage.com/`

## World Transhumanist Association

The World Transhumanist Association is an organization that promotes "the ethical use of technologies to extend human capabilities" including extending the life span.

`http://www.transhumanism.org/index.php/WTA/index/`

## Life Extension Foundation

The Life Extension Foundation is a group that disseminates information and supports research related to anti-aging technology and the life span.

`http://www.lef.org/`

## Scientific American

In 2002 *Scientific American* magazine dealt with the proliferation of anti-aging claims in medical fields by publishing a position statement by 51 prominent scientists. That statement is available on the *Scientific American* Web site.

`http://www.sciam.com/article.cfm?articleID=`
`0004F171-FE1E-1CDF-B4A8809EC588EEDF`

# PART 9

# Later Adulthood

*T*he central question for thinking about later adulthood, the period of life after retirement age, is whether it is an inevitable period of decline or merely a period of adaptation. While we often think of old age as a time of general deterioration, research suggests that most people in this stage actually adjust to the challenges of aging reasonably well. Yet there are unquestionable challenges, including the eventual decline of physical and cognitive functioning. One of the issues in this section considers how people most successfully manage these challenges, while the other considers whether technological intervention in the face of such challenges would be a social good.

- Can We Universally Define "Successful Aging"?

- Is Anti-Aging Technology a Cause for Societal Concern?

# ISSUE 19

## Can We Universally Define "Successful Aging"?

**YES: John W. Rowe and Robert L. Kahn,** from "Successful Aging," *The Gerontologist* (vol. 37, 1997)

**NO: Martha B. Holstein and Meredith Minkler,** from "Self, Society, and the 'New Gerontology'," *The Gerontologist* (vol. 43, 2003)

### ISSUE SUMMARY

**YES:** With a drastically increasing population of the elderly, professors of medicine John W. Rowe and Robert L. Kahn suggest that a unified model of healthy aging is necessary to guide work with the elderly.

**NO:** Martha B. Holstein and Meredith Minkler, professors of religion and public health, respectively, counter that a unified model of successful aging is based on particular values and assumptions that may not be fair to marginalized populations.

The American population and the world population are both aging. People are living longer and spending more time in the stage generally described as old age. With more people living longer and longer, has increased in the field of "gerontology," which is defined as "the comprehensive study of aging and the problems of the aged" (according to the Merriam-Webster Dictionary). This definition points out the traditional emphasis in gerontology on problems, deriving from a general assumption that old age is a period of inevitable decline. The notion of "successful aging" is a direct response to this tendency, and a challenge to the idea that aging has to focus only on problems and decreased well-being.

The concept of "successful aging" owes its popularity largely to the authors of the first selection, John W. Rowe and Robert L. Kahn. Rowe and Kahn are researchers who directed an ambitious 10-year study of aging that was aimed at determining life span factors that correlated with healthy outcomes in old age. Their basic premise, as they articulate in the article, was that most work in the field of gerontology focused on classifying the elderly as either sick or non-sick. There was no room in these classes for thinking about people who go beyond non-sick to be well—people who have not only avoided problems, but actually aged "successfully." Based on their research and previous writing (including the following selection), Rowe and Kahn published a book in 1997 that has been arguably the most influential work in recent gerontology. The shift they helped create was to stop thinking about aging as something that needs to be fixed when it goes wrong, but instead to think about how decisions throughout the life span might create a positive experience of aging. In the second selection, Martha B. Holstein and Meredith Minkler term the changes brought to the study of aging by Rowe and Kahn as a major part of the "new gerontology."

While acknowledging that Rowe and Kahn's research provided useful insight into the characteristics most associated with good health in old age, Holstein and Minkler firmly object to the ideas that underpin one simple definition for "successful aging." They take the perspective of "critical gerontology," which they contrast with more "positivist" models for studying the life span. By associating the idea of one model for successful aging with a tradition of logical positivism, Holstein and Minkler are suggesting that successful aging is a misguided effort at finding a universal truth.

Logical positivism is a tradition of thought suggesting that science is progressing toward one truth—a suggestion that is controversial to many social scientists who assert that the complex and changing nature of the social world does not allow for simple single truth. Note, for example, that Rowe and Kahn use extensive data from research with twins to support their claims about successful aging. Twin studies are important to the study of life span development, because identical twins share 100 percent of their genetic material and thus provide researchers a chance to control for genetic variation. The assumption is that any differences between identical twins must be environmental, and by comparing those differences with average differences between other related people researchers can statistically estimate "heritability"—or the numerical estimate of how much of a trait or behavior is due to genetic inheritance. Rowe and Kahn present heritability as a tidy, clean statistical estimate, allowing us to appreciate the role life choices make in later life outcomes. But such a presentation requires a reliance on logical positivist assumptions: By statistically modeling influences on development, we can know something universal and true about the human experience. Not all scholars are comfortable with this assumption. As such, this controversy is embedded in a much larger controversy about the philosophy and practice of science: Will research and scholarship lead us to one clear "best" model of the human experience?

While Rowe and Kahn present their model of successful aging in a relatively straightforward manner, the criticism of their model illustrates several subtle but important points of controversy. One important point is about diversity: Does defining only one version of successful aging deny the diversity that is inherent in life span development? A second important point is about how much control individuals have in determining their own life span: Suggesting that "success" in aging is due to good individual choices denies the impact of social and cultural forces that are beyond individual control. As such, key questions to think about when reading these selections are whether defining "successful aging" allows for individual diversity, and whether it allows for diverse experiences in the social world.

John W. Rowe and
Robert L. Kahn

 **YES**

# Successful Aging

In an earlier article, we proposed the distinction between usual and successful aging as nonpathologic states. Our purpose in doing so was to counteract the longstanding tendency of gerontology to emphasize only the distinction between the pathologic and nonpathologic, that is, between older people with diseases or disabilities and those suffering from neither. The implicit assumption of that earlier gerontology was that, in the absence of disease and disability, other age-related alterations in physical function (such as increases in blood pressure and blood glucose) and cognitive function (such as modest memory impairment) were "normal," determined by intrinsic aging processes, primarily genetic, and not associated with risk.

We hoped that the distinction between two groups of nondiseased older persons—usual (nonpathologic but high risk) and successful (low risk and high function)—would help to correct those tendencies, stimulate research on the criteria and determinants of successful aging, and identify proper targets for interventions with "normal" elderly. In recent years, "successful aging" has become a familiar term among gerontologists and a considerable body of research has accumulated on its characteristics. Much of this work was supported by the MacArthur Foundation Research Network on Successful Aging. In this article we summarize the central findings of that work, propose a conceptual framework for successful aging, and consider some pathways or mechanisms that make for successful old age.

## Defining Successful Aging

We define successful aging as including three main components: low probability of disease and disease-related disability, high cognitive and physical functional capacity, and active engagement with life. All three terms are relative and the relationship among them is to some extent hierarchical. As the figure indicates, successful aging is more than absence of disease, important though that is, and more than the maintenance of functional capacities, important as it is. Both are important components of successful aging, but it is their combination with active engagement with life that represents the concept of successful aging most fully.

Each of the three components of successful aging includes subparts. Low probability of disease refers not only to absence or presence of disease itself, but

From *The Gerontologist*, vol. 37, no. 4, 1997, pp. 433–440. Copyright © 1997 by Gerontological Society of America. Reprinted by permission.

also to absence, presence, or severity of risk factors for disease. High functional level includes both physical and cognitive components. Physical and cognitive capacities are potentials for activity; they tell us what a person can do, not what he or she *does* do. Successful aging goes beyond potential; it involves activity. While active engagement with life takes many forms, we are most concerned with two—interpersonal relations and productive activity. Interpersonal relations involve contacts and transactions with others, exchange of information, emotional support, and direct assistance. An activity is productive if it creates societal value, whether or not it is reimbursed. Thus, a person who cares for a disabled family member or works as a volunteer in a local church or hospital is being productive, although unpaid. . . .

## Heritability, Lifestyle, and Age-related Risk

The previously held view that increased risk of diseases and disability with advancing age results from inevitable, intrinsic aging processes, for the most part genetically determined, is inconsistent with a rapidly developing body of information that many usual aging characteristics are due to lifestyle and other factors that may be age-related (i.e., they increase with age) but are not age-dependent (not caused by aging itself).

A major source of such information is the Swedish Adoption/Twin Study of Aging (SATSA), a subset of the Swedish National Twin Registry that includes over 300 pairs of aging Swedish twins, mean age 66 years old, half of whom were reared together and half who were reared apart. About one third are monozygotic, while two thirds are dizygotic. Comparison of usual aging characteristics in twins of differing zygosity and rearing status enables estimation of the relative contributions of heritable and environmental influences.

SATSA-based studies have determined the heritability coefficients (the proportion of total variance attributable to genetic factors) for major risk factors for cardiovascular and cerebrovascular disease in older persons. These are .66–.70 for body mass index, .28–.78 for individual lipids (total cholesterol, low- and high-density lipoprotein cholesterol, apolipoproteins A-1 and B, and triglycerides), .44 for systolic and .34 for diastolic blood pressure.

Heritability trends across decades of advanced age revealed a reduction in the heritability coefficients for apolipoprotein B and triglycerides and for systolic blood pressure (.62 for people under 65 years old and .12 for those over 65). Consistent with these age-related reductions in heritability are mortality data from a 26-year follow-up of the entire Swedish Twin Registry, 21,004 twins born between 1886 and 1925. Among male identical twins, the risk of death from coronary heart disease (CHD) was eightfold greater for those whose twin died before age 55 than for those whose twin did not die before age 55, and among male nonidentical twins the corresponding risk was nearly four times greater. When one female identical twin died before the age of 65, the risk of death for the other twin was 15 times greater than if one's twin did not die before the age of 65, and 2.6 times greater in the case of female nonidentical twins. Overall, the magnitude of the risk associated with one's twin dying of CHD decreased as the age at which the twin died increased, independent of gender and zygosity.

Beyond twin studies, other evidence indicates the importance of lifestyle factors in the emergence of risk in old age. For instance, advancing age is associated with progressive impairment in carbohydrate tolerance, insufficient to meet diagnostic criteria for diabetes mellitus but characterized by increases in basal and post-glucose challenge levels of blood sugar and insulin. The hyperglycemia of aging carries increased risk for coronary heart disease and stroke, with progressive increases in the usual aging range associated with increasing risk. Similarly, the hyperinsulinemia associated with aging is an independent risk factor for coronary heart disease. Several studies have now demonstrated that the dominant determinants of this risk are age-related but potentially avoidable factors, such as the amount and distribution of body fat and reduced physical activity and dietary factors.

Substantial and growing evidence supports the contention that established risk factors for the emergence of diseases in older populations, such as cardiovascular and cerebrovascular disease, can be substantially modified. In a study demonstrating the modifiability of "usual aging," Katzel and colleagues conducted a randomized, controlled, prospective trial comparing the effects of a 9-month diet-induced weight loss (approximately 10% of body weight) to the effects of a constant-weight aerobic exercise program and a control program on a well characterized group of middle-aged and older men at risk for cardiovascular disease. The study participants were nondiabetic and were obese (body mass index 30 kg/m$^2$), with increased waist-hip ratios and modest increases in blood pressure, blood glucose, insulin, and an atherogenic lipid profile. Compared to controls, the reduced-energy intake diet resulted in statistically significant reductions in weight, waist-hip ratio, fasting and post-prandial glucose and insulin levels, blood pressure and plasma levels of triglycerides, low-density lipoprotein/cholesterol, and increases in high-density lipoprotein/cholesterol. While the older weight loss subjects (over 60 years old) lost less weight than the middle-aged subjects and had more modest improvements in carbohydrate tolerance, they participated fully in the reductions in other risk factors. In general, the weight loss intervention had greater effects than the constant-weight aerobic exercise intervention.

Taken together, these reports reveal three consistent findings. First, intrinsic factors alone, while highly significant, do not dominate the determination of risk in advancing age. Extrinsic environmental factors, including elements of lifestyle, play a very important role in determining risk for disease. Second, with advancing age the relative contribution of genetic factors decreases and the force of nongenetic factors increases. Third, usual aging characteristics are modifiable. These findings underline the importance of environmental and behavioral factors in determining the risk of disease late in life.

## Intra-Individual Variability: A Newly Identified Risk Factor in Older Persons

The traditional repertoire of risk factors identified in studies of young and middle-aged populations may not include some additional risk factors unique to, or more easily identified in, elderly populations. In this regard, the MacArthur

Foundation's Studies of Successful Aging point to a previously unrecognized risk factor—altered within-individual variability in physiologic functions—which may be important in determining the usual aging syndrome.

Most gerontological research, and indeed research in all age groups, is not geared to the measurement of short-term variations and changes. Study designs generally focus on the absolute level of a variable, perhaps comparing levels at two or more time points that may be separated by months or years. Nesselroade and colleagues, reasoned that short-term variability in a number of physiological or perhaps psychological characteristics might reflect a loss of underlying physiological reserve and represent a risk factor for emergence of disease or disability. To study the impact of short-term variability, they examined between-person differences in similarly aged residents of a retirement community. They assessed various aspects of biomedical, cognitive, and physical functioning every week for 25 weeks in a group of 31 individuals and a matched group of 30 assessed only at the outset and the end of the 25-week period, and they followed the subjects for several years to ascertain the relationship between within-person variability and its risk.

Within-person variability of a joint index of physical performance and physiological measures (gait, balance, and blood pressure) was an excellent predictor of mortality five years later ($R = 0.70$, $R^2 = 0.49$). Variability of the composite measure was a better predictor of mortality than mean level, which did not represent a statistically significant risk factor. A similar pattern of findings held for the psychological attributes of perceived control and efficacy, for which average level was not a significant predictor of mortality but intra-individual variability scores predicted 30% of the variance in mortality.

It should be emphasized that some functions are highly variable under normal conditions and others much less so. The significant aspect of intra-individual variability as a potential measure of decreased capacity and increased risk must be a change from the normal variability, regardless of whether the change is an increase or decrease. For example, a decline in beat-to-beat variability in heart rate has been shown to be a predictor or mortality in patients who have previously suffered a myocardial infarction. While in the physiological measurement used in this study, an increase in variability was associated with increased risk; in other highly regulated systems, a decrease in variability may be detrimental and represent decreased reserve and increased risk.

## Maximizing Cognitive and Physical Function in Late Life

A second essential component of successful aging is maximization of functional status. One common concern of older people relates to cognitive function, especially learning and short-term memory. Another functional area of major interest is physical performance. Modest reductions in the capacity to easily perform common physical functions may prevent full participation in productive and recreational activities of daily life.

The MacArthur Foundation Research Network on Successful Aging conducted a longitudinal study of older persons to identify those physical, psychological, social, and biomedical characteristics predictive of the maintenance of high function in late life. The 1,189 subjects in this three-site longitudinal study were 70–79 years old at initial evaluation and were functionally in the upper one third of the general aging population. Smaller age- and sex-matched samples (80 subjects in the medium functioning group and 82 subjects in the low functioning group) were selected to represent the middle and lowest tertiles. Initial data included detailed assessments of physical and cognitive performance, health status, and social and psychological characteristics (the MacArthur battery), as well as the collection of blood and urine samples. After a 2.0–2.5 year interval, 1,115 subjects were re-evaluated, providing a 91% follow-up rate for the study.

## Predictors of Cognitive Function

Cognitive ability was assessed with neuropsychological tests of language, non-verbal memory, verbal memory, conceptualization, and visual spatial ability. In the initially high functioning group, four variables—education, strenuous activity in and around the home, peak pulmonary flow rate, and self-efficacy—were found to be direct predictors of change or maintenance of cognitive function, together explaining 40% of the variance in cognitive test performance. Education was the strongest predictor, with greater years of schooling increasing the likelihood of maintaining high cognitive function. This finding is consistent with several cross-sectional studies, which identify education as a major protective factor against reductions in cognitive function. Since all the subjects had high cognitive function at first evaluation, it is unlikely that the observed effect merely reflected ability to perform well on cognitive tests or was the result of individuals with greater innate intelligence having received more education. Instead, the results suggest either or both of two explanatory mechanisms: a direct beneficial effect of education early in life on brain circuitry and function, and the possibility that education is a proxy for life-long intellectual activities (reading, crossword puzzles, etc.) which might serve to maintain cognitive function late in life.

Pulmonary peak expiratory flow rate was the second strongest predictor of maintenance of cognitive function. In previous studies, this function was a predictor of total and cardiovascular mortality and a correlate of cognitive and physical function in elderly populations.

A surprising finding of this study was that the amount of strenuous physical activity at and around the home was an important predictor of maintaining cognitive function. In a follow-up study to evaluate a possible mechanism of this effect, Neeper, Gomez-Pinilla, Choi, and Cotman measured the effect of exercise on central nervous system levels of brain-derived neurotrophic factor (BDNF) in adult rats. These investigators found that increasing exercise was associated with very substantial "dose-related" increases in BDNF in the hippocampus and neocortex, brain areas known to be highly responsive to environmental stimuli. These data provide a potential mechanism whereby exercise might enhance central nervous system function, particularly memory function.

A personality measure, perceived self-efficacy, was also predictive of maintaining cognitive function in old age. The concept of self-efficacy developed by Bandura is defined as "people's beliefs in their capabilities to organize and execute the courses of action required to deal with prospective situations."

In students and young adults, self-efficacy influences persistence in solving cognitive problems, heart rate during performance of cognitive tasks, mathematical performance, and mastery of computer software procedures. Lachman and colleagues have proposed a role for self-efficacy beliefs in maintenance of cognitive function among older people.

In addition to these findings of predictors of maintenance of cognitive function, evidence is accumulating to indicate that it can be enhanced in old age. For example, older people who showed a clear age-related pattern of decline in fluid intelligence (inductive reasoning and spatial orientation) showed substantial improvement after five training sessions that stressed ways of approaching such problems and provided practice in solving them. Moreover, repeated measurement indicated that the improvements were maintained. Studies from the Max Planck Institute in Berlin confirm the finding that cognitive losses among healthy older people are reversible by means of training, although they also shows a substantial age-related training effect in favor of younger subjects. There is a double message in these findings: first, and most important, the capacity for positive change, sometimes called plasticity, persists in old age; appropriate interventions can often bring older people back to (or above) some earlier level of function. Second, the same interventions may be still more effective with younger subjects, which suggests an age-related reduction in reserve functional capacity. These demonstrations of plasticity in old age are encouraging in their own right and tell us that positive change is possible.

## Predictors of Physical Function

In the MacArthur studies, maintenance of high physical performance, including hand, trunk, and lower extremity movements and integrated movements of balance and gait, was predicted by both socio-demographic and health status characteristics. Being older and having an income of less than $10,000 a year increased the likelihood of a decline in physical performance, as did higher body mass index (greater fat), high blood pressure, and lower initial cognitive performance. Behavioral predictors of maintenance of physical function included moderate and/or strenuous leisure activity and emotional support from family and friends. Moderate levels of exercise activity (e.g., walking leisurely) appeared in these studies to convey similar advantages to more strenuous exercise (e.g., brisk walking).

## Continuing Engagement with Life

The third component of successful aging, engagement with life, has two major elements: maintenance of interpersonal relations and of productive activities.

## Social Relations

At least since Durkheim's classic study of suicide, isolation and lack of connectedness to others have been recognized as predictors of morbidity and mortality. Five prospective studies of substantial populations have now demonstrated causality throughout the life course in such associations: being part of a social network is a significant determinant of longevity, especially for men.

Research on the health protective aspect of network membership has emphasized two kinds of supportive transactions: socio-emotional (expressions of affection, respect and the like) and instrumental (direct assistance, such as giving physical help, doing chores, providing transportation, or giving money).

The three-community MacArthur study tested both instrumental and emotional support as predictors of neuroendocrine function and physical performance. Neuroendocrine measures were also studied as possible mediators of the effects of support. Over a three-year period, marital status (being married), presumably a source of emotional support, protected against reduction in productive activity. Men with higher emotional support had significantly lower urine excretion of norepinephrine, epinephrine, and cortisol, and for both men and women, emotional support was a positive predictor of physical performance. Instrumental support, on the other hand, had few significant neuroendocrine relations for men, none for women, and was associated with lower physical performance, probably as an effect rather than a cause.

These varying effects of social support are consistent with research relating the effect of support to the specific situation in which it is offered. For example, instrumental support rather than emotional support influenced the promptness with which older people who experienced cancer-suspicious symptoms actually saw a physician. Opposite results came from a nursing home experiment, however: socio-emotional support (verbal encouragement) had positive performance effects, whereas instrumental support (direct assistance) had negative effects on performance.

Several conclusions seem warranted regarding the properties of social relations and their effects:

a. Isolation (lack of social ties), is a risk factor for health.
b. Social support, both emotional and instrumental, can have positive health-relevant effects.
c. No single type of support is uniformly effective; effectiveness depends on the appropriateness of the supportive acts to the requirements of the situation and the person.

## Productive Activities

Older people are not considered "old" by their families and friends, nor do they think of themselves as "old," so long as they remain active and productive in some meaningful sense. In legislative policy, Congressional discussion as to whether the nation can "afford" its older people is as much a debate about their productivity as their requirements for service, especially medical care.

Part of the confusion stems from lack of clarity about what constitutes a productive activity. Our national statistics define Gross Domestic Product (GDP) in terms of activities that are paid for, and exclude all unpaid activities, however valuable. Several current studies (ACL, MacArthur, HRS) utilize a broader definition that includes all activities, paid or unpaid, that create goods or services of economic value, and these studies have generated age-related patterns very different from those for paid employment alone.

The nationwide Americans Changing Lives (ACL) study found that, contrary to the stereotype of unproductive old age, most older people make productive contributions of some kind, more as informal help-giving and unpaid volunteer work than paid employment. When all forms of productive activity are combined, the amount of work done by older men and women is substantial. Among those aged 60 or more, 39% reported at least 1500 hours of productive activity during the preceding year; 41% reported 500–1499 hours, and 18% reported 1–499 hours. The relationship between age and productive activity depends on the activity. While hours of paid work drop sharply after age 55, hours of volunteer work in organizations peak in the middle years (ages 35–55), and informal help to friends and relatives peaks still later (ages 55–64) and remains significant to age 75 and beyond.

Both the ACL and MacArthur studies address the question of what factors enable sustained productivity in old age. Both include longitudinal as well as cross-sectional data, and in some respects the studies are complementary— national representativeness over the full adult age range in the ACL survey, biomedical and performance measures as well as self-report in the MacArthur research. Three factors emerge as predictors of productive activity: functional capacity, education, and self-efficacy.

*Functional capacity.*   Men and women high in cognitive and physical function are three times as likely to be doing some paid work and more than twice as likely to be doing volunteer work. Moreover, for all forms of productive work except child care, functional status also predicts the amount of such work. Indicators of functional decrement, such as limitations with vision and number of bed days during the three months preceding the data collection, predict lesser productive activity.

*Education.*   Educational level is a well established predictor of sustained productive behavior, paid and unpaid. The possible mechanisms of this effect include the role of education as a major determinant of occupation and income, both of which are major influences on the life course, the selective process in education that probably includes genetic elements and certainly includes parental socioeconomic status, and the tendency of education to inculcate values and establish habits that express themselves in later life as higher functional status and engagement in productive behavior.

*Self-efficacy.*   Self-efficacy and the related concepts of mastery and control are consistent predictors of sustained activity in old age. The ACL study, in addition to identifying a positive relationship between self-efficacy and productive activity, found that two other variables, labeled vulnerability and fatalism, essentially inversions of self-efficacy, were negatively related to productivity. Consistent with these findings, in the MacArthur sample only one factor—mastery—emerged as relevant for both increases and decreases in productivity; increases in mastery led to increased productivity; decreases in mastery had the opposite effect.

*Response to stress.*   If we had continuous rather than occasional measurement of successful aging, we would expect to find that even older people who are aging successfully have not met the criteria at every moment in the past. They have moved "in and out of success," just as healthy people can be said to move in and out of illness. Under the most fortunate circumstances, aging brings with it some repetitive experience of chronic or recurrent stresses, the "daily hassles" of life and their cumulative effects. Most older people have also experienced more acute episodes, the "stressful life events" that have been much-studied. For example, older men and women may have been seriously ill, temporarily disabled by accident or injury, disoriented after a stroke, or depressed by the death of a spouse. Apart from such crises of illness and bereavement, but similarly stressful, are the experiences of forced retirement, sudden reduction in income, mugging, and burglary.

We propose the concept of *resilience* to describe the rapidity and completeness with which people recover from such episodes and return to meeting the criteria of success. Determination of resilience in dealing with a specific stressful event would require assessment of relevant functions before the stressing challenge is encountered and subsequent monitoring the observe the initial decremental effect, the time required to regain stability of function, and the level of function regained. While no research has yet robustly evaluated resilience, a number of studies are relevant to it. The work by Nesselroade and his colleagues, described earlier, demonstrated the importance of short term variability in physical function and blood pressure as a predictor of mortality among elderly subjects. We may interpret low variability in blood pressure as an indicator of resilience, but the interpretation must be tentative; we do not know the challenges or stressors to which these subjects were responding.

*Conclusion.*    Recent and projected substantial increases in the relative and absolute number of older persons in our society pose a significant challenge for biology, social and behavioral science, and medicine. Gerontology is broadening its perspective from a prior preoccupation with disease and disability to a more robust view that includes successful aging. As conceptual and empiric research in this area accelerates, successful aging is seen as multidimensional, encompassing three distinct domains: avoidance of disease and disability, maintenance of high physical and cognitive function, and sustained engagement in social and productive activities. For each of these domains, an interdisciplinary database is coalescing that relates to both reducing the risk of adverse events and enhancing resilience in their presence. Many of the predictors of risk and of both functional and activity levels appear to be potentially modifiable, either by individuals or by changes in their immediate environments. The stage is thus set for intervention studies to identify effective strategies that enhance the proportion of our older population that ages successfully.

# NO

**Martha B. Holstein and
Meredith Minkler**

# Self, Society, and the "New Gerontology"

> The primary task of the critic is to analyze the present and to reveal its fractures and instabilities and the ways in which it at once limits us and points to the transgressions of those limits.

One of gerontology's great strengths has been its multidisciplinary perspective. To date, biology and the social sciences have provided the primary filters through which gerontologists have studied aging and old age. These disciplines have deepened our understanding of the processes of aging, contributed to policy and program development, and influenced new generations of gerontologists. In the past several years, a new paradigm has assumed pride of place. Although linguistically similar to (but quite different in content from) earlier work on successful aging, this paradigm, firmly grounded in the 10-year, $10 million MacArthur Foundation Study of Successful Aging, is hailed as the "new gerontology." It is part of a larger movement in gerontology and geriatrics—a vigorous emphasis on the potential for and indeed the likelihood of a healthy and engaged old age. This view seeks to counteract and replace the old "decline and loss" paradigm that views aging as a series of individual decrements or losses to which both elders and society needed to adapt or adjust. In contrast, the new gerontology adopts a prevention model—modify individual behaviors throughout your life and so avoid these decrements and losses.

In addition to publishing in academic journals, Rowe and Kahn presented their model and a wealth of evidence-based health promotion and disease and disability prevention advice in the form of a book geared at a lay audience. In the years since the publication of *Successful Aging,* this volume has attracted an articulate, popular, and professional following. Greeted as a lodestar for moving the field of aging toward a new understanding of what permits effective functioning in old age and drawing on the contributions of many leading scientists in the field of aging, *Successful Aging* is perhaps the single most recognized work in recent gerontology. Intended to stimulate this wide recognition, the major public relations effort that followed the book's publication and the resulting media attention have deepened its cultural resonance while also influencing the nation's research agenda on aging.

From *The Gerontologist,* vol. 43, no. 6, 2003, pp. 787–789, 791–795. Copyright © 2003 by Gerontological Society of America. Reprinted by permission.

Time and popularity have not, however, erased our concerns about this paradigm and the associated use of the implicitly normative phrase "successful aging." Its very simplicity and apparent clarity mask vital differences and many critical dimensions of what may be described as a liminal state—"the condition of moving from one state to another"—under circumstances marked by change and uncertainty. It is thus timely, we believe, to take another look at the new gerontology. In particular, we want to apply to the successful aging paradigm and its popular manifestations critical and feminist perspectives, whose standpoints can unsettle familiar and conventional ways of thinking by revealing their often-unrecognized underlying values and consequences. To be critical means to engage in "historically and socially situated normative reflection about research methodologies, assumptions and directions." Critical practices reformulate the questions that research asks, insist on broad sources of knowledge generation, and urge asking traditional "subjects" normative questions—what ought to be—as a way of uncovering hidden normative possibilities. As interested in the particular as in the general, in understanding as well as generalizing, a critical approach enlarges our perceptions and so calls attention to what more positivist approaches cannot or do not notice. . . .

## Successful Aging and the New Gerontology

Ironically, the new gerontology has much in common with the century-old Victorian view of successful aging in which good health signaled a life lived according to the strict dictates of Victorian convention. Albeit without today's scientific foundation and inclined to view "vices," such as vigorous sexual activity, as the cause of an unhealthy old age, it still distinguished between positive and negative experiences of aging rooted in individual action over a lifetime. Even in the 19th century, America scientists "sought a 'normal' old age that contained an unstated ideal of health or maximum functioning—the 'good' old age of Victorian morality."

For many years, the modern gerontological enterprise similarly has sought to understand what can make old age better—healthier, financially more secure, and a period of fulfillment and even growth. In the classic edited, work, *Problems of Aging,* published in 1937, Edmund Cowdry invited a stellar group of scientists to bring to the multifaceted problem of aging an "understanding of how things worked" from the perspective of several scientific disciplines. In the years since the publication of this first handbook on aging, we have come a long way toward understanding what that early volume called the "problem of senescence." With improved economic conditions, positive changes in physical and often social environments, and improvements in health care and health care access, many more—though certainly not all—older people can have a relatively satisfactory old age. Since the early 1980s, declining poverty and the mitigation of many diseases of old age have facilitated interest in health promotion and wellness and have contributed to richer, more open perceptions about old age.

The new gerontology is in this tradition. It describes, in detail and with carefully documented scientific support, how individuals can contribute to their continued good health. In this way it provides younger people with an important message about making choices (albeit, as we will discuss, without sufficient attention to the contexts and constraints influencing those choices). Commenting on the impressive scientific grounding of the successful aging model, Scheidt, Humphreys, and Yorgason noted that "at least a hundred studies have shown the efficacy of modifications to environmental and lifestyle factors for increasing the likelihood that older individuals might achieve success under this triarchic definition. So what's not to like?" We will return to that question after briefly reviewing the premises of successful aging.

Rowe and Kahn argued that three conditions or characteristics are necessary preconditions for successful aging: (a) the avoidance of disease and disability; (b) the maintenance of high physical and cognitive functional capacity; and (c) "active engagement in life." They further suggested that these three components are hierarchically ordered:

> The absence of disease and disability makes it easier to maintain mental and physical function. And maintenance of mental and physical function in turn enables (but does not guarantee) active engagement with life. It is the *combination* [emphasis in the original] of all three—avoidance of disease and disability, maintenance of cognitive and physical function and sustained engagement with life—that *represents the concept of successful aging most fully* [italics added].

While Rowe and Kahn have refined their model over the years, reaffirming more strongly, for example, an emphasis on the importance of "active engagement with life," the instrumental or preconditions for successful aging have become transformed, as the aforementioned quote suggests, into the concept itself. In a few short years, this model has become a central theoretical paradigm within the fields of geriatrics and gerontology. Despite its many strengths and contributions, however, the successful aging model and its attendant publicity are problematic. Following a brief review of the critical gerontology framework, we will use these perspectives as lenses through which to more critically examine successful aging and the new gerontology. . . .

# Applying These Perspectives to the New Gerontology

## The Issue of Normativity

Because critical perspectives are concerned about hidden value premises, we turn to the new gerontology's implicit (and thus unacknowledged) normatively. Understood as an objective, scientific discourse, the new gerontology upholds a certain status, defined primarily in terms of health, and labels those who exemplify these standards as aging successfully. This stance affirms normative value commitments, offering ways to think about—and judge—our choices (now and in the past), actions, and their results.

Historians, literary scholars, sociologists, and philosophers, among others, suggest reasons why cultural norms matter. Cultural images, representations, symbols, and metaphors are important means to withhold or to express social recognition; they offer the cultural imagery from which we construct identities. Central to this understanding are notions of the self. Mediating between individuals and their environment, the self is a "biographically anchored and reflexive project," realized in conversations with others and oneself. Norms matter because we are situated selves, embedded in society and culture and resonating with what is valued in the environment. Although resistance is possible, indeed probable, as situated selves, we can rarely ignore cultural norms in the construction of a self. Nor are we able to easily dissent, as individuals, from culture. The theologian Rosemary Reuther observed, "alternate cultures and communities must be built up to support the dissenting consciousness." To date, alternative perspectives tend to be ghettoized while the dominant culture accepts as the desired norm the tanned, vigorous couple who are bicycle riding on gently rolling hills and dining in the warm glow of candles.

Even if we put aside the publicity the new gerontology has received, and the strong scientific base of the MacArthur Foundation Study, it is not surprising that the new paradigm has gained popular approbation. Success, a valued attribute in American society, is generally visible and measurable, perhaps countable in dollars, degrees, gold medals, and so on. Evidence of success is commendable, to the individual's credit, and therefore praiseworthy. The new gerontology offers another measurable variable to define success, another source of praiseworthy behavior that has currency in a competitive society.

However, normative terms such as successful aging are not neutral; they are laden with comparative, either-or, hierarchically ordered dimensions. Unfortunately, too many people—most often the already marginalized—come up on the wrong side of the hierarchy and the either–or divide. Its reductionist qualities are revealed by a different sort of comparison: How would it seem to describe a particular kind of childhood or midlife—as such—as successful because the person rarely became ill and participate in many social events? Why then is it is desirable to describe this kind of aging (or more accurately, old age) as successful?

Even if we bracket for a moment our reluctance to apply the term "successful" to aging, the specific norms the new gerontology identifies as measures of success are also problematic. As we discuss in more detail in the paragraphs that follow, if how we live determines how we age, and if how we live is shaped by many factors beyond individual choice, then success is far harder to come by for some than for others.

Hence, because normative concepts are important, dominant cultural images can easily make individual efforts to transform themselves as their lives and bodies change more difficult. These concepts tell us what is worthwhile (on different levels of our lives) and give us criteria by which to evaluate our lives. Thus, the power to identify such normative concepts is pivotal. For this reason, in particular, the authority to create cultural views and images about aging can only rest in an interactive research process, and in a critical awareness of how context and particularities influence how we grow old and what we value once we get there. Exchanges between older people and academic researchers, for example, are unlikely to accept uncritically that a disease-resistant 80-year-old man playing golf at Augusta or skiing at Aspen is aging more successfully than a woman in a wheelchair who tutors inner city children or writes poetry or feels a passionate energy that she is too fragile to enact.

Health, as a normative standard, calls for certain virtues—diligence, caution, and perhaps a touch of solipsism. We must be ever wary of how we govern our lives. This view omits the natural lottery imposed by genetics, the general contingencies of human life, and the more specific damages (and often strengths) that marginalization and oppression bequeath to many individuals.

In raising these concerns about normativity, we are not suggesting that Rowe and Kahn intended to launch what can appear to be a coercive standard that affects individuals and groups in different and, in some cases, potentially damaging ways (see the paragraphs that follow). In an interesting irony, had Rowe and Kahn not labeled their landmark work as "successful aging," it may well have remained what it in essence is—a careful, empirically grounded account of how to help individuals stay as healthy as possible for as long as possible. On this foundation, they would be free, within inevitable limits, to construct the kind of life they choose. The use of the term "successful," however, shifts that intention to help people stay as well as possible to something much larger. What was initially affirmed as the preconditions for effective functioning in old age—the *foundation* on which many varieties of life choices may flourish—in an almost imperceptible move became the concept of successful aging. The foundation became the entirety. The concept does not say, These are guidelines to preserve your health and well-being in old age, all things being equal. Although such a statement gives health a high status, it does not equate good health with success. Eating properly, exercising regularly, and not smoking are connected directly to a goal of good health, a goal that, we suspect, most would treasure. However, we suggest throughout this essay, despite its wide appeal, attaining a healthy old age on the individual level should not be universally equated with the attainment of a good or successful old age.

## The "Problems" of Feasibility and Disability

Although our discussion raises broad questions about why both the phrase "successful aging," and the model bearing that name are problematic from a normative standpoint, there are other, more specific concerns that challenge its acceptability as an ideal. A major contribution of Rowe and Kahn's paradigm lay in its message that many of the losses associated with "usual aging" are not "normal" aspects of aging at all but are caused primarily by extrinsic factors, such as poor diet and lack of exercise, and therefore are subject to alteration. However, the value of this message from a health promotion perspective is tempered by another, as the authors go on to suggest that "successful aging is dependent upon individual choices and behaviors. *It can be attained through individual choice and effort* [italics added]." The single endpoint is effective physical and mental functioning. In Rowe and Kahn's words: "We were trying to pinpoint the many factors that conspire to put one octogenarian on cross-country skis and another in a wheelchair."

Such a statement is problematic on several counts; key among them is its implication that had the elder who is disabled but tried harder and made different (health-promoting) choices, he or she might also be enjoying a physically vigorous and able-bodied old age. This individualistic analysis doesn't ask if the 80-year-old skier had county club privileges and a winter home in Colorado, or the 80-year-old in the wheelchair had cleaned houses for a living while holding down a second job as a nurses' aide on the graveyard shift in a nursing home. Nor does this analysis inquire about the inner or family life of our 80-year-old in the wheelchair. These contextual features, at a minimum, shape the conditions of possibility for individuals and determine how they choose what to value. If the ideal is not practically feasible for all, or even most, people—even with the best intentions—then it serves to further privilege the already privileged, a danger that a feminist perspective identifies.

The "problem" of disability also looms. Within the successful aging paradigm, and with a few notable exceptions, disability, even visible "oldness," signifies failure or, at best, "usual" aging. "With midlife the universal ideal, older people meet the stringent criteria of successful aging only insofar as they are not 'old.' If the young body is . . . projected into old age as the norm," all will ultimately fail. This end is particularly troubling. When norms consider frailty and disability as reflections of failure, they reinforce "cultural fears of bodily suffering (and thus of people who are 'old') and [promote] inadequate policy responses" at the same time that they blame people whose bodies are proverbially "out of control." As was the case with its Victorian era predecessors, illness, especially because it prevents active engagement with life," becomes a transgression of cultural rules.

This exaggerated emphasis on the degree to which we can control the body contributes to and denies older people with functional limitations, most of whom are women, the dignity of their struggle to accept what they cannot change. On a broader level, it contributes as well to the cultural denial of disability, dependency, and ultimately death. That struggle, social ethicist Frida Furman says, "is a struggle of the soul to affirm what is yet possible, to let go of what is not."

Similarly, the "new ageism" inadvertently promoted though the skis versus wheelchair analogy simply replaces an earlier generalized dread of aging with a more specific fear of aging with a disability. Frequently internalized by older people themselves, this new variant of ageism ironically can mitigate against the very proactive health promotion and healthy maintenance activities advocated by proponents of successful aging by "substantially lowering the bar of dreams and expectations for and by elders with disabilities." Looking old and suffering from disabling conditions become personal failures, thereby compounding the "problem" of aging and contributing to often self-defeating strategies to preserve "youthfulness" and so appear "not old."

Once an individual strategy—staying fit and vigorous—becomes a societal vision, then "whole social groups and areas of life become marginalized." As already noted, such marginalization can elicit damaging and invidious comparisons, particularly if one is disabled, or simply old and "not well preserved."

As Blaikie has argued, the "constant quest for youth, in stigmatizing [sic] the old and sick, casts off these people as human failures."

## Devaluing of Women's Roles and Acts of Resistance

The cultural scripts that the new gerontology extols particularly affect older women. The greater burden of chronic illness and functional limitations they experience and their far higher poverty rates couple with differential societal norms that continue to assign a higher value to physical appearance and "youthful physical attractiveness" among women. However, many women have lived by the norms of their own more intimate society, being responsible for others and attending to the everyday business of life, whether that meant scrubbing floors or caring for a dying parent or a grandchild. These features that mark many a woman's moral life neither gain approbation from the wider society nor give her the leisure to tend to the specifics of health maintenance that contribute to successful aging by the criterion that Rowe and Kahn set forth. Hence, as life course and political economy perspectives remind us, the burden on older women—especially women who live on limited incomes and have experienced exclusions based on color, ethnicity, or class—is often particularly heavy.

The new gerontology can render invisible important adaptive and other actions that allow people to cope with change. Many people, for example, particularly older women, with their less than perfect bodies and with one or more chronic illnesses, confront cultural narratives of decline on their own terms. Rarely noted and seldom valued even if noticed, their acts of resistance—"going gray," choosing to live a simpler, less busy life, taking the time to give concentrated care to a parent, a spouse, or a grandchild, accepting "old" as a way to describe oneself—are less a bulwark against the loss of self-esteem than they might be if different cultural norms prevailed. Successful aging, for example, only tangentially—through its attention to active engagement with life—attends to aspects of the moral life such as nurturing, caring, friendship, love, and social activism that have been primary in the lives of many women. Such aspects of life that are publicly underestimated and undervalued become vulnerable as sources of self-worth if they lack sustenance and recognition. Instead of creating conditions that lessen important aspects of women's lives, does society not have a responsibility to "examine, evaluate, condemn, and change . . . expectations . . . that harm some, and militate against the well-being of all, women?"

## Potential Problems for Policy

In the policy arena, the notion that health and well-being in old age are largely in the hands of individuals can do further damage. Ironically, we are successfully old when we conform to society's needs; placing responsibility on the individual mitigates demands on social resources across our lives. Exceptionalism—"I made it, why can't you"—is, in our minds, a failing strategy. It does nothing to eliminate larger patterns of oppression, in which certain individuals and groups lack the advantages privileged groups possess by virtue of their social location. When the tasks essential to aging successfully are vested in the individual aging person, the young and the middle-aged hear about these splendid people who have aged so well and wonder why all the fuss about old age in America. Policies promoting increased Medicare coverage for home modifications and assistive devices, as well as increased Supplemental Social Security Income payments that would bring elderly and disabled recipients above the poverty line, may well suffer at the hands of a populace and a legislature that has bought the stereotypes of a new breed of successfully aging seniors who no longer need much in the way of government support. Particularly in the current political climate of major government cutbacks in the face of economic downturns and military buildups, overly optimistic images of "successful agers" may make even more vulnerable the position of many older women for whom more, rather than less, government assistance is vital.

The new gerontology can hinder the development of a thoughtful and morally rich account of dependency and interdependency. The often implicit singling out of disabled elderly persons as unsuccessful agers also allows us to evade the inevitable confrontation with sickness and death. In this way, it may further diminish policy attention to the need for greater engagement with these issues in a rapidly aging society. . . .

# Conclusion

Growing old in a society that not only valorizes youth but informs people *whoever they are* that successful aging—defined almost exclusively in terms of health status—"can be attained through individual choice and effort" is potentially damaging personally and politically. Such a perspective tends to trivialize the role of gender, race, socioeconomic status, and genetics in influencing both health and broader life chances both throughout life and in old age. At the same time, and precisely through its failure to take into account the unacknowledged role of broader sociostructural and environmental forces, this viewpoint transforms the particular into the universal and absolves social and political institutions of their responsibilities for the health and well-being of residents. By suggesting that the great majority of those elders in wheelchairs could indeed have been on cross-country skis had they but made the right choices and practiced the right behaviors can burden rather than liberate older people. Hence, we emphasize that concepts such as successful aging are marked by important and unacknowledged class, race, and gender concerns that result in further marginalizing the already marginalized. The perpetuation of privilege is not a desirable end.

However, even setting aside these concerns, the new gerontology offers an impoverished view of what a "good" old age can be. As suggested earlier, the MacArthur Foundation Study of Successful Aging led by Rowe and Kahn made a critical contribution in helping to provide a strong empirical base for the utility of a variety of health-promoting practices and behaviors throughout life and in old age. Nevertheless, the equation of good health with successful aging (and by extension, disability and poor health with failure) together with the simplistic popularization of these proscriptive views in the mass and popular culture fail to honor the many ways in which individuals face the physiological, emotional, or contextual changes that accompany aging.

We end with some ideas about how to alter the problematic aspects of the successful aging model's foundational assumptions. Act of resistance, already touched on, are beginning points. The tyranny of youth-preserving technologies and lifestyles that demand more and more time and money hinders a respectful attitude toward old age. How can we respect age if we do everything in our power to deny it? What most assume as a matter of course in youth and middle age—that is, health and activity—cannot be the critical measure of success in old age. At a minimum, it reduces old age to the most basic norms, less than we would accept at other times of our lives. It offers continuity, but old age is also importantly about transformation as we learn to accept what we cannot change, rage when we must, and adopt new ways of life as needed. Writing in her 60s, the late May Sarton, poet, essayist, and novelist, reflecting on the imminence of death, noted that "preparing to die we shed our leaves, without regret, so that the essential person may be alive and well at the end." Biomedicine, as important as it is, does not see the luminous moments that offer promise despite uncertainty and the proximity of death. Its tools cannot diagnose the mischief the very term "successful" can do, particularly in a competitive, youth-driven society.

We might return to the ancient question: What is the good life—for the whole of life—and what does it take to live a good old age? What virtues do we strive for and how do we honor difference? Germain Greer said it well: "Liberation struggles are not about assimilation but about asserting difference, endowing that difference with dignity and prestige, and insisting on it as a condition of self-definition and self-determination."

# POSTSCRIPT

## Can We Universally Define "Successful Aging"?

$\mathbf{T}$he popularity of Rowe and Kahn's concept of "successful aging" is easy to appreciate. It makes intuitive sense that we should not just focus on deficits in old age, but also consider positive outcome of aging. Further, as noted in the second reading by Holstein and Minkler, the concept of "successful aging" fulfills two important criteria for academic popularity: It is parsimonious and practical. It is parsimonious in that it takes the complex and challenging process of aging and makes that process seem manageable and understandable. It is practical in that it offers tangible suggestions for both gerontologists and for the elderly as to how they might contribute to good health and active engagement in later life. But, as Holstein and Minkler emphasize, parsimony and practicality do not always equate with truth.

For Holstein and Minkler, aging is a complex process guided by much more than just individual decisions. Depending on class, race, and gender, people's experience of old age derives from their opportunities and constraints throughout the life span. The vision of all senior citizens frolicking at golf courses and ski areas is embedded with bias toward those who have access to such recreation, and those who have not had to spend their lives exhausting their bodies with hard physical labor. In their view, promoting a simple version of successful aging implicitly and unfairly promotes one exclusive idea of what a body and a life should become.

In their general perspectives on the last stage of the life span, these two readings offer different perspectives on what matters most for determining the outcomes of old age. For Rowe and Kahn, what matters most is the individual choices and behaviors accumulated through the life span. Their message is that we are in control of our old age. For Holstein and Minkler, what matters most is the structures and expectations of society. Their message is that society dictates old age, creating and recycling inequalities. In its essence, this is an important question for the study of life span development at any stage: Do we have individual agency, or are we subject to larger social forces?

Perspectives on that question have significant implications for both how we understand the life span, and how we think about trying to "improve" development. With a rapidly aging population, there is great interest in trying to make old age pleasant. Some of the fastest growing professions and industries cater to geriatric populations. So how should such professionals and industries focus their attention? Should they address individual choices, assuming with Rowe and Kahn that our personal actions craft our later life outcomes? Or should they address societal structures, assuming with Holstein and Minkler that the inequalities of society are reproduced and accentuated by valuing one model of "successful aging" as a universal good?

# Suggested Readings

P. Baltes and M. Baltes, "Savoir Vivre in Old Age," *National Forum* (Spring 1998).

P. Baltes and J. Smith, "New Frontiers in the Future of Aging: From Successful Aging of the Young Old to the Dilemmas of the Fourth Age," *Gerontology* (March/April 2003).

J. Birren and K. Schaie, *Handbook of the Psychology of Aging* (San Diego Academic Press, 1990).

R. Kahn, "On 'Successful Aging' and Well-Being: Self Rated Compared with Rowe and Kahn," *Gerontologist* (December 2002).

E. Phalon and E. Larson, "'Successful Aging'—Where Next?" *Journal of the American Geriatrics Society* (July 2002).

E. Phelan, L. Anderson, A. LaCroix, and E. Larson, "Older Adults' Views of 'Successful Aging'—How Do They Compare with Researchers' Definitions?" *Journal of the American Geriatrics Society* (February 2004).

J.W. Rowe and R.L. Kahn, *Successful Aging* (Pantheon, 1998).

W. Strawbridge, M. Wallhagen, and R. Cohen, "Successful Aging and Well-Being: Self-Rated Compared with Rowe and Kahn," *Gerontologist* (December 2002).

G.E. Vaillant, *Aging Well: Surprising Guideposts to a Happier Life from the Landmark Harvard Study of Adult Development* (Little, Brown, 2002).

# ISSUE 20

## Is Anti-Aging Technology a Cause for Societal Concern?

**YES: Chris Hackler,** from "Troubling Implications of Doubling the Human Lifespan," *Generations* (Winter 2001/2002)

**NO: Ronald Klatz,** from "Anti-Aging Medicine: Resounding, Independent Support for Expansion of an Innovative Medical Specialty," *Generations* (Winter 2001/2002)

### ISSUE SUMMARY

**YES:** Chris Hackler, professor of medical humanities, argues that advances in medical technology raise as many dilemmas as they solve. If we were able to extend the life span for many years, both society and individuals would face dramatic new challenges.

**NO:** Ronald Klatz, a medical doctor promoting anti-aging technology, asserts that any technology to extend the life span will be both welcome and safe.

The idea of extending the life span, creating technology that would allow people to live for years beyond the "natural" life expectancy, is often the stuff of science fiction. Technological enhancement of the life span is not currently a viable option, other than the occasional story about overly optimistic celebrities trying to use cryogenic compartments to extend and revive life. Using technology to significantly extend the life span, however, is a popular idea and something scientists both imagine and work to create.

The current estimate of the maximum life span, as calculated by doctors using knowledge about the durability of the human organism, is about 110 years. While few people actually reach their 110th birthday, the average life expectancy has been consistently increasing. A baby born this year, for example, could expect to live nearly 80 years based on statistical estimates. In contrast, a baby born in 1930 had a life expectancy of merely 60 years. Through the twentieth century, life expectancy in the United States increased by an amazing 50 percent.

The main reason for this increase is advances in public health. In past centuries, infectious diseases, some as simple as the flu, commonly took lives.

Today infectious diseases are much less common killers than chronic and degenerative diseases having to do with deterioration of the organs—heart disease, lung disease, cancer, etc. While there is still a desperate need for medical advances in these areas, Western medical technology is approaching a point where the focus can shift from developing more capacity to stop premature death, to focusing on ways of extending the "normal" life span.

Most serious research toward extending the life span has to this point focused on animal models. Making genetic manipulations to animals, which would be unethical in humans, scientists have been able to dramatically lengthen the life span of animals, including fruit flies and worms. There has also been much research attention devoted to the role of diet in longevity, with a suggestion that limiting certain types of caloric intake can extend the body's ability to function. While there does not seem to be any impending breakthrough that would offer individuals the opportunity to scientifically extend their own life span, the power of modern technology makes that offer a realistic possibility in the next century.

The mere possibility that we could use medical technology to artificially extend the life span raises a number of fascinating intellectual questions about human development. Many of the most important such questions are raised by Chris Hackler in his article. He raises provocative possibilities about what might happen to the family, marriage, work, politics, and more if scientists were able to develop ways of artificially extending life by several decades. At a general level, the potential implications raised by Hackler demonstrate how central our conception of the life span is to the institutions that matter for our lives. Our jobs, our personal lives, and our society depend heavily on an expectation that most people will progress through seven or eight decades of life in a relatively orderly fashion. Altering that expectation has the potential to alter not just the quantity of years we live, but the quality and content of those years. For Hackler, this possibility is troubling; while he recognizes that we would likely adapt to a significantly longer life span, he suggests that adaptation would not come without its challenges.

Ronald Klatz, on the other hand, sees nothing but excitement and promise in anti-aging technology. A medical doctor who has worked to encourage and support anti-aging research, Klatz suggests that the fundamental idea of extending the life span has moved from the fringes of medical science to the mainstream. He claims that researchers and society have come to recognize the potential of extending the life span and, in his mind, minimizing the suffering associated with old age. Note that much of Klatz's argument relates to potential benefits to the health care system—which seems overwhelmed by the growing legions of old people.

As you read these selections, think about these claims in the way they redefine old age. Is old age defined by years? Or is old age defined by health and productivity?

Chris Hackler  **YES**

# Troubling Implications of Doubling the Human Lifespan

**T**o live longer with fewer infirmities of old age is a nearly universal human desire. Several recent announcements have revived speculation that a significantly longer lifespan may finally be within reach. The demand for the technology that could accomplish this lengthening would be unprecedented—so also the problems it would create. Here, after a brief look at the reasons that lifespan extension may well be near, is an attempt to sketch in broad strokes some of the social displacement it might create.

## Increasing the Maximum Lifespan

Of course the average length of life, or life expectancy, has increased steadily over the past two centuries in Europe and North America, largely because of improvements in living standards, nutrition, and public health. Nevertheless, the maximum lifespan has remained fairly constant. With rare exceptions, the longest humans can live is about 110 years. Most animals face a similar limit, though it varies widely from species to species.

*Caloric reduction.* The maximum lifespan of laboratory animals is currently being expanded by a number of methods. An established and widely reproduced technique is reduction of the number of calories the animals are fed by about 40 percent. Lifespans have been lengthened by 30 percent to 50 percent or more in several species of short-lived animals such as fruit flies and nematodes (worms). Experiments with longer-lived primates are yielding preliminary results that suggest a similar effect. Experiments with humans have been considered, though it is difficult to imagine the general population practicing severe dietary restrictions over an entire lifetime.

*Genetic manipulation.* The diet itself may be unnecessary, however, if the effects of caloric restriction can be produced by genetic manipulation. A large step in this direction was announced in December of 2000 in the journal *Science.* Under the direction of Stephen L. Helfand of the University of Connecticut Health Center in Farmington, researchers accidentally disabled a gene

From *Generations,* Winter 2001-02, pp. 15–19. Copyright © 2001 by American Society on Aging. Reprinted by permission.

that they then learned directs cells to make a protein that helps move nutrients across the cell membrane. The average lifespans of the fruit flies with the altered gene, which the researchers dubbed "indy," for I'm Not Dead Yet, almost doubled, from 37 to 71 days, and the maximum span increased from 70 to 110 days. It appears that they "inadvertently created the effect of caloric restriction genetically," Helfand said in *The New York Times*. If this proves to be correct, he added, a drug could be produced that would retard aging without the necessity of a restricted diet. The fact that only a single gene is involved is especially exciting Steven Austad of the University of Iowa told the reporter, since "it gives us something quite specific that we can look at quite easily."

*Doubling the lifespan.* Impressive results are being produced in several other laboratories using different methods. Thomas Johnson at the University of Colorado has produced strains of the transparent roundworm *C elegans* that live twice the normal lifespan. At McGill University, in the lab of Siegfried Hekemi, roundworms have been produced that live five times the normal lifespan. To translate that into human terms, it would be comparable to a human lifespan of 400 to 500 years. Of course, the possibility of transferring such results to humans is uncertain and attempts to do so would raise complex ethical issues of experimentation with human subjects. Nevertheless, several leading researchers believe that we will eventually be able to double the human lifespan. This figure, though certainly speculative, appears to be the one most commonly accepted as possible within a few generations and is the one we will assume for the present discussion.

*Slowing aging.* For simplicity of illustration, we are assuming the longevity intervention to be a form of germ-line enhancement or at least an intervention delivered early in life. (The issue of timing of the intervention is interesting but will not be explored here.) Because it is the rate of aging that such an intervention affects, at age 100 one would presumably look and feel much the same as one does now at 50 or 60, if not better. Genetically altered fruit flies that live the equivalent of 150 human years are remarkably active and robust in their old age. In addition, research on aging is telling us much about age-related disorders. Learning why normal cells age should also tell us why malignant ones do not—meaning a cure for cancer might finally be possible. There is also much optimism about chronic and degenerative diseases such as arthritis and dementia.

*Mythic desire.* Gaining control over the aging process is a goal that is expressed in the myths and legends of many cultures, beginning with the first known epic, *Gilgamesh,* and typified in modern times by the search for a fountain of youth. Undoubtedly, significantly prolonged life would be highly desired. A little reflection also suggests that it would produce profound consequences in every aspect of life, requiring social adjustments unprecedented in their scope and complexity. It is hard to think of a single human institution that would be unaffected, from family life through government and international relations.

# Potential Social Issues and Consequences

We must be circumspect in developing a technology with the potential for such pervasive cultural dislocation. Some theologians see danger in attempts to assume godlike powers and refashion the natural order. Do we have the wisdom to tamper with the exquisite balance of nature that has evolved over the ages? Can we possibly foresee the consequences of altering our genetic inheritance? Do we have the right to unsettle so profoundly the social conditions under which succeeding generations will live? Will individuals be happier on balance if they live longer, or might life become less precious and meaningful with death further removed? Would boredom and ennui become common after 100 years? Would suicide be an option if chronic disease, stroke, or personal misfortune were to destroy the quality of a much longer life? These are some of the compelling issues that must be addressed as we are developing the means to extend life significantly. Following is a brief look at some of the issues that might arise and some of the social institutions that would be affected by doubling the human lifespan.

*Access.*   One of the most basic ethical and legal questions is, Would access to life-extending technology be a right that individuals could assert or a privilege that society cold confer or withhold? How would we make decisions about who would receive this benefit? Would it be included in medical insurance plans? If so, in Medicaid? We are committed to saving every life in the emergency room without regard to ability to pay; would this commitment entail extending every life? Would this issue become a new cause of the right-to-life movement, with a potential for social divisiveness even greater than abortion and euthanasia?

*Marriage.*   The nuclear family would face stress from several directions. As life expectancy has risen over the past century, so has the divorce rate. There is reason to think that this trend would continue or even accelerate with lifespan extension. The birthrate would have to be controlled, and a longer life would remain after child rearing, further loosening the bond of children. Women facing a longer lifetime of potential dependency would want careers of their own, making it easier for them to leave an inadequate marriage. Tolerable marriages that have grown unsatisfying are sometimes preserved out of inertia or because they provide comfort and predictability, but if forty to fifty years remain, more of these marriages will be ended. Slowing the rate of aging should prolong the period of sexual attractiveness and desire, while at the same time giving boredom and overfamiliarity longer to develop, posing a threat to marital fidelity. Since short-term relationships of four or five years are usually unsatisfying and do not allow for the time necessary to rear children, marriage may survive as a long-term commitment of thirty years or so, but its future would be unclear to say the least.

*The family.*   Doubling the lifespan would change several other aspects of family life as well. Since the period of fertility would presumably be extended, siblings or half siblings could be forty or fifty years apart in age. The sibling relationship would be profoundly altered by such age differentials. The same can be said of the parent-child relationship, which changes as the relative age difference narrows. A son or daughter of 50 relates to a parent of 75 in a much different manner than a child of 15 relates to a parent of 40. The relationship would certainly undergo further evolution as their respective ages reached 100 and 125 and each was married to a third spouse. Transfers of wealth across the generations would probably become more complicated, with an inheritance coming only in one's old age, if at all. Families have already changed significantly in the past fifty years, and the pace of change will only accelerate as more people live longer.

*Work.* Work is an important source of identity and status as well as income. It is doubtful that many would want to retire at 70 if they could expect to be healthy and active for another 70 years. Those who did could not be supported for their remaining life by Social Security and pension payments. Much longer careers seem inevitable but will present a number of problems. Assuming that significant numbers of executives, managers, and professionals remain in their chosen careers, they may be able to amass great wealth and come to dominate corporations, universities, and other institutions. Without significant economic expansion, there would be fewer openings for individuals entering the workforce. Those able to secure a position could find promotional ladders blocked. A shorter workweek would be helpful, but only if overall productivity and growth did not suffer as a result.

*New careers.* Policies and programs would possibly be needed to induce workers to change positions voluntarily every fifteen years or so and even to adopt a new career every forty years. Such policies would provide hope for advancement throughout the workforce, would promote new ideas and fresh approaches in the workplace, and would forestall boredom and burnout in the workers themselves. Clearly there would have to be much more lateral mobility than we are accustomed to today. It is hard to imagine enough strata of status and responsibility to accommodate continual upward mobility through a work life of 80 to 100 years. It would be especially challenging to devise a system that encouraged starting entirely new careers, presumably at the bottom of the career ladder, at no reduction in salary.

*Consolidation of power.* We have seen that extreme longevity in the workplace could allow some people to amass great wealth and power while distorting the normal pace of institutional growth and change. Similar dangers may exist in the political arena. Individuals would have more than a century to consolidate political power, which could pose a threat to good government or even to democracy itself. Some states might prosper while others were neglected if the chairs of congressional committees such as Appropriations were occupied for decades. Under the U.S. Constitution, federal judges serve for life. Justices of the Supreme Court sitting on the bench for a hundred years would have a powerful influence on the shape of social institutions. Term limitations would surely become more popular if politicians lived twice as long!

*Penal system.* We will also need to consider our system of judicial punishment. With twice as long to get into trouble, overcrowding could be a serious problem in our jails and prisons. A life sentence would be a much harsher punishment to the criminal and much more costly to society. Pressure for capital punishment might increase. It is conceivable that age-retarding technology would only be provided to those who had stayed out of trouble until their eighteenth birthday, to avoid producing long-lived sociopaths.

*Right to die.* From the individual perspective, would it be a duty to continue the long journey once it is begun? Genetic medicine hopes to cure or prevent the diseases and infirmities of old age but surely will not rid us entirely of them. Must we live twice as long with strokes, arthritis, or Alzheimer's disease, or could we cut short the prolonged suffering? The claim was made, erroneously it turns out, that the first artificial heart recipient, Barney Clark, was given a key to turn off his new artificial heart in the event that his prolonged life turned out to be unacceptable to him. We might have to consider a similar way out for people who find that they have purchased a double dose of misery rather than prolonged happiness.

# Global Concerns

All of the preceding issues are complex and of great importance for our individual and collective well-being, but we are an ingenious species and have adapted to many changes in the past. There is some basis for optimism that we could meet these challenges and devise a new order of family, commercial, and social relationships that would be rich and satisfying. But we are not talking about a few people, or a few wealthy and under populated countries. The most serious concern can be expressed as a stark dilemma: Overpopulation would be an overwhelming problem if all have access to the technology; injustice would be a burning issue, and armed conflict a possibility, if some did not. Herein lie the most complex, grave, and truly recalcitrant social, ethical, and political problems.

*Population pressures.* It seems obvious that if people lived twice as long and continued their current procreative behavior, we would face an ecological catastrophe. Deforestation and overuse of land and water supplies could result in mass starvation and pandemics of infectious diseases. The Earth's resources simply could not support such numbers. Surely we would devastate the environment within three generations (old-scale generations, that is) if access to the technology were unrestricted. Attitudes and patterns of behavior do change, but a quick change in reproductive behavior is a risky bet. There are deep cultural and especially religious influences on these patterns of behavior that so far have shown great resistance to change, even in the face of current population pressures and ecological nightmares.

*Restricting access.* Hoe might we consider controlling global access to age-retarding technology? Well, we might just restrict it to ourselves and our friends in other developed countries with stable populations, much as we currently restrict (or try to) the export of sensitive scientific and technological information. Such a policy would surely be excoriated as genetic elitism, and whatever moral leadership we had been able to earn in the New World Order would be dissipated on this one issue. After all, we are talking about desires of mythic proportions, expressed in the myths of many cultures, not just our own.

A second possibility would be to make the technology available only to those countries that adopt vigorous population controls, or alternatively to offer it without regard to nationality, but to condition access upon accepting some norm of procreation—no children, say, or perhaps one. Surgical sterilization could even be made a prerequisite. Such a policy would have some rational basis in attempting to control the clearly foreseeable consequences of universal access while making its benefits available to those who would not produce those consequences. I believe it is debatable whether or not such a policy would be just, but there is little doubt that it would be perceived as unjust by those denied access, in their view denied access because they will not defy cultural attitudes or religious teachings.

*Enforcement of restrictions.*   We have been considering ways to restrict access to age-retarding technology, but we should ask whether any restrictions could be enforced. Our past experience with prohibition and our current problems with illegal drugs illustrate how difficult it can be to restrict access to strongly desired goods. One can imagine moonshine youth stills in the rain forests with networks of bootleggers supplying the rich and adventuresome of all countries. One can imagine offshore destinations where "youth treatments" are legal, or cruise ships that offer anti-aging interventions much as they offer gambling in international waters.

*Prohibition.*   One initially plausible position would be that we should not allow technology to be developed to double the human lifespan until population pressures are clearly under control or we have established colonies in outer space. The reasoning could be distilled as follows: (1) the consequences of widespread access to the technology would be an ecological disaster of unparalleled magnitude, (2) there is no ethically and politically acceptable way to restrict access to the technology. Therefore (3) nobody should have access to it. But (4) if it is developed there is no practically effective way to prohibit access to it. This, (5) it should not be developed.

*Reality.*   This is without doubt an overly simple and even quixotic argument. We certainly do not want to stop all research on aging. The same studies that might eventually provide us with the means to double the human lifespan will also produce more immediate benefits: greater control over disease and disability in the later years, perhaps modest increases in life expectancy. We do not want to jeopardize these incremental gains by banning the research that would produce them. Banning scientific research is intrinsically repugnant anyway.

*Compromise.*   The wisest course is usually a compromise, and I suspect it will be here as well. We could continue basic research into aging and allow future applied research with the stipulation that any human intervention would be incremental, aimed only at, say, a twenty-year extension for the first two or three generations. Individuals and institutions would have more time to adapt to longer lifespans, and if there is too much stress, the damage would be limited. If adaptation is successful and large-scale social and ethical problems are avoided, the span could be increased by another increment. It is not at all clear who might design and administer these controls or how they could be enforced, or who would make the decision about proceeding, but the general approach seems sound. Even a modest initial gain in lifespan should be seen as a great benefit to the first generations to receive it.

# NO

Ronald Klatz

## Anti-Aging Medicine: Resounding, Independent Support for Expansion of an Innovative Medical Specialty

The World Health Organization estimates that by the year 2025, we will be a planet of 8 billion residents. At that time, the number of people age 65 and older will reach 800 million—one of every ten persons. We will also enjoy, worldwide, an average life expectancy of 73 years. In order to avert the financially, socially, and medically burdensome task of caring for the swelling aged population, rapid adoption of safe and effective diagnostic and treatment processes that can improve the quality of life in these extended years is a critical imperative to maintain the well-being of society in the twenty-second century.

In 1993, a dozen pioneering physicians and scientists met to create the medical specialty of anti-aging medicine. To accomplish a compaign of education and advocacy to advance the acceptance of anti-aging medicine around the globe, we formed the American Academy of Anti-Aging Medicine. As the academy founder, I present to you the original, official definition of anti-aging medicine:

> Anti aging medicine is a medical specialty founded on the application of advanced scientific and medical technologies for the early detection, prevention, treatment, and reversal of age-related dysfunction, disorders, and diseases. It is a healthcare model promoting innovative science and research to prolong the healthy lifespan in humans. As such, anti-aging medicine is based on principles of sound and responsible medical care that are consistent with those applied in other preventive health specialties.

Anti-aging medicine has matured into a prestigious medical field that has become recognized by independent public policy organizations. In 2001, the World Future Society—a nonprofit educational and scientific organization founded in 1966 as a neutral clearinghouse exploring the impact of social and technological developments on the future—heralded anti-aging medicine as an effective solution to the growing aging population worldwide. The World Future Society notes that "geriatrics may . . . be suffering from competition arising in a new health-care subspecialty: anti-aging." Citing an "aging baby-boom generation [that] is bringing a potential medical crisis to the fore and a critical

From *Generations*, Winter 2001-02, pp. 59–62. Copyright © 2001 by American Society on Aging. Reprinted by permission.

lack of doctors who specialize in treating elderly patients," the World Future Society refers to anti-aging medicine as a potential answer, embracing "a realignment of priorities from the problems of the elderly to the opportunities of longer lives." The society also notes that the number of members of the American Academy of Anti-Aging Medicine and certified anti-aging physicians and health practitioners is rising steadily, while the number of certified geriatricians is on the decline.

Similarly, the highly respected Global Aging Initiative of the Center for Strategic and International Studies proclaimed its support of anti-aging medicine in its "Summary Report of the Co-chairmen and Findings and Recommendations of the CSIS Commission on Global Aging." Among the report's conclusions were that governments should "pursue an integrated strategy designed to raise productivity by . . . providing financial support, and creating a favorable tax and regulatory environment for research and development in the new services and health sectors, including disease prevention, anti-aging medicine, and other innovative technology."

Indeed, the utilization of advanced medical technologies is a cornerstone of anti-aging medicine. The American Academy of Anti-Aging Medicine offers a hopeful and attainable model for medicine in the new millennium founded on the dramatic advancements offered by the biotech revolution. The model identifies a continued and expanding arena of discovery and advancement in our understanding of ways to mitigate age-related disability and disease and is based on what the academy calls "technodemography." As conceived by the organization, technodemography is the application of modern biotechnology to the issues of diagnosis, prevention, and intervention in aging, such that one may extrapolate future progress in human aging based on the application of innovative medical interventions. The model incorporates the impact that five key areas in biomedical technology can be expected to exert on gains in human longevity and assumes a doubling of the amount of medical technology and knowledge in this area every three and one-half years after the year 2000. The five key areas are as follows:

- Genetic engineering, including work with stem cells. Advancements would allow scientists to alter genetic make-up to eradicate disease and would permit development of a supply source for human cells, tissues, and organs for use in acute emergency care as well as treatment of chronic, debilitating disease.
- Cloning. This technique holds tremendous promise in producing consistent sources of organs, tissues, and proteins for biomedical use and transplantation in humans.
- "Nanotechnology." This form of technology would enable scientists to use tiny tools to manipulate human biology at its most basic levels.
- Artificial organs. Advancement in this area would make replacement body parts readily available.
- Nerve-impulse continuity (brain and spinal cord). Progress in this area would allow nerve signal transmission to be maintained without interruption, despite physical trauma.

Recently, ardent critics have actually begun to gravitate toward adoption of anti-aging medicine—first, by renaming it so that the concept appears to be their original creation. *Longevity medicine, successful aging, healthy aging, optimal aging,* and *aging gracefully,* among other synonyms, are being substituted by conventional gerontologists for the term *anti-aging.* The medical premise of these alternative terms—incorporating "all means that would extend healthy life . . . as well as advanced medical care and new discoveries . . . and even manipulating . . . genetic factors"—is completely identical to the original model of anti-aging medicine established nine years ago by the founders of anti-aging medicine, the physicians, health professionals, and scientists of the American Academy of Anti-Aging Medicine.

In its continued effort to absorb what it cannot deny, the gerontological establishment has expressed a number of conclusions about anti-aging medicine that are presented below, along with a response to each that represents the position of the American Academy of Anti-Aging Medicine:

- "Some people may prefer to trivialize 'anti-aging,' but it has been a very important part of medical research. . . . Many of today's anti-aging therapies are the same ones that physicians and scientists were developing in the 1920s and 1930s."

*Response.* This statement indicates the important presence of the anti-aging specialty in the healthcare spectrum. In the past, the gerontological establishment has gone to great lengths to misrepresent the scientific validity of hormone replacement therapy, which has been used in one approach or another for the past seventy years. In actuality, hormone replacement therapy, performed judiciously and administered in appropriate doses by qualified anti-aging physicians, has been found to improve health by thousands of peer-reviewed research studies.

- "Anti-aging' medicine could be simply defined as any intervention that delays the development of age-dependent pathology and other adverse age-related changes that are not officially listed as diseases."

*Response.* This variant definition of anti-aging medicine is consistent with the original, official definition stated above. We are pleased that the gerontological establishment has at last grasped this concept.

- "Further extension [of human life expectancy] will almost certainly require biomedical intervention to delay age-related pathology and disease. . . . Clearly, modern technology has made great strides toward improving human health and enabling greater numbers of people to survive into old age."

*Response.* A statement by the Board of Editors of *Scientific American* makes the point well: "Thanks to modern technology and medicine, people have taken much more control over their differential survival. Ills are not the barriers they once were. Our technology may exert the greatest influence."

All diseases fall into three categories. The first two—inherited genetic disease and infectious disease—account for only to percent of the cost for treating all disease in America. Ninety percent of all healthcare dollars are spent on extraordinary care in the last two to three years of life. Indeed, the leading causes of death have undergone a profound shift. Because of improvements in sanitation and infection control since the turn of the twentieth century, Americans are now losing their health and lives to heart disease (31.4 percent), cancer (23.3 percent), and stroke (6.9 percent). These three diseases, known collectively as the degenerative diseases of aging, swallow 50 percent of the U.S. healthcare budget. One hundred million Americans are currently being treated for one or another degenerative disease at a healthcare cost of more than $700 billion per year. If we really want to make an impact on healthcare in this country and in the world, we must focus on the degenerative diseases of aging. If we can slow aging, we can eliminate more than 50 percent of all diseases overnight. We can alter this dreadful course by preventing, delaying, or reversing the diseases associated with aging.

Anti-aging medicine—the application of any therapy or modality that delivers very early detection, prevention, treatment, or reversal of aging-related dysfunction and disease, thus enhancing the quality and extending the length of the human lifespan—is the most important new model for healthcare for this new millennium. Anti-aging medicine is the following:

- It is scientific. Anti-aging diagnostic and treatment practices are supported by scientific evidence and therefore cannot be branded as anecdotal.
- It is evidence-based. Anti-aging medicine is based on an orderly process for acquiring data in order to formulate a scientific and objective assessment upon which effective treatment is assigned.
- Is well-documented by peer-reviewed journals such as *Aging, American Journal of Cardiology, Journal of the American Geriatrics Society,* and *Journal of the American Medical Association,* among many others.

The benefits of anti-aging medicine are resounding and clear. As a global population, we are experiencing leaps in life expectancy, decreases in death rates from the leading causes of death (heart disease, cancer, and stroke), and, in the United States, we are seeing a decrease in the use of nursing home care. Most important, accessibility to quality medical care is improving. Clearly, anti-aging medicine has made a distinct impression on evolving healthcare to the betterment of the public at large.

As the German physicist and Nobel Laureate Max Planck once remarked, "An important scientific innovation rarely makes its way by gradually winning over and converting its opponents. . . . Its opponents gradually die out and the growing generation is familiar with the idea from the beginning."

It is gratifying that, in the ninth year since its formal beginnings, anti-aging medicine is gaining recognition from the gerontological establishment. For 2002, the proponents of anti-aging medicine—physicians, health professionals, scientists, and academics—are hopeful that we will continue to close the philosophical gap between us and our gerontology colleagues. Our goal is to create widespread adoption of an innovative model of healthcare that demonstrates near-term potential to elevate the quality of life, and extend the length of life, for all.

# POSTSCRIPT

## Is Anti-Aging Technology a Cause for Societal Concern?

In Erik Erikson's well-known representation of the life span as a series of psychosocial crises, old age is defined by the struggle between integrity and despair. This intuitively appealing idea is that in our later years we move toward accepting the inevitability of death by undertaking a life review, looking back and feeling integrity based on one's life experience or feeling despair based on disappointment and regret. Does our fascination with the possibility of extending the life span signify a collective integrity—wanting more of what we feel good about? Or does it represent a social despair—a feeling of regret such that life needs something more?

These existential questions nicely dovetail with issues that overlap all stages of the life span. Hackler raises practical questions about marriage and the family—demonstrating that controversies about traditional marriage and family structure may be about more than just values. He also provocatively notes that power and privilege in society are managed, to some degree, by the nature of the human organism. He even cites implications for globalization, noting that technology to extend life expectancy would likely provide further advantages to wealthy citizens and nations. Extending the life span would change the structures of society, which would change the way we think, which would change the way we develop.

For Katz, however, the only considered changes are positive. Yes, he acknowledges, society would change. But from his perspective, society—particularly in the challenge of dealing with an increasingly elderly population—needs to change. He suggests that current health care capacity is in the process of being overwhelmed by increasingly life expectancy. His solution is to focus on technologies that will resist aging.

But one must assume that even if we are able to significantly lengthen life, people would still get old at some point. Would anti-aging technology just delay the inevitable? And would that delay be worth profoundly disrupting the fine balance of contemporary society? Or is the balance of life span development always about dealing with change?

Certainly the study of life span development is always changing. At a practical level, what is defined as old age has already shifted due to the gradual improvement in public health. Further, the field of gerontology, devoted to studying the final stages of the life span, has become an essential contributor to the way we do and will live. At a more abstract level, the meanings we assign to old age are also changing. As scientific advances make life extension an intriguingly realistic possibility, we no longer are allowed the assumption that our lives are part of a larger cycle. Perhaps the study of life span development will itself change to focus more on the quantity, rather than the qualities, of life. Depending on your perspective in thinking about this controversy, it is important to ask whether such a change could be a good thing.

## Suggested Readings

P. Baltes, "The Aging Mind: Potential Limits," *Gerontologist* (October 1993).

D. Callahan, "A New Debate on an Old Topic," *Hastings Center Report* (July–August 2003).

D. Gems, "Is More Life Always Better? The New Biology of Aging and the Meaning of Life," *Hastings Center Report* (July–August 2003).

E. Juengst, R. Binstock, M. Mehlman, S. Post, and P. Whitehouse, "Biogerontology, 'Anti-Aging Medicine,' and the Challenges of Human Enhancement," *Hastings Center Report* (July–August 2003).

S. Katz, "Growing Older Without Aging? Positive Aging, Anti-Ageism, and Anti-Aging," *Generations* (Winter 2001).

H. Moody, "Who's Afraid of Life Extension?" *Generations* (Winter 2001).

# Contributors to This Volume

## EDITOR

**ANDREW M. GUEST** is a developmental psychologist and faculty member in the department of social and behavioral sciences at the University of Portland. He has research experience investigating development in impoverished communities, studying culture in relation to social development during middle childhood, and evaluating the influence of extracurricular activities during adolescence. He also has experience working with programs focused on enhancing life span development for disadvantaged populations in the United States, Malawi, Mexico, and Angola. He received a B.A. from Kenyon College in psychology, an M.S. from Miami University in sports studies, and a M.A. and Ph.D. from the University of Chicago's Committee on Human Development.

## STAFF

| | |
|---|---|
| Larry Loeppke | Managing Editor |
| Jill Peter | Senior Developmental Editor |
| Nichole Altman | Developmental Editor |
| Beth Kundert | Production Manager |
| Jane Mohr | Project Manager |
| Tara McDermott | Design Coordinator |
| Bonnie Coakley | Editorial Assistant |
| Lori Church | Permissions |
| Julie J. Keck | Senior Marketing Manager |
| Mary S. Klein | Marketing Communications Specialist |
| Alice M. Link | Marketing Coordinator |
| Tracie A. Kammerude | Senior Marketing Assistant |

# AUTHORS

**ROY F. BAUMEISTER** is a member of the social psychology faculty at Florida State University. A Ph.D. from Princeton University, Baumeister is an expert in self and identity and the author of several texts, including the recently published *The Cultural Animal: Human Nature, Meaning, and Social Life.*

**MARIAH BLAKE** is an assistant editor at the Columbia Journalism Review.

**JOHN T. BRUER** is president of the James McDonnell Foundation, which awards millions of dollars annually in support of biomedical, science, education, and international projects. He has a Ph.D. in philosophy from Rockefeller University.

**GWEN BROUDE** is a professor of psychology at Vassar College, and has a Ph.D. in social anthropology from Harvard University. Her books include *Growing Up: A Cross-Cultural Encyclopedia.*

**JENNIFER D. CAMPBELL** is a professor in the department of psychology at the University of British Columbia. Her research touches topics related to self-concept, perfectionism, and adjustment.

**PAUL EHRLICH** is a professor of population studies at Stanford University, president of the Center for Conservation Biology, co-founder of the field of coevolution, and a pioneer in the development of cultural considerations for growing concerns about overpopulation.

**JULIE JUOLA EXLINE** is a member of the department of psychology at Case Western Reserve University. Dr. Exline specializes in research about religious and spiritual struggles as they relate to morality and humanity's relationship with God.

**MARCUS FELDMAN** is a professor of biological sciences at Stanford University, with primary research focusing on the interaction of biological and cultural evolution.

**JONATHAN L. FREEDMAN** is a psychology professor at the University of Toronto and has focused a great deal of his work on the affects of media violence on aggression.

**MICHAEL FUMENTO** is an author, journalist, and attorney specializing in science and health issues. He has written for numerous newspapers and magazines, and his work has been nominated for the National Magazine Award.

**FRANK F. FURSTENBERG, JR.,** is a professor of sociology and a research associate in the Population Studies Center at the University of Pennsylvania. He is chair of the MacArthur Foundation Research Network on the Transition to Adulthood and co-editor of *On the Frontiers of Adulthood: Theory, Research, and Public Policy.*

**HOWARD GARDNER** is professor of cognition and education at the Harvard Graduate School of Education and founder of Project Zero, a research group to aid development of personalized curriculum designed for multiple intelligences (the theory Gardner is most known for). Winner of numerous honors in the fields of education and psychology, Garner is also the author of more than 20 books.

LINDA S. GOTTFREDSON is a professor of education and co-director of the Delaware-Johns Hopkins Project for the Study of Intelligence and Society. She has published for more than 30 years on the topics of intelligence and health and intelligence and social equality.

GILBERT J. GRANT, M.D., is associate professor at the New York University School of Medicine and director of obstetric anesthesia at New York University Medical Center.

DAVE GROSSMAN, a lieutenant colonel, is a former West Point psychology instructor, professor of military science, director of the Killology Research Group, and an expert in the field of human aggression and the roots of violence.

CHRIS HACKLER is a professor and the first director of the division of medical humanities at the University of Arkansas for Medical Sciences. He has a Ph.D. in philosophy from the University of North Carolina and has written and lectured extensively on the topic of advance directives and end-of-life decisions.

JUDITH RICH HARRIS has psychology degrees from Brandeis and Harvard Universities and has authored several textbooks in developmental psychology, most notably *The Child* and *Infant and Child*. She is an expert in child environments, parenting and the nature vs. nurture question.

JENNIFER HEDLUND teaches criminology and criminal justice at Central Connecticut State University and has a Ph.D. from Michigan State University. She specializes in theories of intelligence.

MARTHA B. HOLSTEIN has taught at DePaul University and has a Ph.D. in medical ethics from the University of Texas Medical Branch.

BRUCE HOOD is a professor in experimental psychology at the University of Bristol and a previous associate professor in the department of psychology at Harvard University. Dr. Hood's primary research addresses cognitive development from a neuroscience perspective.

NEIL HUMPHREY is the program director of the master's degree in educational psychology at the University of Manchester and has published especially on the role of self-esteem and self-concept in managing developmental dyslexia.

JOLI JENSEN is a professor in communications at the University of Tulsa and has researched American culture and social thought, most recently in her book *Is Art Good for Us?*

ROBERT L. KAHN is a professor emeritus in psychology and public health at the University of Michigan, where he also founded the Institute for Social Research. A former fellow at the Center for Advanced Study in the Behavioral Sciences at Stanford University, Dr. Kahn's research has concentrated on organizational behavior and aging.

MICHAEL KIMMEL is a sociologist who is well known for his work on men and masculinity. His most recent book is *Manhood in America: A Cultural History,* and he is the national spokesperson for the National Organization for Men Against Sexism. Dr. Kimmel is a professor in the department of sociology at the State University of New York at Stony Brook.

RONALD KLATZ, M.D., is the physician founder and president of the American Academy of Anti-Aging Medicine and author of several texts about life-enhancing medical care.

HAROLD S. KOPLEWICZ, M.D., is professor of child and adolescent psychiatry and professor of pediatrics at the New York University Medical Center. Dr. Koplewicz is known as an advocate for children with mental illness and serves as editor-in-chief of the *Journal of Child and Adolescent Psychopharmacology.*

JOACHIM I. KRUEGER is on faculty in the department of psychology at Brown University and specializes in self-perception, particularly as it relates to the egocentric processes of self-enhancement and social projection.

JONATHAN LEO is associate professor of anatomy at the College of Osteopathic Medicine of the Pacific. He is editor-in-chief of *Human Sciences and Services.*

MEL LEVINE is founder of All Kinds of Minds, an institute for understanding different types of learning. Formerly an associate professor of pediatrics at Harvard Medical School, Dr. Levine is currently a professor and director of the Clinical Center for the Study of Development and Learning at the University of North Carolina School of Medicine.

MICHAEL LINTON is head of the division of music theory and composition at Middle Tennessee State University. He writes on issues of contemporary music and culture.

GARY MARCUS is a faculty member in psychology and neural science at New York University and an advocate for the developing field of cognitive neuroscience. His forthcoming book is *The Algebraic Mind.*

SHERRI McCARTHY is professor of educational psychology at Northern Arizona University and a former Fulbright scholar.

MARSHALL MILLER, a speaker, trainer, and writer, is the founder of the Alternatives to Marriage Project and co-author of *Unmarried to Each Other.*

MEREDITH MINKLER is a faculty member in the School of Public Health at the University of California, Berkeley, with a specialty in health and social behavior.

DAVID G. MYERS is a social psychologist with research interests in happiness and spiritual well-being. A professor of psychology at Hope College, Meyers has written several popular psychology textbooks and multiple other scholarly books.

STEVEN PINKER is a specialist in language and cognition and professor of psychology at Harvard University. His books include *How the Mind Works* and *The Blank Slate.*

**C. CYBELE RAVER** is a developmental psychologist, professor at The Harris School for Public Policy at the University of Chicago and director of the school's Center for Human Potential and Public Policy. Dr. Raver's research focuses primarily on the well-being of children and families.

**LENNART RIGHARD** is a former senior pediatrician at the University of Lund in Sweden.

**JOHN W. ROWE, M.D.,** was formerly a professor of medicine and founding director of the Division on Aging at Harvard Medical School. He is currently chairman and CEO of Aetna, Inc., one of the nation's leading health care organizations.

**CYNTHIA RUSSETT** is professor of history at Yale University and an expert on the history of American women and intellectual life in the twentieth century.

**GORDON L. SHAW** is professor emeritus in physics at the University of California, Irvine, and a member of the MIND Institute. He is the author of *Keeping Mozart in Mind*.

**DORIAN SOLOT,** a speaker, educator, writer, and doula is the executive director of the Alternatives to Marriage Project and co-author of *Unmarried to Each Other*.

**CHRISTINA HOFF SOMMERS** is a former professor at Clark University with a Ph.D. in philosophy from Brandeis University. Hoff Sommers is a resident scholar at the American Enterprise Institute and has written widely about feminism, psychology, and American culture.

**ELIZABETH S. SPELKE** is the Marshall L. Berkman Professor of Psychology at Harvard University, and is an award winning scholar with particular expertise in infant cognitive development.

**ROBERT J. STERNBERG** is dean of the School of Arts and Sciences at Tufts University, and a former professor of psychology and education in the department of psychology at Yale University. His many books include *Practical Intelligence, Successful Intelligence,* and *Satisfaction in Close Relationships*.

**THE U.S. DEPARTMENT OF HEALTH AND HUMAN SERVICES** is the U.S. government agency responsible for protecting the health of all Americans and providing essential human services, especially for those who are least able to help themselves. The department funds and facilitates more than 300 programs designed to serve these aims.

**KATHLEEN D. VOHS** is a research chair in marketing science and consumer psychology at the University of British Columbia and holds a Ph.D. in social psychology from Dartmouth College.

**LINDA J. WAITE** is professor of sociology, director of the Center on Aging, and co-director of the Center on Parents, Children and Work at the University of Chicago. Dr. Waite has done extensive demographic research in the areas of family structure and aging.

**THOMAS FRANKLIN WATERS** is a faculty member teaching criminal justice at Northern Arizona University.

**ZERO TO THREE** is a not-for-profit organization working to promote the healthy development of infants and toddlers.

**EDWARD F. ZIGLER** is emeritus director of the Zigler Center in Child Development and Social Policy at Yale University. Zigler is the author of several books, including *Children's Play* and *The First Three Years and Beyond*, and was closely involved with developing the federal Head Start preschool program.

# Index

AAUW. *See* American Association of University Women
Abecedarian Project, 164
academic skills: emphasis on, in at-risk preschool children, 154–72; and self-esteem, in school-age children, 180–202
achievement gap, 159–61, 168
ACL. *See* Americans Changing Lives
activity level, in later adulthood, 380–82
ADD/ADHD. *See* attention deficit disorder/attention deficit hyperactivity disorder
adolescence: risks for boys versus girls during, 232–46; violent media and aggressive behavior during, 251–63
Adorno, Theodor, 283
adulthood: antidepressant use during, 270–83; career success in, 323–41; changing notions of, 294–95; marriage during, 306–18; preparation for/transition to, 288–98; religion in, 346–66. *See also* later adulthood
aggression, during adolescence, violent media and, 251–63
aging: anti-aging technology and, 396–406; successful, 374–91
Allman, John, 11
Alternatives to Marriage Project, 315
altruism, religion and, 352–54
American Academy of Anti-Aging Medicine, 403, 404, 405
American Association of University Women (AAUW), 236–37
Americans Changing Lives (ACL), 381
anti-aging technology, 396–406
antidepressants, use during young adulthood, 270–83

Aquinas, Thomas, on differences between men and women, 57–58
Ardrey, Robert, 4
Aristotle, on differences between men and women, 57
Armstrong, Thomas, 207
at-risk children: academic skills emphasized in preschool for, 154–72; during adolescence, 232–46
attention deficit disorder/attention deficit hyperactivity disorder (ADD/ADHD), 207–24; brain scan for, 215–17; case studies of, 222; diagnosis of, 218, 222–23; feminism and, 208; gene therapy for, 223–24; lack of medical evidence for, 217–20; maternal cocaine use and, 72–73; as medical disorder, 207–8; medications for, 209–24; public school system and, 209
Atwater, Lee, 347

Bailey, Susan McGee, 246
Barkley, Russell, 208, 209, 210, 211, 217
Barth, Hilary, 119
Baumeister, Roy F., on self-esteem in school-age children, 180–95
behavior: attention deficit disorder/attention deficit hyperactivity disorder and, 207–24; proper, 34; situational, 29–30
behavioral genetics, and childhood behavior, 38, 41
behavioral phenome, 4–12
Benzer, Seymour, 219
beta-endorphins, in childbirth, 89
Biederman, Joseph, 218
Blake, Mariah, on "crack babies," 80–82

Boettcher, Wendy, 140
brain: in attention deficit hyperactivity disorder, 215–17; development and functions of, 14–16; differences between male and female, 53, 59–60; effects of music on, 142–43
brain plasticity, 13–14
Branden, Nathaniel, 182–83
breastfeeding, 89
Bridwell, Maggie, 275, 276
Broca, Paul, 59
Bronfenbrenner, Urie, 44
Broude, Gwen J., on "myth of the first three years," 104–7
Brownridge, Peter, 96
Bruer, John T., on "myth of the first three years," 104–12
brutalization, 252–53
Burt, Cyril, 5

cafeteria-style religion, 363
Calgary, Alberta, school shooting in, 257
calorie reduction, for increasing lifespan, 396
Campbell, Don, 144
Campbell, Jennifer D., on self-esteem in school-age children, 180–95
Campbell, Patricia, 246
Canfield, Jack, 184
career: general intelligence (g) factor in, 323–41; and life expectancy, 399; marriage and, 310–11, 317–18
career placement services, in college, 288–98
Carey, George, 354
categorization, by children, 31–32
CHADD. See Children and Adults with Attention Deficit Disorder
character, religion and, 351
Charen, Mona, 209, 213
Charles IX (king), 147
Chasnoff, Ira, 80
chess, spatial-temporal reasoning in, 139–40

Chicago Child-Parent Center (CPC) Program, 163–64
child-rearing, culture and, 27–48
childbirth, natural, effects on childhood development, 88–96
children: categorization by, 31–32; compartmentalization in, 29–30; goals of, 28–29; learning in, 29–30; marriage of parents and, 306, 307, 309–10, 315–16; of maternal cocaine users, 70–82; "myth of the first three years," 104–12; religion and, 351. See also early childhood; infancy; school-age children
Children and Adults with Attention Deficit Disorder (CHADD), 216, 222–23
Chira, Susan, 237
classical conditioning, and violence, 253
Clinton, Bill, 254
cocaine, use during pregnancy, effects on children, 70–82
cognitive functions, in later adulthood, 377–79
cohabitation, versus marriage, 306–18
Cole, Nancy, 234
college: antidepressant use during, 270–83; career placement services in, 288–98; freshman year, 272–73; mental health services available in, 275–76; middle years, 274; preparation for life after graduation from, 288–98; senior year, 274–75
compression schemes, 20–21
conditioning: classical, 253; operant, 254
core knowledge, 117–29
Corsaro, William, 33
counting, learning of, 120–22
Cowdry, Edmund, 384
CPC Program. See Chicago Child-Parent Center Program

"crack kids," 70–82; case study of, 74–78; cognitive effects in, 73, 76–77, 81; physical effects in, 70–71, 75; socioemotional effects in, 71–73, 75–76, 79; vocational and life skills implications for, 77
craniology, 59–60
crime: religion and, 351; violent media and, 251–52
Cronin, Helena, 5
Csikzentmihalyi, Mihaly, 44
culture: and child-rearing, 27–48; defining, 42–43; and differences between men and women, 53; versus genetics, as influence on development, 4–22; and religion, 346–66; and self-esteem, 183
Curry, Oliver, 5

Damon, William, 351
Daniel, Kermit, 310
Dawkins, Richard, 350
depression, medication for, in young adulthood, 270–83
Deukmeijian, George, 183
development, parents versus peers in process of, 27–48
developmental problems, in college students, 289–90
d'Holbach, Baron, on differences between men and women, 58
Diamond, Jared, 6–7
Diller, Lawrence, 218
disadvantaged children. See at-risk children
discrimination: sex, 51–52, 232–46; against unmarried people, 317
doctrine of ethos, of Plato, 146–47
domestic partnerships, versus marriage, 306–18
Douvan, Elizabeth, 294
drug use, maternal, effects on children, 70–82

early childhood: academic skills emphasized in, for at-risk preschool children, 154–72; music exposure during, 136–49
Early Head Start, 158
Eberstadt, Mary, 210, 211
economics: and marriage, 309; and transition to adulthood, 297–98
Edell, Dean, 221
education, inclusive, and self-esteem, 200–202
Egeland, Byron, 110
Ehrlich, Paul, on nature versus nurture, 4–12, 13
Eibl-Eibesfeldt, Irenäus, 30
Einstein, Albert, 137, 139
elementary school, achievement gap in, 161
Ellis, Albert, 183
Ellis, Bruce, 7
Ellis, Havelock, 60
emotions, and learning, 110–11
endorphins, in childbirth, 89
environment, versus genetics, as influence on development, 4–22
epidural analgesia, in childbirth, 88, 90, 93
Epstein, Cynthia Fuchs, 243–44
Escher, M. C., 137
Estrich, Susan, 52
evolution: and differences between men and women, 54; and nature versus nurture, 4–12
evolutionary psychology, 6–8
Exline, Julie Juola, on importance of religion in adulthood, 355–66
experience, tacit knowledge and, 337–38

faith, religious, in adulthood, 346–66
family, and life expectancy, 398–99
Fantz, Robert, 126
Feldman, Marcus, on nature versus nurture, 4–12
feminism: on attention deficit hyperactivity disorder, 208; on schooling of boys versus girls, 232–46

Fisher, Bobby, 140
Fisher, R. A., 11
Foley, Robert, 6
Ford, Maggie, 239
Fortner, Lewis, 274
Fraiberg, Selma, 28
Freedman, Jonathan L., on violent media and aggression in adolescence, 257–63
Freud, Sigmund, 27–28, 37, 42
Fukuyama, Francis, 207
Fumento, Michael, on attention deficit disorder, 207–13
Furstenberg, Frank F., Jr., on preparation for life after college, 293–98

g. See general intelligence factor
Gallup, George, Jr., 348
Galton, Francis, 61
Garcia, Antwaun, 80, 81
Gardner, Howard, on parents versus peers in development process, 36–48
gay and lesbian marriage, 316
Gehring, Walter, 20
gender differences, 51–62
gene therapy, for attention deficit hyperactivity disorder, 223–24
general intelligence (g) factor: and career success, 323–41; as construct, 324–27; racial disparities in, 329–32; and tacit knowledge, 338–39
genetic determinism, 4
genetic engineering, for increasing lifespan, 396–97, 404
genetics: and attention deficit hyperactivity disorder, 218–19; behavioral, and childhood behavior, 38, 41; and differences between men and women, 53; versus environment, as influence on development, 4–22; and successful aging, 375–76
genotype, versus phenotype, 4
Gilligan, Carol, 236, 237, 242

Goldberg, Jonah, 207
Goodman, Ellen, 349
goodness, religion and, 350
Gore, Al, 347
Gottfredson, Linda S., on general intelligence factor and career success, 323–32
Gottman, John, 110
Gould, Stephen Jay, 40
government policy, influences on later adulthood, 389–90
Grant, Gilbert J., on pain relief during childbirth, 93–96
Greene, David, 235
Greer, Germain, 391
Grossman, Dave, on violent media and aggression in adolescence, 251–56
group contrast effect, 32, 33–34
group socialization, 31–35
groupness, 33–34
growth cones, 15–16
guilt, over pain relief during childbirth, 96
Gurian, Michael, 242

habituation-recovery technique, 126, 127
Hackler, Chris, on anti-aging technology, 396–402
Hahn, Sabrina, 140
Hardy, G. H., 138
Harris, Eric, 246
Harris, Judith Rich: Gardner's (Howard) response to, 36–46; on parents versus peers in development process, 27–35
Hassler, Marianne, 136
Head Start, 154–72
health: aging and, 374–91; anti-aging technology and, 396–406; marriage and, 307–8
Hedges, Larry V., 235
Hedlund, Jennifer, on general intelligence factor and career success, 333–41
Helfand, Stephen L., 396–97

Hernandez, Donald, 310
heroin addicts, and childbirth, 89–90
high school, achievement gap in, 161
Holstein, Martha B., on successful aging, 383–91
Hood, Bruce, on symbolic representation of objects, 125–29
Hopkins, Nancy, 51
Horatio Alger Association, 238
Horkheimer, Max, 283
Houston, Kerri, 209, 212, 213
Huichol Indians, birthing practices of, 95
Human Genome Project, and nature versus nurture, 4–12
Humphrey, Neil, on self-esteem in school-age children, 196–202
Hurley, Kendra, 81

IF-THEN theory, of genes, 17–20
immigrants, childhood development in, 30
inclusive education, and self-esteem, 200–202
infancy: "myth of the first three years," 104–12; object representation in, 117–29
Inglehart, Ronald, 347
intelligence: in "crack kids," 81; difference between men and women, 60–61; general intelligence factor, 323–41; practical, 334–35; racial disparities in, 329–31
intra-individual variability, and successful aging, 376–77

Jacob, François, 17
Jensen, Arthur, 4–5
Jensen, Joli, on antidepressant use during college, 281–83
Johnson, Byron, 351
Jones, Steven, 40–41
Jonesboro school shooting, 253, 255
juvenile delinquency, 33, 351

Kahn, Robert L.: response to, 383–91; on successful aging, 374–82
Kasparov, Garry, 140
Kelley, Jim, 141
Kimmel, Michael, on schooling of boys versus girls during adolescence, 241–46
kindergarten, achievement gap in, 160, 161
Kindlon, Dan, 241
Klatz, Ronald, on anti-aging technology, 403–6
Kleinfeld, Judith, 238–39
knowledge, tacit, 334–41
Koplewicz, Harold S., on antidepressant use during college, 270–80
Krauthammer, Charles, 81
Krebs, Dennis, 353
Krueger, Joachim I., on self-esteem in school-age children, 180–95
Kulka, Richard, 294
Ky, Katherine, 144

language: learning, 41; in preschool-aged children, 162
language-analytic reasoning, 139
later adulthood: anti-aging technology in, 396–406; successful aging in, 374–91
learning: in children, 29–30; of counting, 120–22; emotional foundations of, 110–11; in first three years of life, 104–12; of language, 41; of number words, 120–22
learning disorders, in college students, 290
LeFever, Gretchen, 211
Leffert, Nancy, 238
Leng, Xiao, 141
Leo, Jonathan, on attention deficit disorder, 214–24
Levine, Mel, on preparation for life after college, 288–92
Lewin, Tamar, 237

life expectancy, increasing, 396–406
lifestyle, and successful aging, 375–76
Lillard, Lee, 308
Limbaugh, Rush, 207, 209
Linton, Michael, on exposure to music during early childhood, 136–43
Lipset, Seymour Martin, 351
Lipton, Jennifer, 119
Littleton, Colorado, school shooting in, 254, 256, 357
Longhurst, Maren, 141
Lye, Diane, 310
Lytton, Hugh, 53

MacArthur Foundation Research Network on Successful Aging, 374, 376–77, 380, 381, 383, 386, 390
Maccoby, Eleanor, 38, 43
magic tricks, 127
Marcus, Gary, on nature versus nurture, 13–22
marriage: career and, 310–11, 317–18; economics and, 309; gay and lesbian, 316; and health, 307–8; importance of, 306–18; interfaith, 357; and life expectancy, 398; and mortality, 308; and sexual satisfaction, 308–9; social responsibility of, 311–12
Martino, Wayne, 245
maternal drug use, effects on children, 70–82
mathematics: and music, 136, 137, 138–39, 140–41, 145–46; in preschool-aged children, 162, 163
mating behavior, evolutionary psychology on, 7–8
Maudsley, Henry, 61
McCarthy, Nora, 81
McCarthy, Sherri, on "crack kids," 70–79
McLanahan, Sara, 309–10
Mecca, Andrew, 183
Medawar, Peter, 223

media, violence in, and aggression during adolescence, 251–63
medication: for attention deficit hyperactivity disorder, 209–13; for depression, in young adulthood, 270–83
men: during adolescence, 232–46; differences from women, 51–62
mental health services, on college campuses, 275–76
MetLife study, on gender equity, 238
military, training methods of, 252–55
Mill, John Stuart, 62
Miller, George, 37
Miller, Marshall, on importance of marriage, 313–18
Miller, Zell, 105
Minkler, Meredith., on successful aging, 383–91
Modell, John, 296
Monod, Jacques, 17
Moonves, Leslie, 256
Morris, Desmond, 4
mortality, marriage and, 308
motivation, source of, 110
Mozart, Wolfgang Amadeus, exposure to music of during early childhood, 136–49
music, exposure to during early childhood, 136–49
Myers, David G., on importance of religion in adulthood, 346–54
"myth of the first three years," 104–12

NALS. See National Adult Literacy Survey
NASE. See National Association for Self-Esteem
National Adult Literacy Survey (NALS), 326
National Assessment of Educational Progress, 234–35
National Association for Self-Esteem (NASE), 184
National Center for Infants, Toddlers and Families, on "myth of the first three years," 108–12

National Institute of Mental Health, on attention deficit hyperactivity disorder, 216–17
natural childbirth, effects on childhood development, 88–96
nature versus nurture: and attention deficit hyperactivity disorder, 218–19; in childhood development, 4–22
Nelson, Charles, 262
"new gerontology," 383–91
New Guinea, evolutionary psychology in, 6–7
normativity, in later adulthood, 385–87
Nowell, Amy, 235
number words, learning of, 120–22
numerosity, core knowledge of, 119–20

object representation, in infancy, 117–29
Oedipal period, 28, 37
operant conditioning, and violence, 254
O'Reilly, Patricia, 232

Paducah, Kentucky, school shooting in, 251, 254, 257
Paglia, Camille, 244
pain relief, during childbirth, 88–96
parents: married versus unmarried, 306, 307, 309–10, 315–16; versus peers, in development process, 27–48
peers, versus parents, in development process, 27–48
PEN. See Public Education Network
penal system, life expectancy and, 400
Perry Preschool Study, 164–65
Personal Attributes Questionnaire, 40
personality-type tests, tacit knowledge and, 340–41
phenome, behavioral, 4–12
phenotype, versus genotype, 4
Phillips, Katherin Ross, 297

phrenology, 59
physical functions, in later adulthood, 377–78, 379
Piaget, Jean, 126, 128
Pinker, Steven, 6, 29; on differences between men and women, 51–55
Pisan, Christine de, on differences between men and women, 58
Pitocin, in childbirth, 88, 89, 90
Planck, Max, 406
Plato: on differences between men and women, 56–57; doctrine of ethos of, 146–47
Pollack, William, 241, 242
population growth, anti-aging technology and, 400
Postman, Neil, 36
power, and life expectancy, 399
practical intelligence, 334–35
Prager, Dennis, 351
Prechtl, Heinz, 143
preferential looking method, 117–18
pregnancy, drug use during, 70–82
preschool children. See early childhood
proportional math, 137, 145–46
Provence, Sally, 111
Prozac, use during young adulthood, 278–80
psychology, evolutionary, 6–8
Public Education Network (PEN), 237–38
public school system, and attention deficit hyperactivity disorder, 209, 220–21
Pythagoras, 137, 145–46

racial disparities, in general intelligence factor, 329–32
Ramanujan, Srinivasa, 138–39
Rapoport, Judith, 208, 209, 219–20, 224
Rauscher, Frances, 144
Raver, C. Cybele, on academic skills in at-risk preschool children, 166–72
Ravitch, Diane, 237

reading, in preschool-aged children, 162, 163
reasoning: language-analytic, 139; spatial-temporal, 139–40
Reich, Robert, 39
religion, 346–66; and altruism, 352–54; cafeteria-style, 363; and character, 351; conflicts over, 357–59; and goodness, 350; intellectual barriers to, 361–63; mistrust of, 359–61; and virtue, 363–65
Rief, Sandra, 212
Righard, Lennart, on natural childbirth, 88–92
right to die, 400
Ritalin, for attention deficit hyperactivity disorder, 209–24
Robber's Cave study, 32–33
Robbins, Anthony, 184
role models, and teenage violence, 254–55
Romanes, George John, 60
Romney, David, 53
Ross, Karen, 298
Rossi, Alice, 294
Rousseau, Jacques, on differences between men and women, 58
Rovee-Collier, Carolyn, 29
Rowe, John W.: response to, 383–91; on successful aging, 374–82
Russett, Cynthia, on differences between men and women, 56–62

Sacks, Jonathan, 354
Sadker, David, 234
Sadker, Myra, 234
Sandefur, Gary, 309–10
Sarton, May, 391
SAT. *See* Scholastic Assessment Test
SATSA. *See* Swedish Adoption/Twin Study of Aging
Scarsdale High School (New York), gender equity in, 235
Schervish, Paul, 353
Schlafly, Phyllis, 207, 209, 210

Schoeni, Robert, 298
Scholastic Assessment Test (SAT), gender differences in scores of, 234
school: differences of boys versus girls in, 232–46; readiness for, 154–72; and successful aging, 381
school-age children: attention deficit hyperactivity disorder in, 207–24; self-esteem in, 180–202
school shootings, 251–63
Search Institute, 238
self-control: development of, 110; and early learning, 170
self-efficacy, and successful aging, 381
self-esteem: American Association of University Women's study of, 236–37; appeal of, 182–85; development of, 196–98; and inclusive education, 200–202; reasons for studying, 181–82; in school-age children, 180–202; and school performance, 186–93
sex discrimination, 51–52, 232–46
sexual satisfaction, marriage and, 308–9
Shaw, Gordon, 144
Shaw, Gordon L., on exposure to music during early childhood, 136–43
Sherif, Muzafer, 32
Shipp, E. R., 82
SIDS. *See* Sudden Infant Death Syndrome
Siegal, Allan, 82
Siegel, Bernie, 184
Silber, John, 212
Simmons, Roberta, 237
situational judgment tests (SJTs), 336
SJTs. *See* situational judgment tests
sleep dysfunction, in "crack kids," 75
Smeeding, Timothy, 297
Smith, James, 309
Sober, Elliott, 10

socialization: group, 31–35; in later adulthood, 379–80; parents versus peer groups in, 27–46
society: and child-rearing, 27–48; impact of anti-aging technology on, 396–406; marriage and, 311–12
Solot, Dorian, on importance of marriage, 313–18
Sommers, Christina Hoff: Kimmel's (Michael) response to, 241–46; on schooling of boys versus girls during adolescence, 232–40
Sowell, Thomas, 207, 209
spatial-temporal reasoning: in chess, 139–40; music and, 137
Spearman, Charles, 60
Spelke, Elizabeth, on symbolic representation of objects, 117–24
spirituality, in adulthood, 346–66
Spurzheim, J. G., 59
Sroufe, Alan, 110
standardized testing: and general intelligence factor, 323–32; scores of, gender differences in, 233–35, 245
Steinem, Gloria, 184, 239, 242, 246
Sternberg, Robert J., on general intelligence factor and career success, 333–41
Stimpson, Catharine, 245
Stone, Lawrence, 224
stress, response to, and successful aging, 381–82
Sudden Infant Death Syndrome (SIDS), maternal cocaine use and, 71
Sulloway, Frank, 36
Summers, Lawrence, 51, 52, 53, 56, 61
Sustad, Steven, 397
Swanson, James, 222
Swedish Adoption/Twin Study of Aging (SATSA), 375
Swift, Jonathan, 352
symbolic representation, of objects, innate ability for, 117–29

taboo, psychology of, 54–55
tacit knowledge, 334–41
Tajfel, Henri, 32, 33
test scores: gender differences in, 233–35, 245; and general intelligence factor, 323–32
Tetlock, Philip, 54
Thompson, Helen Bradford, 60
Thompson, Michael, 241
Thompson, Peter, 125
Thompson, Tommy, 167, 169
Tocqueville, Alexis de, 43
training methods, of military, 252–55
Trueblood, Elton, 350
trust, development of, 109–10
twin studies: on aging, 375; in behavioral genetics, 41

Umberson, Debra, 307
U.S. Department of Health and Human Services, on academic skills in at-risk preschool children, 154–65

values inculcation, 252–53
Van Hesteren, Frank, 353
Vasconcellos, John, 183, 184
Veroff, Joseph, 294
Vickers, Melana Zyla, 211
video games, violence in, and aggressive behavior, 251–63
violence, in media, and aggression during adolescence, 251–63
virtue, religion and, 363–65
Vohs, Kathleen D., on self-esteem in school-age children, 180–95
Voltaire, 350

Waite, Linda J., on importance of marriage, 306–12
Waters, Thomas Franklin, on "crack kids," 70–79
Wellesley College Center for Research on Women, 237
Whiting, Beatrice, 43
Whiting, John, 43
Williams, Armstrong, 210

Wilson, E. O., 350
Wilson, James Q., 234
Winkle, Lenny, 211
Winn, Marie, 36
Wollstonecraft, Mary, on
    differences between men
    and women, 58
women: during adolescence, 232–46;
    differences from men, 51–62; in
    later adulthood, 389

work, preparation for, 288–98
Wynn, Karen, 117

Xu, Fei, 119

Zametkin, Alan, 215–16, 218–19
Zero to Three, on "myth of the first
    three years," 108–12
Zigler, Edward F., on academic skills in
    at-risk preschool children, 166–72